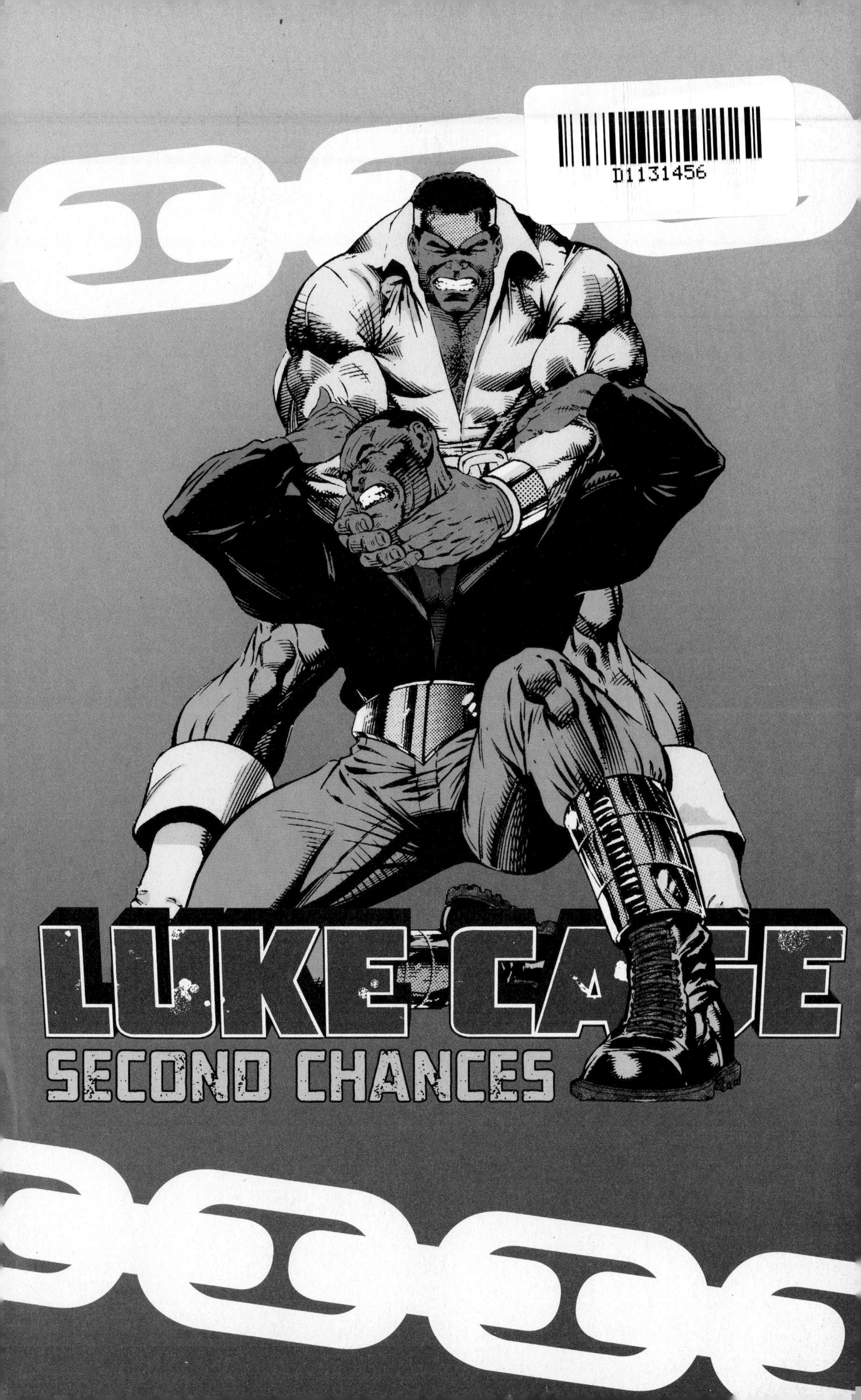
LUKE CAGE
SECOND CHANCES

COLLECTION EDITOR: **MARK D. BEAZLEY**
ASSISTANT MANAGING EDITOR: **JOE HOCHSTEIN**
ASSOCIATE MANAGING EDITOR: **ALEX STARBUCK**
EDITOR, SPECIAL PROJECTS: **JENNIFER GRÜNWALD**
SENIOR EDITOR, SPECIAL PROJECTS: **JEFF YOUNGQUIST**
RESEARCH: **STUART VANDAL**
LAYOUT: **JEPH YORK**
PRODUCTION: **COLORTEK & JOE FRONTIRRE**
BOOK DESIGNER: **ADAM DEL RE**
SVP PRINT, SALES & MARKETING: **DAVID GABRIEL**

EDITOR IN CHIEF: **AXEL ALONSO**
CHIEF CREATIVE OFFICER: **JOE QUESADA**
PUBLISHER: **DAN BUCKLEY**
EXECUTIVE PRODUCER: **ALAN FINE**

SPECIAL THANKS TO **MIKE HANSEN &
DOUG SHARK OF MYCOMICSHOP.COM**

LUKE CAGE: SECOND CHANCES VOL. 1. Contains material originally published in magazine form as CAGE #1-12 and MARVEL COMICS PRESENTS #82. First printing 2015. ISBN# 978-0-7851-9298-5. Published by MARVEL WORLDWIDE, INC., a subsidiary of MARVEL ENTERTAINMENT, LLC. OFFICE OF PUBLICATION: 135 West 50th Street, New York, NY 10020. Copyright © 2015 MARVEL No similarity between any of the names, characters, persons, and/or institutions in this magazine with those of any living or dead person or institution is intended, and any such similarity which may exist is purely coincidental. **Printed in the U.S.A.** ALAN FINE, President, Marvel Entertainment; DAN BUCKLEY, President, TV, Publishing and Brand Management; JOE QUESADA, Chief Creative Officer; TOM BREVOORT, SVP of Publishing; DAVID BOGART, SVP of Operations & Procurement, Publishing; C.B. CEBULSKI, VP of International Development & Brand Management; DAVID GABRIEL, SVP Print, Sales & Marketing; JIM O'KEEFE, VP of Operations & Logistics; DAN CARR, Executive Director of Publishing Technology; SUSAN CRESPI, Editorial Operations Manager; ALEX MORALES, Publishing Operations Manager; STAN LEE, Chairman Emeritus. For information regarding advertising in Marvel Comics or on Marvel.com, please contact Jonathan Rheingold, VP of Custom Solutions & Ad Sales, at jrheingold@marvel.com. For Marvel subscription inquiries, please call 800-217-9158. **Manufactured between 7/17/2015 and 8/24/2015 by R.R. DONNELLEY, INC., SALEM, VA, USA.**
10 9 8 7 6 5 4 3 2 1

LUKE CAGE
SECOND CHANCES

WRITER
MARC McLAURIN

PENCILERS
**DWAYNE TURNER, RURIK TYLER
& GORDON PURCELL** with **SAL VELLUTO**

INKERS
**CHRIS IVY, JOSEF RUBINSTEIN
& ANDREW PEPOY** with **BRAD VANCATA**

COLORISTS
MIKE THOMAS & KRIS RENKEWITZ
with **MARC McLAURIN**

LETTERERS
**CHRIS ELIOPOULOS, RICHARD STARKINGS
& JANICE CHIANG** with **TODD KLEIN**

ASSISTANT EDITORS
JAYE GARDNER with **MARK POWERS**

EDITORS
KELLY CORVESE with **TERRY KAVANAGH**

FRONT COVER ARTISTS: **DWAYNE TURNER, CHRIS IVY & MATT MILLA**

BACK COVER ARTISTS: **DWAYNE TURNER & CHRIS IVY**

MARVEL COMICS PRESENTS #82

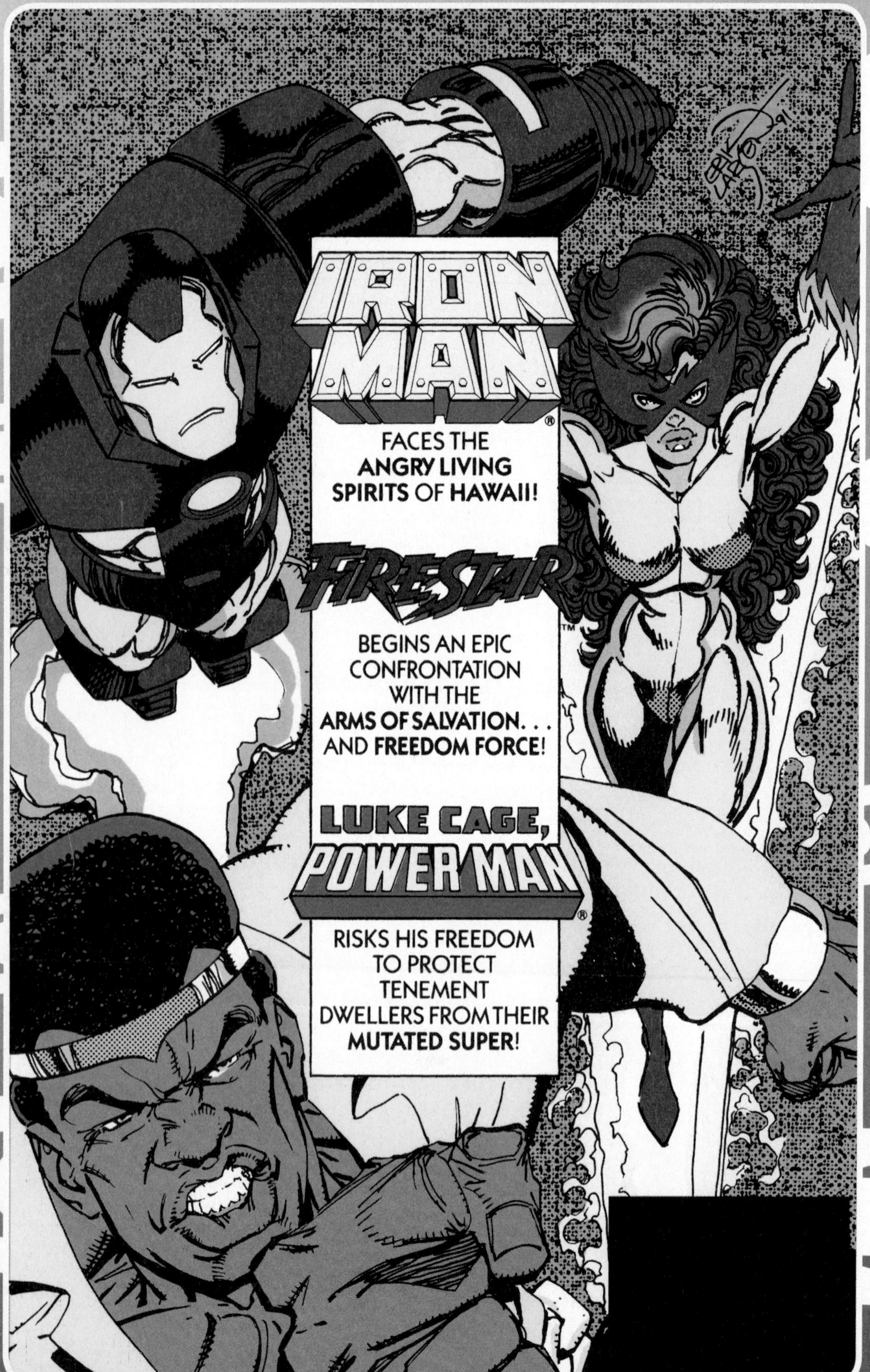
IRON MAN®
FACES THE ANGRY LIVING SPIRITS OF HAWAII!
FIRESTAR™
BEGINS AN EPIC CONFRONTATION WITH THE ARMS OF SALVATION. . . AND FREEDOM FORCE!
LUKE CAGE, POWER MAN®
RISKS HIS FREEDOM TO PROTECT TENEMENT DWELLERS FROM THEIR MUTATED SUPER!

WRITER & COLORIST: MARC MCLAURIN • PENCILER: SAL VELLUTO • INKER: BRAD VANCATA
LETTERER: TODD KLEIN • ASSISTANT EDITOR: MARK POWERS • EDITOR: TERRY KAVANAGH

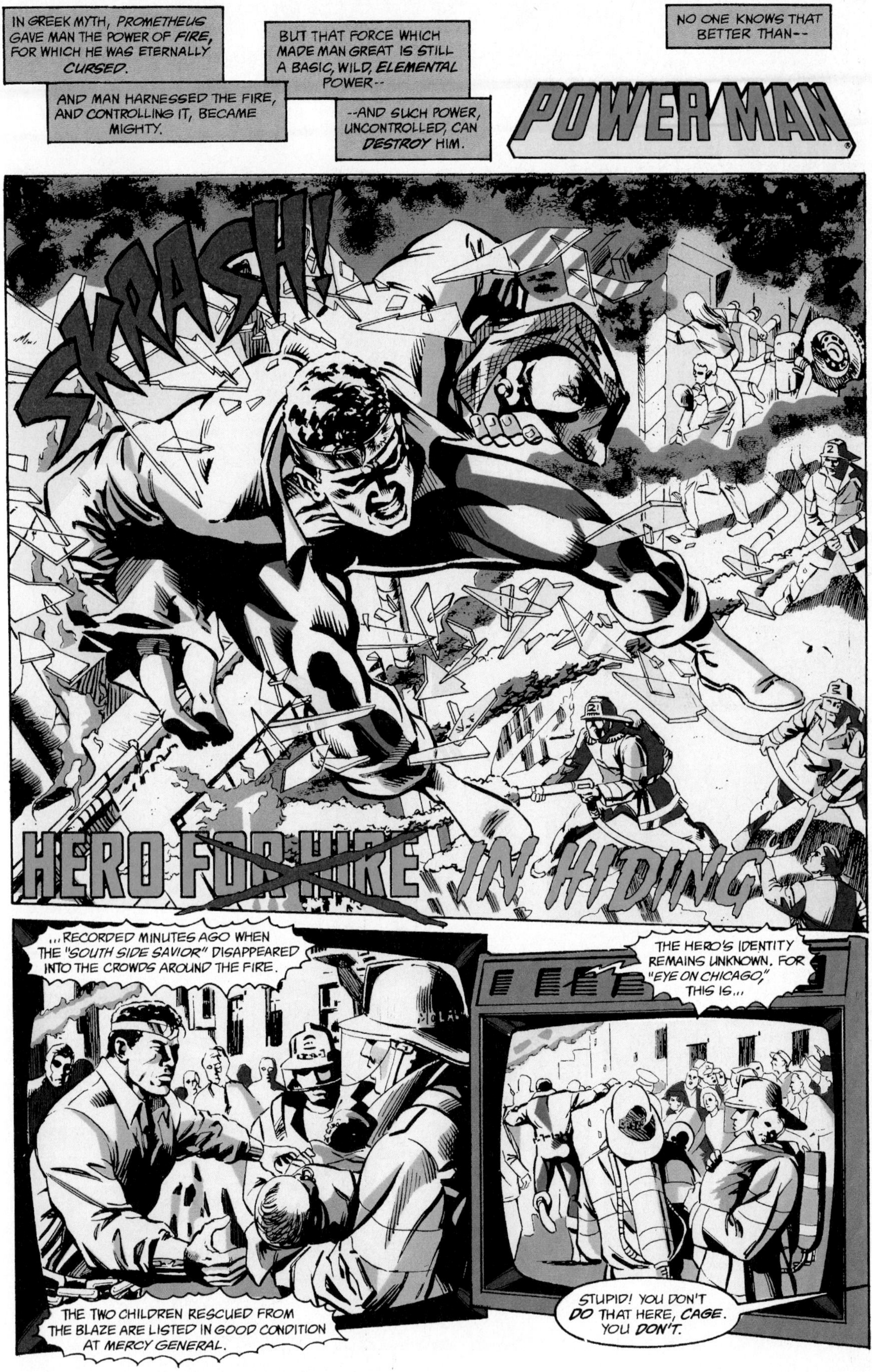

IN GREEK MYTH, PROMETHEUS GAVE MAN THE POWER OF FIRE, FOR WHICH HE WAS ETERNALLY CURSED.
AND MAN HARNESSED THE FIRE, AND CONTROLLING IT, BECAME MIGHTY.
BUT THAT FORCE WHICH MADE MAN GREAT IS STILL A BASIC, WILD, ELEMENTAL POWER--
--AND SUCH POWER, UNCONTROLLED, CAN DESTROY HIM.
NO ONE KNOWS THAT BETTER THAN--
POWER MAN
SKRASH!
HERO FOR HIRE IN HIDING
...RECORDED MINUTES AGO WHEN THE "SOUTH SIDE SAVIOR" DISAPPEARED INTO THE CROWDS AROUND THE FIRE.
THE TWO CHILDREN RESCUED FROM THE BLAZE ARE LISTED IN GOOD CONDITION AT MERCY GENERAL.
THE HERO'S IDENTITY REMAINS UNKNOWN. FOR "EYE ON CHICAGO," THIS IS...
STUPID! YOU DON'T DO THAT HERE, CAGE. YOU DON'T.

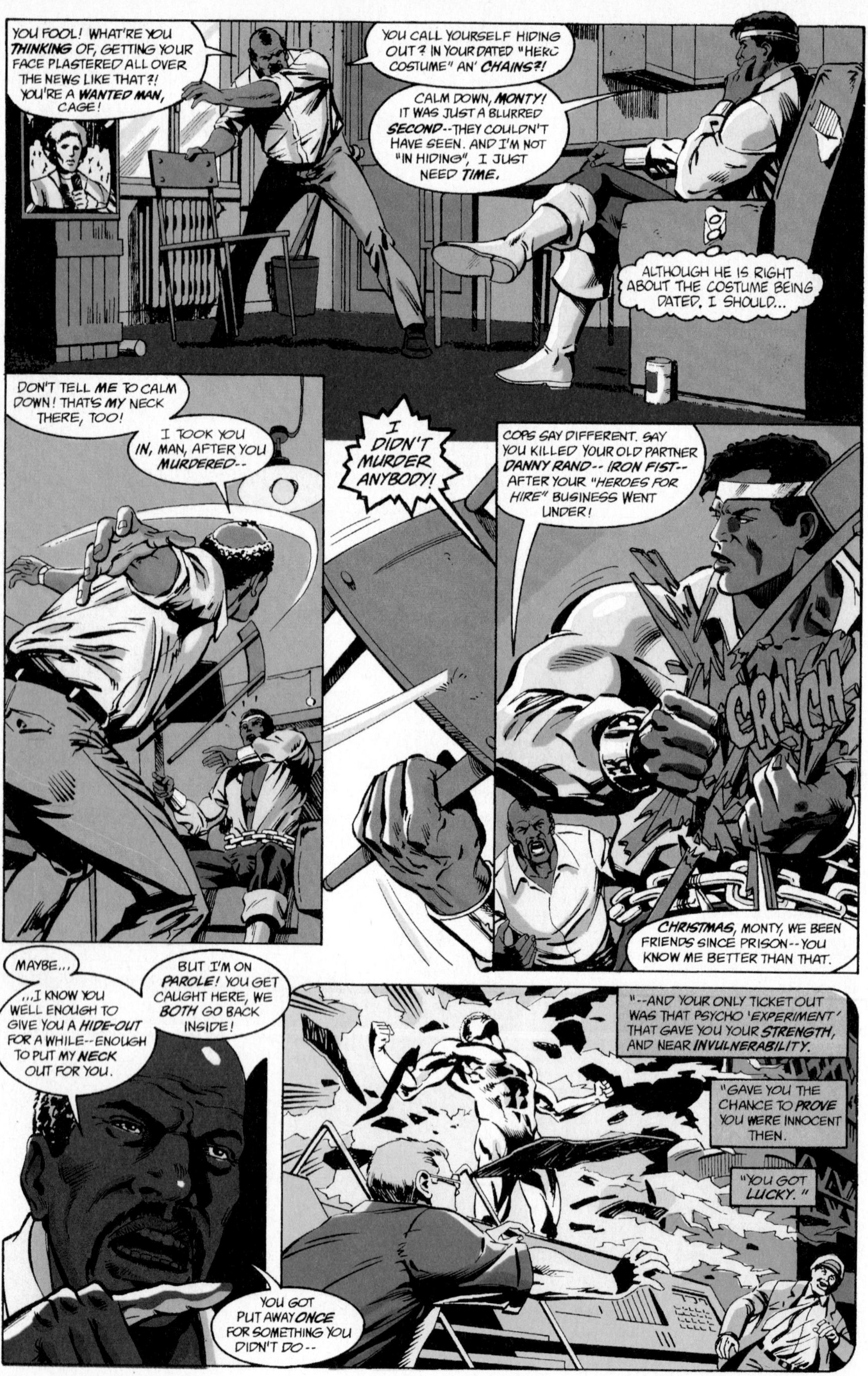
YOU FOOL! WHAT'RE YOU THINKING OF, GETTING YOUR FACE PLASTERED ALL OVER THE NEWS LIKE THAT?! YOU'RE A WANTED MAN, CAGE!
YOU CALL YOURSELF HIDING OUT? IN YOUR DATED "HERO COSTUME" AN' CHAINS?!
CALM DOWN, MONTY! IT WAS JUST A BLURRED SECOND--THEY COULDN'T HAVE SEEN. AND I'M NOT "IN HIDING", I JUST NEED TIME.
ALTHOUGH HE IS RIGHT ABOUT THE COSTUME BEING DATED. I SHOULD...
DON'T TELL ME TO CALM DOWN! THAT'S MY NECK THERE, TOO!
I TOOK YOU IN, MAN, AFTER YOU MURDERED--
I DIDN'T MURDER ANYBODY!
COPS SAY DIFFERENT. SAY YOU KILLED YOUR OLD PARTNER DANNY RAND-- IRON FIST-- AFTER YOUR "HEROES FOR HIRE" BUSINESS WENT UNDER!
CRNCH
CHRISTMAS, MONTY, WE BEEN FRIENDS SINCE PRISON--YOU KNOW ME BETTER THAN THAT.
MAYBE...
...I KNOW YOU WELL ENOUGH TO GIVE YOU A HIDE-OUT FOR A WHILE--ENOUGH TO PUT MY NECK OUT FOR YOU.
BUT I'M ON PAROLE! YOU GET CAUGHT HERE, WE BOTH GO BACK INSIDE!
YOU GOT PUT AWAY ONCE FOR SOMETHING YOU DIDN'T DO--
"--AND YOUR ONLY TICKET OUT WAS THAT PSYCHO 'EXPERIMENT' THAT GAVE YOU YOUR STRENGTH, AND NEAR INVULNERABILITY.
"GAVE YOU THE CHANCE TO PROVE YOU WERE INNOCENT THEN.
"YOU GOT LUCKY."

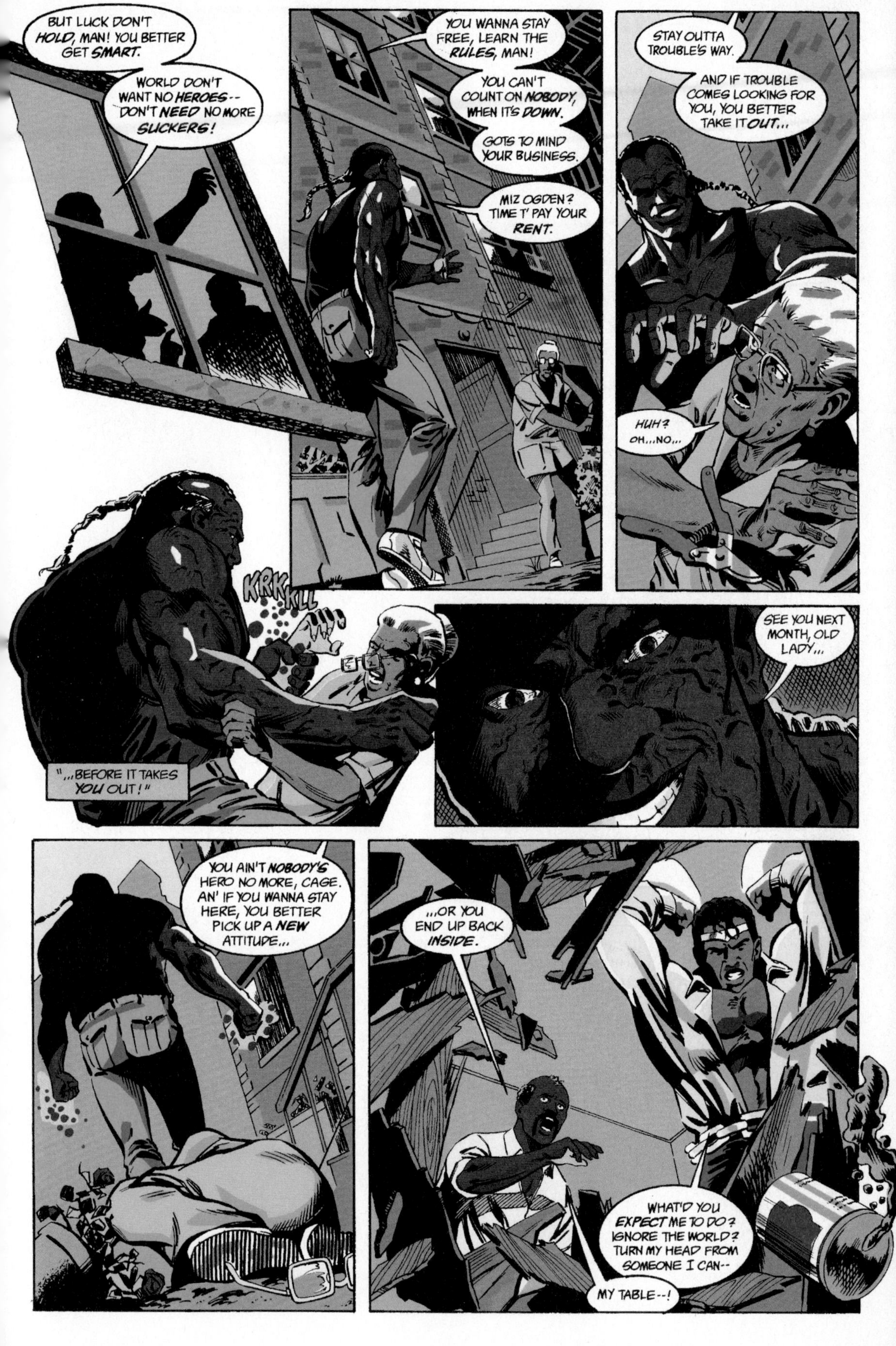
BUT LUCK DON'T HOLD, MAN! YOU BETTER GET SMART.
WORLD DON'T WANT NO HEROES-- DON'T NEED NO MORE SUCKERS!
YOU WANNA STAY FREE, LEARN THE RULES, MAN!
YOU CAN'T COUNT ON NOBODY, WHEN IT'S DOWN.
GOTS TO MIND YOUR BUSINESS.
MIZ OGDEN? TIME T' PAY YOUR RENT.
STAY OUTTA TROUBLE'S WAY.
AND IF TROUBLE COMES LOOKING FOR YOU, YOU BETTER TAKE IT OUT...
HUH? OH...NO...
KRKKLL
"...BEFORE IT TAKES YOU OUT!"
SEE YOU NEXT MONTH, OLD LADY...
YOU AIN'T NOBODY'S HERO NO MORE, CAGE. AN' IF YOU WANNA STAY HERE, YOU BETTER PICK UP A NEW ATTITUDE...
...OR YOU END UP BACK INSIDE.
WHAT'D YOU EXPECT ME TO DO? IGNORE THE WORLD? TURN MY HEAD FROM SOMEONE I CAN--
MY TABLE--!

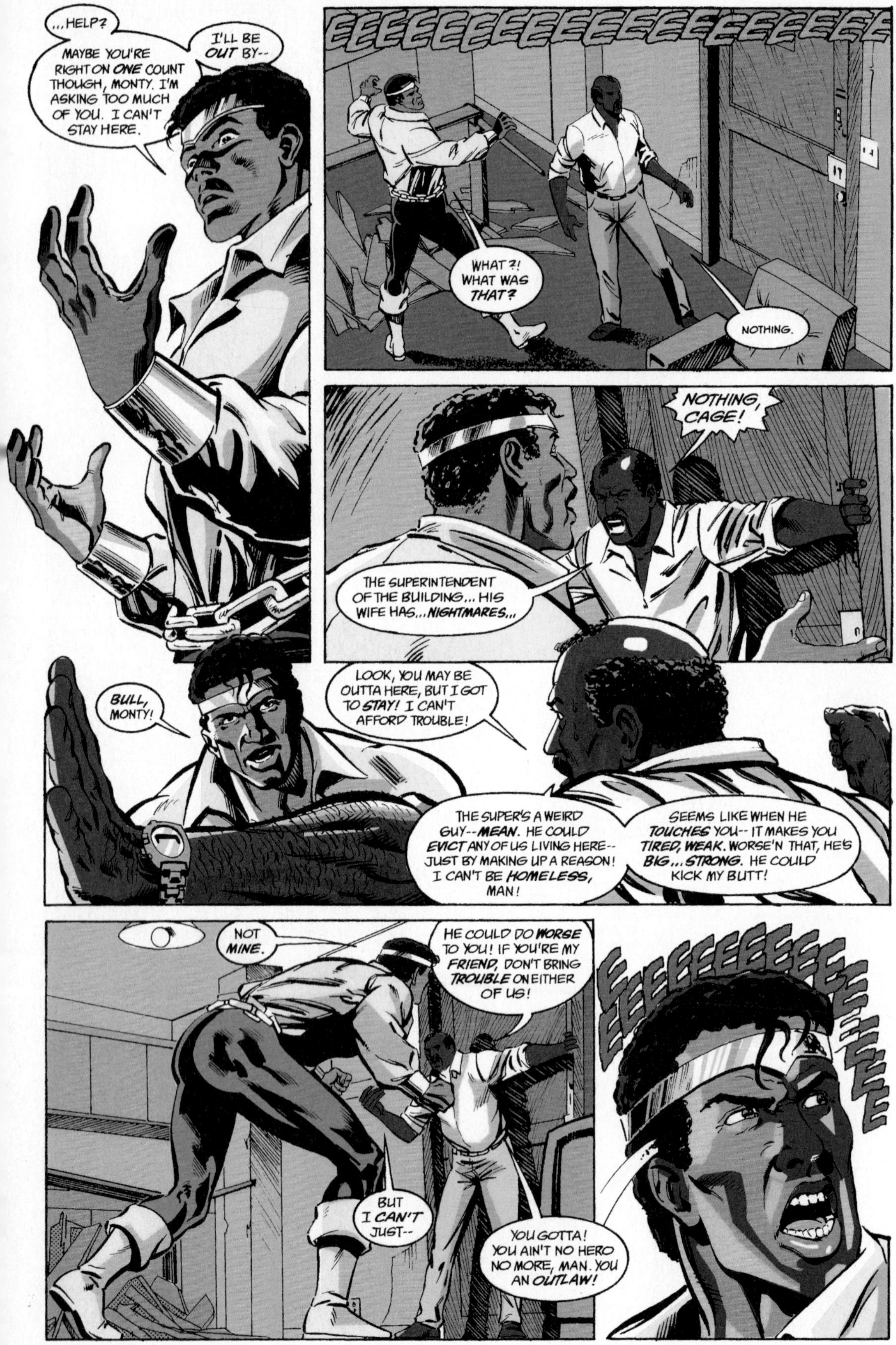
...HELP?
MAYBE YOU'RE RIGHT ON ONE COUNT THOUGH, MONTY. I'M ASKING TOO MUCH OF YOU. I CAN'T STAY HERE.
I'LL BE OUT BY--
EEEEEEEEEEEEEEEEEEEEEEE
WHAT?! WHAT WAS THAT?
NOTHING.
NOTHING, CAGE!
THE SUPERINTENDENT OF THE BUILDING... HIS WIFE HAS... NIGHTMARES...
BULL, MONTY!
LOOK, YOU MAY BE OUTTA HERE, BUT I GOT TO STAY! I CAN'T AFFORD TROUBLE!
THE SUPER'S A WEIRD GUY--MEAN. HE COULD EVICT ANY OF US LIVING HERE--JUST BY MAKING UP A REASON! I CAN'T BE HOMELESS, MAN!
SEEMS LIKE WHEN HE TOUCHES YOU-- IT MAKES YOU TIRED, WEAK. WORSE'N THAT, HE'S BIG... STRONG. HE COULD KICK MY BUTT!
NOT MINE.
HE COULD DO WORSE TO YOU! IF YOU'RE MY FRIEND, DON'T BRING TROUBLE ON EITHER OF US!
BUT I CAN'T JUST--
YOU GOTTA! YOU AIN'T NO HERO NO MORE, MAN. YOU AN OUTLAW!
EEEEEEEEEEEEEEEEEEEE

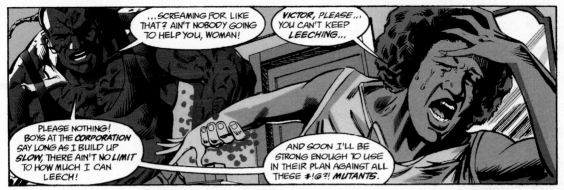

...SCREAMING FOR LIKE THAT? AIN'T NOBODY GOING TO HELP YOU, WOMAN!

VICTOR, PLEASE... YOU CAN'T KEEP LEECHING...

PLEASE NOTHING! BOYS AT THE *CORPORATION* SAY LONG AS I BUILD UP *SLOW*, THERE AIN'T NO *LIMIT* TO HOW MUCH I CAN LEECH!

AND SOON I'LL BE STRONG ENOUGH TO USE IN THEIR PLAN AGAINST ALL THESE #!*G*?! MUTANTS.

THEN ALL THE TIME AND MONEY'LL PAY OFF, FOR THEM *AND ME* ... SOON--

SOON YOU'LL BE ON THE FLOOR, MISTER, IF YOU DON'T LET HER *GO*!

CRASH

WHO--?

BOY, YOU DON'T KNOW *WHAT* YOU'RE MESSING WITH!

OH YES I DO... *AND* WHAT IT'S COSTING ME!

FROM THIS ANGLE, IT LOOKS LIKE A STINKING *WIFE-BEATER*!

SMELLS LIKE ONE, TOO!

YOU'LL SMELL *BLOOD* IN A MINUTE, BOY!

EEEEEE

ZZZKKKK

WHOOM

9

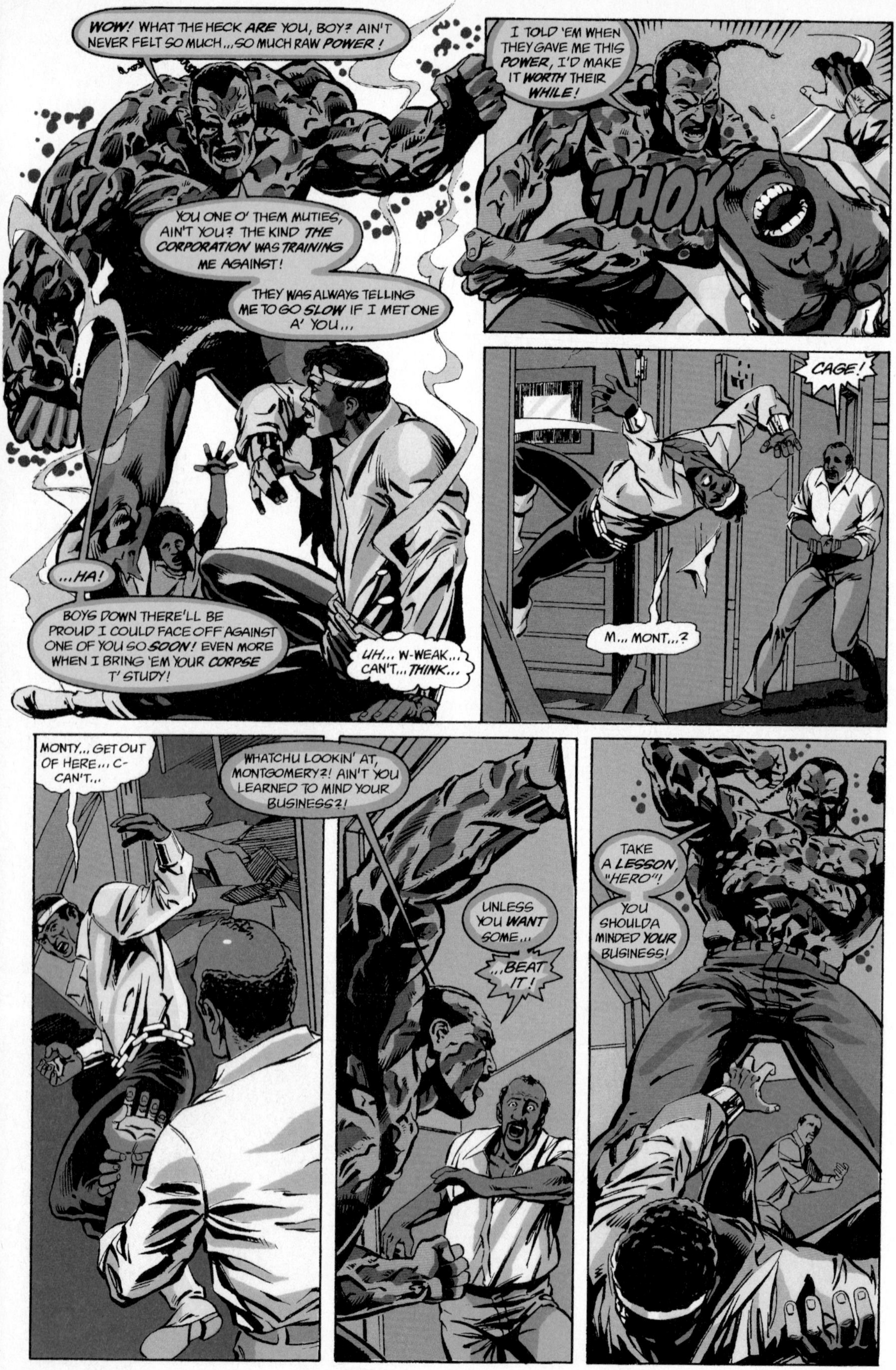
WOW! WHAT THE HECK ARE YOU, BOY? AIN'T NEVER FELT SO MUCH... SO MUCH RAW POWER!
YOU ONE O' THEM MUTIES, AIN'T YOU? THE KIND THE CORPORATION WAS TRAINING ME AGAINST!
THEY WAS ALWAYS TELLING ME TO GO SLOW IF I MET ONE A' YOU...
...HA!
BOYS DOWN THERE'LL BE PROUD I COULD FACE OFF AGAINST ONE OF YOU SO SOON! EVEN MORE WHEN I BRING 'EM YOUR CORPSE T' STUDY!
UH... W-WEAK... CAN'T... THINK...
I TOLD 'EM WHEN THEY GAVE ME THIS POWER, I'D MAKE IT WORTH THEIR WHILE!
THOK
CAGE!
M... MONT...?
MONTY... GET OUT OF HERE... C-CAN'T...
WHATCHU LOOKIN' AT, MONTGOMERY?! AIN'T YOU LEARNED TO MIND YOUR BUSINESS?!
UNLESS YOU WANT SOME...
...BEAT IT!
TAKE A LESSON, "HERO"!
YOU SHOULDA MINDED YOUR BUSINESS!

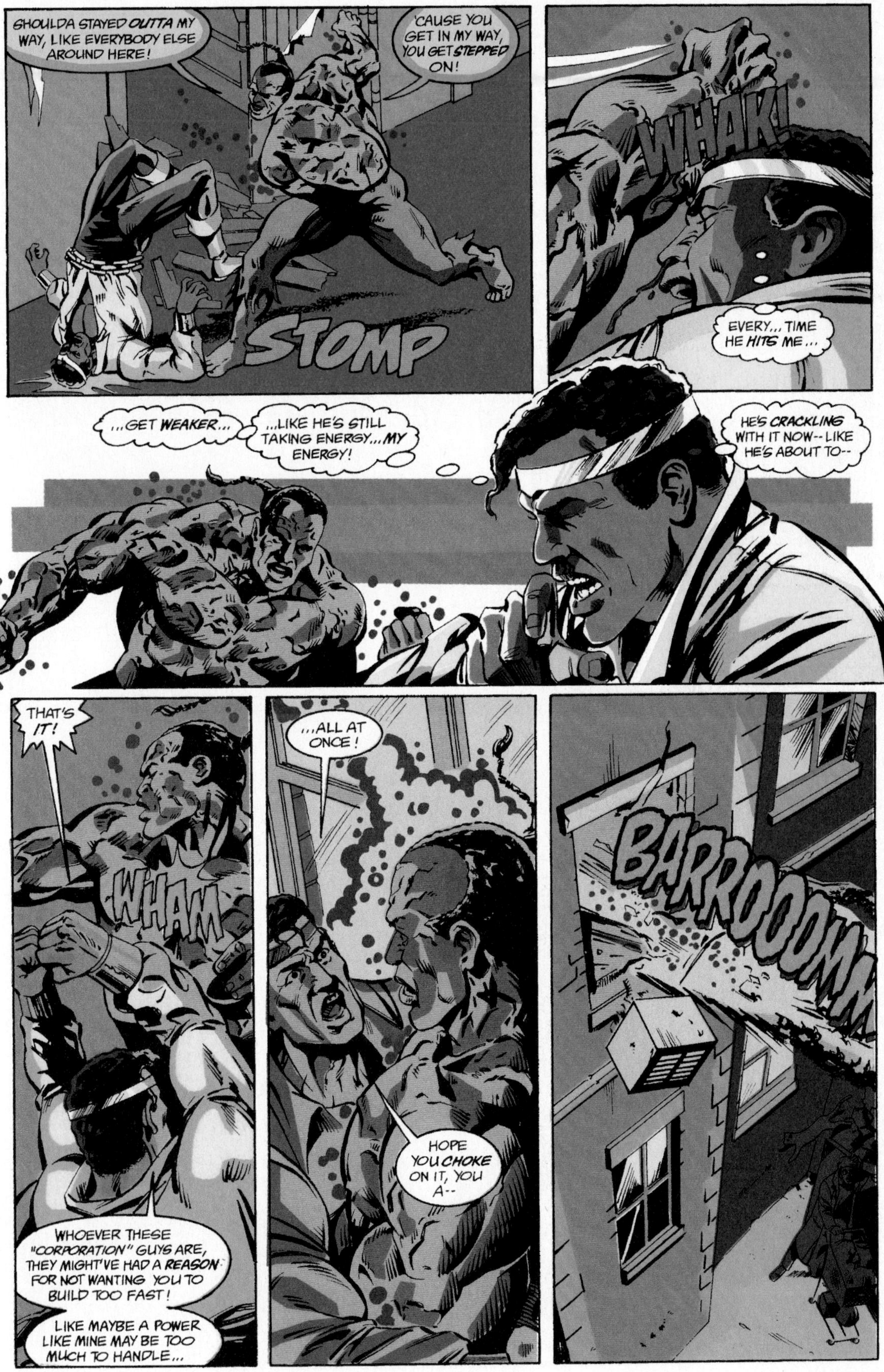

SHOULDA STAYED OUTTA MY WAY, LIKE EVERYBODY ELSE AROUND HERE!
'CAUSE YOU GET IN MY WAY, YOU GET STEPPED ON!
STOMP
WHAK!
EVERY... TIME HE HITS ME...
...GET WEAKER...
...LIKE HE'S STILL TAKING ENERGY... MY ENERGY!
HE'S CRACKLING WITH IT NOW-- LIKE HE'S ABOUT TO--
THAT'S IT!
WHAM
WHOEVER THESE "CORPORATION" GUYS ARE, THEY MIGHT'VE HAD A REASON FOR NOT WANTING YOU TO BUILD TOO FAST!
LIKE MAYBE A POWER LIKE MINE MAY BE TOO MUCH TO HANDLE...
...ALL AT ONCE!
HOPE YOU CHOKE ON IT, YOU A--
BARROOOMM

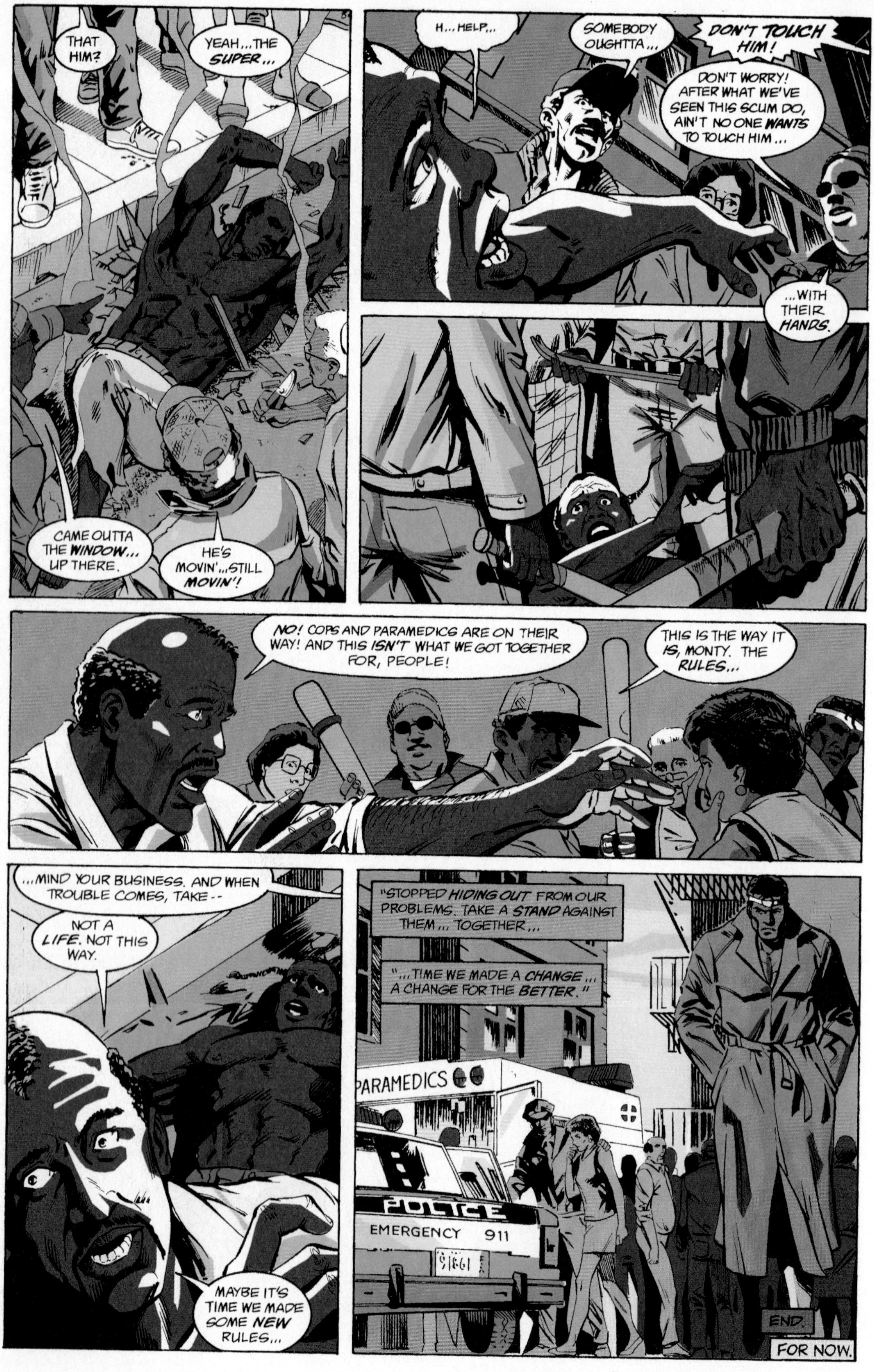
THAT HIM?
YEAH,...THE SUPER...
CAME OUTTA THE WINDOW... UP THERE.
HE'S MOVIN'...STILL MOVIN'!
H...HELP...
SOMEBODY OUGHTTA...
DON'T TOUCH HIM!
DON'T WORRY! AFTER WHAT WE'VE SEEN THIS SCUM DO, AIN'T NO ONE WANTS TO TOUCH HIM...
...WITH THEIR HANDS.
NO! COPS AND PARAMEDICS ARE ON THEIR WAY! AND THIS ISN'T WHAT WE GOT TOGETHER FOR, PEOPLE!
THIS IS THE WAY IT IS, MONTY. THE RULES...
...MIND YOUR BUSINESS. AND WHEN TROUBLE COMES, TAKE --
NOT A LIFE. NOT THIS WAY.
MAYBE IT'S TIME WE MADE SOME NEW RULES...
"STOPPED HIDING OUT FROM OUR PROBLEMS. TAKE A STAND AGAINST THEM... TOGETHER...
"...TIME WE MADE A CHANGE... A CHANGE FOR THE BETTER."
PARAMEDICS
POLICE
EMERGENCY 911
END.
FOR NOW.

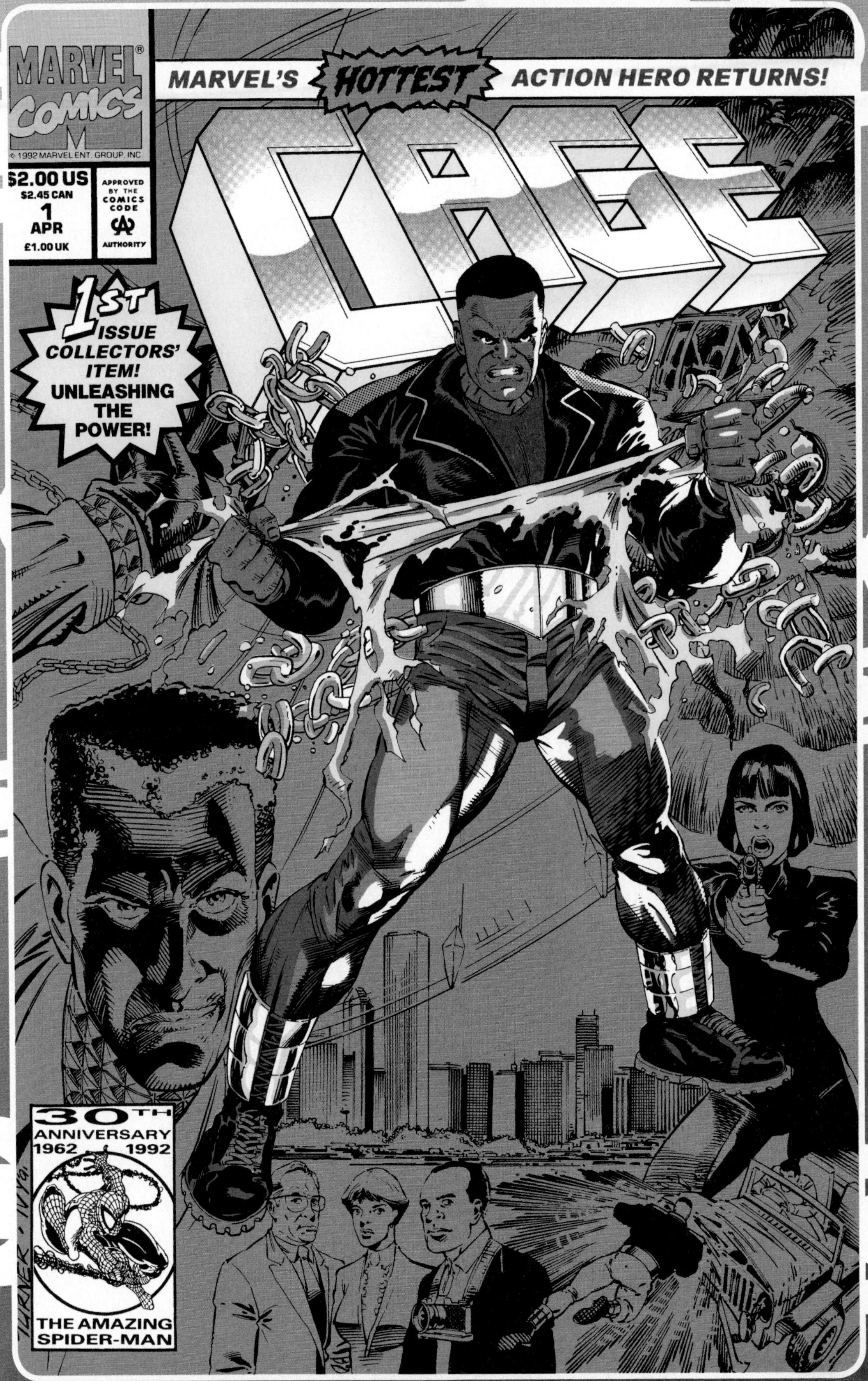

MARVEL COMICS
© 1992 MARVEL ENT. GROUP, INC.
MARVEL'S HOTTEST ACTION HERO RETURNS!
CAGE
$2.00 US
$2.45 CAN
1
APR
£1.00 UK
APPROVED BY THE COMICS CODE AUTHORITY
1ST ISSUE COLLECTORS' ITEM! UNLEASHING THE POWER!
30TH ANNIVERSARY
1962 1992
THE AMAZING SPIDER-MAN

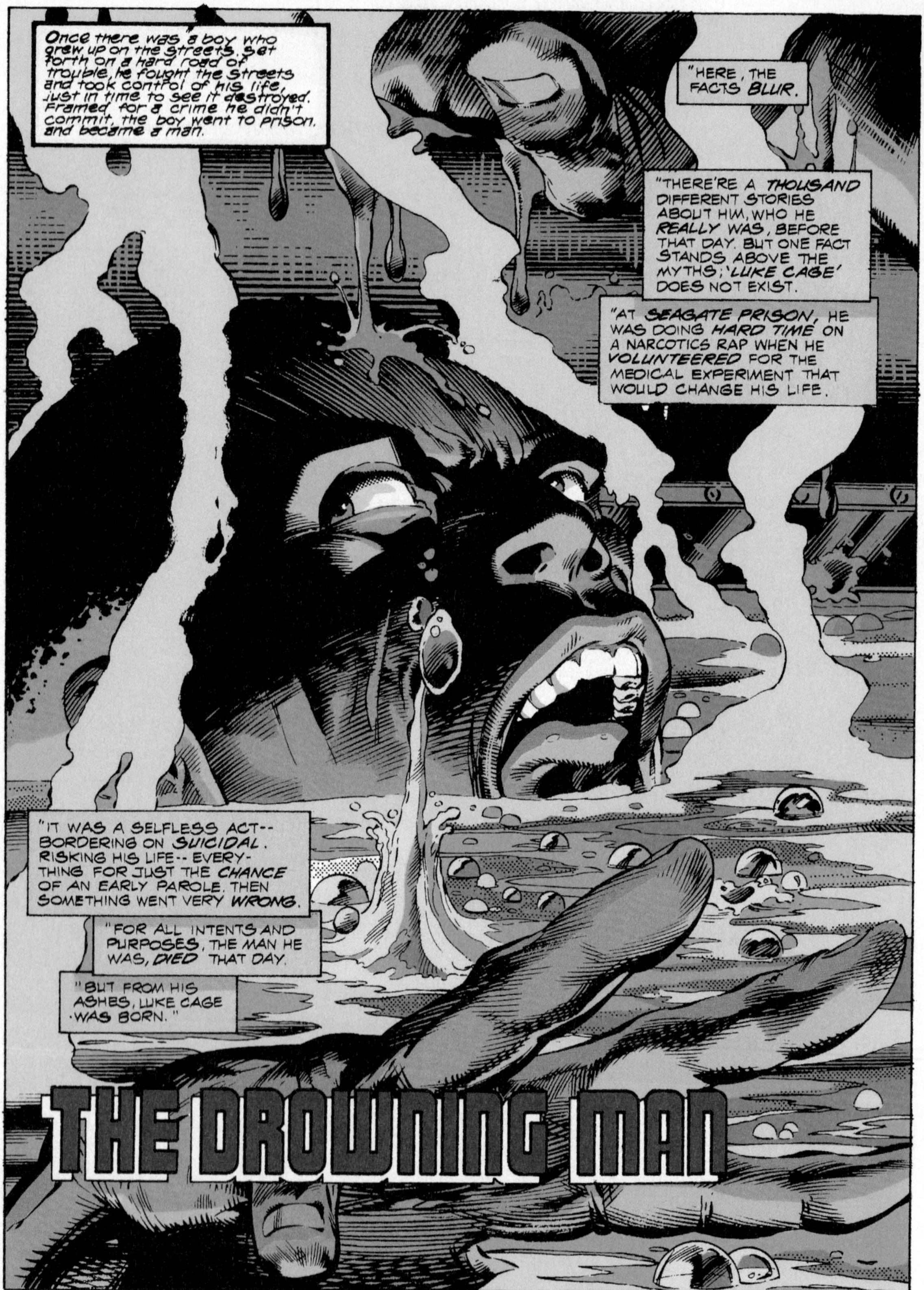

Once there was a boy who grew up on the streets. Set forth on a hard road of trouble, he fought the streets and took control of his life, just in time to see it destroyed. Framed for a crime he didn't commit, the boy went to prison, and became a man.
"HERE, THE FACTS BLUR.
"THERE'RE A THOUSAND DIFFERENT STORIES ABOUT HIM, WHO HE REALLY WAS, BEFORE THAT DAY. BUT ONE FACT STANDS ABOVE THE MYTHS; 'LUKE CAGE' DOES NOT EXIST.
"AT SEAGATE PRISON, HE WAS DOING HARD TIME ON A NARCOTICS RAP WHEN HE VOLUNTEERED FOR THE MEDICAL EXPERIMENT THAT WOULD CHANGE HIS LIFE.
"IT WAS A SELFLESS ACT--BORDERING ON SUICIDAL. RISKING HIS LIFE-- EVERYTHING FOR JUST THE CHANCE OF AN EARLY PAROLE. THEN SOMETHING WENT VERY WRONG.
"FOR ALL INTENTS AND PURPOSES, THE MAN HE WAS, DIED THAT DAY.
"BUT FROM HIS ASHES, LUKE CAGE WAS BORN."
THE DROWNING MAN

MARC McLAURIN WRITER · DWAYNE TURNER PENCILER · CHRISTOPHER IVY INKER · CHRIS ELIOPOULOS LETTERER · MIKE THOMAS COLORIST · KELLY CORVESE EDITOR · TOM DEFALCO CHIEF

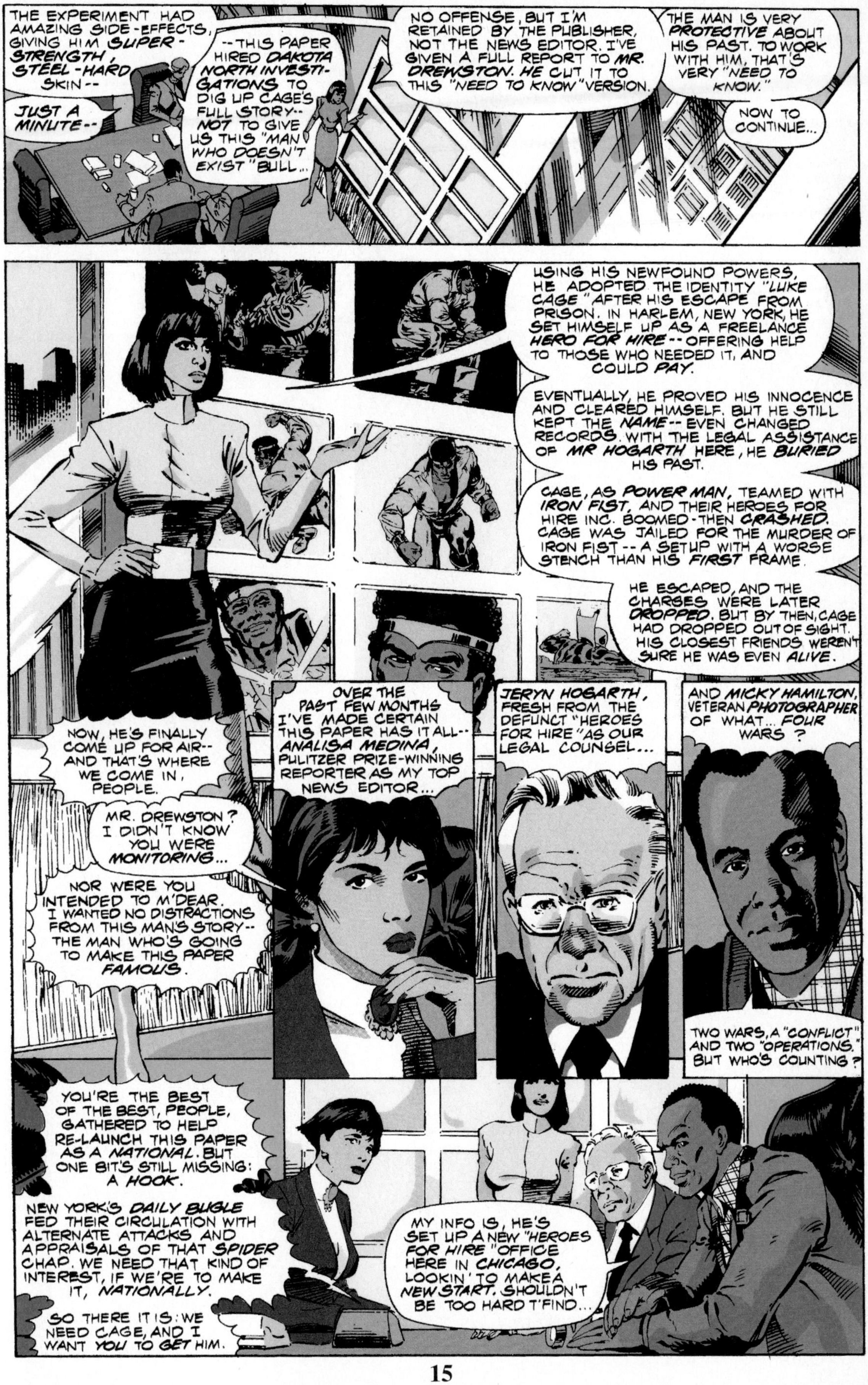
THE EXPERIMENT HAD AMAZING SIDE-EFFECTS, GIVING HIM SUPER-STRENGTH, STEEL-HARD SKIN--
JUST A MINUTE--
--THIS PAPER HIRED DAKOTA NORTH INVESTIGATIONS TO DIG UP CAGE'S FULL STORY-- NOT TO GIVE US THIS "MAN WHO DOESN'T EXIST" BULL...
NO OFFENSE, BUT I'M RETAINED BY THE PUBLISHER, NOT THE NEWS EDITOR. I'VE GIVEN A FULL REPORT TO MR. DREWSTON. HE CUT IT TO THIS "NEED TO KNOW" VERSION.
THE MAN IS VERY PROTECTIVE ABOUT HIS PAST. TO WORK WITH HIM, THAT'S VERY "NEED TO KNOW."
NOW TO CONTINUE...
USING HIS NEWFOUND POWERS, HE ADOPTED THE IDENTITY "LUKE CAGE" AFTER HIS ESCAPE FROM PRISON. IN HARLEM, NEW YORK, HE SET HIMSELF UP AS A FREELANCE HERO FOR HIRE-- OFFERING HELP TO THOSE WHO NEEDED IT, AND COULD PAY.
EVENTUALLY, HE PROVED HIS INNOCENCE AND CLEARED HIMSELF. BUT HE STILL KEPT THE NAME-- EVEN CHANGED RECORDS. WITH THE LEGAL ASSISTANCE OF MR HOGARTH HERE, HE BURIED HIS PAST.
CAGE, AS POWER MAN, TEAMED WITH IRON FIST, AND THEIR HEROES FOR HIRE INC. BOOMED-THEN CRASHED. CAGE WAS JAILED FOR THE MURDER OF IRON FIST -- A SETUP WITH A WORSE STENCH THAN HIS FIRST FRAME.
HE ESCAPED, AND THE CHARGES WERE LATER DROPPED. BUT BY THEN, CAGE HAD DROPPED OUT OF SIGHT. HIS CLOSEST FRIENDS WEREN'T SURE HE WAS EVEN ALIVE.
NOW, HE'S FINALLY COME UP FOR AIR-- AND THAT'S WHERE WE COME IN, PEOPLE.
OVER THE PAST FEW MONTHS I'VE MADE CERTAIN THIS PAPER HAS IT ALL-- ANALISA MEDINA, PULITZER PRIZE-WINNING REPORTER AS MY TOP NEWS EDITOR...
JERYN HOGARTH, FRESH FROM THE DEFUNCT "HEROES FOR HIRE" AS OUR LEGAL COUNSEL...
AND MICKY HAMILTON, VETERAN PHOTOGRAPHER OF WHAT... FOUR WARS?
MR. DREWSTON? I DIDN'T KNOW YOU WERE MONITORING...
NOR WERE YOU INTENDED TO M'DEAR. I WANTED NO DISTRACTIONS FROM THIS MAN'S STORY-- THE MAN WHO'S GOING TO MAKE THIS PAPER FAMOUS.
TWO WARS, A "CONFLICT" AND TWO "OPERATIONS." BUT WHO'S COUNTING?
YOU'RE THE BEST OF THE BEST, PEOPLE, GATHERED TO HELP RE-LAUNCH THIS PAPER AS A NATIONAL. BUT ONE BIT'S STILL MISSING: A HOOK.
NEW YORK'S DAILY BUGLE FED THEIR CIRCULATION WITH ALTERNATE ATTACKS AND APPRAISALS OF THAT SPIDER CHAP. WE NEED THAT KIND OF INTEREST, IF WE'RE TO MAKE IT, NATIONALLY.
SO THERE IT IS: WE NEED CAGE, AND I WANT YOU TO GET HIM.
MY INFO IS, HE'S SET UP A NEW "HEROES FOR HIRE" OFFICE HERE IN CHICAGO, LOOKIN' TO MAKE A NEW START. SHOULDN'T BE TOO HARD T'FIND...

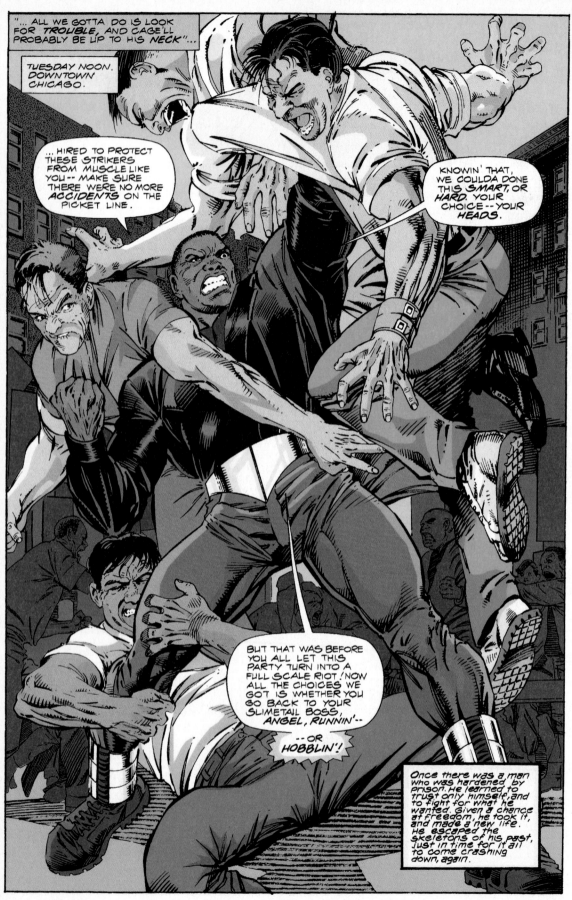

"...ALL WE GOTTA DO IS LOOK FOR *TROUBLE*, AND CAGE'LL PROBABLY BE *UP* TO HIS *NECK*"...

TUESDAY NOON. DOWNTOWN CHICAGO.

...HIRED TO PROTECT THESE STRIKERS FROM MUSCLE LIKE YOU -- MAKE SURE THERE WERE NO MORE *ACCIDENTS* ON THE PICKET LINE.

KNOWIN' THAT, WE COULDA DONE THIS *SMART*, OR *HARD*. YOUR CHOICE -- YOUR *HEADS*.

BUT THAT WAS BEFORE YOU ALL LET THIS PARTY TURN INTO A FULL SCALE RIOT! NOW ALL THE CHOICES WE GOT IS WHETHER YOU GO BACK TO YOUR SLIMETAIL BOSS, ANGEL, RUNNIN'--

--OR *HOBBLIN'!*

Once there was a man who was hardened by prison. He learned to trust only himself, and to fight for what he wanted. Given a chance at freedom, he took it, and made a new life. He escaped the skeletons of his past, just in time for it all to come crashing down, again.

16

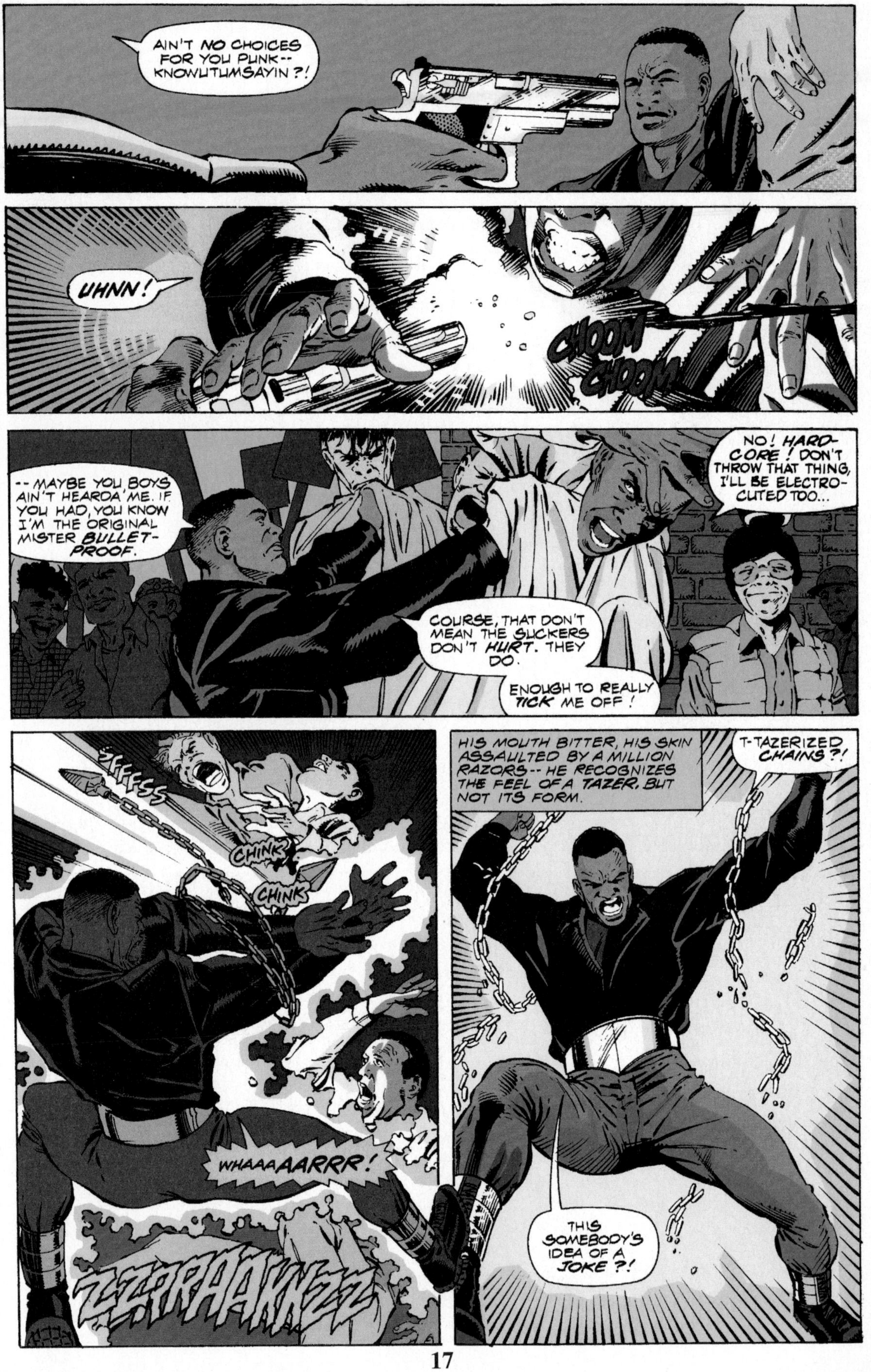

AIN'T NO CHOICES FOR YOU PUNK-- KNOWUTUMSAYIN?!
UHNN!
CHOOM CHOOM
--MAYBE YOU BOYS AIN'T HEARDA' ME. IF YOU HAD, YOU KNOW I'M THE ORIGINAL MISTER BULLET-PROOF.
NO! HARD-CORE! DON'T THROW THAT THING, I'LL BE ELECTRO-CUTED TOO...
COURSE, THAT DON'T MEAN THE SUCKERS DON'T HURT. THEY DO.
ENOUGH TO REALLY TICK ME OFF!
SFFFSS
CHINK
CHINK
WHAAAAARRR!
ZZZRAAKKZZ
HIS MOUTH BITTER, HIS SKIN ASSAULTED BY A MILLION RAZORS-- HE RECOGNIZES THE FEEL OF A TAZER. BUT NOT ITS FORM.
T-TAZERIZED CHAINS?!
THIS SOMEBODY'S IDEA OF A JOKE?!

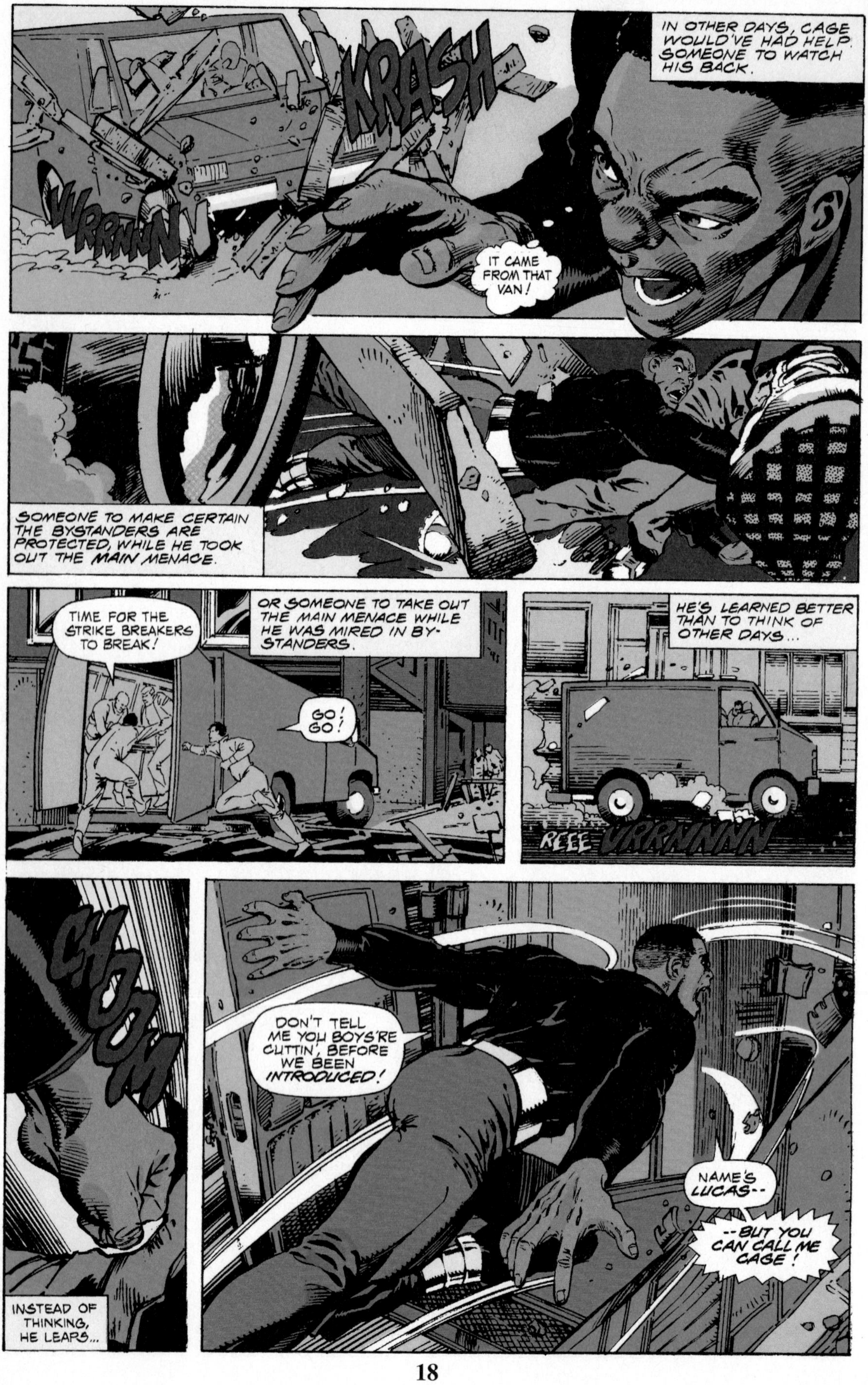

IN OTHER DAYS, CAGE WOULD'VE HAD HELP. SOMEONE TO WATCH HIS BACK.
KRASH
VRRRNNN
IT CAME FROM THAT VAN!
SOMEONE TO MAKE CERTAIN THE BYSTANDERS ARE PROTECTED, WHILE HE TOOK OUT THE MAIN MENACE.
TIME FOR THE STRIKE BREAKERS TO BREAK!
OR SOMEONE TO TAKE OUT THE MAIN MENACE WHILE HE WAS MIRED IN BY-STANDERS.
GO! GO!
HE'S LEARNED BETTER THAN TO THINK OF OTHER DAYS...
REEE VRRNNNN
CHOOM
INSTEAD OF THINKING, HE LEAPS...
DON'T TELL ME YOU BOYS'RE CUTTIN', BEFORE WE BEEN INTRODUCED!
NAME'S LUCAS--
--BUT YOU CAN CALL ME CAGE!

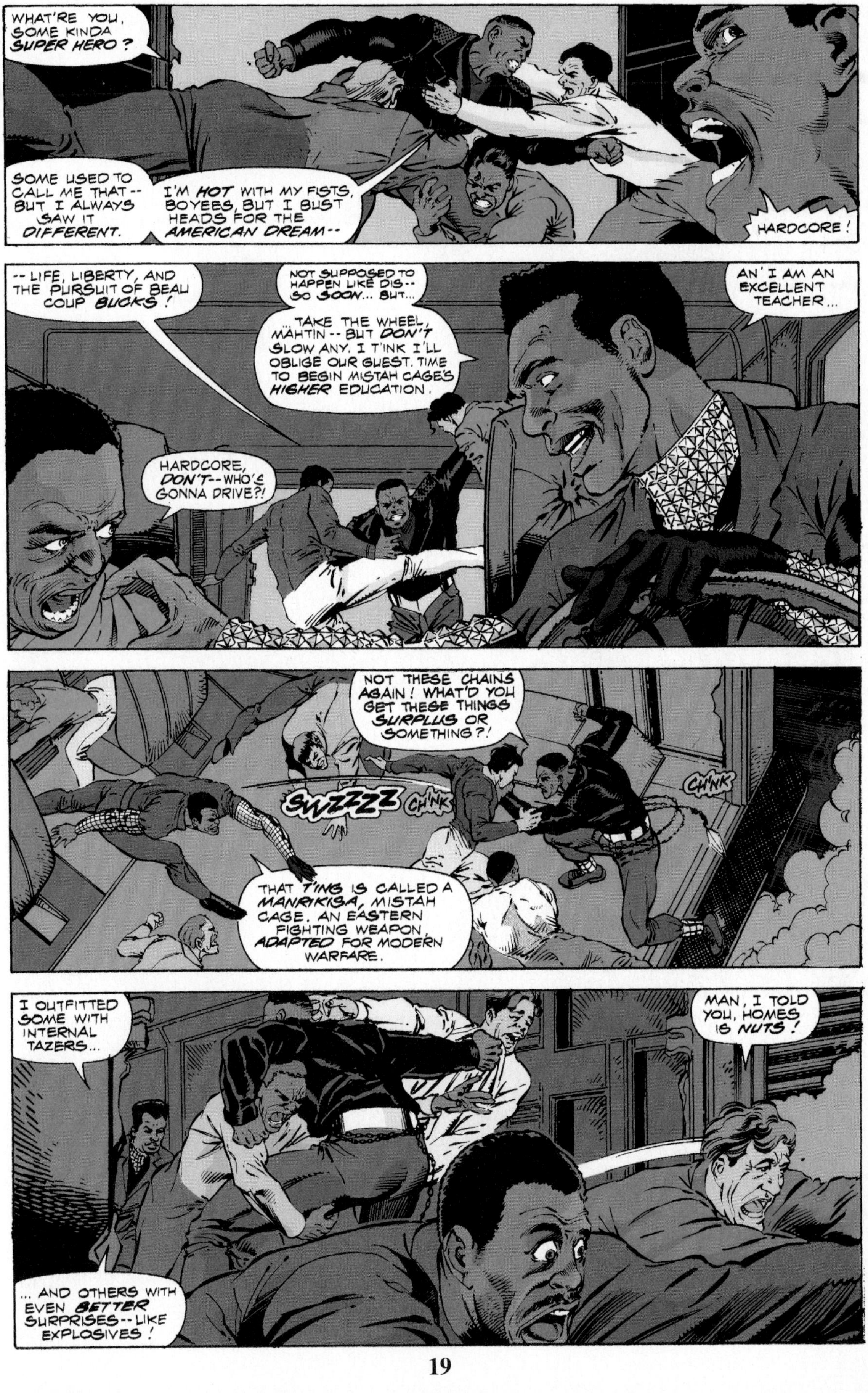
WHAT'RE YOU, SOME KINDA SUPER HERO?
SOME USED TO CALL ME THAT-- BUT I ALWAYS SAW IT DIFFERENT.
I'M HOT WITH MY FISTS, BOYEES, BUT I BUST HEADS FOR THE AMERICAN DREAM--
HARDCORE!
--LIFE, LIBERTY, AND THE PURSUIT OF BEAU COUP BUCKS!
NOT SUPPOSED TO HAPPEN LIKE DIS-- SO SOON... BUT...
...TAKE THE WHEEL, MAHTIN-- BUT DON'T SLOW ANY. I T'INK I'LL OBLIGE OUR GUEST. TIME TO BEGIN MISTAH CAGE'S HIGHER EDUCATION.
AN' I AM AN EXCELLENT TEACHER...
HARDCORE, DON'T--WHO'S GONNA DRIVE?!
NOT THESE CHAINS AGAIN! WHAT'D YOU GET THESE THINGS SURPLUS OR SOMETHING?!
SWZZZZ
CH'NK
CH'NK
THAT T'ING IS CALLED A MANRIKISA, MISTAH CAGE. AN EASTERN FIGHTING WEAPON, ADAPTED FOR MODERN WARFARE.
I OUTFITTED SOME WITH INTERNAL TAZERS...
MAN, I TOLD YOU, HOMES IS NUTS!
...AND OTHERS WITH EVEN BETTER SURPRISES--LIKE EXPLOSIVES!

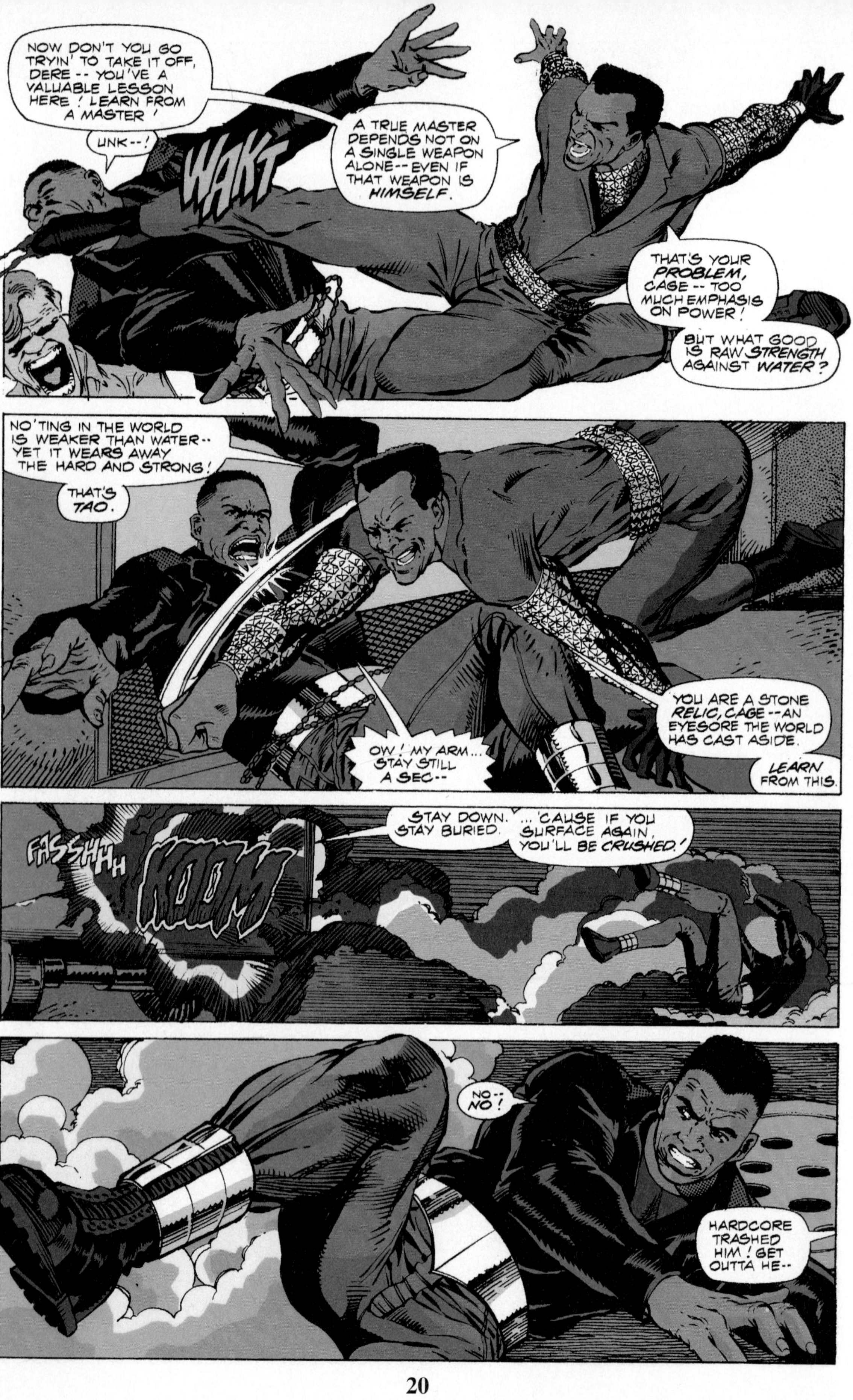
NOW DON'T YOU GO TRYIN' TO TAKE IT OFF, DERE -- YOU'VE A VALUABLE LESSON HERE! LEARN FROM A MASTER!
UNK--!
WAKT
A TRUE MASTER DEPENDS NOT ON A SINGLE WEAPON ALONE--EVEN IF THAT WEAPON IS HIMSELF.
THAT'S YOUR PROBLEM, CAGE -- TOO MUCH EMPHASIS ON POWER!
BUT WHAT GOOD IS RAW STRENGTH AGAINST WATER?
NO'TING IN THE WORLD IS WEAKER THAN WATER-- YET IT WEARS AWAY THE HARD AND STRONG!
THAT'S TAO.
YOU ARE A STONE RELIC, CAGE--AN EYESORE THE WORLD HAS CAST ASIDE.
LEARN FROM THIS.
OW! MY ARM... STAY STILL A SEC--
FASSHHH
KOOM
STAY DOWN. STAY BURIED.
...'CAUSE IF YOU SURFACE AGAIN, YOU'LL BE CRUSHED!
NO-- NO!
HARDCORE TRASHED HIM! GET OUTTA HE--

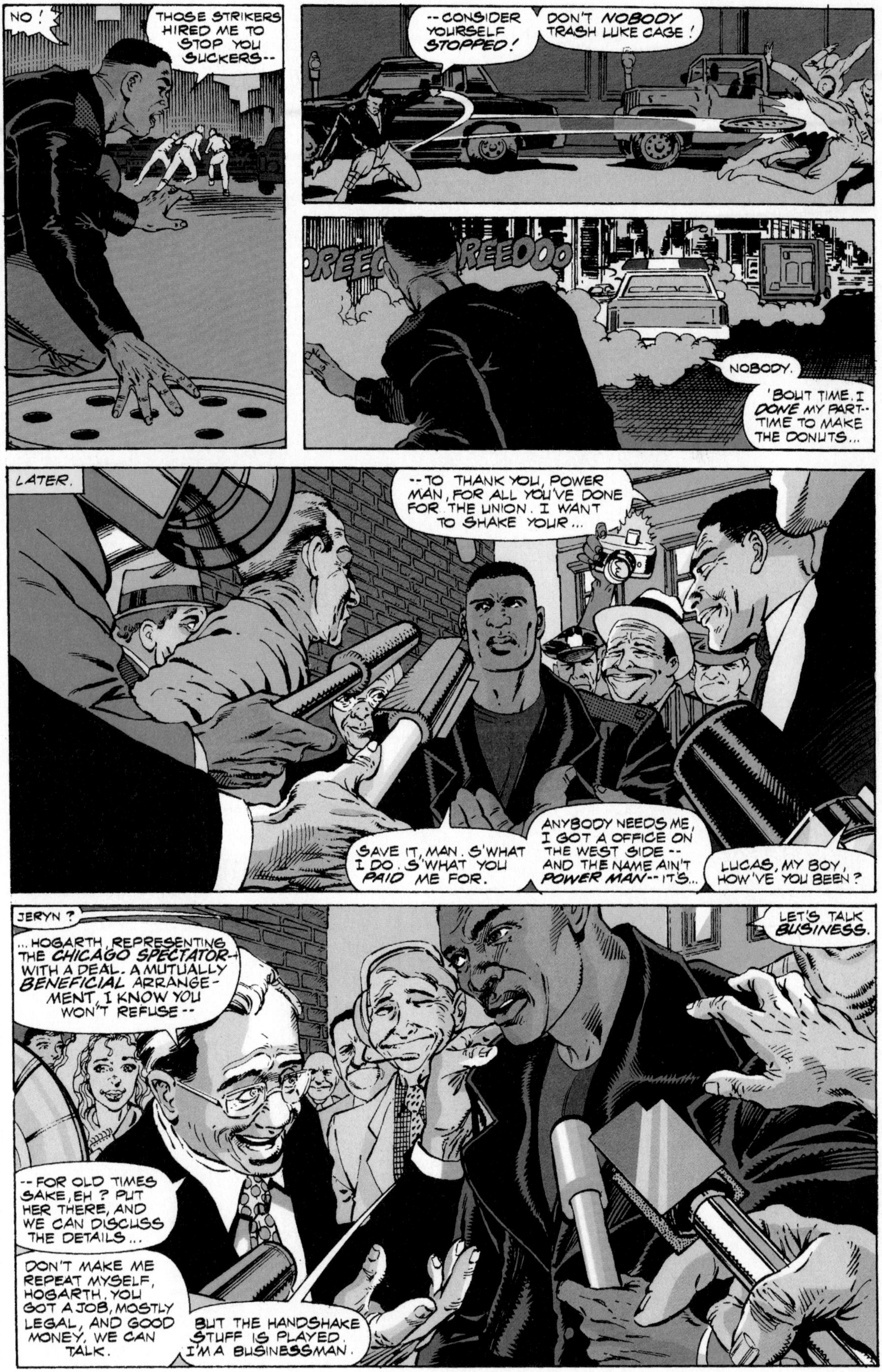
NO!
THOSE STRIKERS HIRED ME TO STOP YOU SUCKERS--
--CONSIDER YOURSELF STOPPED!
DON'T NOBODY TRASH LUKE CAGE!
REEEC
REEDOOO
NOBODY.
'BOUT TIME. I DONE MY PART--TIME TO MAKE THE DONUTS...
LATER.
--TO THANK YOU, POWER MAN, FOR ALL YOU'VE DONE FOR THE UNION. I WANT TO SHAKE YOUR...
SAVE IT, MAN. S'WHAT I DO. S'WHAT YOU PAID ME FOR.
ANYBODY NEEDS ME, I GOT A OFFICE ON THE WEST SIDE--AND THE NAME AIN'T POWER MAN--IT'S...
LUCAS, MY BOY, HOW'VE YOU BEEN?
JERYN?
...HOGARTH, REPRESENTING THE CHICAGO SPECTATOR--WITH A DEAL. A MUTUALLY BENEFICIAL ARRANGEMENT, I KNOW YOU WON'T REFUSE--
LET'S TALK BUSINESS.
--FOR OLD TIMES SAKE, EH? PUT HER THERE, AND WE CAN DISCUSS THE DETAILS...
DON'T MAKE ME REPEAT MYSELF, HOGARTH. YOU GOT A JOB, MOSTLY LEGAL, AND GOOD MONEY, WE CAN TALK.
BUT THE HANDSHAKE STUFF IS PLAYED. I'M A BUSINESSMAN.

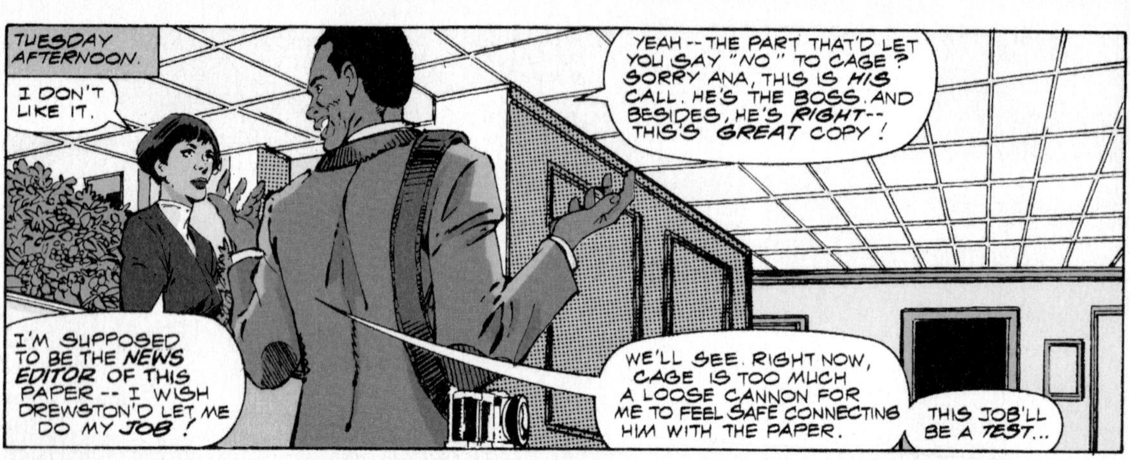
TUESDAY AFTERNOON.
I DON'T LIKE IT.
YEAH -- THE PART THAT'D LET YOU SAY "NO" TO CAGE? SORRY ANA, THIS IS HIS CALL. HE'S THE BOSS. AND BESIDES, HE'S RIGHT -- THIS'S GREAT COPY!
I'M SUPPOSED TO BE THE NEWS EDITOR OF THIS PAPER -- I WISH DREWSTON'D LET ME DO MY JOB!
WE'LL SEE. RIGHT NOW, CAGE IS TOO MUCH A LOOSE CANNON FOR ME TO FEEL SAFE CONNECTING HIM WITH THE PAPER.
THIS JOB'LL BE A TEST...

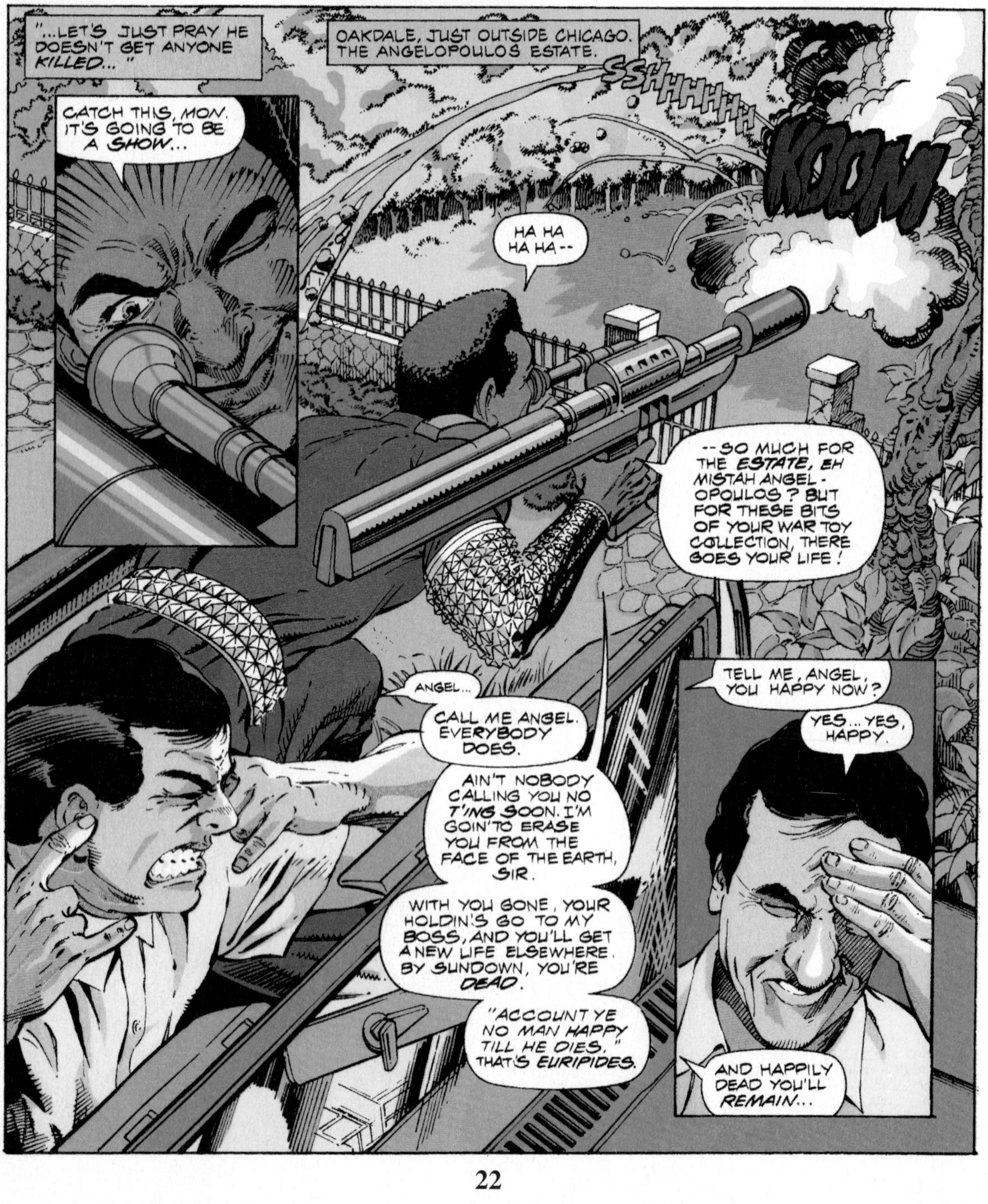
"...LET'S JUST PRAY HE DOESN'T GET ANYONE KILLED..."
OAKDALE, JUST OUTSIDE CHICAGO. THE ANGELOPOULOS ESTATE.
SSHHHHHH
KOOM
CATCH THIS, MON. IT'S GOING TO BE A SHOW...
HA HA HA HA --
-- SO MUCH FOR THE ESTATE, EH MISTAH ANGEL-OPOULOS? BUT FOR THESE BITS OF YOUR WAR TOY COLLECTION, THERE GOES YOUR LIFE!
ANGEL...
CALL ME ANGEL. EVERYBODY DOES.
AIN'T NOBODY CALLING YOU NO T'ING SOON. I'M GOIN' TO ERASE YOU FROM THE FACE OF THE EARTH, SIR.
WITH YOU GONE, YOUR HOLDIN'S GO TO MY BOSS, AND YOU'LL GET A NEW LIFE ELSEWHERE. BY SUNDOWN, YOU'RE DEAD.
"ACCOUNT YE NO MAN HAPPY TILL HE DIES." THAT'S EURIPIDES.
TELL ME, ANGEL, YOU HAPPY NOW?
YES... YES, HAPPY.
AND HAPPILY DEAD YOU'LL REMAIN...

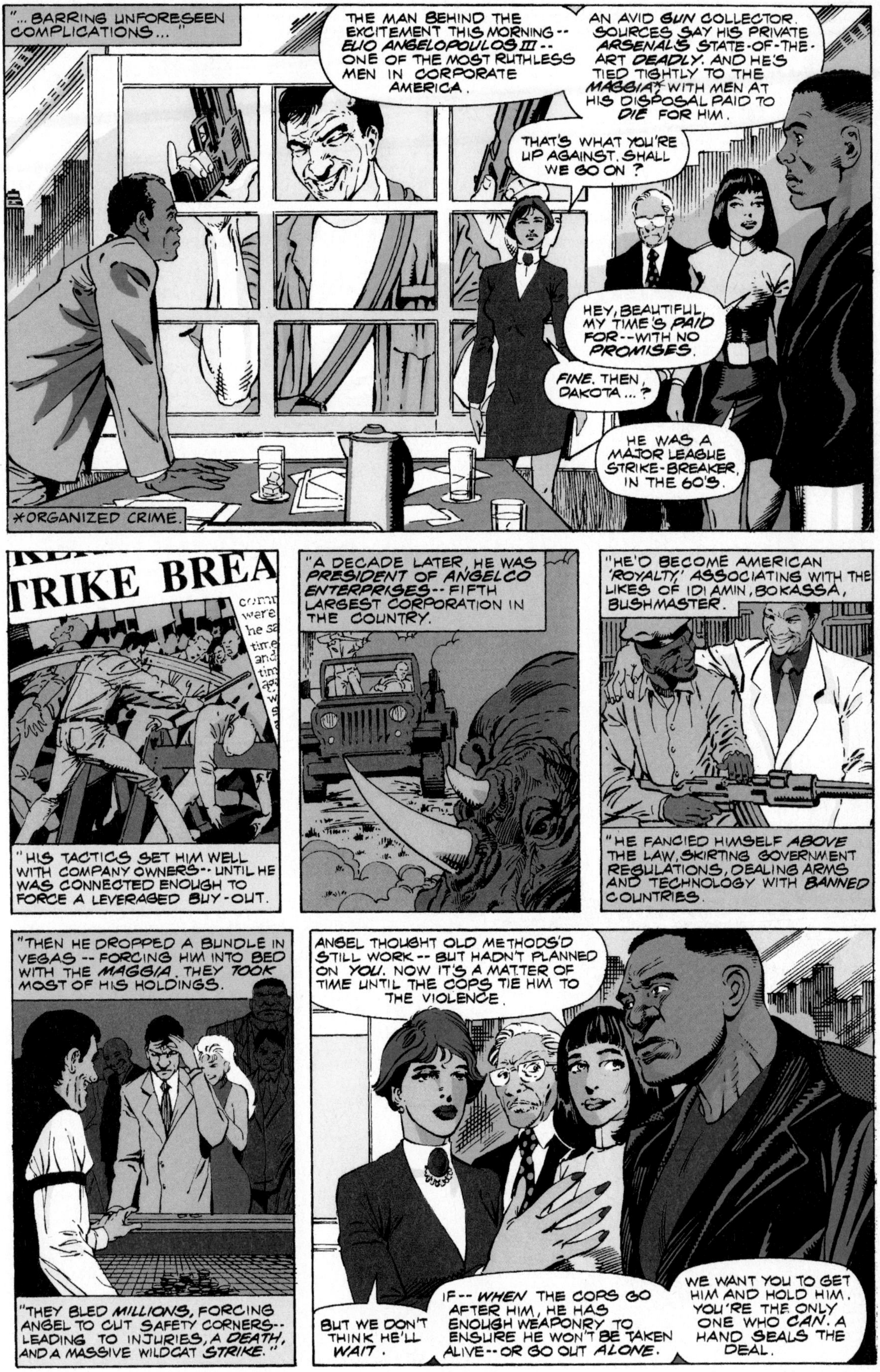
"... BARRING UNFORESEEN COMPLICATIONS ..."
THE MAN BEHIND THE EXCITEMENT THIS MORNING -- ELIO ANGELOPOULOS III -- ONE OF THE MOST RUTHLESS MEN IN CORPORATE AMERICA.
AN AVID GUN COLLECTOR. SOURCES SAY HIS PRIVATE ARSENAL'S STATE-OF-THE-ART DEADLY. AND HE'S TIED TIGHTLY TO THE MAGGIA* WITH MEN AT HIS DISPOSAL PAID TO DIE FOR HIM.
THAT'S WHAT YOU'RE UP AGAINST. SHALL WE GO ON?
HEY, BEAUTIFUL, MY TIME'S PAID FOR--WITH NO PROMISES.
FINE. THEN, DAKOTA ...?
HE WAS A MAJOR LEAGUE STRIKE-BREAKER, IN THE 60'S.
*ORGANIZED CRIME.
TRIKE BREA
"HIS TACTICS SET HIM WELL WITH COMPANY OWNERS-- UNTIL HE WAS CONNECTED ENOUGH TO FORCE A LEVERAGED BUY-OUT.
"A DECADE LATER, HE WAS PRESIDENT OF ANGELCO ENTERPRISES-- FIFTH LARGEST CORPORATION IN THE COUNTRY.
"HE'D BECOME AMERICAN 'ROYALTY,' ASSOCIATING WITH THE LIKES OF IDI AMIN, BOKASSA, BUSHMASTER.
"HE FANCIED HIMSELF ABOVE THE LAW, SKIRTING GOVERNMENT REGULATIONS, DEALING ARMS AND TECHNOLOGY WITH BANNED COUNTRIES.
"THEN HE DROPPED A BUNDLE IN VEGAS -- FORCING HIM INTO BED WITH THE MAGGIA. THEY TOOK MOST OF HIS HOLDINGS.
"THEY BLED MILLIONS, FORCING ANGEL TO CUT SAFETY CORNERS-- LEADING TO INJURIES, A DEATH, AND A MASSIVE WILDCAT STRIKE."
ANGEL THOUGHT OLD METHODS'D STILL WORK -- BUT HADN'T PLANNED ON YOU. NOW IT'S A MATTER OF TIME UNTIL THE COPS TIE HIM TO THE VIOLENCE.
BUT WE DON'T THINK HE'LL WAIT.
IF -- WHEN THE COPS GO AFTER HIM, HE HAS ENOUGH WEAPONRY TO ENSURE HE WON'T BE TAKEN ALIVE -- OR GO OUT ALONE.
WE WANT YOU TO GET HIM AND HOLD HIM. YOU'RE THE ONLY ONE WHO CAN. A HAND SEALS THE DEAL.

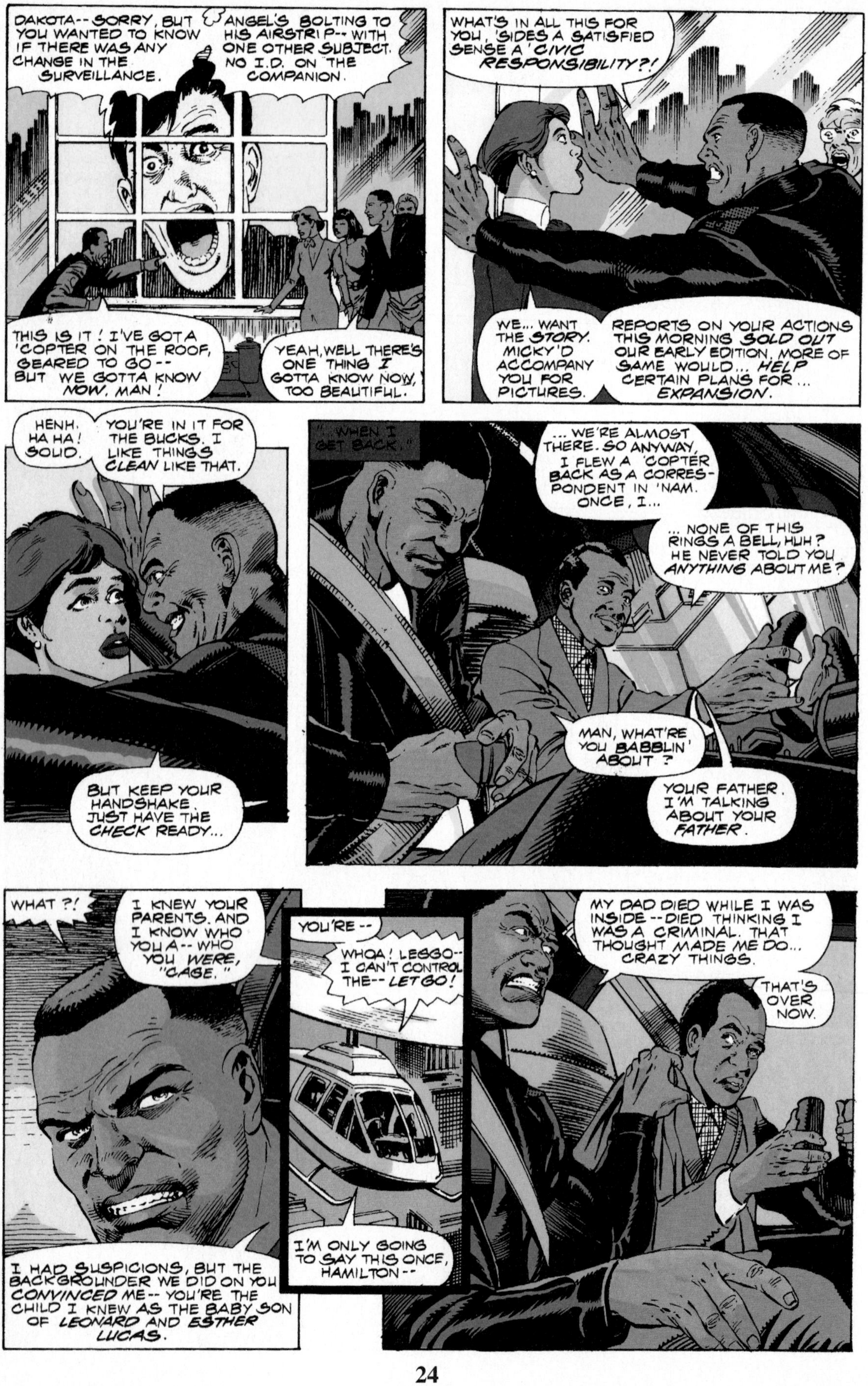
DAKOTA-- SORRY, BUT YOU WANTED TO KNOW IF THERE WAS ANY CHANGE IN THE SURVEILLANCE.
ANGEL'S BOLTING TO HIS AIRSTRIP-- WITH ONE OTHER SUBJECT. NO I.D. ON THE COMPANION.
THIS IS IT! I'VE GOT A 'COPTER ON THE ROOF, GEARED TO GO -- BUT WE GOTTA KNOW NOW, MAN!
YEAH, WELL THERE'S ONE THING I GOTTA KNOW NOW, TOO BEAUTIFUL.
WHAT'S IN ALL THIS FOR YOU, 'SIDES A SATISFIED SENSE A 'CIVIC RESPONSIBILITY?!
WE... WANT THE STORY. MICKY'D ACCOMPANY YOU FOR PICTURES.
REPORTS ON YOUR ACTIONS THIS MORNING SOLD OUT OUR EARLY EDITION. MORE OF SAME WOULD... HELP CERTAIN PLANS FOR... EXPANSION.
HENH. HA HA! SOLID.
YOU'RE IN IT FOR THE BUCKS. I LIKE THINGS CLEAN LIKE THAT.
BUT KEEP YOUR HANDSHAKE. JUST HAVE THE CHECK READY...
"...WHEN I GET BACK."
...WE'RE ALMOST THERE. SO ANYWAY, I FLEW A 'COPTER BACK AS A CORRESPONDENT IN 'NAM. ONCE, I...
...NONE OF THIS RINGS A BELL, HUH? HE NEVER TOLD YOU ANYTHING ABOUT ME?
MAN, WHAT'RE YOU BABBLIN' ABOUT?
YOUR FATHER. I'M TALKING ABOUT YOUR FATHER.
WHAT?!
I KNEW YOUR PARENTS. AND I KNOW WHO YOU A-- WHO YOU WERE, "CAGE."
I HAD SUSPICIONS, BUT THE BACKGROUNDER WE DID ON YOU CONVINCED ME-- YOU'RE THE CHILD I KNEW AS THE BABY SON OF LEONARD AND ESTHER LUCAS.
YOU'RE --
WHOA! LEGGO-- I CAN'T CONTROL THE-- LET GO!
I'M ONLY GOING TO SAY THIS ONCE, HAMILTON --
MY DAD DIED WHILE I WAS INSIDE -- DIED THINKING I WAS A CRIMINAL. THAT THOUGHT MADE ME DO... CRAZY THINGS.
THAT'S OVER NOW.

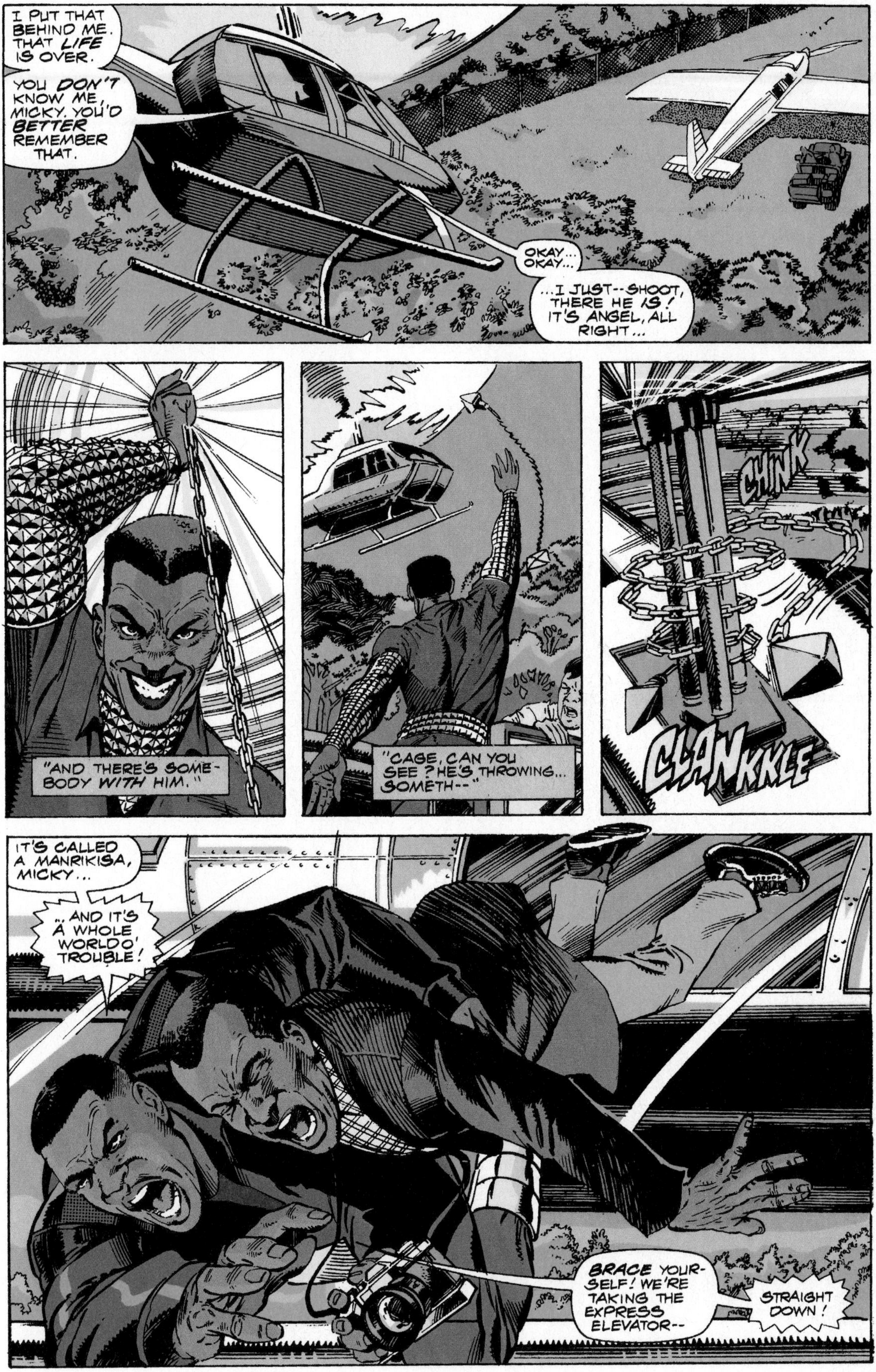
I PUT THAT BEHIND ME. THAT LIFE IS OVER.
YOU DON'T KNOW ME, MICKY. YOU'D BETTER REMEMBER THAT.
OKAY... OKAY...
...I JUST--SHOOT, THERE HE IS! IT'S ANGEL, ALL RIGHT...
"AND THERE'S SOME-BODY WITH HIM."
"CAGE, CAN YOU SEE? HE'S THROWING... SOMETH--"
CHINK
CLANKKLE
IT'S CALLED A MANRIKISA, MICKY...
...AND IT'S A WHOLE WORLD O' TROUBLE!
BRACE YOUR-SELF! WE'RE TAKING THE EXPRESS ELEVATOR--
STRAIGHT DOWN!

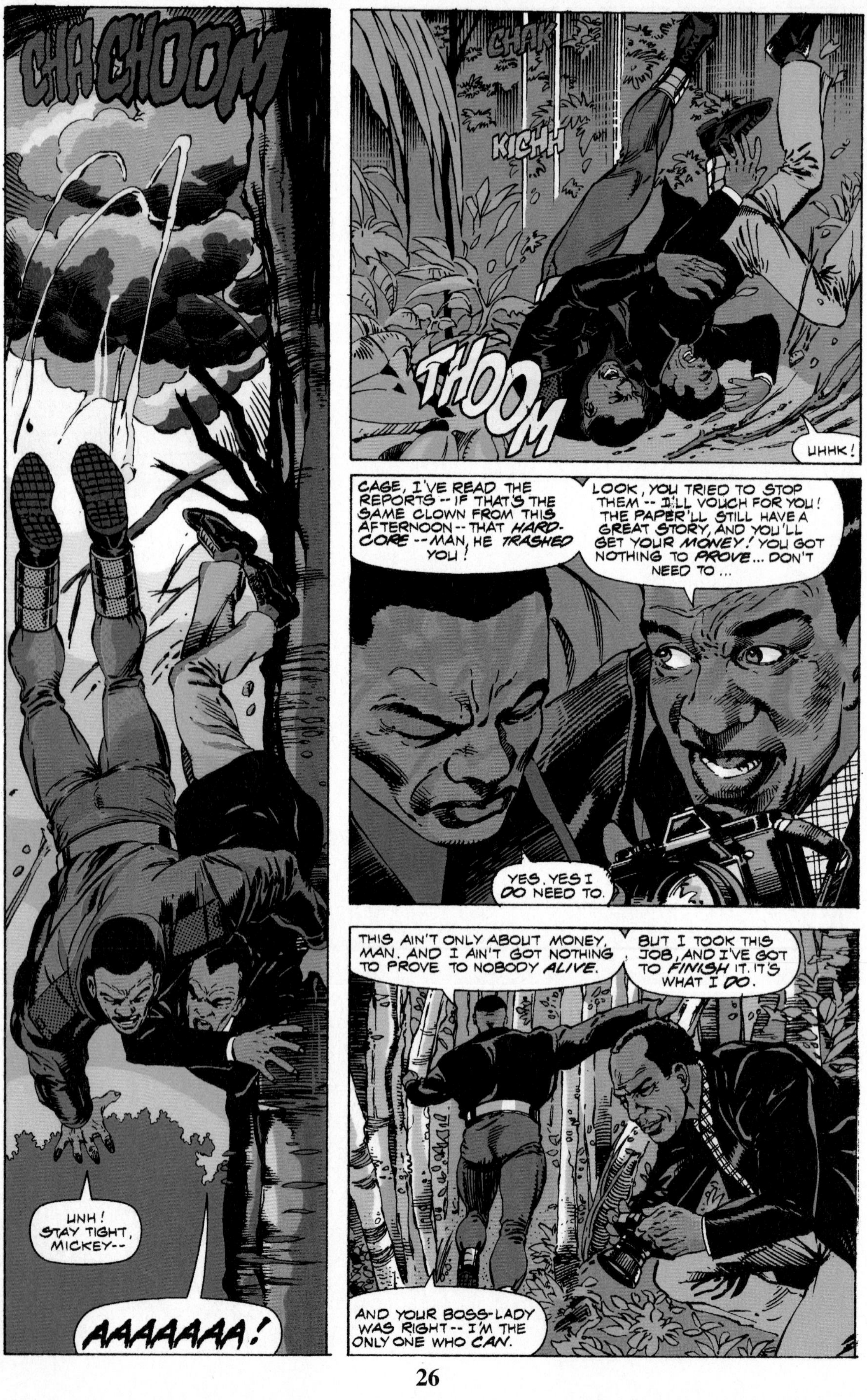
CHACHOOM
UNH! STAY TIGHT, MICKEY--
AAAAAAA!
CHAK
KICHH
THOOM
UHHK!
CAGE, I'VE READ THE REPORTS -- IF THAT'S THE SAME CLOWN FROM THIS AFTERNOON -- THAT HARD-CORE -- MAN, HE TRASHED YOU!
LOOK, YOU TRIED TO STOP THEM -- I'LL VOUCH FOR YOU! THE PAPER'LL STILL HAVE A GREAT STORY, AND YOU'LL GET YOUR MONEY! YOU GOT NOTHING TO PROVE... DON'T NEED TO...
YES. YES I DO NEED TO.
THIS AIN'T ONLY ABOUT MONEY, MAN. AND I AIN'T GOT NOTHING TO PROVE TO NOBODY ALIVE.
BUT I TOOK THIS JOB, AND I'VE GOT TO FINISH IT. IT'S WHAT I DO.
AND YOUR BOSS-LADY WAS RIGHT -- I'M THE ONLY ONE WHO CAN.

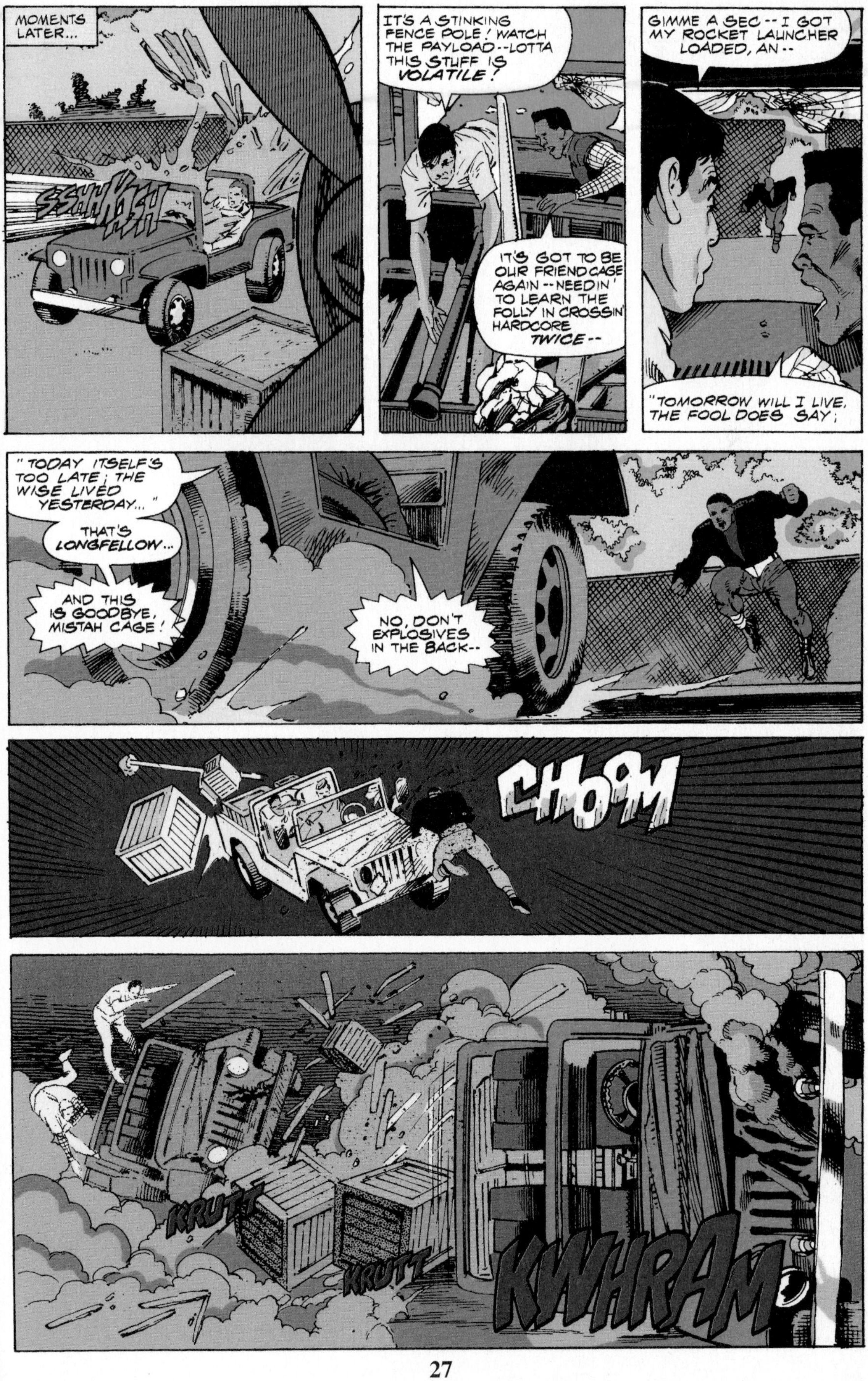
MOMENTS LATER...
SSHHKKSH
IT'S A STINKING FENCE POLE! WATCH THE PAYLOAD--LOTTA THIS STUFF IS VOLATILE!
IT'S GOT TO BE OUR FRIEND CAGE AGAIN--NEEDIN' TO LEARN THE FOLLY IN CROSSIN' HARDCORE TWICE--
GIMME A SEC--I GOT MY ROCKET LAUNCHER LOADED, AN--
"TOMORROW WILL I LIVE, THE FOOL DOES SAY;
"TODAY ITSELF'S TOO LATE; THE WISE LIVED YESTERDAY..."
THAT'S LONGFELLOW...
AND THIS IS GOODBYE, MISTAH CAGE!
NO, DON'T EXPLOSIVES IN THE BACK--
CHOOM
KRUTT
KRUTT
KWHRAM

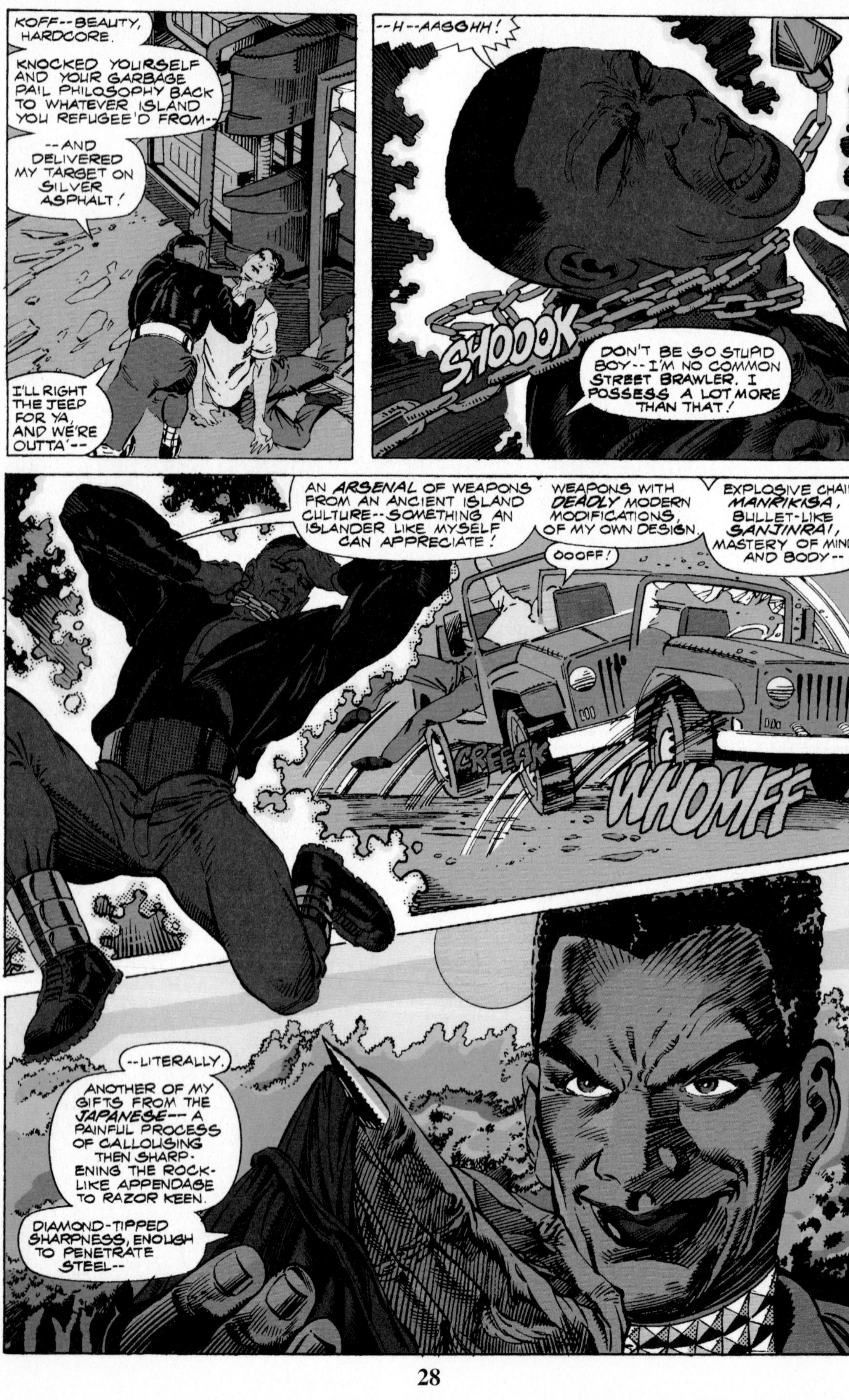
KOFF--BEAUTY, HARDCORE.
KNOCKED YOURSELF AND YOUR GARBAGE PAIL PHILOSOPHY BACK TO WHATEVER ISLAND YOU REFUGEE'D FROM--
--AND DELIVERED MY TARGET ON SILVER ASPHALT!
I'LL RIGHT THE JEEP FOR YA, AND WE'RE OUTTA'--
--H--AASGHH!
SHOOOK
DON'T BE SO STUPID BOY--I'M NO COMMON STREET BRAWLER. I POSSESS A LOT MORE THAN THAT!
AN ARSENAL OF WEAPONS FROM AN ANCIENT ISLAND CULTURE--SOMETHING AN ISLANDER LIKE MYSELF CAN APPRECIATE!
WEAPONS WITH DEADLY MODERN MODIFICATIONS, OF MY OWN DESIGN.
EXPLOSIVE CHAIN MANRIKISA, BULLET-LIKE SANJINRAI, MASTERY OF MIND AND BODY--
OOOFF!
CREEAK
WHOMFF
--LITERALLY.
ANOTHER OF MY GIFTS FROM THE JAPANESE-- A PAINFUL PROCESS OF CALLOUSING THEN SHARPENING THE ROCK-LIKE APPENDAGE TO RAZOR KEEN.
DIAMOND-TIPPED SHARPNESS, ENOUGH TO PENETRATE STEEL--

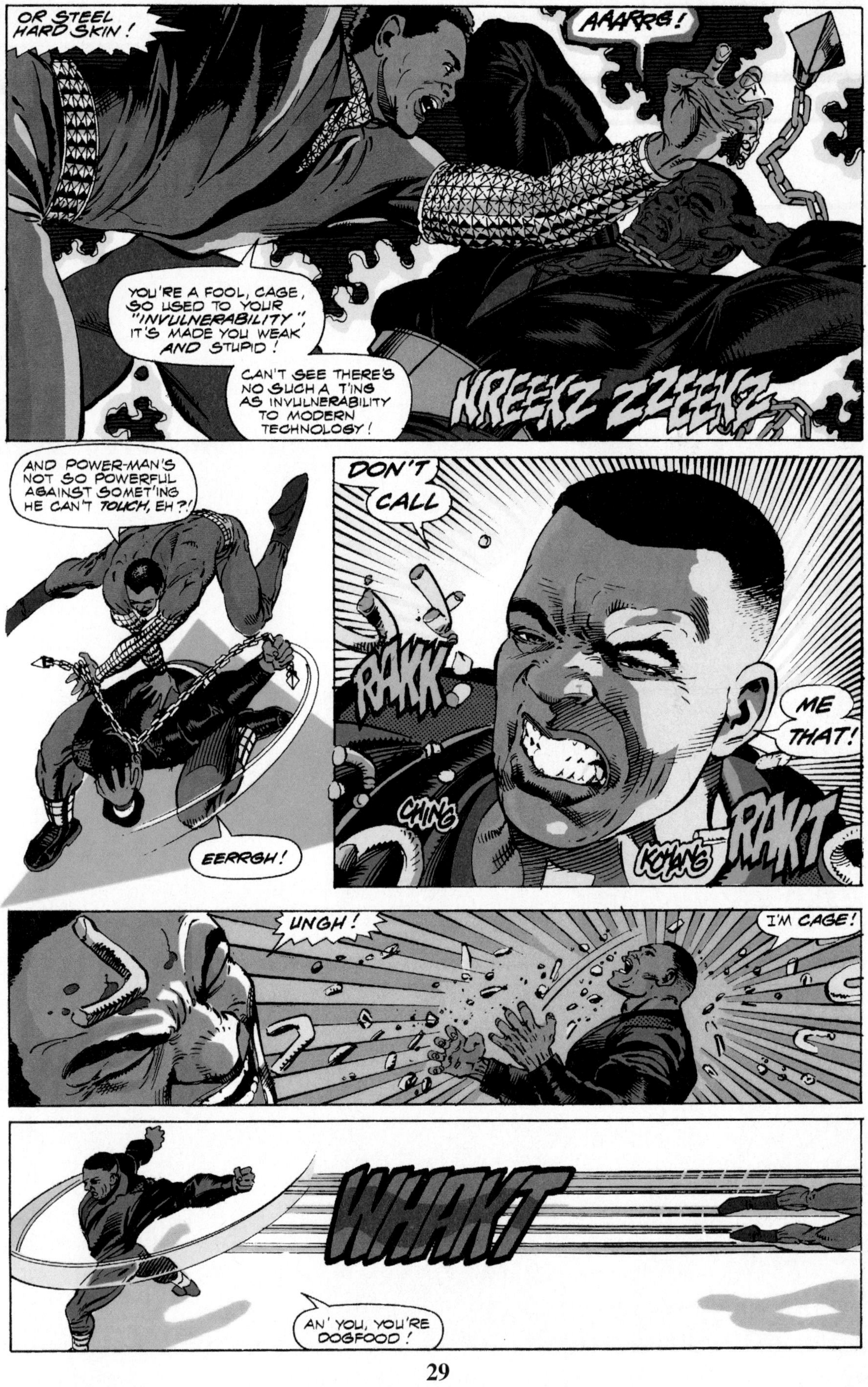
OR STEEL HARD SKIN!
AAARRG!
YOU'RE A FOOL, CAGE, SO USED TO YOUR "INVULNERABILITY", IT'S MADE YOU WEAK AND STUPID!
CAN'T SEE THERE'S NO SUCH A T'ING AS INVULNERABILITY TO MODERN TECHNOLOGY!
KREEKZ ZZEEKZ
AND POWER-MAN'S NOT SO POWERFUL AGAINST SOMET'ING HE CAN'T TOUCH, EH?!
EERRGH!
DON'T
CALL
RAKK
ME
THAT!
CHING
KCHANG
RAKT
UNGH!
I'M CAGE!
WHAKT
AN' YOU, YOU'RE DOGFOOD!

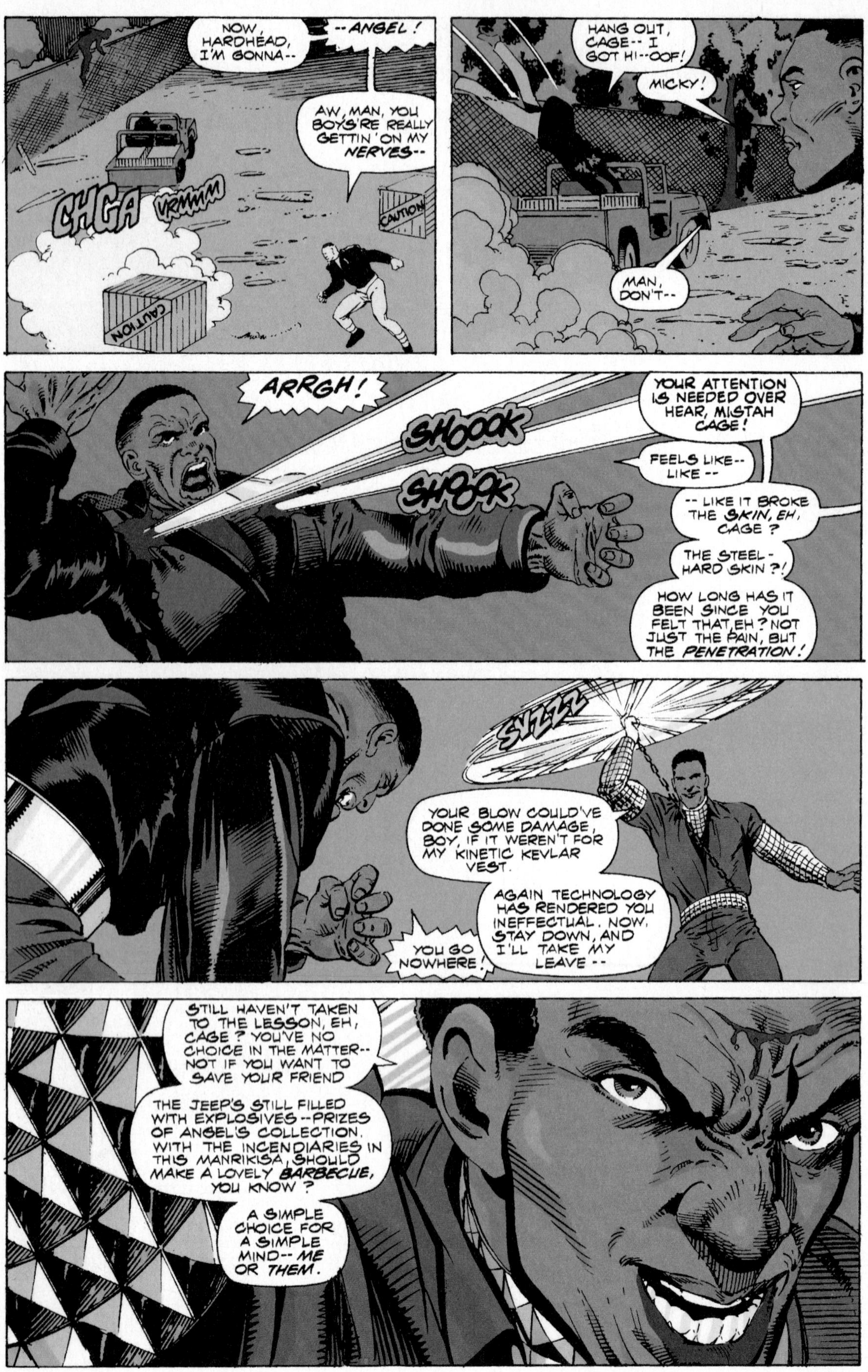
NOW, HARDHEAD, I'M GONNA--
--ANGEL!
AW, MAN, YOU BOYS'RE REALLY GETTIN' ON MY NERVES--
CHGA
VRMMM
CAUTION
CAUTION
HANG OUT, CAGE-- I GOT HI--OOF!
MICKY!
MAN, DON'T--
ARRGH!
SHOOOK
SHOOK
YOUR ATTENTION IS NEEDED OVER HEAR, MISTAH CAGE!
FEELS LIKE-- LIKE --
-- LIKE IT BROKE THE SKIN, EH, CAGE?
THE STEEL-HARD SKIN?!
HOW LONG HAS IT BEEN SINCE YOU FELT THAT, EH? NOT JUST THE PAIN, BUT THE PENETRATION!
SYZZZ
YOUR BLOW COULD'VE DONE SOME DAMAGE, BOY, IF IT WEREN'T FOR MY KINETIC KEVLAR VEST.
AGAIN TECHNOLOGY HAS RENDERED YOU INEFFECTUAL. NOW, STAY DOWN, AND I'LL TAKE MY LEAVE --
YOU GO NOWHERE!
STILL HAVEN'T TAKEN TO THE LESSON, EH, CAGE? YOU'VE NO CHOICE IN THE MATTER-- NOT IF YOU WANT TO SAVE YOUR FRIEND
THE JEEP'S STILL FILLED WITH EXPLOSIVES--PRIZES OF ANGEL'S COLLECTION. WITH THE INCENDIARIES IN THIS MANRIKISA, SHOULD MAKE A LOVELY BARBECUE, YOU KNOW?
A SIMPLE CHOICE FOR A SIMPLE MIND-- ME OR THEM.

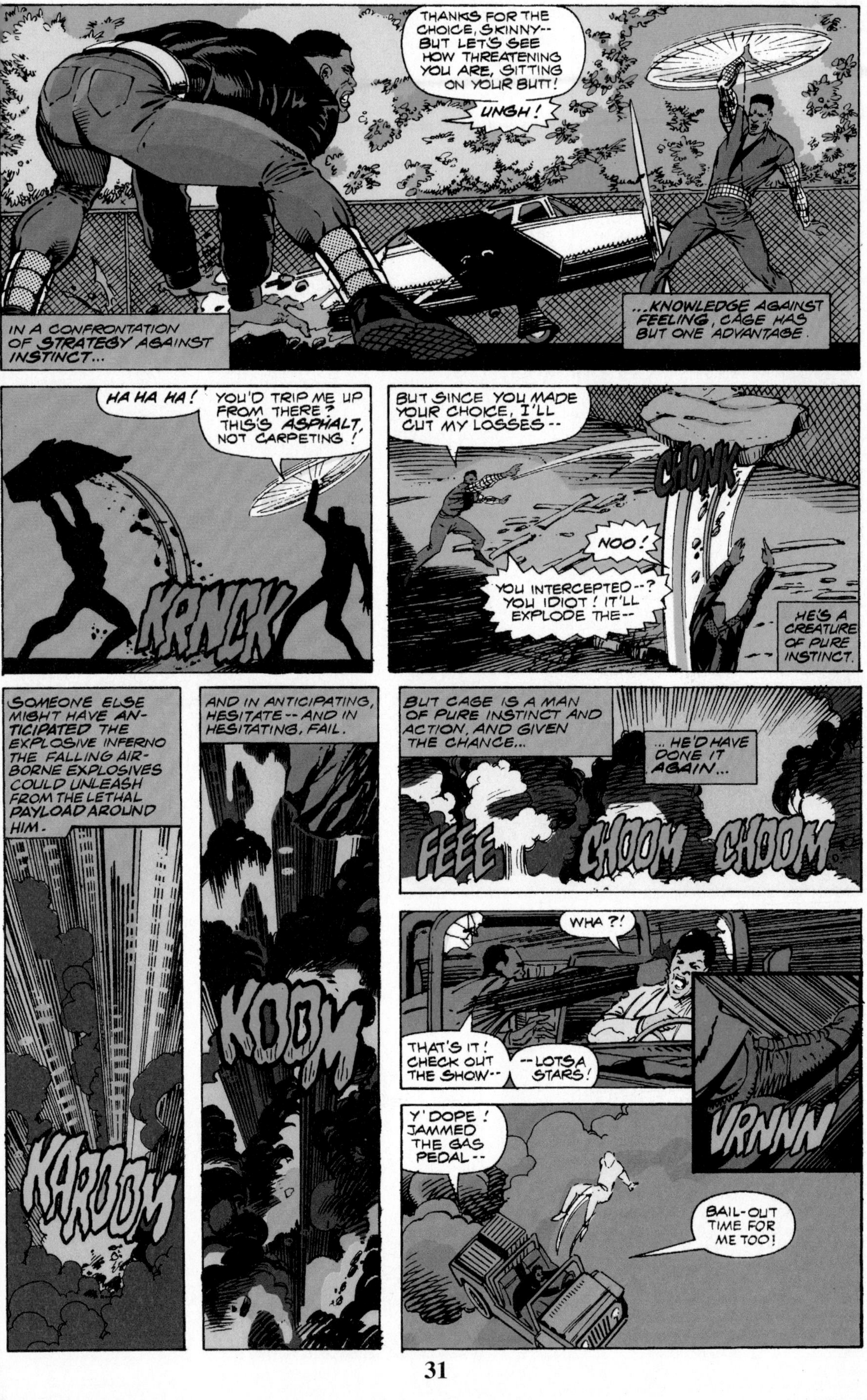
THANKS FOR THE CHOICE, SKINNY-- BUT LET'S SEE HOW THREATENING YOU ARE, SITTING ON YOUR BUTT!
UNGH!
IN A CONFRONTATION OF STRATEGY AGAINST INSTINCT...
...KNOWLEDGE AGAINST FEELING, CAGE HAS BUT ONE ADVANTAGE.
HA HA HA!
YOU'D TRIP ME UP FROM THERE? THIS'S ASPHALT, NOT CARPETING!
KRNCK
BUT SINCE YOU MADE YOUR CHOICE, I'LL CUT MY LOSSES --
CHONK
NOO!
YOU INTERCEPTED--? YOU IDIOT! IT'LL EXPLODE THE--
HE'S A CREATURE OF PURE INSTINCT.
SOMEONE ELSE MIGHT HAVE ANTICIPATED THE EXPLOSIVE INFERNO THE FALLING AIRBORNE EXPLOSIVES COULD UNLEASH FROM THE LETHAL PAYLOAD AROUND HIM.
KAROOM
AND IN ANTICIPATING, HESITATE-- AND IN HESITATING, FAIL.
KOOM
BUT CAGE IS A MAN OF PURE INSTINCT AND ACTION, AND GIVEN THE CHANCE...
...HE'D HAVE DONE IT AGAIN...
FEEE
CHOOM
CHOOM
WHA?!
THAT'S IT! CHECK OUT THE SHOW--
--LOTSA STARS!
VRNNN
Y'DOPE! JAMMED THE GAS PEDAL--
BAIL-OUT TIME FOR ME TOO!

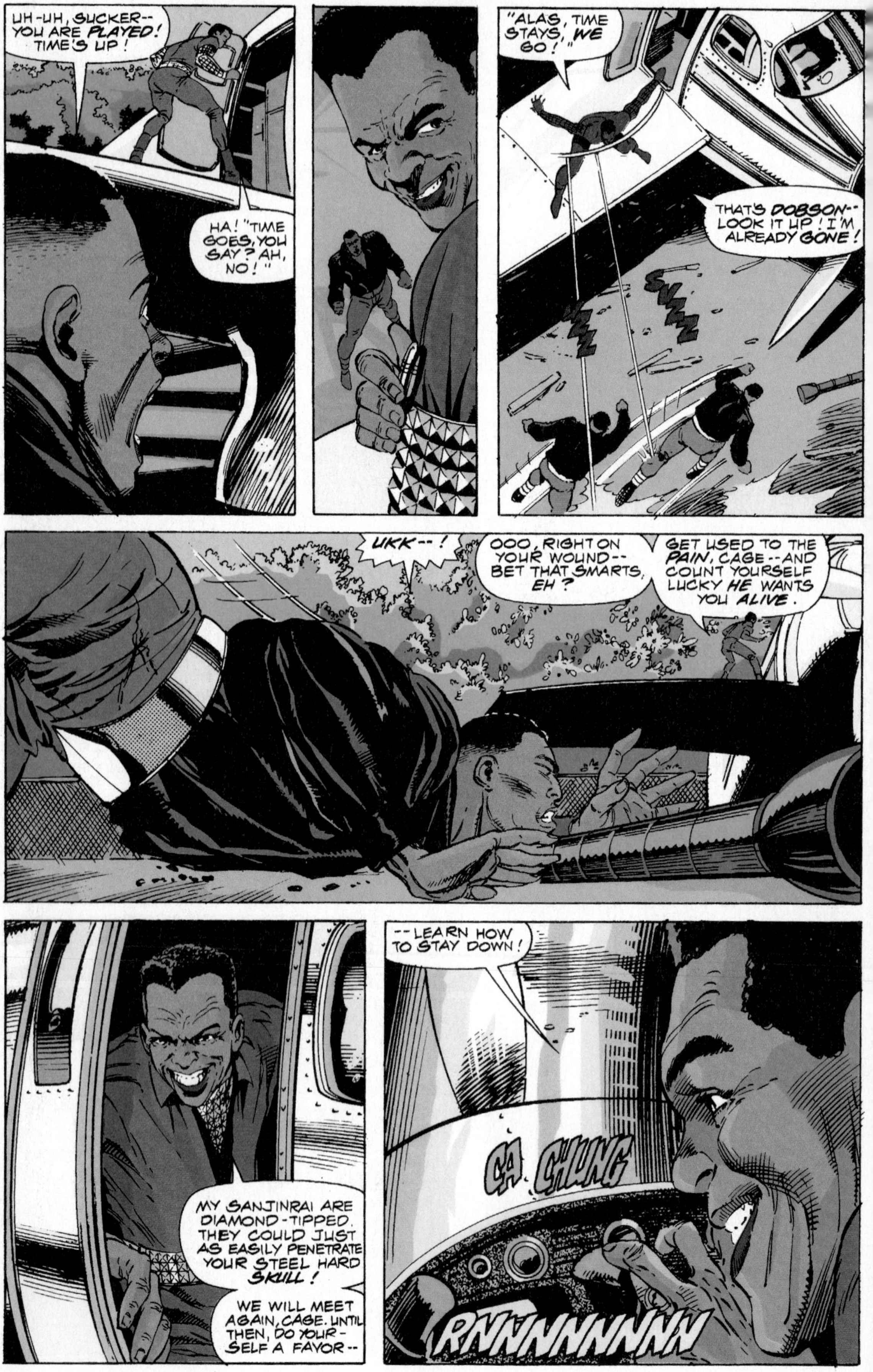
UH-UH, SUCKER-- YOU ARE PLAYED! TIME'S UP!
HA! "TIME GOES, YOU SAY? AH, NO!"
"ALAS, TIME STAYS, WE GO!"
THAT'S DOBSON-- LOOK IT UP! I'M ALREADY GONE!
SNNN
UKK--!
OOO, RIGHT ON YOUR WOUND-- BET THAT SMARTS, EH?
GET USED TO THE PAIN, CAGE--AND COUNT YOURSELF LUCKY HE WANTS YOU ALIVE.
MY SANJINRAI ARE DIAMOND-TIPPED. THEY COULD JUST AS EASILY PENETRATE YOUR STEEL HARD SKULL!
WE WILL MEET AGAIN, CAGE. UNTIL THEN, DO YOURSELF A FAVOR--
--LEARN HOW TO STAY DOWN!
CA CHUNG
RNNNNNNNNN

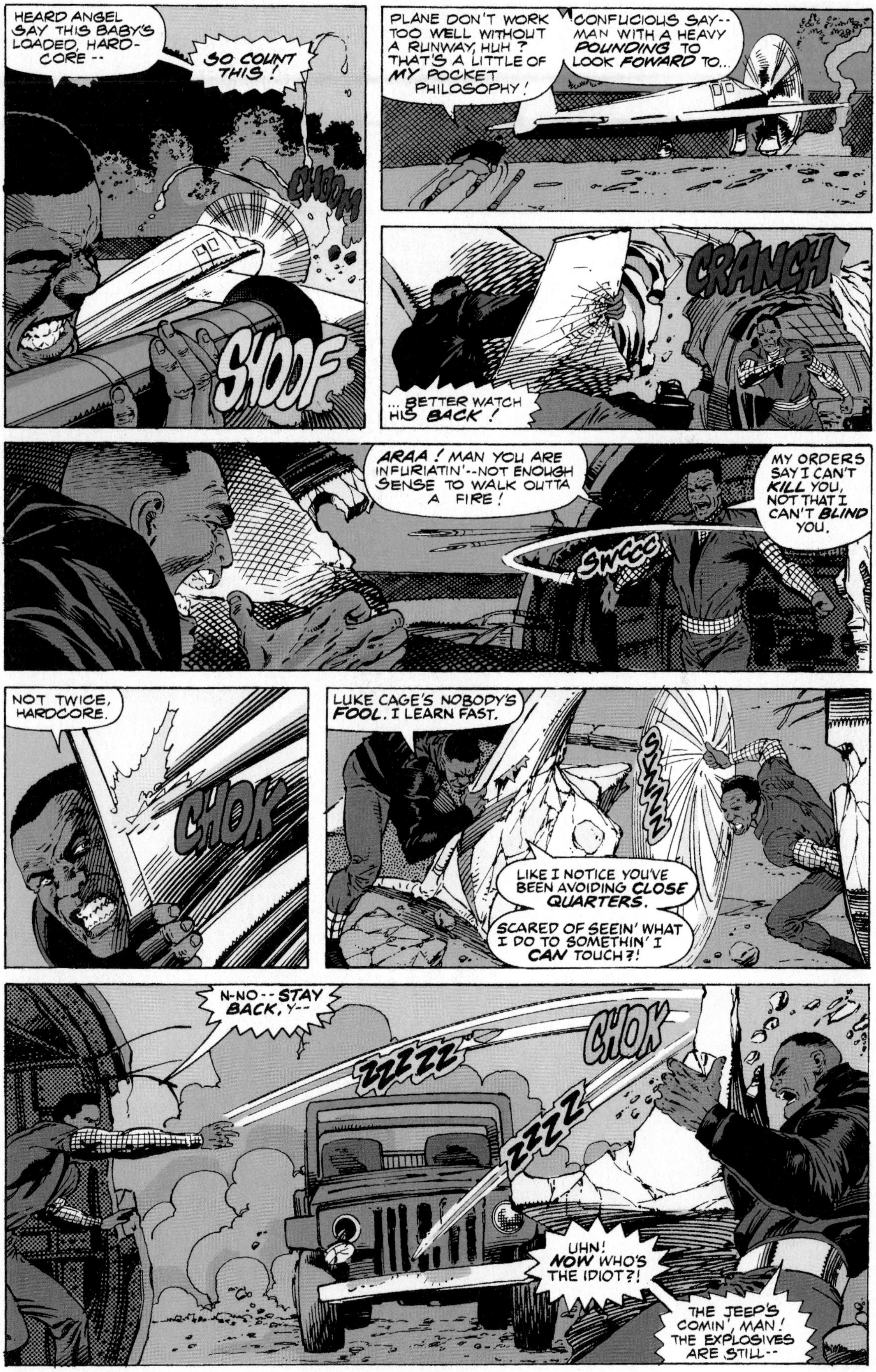
HEARD ANGEL SAY THIS BABY'S LOADED, HARDCORE --
SO COUNT THIS!
CHOOM
SHOOF
PLANE DON'T WORK TOO WELL WITHOUT A RUNWAY, HUH? THAT'S A LITTLE OF MY POCKET PHILOSOPHY!
CONFUCIOUS SAY-- MAN WITH A HEAVY POUNDING TO LOOK FOWARD TO...
CRANCH
...BETTER WATCH HIS BACK!
ARAA! MAN YOU ARE INFURIATIN'--NOT ENOUGH SENSE TO WALK OUTTA A FIRE!
MY ORDERS SAY I CAN'T KILL YOU, NOT THAT I CAN'T BLIND YOU.
SWCCC
NOT TWICE, HARDCORE.
CHOK
LUKE CAGE'S NOBODY'S FOOL. I LEARN FAST.
LIKE I NOTICE YOU'VE BEEN AVOIDING CLOSE QUARTERS.
SCARED OF SEEIN' WHAT I DO TO SOMETHIN' I CAN TOUCH?!
N-NO--STAY BACK, Y--
CHOK
ZZZZZ
ZZZZ
UHN! NOW WHO'S THE IDIOT?!
THE JEEP'S COMIN', MAN! THE EXPLOSIVES ARE STILL--

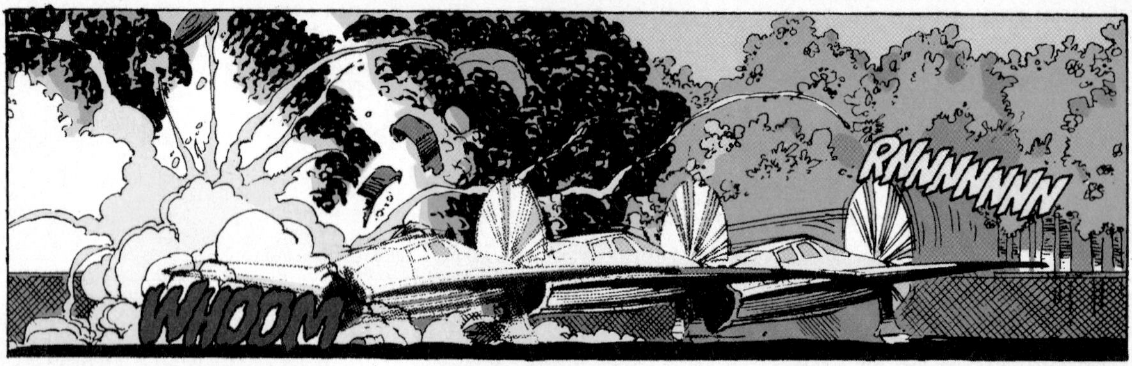
RNNNNNNN
WHOOM

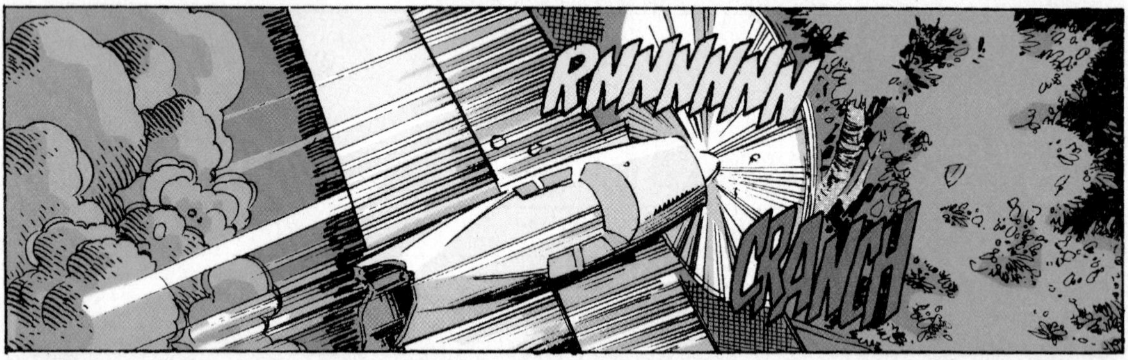
RNNNNNN
CRANCH

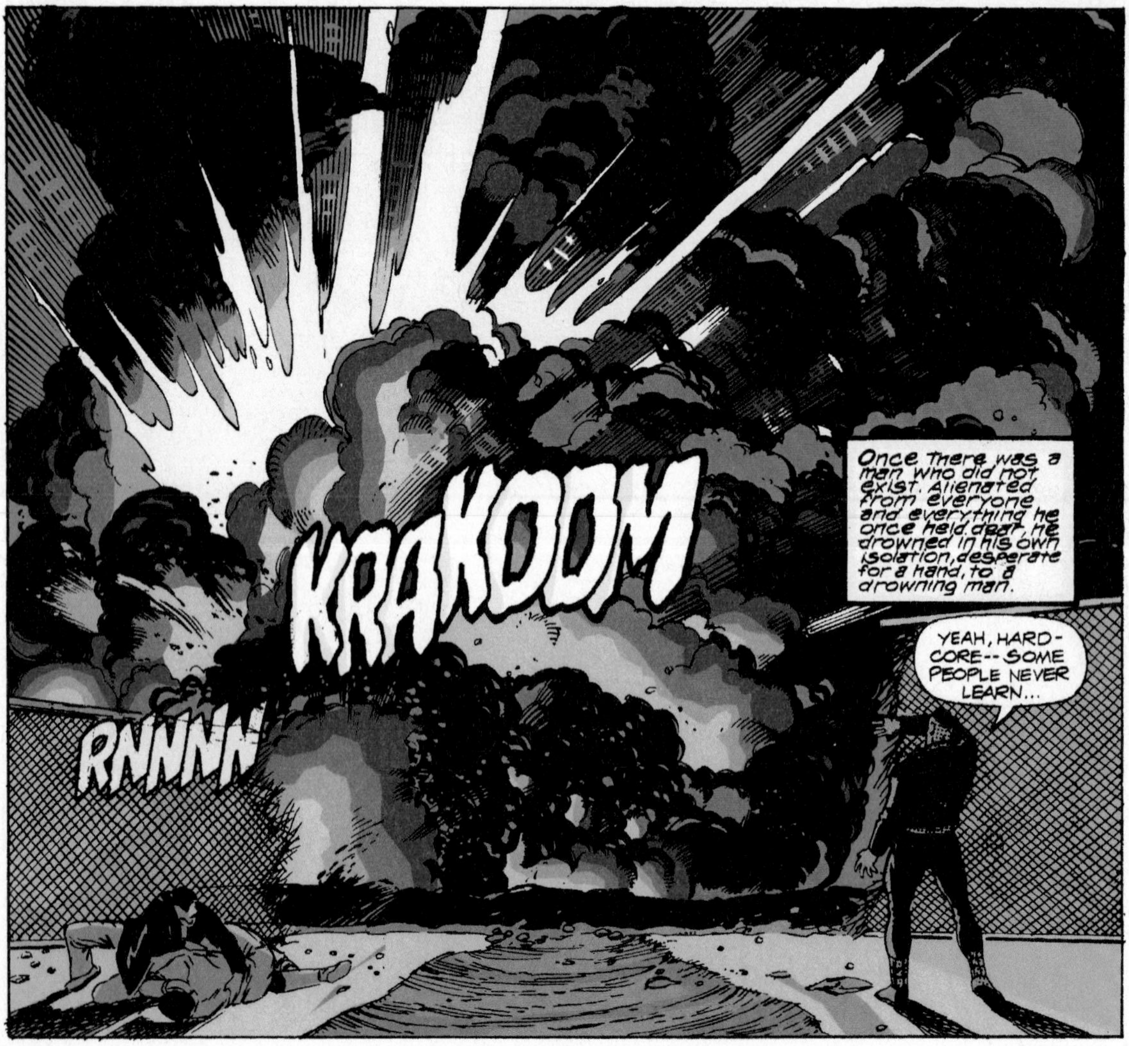
KRAKOOM
Once there was a man who did not exist. Alienated from everyone and everything he once held dear, he drowned in his own isolation, desperate for a hand, to a drowning man.
YEAH, HARD-CORE-- SOME PEOPLE NEVER LEARN...
RNNNN

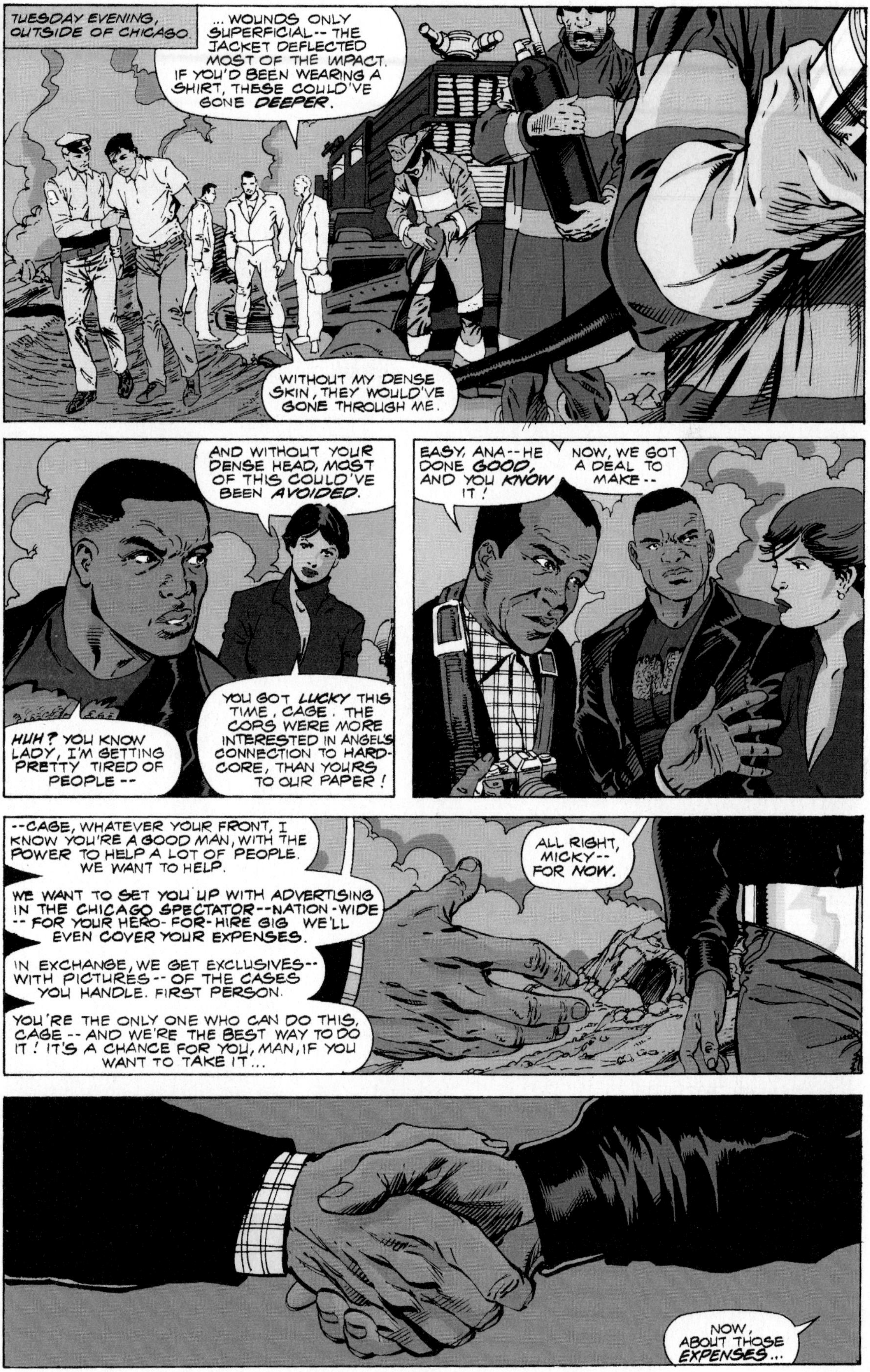
TUESDAY EVENING, OUTSIDE OF CHICAGO.
... WOUNDS ONLY SUPERFICIAL -- THE JACKET DEFLECTED MOST OF THE IMPACT. IF YOU'D BEEN WEARING A SHIRT, THESE COULD'VE GONE DEEPER.
WITHOUT MY DENSE SKIN, THEY WOULD'VE GONE THROUGH ME.
AND WITHOUT YOUR DENSE HEAD, MOST OF THIS COULD'VE BEEN AVOIDED.
HUH? YOU KNOW LADY, I'M GETTING PRETTY TIRED OF PEOPLE --
YOU GOT LUCKY THIS TIME, CAGE. THE COPS WERE MORE INTERESTED IN ANGEL'S CONNECTION TO HARD-CORE, THAN YOURS TO OUR PAPER!
EASY, ANA -- HE DONE GOOD, AND YOU KNOW IT!
NOW, WE GOT A DEAL TO MAKE --
-- CAGE, WHATEVER YOUR FRONT, I KNOW YOU'RE A GOOD MAN, WITH THE POWER TO HELP A LOT OF PEOPLE. WE WANT TO HELP.
WE WANT TO SET YOU UP WITH ADVERTISING IN THE CHICAGO SPECTATOR -- NATION-WIDE -- FOR YOUR HERO-FOR-HIRE GIG. WE'LL EVEN COVER YOUR EXPENSES.
IN EXCHANGE, WE GET EXCLUSIVES -- WITH PICTURES -- OF THE CASES YOU HANDLE. FIRST PERSON.
YOU'RE THE ONLY ONE WHO CAN DO THIS, CAGE -- AND WE'RE THE BEST WAY TO DO IT! IT'S A CHANCE FOR YOU, MAN, IF YOU WANT TO TAKE IT...
ALL RIGHT, MICKY -- FOR NOW.
NOW, ABOUT THOSE EXPENSES...

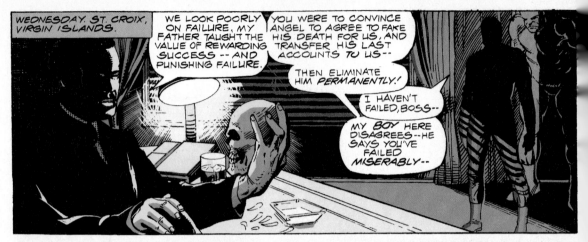

WEDNESDAY. ST. CROIX, VIRGIN ISLANDS.

WE LOOK POORLY ON FAILURE, MY FATHER TAUGHT THE VALUE OF REWARDING SUCCESS -- AND PUNISHING FAILURE.

YOU WERE TO CONVINCE ANGEL TO AGREE TO FAKE HIS DEATH FOR US, AND TRANSFER HIS LAST ACCOUNTS TO US--

THEN ELIMINATE HIM PERMANENTLY!

I HAVEN'T FAILED, BOSS--

MY BOY HERE DISAGREES--HE SAYS YOU'VE FAILED MISERABLY--

KRONK

UNK--

--HARDCORE!

ANGEL'S SURVIVAL IS A LOOSE END I'LL TIE LATER! MEANWHILE CAGE BELIEVES I AM DEAD!

AND THE CAGE OBJECTIVE--

CAGE WAS NOT TO BE OUR OBJECTIVE FOR SOME TIME!

THAT PLAN REQUIRES CAGE BE HUMBLED-- BROKEN TO OUR PURPOSE! THIS EXERCISE HAS GIVEN HIM A HANDHOLD AT REBUILDING HIS LIFE!

HE MAY EVEN RISE TO THREATEN MY LARGER PLANS -- WHICH MUST NOT HAPPEN!

AND WILL NOT. PLANS INTERSECTED FORCING GREATER STRATEGY, BUT NO HARM'S BEEN DONE. GIVING HIM TIME TO ESTABLISH NEW BONDS WILL WORK FOR US--

FOR TO CRUSH THE MAN, FINALLY,...

NUH-- BOSS--

...WE NEED ONLY TO CUT THE BONDS!

AND WHEN THAT HAPPENS, I PROMISE YOU--

--HE WILL NEVER GET UP AGAIN!

NEXT: CREATIVE HATE

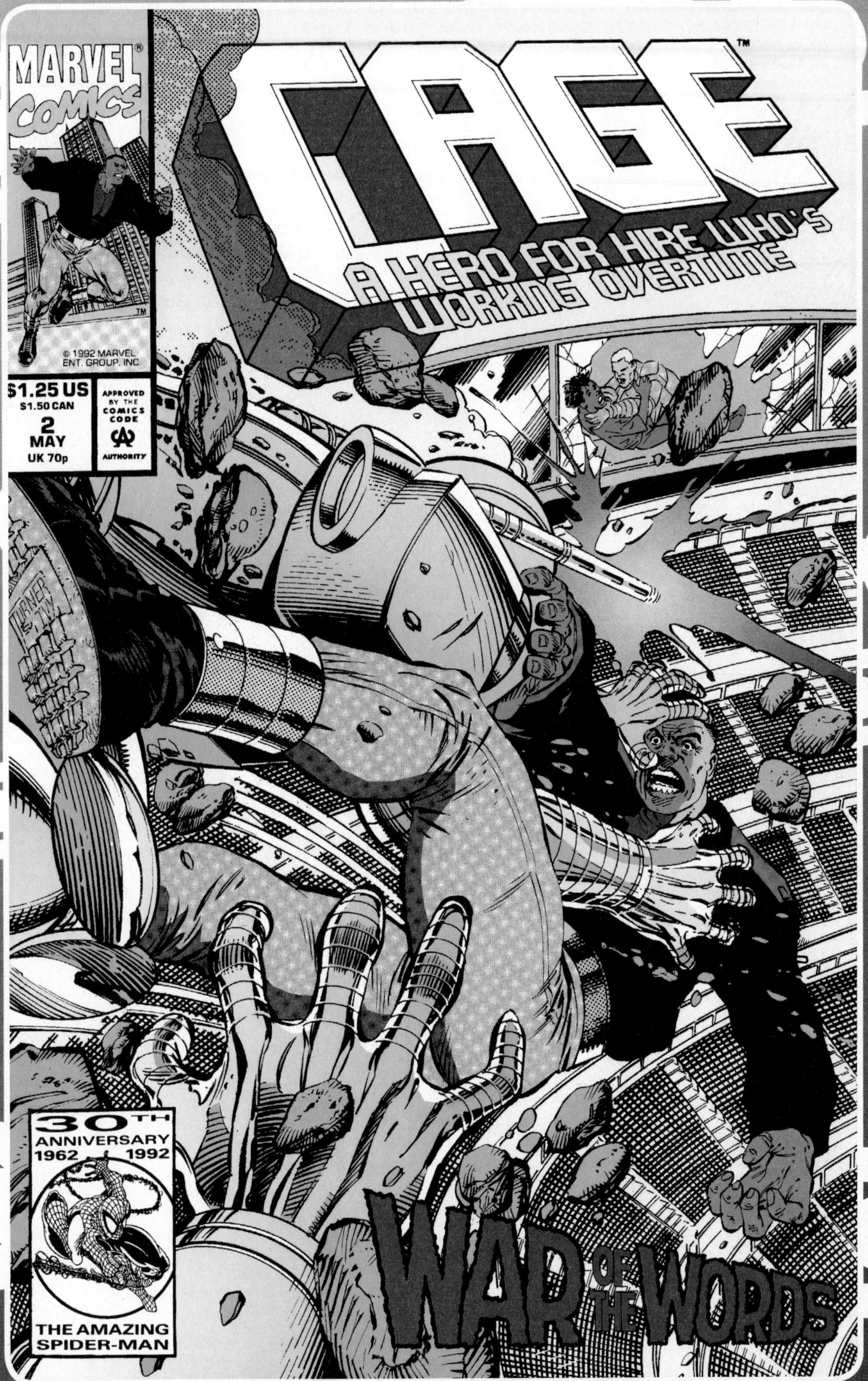
MARVEL® COMICS
CAGE™
A HERO FOR HIRE WHO'S WORKING OVERTIME
© 1992 MARVEL ENT. GROUP, INC.
$1.25 US
$1.50 CAN
2
MAY
UK 70p
APPROVED BY THE COMICS CODE AUTHORITY
30TH ANNIVERSARY 1962 1992
THE AMAZING SPIDER-MAN
WAR OF THE WORDS

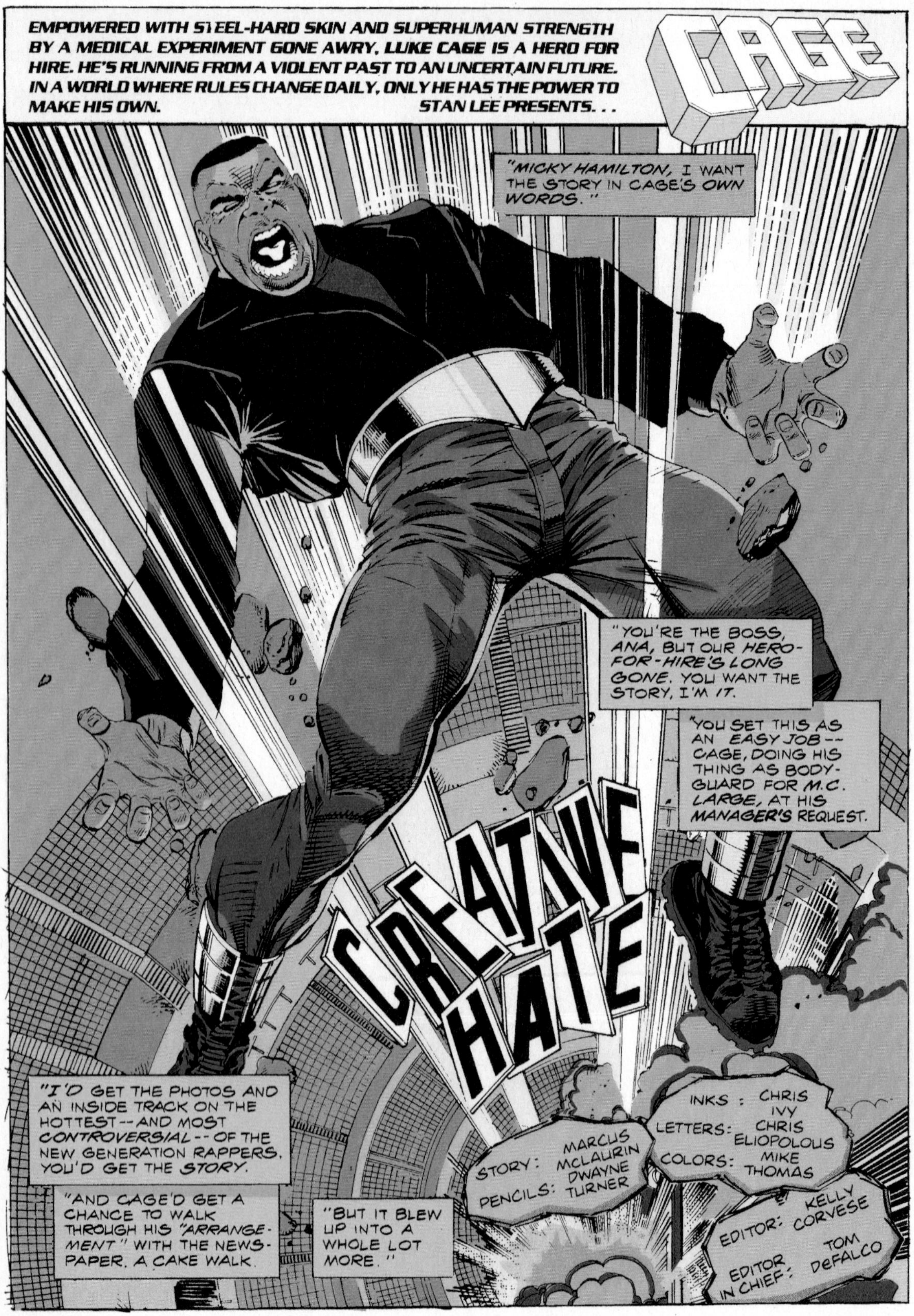
EMPOWERED WITH STEEL-HARD SKIN AND SUPERHUMAN STRENGTH BY A MEDICAL EXPERIMENT GONE AWRY, LUKE CAGE IS A HERO FOR HIRE. HE'S RUNNING FROM A VIOLENT PAST TO AN UNCERTAIN FUTURE. IN A WORLD WHERE RULES CHANGE DAILY, ONLY HE HAS THE POWER TO MAKE HIS OWN.
STAN LEE PRESENTS. . .
CAGE
"MICKY HAMILTON, I WANT THE STORY IN CAGE'S OWN WORDS."
"YOU'RE THE BOSS, ANA, BUT OUR HERO-FOR-HIRE'S LONG GONE. YOU WANT THE STORY, I'M IT.
"YOU SET THIS AS AN EASY JOB -- CAGE, DOING HIS THING AS BODY-GUARD FOR M.C. LARGE, AT HIS MANAGER'S REQUEST.
CREATIVE HATE
"I'D GET THE PHOTOS AND AN INSIDE TRACK ON THE HOTTEST -- AND MOST CONTROVERSIAL -- OF THE NEW GENERATION RAPPERS. YOU'D GET THE STORY.
"AND CAGE'D GET A CHANCE TO WALK THROUGH HIS "ARRANGEMENT" WITH THE NEWSPAPER. A CAKE WALK.
"BUT IT BLEW UP INTO A WHOLE LOT MORE."
STORY: MARCUS McLAURIN
PENCILS: DWAYNE TURNER
INKS: CHRIS IVY
LETTERS: CHRIS ELIOPOLOUS
COLORS: MIKE THOMAS
EDITOR: KELLY CORVESE
EDITOR IN CHIEF: TOM DeFALCO

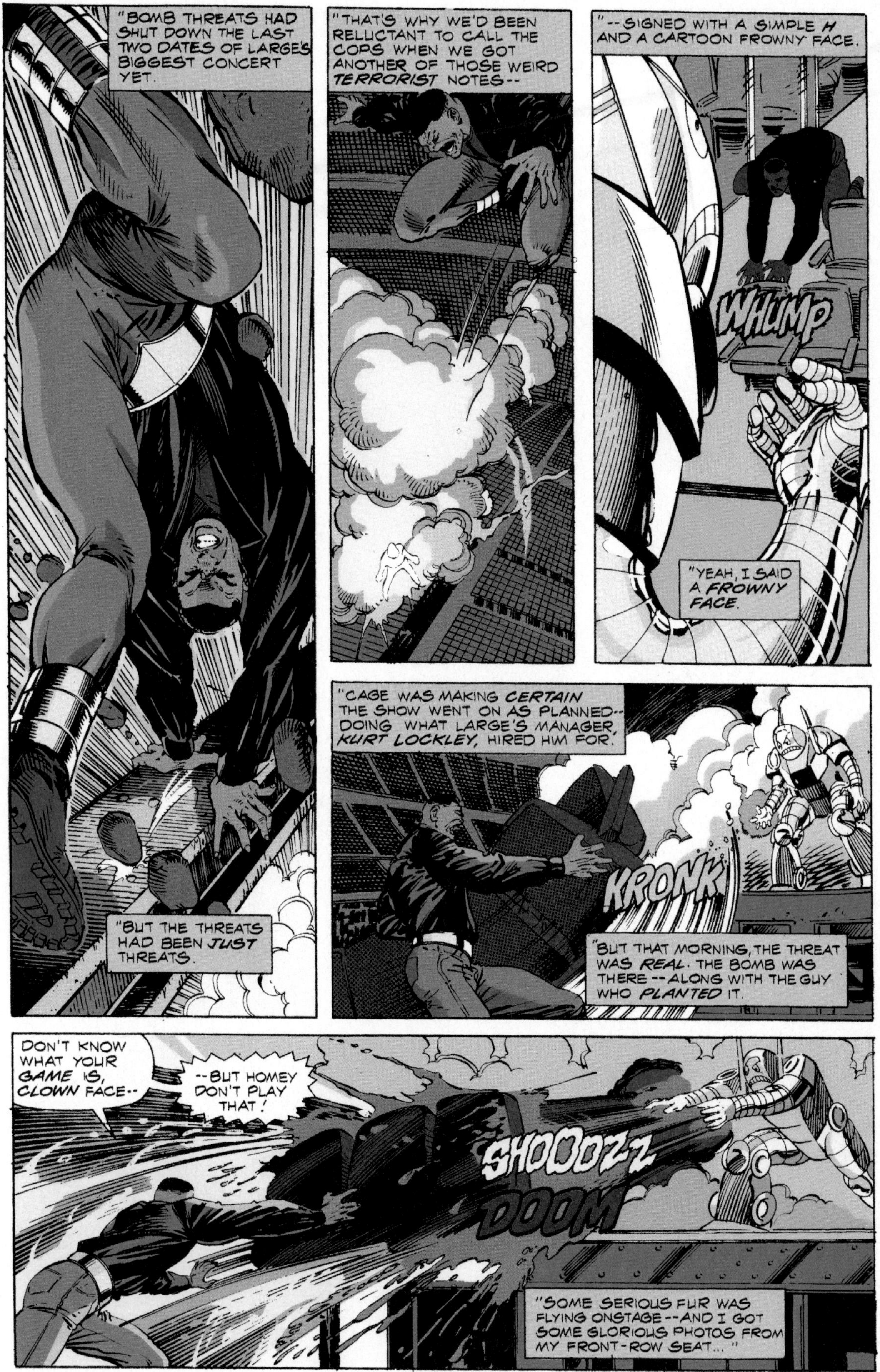
"BOMB THREATS HAD SHUT DOWN THE LAST TWO DATES OF LARGE'S BIGGEST CONCERT YET.
"BUT THE THREATS HAD BEEN JUST THREATS.
"THAT'S WHY WE'D BEEN RELUCTANT TO CALL THE COPS WHEN WE GOT ANOTHER OF THOSE WEIRD TERRORIST NOTES--
"--SIGNED WITH A SIMPLE H AND A CARTOON FROWNY FACE.
WHUMP
"YEAH, I SAID A FROWNY FACE.
"CAGE WAS MAKING CERTAIN THE SHOW WENT ON AS PLANNED--DOING WHAT LARGE'S MANAGER, KURT LOCKLEY, HIRED HIM FOR.
KRONK
"BUT THAT MORNING, THE THREAT WAS REAL. THE BOMB WAS THERE --ALONG WITH THE GUY WHO PLANTED IT.
DON'T KNOW WHAT YOUR GAME IS, CLOWN FACE--
--BUT HOMEY DON'T PLAY THAT!
SHOOOZZ
DOOM
"SOME SERIOUS FUR WAS FLYING ONSTAGE--AND I GOT SOME GLORIOUS PHOTOS FROM MY FRONT-ROW SEAT..."

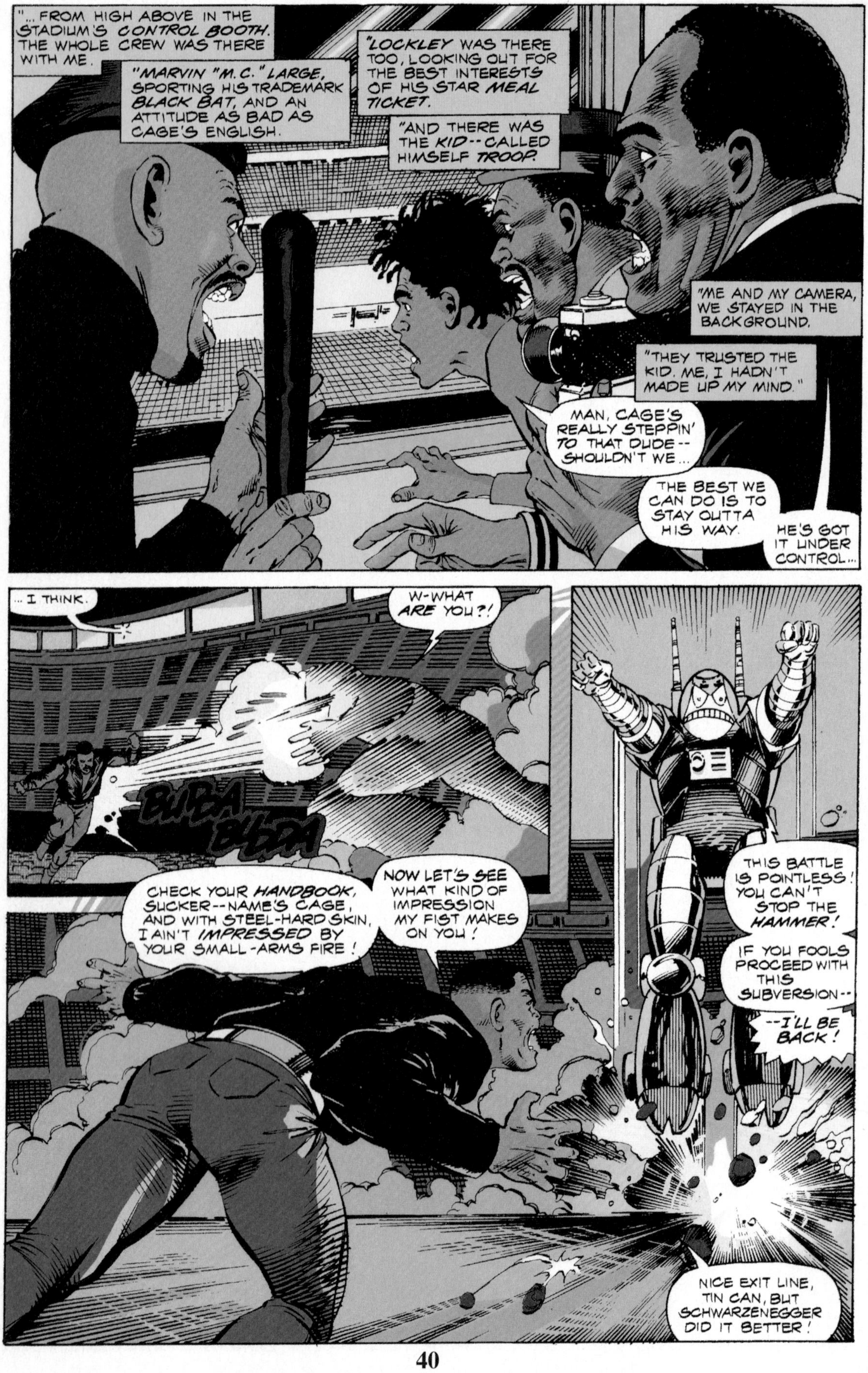
"... FROM HIGH ABOVE IN THE STADIUM'S CONTROL BOOTH. THE WHOLE CREW WAS THERE WITH ME.
"MARVIN "M.C." LARGE, SPORTING HIS TRADEMARK BLACK BAT, AND AN ATTITUDE AS BAD AS CAGE'S ENGLISH.
"LOCKLEY WAS THERE TOO, LOOKING OUT FOR THE BEST INTERESTS OF HIS STAR MEAL TICKET.
"AND THERE WAS THE KID--CALLED HIMSELF TROOP.
"ME AND MY CAMERA, WE STAYED IN THE BACKGROUND.
"THEY TRUSTED THE KID. ME, I HADN'T MADE UP MY MIND."
MAN, CAGE'S REALLY STEPPIN' TO THAT DUDE-- SHOULDN'T WE...
THE BEST WE CAN DO IS TO STAY OUTTA HIS WAY.
HE'S GOT IT UNDER CONTROL...
... I THINK.
W-WHAT ARE YOU?!
BUDDA BUDDA
CHECK YOUR HANDBOOK, SUCKER--NAME'S CAGE, AND WITH STEEL-HARD SKIN, I AIN'T IMPRESSED BY YOUR SMALL-ARMS FIRE!
NOW LET'S SEE WHAT KIND OF IMPRESSION MY FIST MAKES ON YOU!
THIS BATTLE IS POINTLESS! YOU CAN'T STOP THE HAMMER!
IF YOU FOOLS PROCEED WITH THIS SUBVERSION--
--I'LL BE BACK!
NICE EXIT LINE, TIN CAN, BUT SCHWARZENEGGER DID IT BETTER!

TRY THIS ONE--

--HASTA LA VISTA *THIS*, BABY!

ZHOOSH

NO! THOSE'RE MY GYRO STABLIZERS-- WITHOUT THOSE, I CAN'T STAY UP!

I'M OUT OF CONTROL!

VRREEEEEE

"FROM OUR VANTAGE, WE COULDN'T TELL WHO WAS *WINNING*--

YO, I DON'T CARE *WHAT* YOU SAY, OLD DUDE-- I'M *THERE!*

"BUT WE KNEW WHERE WE'D BETTER BE IF WE WANTED ANY PIECE OF DECIDING."

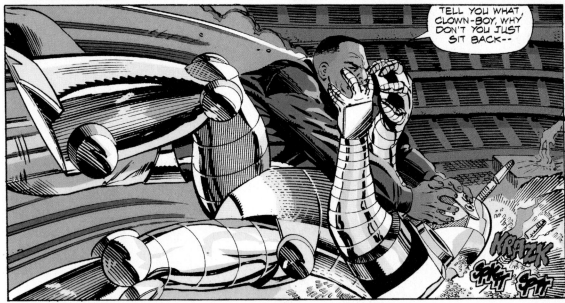

TELL YOU WHAT, CLOWN-BOY, WHY DON'T YOU JUST SIT BACK--

KRAZK
SPKT SPTT

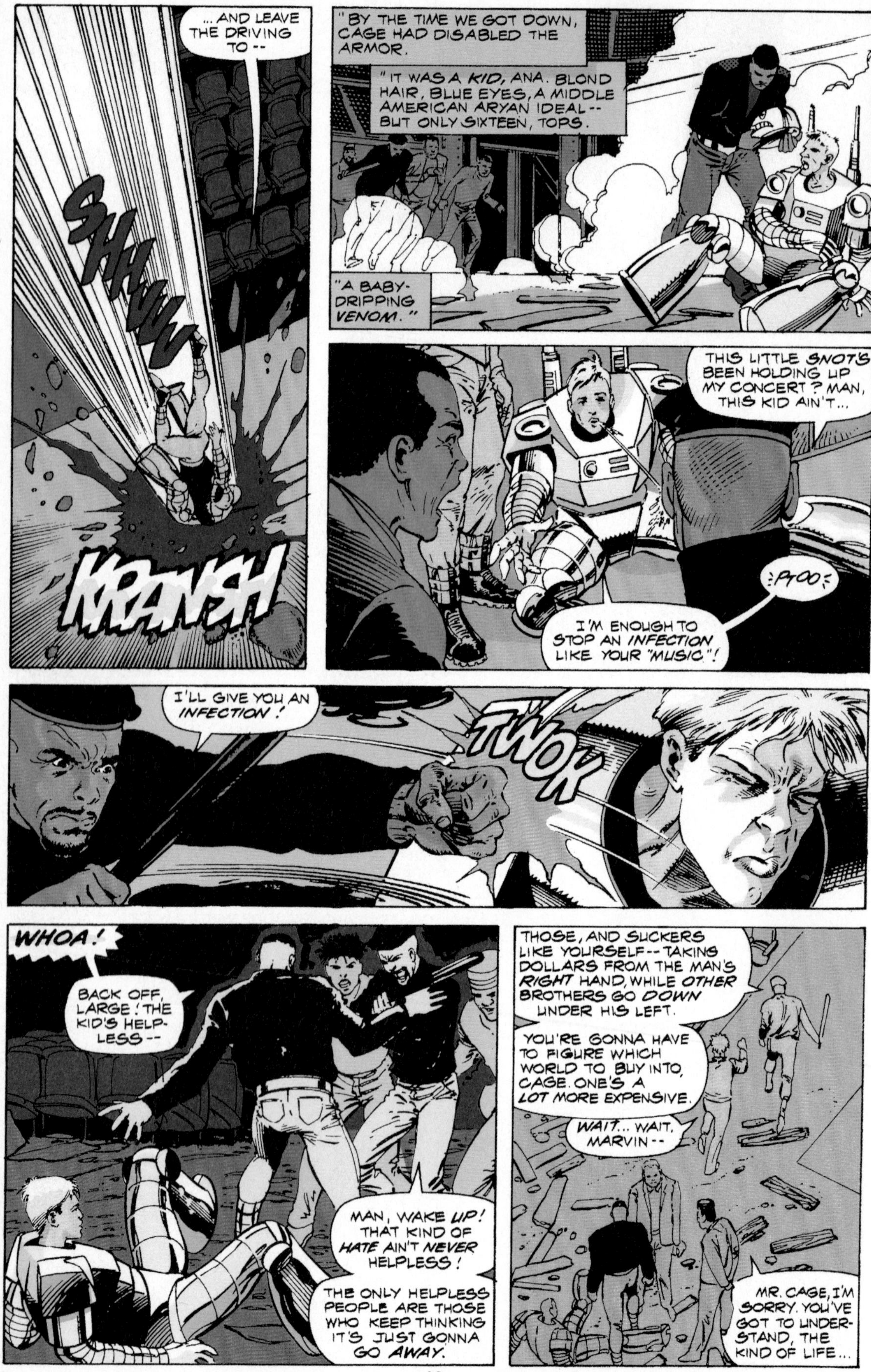

... AND LEAVE THE DRIVING TO --
SHHWW
KRANSH
"BY THE TIME WE GOT DOWN, CAGE HAD DISABLED THE ARMOR.
"IT WAS A KID, ANA. BLOND HAIR, BLUE EYES, A MIDDLE AMERICAN ARYAN IDEAL -- BUT ONLY SIXTEEN, TOPS.
"A BABY-DRIPPING VENOM."
THIS LITTLE SNOT'S BEEN HOLDING UP MY CONCERT? MAN, THIS KID AIN'T...
PTOO
I'M ENOUGH TO STOP AN INFECTION LIKE YOUR "MUSIC"!
I'LL GIVE YOU AN INFECTION!
TWOK
WHOA!
BACK OFF, LARGE! THE KID'S HELPLESS --
MAN, WAKE UP! THAT KIND OF HATE AIN'T NEVER HELPLESS!
THE ONLY HELPLESS PEOPLE ARE THOSE WHO KEEP THINKING IT'S JUST GONNA GO AWAY.
THOSE, AND SUCKERS LIKE YOURSELF -- TAKING DOLLARS FROM THE MAN'S RIGHT HAND, WHILE OTHER BROTHERS GO DOWN UNDER HIS LEFT.
YOU'RE GONNA HAVE TO FIGURE WHICH WORLD TO BUY INTO, CAGE. ONE'S A LOT MORE EXPENSIVE.
WAIT... WAIT, MARVIN --
MR. CAGE, I'M SORRY. YOU'VE GOT TO UNDERSTAND, THE KIND OF LIFE...

THE LIFE YOU *ALL* COME FROM-- THE USUAL EXCUSE, *ISN'T* IT?

NO EXCUSE, *BOY*-- A POINT OF *UNDER- STANDING.*

THE 'HOODS OF *EAST LA.* DON'T HAVE MANY SHADES OF GREY. YOU CHOOSE SIDES, AND STICK WITH THEM.

BUT WE GOT *OUT.* AND WE'RE HELPING OTHER BROTHERS DO THE SAME. THAT'S HIS MESSAGE, AND OUR *GOAL.*

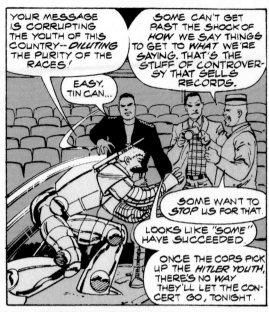

YOUR MESSAGE IS CORRUPTING THE YOUTH OF THIS COUNTRY-- *DILUTING* THE PURITY OF THE RACES!

SOME CAN'T GET PAST THE SHOCK OF *HOW* WE SAY THINGS TO GET TO *WHAT* WE'RE SAYING. THAT'S THE STUFF OF CONTROVER- SY THAT *SELLS* RECORDS.

EASY, *TIN CAN...*

SOME WANT TO *STOP* US FOR THAT.

LOOKS LIKE *"SOME"* HAVE *SUCCEEDED.*

ONCE THE COPS PICK UP THE *HITLER YOUTH,* THERE'S NO *WAY* THEY'LL LET THE CON- CERT GO, TONIGHT.

YOU *SEE?!* YOU *SEE?!* THE HAMMER'S *WON!*

NO! MR. CAGE, THIS BOY--THIS *"HAMMER"* IS *DOWN.* THREAT'S *OVER.*

WHAT'S YOUR *POINT?*

A POINT OF *UNDERSTANDING,* MR. CAGE. YOU DON'T HAVE TO CALL THE COPS... *YET.* GIVE US A *CHANCE!*

HAVEN'T YOU EVER NEEDED THAT *ONE* BREAK?

"CAGE WAS A CON WHO CLEARED HIMSELF, THANKS TO THE FREAK *EXPERIMENT* THAT GAVE HIM HIS POWERS. *HIS* BIG BREAK.

"LOCKLEY WAS PUSHING THE RIGHT BUTTONS, TOO WELL. CAGE NEEDED A VOICE OF *REASON.*

"UNFORTUNATELY, I WAS THE ONLY ONE *THERE.*

YOU *CAN'T* BE SERIOUS! YOU CAN'T JUST *SIT* ON THIS GUY ALL DAY!

YOU'VE GOT TO--

THAT'S WHAT YOU KEEP FORGETTIN', MICKY. I DON'T *GOTTA* NOTHING. I'M NO COP-- I FOLLOW MY *OWN* RULES.

LOCKLEY, YOU GOT TILL *AFTER* THE CONCERT. NO MORE.

"CAGE HAD NO *CLUE* WHAT HE WAS IN FOR."

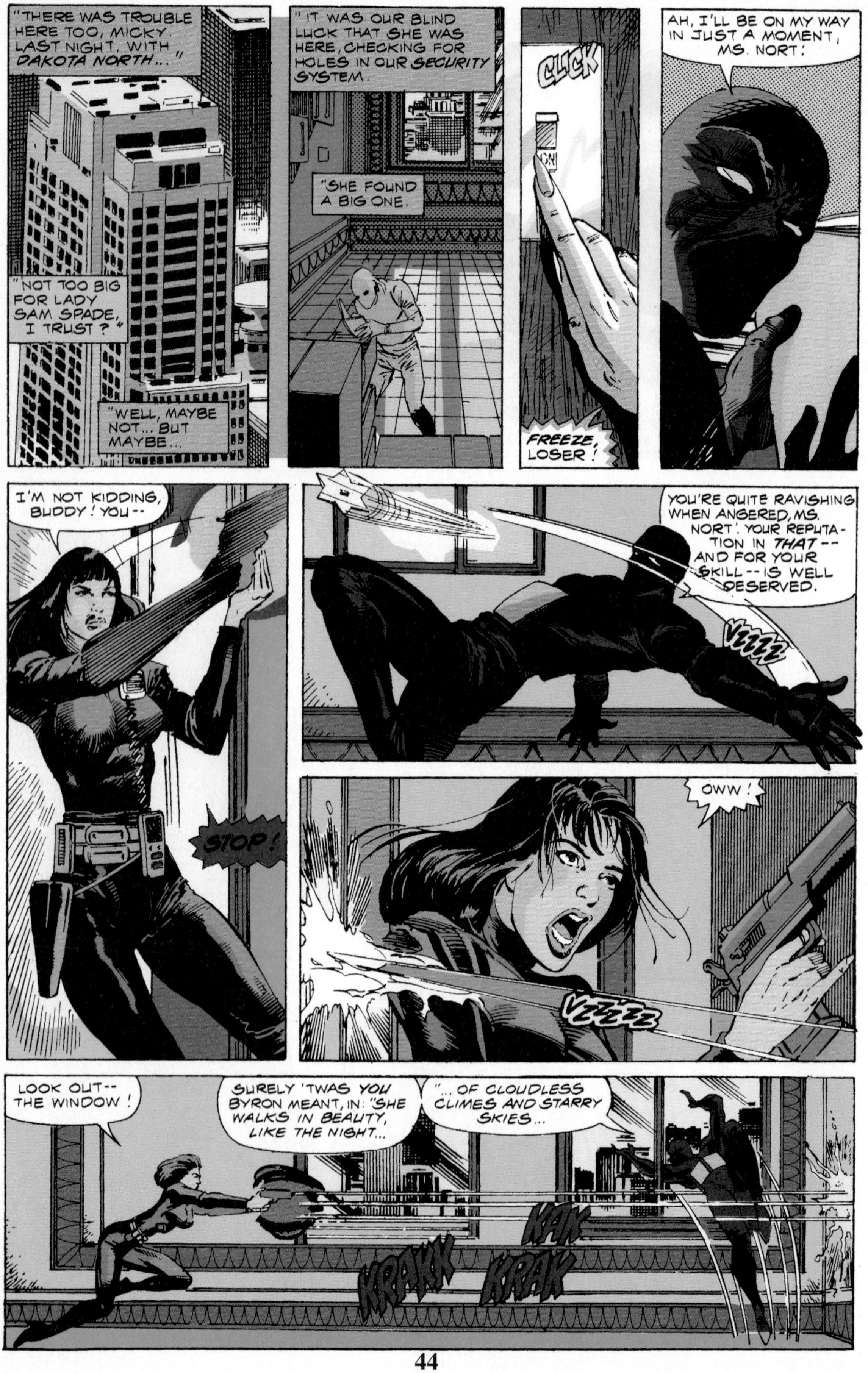
"THERE WAS TROUBLE HERE TOO, MICKY. LAST NIGHT, WITH DAKOTA NORTH..."
"NOT TOO BIG FOR LADY SAM SPADE, I TRUST?"
"WELL, MAYBE NOT... BUT MAYBE...
"IT WAS OUR BLIND LUCK THAT SHE WAS HERE, CHECKING FOR HOLES IN OUR SECURITY SYSTEM.
"SHE FOUND A BIG ONE.
CLICK
FREEZE, LOSER!
AH, I'LL BE ON MY WAY IN JUST A MOMENT, MS. NORT!
I'M NOT KIDDING, BUDDY! YOU--
STOP!
YOU'RE QUITE RAVISHING WHEN ANGERED, MS. NORT! YOUR REPUTATION IN THAT--AND FOR YOUR SKILL--IS WELL DESERVED.
VZZZZ
OWW!
VZZZZZ
LOOK OUT--THE WINDOW!
SURELY 'TWAS YOU BYRON MEANT, IN: "SHE WALKS IN BEAUTY, LIKE THE NIGHT...
"...OF CLOUDLESS CLIMES AND STARRY SKIES...
KAK
KRAKK
KRAK

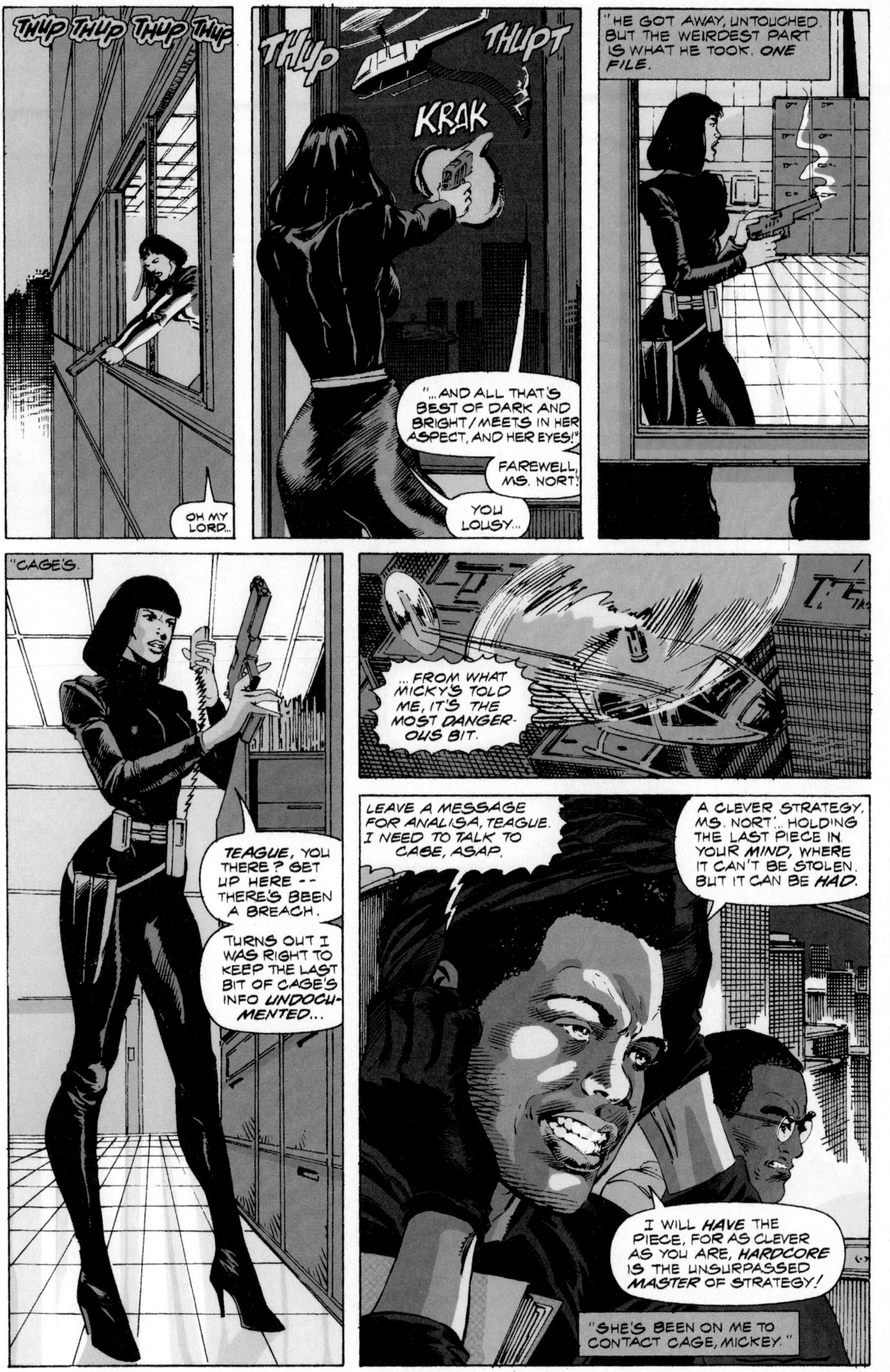

THUP THUP THUP THUP
OH MY LORD...
THUP
THUPT
KRAK
"...AND ALL THAT'S BEST OF DARK AND BRIGHT / MEETS IN HER ASPECT, AND HER EYES!"
FAREWELL, MS. NORT!
YOU LOUSY...
"HE GOT AWAY, UNTOUCHED. BUT THE WEIRDEST PART IS WHAT HE TOOK. ONE FILE.
"CAGE'S.
TEAGUE, YOU THERE? GET UP HERE -- THERE'S BEEN A BREACH.
TURNS OUT I WAS RIGHT TO KEEP THE LAST BIT OF CAGE'S INFO UNDOCUMENTED...
... FROM WHAT MICKY'S TOLD ME, IT'S THE MOST DANGEROUS BIT.
LEAVE A MESSAGE FOR ANALISA, TEAGUE. I NEED TO TALK TO CAGE, ASAP.
A CLEVER STRATEGY, MS. NORT... HOLDING THE LAST PIECE IN YOUR MIND, WHERE IT CAN'T BE STOLEN. BUT IT CAN BE HAD.
I WILL HAVE THE PIECE, FOR AS CLEVER AS YOU ARE, HARDCORE IS THE UNSURPASSED MASTER OF STRATEGY!
"SHE'S BEEN ON ME TO CONTACT CAGE, MICKEY."

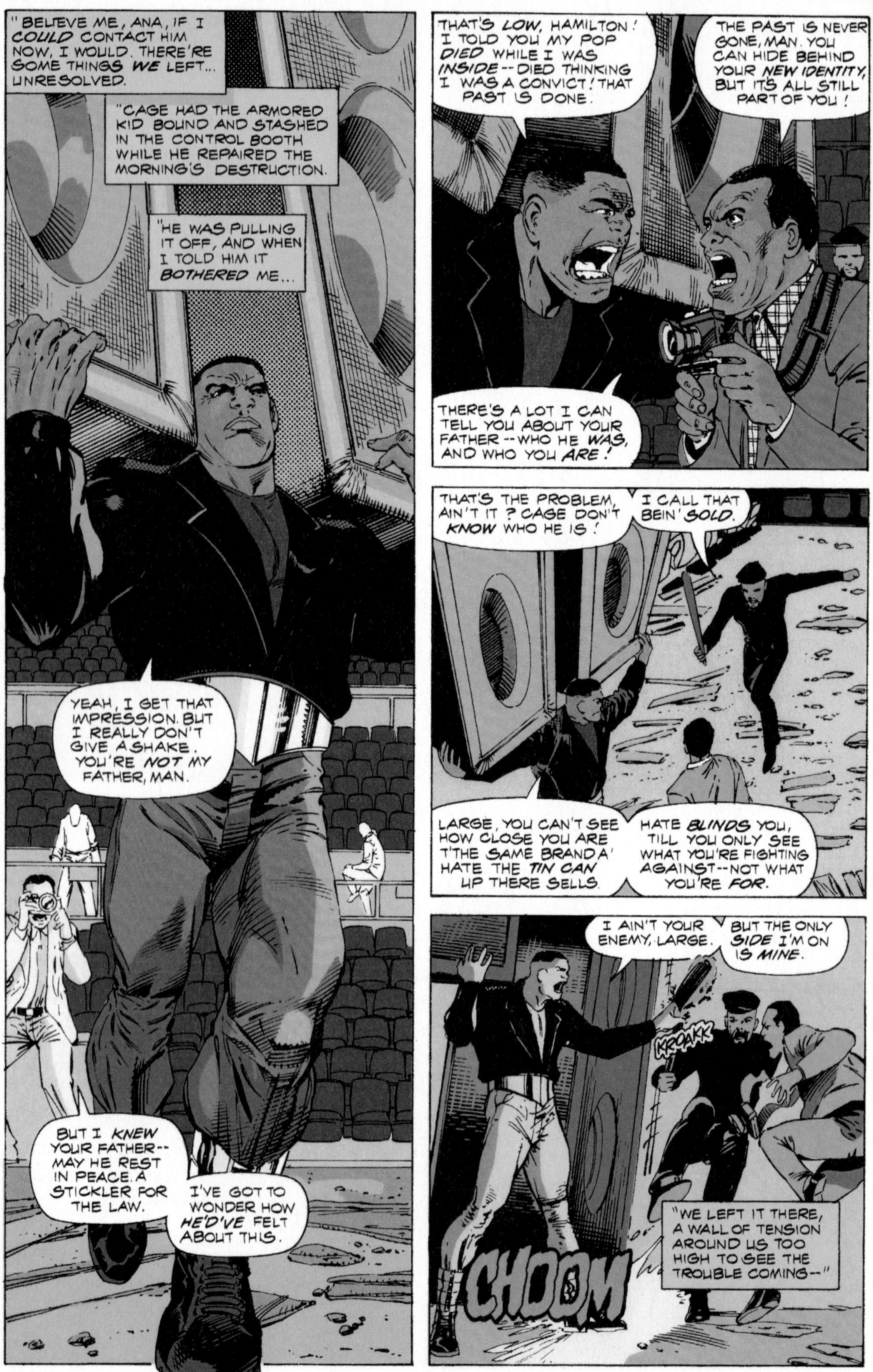
"BELIEVE ME, ANA, IF I COULD CONTACT HIM NOW, I WOULD. THERE'RE SOME THINGS WE LEFT... UNRESOLVED.
"CAGE HAD THE ARMORED KID BOUND AND STASHED IN THE CONTROL BOOTH WHILE HE REPAIRED THE MORNING'S DESTRUCTION.
"HE WAS PULLING IT OFF, AND WHEN I TOLD HIM IT BOTHERED ME...
YEAH, I GET THAT IMPRESSION. BUT I REALLY DON'T GIVE A SHAKE. YOU'RE NOT MY FATHER, MAN.
BUT I KNEW YOUR FATHER-- MAY HE REST IN PEACE. A STICKLER FOR THE LAW.
I'VE GOT TO WONDER HOW HE'D'VE FELT ABOUT THIS.
THAT'S LOW, HAMILTON! I TOLD YOU MY POP DIED WHILE I WAS INSIDE--DIED THINKING I WAS A CONVICT! THAT PAST IS DONE.
THE PAST IS NEVER GONE, MAN. YOU CAN HIDE BEHIND YOUR NEW IDENTITY, BUT IT'S ALL STILL PART OF YOU!
THERE'S A LOT I CAN TELL YOU ABOUT YOUR FATHER --WHO HE WAS, AND WHO YOU ARE!
THAT'S THE PROBLEM, AIN'T IT? CAGE DON'T KNOW WHO HE IS!
I CALL THAT BEIN' SOLD.
LARGE, YOU CAN'T SEE HOW CLOSE YOU ARE T'THE SAME BRAND A' HATE THE TIN CAN UP THERE SELLS.
HATE BLINDS YOU, TILL YOU ONLY SEE WHAT YOU'RE FIGHTING AGAINST--NOT WHAT YOU'RE FOR.
I AIN'T YOUR ENEMY, LARGE.
BUT THE ONLY SIDE I'M ON IS MINE.
KROAKK
CHOOM
"WE LEFT IT THERE, A WALL OF TENSION AROUND US TOO HIGH TO SEE THE TROUBLE COMING--"

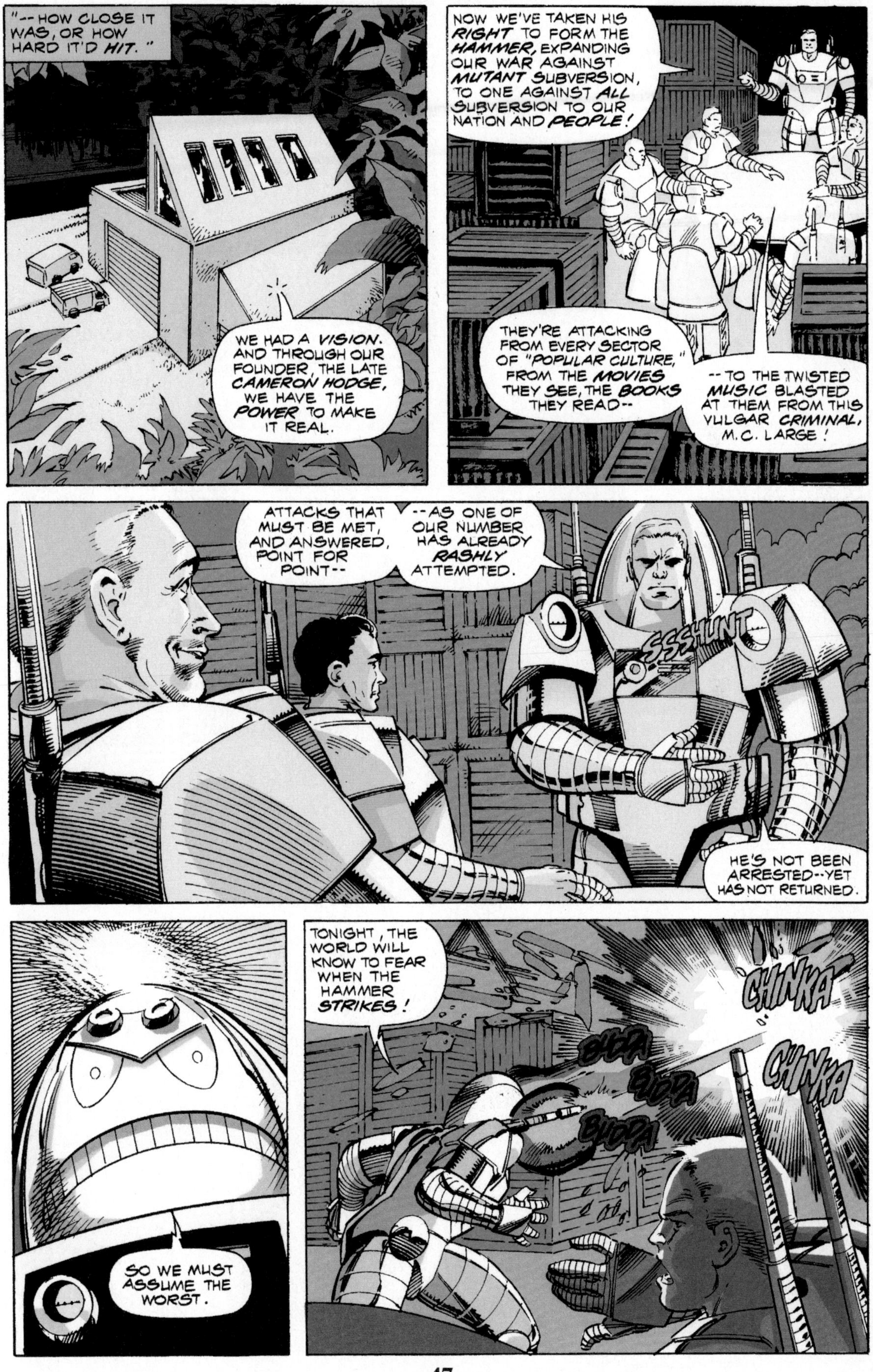
"--HOW CLOSE IT WAS, OR HOW HARD IT'D *HIT*."
WE HAD A *VISION*. AND THROUGH OUR FOUNDER, THE LATE *CAMERON HODGE*, WE HAVE THE *POWER* TO MAKE IT REAL.
NOW WE'VE TAKEN HIS *RIGHT* TO FORM THE *HAMMER*, EXPANDING OUR WAR AGAINST *MUTANT* SUBVERSION, TO ONE AGAINST *ALL* SUBVERSION TO OUR NATION AND *PEOPLE*!
THEY'RE ATTACKING FROM EVERY SECTOR OF "*POPULAR CULTURE*," FROM THE *MOVIES* THEY SEE, THE *BOOKS* THEY READ--
--TO THE TWISTED *MUSIC* BLASTED AT THEM FROM THIS VULGAR *CRIMINAL*, M.C. LARGE!
ATTACKS THAT MUST BE MET, AND ANSWERED, POINT FOR POINT--
--AS ONE OF OUR NUMBER HAS ALREADY *RASHLY* ATTEMPTED.
SSSHUNT
HE'S NOT BEEN ARRESTED--YET HAS NOT RETURNED.
SO WE MUST ASSUME THE WORST.
TONIGHT, THE WORLD WILL KNOW TO FEAR WHEN THE HAMMER *STRIKES*!
CHINKA
CHINKA
BUDDA
BUDDA
BUDDA

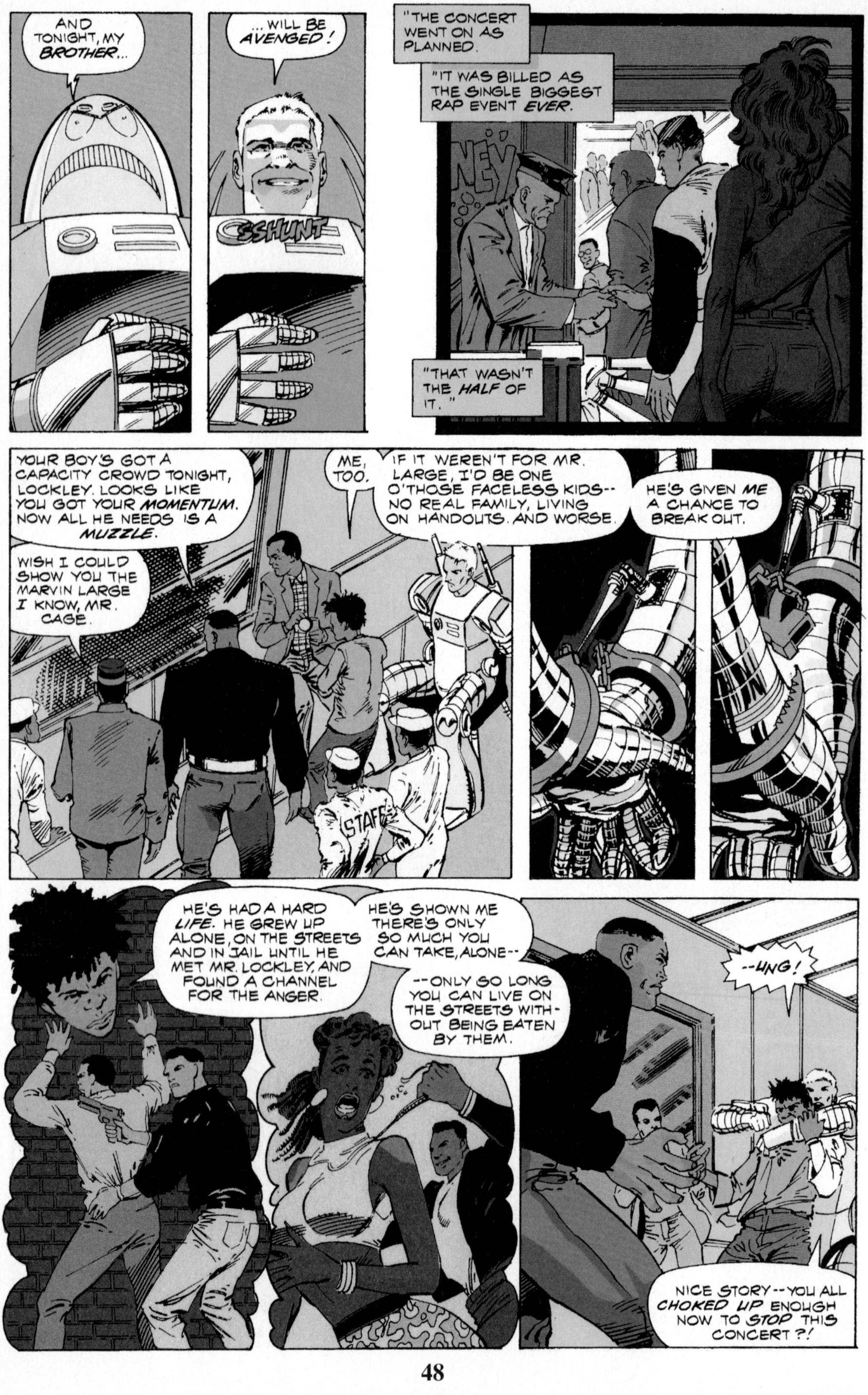
AND TONIGHT, MY BROTHER...
...WILL BE AVENGED!
SSHUNT
"THE CONCERT WENT ON AS PLANNED.
"IT WAS BILLED AS THE SINGLE BIGGEST RAP EVENT EVER.
"THAT WASN'T THE HALF OF IT."
YOUR BOY'S GOT A CAPACITY CROWD TONIGHT, LOCKLEY. LOOKS LIKE YOU GOT YOUR MOMENTUM. NOW ALL HE NEEDS IS A MUZZLE.
WISH I COULD SHOW YOU THE MARVIN LARGE I KNOW, MR. CAGE.
ME, TOO.
IF IT WEREN'T FOR MR. LARGE, I'D BE ONE O'THOSE FACELESS KIDS-- NO REAL FAMILY, LIVING ON HANDOUTS. AND WORSE.
STAFF
HE'S GIVEN ME A CHANCE TO BREAK OUT.
HE'S HAD A HARD LIFE. HE GREW UP ALONE, ON THE STREETS AND IN JAIL UNTIL HE MET MR. LOCKLEY, AND FOUND A CHANNEL FOR THE ANGER.
HE'S SHOWN ME THERE'S ONLY SO MUCH YOU CAN TAKE, ALONE--
--ONLY SO LONG YOU CAN LIVE ON THE STREETS WITH-OUT BEING EATEN BY THEM.
--UNG!
NICE STORY--YOU ALL CHOKED UP ENOUGH NOW TO STOP THIS CONCERT?!

UH-UHN! CHECK THAT, SUCKER!

I MAY BE *DOMESTICATED,* BUT I STILL GOT M'STREET MOVES!

UNG!

"YOU SHOULD'VE SEEN THE KID, ANA. A REAL *BRUCE LEROY.*

IT'S IMPORTANT NOT TO LOSE WHERE YOU COME FROM, YOU KNOW?

SLANG

STEP BACK, OLD DUDE--

"STILL A *SMART* MOUTH, THOUGH.

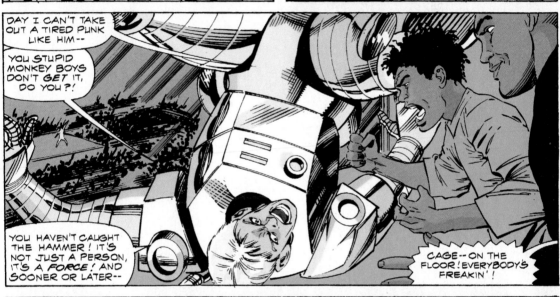

DAY I CAN'T TAKE OUT A TIRED PUNK LIKE HIM--

YOU STUPID MONKEY BOYS DON'T *GET* IT, DO YOU?!

YOU HAVEN'T CAUGHT THE HAMMER! IT'S NOT JUST A PERSON, IT'S A *FORCE!* AND SOONER OR LATER--

CAGE-- ON THE FLOOR! EVERYBODY'S FREAKIN'!

"THAT'S WHEN THE SKY FELL IN.

CHOKA

CHOKA CHOKA CHOKA

"THEY BLASTED IN THROUGH THE ROOF, RAINING DEBRIS AND DEATH ON THE HAPLESS SOULS BELOW.

"OKAY, *YOU* REWORD IT ANA. POINT IS, IT WAS *BAD.* "

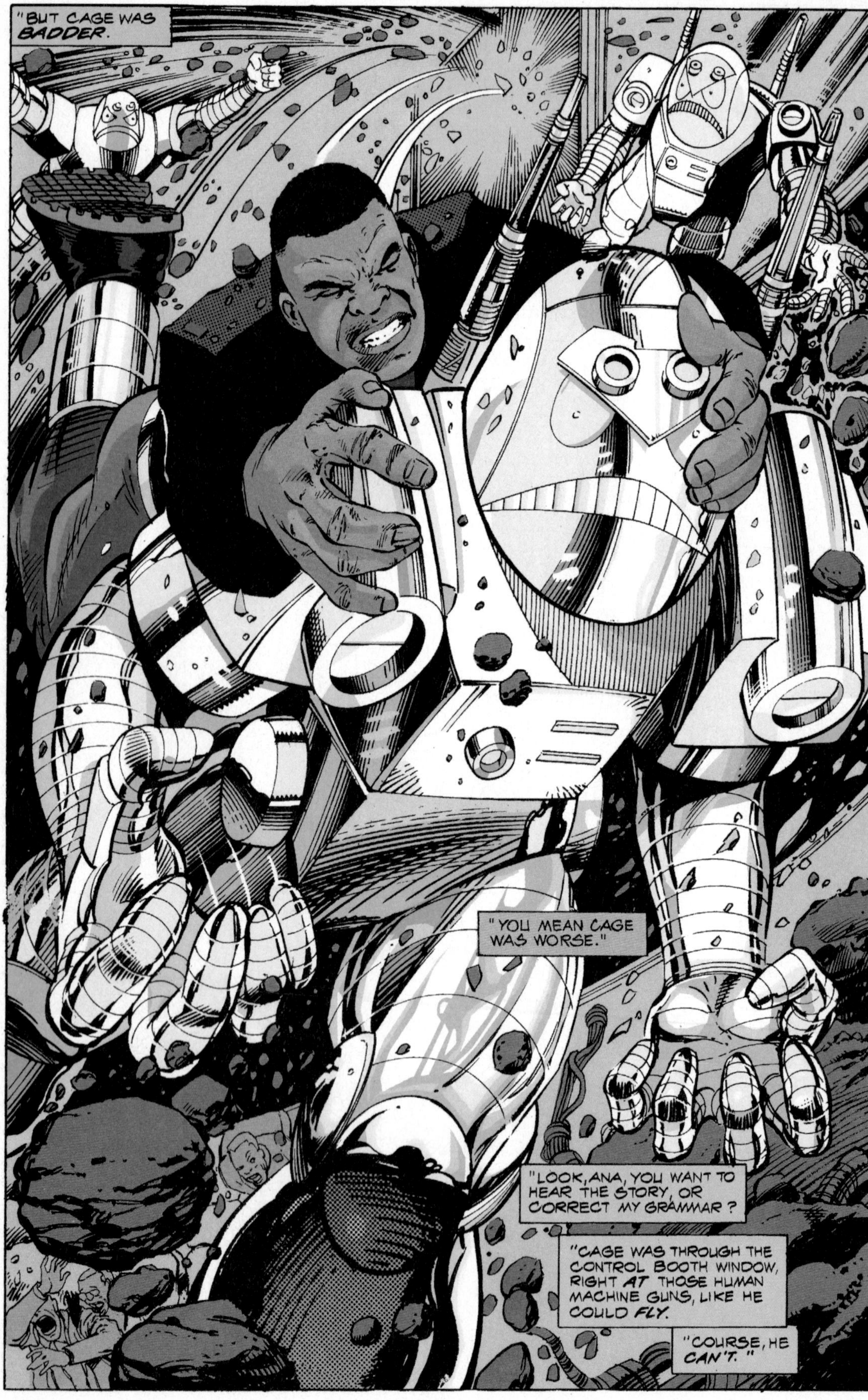
"BUT CAGE WAS BADDER.
"YOU MEAN CAGE WAS WORSE."
"LOOK, ANA, YOU WANT TO HEAR THE STORY, OR CORRECT MY GRAMMAR?
"CAGE WAS THROUGH THE CONTROL BOOTH WINDOW, RIGHT AT THOSE HUMAN MACHINE GUNS, LIKE HE COULD FLY.
"COURSE, HE CAN'T."

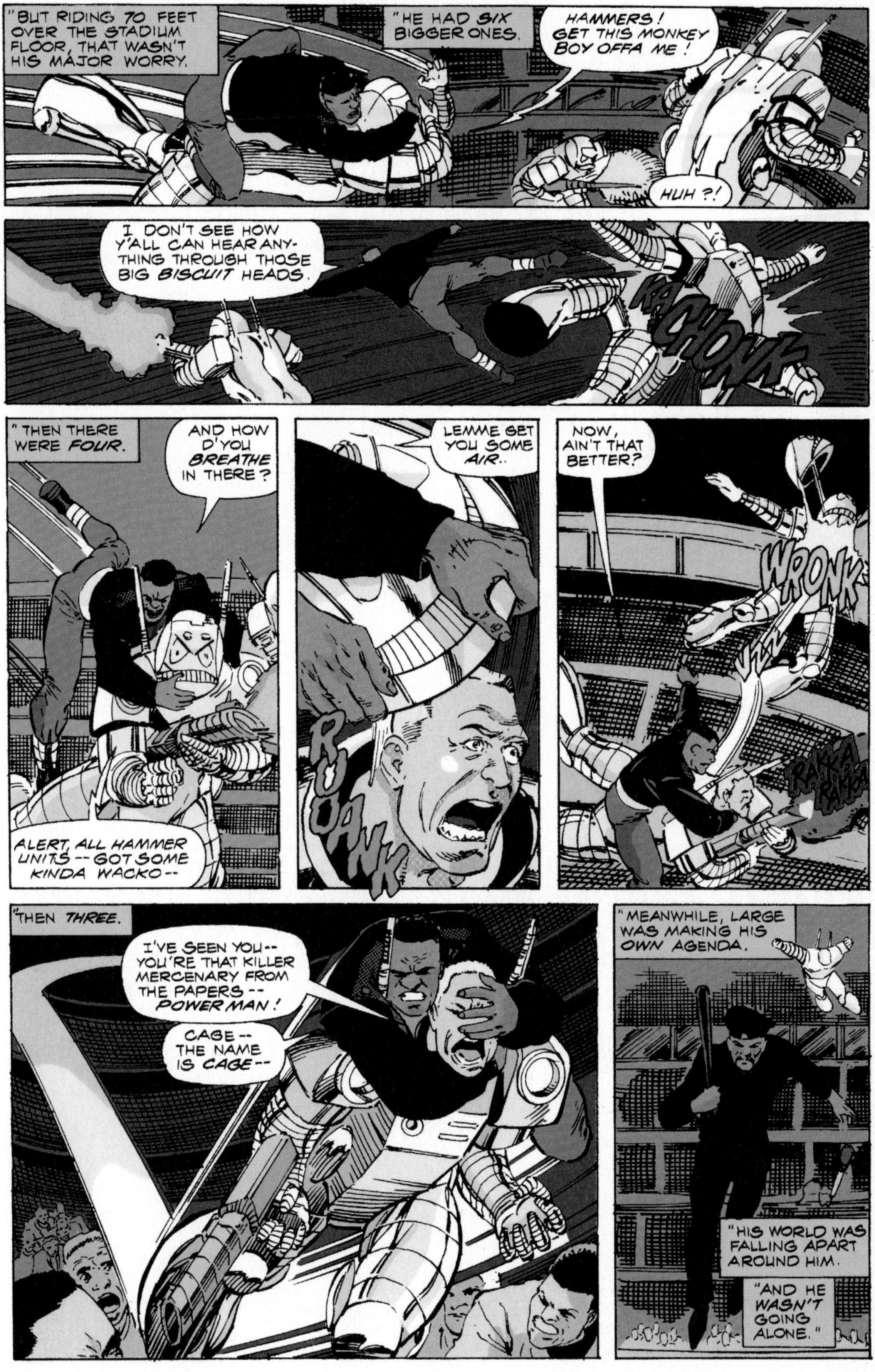
"BUT RIDING 70 FEET OVER THE STADIUM FLOOR, THAT WASN'T HIS MAJOR WORRY.
"HE HAD SIX BIGGER ONES.
HAMMERS! GET THIS MONKEY BOY OFFA ME!
HUH ?!
I DON'T SEE HOW Y'ALL CAN HEAR ANYTHING THROUGH THOSE BIG BISCUIT HEADS.
KACHONK
"THEN THERE WERE FOUR.
AND HOW D'YOU BREATHE IN THERE?
ALERT, ALL HAMMER UNITS -- GOT SOME KINDA WACKO --
LEMME GET YOU SOME AIR..
RUUANK
NOW, AIN'T THAT BETTER?
WRONK
RAKKA RAKKA
"THEN THREE.
I'VE SEEN YOU -- YOU'RE THAT KILLER MERCENARY FROM THE PAPERS -- POWER MAN!
CAGE -- THE NAME IS CAGE --
"MEANWHILE, LARGE WAS MAKING HIS OWN AGENDA.
"HIS WORLD WAS FALLING APART AROUND HIM.
"AND HE WASN'T GOING ALONE."

TAKE HIM! WE'LL **TEST** HOW HARD HE IS--

WHAT'D YOU WANT ME TO DO, HAMMER ONE?

JUST **HOLD** HIM. LET'S SEE HOW HE HOLDS UP AGAINST TWO 3/4" ROCKETS!

ROCKET? T-THAT GO RIGHT THROUGH **ME!**

SSHH

CHOOM

NO! YOU IDIOT, HE'S BULLETPROOF!!

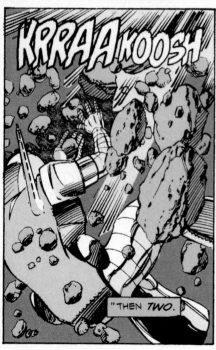

KRRAAKOOSH

"THEN **TWO.**

" WE ALL CUT OUT OF THE CONTROL BOOTH FOR THE FLOOR-- TRYING TO GET EVERYONE OUT OF WHAT HAD BECOME A **WAR ZONE.**

"WE'D LEFT THE ARMORED KID BEHIND, LOCKED UP TIGHT.

"OR SO WE THOUGHT."

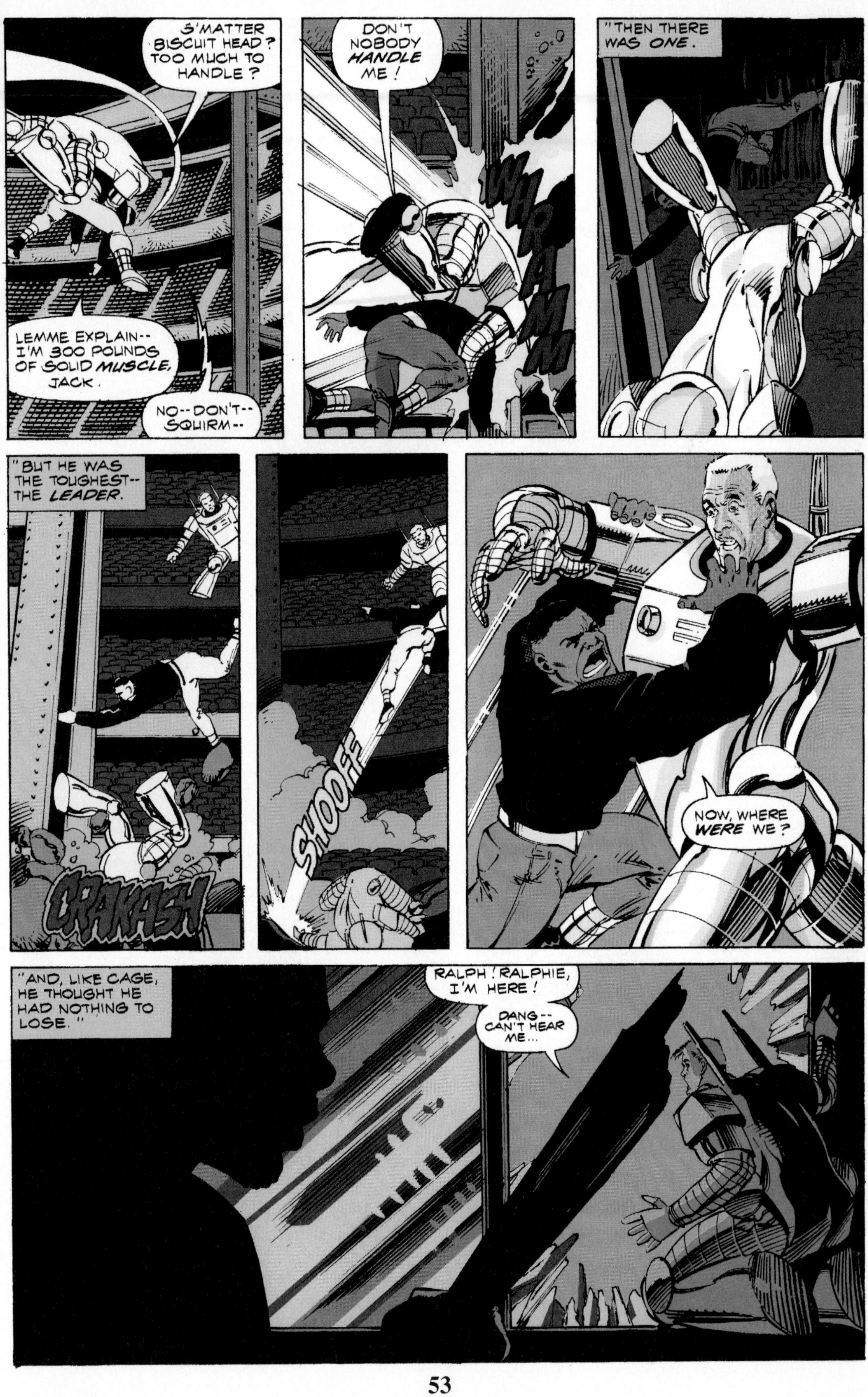
S'MATTER BISCUIT HEAD? TOO MUCH TO HANDLE?
LEMME EXPLAIN-- I'M 300 POUNDS OF SOLID MUSCLE, JACK.
NO--DON'T--SQUIRM--
DON'T NOBODY HANDLE ME!
WHRAMM
"THEN THERE WAS ONE.
"BUT HE WAS THE TOUGHEST--THE LEADER.
CRAKASH
SHOOFF
NOW, WHERE WERE WE?
"AND, LIKE CAGE, HE THOUGHT HE HAD NOTHING TO LOSE."
RALPH! RALPHIE, I'M HERE!
DANG--CAN'T HEAR ME...

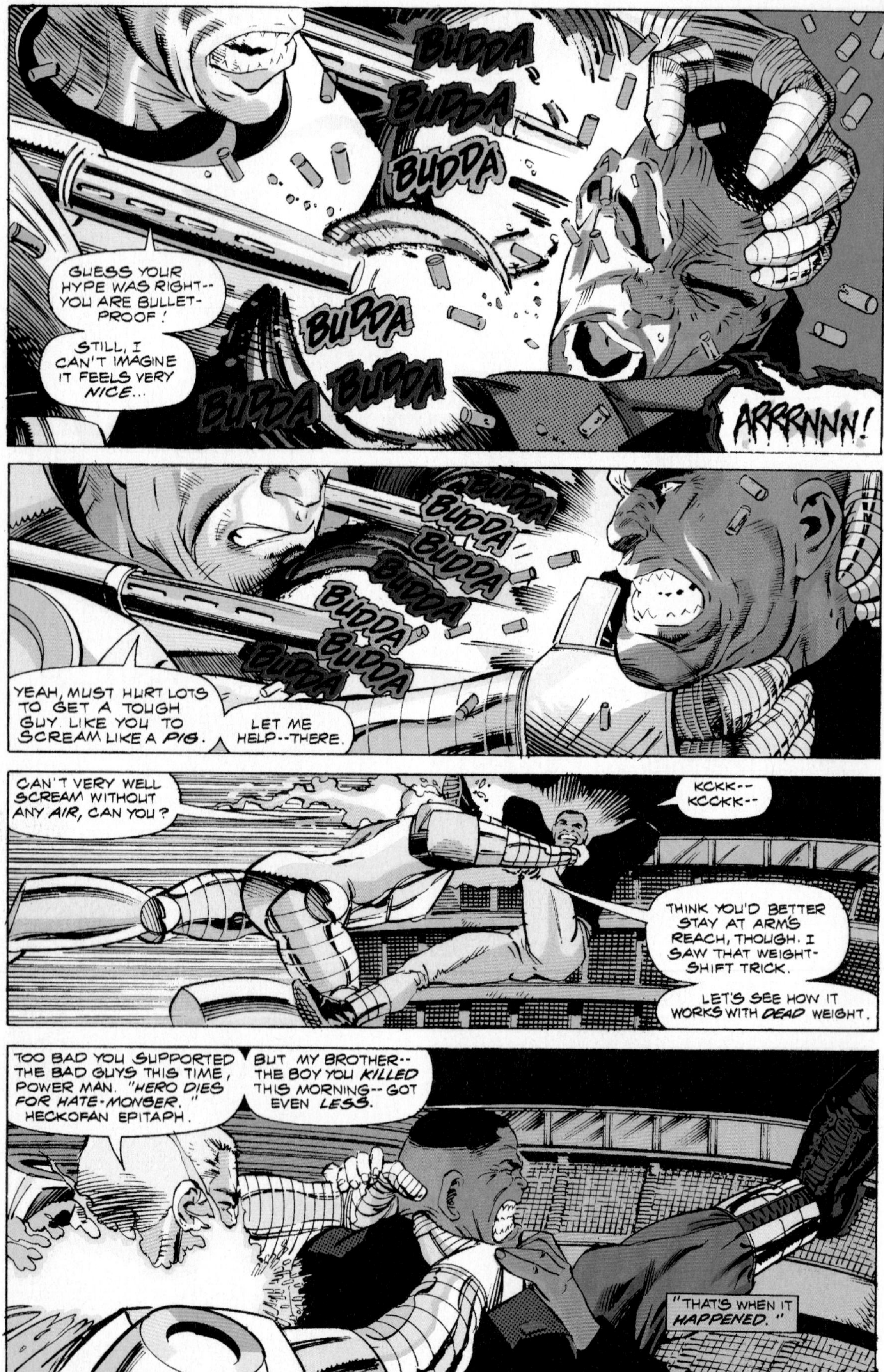
BUDDA BUDDA BUDDA
GUESS YOUR HYPE WAS RIGHT-- YOU ARE BULLET-PROOF!
STILL, I CAN'T IMAGINE IT FEELS VERY NICE...
BUDDA BUDDA BUDDA
ARRRNNN!
BUDDA BUDDA BUDDA BUDDA BUDDA BUDDA BUDDA
YEAH, MUST HURT LOTS TO GET A TOUGH GUY LIKE YOU TO SCREAM LIKE A PIG.
LET ME HELP--THERE.
CAN'T VERY WELL SCREAM WITHOUT ANY AIR, CAN YOU?
KCKK-- KCCKK--
THINK YOU'D BETTER STAY AT ARM'S REACH, THOUGH. I SAW THAT WEIGHT-SHIFT TRICK.
LET'S SEE HOW IT WORKS WITH DEAD WEIGHT.
TOO BAD YOU SUPPORTED THE BAD GUYS THIS TIME, POWER MAN. "HERO DIES FOR HATE-MONGER." HECKOFAN EPITAPH.
BUT MY BROTHER-- THE BOY YOU KILLED THIS MORNING-- GOT EVEN LESS.
"THAT'S WHEN IT HAPPENED."

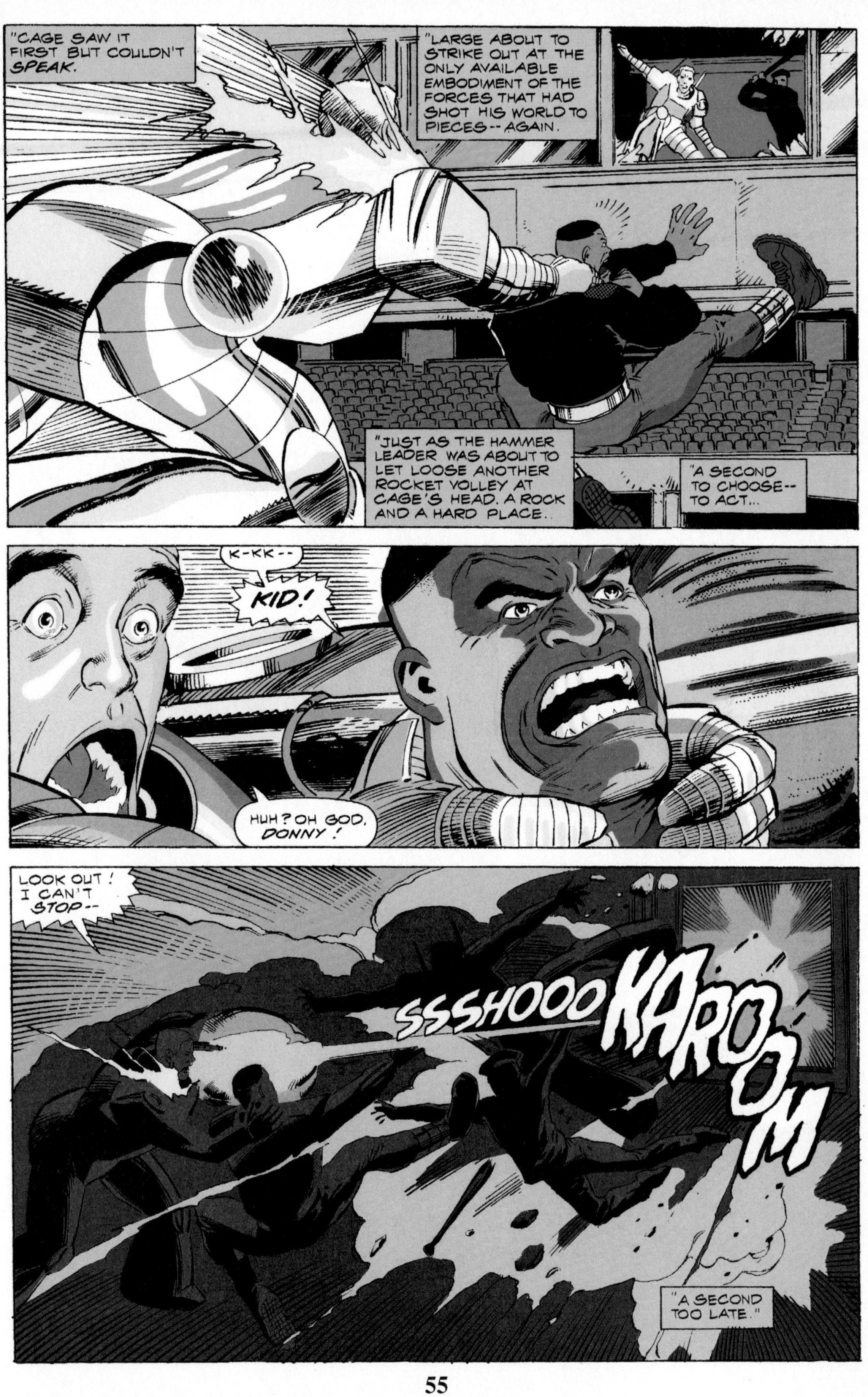
"CAGE SAW IT FIRST BUT COULDN'T *SPEAK*.
"LARGE ABOUT TO STRIKE OUT AT THE ONLY AVAILABLE EMBODIMENT OF THE FORCES THAT HAD SHOT HIS WORLD TO PIECES--AGAIN.
"JUST AS THE HAMMER LEADER WAS ABOUT TO LET LOOSE ANOTHER ROCKET VOLLEY AT CAGE'S HEAD. A ROCK AND A HARD PLACE.
"A SECOND TO CHOOSE--TO ACT...
K-KK--
KID!
HUH? OH GOD, *DONNY*!
LOOK OUT! I CAN'T *STOP*--
SSSHOOO KAROOM
"A SECOND TOO LATE."

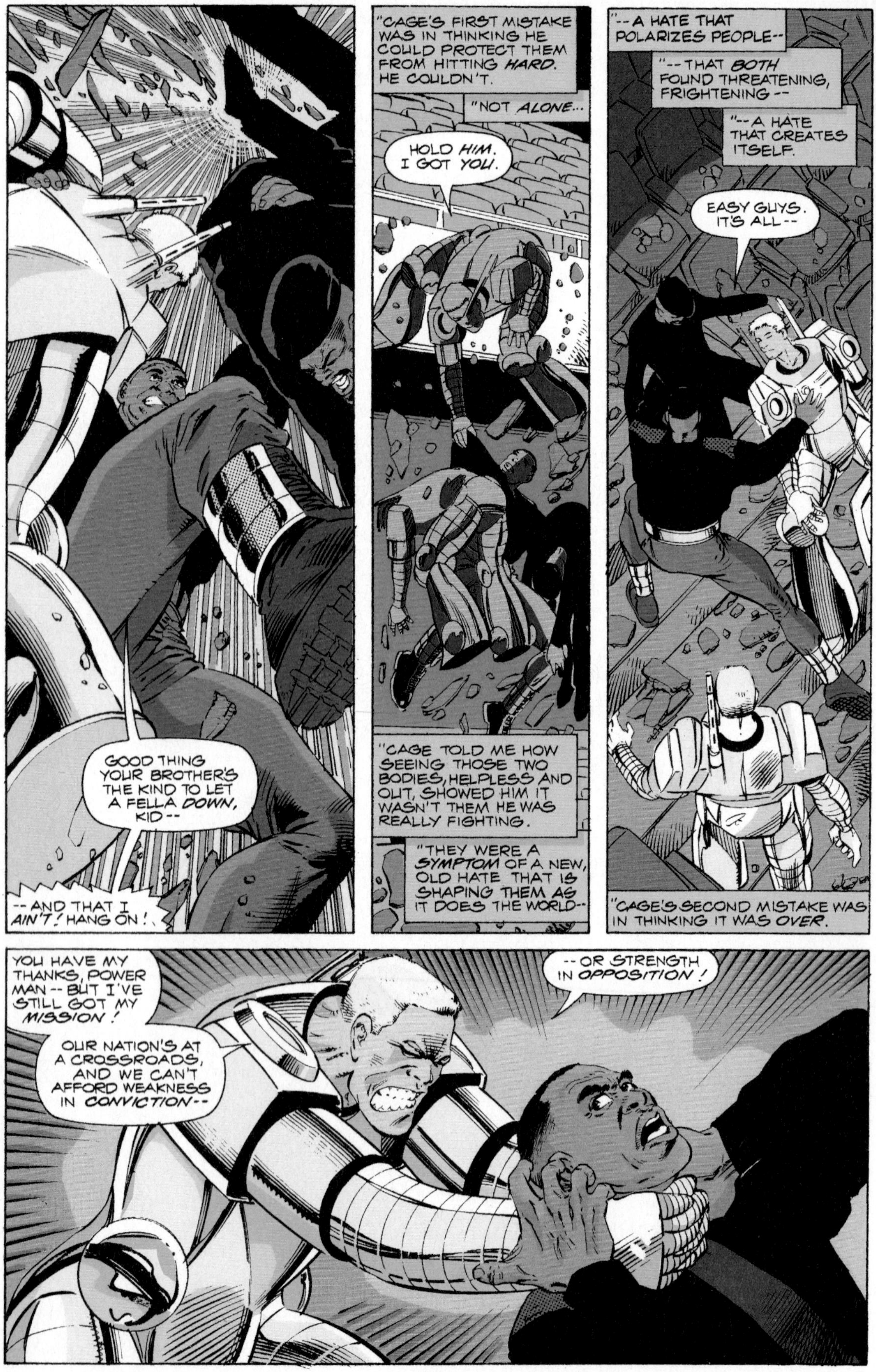
GOOD THING YOUR BROTHER'S THE KIND TO LET A FELLA DOWN, KID --
-- AND THAT I AIN'T! HANG ON!
"CAGE'S FIRST MISTAKE WAS IN THINKING HE COULD PROTECT THEM FROM HITTING HARD. HE COULDN'T.
"NOT ALONE...
HOLD HIM. I GOT YOU.
"CAGE TOLD ME HOW SEEING THOSE TWO BODIES, HELPLESS AND OUT, SHOWED HIM IT WASN'T THEM HE WAS REALLY FIGHTING.
"THEY WERE A SYMPTOM OF A NEW, OLD HATE THAT IS SHAPING THEM AS IT DOES THE WORLD--
"-- A HATE THAT POLARIZES PEOPLE--
"-- THAT BOTH FOUND THREATENING, FRIGHTENING --
"-- A HATE THAT CREATES ITSELF.
EASY GUYS. IT'S ALL --
"CAGE'S SECOND MISTAKE WAS IN THINKING IT WAS OVER.
YOU HAVE MY THANKS, POWER MAN -- BUT I'VE STILL GOT MY MISSION!
OUR NATION'S AT A CROSSROADS, AND WE CAN'T AFFORD WEAKNESS IN CONVICTION--
-- OR STRENGTH IN OPPOSITION!

THAT'S HOW IT IS, HUH? MAN, LARGE WAS *RIGHT*.

UNGH!

MAYBE HE WAS, BOY.

IT'S CALLED *SURVIVAL*-- TO *KNOW* YOUR FRIENDS, HATE YOUR ENEMIES--

--AND ALWAYS STAND WITH YOUR *OWN*.

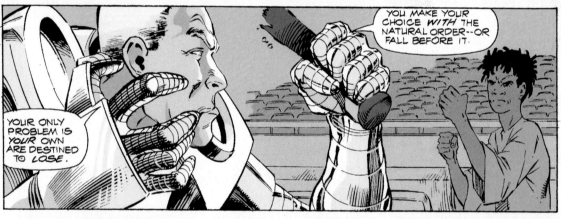

YOUR ONLY PROBLEM IS *YOUR* OWN ARE DESTINED TO *LOSE*.

YOU MAKE YOUR CHOICE *WITH* THE NATURAL ORDER--OR FALL BEFORE IT.

CHOICES. YEAH.

MAYBE IT IS TIME I CHOSE A SIDE.

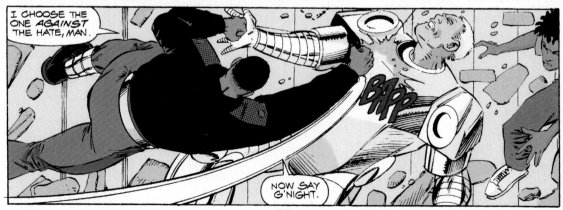

I CHOOSE THE ONE *AGAINST* THE HATE, MAN.

BAPP

NOW SAY G'NIGHT.

57

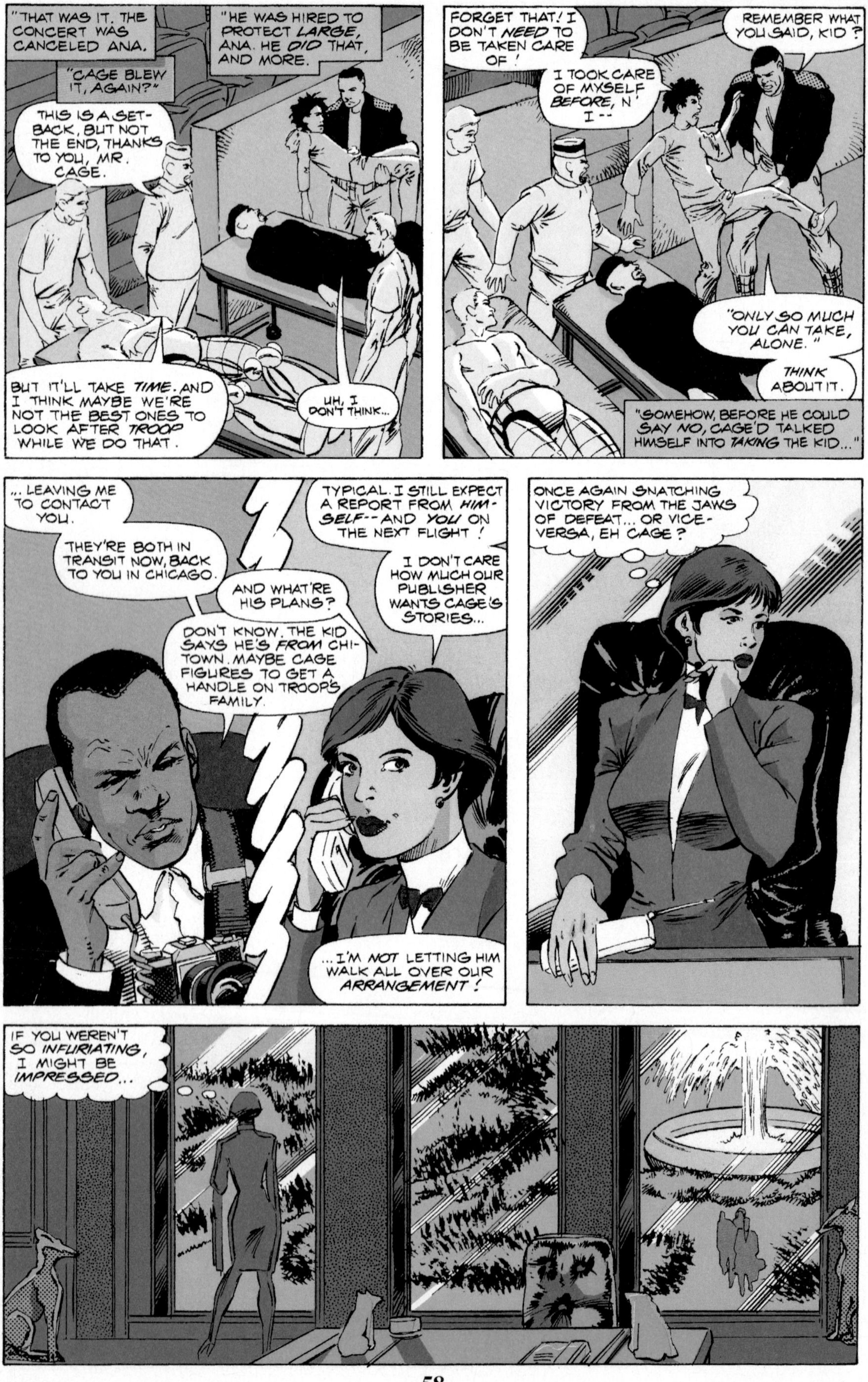

"THAT WAS IT. THE CONCERT WAS CANCELED ANA.
"CAGE BLEW IT, AGAIN?"
"HE WAS HIRED TO PROTECT LARGE, ANA. HE DID THAT, AND MORE.
THIS IS A SET-BACK, BUT NOT THE END, THANKS TO YOU, MR. CAGE.
BUT IT'LL TAKE TIME. AND I THINK MAYBE WE'RE NOT THE BEST ONES TO LOOK AFTER TROOP WHILE WE DO THAT.
UH, I DON'T THINK...
FORGET THAT! I DON'T NEED TO BE TAKEN CARE OF!
I TOOK CARE OF MYSELF BEFORE, N' I --
REMEMBER WHAT YOU SAID, KID?
"ONLY SO MUCH YOU CAN TAKE, ALONE."
THINK ABOUT IT.
"SOMEHOW, BEFORE HE COULD SAY NO, CAGE'D TALKED HIMSELF INTO TAKING THE KID..."
... LEAVING ME TO CONTACT YOU.
THEY'RE BOTH IN TRANSIT NOW, BACK TO YOU IN CHICAGO.
TYPICAL. I STILL EXPECT A REPORT FROM HIM-SELF--AND YOU ON THE NEXT FLIGHT!
AND WHAT'RE HIS PLANS?
DON'T KNOW. THE KID SAYS HE'S FROM CHI-TOWN. MAYBE CAGE FIGURES TO GET A HANDLE ON TROOP'S FAMILY.
I DON'T CARE HOW MUCH OUR PUBLISHER WANTS CAGE'S STORIES...
... I'M NOT LETTING HIM WALK ALL OVER OUR ARRANGEMENT!
ONCE AGAIN SNATCHING VICTORY FROM THE JAWS OF DEFEAT... OR VICE-VERSA, EH CAGE?
IF YOU WEREN'T SO INFURIATING, I MIGHT BE IMPRESSED...

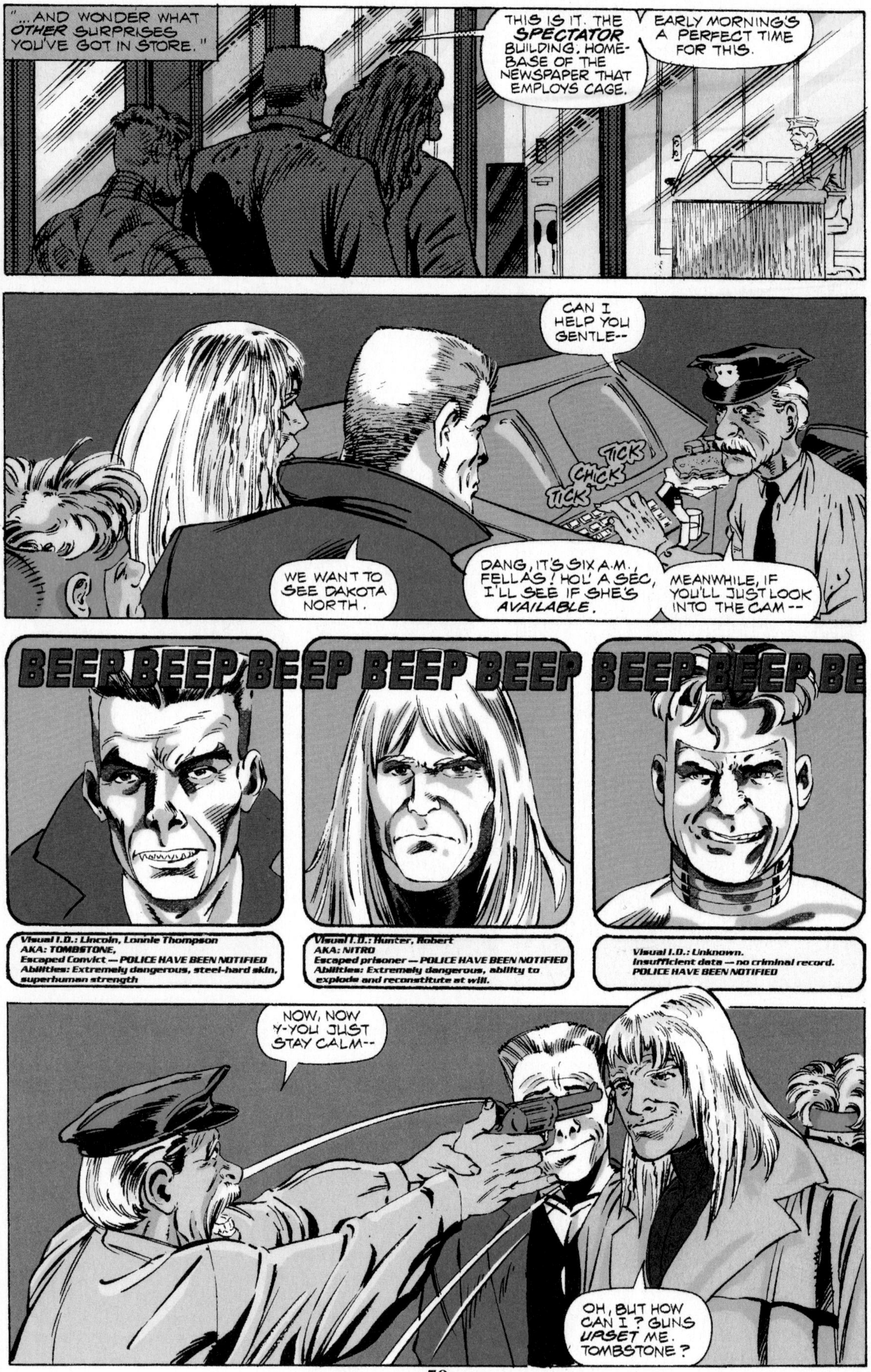
"...AND WONDER WHAT OTHER SURPRISES YOU'VE GOT IN STORE."
THIS IS IT. THE SPECTATOR BUILDING. HOME-BASE OF THE NEWSPAPER THAT EMPLOYS CAGE.
EARLY MORNING'S A PERFECT TIME FOR THIS.
CAN I HELP YOU GENTLE--
TICK CHICK TICK
WE WANT TO SEE DAKOTA NORTH.
DANG, IT'S SIX A.M., FELLAS! HOL' A SEC, I'LL SEE IF SHE'S AVAILABLE.
MEANWHILE, IF YOU'LL JUST LOOK INTO THE CAM--
BEEP BEEP BEEP BEEP BEEP BEEP BEEP BE
Visual I.D.: Lincoln, Lonnie Thompson
AKA: TOMBSTONE,
Escaped Convict — POLICE HAVE BEEN NOTIFIED
Abilities: Extremely dangerous, steel-hard skin, superhuman strength
Visual I.D.: Hunter, Robert
AKA: NITRO
Escaped prisoner — POLICE HAVE BEEN NOTIFIED
Abilities: Extremely dangerous, ability to explode and reconstitute at will.
Visual I.D.: Unknown.
Insufficient data — no criminal record.
POLICE HAVE BEEN NOTIFIED
NOW, NOW Y-YOU JUST STAY CALM--
OH, BUT HOW CAN I? GUNS UPSET ME. TOMBSTONE?

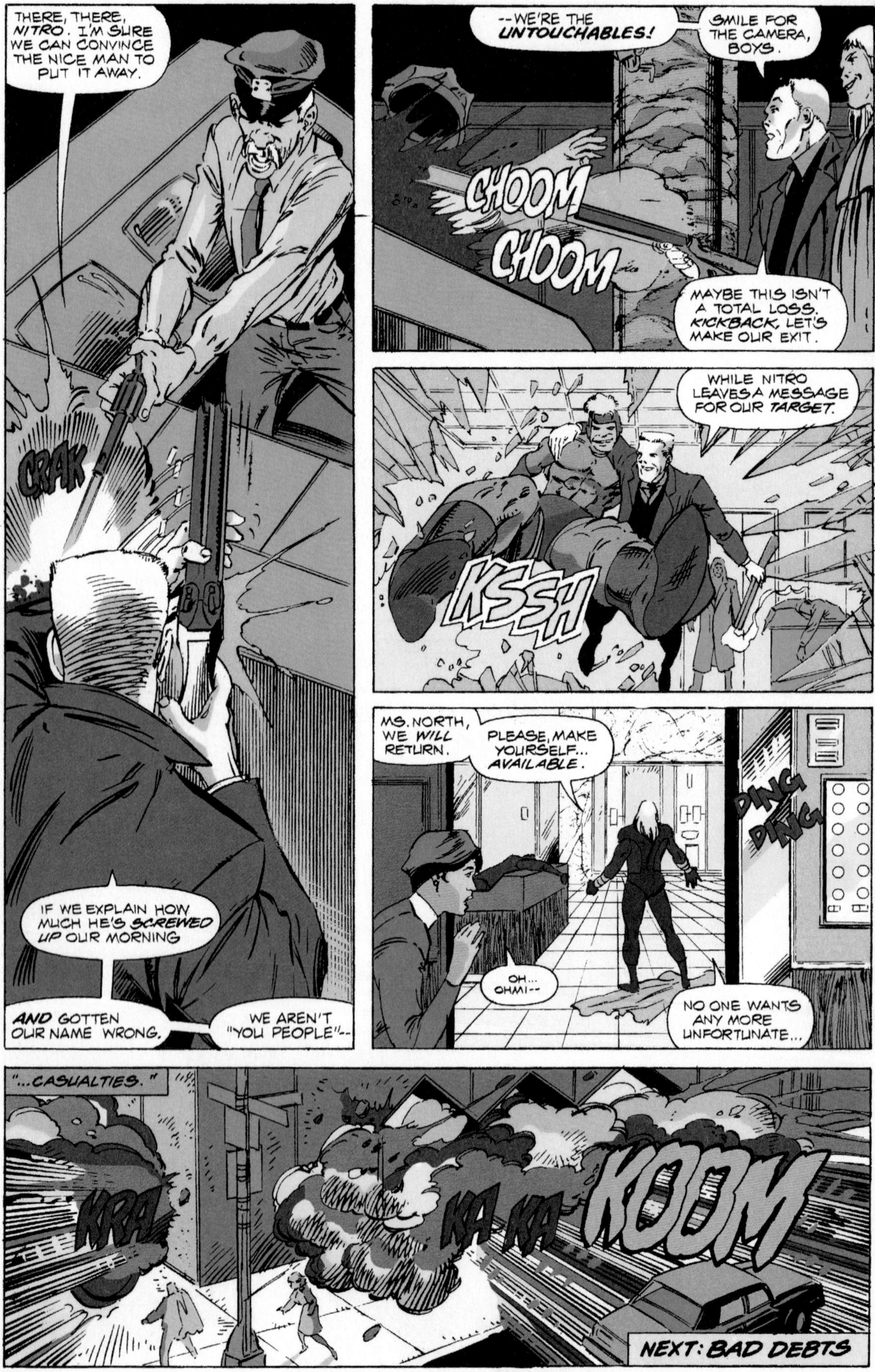

THERE, THERE, NITRO. I'M SURE WE CAN CONVINCE THE NICE MAN TO PUT IT AWAY.
CRAK
IF WE EXPLAIN HOW MUCH HE'S SCREWED UP OUR MORNING
AND GOTTEN OUR NAME WRONG.
WE AREN'T "YOU PEOPLE"--
--WE'RE THE UNTOUCHABLES!
SMILE FOR THE CAMERA, BOYS.
CHOOM
CHOOM
MAYBE THIS ISN'T A TOTAL LOSS. KICKBACK, LET'S MAKE OUR EXIT.
WHILE NITRO LEAVES A MESSAGE FOR OUR TARGET.
KSSH
MS. NORTH, WE WILL RETURN.
PLEASE, MAKE YOURSELF... AVAILABLE.
DING DING
OH... OHMI--
NO ONE WANTS ANY MORE UNFORTUNATE...
"...CASUALTIES."
KRA
KA KA
KOOM
NEXT: BAD DEBTS

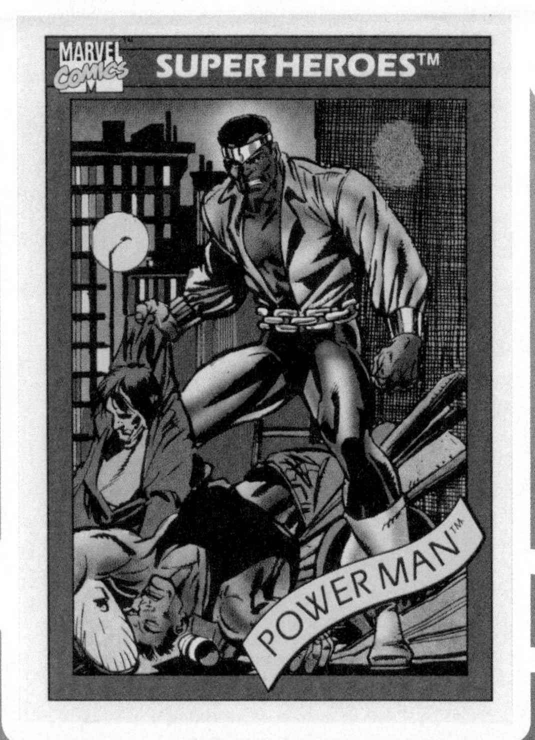
MARVEL COMICS
SUPER HEROES™
POWER MAN™

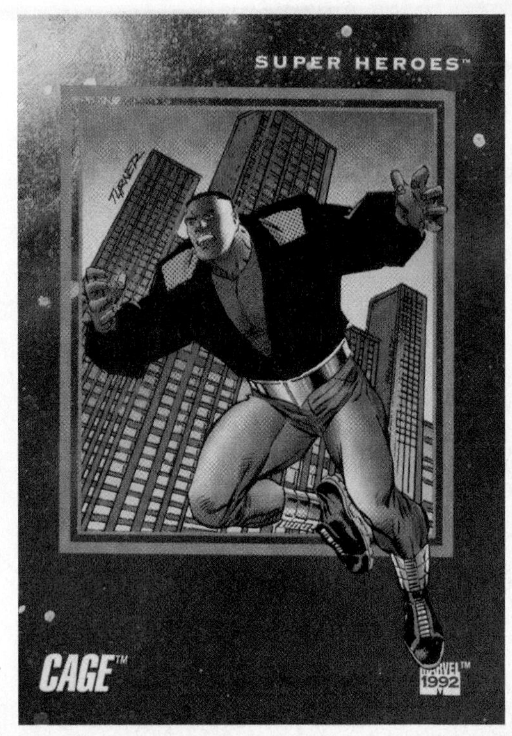
SUPER HEROES™
CAGE™
MARVEL™ 1992

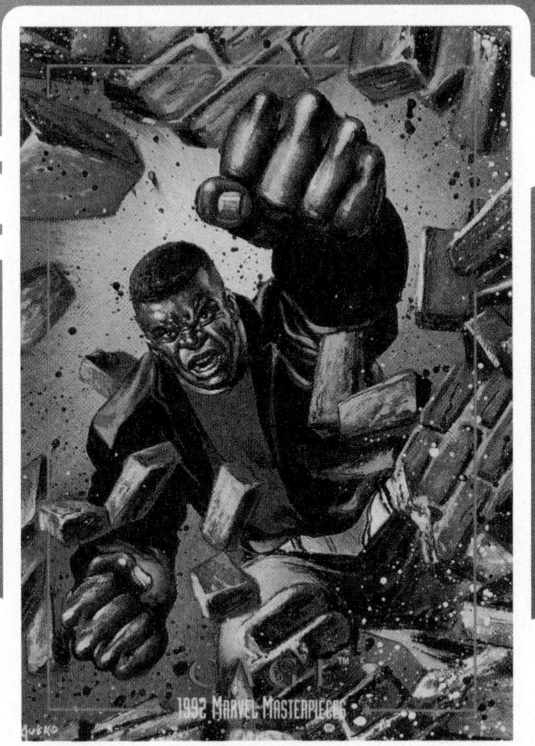
1992 Marvel Masterpieces

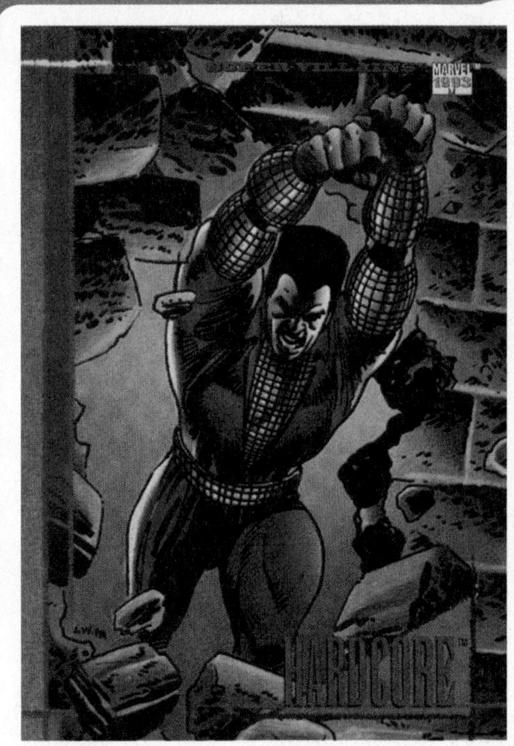
MARVEL™ 1993
HARDCORE™

1990–1993 TRADING-CARD ART BY MARK BAGLEY, DWAYNE TURNER, JOE JUSKO, LEE WEEKS & PAUL MOUNTS

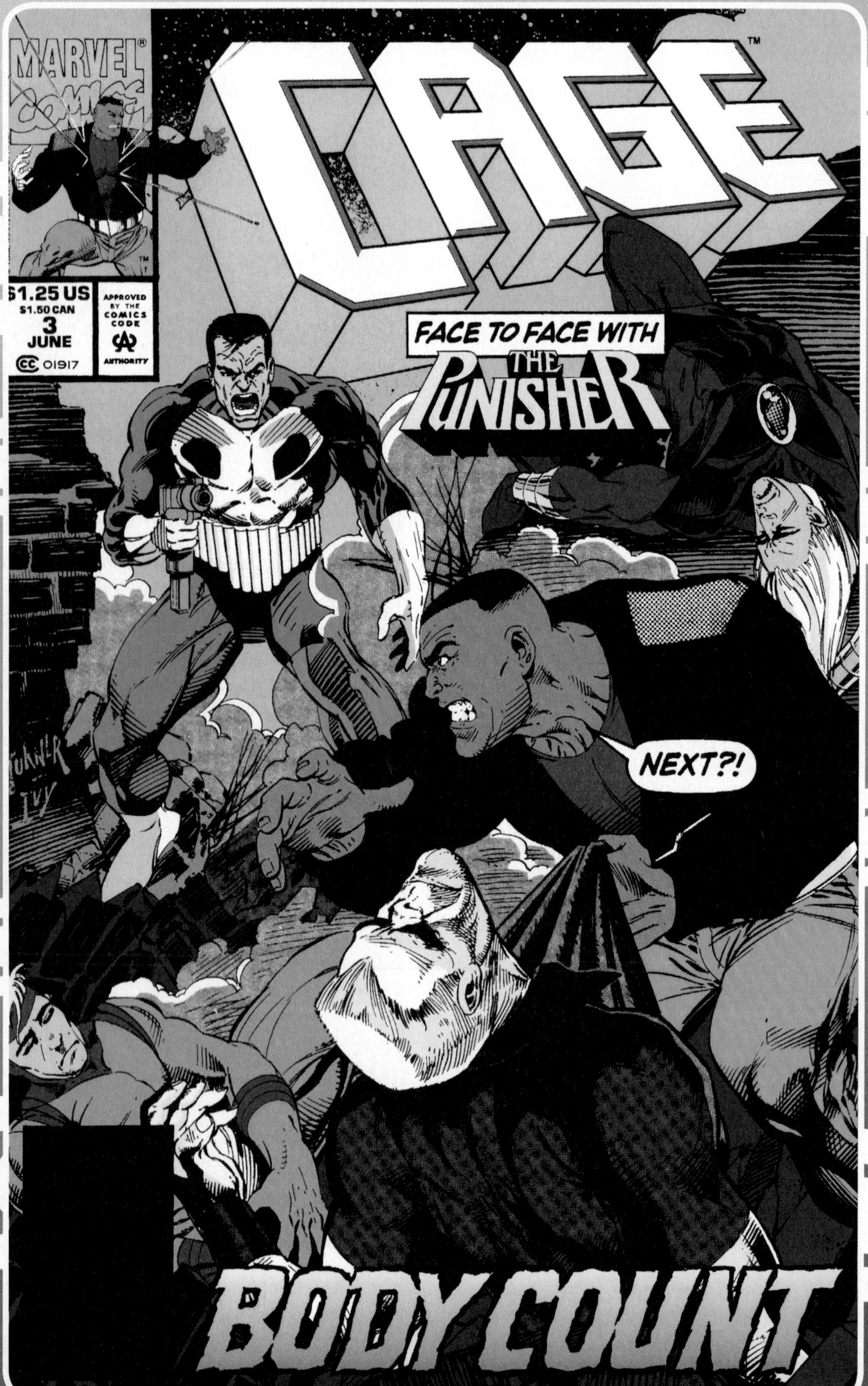
MARVEL COMICS
CAGE
$1.25 US
$1.50 CAN
3
JUNE
CC 01917
APPROVED BY THE COMICS CODE AUTHORITY
FACE TO FACE WITH
THE PUNISHER
NEXT?!
BODY COUNT

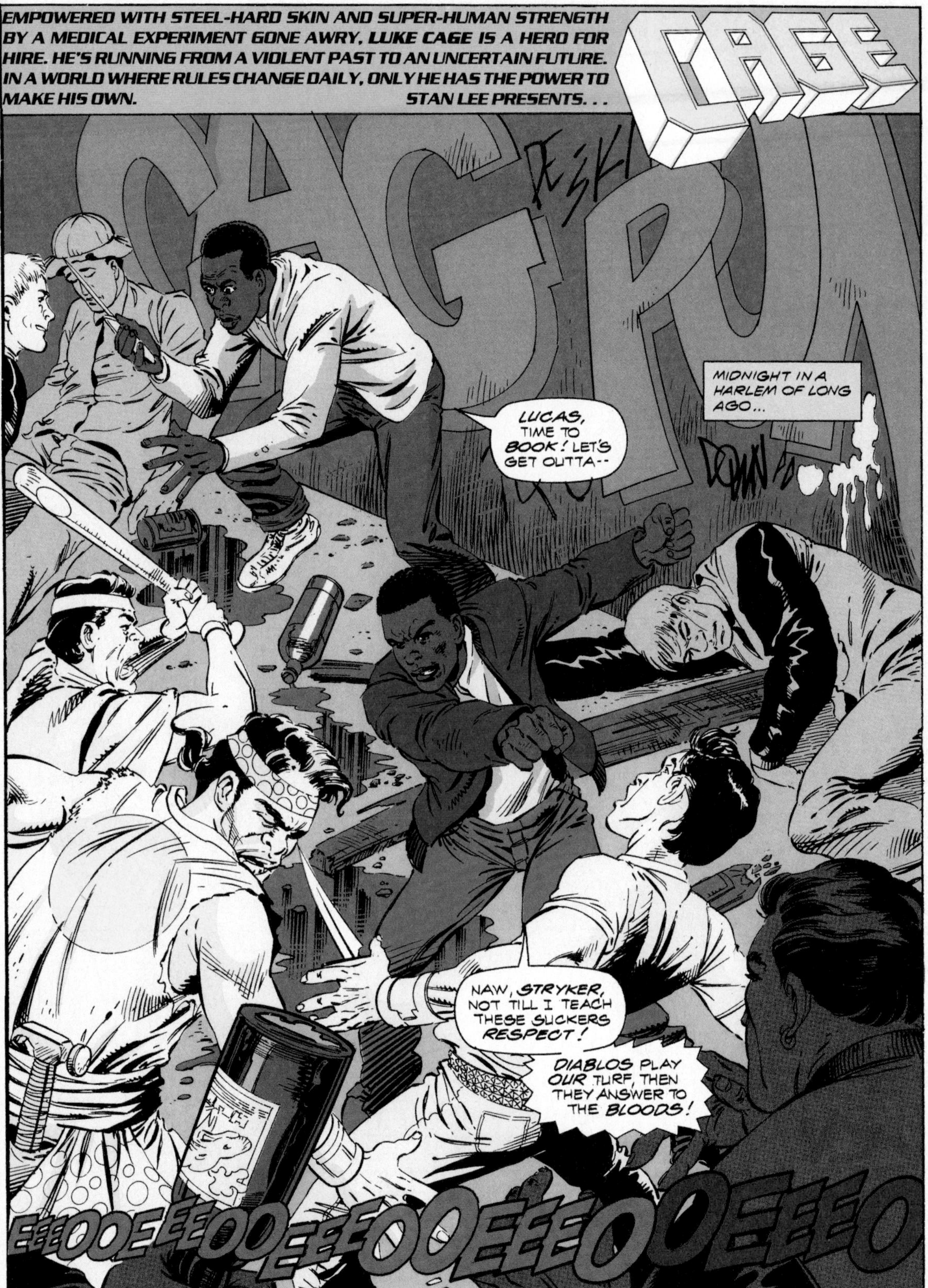
EMPOWERED WITH STEEL-HARD SKIN AND SUPER-HUMAN STRENGTH BY A MEDICAL EXPERIMENT GONE AWRY, LUKE CAGE IS A HERO FOR HIRE. HE'S RUNNING FROM A VIOLENT PAST TO AN UNCERTAIN FUTURE. IN A WORLD WHERE RULES CHANGE DAILY, ONLY HE HAS THE POWER TO MAKE HIS OWN.
STAN LEE PRESENTS. . .
CAGE
MIDNIGHT IN A HARLEM OF LONG AGO...
LUCAS, TIME TO BOOK! LET'S GET OUTTA--
NAW, STRYKER, NOT TILL I TEACH THESE SUCKERS RESPECT!
DIABLOS PLAY OUR TURF, THEN THEY ANSWER TO THE BLOODS!

DWAYNE TURNER PENCILER | MARC McLAURIN WRITER | CHRISTOPHER IVY INKER | CHRIS ELIOPOULOS LETTERER | MIKE THOMAS COLORIST | KELLY CORVESE EDITOR | TOM DEFALCO CHIEF

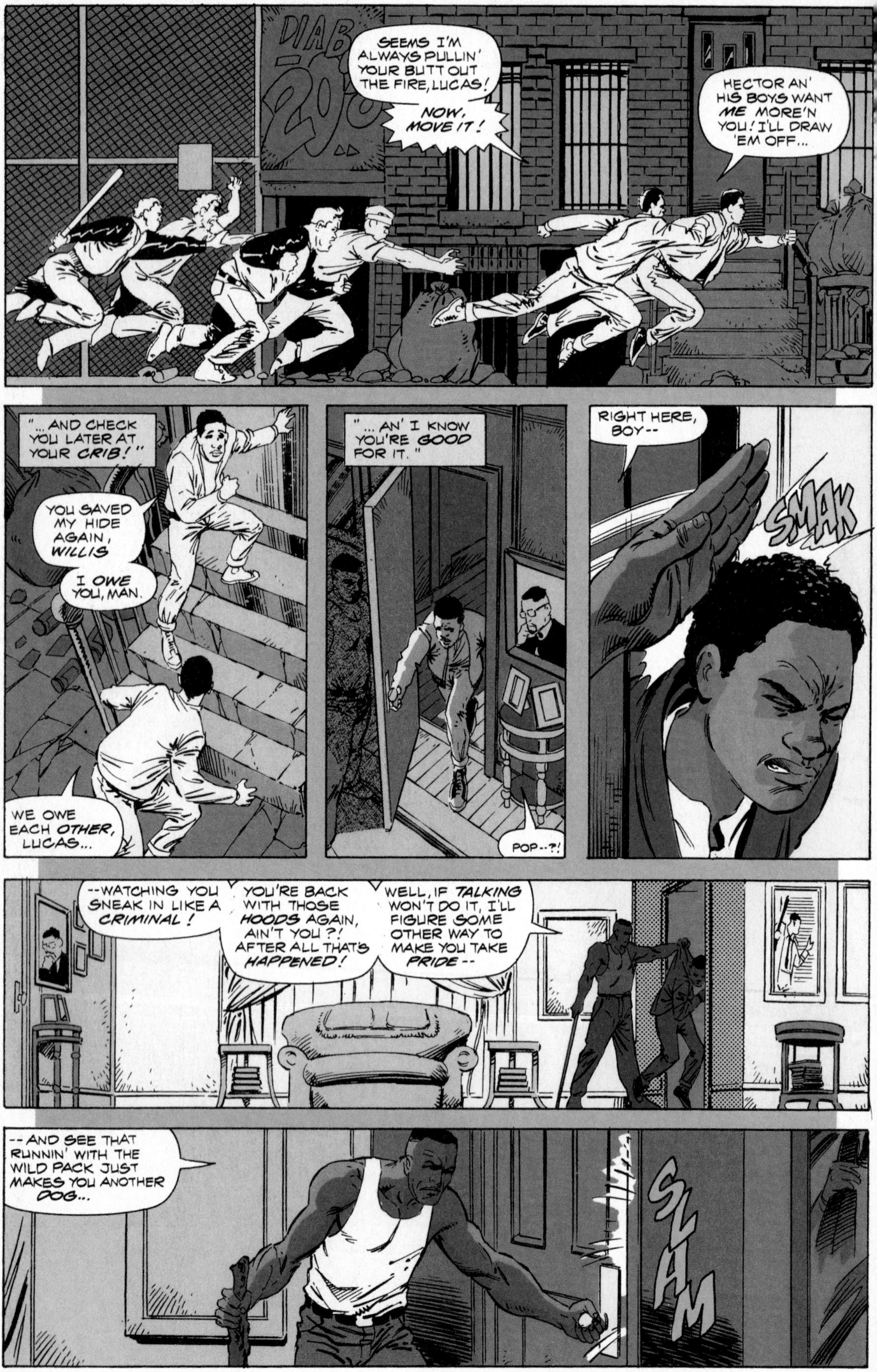
DIAB-20
SEEMS I'M ALWAYS PULLIN' YOUR BUTT OUT THE FIRE, LUCAS!
NOW, MOVE IT!
HECTOR AN' HIS BOYS WANT ME MORE'N YOU! I'LL DRAW 'EM OFF...
"...AND CHECK YOU LATER AT YOUR CRIB!"
YOU SAVED MY HIDE AGAIN, WILLIS
I OWE YOU, MAN.
WE OWE EACH OTHER, LUCAS...
"...AN' I KNOW YOU'RE GOOD FOR IT."
POP--?!
RIGHT HERE, BOY--
SMAK
--WATCHING YOU SNEAK IN LIKE A CRIMINAL!
YOU'RE BACK WITH THOSE HOODS AGAIN, AIN'T YOU?! AFTER ALL THAT'S HAPPENED!
WELL, IF TALKING WON'T DO IT, I'LL FIGURE SOME OTHER WAY TO MAKE YOU TAKE PRIDE--
--AND SEE THAT RUNNIN' WITH THE WILD PACK JUST MAKES YOU ANOTHER DOG...
SLAM

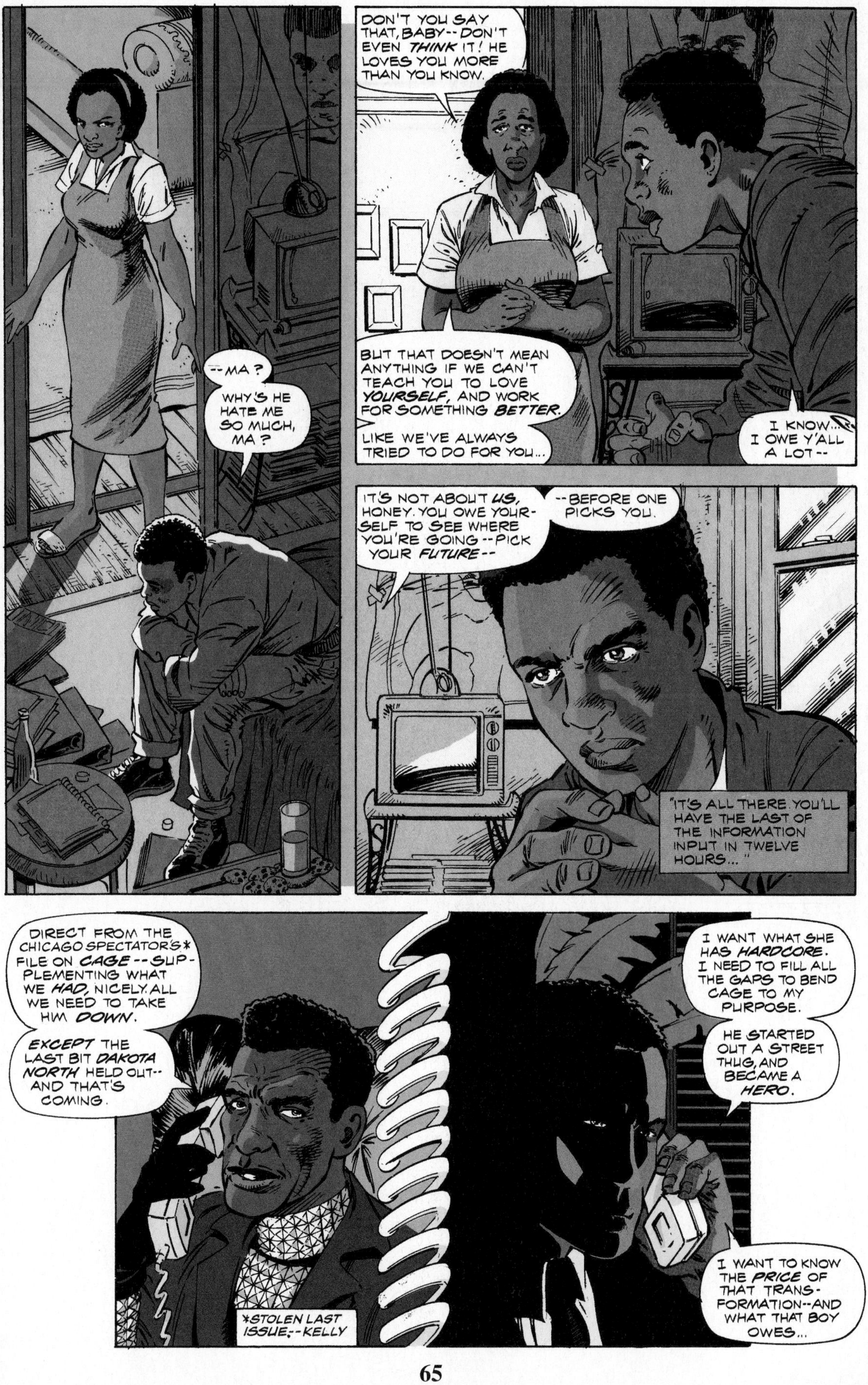

--MA?
WHY'S HE HATE ME SO MUCH, MA?
DON'T YOU SAY THAT, BABY--DON'T EVEN THINK IT! HE LOVES YOU MORE THAN YOU KNOW.
BUT THAT DOESN'T MEAN ANYTHING IF WE CAN'T TEACH YOU TO LOVE YOURSELF, AND WORK FOR SOMETHING BETTER.
LIKE WE'VE ALWAYS TRIED TO DO FOR YOU...
I KNOW... I OWE Y'ALL A LOT--
IT'S NOT ABOUT US, HONEY. YOU OWE YOURSELF TO SEE WHERE YOU'RE GOING--PICK YOUR FUTURE--
--BEFORE ONE PICKS YOU.
"IT'S ALL THERE. YOU'LL HAVE THE LAST OF THE INFORMATION INPUT IN TWELVE HOURS..."
DIRECT FROM THE CHICAGO SPECTATOR'S* FILE ON CAGE--SUPPLEMENTING WHAT WE HAD, NICELY. ALL WE NEED TO TAKE HIM DOWN.
EXCEPT THE LAST BIT DAKOTA NORTH HELD OUT--AND THAT'S COMING.
I WANT WHAT SHE HAS HARDCORE. I NEED TO FILL ALL THE GAPS TO BEND CAGE TO MY PURPOSE.
HE STARTED OUT A STREET THUG, AND BECAME A HERO.
I WANT TO KNOW THE PRICE OF THAT TRANSFORMATION--AND WHAT THAT BOY OWES...
*STOLEN LAST ISSUE.--KELLY

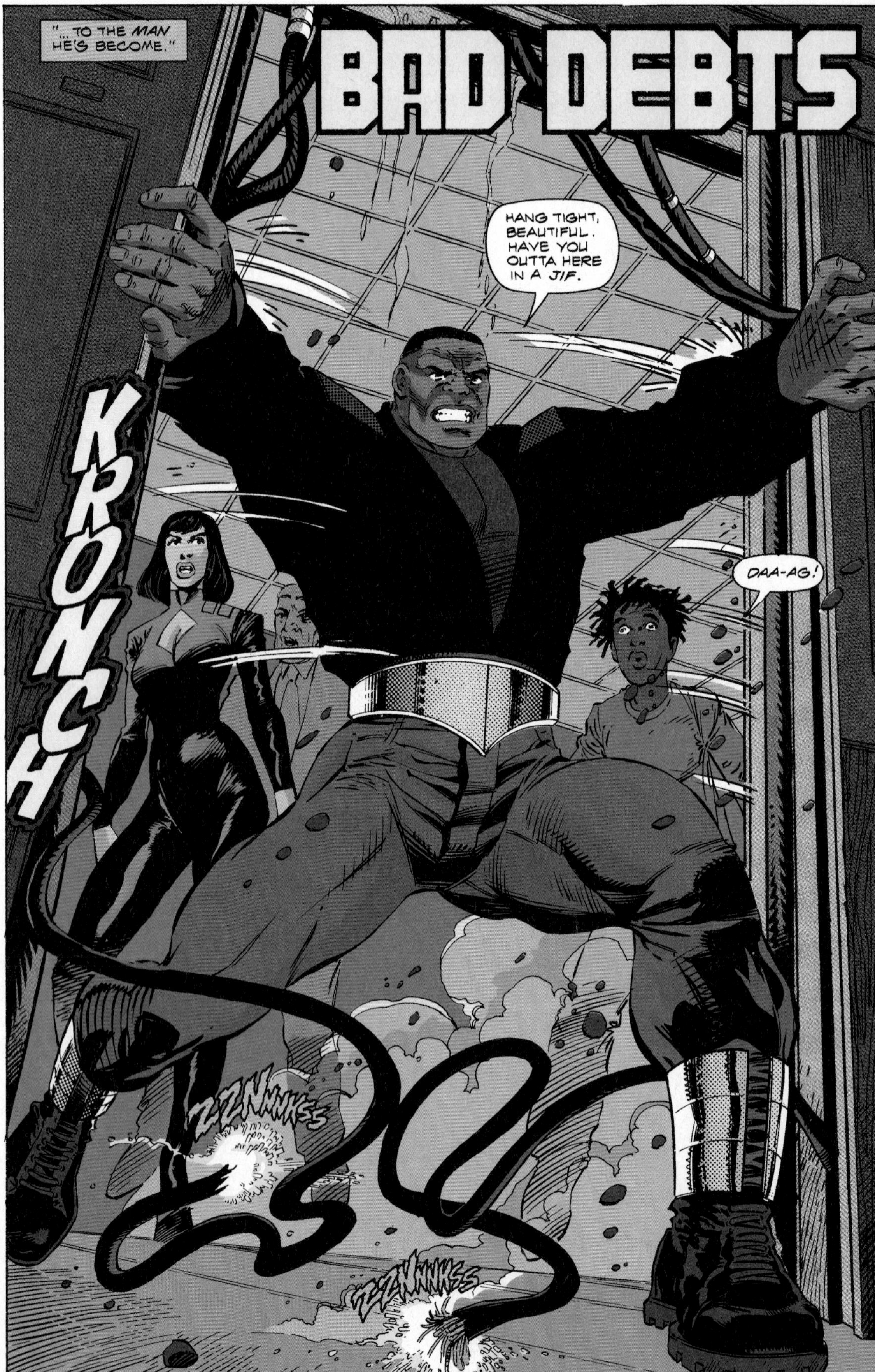
"... TO THE MAN HE'S BECOME."
BAD DEBTS
HANG TIGHT, BEAUTIFUL. HAVE YOU OUTTA HERE IN A JIF.
KRONCH
DAA-AG!
ZZNNNKSS
ZZZNNNKSS

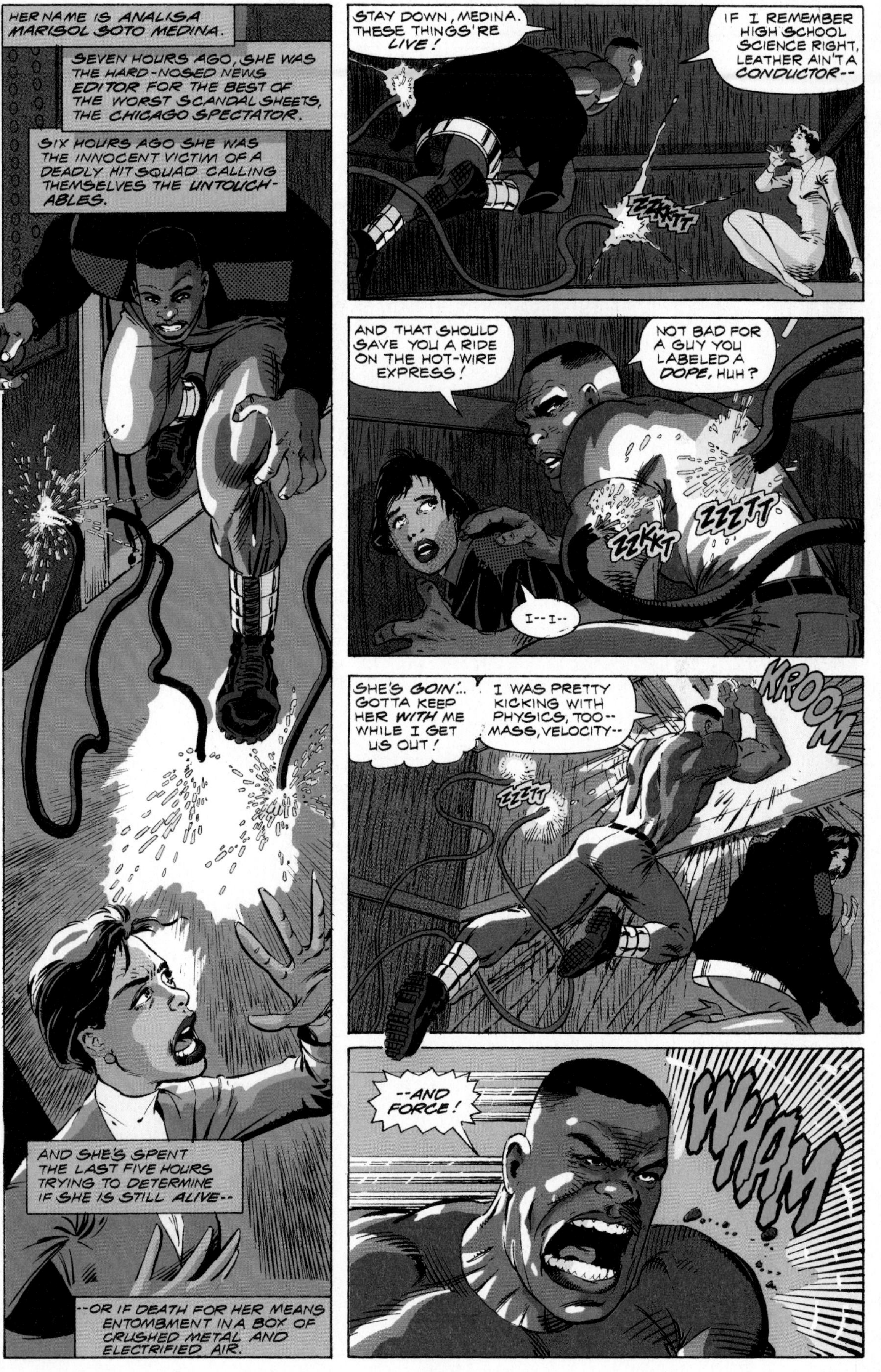
HER NAME IS ANALISA MARISOL SOTO MEDINA.
SEVEN HOURS AGO, SHE WAS THE HARD-NOSED NEWS EDITOR FOR THE BEST OF THE WORST SCANDAL SHEETS, THE CHICAGO SPECTATOR.
SIX HOURS AGO SHE WAS THE INNOCENT VICTIM OF A DEADLY HIT SQUAD CALLING THEMSELVES THE UNTOUCH-ABLES.
AND SHE'S SPENT THE LAST FIVE HOURS TRYING TO DETERMINE IF SHE IS STILL ALIVE--
--OR IF DEATH FOR HER MEANS ENTOMBMENT IN A BOX OF CRUSHED METAL AND ELECTRIFIED AIR.
STAY DOWN, MEDINA. THESE THINGS'RE LIVE!
IF I REMEMBER HIGH SCHOOL SCIENCE RIGHT, LEATHER AIN'T A CONDUCTOR--
ZZZKKTT
AND THAT SHOULD SAVE YOU A RIDE ON THE HOT-WIRE EXPRESS!
NOT BAD FOR A GUY YOU LABELED A DOPE, HUH?
ZZZTT
ZZKKT
I-- I--
SHE'S GOIN'... GOTTA KEEP HER WITH ME WHILE I GET US OUT!
I WAS PRETTY KICKING WITH PHYSICS, TOO-- MASS, VELOCITY--
KROOM
ZZZTT
--AND FORCE!
WHAM

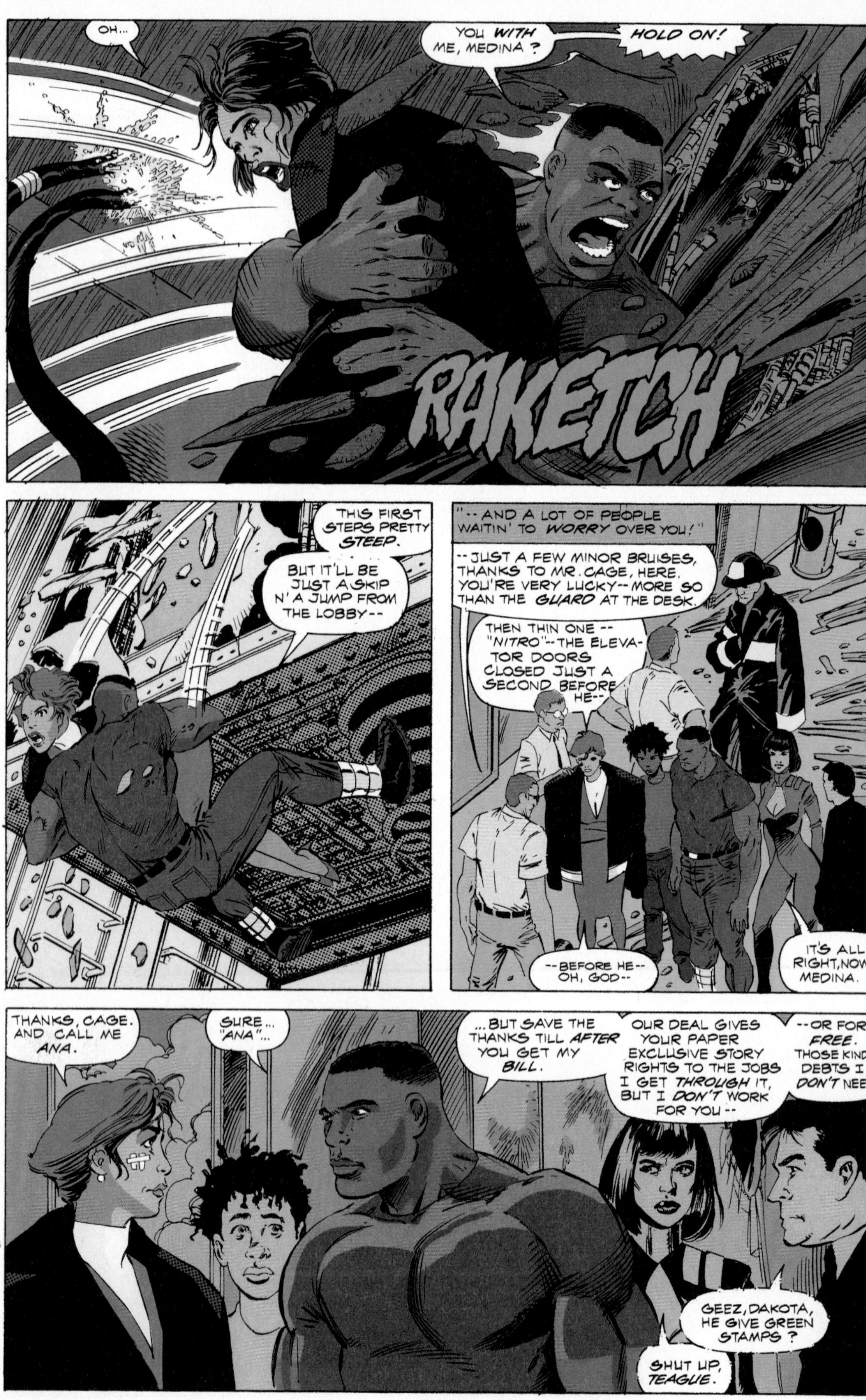
OH...
YOU WITH ME, MEDINA?
HOLD ON!
RAKETCH
THIS FIRST STEPS PRETTY STEEP.
BUT IT'LL BE JUST A SKIP N' A JUMP FROM THE LOBBY--
"--AND A LOT OF PEOPLE WAITIN' TO WORRY OVER YOU!"
--JUST A FEW MINOR BRUISES, THANKS TO MR. CAGE, HERE. YOU'RE VERY LUCKY--MORE SO THAN THE GUARD AT THE DESK.
THEN THIN ONE -- "NITRO"--THE ELEVATOR DOORS CLOSED JUST A SECOND BEFORE HE--
--BEFORE HE-- OH, GOD--
IT'S ALL RIGHT, NOW, MEDINA.
THANKS, CAGE. AND CALL ME ANA.
SURE... "ANA"...
...BUT SAVE THE THANKS TILL AFTER YOU GET MY BILL.
OUR DEAL GIVES YOUR PAPER EXCLUSIVE STORY RIGHTS TO THE JOBS I GET THROUGH IT, BUT I DON'T WORK FOR YOU--
--OR FOR FREE. THOSE KINDA DEBTS I DON'T NEED.
GEEZ, DAKOTA, HE GIVE GREEN STAMPS?
SHUT UP, TEAGUE.

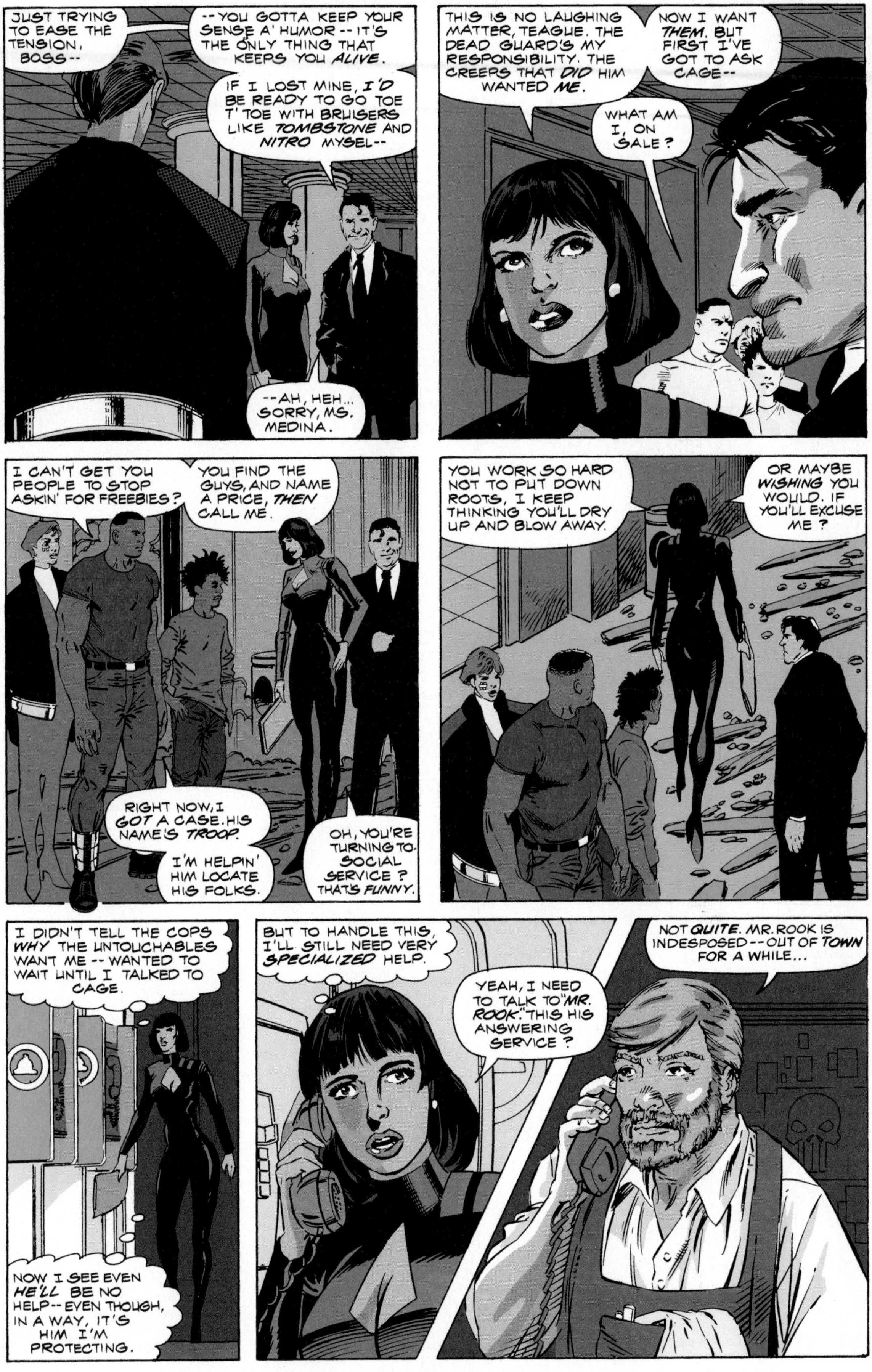
JUST TRYING TO EASE THE TENSION, BOSS--
--YOU GOTTA KEEP YOUR SENSE A' HUMOR -- IT'S THE ONLY THING THAT KEEPS YOU ALIVE.
IF I LOST MINE, I'D BE READY TO GO TOE T' TOE WITH BRUISERS LIKE TOMBSTONE AND NITRO MYSEL--
--AH, HEH... SORRY, MS. MEDINA.
THIS IS NO LAUGHING MATTER, TEAGUE. THE DEAD GUARD'S MY RESPONSIBILITY. THE CREEPS THAT DID HIM WANTED ME.
NOW I WANT THEM. BUT FIRST I'VE GOT TO ASK CAGE--
WHAT AM I, ON SALE?
I CAN'T GET YOU PEOPLE TO STOP ASKIN' FOR FREEBIES?
YOU FIND THE GUYS, AND NAME A PRICE, THEN CALL ME.
RIGHT NOW, I GOT A CASE. HIS NAME'S TROOP.
I'M HELPIN' HIM LOCATE HIS FOLKS.
OH, YOU'RE TURNING TO SOCIAL SERVICE? THAT'S FUNNY.
YOU WORK SO HARD NOT TO PUT DOWN ROOTS, I KEEP THINKING YOU'LL DRY UP AND BLOW AWAY.
OR MAYBE WISHING YOU WOULD. IF YOU'LL EXCUSE ME?
I DIDN'T TELL THE COPS WHY THE UNTOUCHABLES WANT ME -- WANTED TO WAIT UNTIL I TALKED TO CAGE.
NOW I SEE EVEN HE'LL BE NO HELP -- EVEN THOUGH, IN A WAY, IT'S HIM I'M PROTECTING.
BUT TO HANDLE THIS, I'LL STILL NEED VERY SPECIALIZED HELP.
YEAH, I NEED TO TALK TO "MR. ROOK." THIS HIS ANSWERING SERVICE?
NOT QUITE. MR. ROOK IS INDESPOSED -- OUT OF TOWN FOR A WHILE...

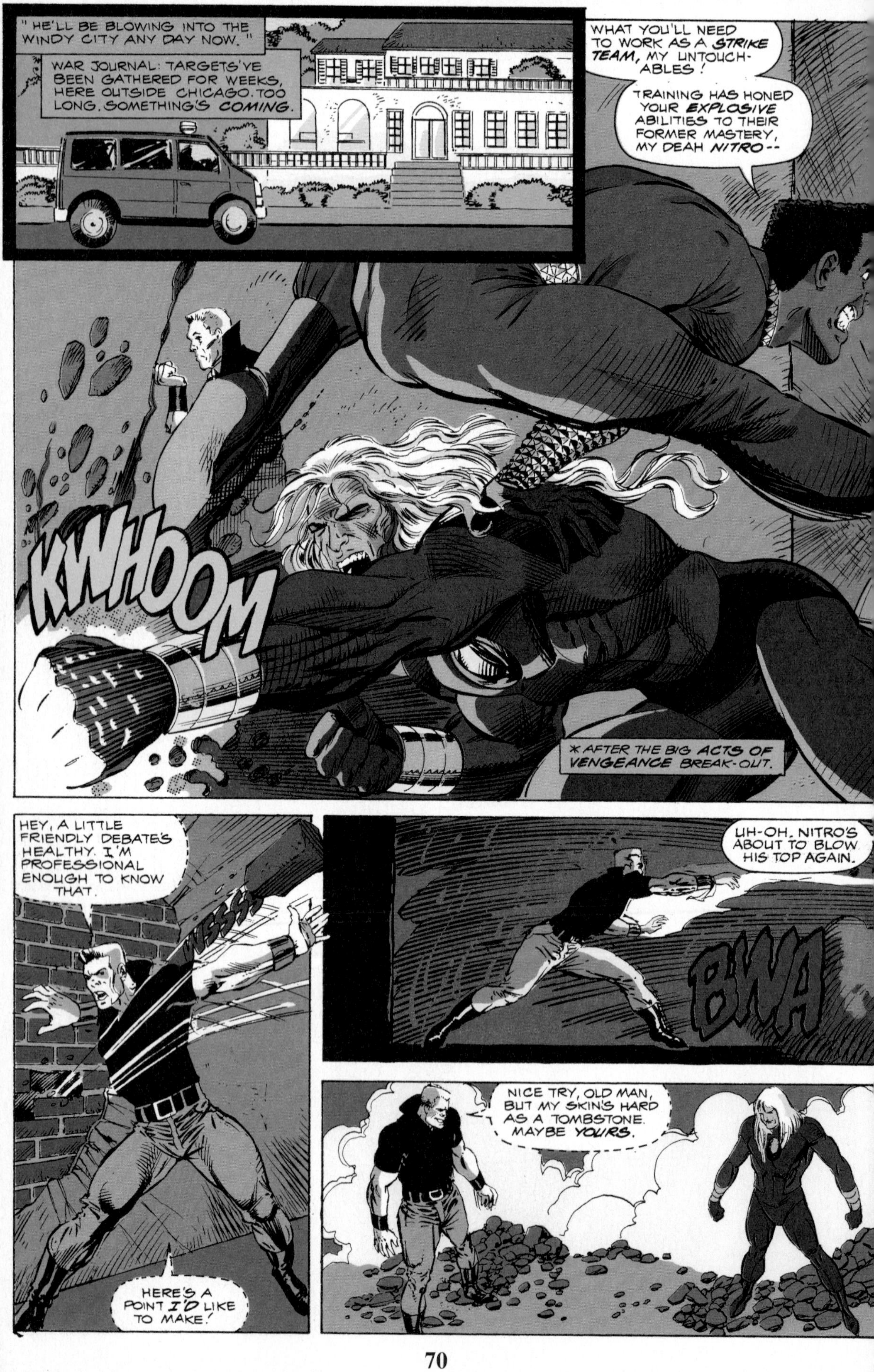
"HE'LL BE BLOWING INTO THE WINDY CITY ANY DAY NOW."
WAR JOURNAL: TARGETS'VE BEEN GATHERED FOR WEEKS, HERE OUTSIDE CHICAGO. TOO LONG. SOMETHING'S COMING.
WHAT YOU'LL NEED TO WORK AS A STRIKE TEAM, MY UNTOUCH-ABLES!
TRAINING HAS HONED YOUR EXPLOSIVE ABILITIES TO THEIR FORMER MASTERY, MY DEAH NITRO--
KWHOOM
*AFTER THE BIG ACTS OF VENGEANCE BREAK-OUT.
HEY, A LITTLE FRIENDLY DEBATE'S HEALTHY. I'M PROFESSIONAL ENOUGH TO KNOW THAT.
HERE'S A POINT I'D LIKE TO MAKE!
UH-OH. NITRO'S ABOUT TO BLOW HIS TOP AGAIN.
BWA
NICE TRY, OLD MAN, BUT MY SKIN'S HARD AS A TOMBSTONE. MAYBE YOURS.

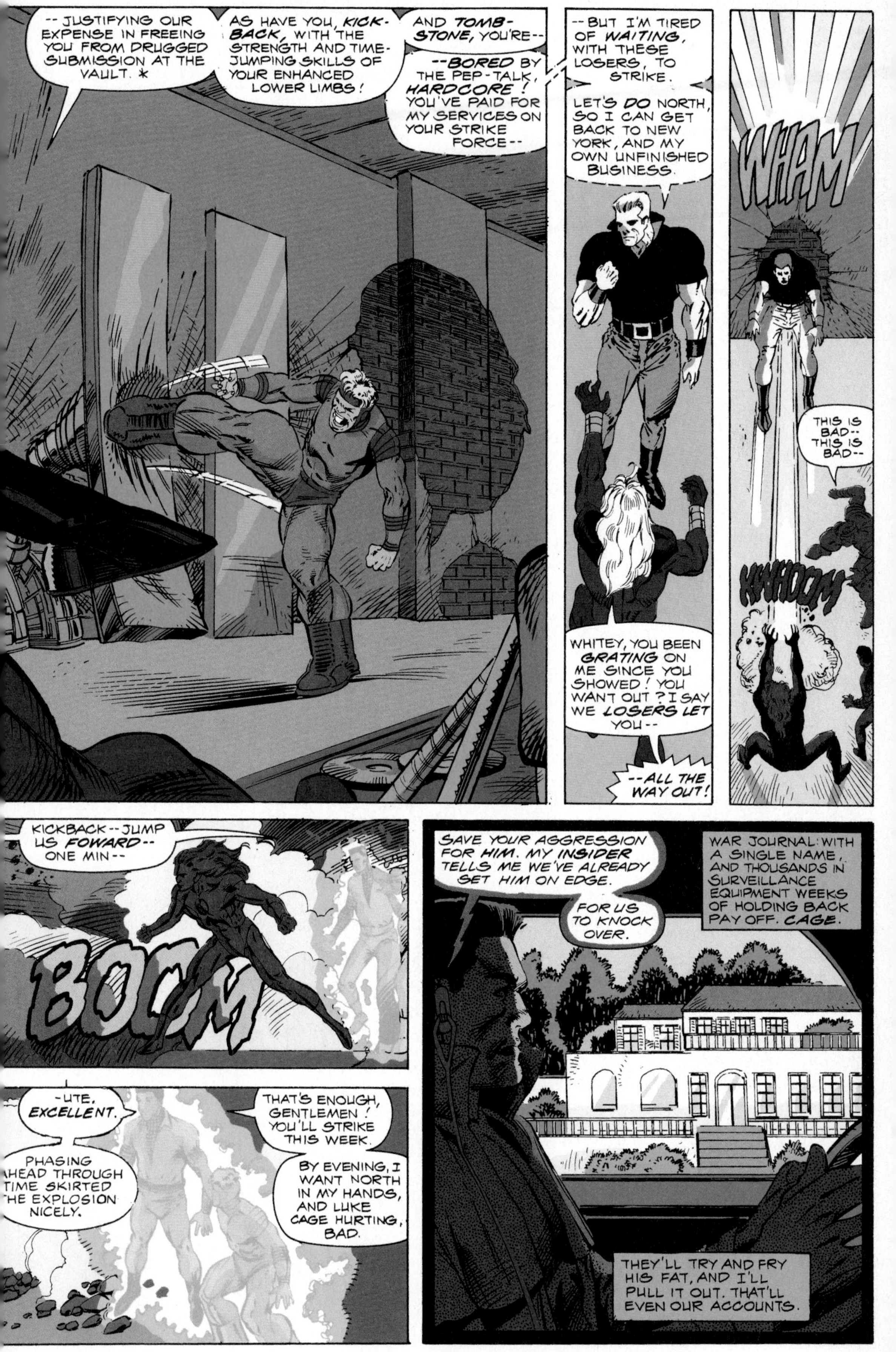

-- JUSTIFYING OUR EXPENSE IN FREEING YOU FROM DRUGGED SUBMISSION AT THE VAULT. *
AS HAVE YOU, KICK-BACK, WITH THE STRENGTH AND TIME-JUMPING SKILLS OF YOUR ENHANCED LOWER LIMBS!
AND TOMBSTONE, YOU'RE--
--BORED BY THE PEP-TALK, HARDCORE! YOU'VE PAID FOR MY SERVICES ON YOUR STRIKE FORCE--
--BUT I'M TIRED OF WAITING, WITH THESE LOSERS, TO STRIKE.
LET'S DO NORTH, SO I CAN GET BACK TO NEW YORK, AND MY OWN UNFINISHED BUSINESS.
WHITEY, YOU BEEN GRATING ON ME SINCE YOU SHOWED! YOU WANT OUT? I SAY WE LOSERS LET YOU--
--ALL THE WAY OUT!
WHAM
THIS IS BAD-- THIS IS BAD--
KAHDOOM
KICKBACK--JUMP US FOWARD-- ONE MIN--
BOOM
-UTE. EXCELLENT.
PHASING AHEAD THROUGH TIME SKIRTED THE EXPLOSION NICELY.
THAT'S ENOUGH, GENTLEMEN! YOU'LL STRIKE THIS WEEK.
BY EVENING, I WANT NORTH IN MY HANDS, AND LUKE CAGE HURTING, BAD.
SAVE YOUR AGGRESSION FOR HIM. MY INSIDER TELLS ME WE'VE ALREADY SET HIM ON EDGE.
FOR US TO KNOCK OVER.
WAR JOURNAL: WITH A SINGLE NAME, AND THOUSANDS IN SURVEILLANCE EQUIPMENT WEEKS OF HOLDING BACK PAY OFF. CAGE.
THEY'LL TRY AND FRY HIS FAT, AND I'LL PULL IT OUT. THAT'LL EVEN OUR ACCOUNTS.

NOON, NEAR CHICAGO'S STATE STREET MALL. SCHOOL'S IN SESSION.

...AND WE'LL FIND YOUR PEOPLE "YOU CAN DO IT IF YOU NEED TO." FIRST OF "CAGE'S ADVANCED LAWS OF SURVIVAL."

SECOND, "A STRONG MAN WORKS FOR HIS MONEY."

CHANGE, BUDDY? SPARAQUARTA?

THIRD, "A SMART MAN PUTS HIS MONEY TO WORK FOR HIM."

FOURTH --

NOBODY MOVES, NOBODY GETS HURT!

LET'S KEEP THIS SIMPLE!

AW, MAN, I DON'T HAVE TIME FOR THIS...

...SO IT'S GONNA GET REAL COMPLICATED!

SHEE-- THE BULLETS BOUNCE!

NRAKK

BRAKK
BRAKK

THIS IS --IT'S THAT POWER MAN GUY, FROM THE PAPER!

I GOTTA GET A --:SLING: PUBLICIST.

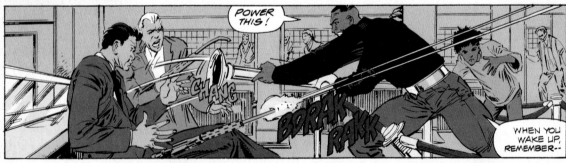

POWER THIS!

CHANG

BDRAKK RAKK

WHEN YOU WAKE UP, REMEMBER--

--THE NAME IS CAGE. I BELIEVE THIS MESS IS YOURS.

BUT IT'S NOTHIN' LIKE THE MESS THIS BANK'LL BE, WHEN IT BLOWS!

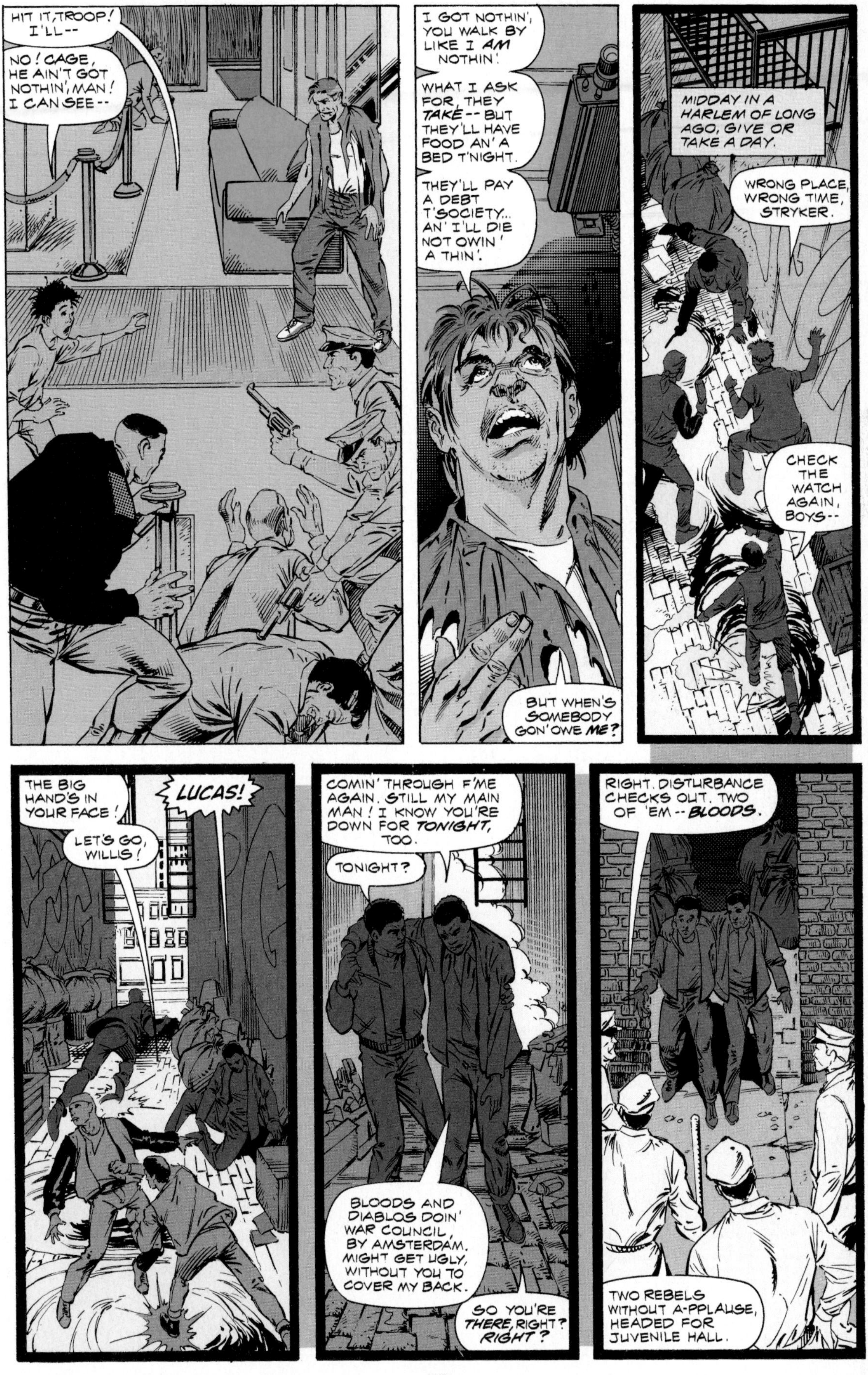
HIT IT, TROOP! I'LL--
NO! CAGE, HE AIN'T GOT NOTHIN', MAN! I CAN SEE--
I GOT NOTHIN', YOU WALK BY LIKE I AM NOTHIN'.
WHAT I ASK FOR, THEY TAKE-- BUT THEY'LL HAVE FOOD AN' A BED T'NIGHT.
THEY'LL PAY A DEBT T'SOCIETY... AN' I'LL DIE NOT OWIN' A THIN'.
BUT WHEN'S SOMEBODY GON' OWE ME?
MIDDAY IN A HARLEM OF LONG AGO, GIVE OR TAKE A DAY.
WRONG PLACE, WRONG TIME, STRYKER.
CHECK THE WATCH AGAIN, BOYS--
THE BIG HAND'S IN YOUR FACE!
LUCAS!
LET'S GO, WILLIS!
COMIN' THROUGH F'ME AGAIN. STILL MY MAIN MAN! I KNOW YOU'RE DOWN FOR TONIGHT, TOO.
TONIGHT?
BLOODS AND DIABLOS DOIN' WAR COUNCIL, BY AMSTERDAM. MIGHT GET UGLY, WITHOUT YOU TO COVER MY BACK.
SO YOU'RE THERE, RIGHT? RIGHT?
RIGHT. DISTURBANCE CHECKS OUT. TWO OF 'EM-- BLOODS.
TWO REBELS WITHOUT A-PPLAUSE, HEADED FOR JUVENILE HALL.

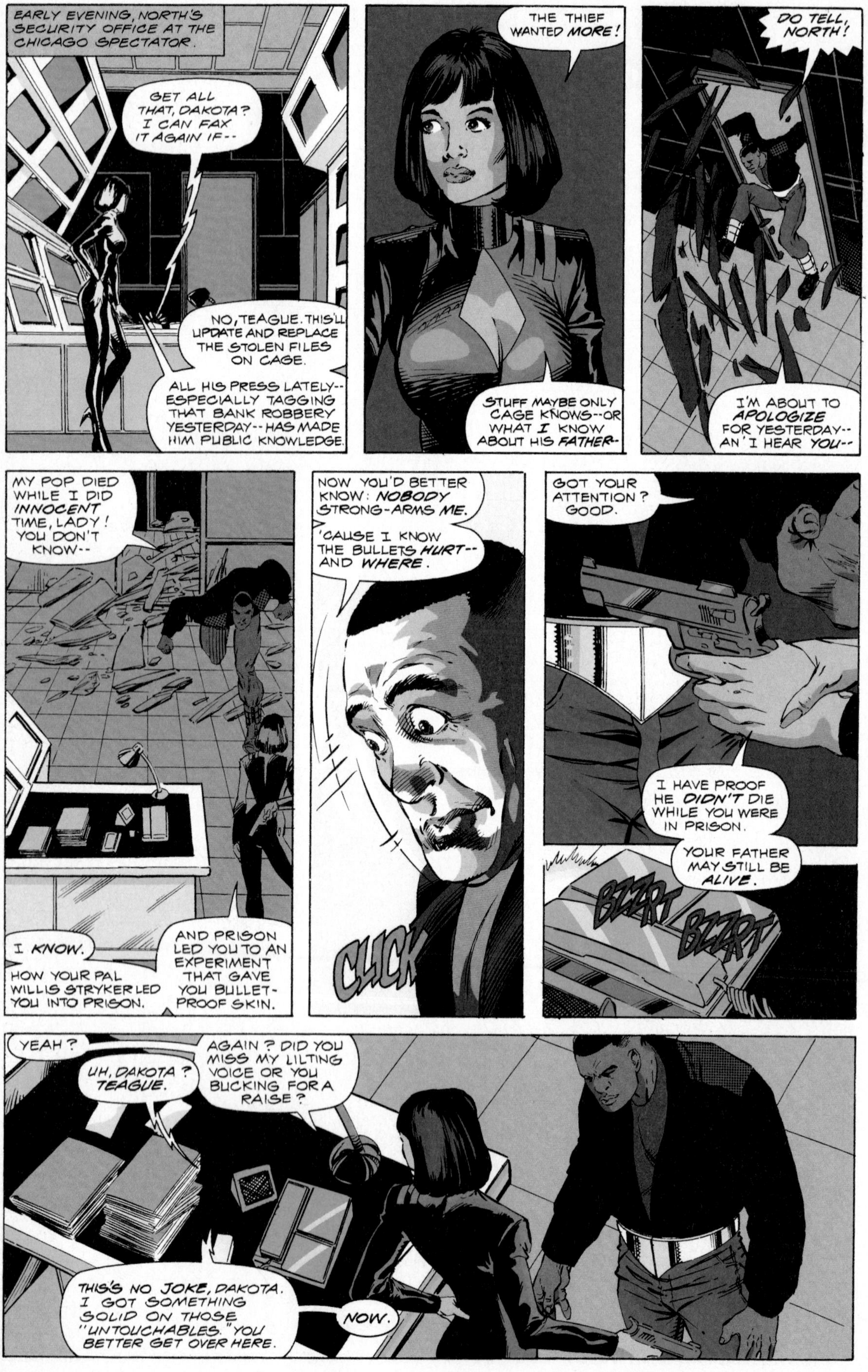
EARLY EVENING, NORTH'S SECURITY OFFICE AT THE CHICAGO SPECTATOR.
GET ALL THAT, DAKOTA? I CAN FAX IT AGAIN IF--
NO, TEAGUE. THIS'LL UPDATE AND REPLACE THE STOLEN FILES ON CAGE.
ALL HIS PRESS LATELY--ESPECIALLY TAGGING THAT BANK ROBBERY YESTERDAY--HAS MADE HIM PUBLIC KNOWLEDGE.
THE THIEF WANTED MORE!
STUFF MAYBE ONLY CAGE KNOWS--OR WHAT I KNOW ABOUT HIS FATHER-
DO TELL, NORTH!
I'M ABOUT TO APOLOGIZE FOR YESTERDAY--AN' I HEAR YOU--
MY POP DIED WHILE I DID INNOCENT TIME, LADY! YOU DON'T KNOW--
I KNOW.
HOW YOUR PAL WILLIS STRYKER LED YOU INTO PRISON.
AND PRISON LED YOU TO AN EXPERIMENT THAT GAVE YOU BULLET-PROOF SKIN.
NOW YOU'D BETTER KNOW: NOBODY STRONG-ARMS ME.
'CAUSE I KNOW THE BULLETS HURT--AND WHERE.
CLICK
GOT YOUR ATTENTION? GOOD.
I HAVE PROOF HE DIDN'T DIE WHILE YOU WERE IN PRISON.
YOUR FATHER MAY STILL BE ALIVE.
BZZRT BZZRT
YEAH?
UH, DAKOTA? TEAGUE.
AGAIN? DID YOU MISS MY LILTING VOICE OR YOU BUCKING FOR A RAISE?
THIS'S NO JOKE, DAKOTA. I GOT SOMETHING SOLID ON THOSE "UNTOUCHABLES." YOU BETTER GET OVER HERE.
NOW.

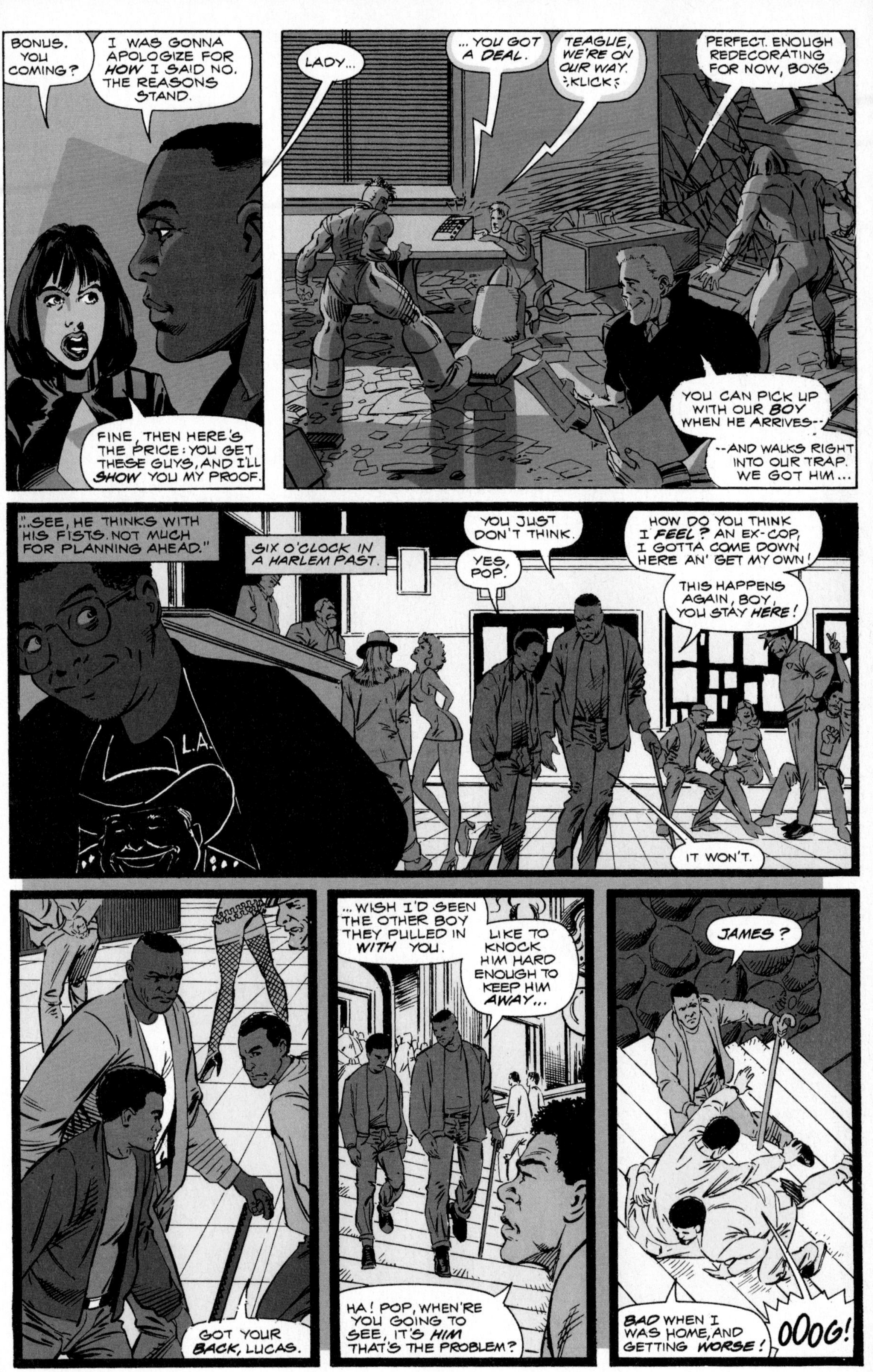
BONUS. YOU COMING?
I WAS GONNA APOLOGIZE FOR HOW I SAID NO. THE REASONS STAND.
FINE, THEN HERE'S THE PRICE: YOU GET THESE GUYS, AND I'LL SHOW YOU MY PROOF.
LADY...
...YOU GOT A DEAL.
TEAGUE, WE'RE ON OUR WAY. KLICK
PERFECT. ENOUGH REDECORATING FOR NOW, BOYS.
YOU CAN PICK UP WITH OUR BOY WHEN HE ARRIVES--
--AND WALKS RIGHT INTO OUR TRAP. WE GOT HIM...
"...SEE, HE THINKS WITH HIS FISTS. NOT MUCH FOR PLANNING AHEAD."
SIX O'CLOCK IN A HARLEM PAST.
L.A.
YOU JUST DON'T THINK.
YES, POP.
HOW DO YOU THINK I FEEL? AN EX-COP, I GOTTA COME DOWN HERE AN' GET MY OWN!
THIS HAPPENS AGAIN, BOY, YOU STAY HERE!
IT WON'T.
GOT YOUR BACK, LUCAS.
...WISH I'D SEEN THE OTHER BOY THEY PULLED IN WITH YOU.
LIKE TO KNOCK HIM HARD ENOUGH TO KEEP HIM AWAY...
HA! POP, WHEN'RE YOU GOING TO SEE, IT'S HIM THAT'S THE PROBLEM?
JAMES?
BAD WHEN I WAS HOME, AND GETTING WORSE!
OOOG!

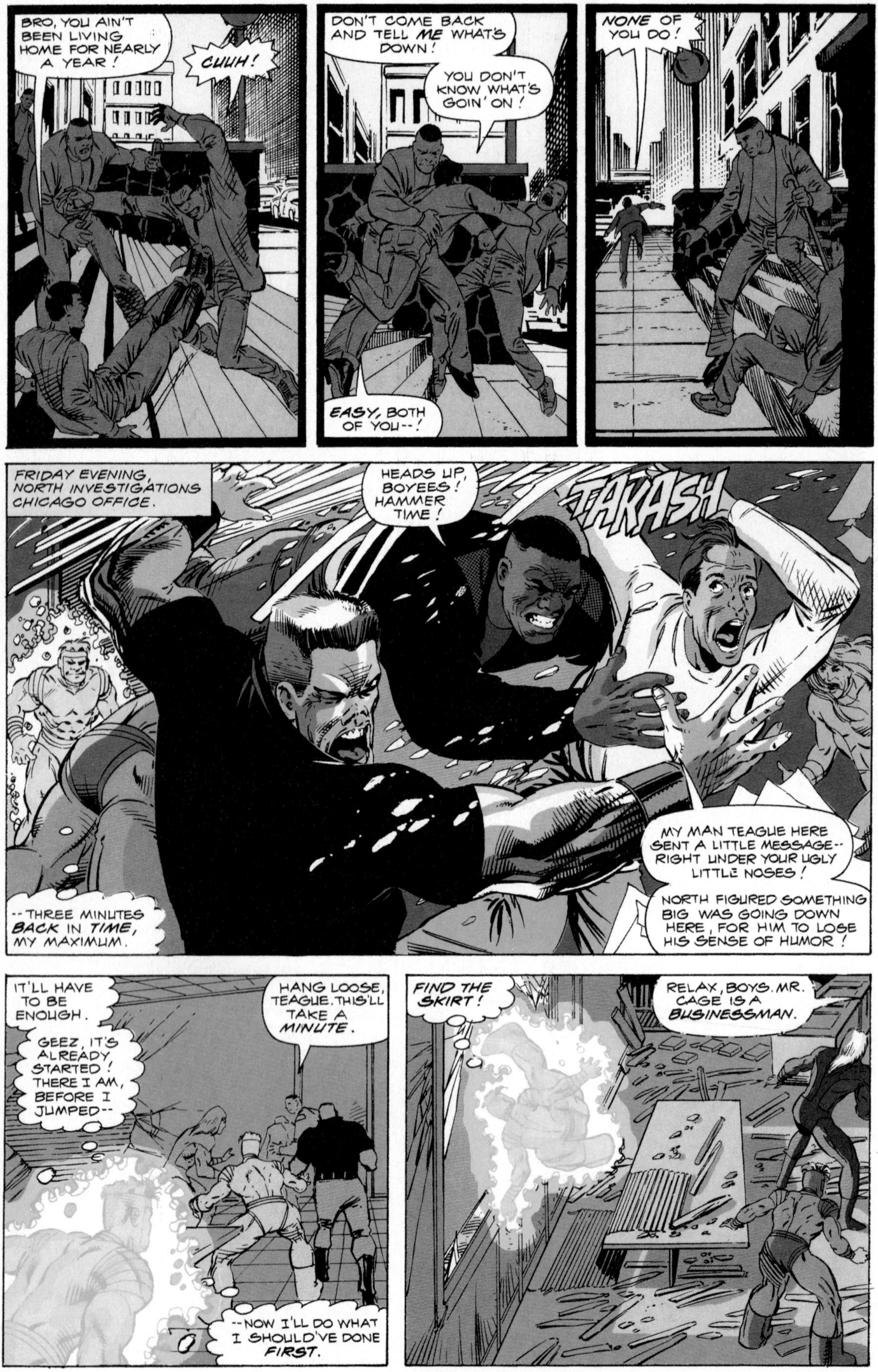
BRO, YOU AIN'T BEEN LIVING HOME FOR NEARLY A YEAR!
CUUH!
DON'T COME BACK AND TELL ME WHAT'S DOWN!
YOU DON'T KNOW WHAT'S GOIN' ON!
EASY, BOTH OF YOU--!
NONE OF YOU DO!
FRIDAY EVENING, NORTH INVESTIGATIONS CHICAGO OFFICE.
HEADS UP, BOYEES! HAMMER TIME!
TAKASH
MY MAN TEAGUE HERE SENT A LITTLE MESSAGE--RIGHT UNDER YOUR UGLY LITTLE NOSES!
NORTH FIGURED SOMETHING BIG WAS GOING DOWN FOR HIM TO LOSE HIS SENSE OF HUMOR!
--THREE MINUTES BACK IN TIME, MY MAXIMUM.
IT'LL HAVE TO BE ENOUGH.
GEEZ, IT'S ALREADY STARTED! THERE I AM, BEFORE I JUMPED--
HANG LOOSE, TEAGUE. THIS'LL TAKE A MINUTE.
--NOW I'LL DO WHAT I SHOULD'VE DONE FIRST.
FIND THE SKIRT!
RELAX, BOYS. MR. CAGE IS A BUSINESSMAN.

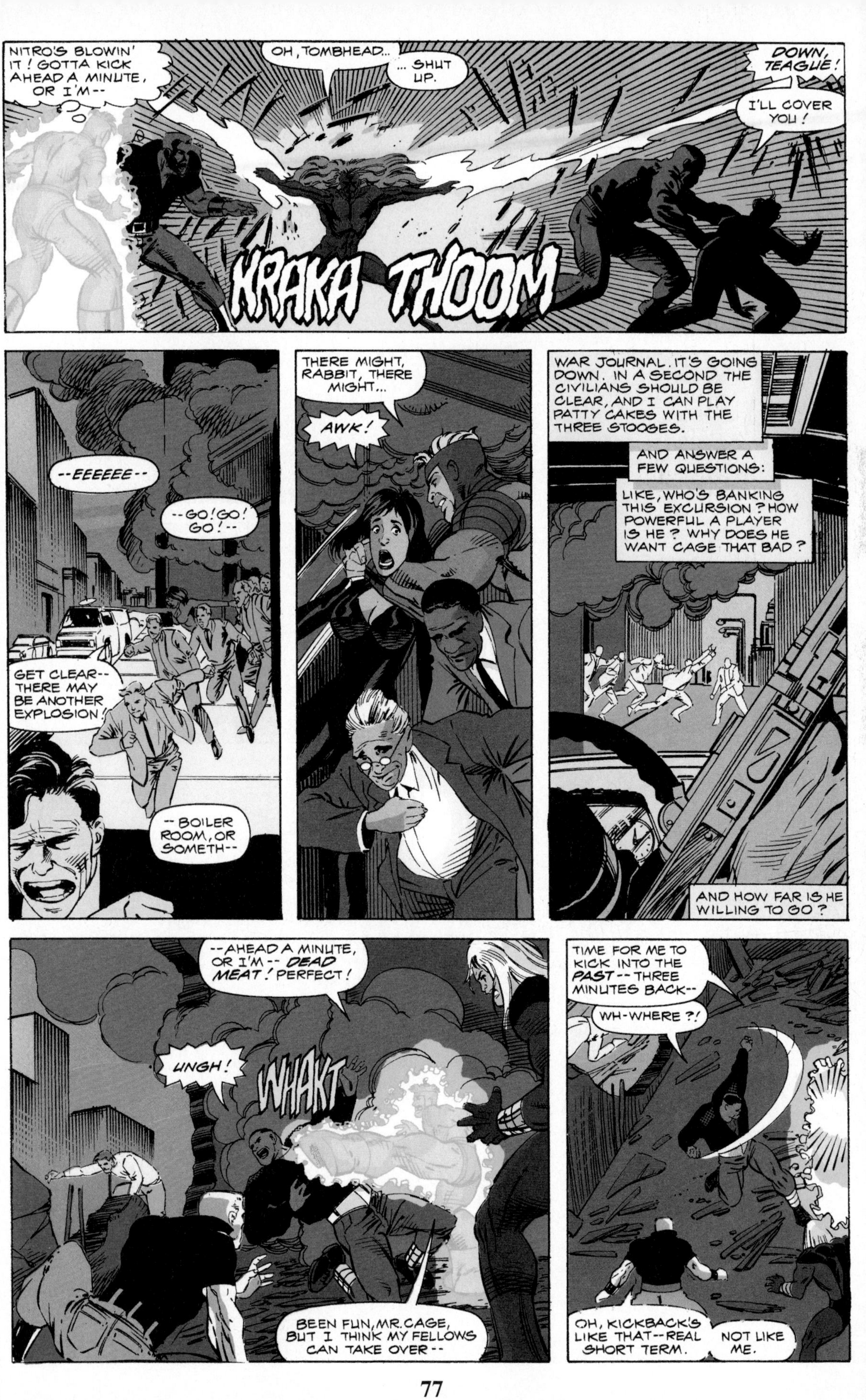

NITRO'S BLOWIN' IT! GOTTA KICK AHEAD A MINUTE, OR I'M--
OH, TOMBHEAD...
... SHUT UP.
DOWN, TEAGUE!
I'LL COVER YOU!
KRAKA THOOM
--EEEEEE--
--GO! GO! GO!--
GET CLEAR-- THERE MAY BE ANOTHER EXPLOSION!
--BOILER ROOM, OR SOMETH--
THERE MIGHT, RABBIT, THERE MIGHT...
AWK!
WAR JOURNAL. IT'S GOING DOWN. IN A SECOND THE CIVILIANS SHOULD BE CLEAR, AND I CAN PLAY PATTY CAKES WITH THE THREE STOOGES.
AND ANSWER A FEW QUESTIONS:
LIKE, WHO'S BANKING THIS EXCURSION? HOW POWERFUL A PLAYER IS HE? WHY DOES HE WANT CAGE THAT BAD?
AND HOW FAR IS HE WILLING TO GO?
--AHEAD A MINUTE, OR I'M-- DEAD MEAT! PERFECT!
UNGH!
WHAKT
BEEN FUN, MR. CAGE, BUT I THINK MY FELLOWS CAN TAKE OVER--
TIME FOR ME TO KICK INTO THE PAST-- THREE MINUTES BACK--
WH-WHERE?!
OH, KICKBACK'S LIKE THAT--REAL SHORT TERM.
NOT LIKE ME.

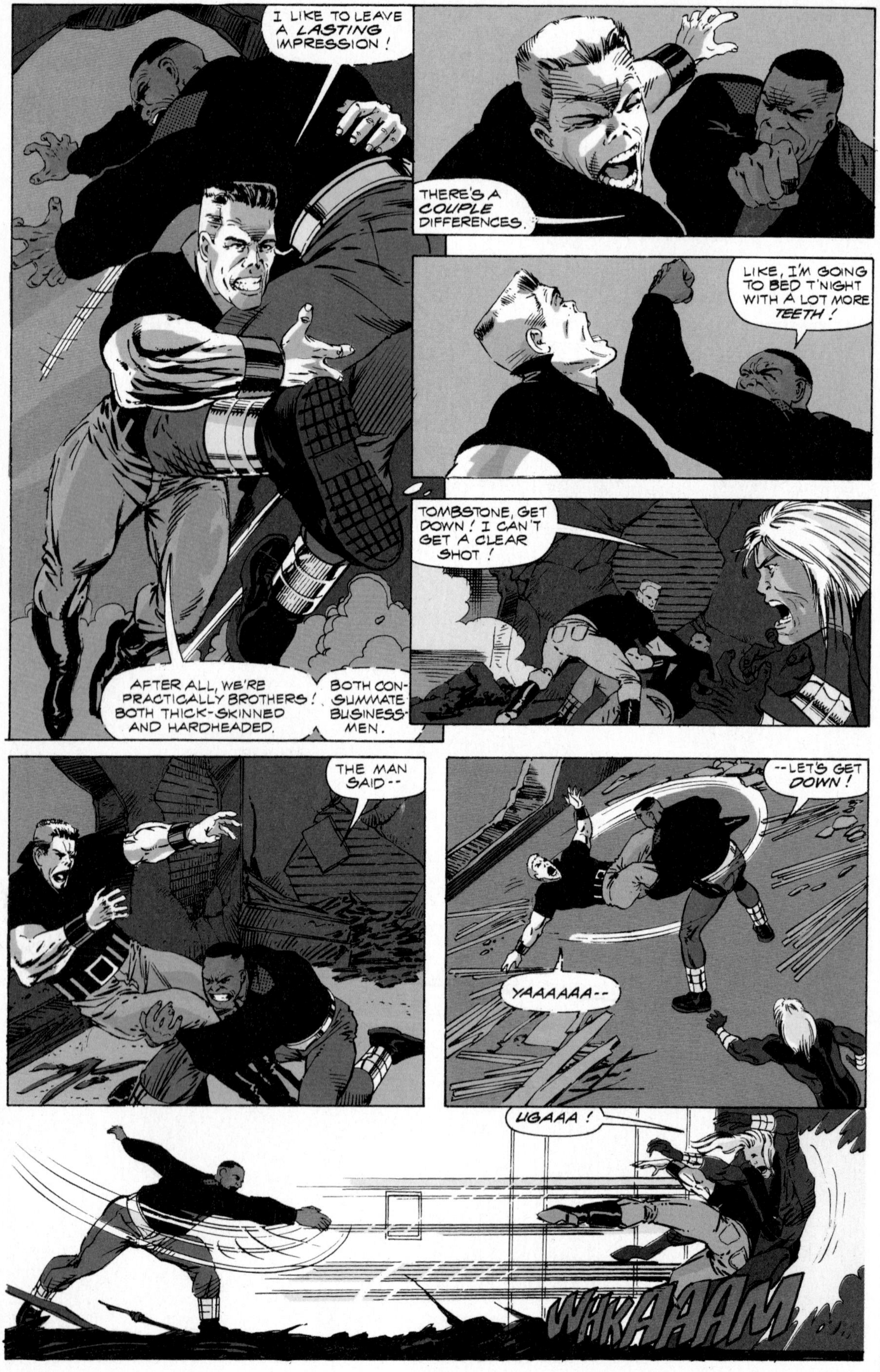
I LIKE TO LEAVE A LASTING IMPRESSION!
AFTER ALL, WE'RE PRACTICALLY BROTHERS! BOTH THICK-SKINNED AND HARDHEADED.
BOTH CON-SUMMATE BUSINESS-MEN.
THERE'S A COUPLE DIFFERENCES.
LIKE, I'M GOING TO BED T'NIGHT WITH A LOT MORE TEETH!
TOMBSTONE, GET DOWN! I CAN'T GET A CLEAR SHOT!
THE MAN SAID--
--LET'S GET DOWN!
YAAAAAA--
UGAAA!
WHKAAAM

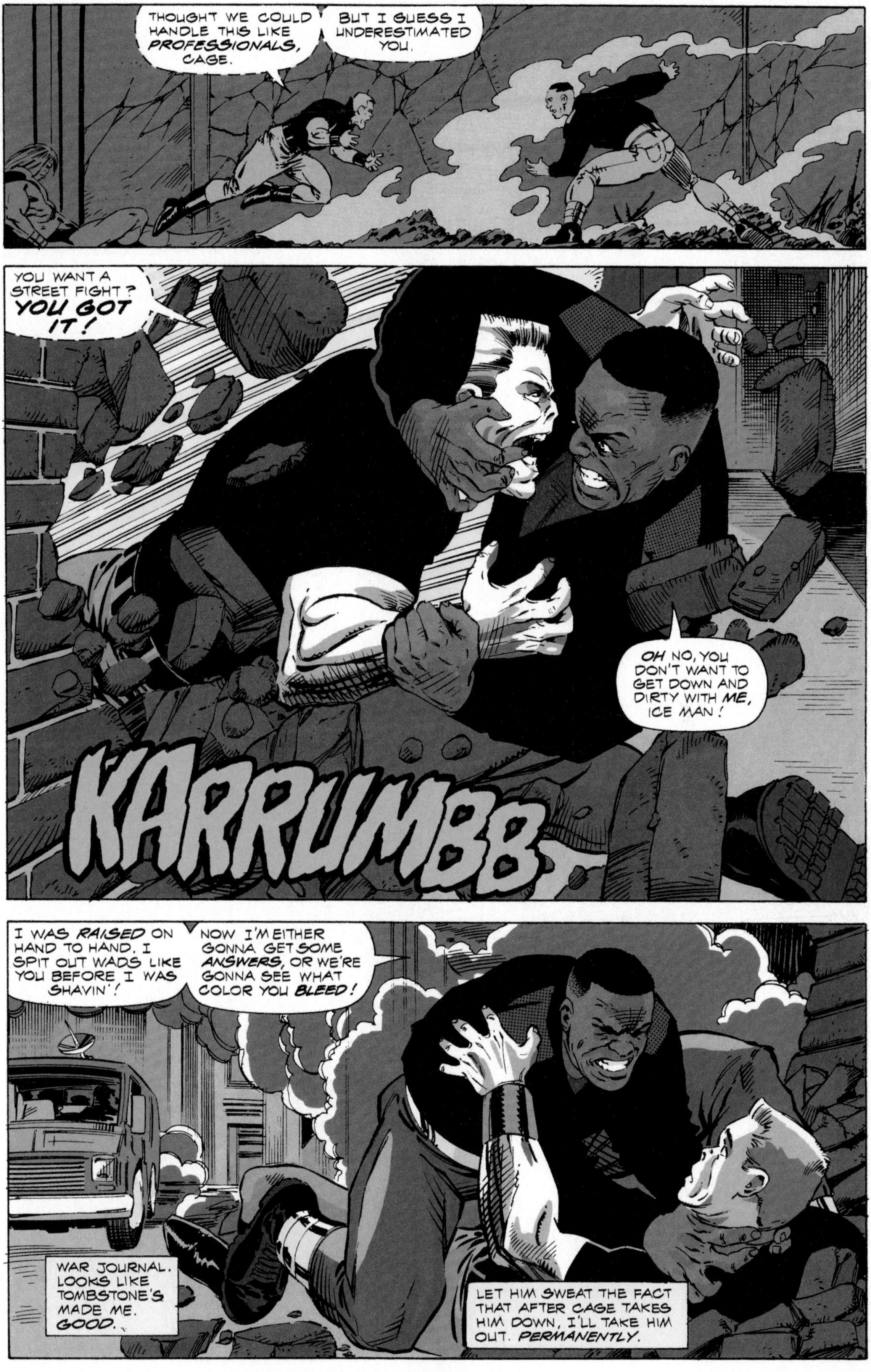
THOUGHT WE COULD HANDLE THIS LIKE PROFESSIONALS, CAGE.
BUT I GUESS I UNDERESTIMATED YOU.
YOU WANT A STREET FIGHT? YOU GOT IT!
OH NO, YOU DON'T WANT TO GET DOWN AND DIRTY WITH ME, ICE MAN!
KARRUMBB
I WAS RAISED ON HAND TO HAND. I SPIT OUT WADS LIKE YOU BEFORE I WAS SHAVIN'!
NOW I'M EITHER GONNA GET SOME ANSWERS, OR WE'RE GONNA SEE WHAT COLOR YOU BLEED!
WAR JOURNAL. LOOKS LIKE TOMBSTONE'S MADE ME. GOOD.
LET HIM SWEAT THE FACT THAT AFTER CAGE TAKES HIM DOWN, I'LL TAKE HIM OUT. PERMANENTLY.

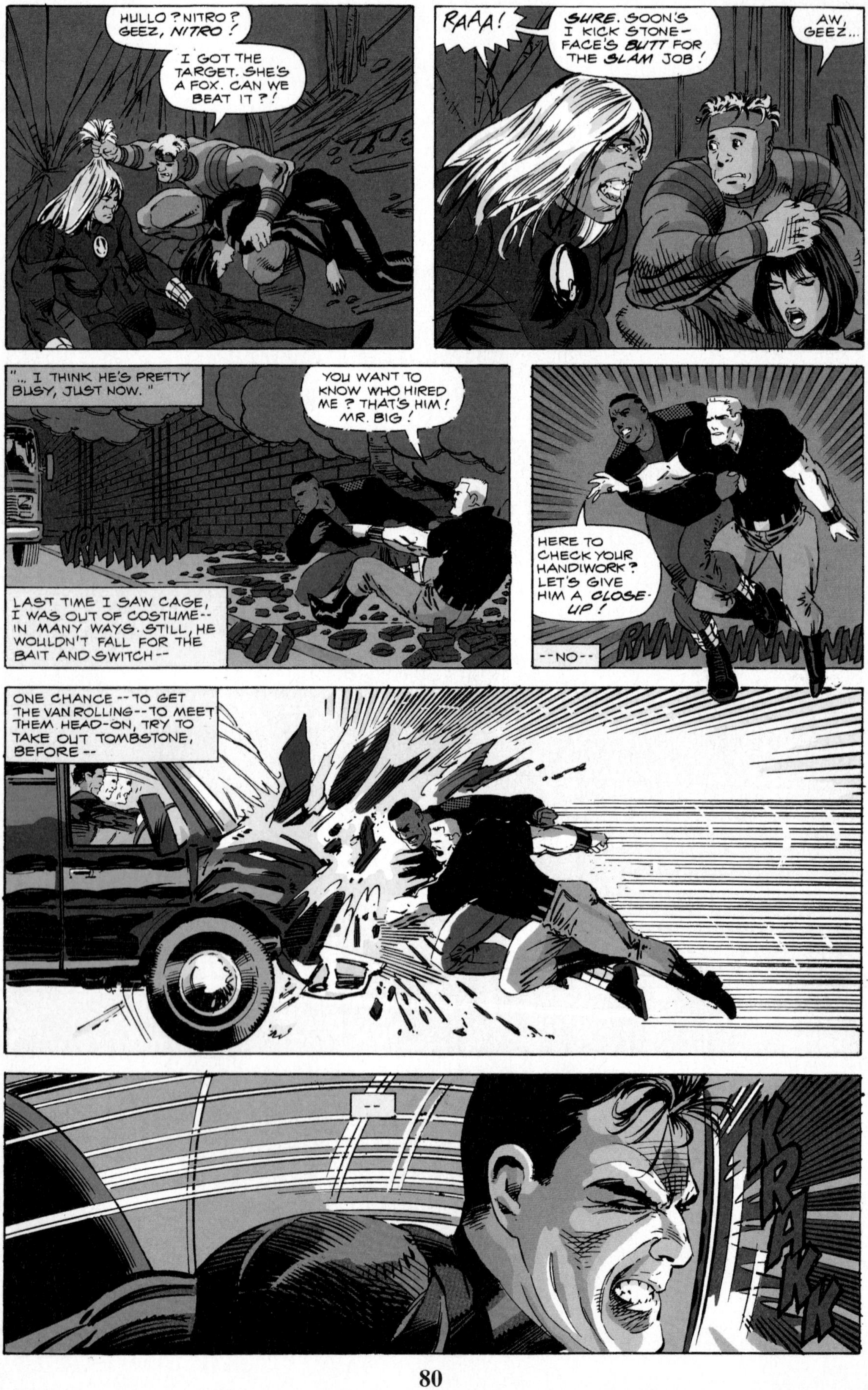
HULLO? NITRO? GEEZ, NITRO!
I GOT THE TARGET. SHE'S A FOX. CAN WE BEAT IT?!
RAAA!
SURE. SOON'S I KICK STONE-FACE'S BUTT FOR THE SLAM JOB!
AW, GEEZ...
"... I THINK HE'S PRETTY BUSY, JUST NOW."
YOU WANT TO KNOW WHO HIRED ME? THAT'S HIM! MR. BIG!
VRNNNNN
LAST TIME I SAW CAGE, I WAS OUT OF COSTUME-- IN MANY WAYS. STILL, HE WOULDN'T FALL FOR THE BAIT AND SWITCH--
HERE TO CHECK YOUR HANDIWORK? LET'S GIVE HIM A CLOSE-UP!
--NO--
RNNNNNNNNNNN
ONE CHANCE--TO GET THE VAN ROLLING--TO MEET THEM HEAD-ON, TRY TO TAKE OUT TOMBSTONE, BEFORE--
--
KRAKK

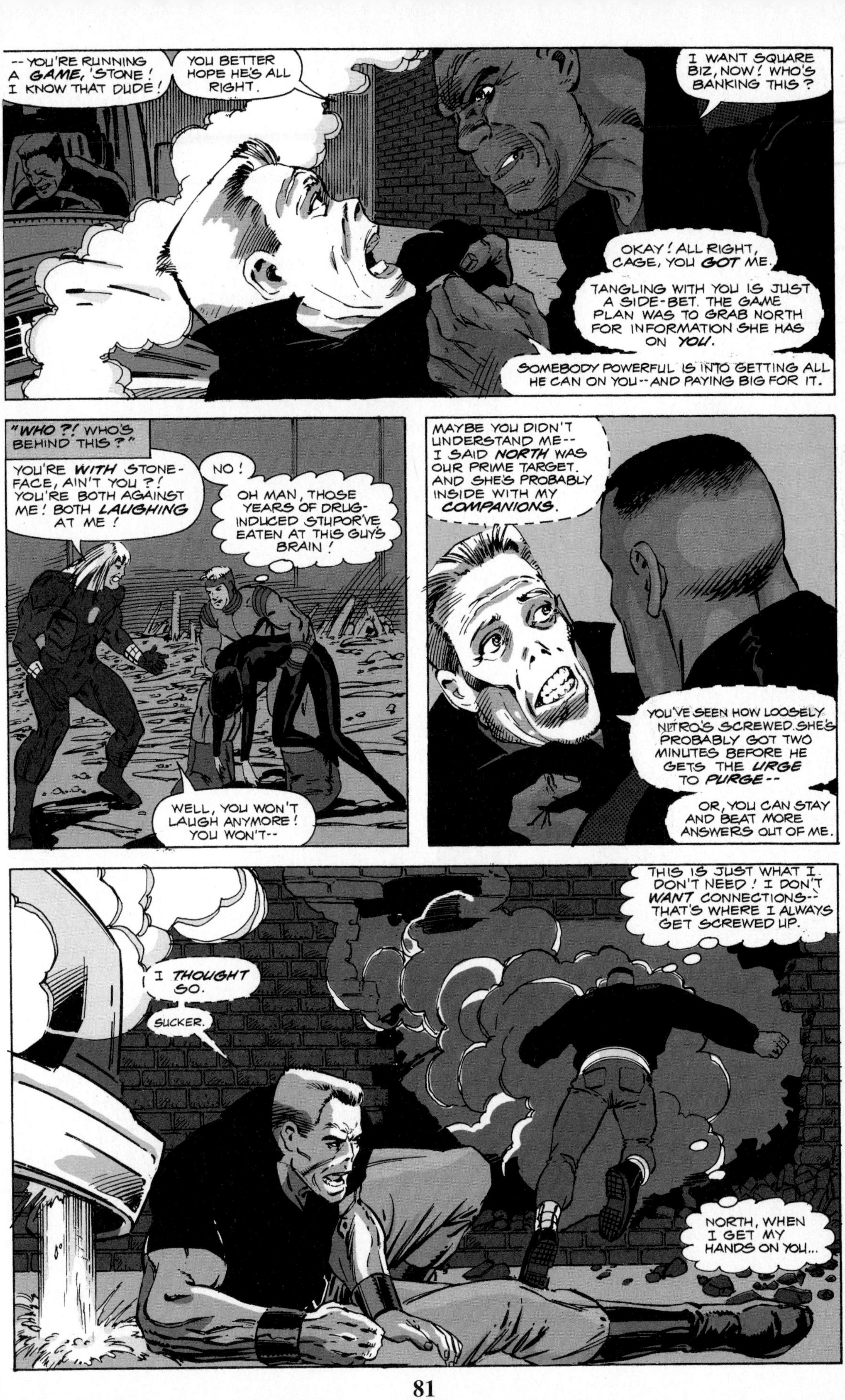

-- YOU'RE RUNNING A GAME, 'STONE! I KNOW THAT DUDE!
YOU BETTER HOPE HE'S ALL RIGHT.
I WANT SQUARE BIZ, NOW! WHO'S BANKING THIS?
OKAY! ALL RIGHT, CAGE, YOU GOT ME.
TANGLING WITH YOU IS JUST A SIDE-BET. THE GAME PLAN WAS TO GRAB NORTH FOR INFORMATION SHE HAS ON YOU.
SOMEBODY POWERFUL IS INTO GETTING ALL HE CAN ON YOU -- AND PAYING BIG FOR IT.
"WHO?! WHO'S BEHIND THIS?"
YOU'RE WITH STONE-FACE, AIN'T YOU?! YOU'RE BOTH AGAINST ME! BOTH LAUGHING AT ME!
NO!
OH MAN, THOSE YEARS OF DRUG-INDUCED STUPOR'VE EATEN AT THIS GUY'S BRAIN!
WELL, YOU WON'T LAUGH ANYMORE! YOU WON'T--
MAYBE YOU DIDN'T UNDERSTAND ME-- I SAID NORTH WAS OUR PRIME TARGET. AND SHE'S PROBABLY INSIDE WITH MY COMPANIONS.
YOU'VE SEEN HOW LOOSELY NITRO'S SCREWED. SHE'S PROBABLY GOT TWO MINUTES BEFORE HE GETS THE URGE TO PURGE--
OR, YOU CAN STAY AND BEAT MORE ANSWERS OUT OF ME.
THIS IS JUST WHAT I DON'T NEED! I DON'T WANT CONNECTIONS-- THAT'S WHERE I ALWAYS GET SCREWED UP.
I THOUGHT SO.
SUCKER.
NORTH, WHEN I GET MY HANDS ON YOU...

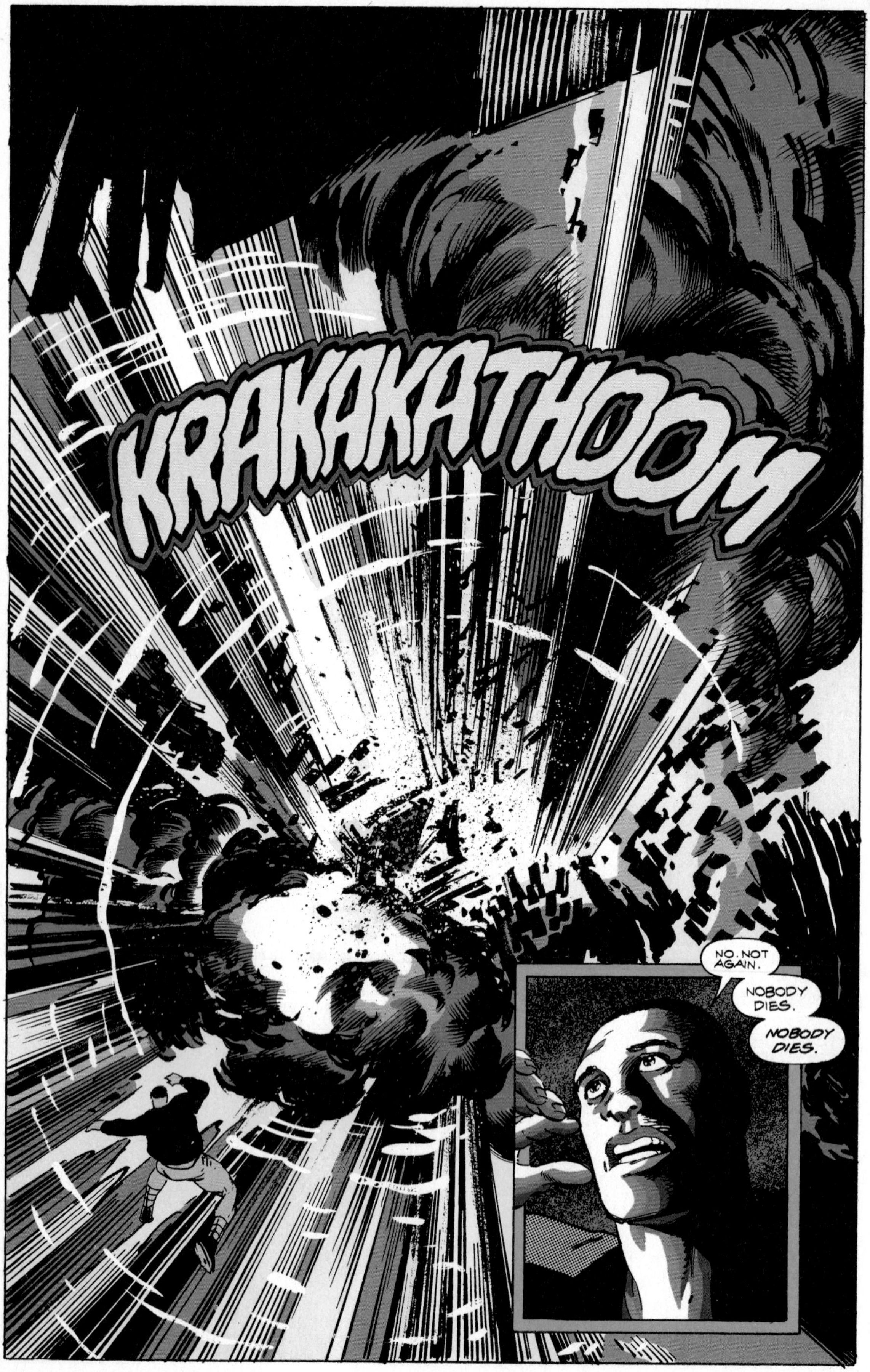
KRAKAKATHOOM
NO. NOT AGAIN.
NOBODY DIES.
NOBODY DIES.

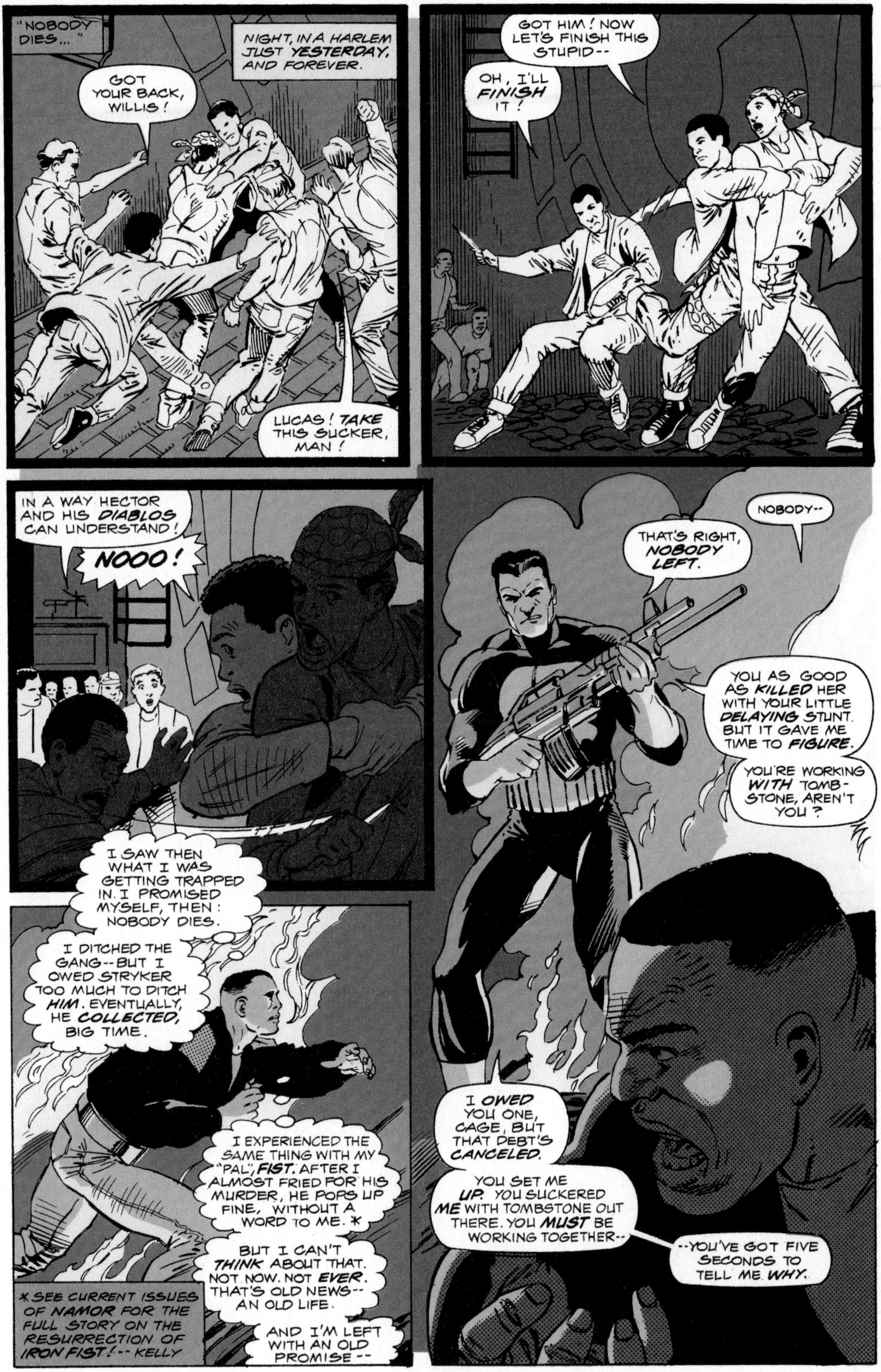
"NOBODY DIES..."
NIGHT, IN A HARLEM JUST YESTERDAY, AND FOREVER.
GOT YOUR BACK, WILLIS!
LUCAS! TAKE THIS SUCKER, MAN!
GOT HIM! NOW LET'S FINISH THIS STUPID--
OH, I'LL FINISH IT!
IN A WAY HECTOR AND HIS DIABLOS CAN UNDERSTAND!
NOOO!
I SAW THEN WHAT I WAS GETTING TRAPPED IN. I PROMISED MYSELF, THEN: NOBODY DIES.
I DITCHED THE GANG--BUT I OWED STRYKER TOO MUCH TO DITCH HIM. EVENTUALLY, HE COLLECTED, BIG TIME.
I EXPERIENCED THE SAME THING WITH MY "PAL", FIST. AFTER I ALMOST FRIED FOR HIS MURDER, HE POPS UP FINE, WITHOUT A WORD TO ME. *
BUT I CAN'T THINK ABOUT THAT. NOT NOW. NOT EVER. THAT'S OLD NEWS-- AN OLD LIFE.
AND I'M LEFT WITH AN OLD PROMISE--
* SEE CURRENT ISSUES OF NAMOR FOR THE FULL STORY ON THE RESURRECTION OF IRON FIST! --KELLY
NOBODY--
THAT'S RIGHT, NOBODY LEFT.
YOU AS GOOD AS KILLED HER WITH YOUR LITTLE DELAYING STUNT. BUT IT GAVE ME TIME TO FIGURE.
YOU'RE WORKING WITH TOMB-STONE, AREN'T YOU?
I OWED YOU ONE, CAGE, BUT THAT DEBT'S CANCELED.
YOU SET ME UP. YOU SUCKERED ME WITH TOMBSTONE OUT THERE. YOU MUST BE WORKING TOGETHER--
--YOU'VE GOT FIVE SECONDS TO TELL ME WHY.

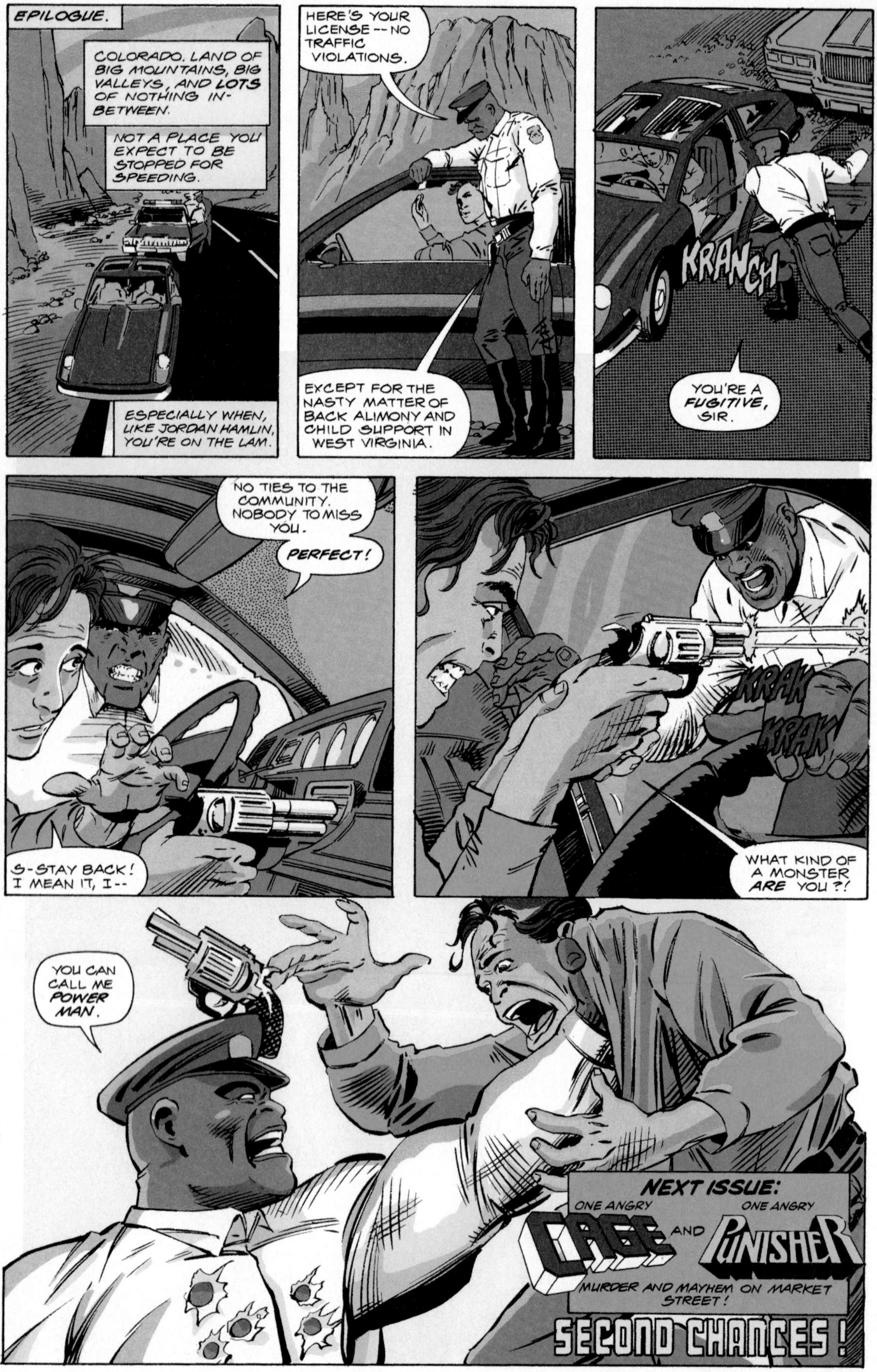
EPILOGUE.
COLORADO. LAND OF BIG MOUNTAINS, BIG VALLEYS, AND LOTS OF NOTHING IN-BETWEEN.
NOT A PLACE YOU EXPECT TO BE STOPPED FOR SPEEDING.
ESPECIALLY WHEN, LIKE JORDAN HAMLIN, YOU'RE ON THE LAM.
HERE'S YOUR LICENSE -- NO TRAFFIC VIOLATIONS.
EXCEPT FOR THE NASTY MATTER OF BACK ALIMONY AND CHILD SUPPORT IN WEST VIRGINIA.
KRANCH
YOU'RE A FUGITIVE, SIR.
NO TIES TO THE COMMUNITY. NOBODY TO MISS YOU.
PERFECT!
S-STAY BACK! I MEAN IT, I--
KRAK
KRAK
WHAT KIND OF A MONSTER ARE YOU?!
YOU CAN CALL ME POWER MAN.
NEXT ISSUE:
ONE ANGRY CAGE AND ONE ANGRY PUNISHER
MURDER AND MAYHEM ON MARKET STREET!
SECOND CHANCES!

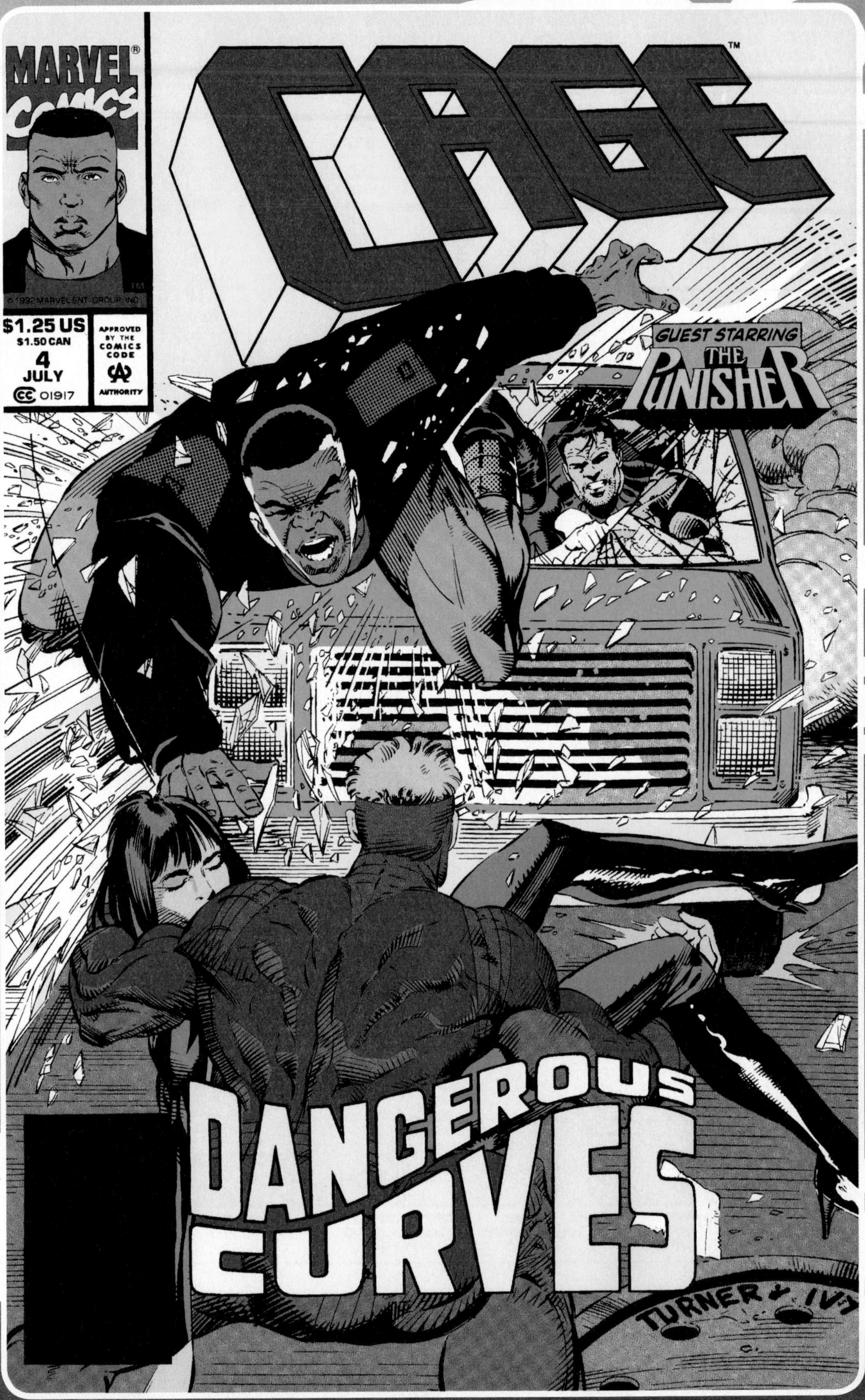

MARVEL COMICS
CAGE™
© 1992 MARVEL ENT. GROUP, INC.
$1.25 US
$1.50 CAN
4
JULY
01917
APPROVED BY THE COMICS CODE AUTHORITY
GUEST STARRING THE PUNISHER
DANGEROUS CURVES
TURNER & IVY

EMPOWERED WITH STEEL-HARD SKIN AND SUPER-HUMAN STRENGTH BY A MEDICAL EXPERIMENT GONE AWRY, LUKE CAGE IS A HERO FOR HIRE. HE'S RUNNING FROM A VIOLENT PAST TO AN UNCERTAIN FUTURE. IN A WORLD WHERE RULES CHANGE DAILY, ONLY HE HAS THE POWER TO MAKE HIS OWN. STAN LEE PRESENTS...

CAGE

MY NAME IS *KICKBACK.*

ACTUALLY, MY NAME'S *RICHARD,* BUT NO ONE'D PAY TOP DOLLAR FOR *DICK, THE ASSASSIN.* MY REP WAS MY *FUTURE.*

I SHOULDA...

MY GIFT IS TIME-JUMPING-- AN' I PAID FOR IT IN *CASH* AND *PAIN.* IT WAS SUPPOSED TO SET ME FOR LIFE--

--AS A KILLER WHO COULDN'T BE CAUGHT; WHO CAN ESCAPE INTO *TIME,* UP TO THREE MINUTES AHEAD OR BACK. *UNSTOPPABLE.*

TILL *THIS* JOB. I SHOULDA...

I *OWED* YOU ONE, *CAGE,* BUT THAT DEBT'S *CANCELED.*

YOU SET ME UP, AND COST *DAKOTA* HER *LIFE.* NOW YOU'RE GOING TO--

--GET *DOWN!*

BRAKKA

BRAKKA

BRAKKA

S'POSED TO HURT *LUKE CAGE,* AND SNATCH HIS LOVELY ASSOCIATE, *DAKOTA NORTH.*

A CINCH, TILL THE PUNISHER SHOWS. *THAT'S* WHERE I WENT WRONG.

I SHOULDA LET 'EM *DIE.*

| DWAYNE TURNER PENCILS | CHRISTOPHER IVY INKS | MARC McLAURIN STORY | CHRISTOPHER ELIOPOULOS LETTERS | MIKE THOMAS COLORS | KELLY CORVESE EDITS | TOM DEFALCO CHIEFS |

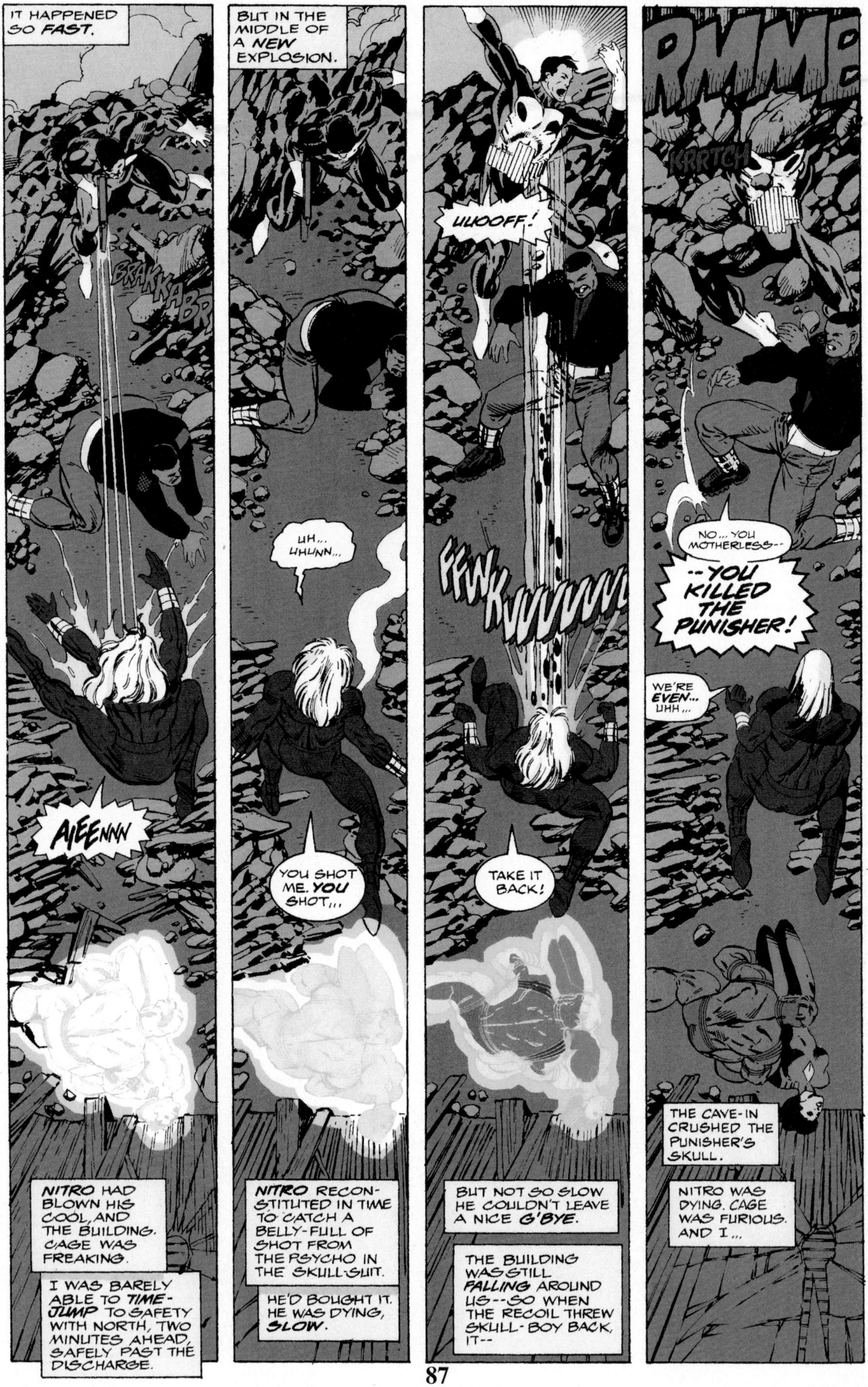
IT HAPPENED SO FAST.
BRAKKA BR
AIEENNN
NITRO HAD BLOWN HIS COOL, AND THE BUILDING. CAGE WAS FREAKING.
I WAS BARELY ABLE TO TIME-JUMP TO SAFETY WITH NORTH, TWO MINUTES AHEAD, SAFELY PAST THE DISCHARGE.
BUT IN THE MIDDLE OF A NEW EXPLOSION.
UH... UHUNN...
YOU SHOT ME. YOU SHOT...
NITRO RECON-STITUTED IN TIME TO CATCH A BELLY-FULL OF SHOT FROM THE PSYCHO IN THE SKULL-SUIT.
HE'D BOUGHT IT. HE WAS DYING, SLOW.
UUOOFF!
FFWKVVVVVVVV
TAKE IT BACK!
BUT NOT SO SLOW HE COULDN'T LEAVE A NICE G'BYE.
THE BUILDING WAS STILL FALLING AROUND US--SO WHEN THE RECOIL THREW SKULL-BOY BACK, IT--
RMMB
KRRTCH
NO... YOU MOTHERLESS--
--YOU KILLED THE PUNISHER!
WE'RE EVEN... UHH...
THE CAVE-IN CRUSHED THE PUNISHER'S SKULL.
NITRO WAS DYING. CAGE WAS FURIOUS. AND I...

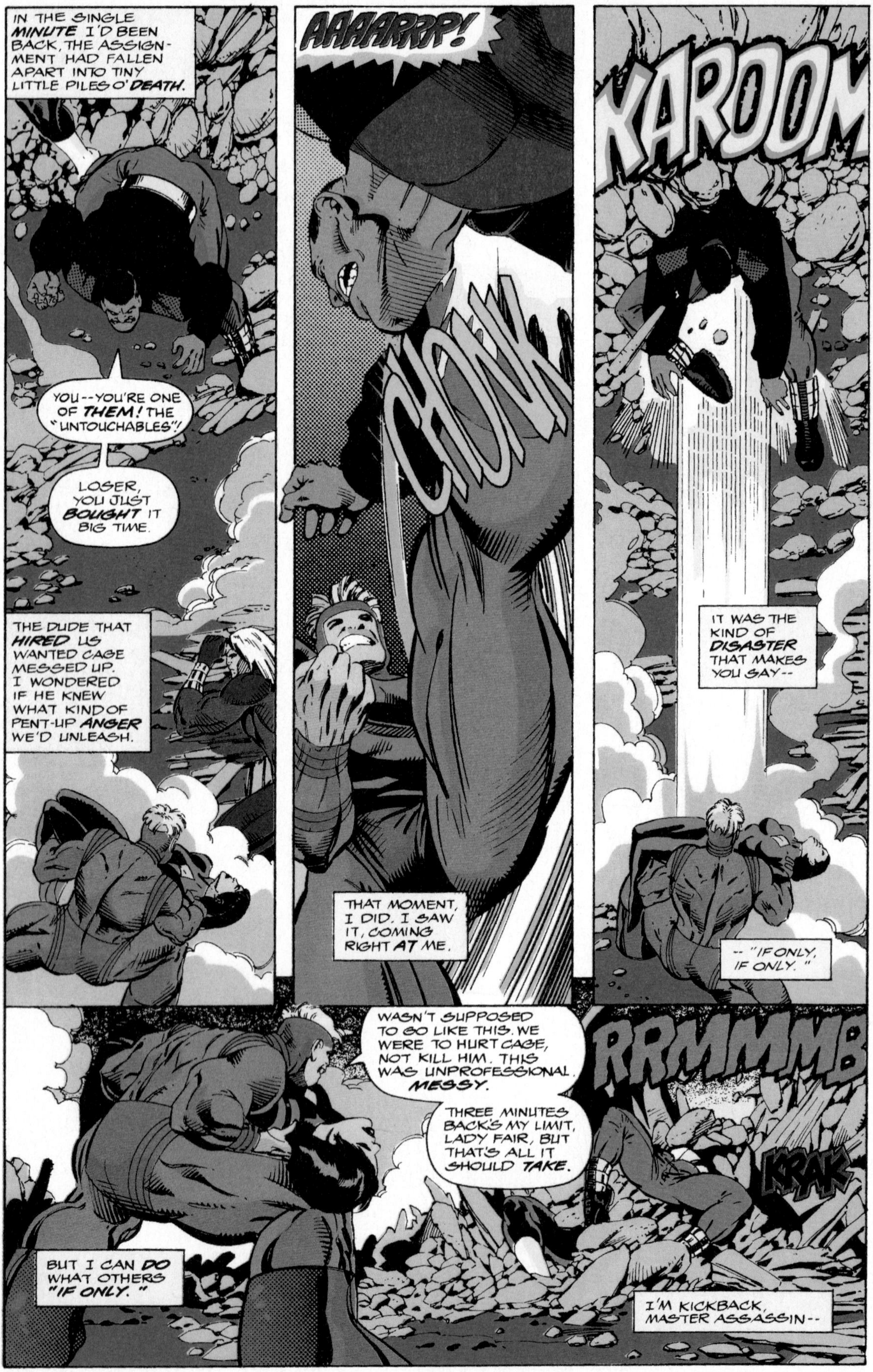
IN THE SINGLE MINUTE I'D BEEN BACK, THE ASSIGN-MENT HAD FALLEN APART INTO TINY LITTLE PILES O' DEATH.
YOU--YOU'RE ONE OF THEM! THE "UNTOUCHABLES"!
LOSER, YOU JUST BOUGHT IT BIG TIME.
THE DUDE THAT HIRED US WANTED CAGE MESSED UP. I WONDERED IF HE KNEW WHAT KIND OF PENT-UP ANGER WE'D UNLEASH.
AAAARRRP!
CHONK
THAT MOMENT, I DID. I SAW IT, COMING RIGHT AT ME.
KAROOM
IT WAS THE KIND OF DISASTER THAT MAKES YOU SAY--
-- "IF ONLY, IF ONLY."
WASN'T SUPPOSED TO GO LIKE THIS. WE WERE TO HURT CAGE, NOT KILL HIM. THIS WAS UNPROFESSIONAL. MESSY.
THREE MINUTES BACK'S MY LIMIT, LADY FAIR, BUT THAT'S ALL IT SHOULD TAKE.
RRMMMB
KRAK
BUT I CAN DO WHAT OTHERS "IF ONLY."
I'M KICKBACK, MASTER ASSASSIN--

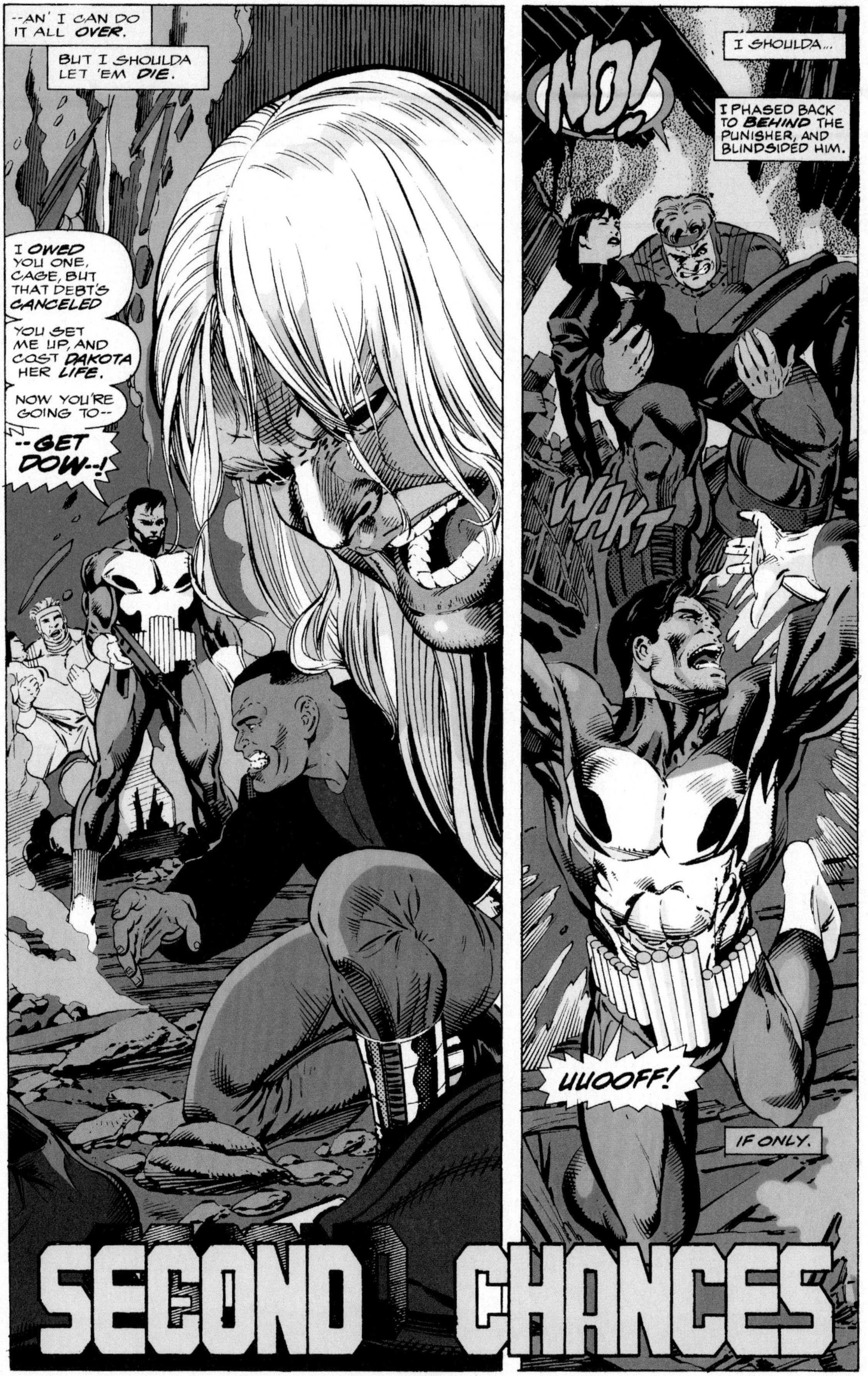

--AN' I CAN DO IT ALL OVER.
BUT I SHOULDA LET 'EM DIE.
I OWED YOU ONE, CAGE, BUT THAT DEBT'S CANCELED
YOU SET ME UP, AND COST DAKOTA HER LIFE.
NOW YOU'RE GOING TO--
--GET DOW--!
I SHOULDA...
NO!
I PHASED BACK TO BEHIND THE PUNISHER, AND BLINDSIDED HIM.
WAKT
UUOOFF!
IF ONLY.
SECOND CHANCES

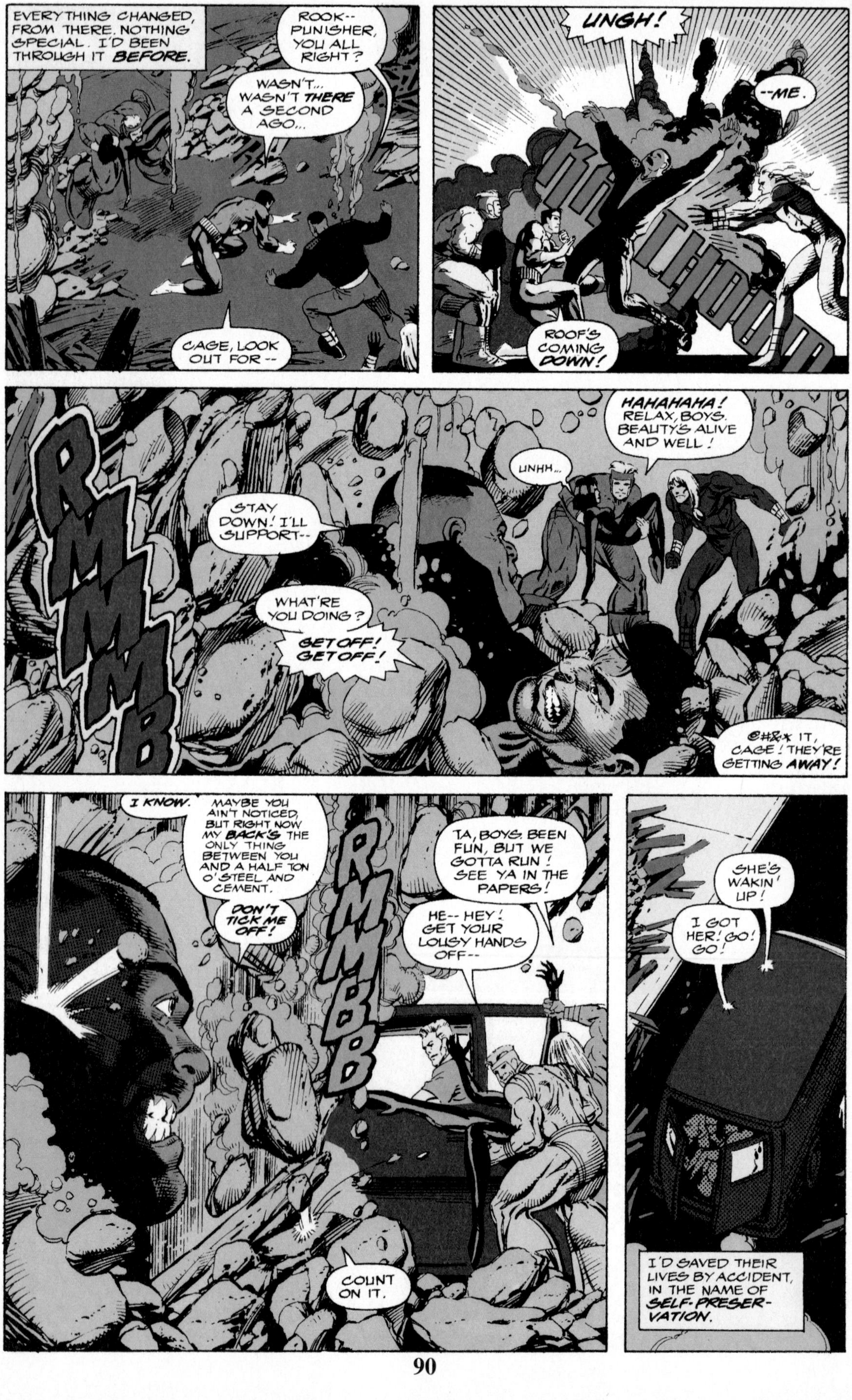
EVERYTHING CHANGED, FROM THERE. NOTHING SPECIAL. I'D BEEN THROUGH IT BEFORE.
ROOK-- PUNISHER, YOU ALL RIGHT?
WASN'T... WASN'T THERE A SECOND AGO...
CAGE, LOOK OUT FOR --
UNGH!
--ME.
ROOF'S COMING DOWN!
HAHAHAHA! RELAX, BOYS. BEAUTY'S ALIVE AND WELL!
UNHH...
STAY DOWN! I'LL SUPPORT--
WHAT'RE YOU DOING?
GET OFF! GET OFF!
@#&* IT, CAGE! THEY'RE GETTING AWAY!
I KNOW.
MAYBE YOU AIN'T NOTICED, BUT RIGHT NOW MY BACK'S THE ONLY THING BETWEEN YOU AND A HALF TON O'STEEL AND CEMENT.
DON'T TICK ME OFF!
TA, BOYS. BEEN FUN, BUT WE GOTTA RUN! SEE YA IN THE PAPERS!
HE-- HEY! GET YOUR LOUSY HANDS OFF--
COUNT ON IT.
SHE'S WAKIN' UP!
I GOT HER! GO! GO!
I'D SAVED THEIR LIVES BY ACCIDENT, IN THE NAME OF SELF-PRESERVATION.

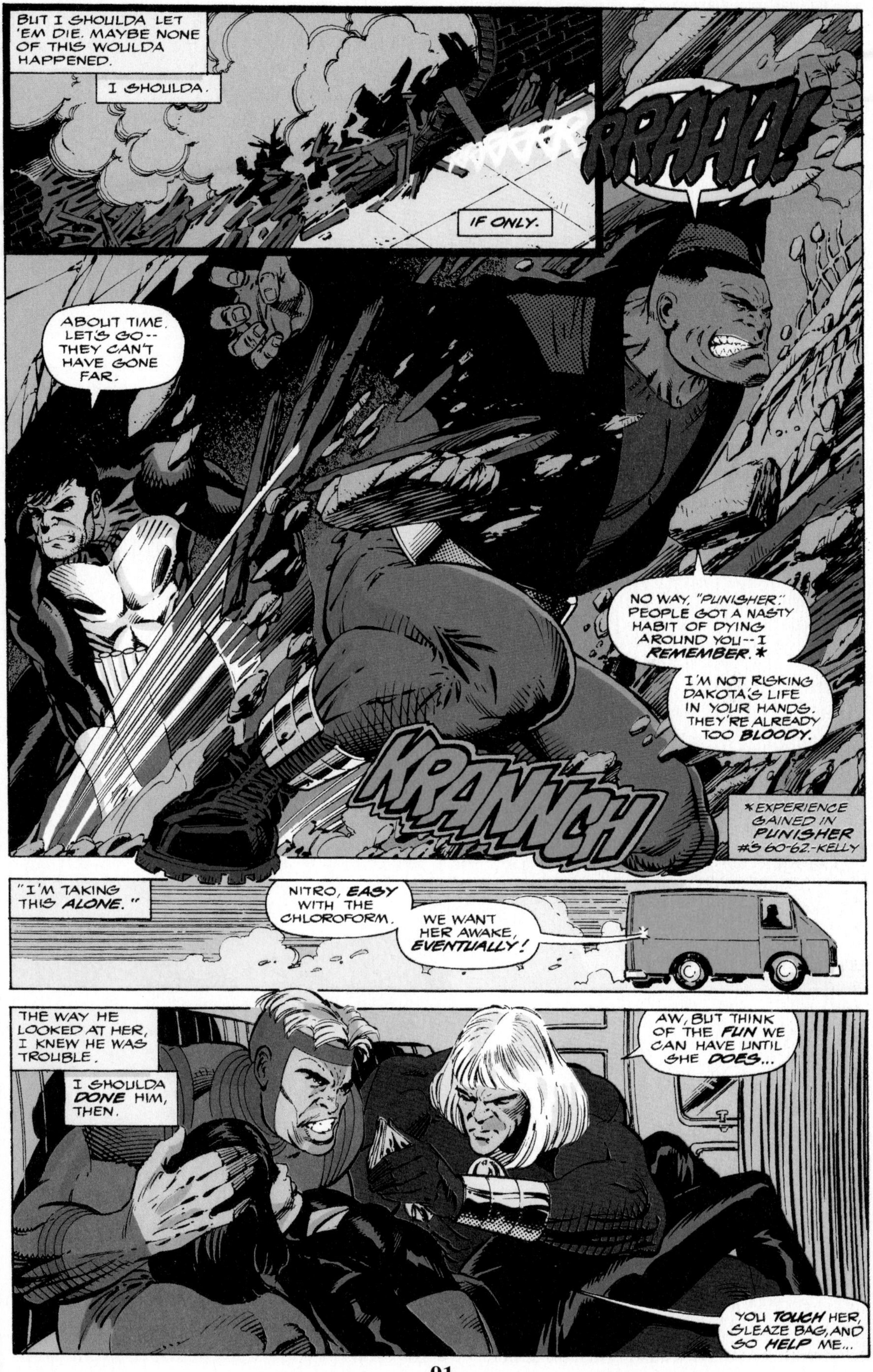
BUT I SHOULDA LET 'EM DIE. MAYBE NONE OF THIS WOULDA HAPPENED.
I SHOULDA.
IF ONLY.
RRAAAA!
ABOUT TIME. LET'S GO-- THEY CAN'T HAVE GONE FAR.
NO WAY, "PUNISHER." PEOPLE GOT A NASTY HABIT OF DYING AROUND YOU-- I REMEMBER.*
I'M NOT RISKING DAKOTA'S LIFE IN YOUR HANDS. THEY'RE ALREADY TOO BLOODY.
KRANNCH
*EXPERIENCE GAINED IN PUNISHER #'S 60-62.-KELLY
"I'M TAKING THIS ALONE."
NITRO, EASY WITH THE CHLOROFORM.
WE WANT HER AWAKE, EVENTUALLY!
THE WAY HE LOOKED AT HER, I KNEW HE WAS TROUBLE.
I SHOULDA DONE HIM, THEN.
AW, BUT THINK OF THE FUN WE CAN HAVE UNTIL SHE DOES...
YOU TOUCH HER, SLEAZE BAG, AND SO HELP ME...

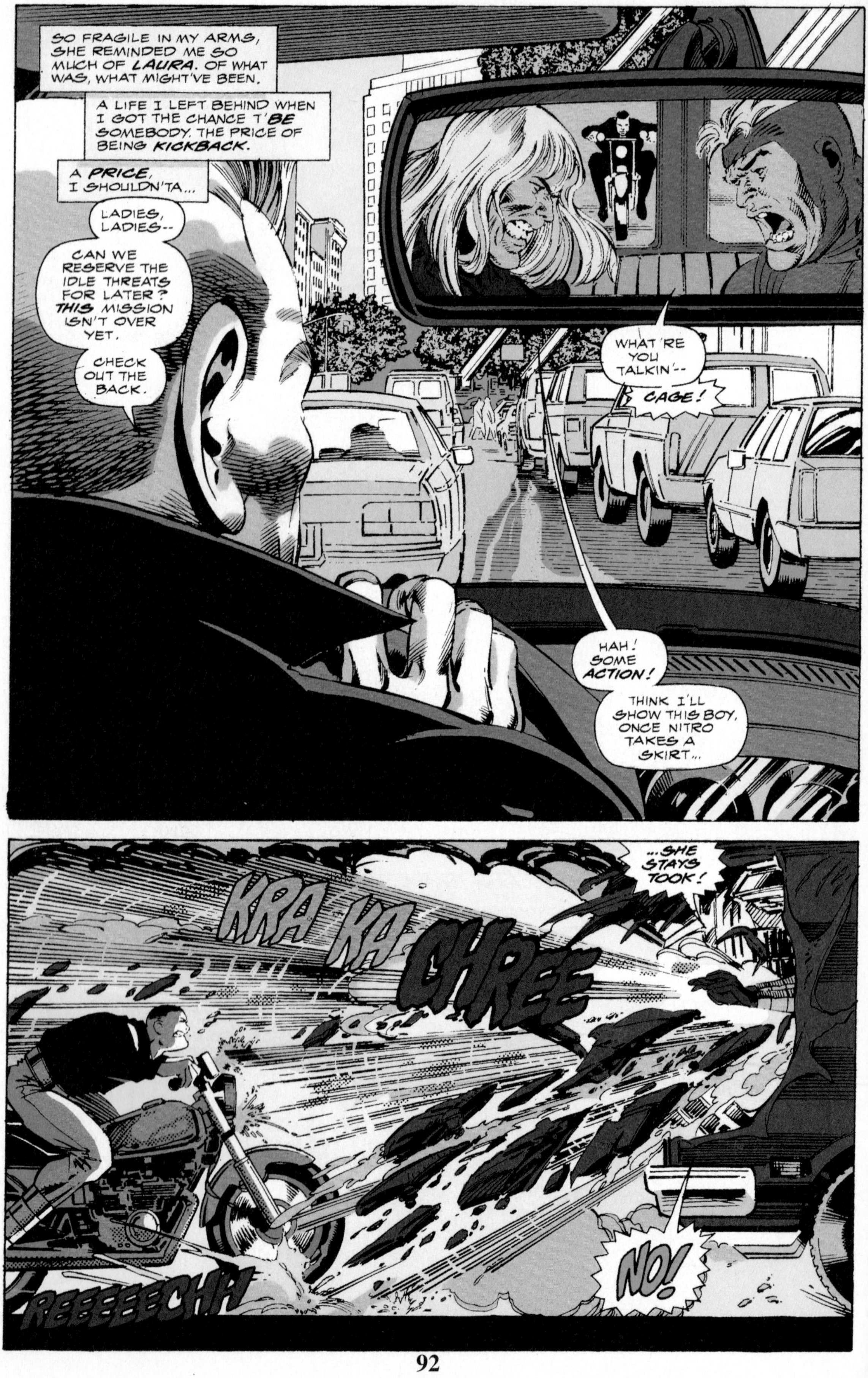
SO FRAGILE IN MY ARMS, SHE REMINDED ME SO MUCH OF LAURA. OF WHAT WAS, WHAT MIGHT'VE BEEN.
A LIFE I LEFT BEHIND WHEN I GOT THE CHANCE T'BE SOMEBODY. THE PRICE OF BEING KICKBACK.
A PRICE, I SHOULDN'TA...
LADIES, LADIES--
CAN WE RESERVE THE IDLE THREATS FOR LATER? THIS MISSION ISN'T OVER YET.
CHECK OUT THE BACK.
WHAT'RE YOU TALKIN'--
CAGE!
HAH! SOME ACTION!
THINK I'LL SHOW THIS BOY, ONCE NITRO TAKES A SKIRT...
...SHE STAYS TOOK!
KRA KA CHREE
NO!
REEEEEECHH

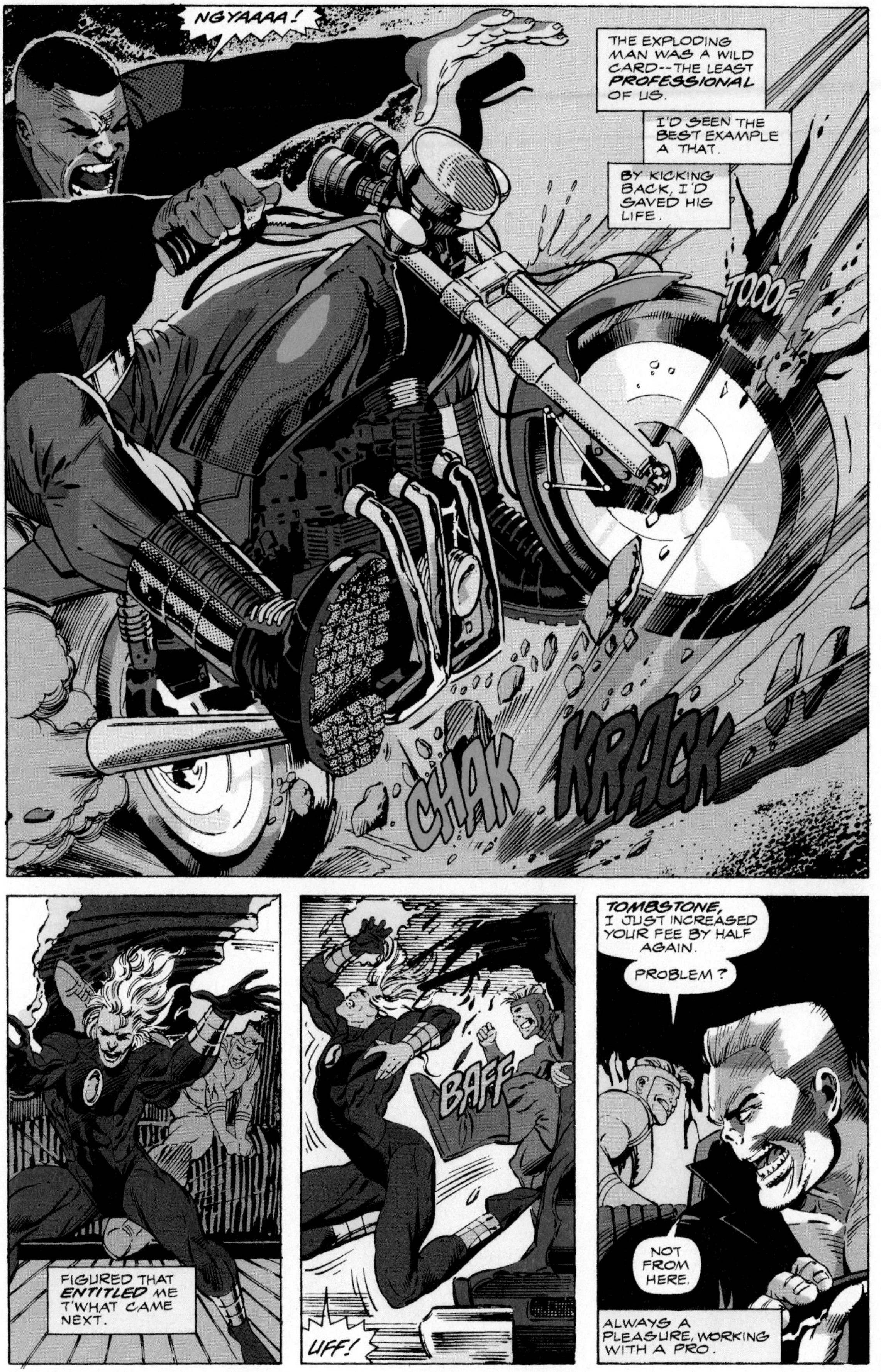
NGYAAAA!
THE EXPLODING MAN WAS A WILD CARD--THE LEAST PROFESSIONAL OF US.
I'D SEEN THE BEST EXAMPLE A THAT.
BY KICKING BACK, I'D SAVED HIS LIFE.
TOOOF
CHAK
KRACK
FIGURED THAT ENTITLED ME T'WHAT CAME NEXT.
BAFF
UFF!
TOMBSTONE, I JUST INCREASED YOUR FEE BY HALF AGAIN.
PROBLEM?
NOT FROM HERE.
ALWAYS A PLEASURE, WORKING WITH A PRO.

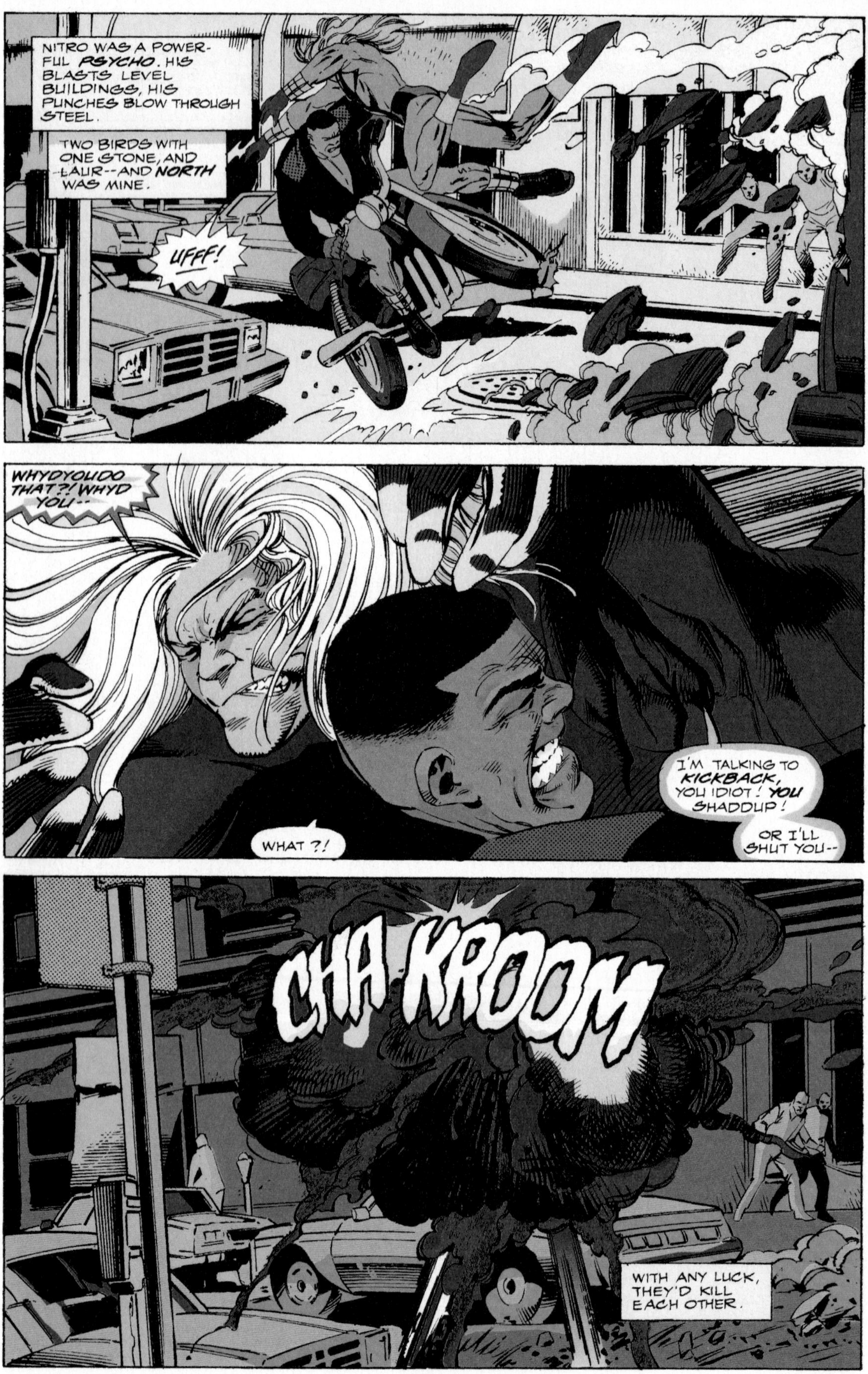
NITRO WAS A POWERFUL *PSYCHO*. HIS BLASTS LEVEL BUILDINGS, HIS PUNCHES BLOW THROUGH STEEL.
TWO BIRDS WITH ONE STONE, AND --LAUR--AND *NORTH* WAS MINE.
UFFF!
WHYDYOUDO THAT?! WHYD YOU--
I'M TALKING TO *KICKBACK*, YOU IDIOT! *YOU* SHADDUP!
OR I'LL SHUT YOU--
WHAT?!
CHA-KROOM
WITH ANY LUCK, THEY'D KILL EACH OTHER.

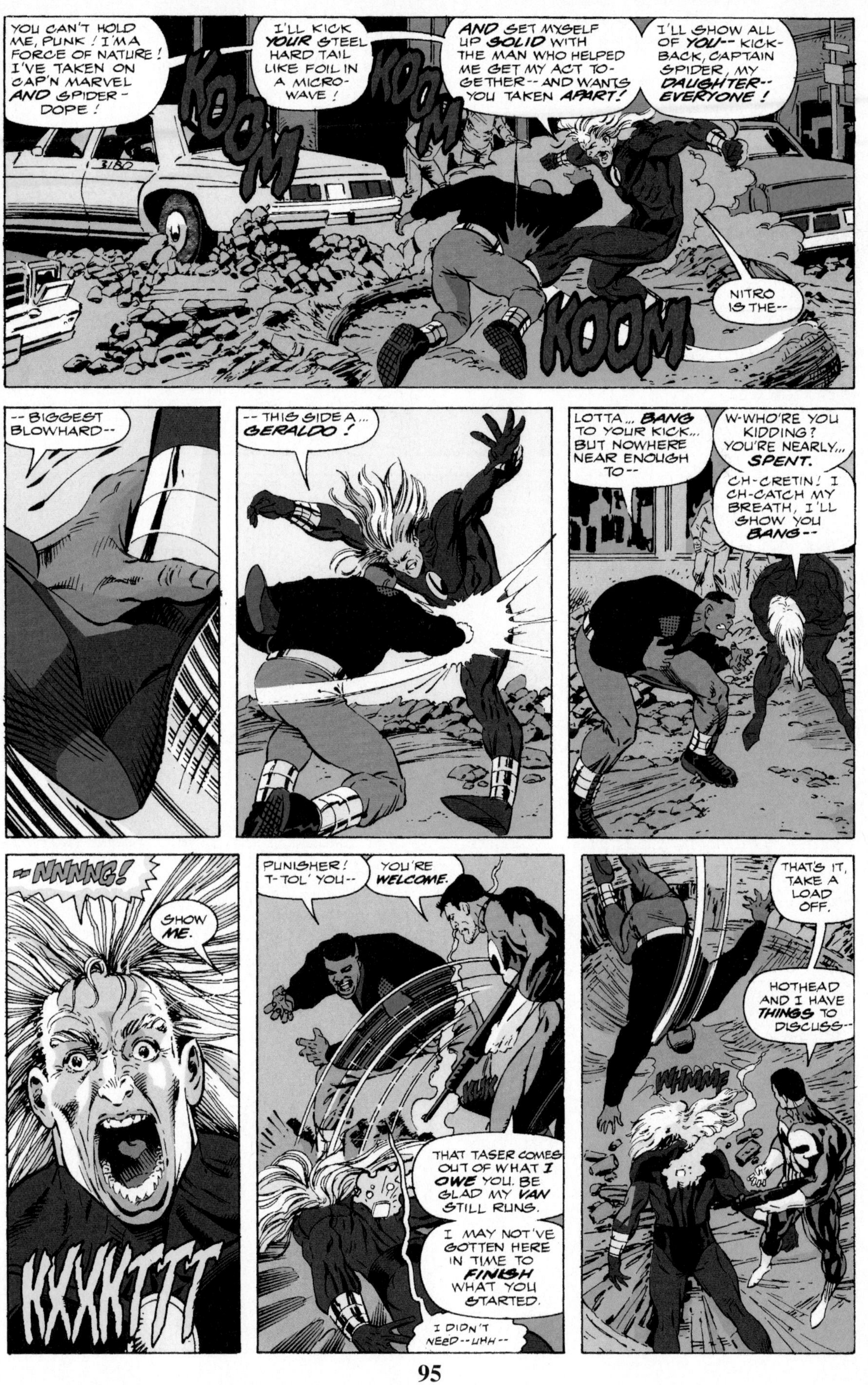
YOU CAN'T HOLD ME, PUNK! I'M A FORCE OF NATURE! I'VE TAKEN ON CAP'N MARVEL AND SPIDER-DOPE!
I'LL KICK YOUR STEEL HARD TAIL LIKE FOIL IN A MICRO-WAVE!
AND SET MYSELF UP SOLID WITH THE MAN WHO HELPED ME GET MY ACT TO-GETHER--AND WANTS YOU TAKEN APART!
I'LL SHOW ALL OF YOU--KICK-BACK, CAPTAIN SPIDER, MY DAUGHTER--EVERYONE!
KOOM
KOOM
KOOM
NITRO IS THE--
--BIGGEST BLOWHARD--
--THIS SIDE A... GERALDO!
LOTTA... BANG TO YOUR KICK... BUT NOWHERE NEAR ENOUGH TO--
W-WHO'RE YOU KIDDING? YOU'RE NEARLY... SPENT.
CH-CRETIN! I CH-CATCH MY BREATH, I'LL SHOW YOU BANG--
--NNNNG!
SHOW ME.
KXXKTTT
PUNISHER! T-TOL' YOU--
YOU'RE WELCOME.
THAT TASER COMES OUT OF WHAT I OWE YOU. BE GLAD MY VAN STILL RUNS.
I MAY NOT'VE GOTTEN HERE IN TIME TO FINISH WHAT YOU STARTED.
I DIDN'T NEED--UHH--
THAT'S IT, TAKE A LOAD OFF.
HOTHEAD AND I HAVE THINGS TO DISCUSS--

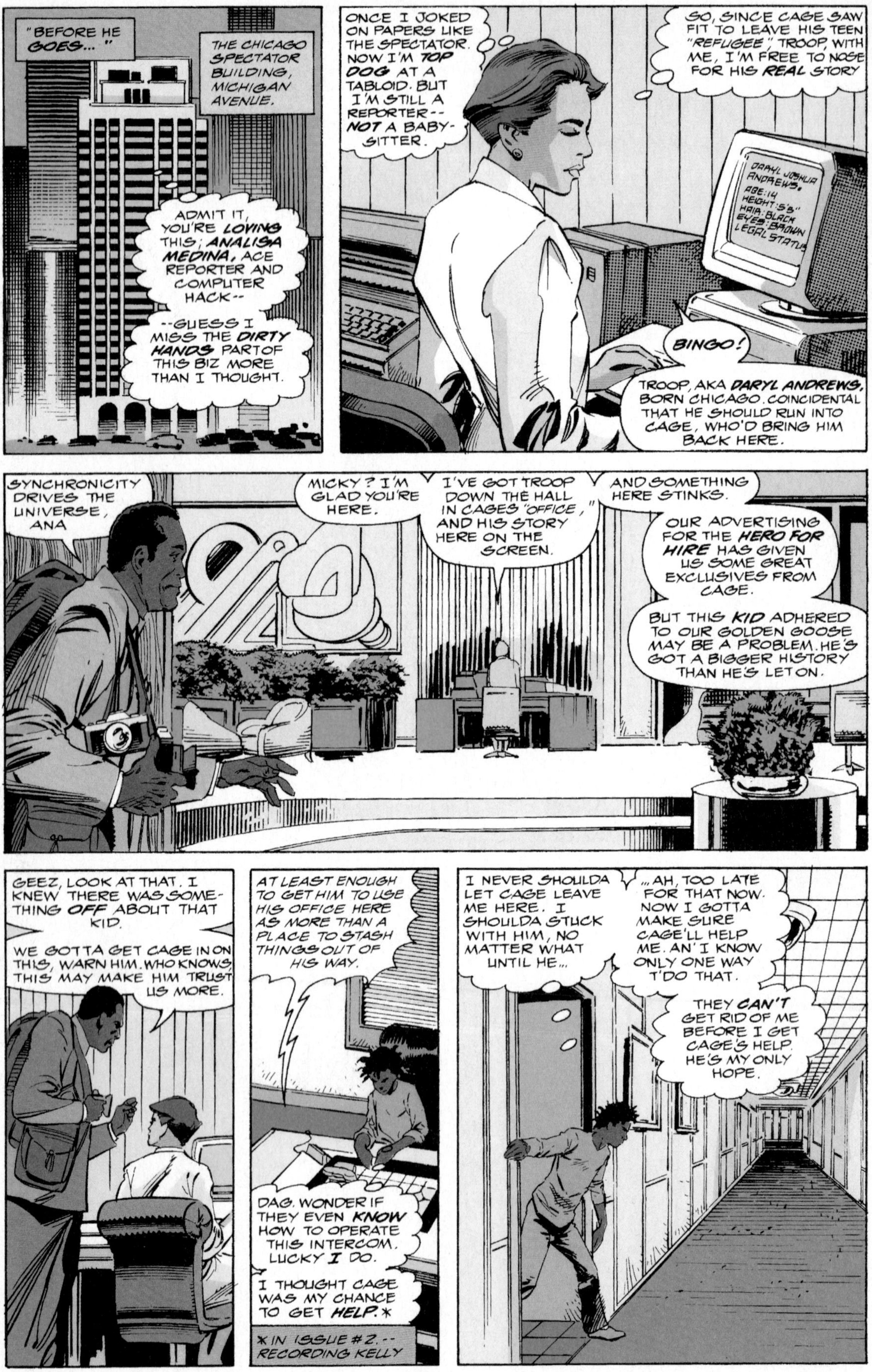
"BEFORE HE GOES..."
THE CHICAGO SPECTATOR BUILDING, MICHIGAN AVENUE.
ADMIT IT, YOU'RE LOVING THIS; ANALISA MEDINA, ACE REPORTER AND COMPUTER HACK--
--GUESS I MISS THE DIRTY HANDS PART OF THIS BIZ MORE THAN I THOUGHT.
ONCE I JOKED ON PAPERS LIKE THE SPECTATOR. NOW I'M TOP DOG AT A TABLOID. BUT I'M STILL A REPORTER-- NOT A BABY-SITTER.
SO, SINCE CAGE SAW FIT TO LEAVE HIS TEEN "REFUGEE", TROOP, WITH ME, I'M FREE TO NOSE FOR HIS REAL STORY
DARYL JOSHUA ANDREWS. AGE: 14 HEIGHT: 5'5" HAIR: BLACK EYES: BROWN LEGAL STATUS
BINGO!
TROOP, AKA DARYL ANDREWS, BORN CHICAGO. COINCIDENTAL THAT HE SHOULD RUN INTO CAGE, WHO'D BRING HIM BACK HERE.
SYNCHRONICITY DRIVES THE UNIVERSE, ANA
MICKY? I'M GLAD YOU'RE HERE.
I'VE GOT TROOP DOWN THE HALL IN CAGES "OFFICE," AND HIS STORY HERE ON THE SCREEN.
AND SOMETHING HERE STINKS.
OUR ADVERTISING FOR THE HERO FOR HIRE HAS GIVEN US SOME GREAT EXCLUSIVES FROM CAGE.
BUT THIS KID ADHERED TO OUR GOLDEN GOOSE MAY BE A PROBLEM. HE'S GOT A BIGGER HISTORY THAN HE'S LET ON.
GEEZ, LOOK AT THAT. I KNEW THERE WAS SOMETHING OFF ABOUT THAT KID.
WE GOTTA GET CAGE IN ON THIS, WARN HIM. WHO KNOWS, THIS MAY MAKE HIM TRUST US MORE.
AT LEAST ENOUGH TO GET HIM TO USE HIS OFFICE HERE AS MORE THAN A PLACE TO STASH THINGS OUT OF HIS WAY.
DAG. WONDER IF THEY EVEN KNOW HOW TO OPERATE THIS INTERCOM. LUCKY I DO.
I THOUGHT CAGE WAS MY CHANCE TO GET HELP.*
*IN ISSUE #2.-- RECORDING KELLY
I NEVER SHOULDA LET CAGE LEAVE ME HERE. I SHOULDA STUCK WITH HIM, NO MATTER WHAT UNTIL HE...
...AH, TOO LATE FOR THAT NOW. NOW I GOTTA MAKE SURE CAGE'LL HELP ME. AN' I KNOW ONLY ONE WAY T'DO THAT.
THEY CAN'T GET RID OF ME BEFORE I GET CAGE'S HELP. HE'S MY ONLY HOPE.

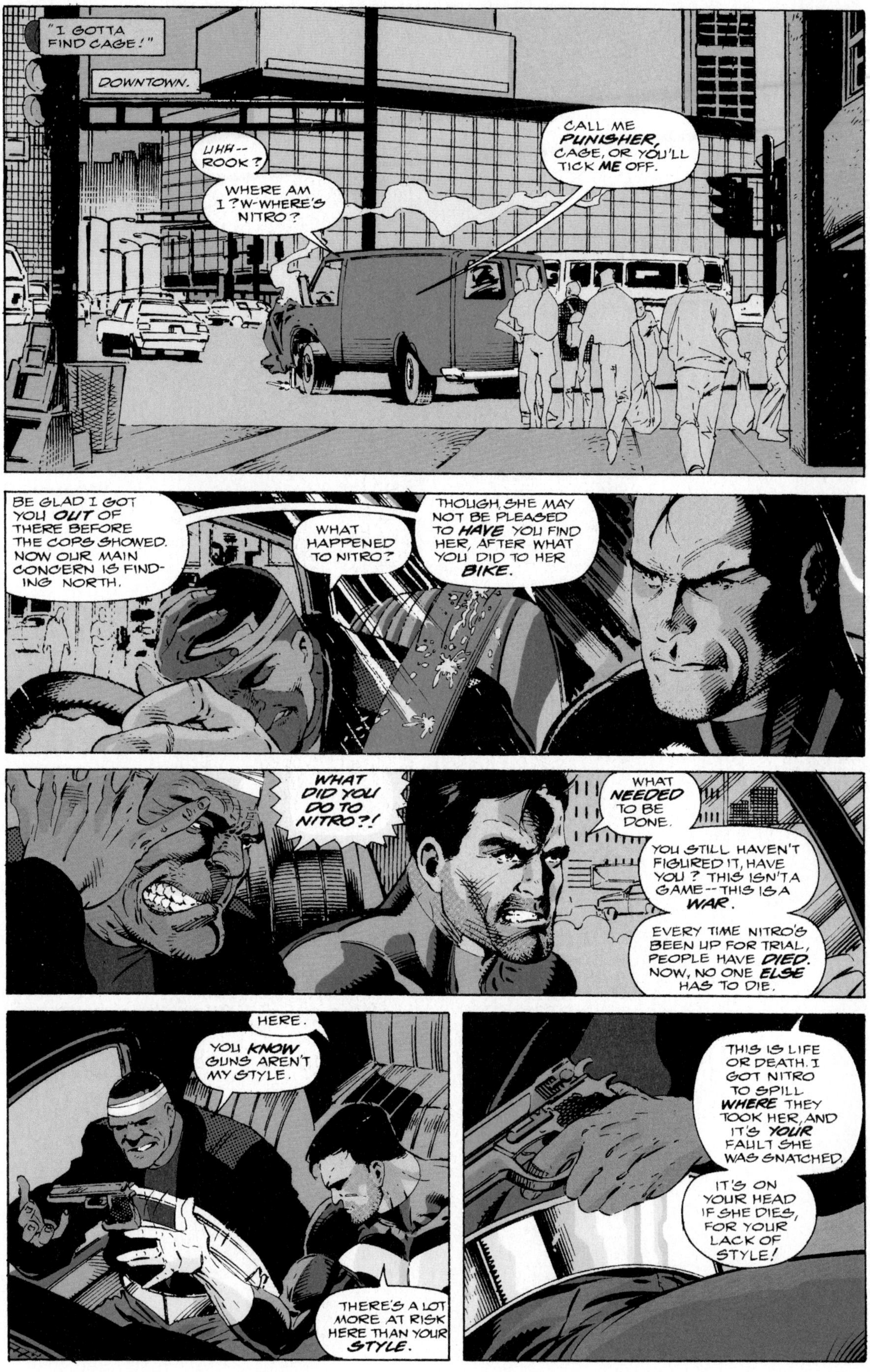

"I GOTTA FIND CAGE!"
DOWNTOWN.
UHH-- ROOK?
WHERE AM I? W-WHERE'S NITRO?
CALL ME PUNISHER, CAGE, OR YOU'LL TICK ME OFF.
BE GLAD I GOT YOU OUT OF THERE BEFORE THE COPS SHOWED. NOW OUR MAIN CONCERN IS FINDING NORTH.
WHAT HAPPENED TO NITRO?
THOUGH, SHE MAY NOT BE PLEASED TO HAVE YOU FIND HER, AFTER WHAT YOU DID TO HER BIKE.
WHAT DID YOU DO TO NITRO?!
WHAT NEEDED TO BE DONE.
YOU STILL HAVEN'T FIGURED IT, HAVE YOU? THIS ISN'T A GAME-- THIS IS A WAR.
EVERY TIME NITRO'S BEEN UP FOR TRIAL, PEOPLE HAVE DIED. NOW, NO ONE ELSE HAS TO DIE.
HERE.
YOU KNOW GUNS AREN'T MY STYLE.
THERE'S A LOT MORE AT RISK HERE THAN YOUR STYLE.
THIS IS LIFE OR DEATH. I GOT NITRO TO SPILL WHERE THEY TOOK HER, AND IT'S YOUR FAULT SHE WAS SNATCHED.
IT'S ON YOUR HEAD IF SHE DIES, FOR YOUR LACK OF STYLE!

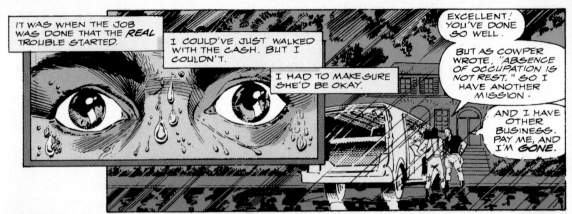

IT WAS WHEN THE JOB WAS DONE THAT THE *REAL* TROUBLE STARTED.

I COULD'VE JUST WALKED WITH THE CASH. BUT I COULDN'T.

I HAD TO MAKE SURE SHE'D BE OKAY.

EXCELLENT! YOU'VE DONE SO WELL.

BUT AS COWPER WROTE, "ABSENCE OF OCCUPATION IS NOT REST." SO I HAVE ANOTHER MISSION.

AND I HAVE OTHER BUSINESS. PAY ME, AND I'M *GONE*.

TACHH TAKKCH

WHAT WAS THAT?

OH, NOT'ING. A MAINTENANCE DEVICE.

I HAVE MORE IMPORTANT CONCERNS -- AND A CHANCE FOR YOU BOTH TO DOUBLE YOUR TAKE.

I ONLY NEED ONE OF YOU-- AND OF COURSE, MS. NORT!

WAIT FOR IT.

NO THANKS. I KNOW WHEN TO CUT, AND THIS DEAL'S TOO HOT, WITH THE PUNISHER IN IT.

FOR ALL YOUR QUOTING, HARD-CORE, YOU OUGHT TO CHECK SUN TZU'S, *THE ART OF WAR*

DON'T *UNDER-ESTIMATE*. CAGE WON'T GO DOWN EASY.

I DON'T BELIEVE IN UNDERESTIMATIN' ANYONE, TOMBSTONE.

GO!

IT'S *ME* THAT PEOPLE NEVER TAKE FULL MEASURE OF. TO *DERE* COST!

UHNN!

DON'T HURT HER!

ZZRRAAKKZZ

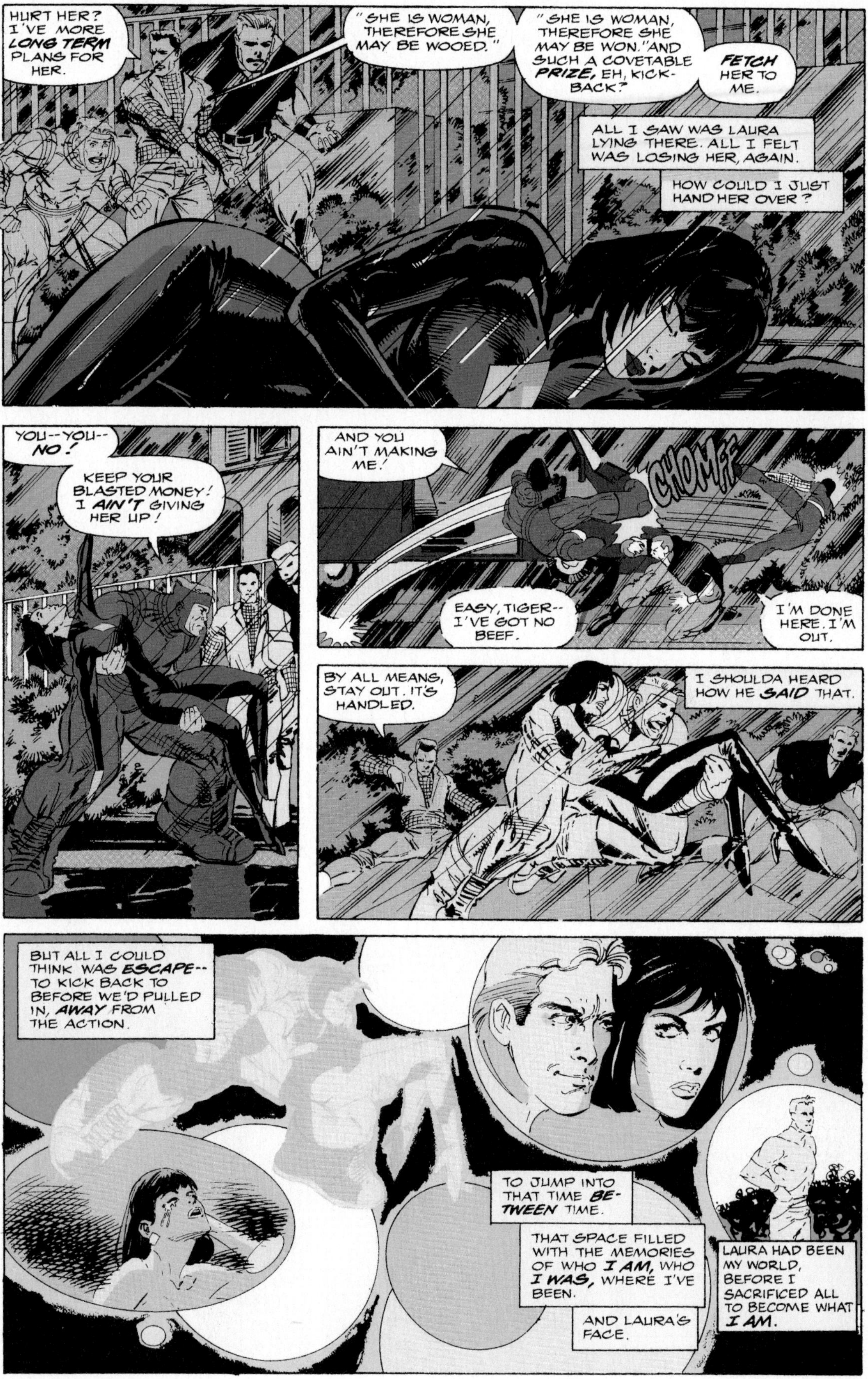
HURT HER? I'VE MORE LONG TERM PLANS FOR HER.
"SHE IS WOMAN, THEREFORE SHE MAY BE WOOED."
"SHE IS WOMAN, THEREFORE SHE MAY BE WON." AND SUCH A COVETABLE PRIZE, EH, KICK-BACK?
FETCH HER TO ME.
ALL I SAW WAS LAURA LYING THERE. ALL I FELT WAS LOSING HER, AGAIN.
HOW COULD I JUST HAND HER OVER?
YOU--YOU-- NO!
KEEP YOUR BLASTED MONEY! I AIN'T GIVING HER UP!
AND YOU AIN'T MAKING ME!
CHOMFF
EASY, TIGER-- I'VE GOT NO BEEF.
I'M DONE HERE. I'M OUT.
BY ALL MEANS, STAY OUT. IT'S HANDLED.
I SHOULDA HEARD HOW HE SAID THAT.
BUT ALL I COULD THINK WAS ESCAPE-- TO KICK BACK TO BEFORE WE'D PULLED IN, AWAY FROM THE ACTION.
TO JUMP INTO THAT TIME BE-TWEEN TIME.
THAT SPACE FILLED WITH THE MEMORIES OF WHO I AM, WHO I WAS, WHERE I'VE BEEN.
AND LAURA'S FACE.
LAURA HAD BEEN MY WORLD, BEFORE I SACRIFICED ALL TO BECOME WHAT I AM.

I KICKED BACK, THE FULL THREE MINUTES, TO FREEDOM.

HA.

EXCELLENT! YOU'VE DONE SO WELL.

BUT AS COWPER WROTE, "ABSENCE OF OCCUPATION IS NOT REST." SO I HAVE ANOTHER MISSION.

AND I HAVE OTHER BUSINESS. PAY ME, AND I'M *GONE*.

I WAS NEVER FREE. I WAS A RAT RUNNING A PRE-ARRANGED MAZE.

AND WHEN I HEARD THE SOUND, I KNEW THE TRAP HAD SPRUNG.

THE SOUND I'D HEARD *BEFORE*.

TACHH

TAKKCH

TAKKCH

"A MAINTENANCE" DEVICE.

IT FIRED TRANQUILIZER DARTS THAT FROZE MY MUSCLES. I COULDN'T MOVE TO KICK BACK.

TAKKCH~

NOW I'VE BEEN IN THE MUD FOR... WHAT SEEMS LIKE *HOURS*, I SEE WHAT I SHOULDA DONE.

IF I'DA LET 'EM ALL DIE, I WOULDN'T NEED TO CONSIDER HARD-CORE'S OFFER.

AND SHE'D BE MINE, NOW.

AFRAID, KICK-BACK? YOU'VE NAUGHT TO FEAR FROM ME. YOU'VE ACTED EXACTLY AS ANTICIPATED.

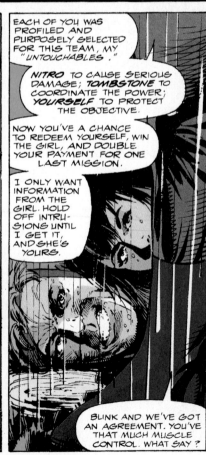

EACH OF YOU WAS PROFILED AND PURPOSELY SELECTED FOR THIS TEAM, MY "UNTOUCHABLES."

NITRO TO CAUSE SERIOUS DAMAGE; *TOMBSTONE* TO COORDINATE THE POWER; *YOURSELF* TO PROTECT THE OBJECTIVE.

NOW YOU'VE A CHANCE TO REDEEM YOURSELF, WIN THE GIRL, AND DOUBLE YOUR PAYMENT FOR ONE LAST MISSION.

I ONLY WANT INFORMATION FROM THE GIRL. HOLD OFF INTRU-SIONS UNTIL I GET IT, AND SHE'S YOURS.

BLINK AND WE'VE GOT AN AGREEMENT. YOU'VE THAT MUCH MUSCLE CONTROL. WHAT SAY?

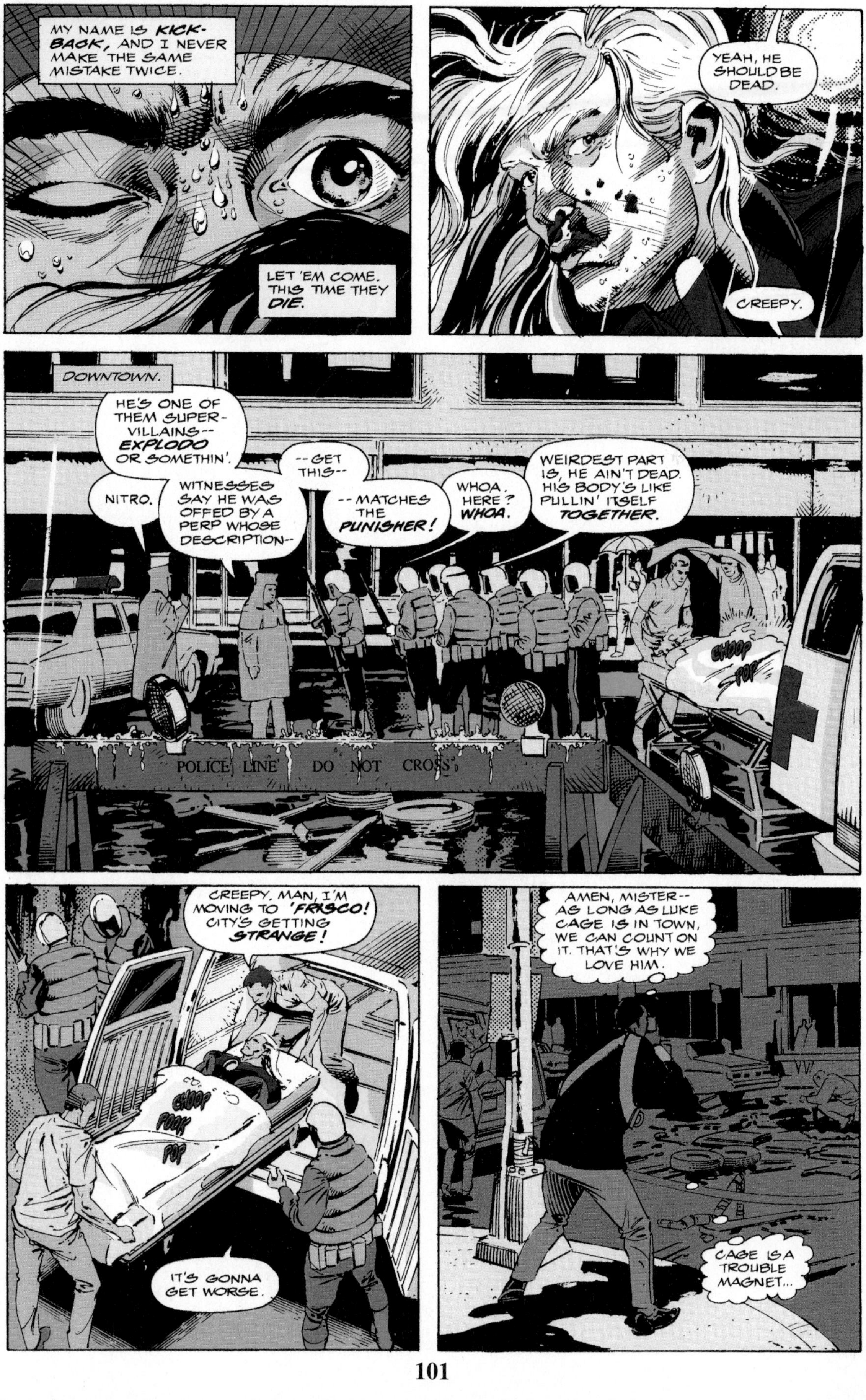

MY NAME IS KICK-BACK, AND I NEVER MAKE THE SAME MISTAKE TWICE.
LET 'EM COME. THIS TIME THEY DIE.
YEAH, HE SHOULD BE DEAD.
CREEPY.
DOWNTOWN.
HE'S ONE OF THEM SUPER-VILLAINS-- EXPLODO OR SOMETHIN'.
NITRO.
WITNESSES SAY HE WAS OFFED BY A PERP WHOSE DESCRIPTION--
--GET THIS--
--MATCHES THE PUNISHER!
WHOA, HERE? WHOA.
WEIRDEST PART IS, HE AIN'T DEAD. HIS BODY'S LIKE PULLIN' ITSELF TOGETHER.
SHOOP
POP
POLICE LINE DO NOT CROSS
CREEPY. MAN, I'M MOVING TO 'FRISCO! CITY'S GETTING STRANGE!
SHOOP
POOK
POP
IT'S GONNA GET WORSE.
AMEN, MISTER-- AS LONG AS LUKE CAGE IS IN TOWN, WE CAN COUNT ON IT. THAT'S WHY WE LOVE HIM.
CAGE IS A TROUBLE MAGNET...

"...AND TROUBLE IS NEWS."

WE'RE HERE. GEAR FOR ACTION, CAGE.

KRAM

REEEEEEEE

I'LL KNOCK.

RNNNNNNN

CHKA CHKA CHKA CHKA

KEEP THEM OCCUPIED. TWENTY MINUTES.

THEN?

THEN SHE'S ALL YOURS. YOU HAVE MY WORD.

OR I'LL HAVE YOUR HEAD.

RNNNNNNNN

AND IN GOOD COMPANY!

CHOOM

CRANCHA

WHERE IS SHE?!

THIS'S THE LAST TIME I'MA ASK NICE!

AREN'T WE ANXIOUS?

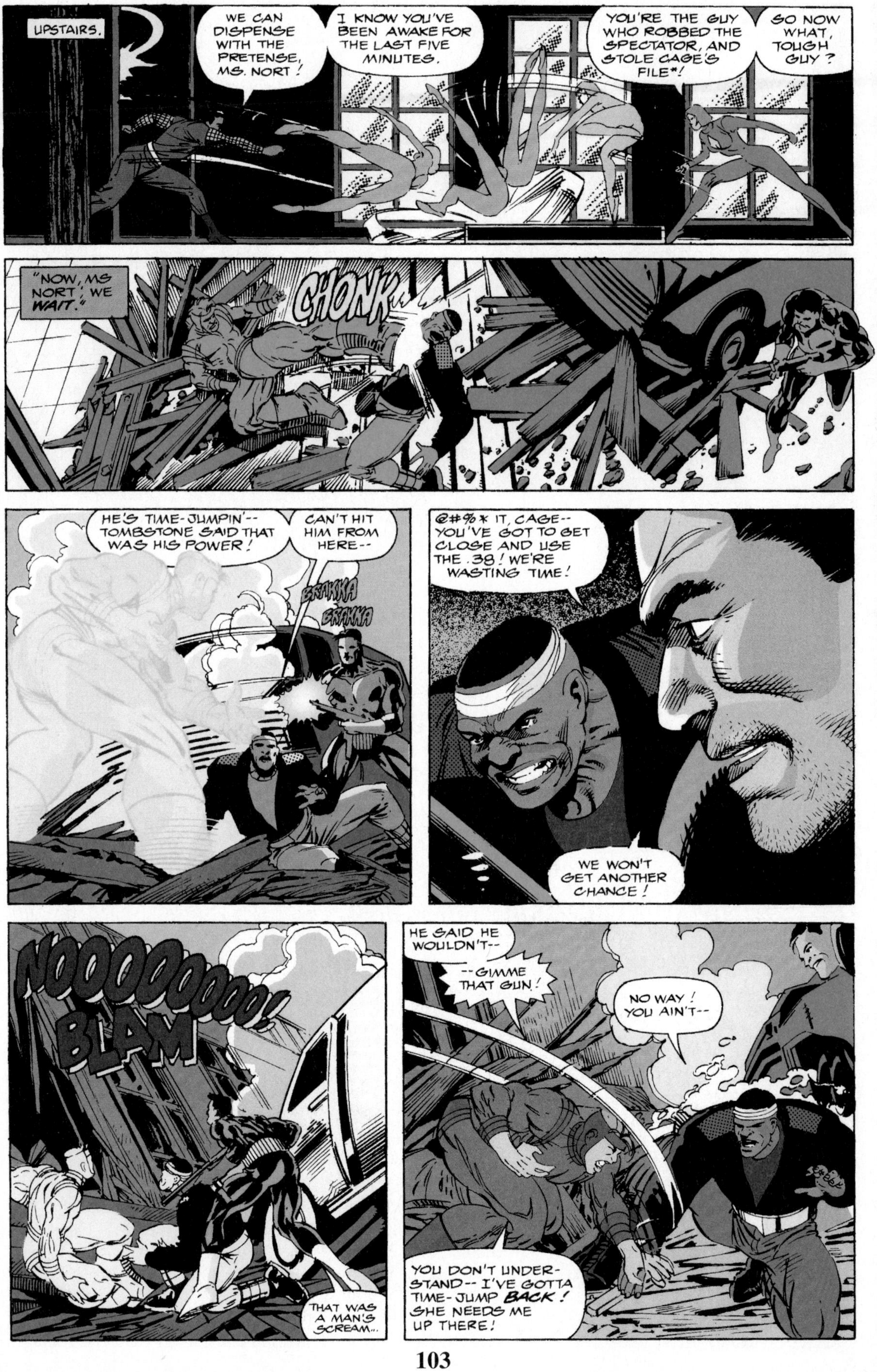
UPSTAIRS.
WE CAN DISPENSE WITH THE PRETENSE, MS. NORT!
I KNOW YOU'VE BEEN AWAKE FOR THE LAST FIVE MINUTES.
YOU'RE THE GUY WHO ROBBED THE SPECTATOR, AND STOLE CAGE'S FILE*!
SO NOW WHAT, TOUGH GUY?
"NOW, MS NORT, WE WAIT."
CHONK
HE'S TIME-JUMPIN'-- TOMBSTONE SAID THAT WAS HIS POWER!
CAN'T HIT HIM FROM HERE--
BRAKKA
BRAKKA
@#%* IT, CAGE-- YOU'VE GOT TO GET CLOSE AND USE THE .38! WE'RE WASTING TIME!
WE WON'T GET ANOTHER CHANCE!
NOOOOOOOOO!
BLAM
THAT WAS A MAN'S SCREAM...
HE SAID HE WOULDN'T--
--GIMME THAT GUN!
NO WAY! YOU AIN'T--
YOU DON'T UNDERSTAND-- I'VE GOTTA TIME-JUMP BACK! SHE NEEDS ME UP THERE!

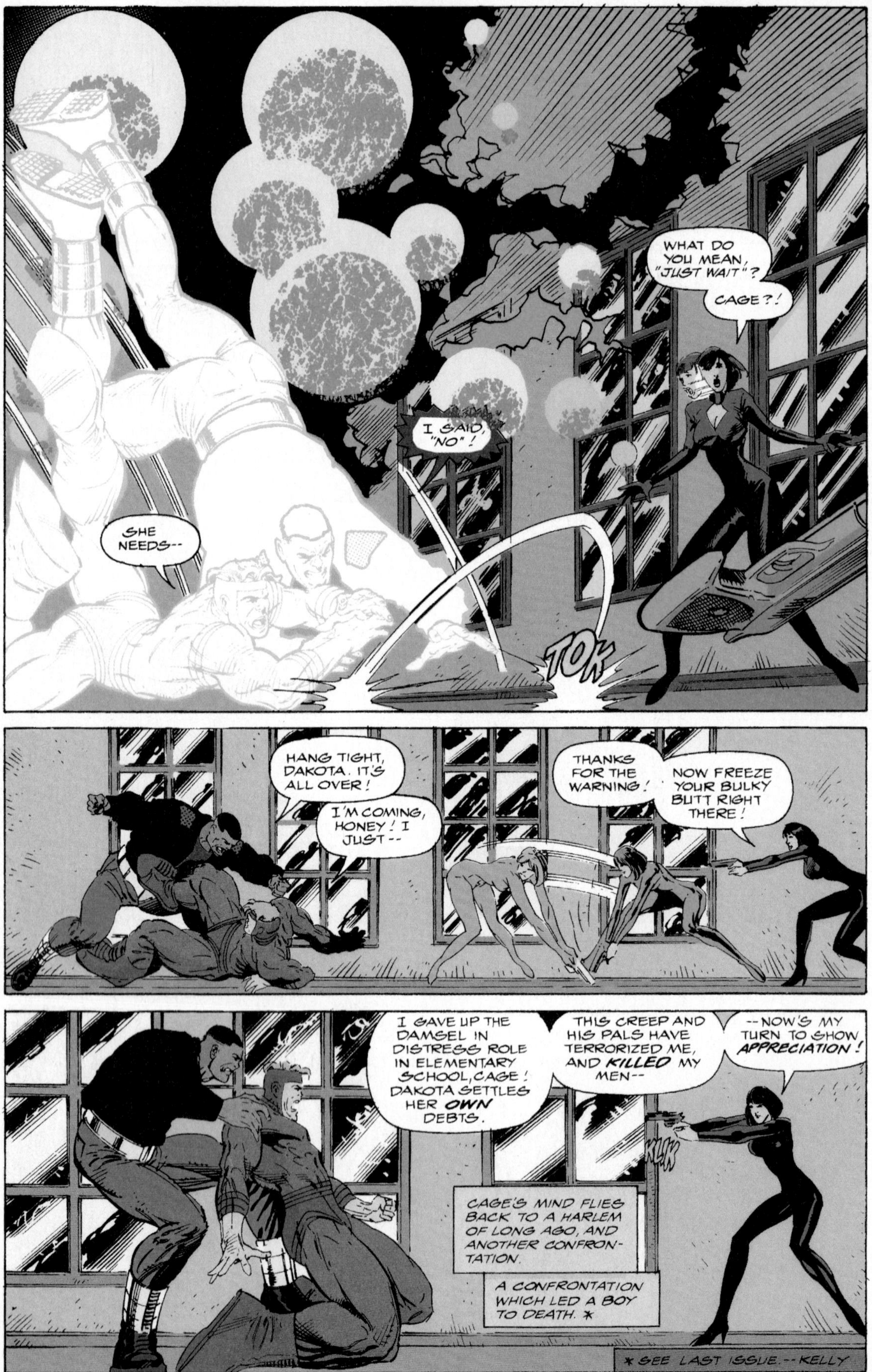
WHAT DO YOU MEAN, "JUST WAIT"?
CAGE?!
I SAID, "NO"!
SHE NEEDS--
TOK
HANG TIGHT, DAKOTA. IT'S ALL OVER!
I'M COMING, HONEY! I JUST--
THANKS FOR THE WARNING!
NOW FREEZE YOUR BULKY BUTT RIGHT THERE!
I GAVE UP THE DAMSEL IN DISTRESS ROLE IN ELEMENTARY SCHOOL, CAGE! DAKOTA SETTLES HER OWN DEBTS.
THIS CREEP AND HIS PALS HAVE TERRORIZED ME, AND KILLED MY MEN--
--NOW'S MY TURN TO SHOW APPRECIATION!
KLIK
CAGE'S MIND FLIES BACK TO A HARLEM OF LONG AGO, AND ANOTHER CONFRONTATION.
A CONFRONTATION WHICH LED A BOY TO DEATH. *
* SEE LAST ISSUE. --KELLY

Ioooooooooo

BLAM

CHAK

AND A **MAN** TO A VOW.

NOBODY DIES.

Y-YA **SHOT** AT ME.

YOU'RE **AFRAID** A'ME.

JUST LIKE **LAURA** WAS.

WHEN I'D DONE IT ALL FOR YOU...

I **SHOULDA**... I...

WAIT A SECOND. DON'T **GO OUT** THERE! HE'LL THINK YOU'RE--

WAIT! **ROOK,** DON'T--

BLAM
BLAM
BLAM

NOW IT'S OVER.

YEAH....

...YEAH..

neigh the city ye and the death o Chicago attributed Castle, infamous vigila known as The Punisher. Ca ledgedly tracking an elusive ga lance operatives who called themse the Untouchables, responsible for the de struction of the lobby of this newspaper, and the murder of a security guard em- ployed by Dakota North Security and Investig ions, Inc. The Untouchables as allegedly acc ...hire, Luk .inning t ime in i

"EXCEPT FOR THE FIREWORKS."

105

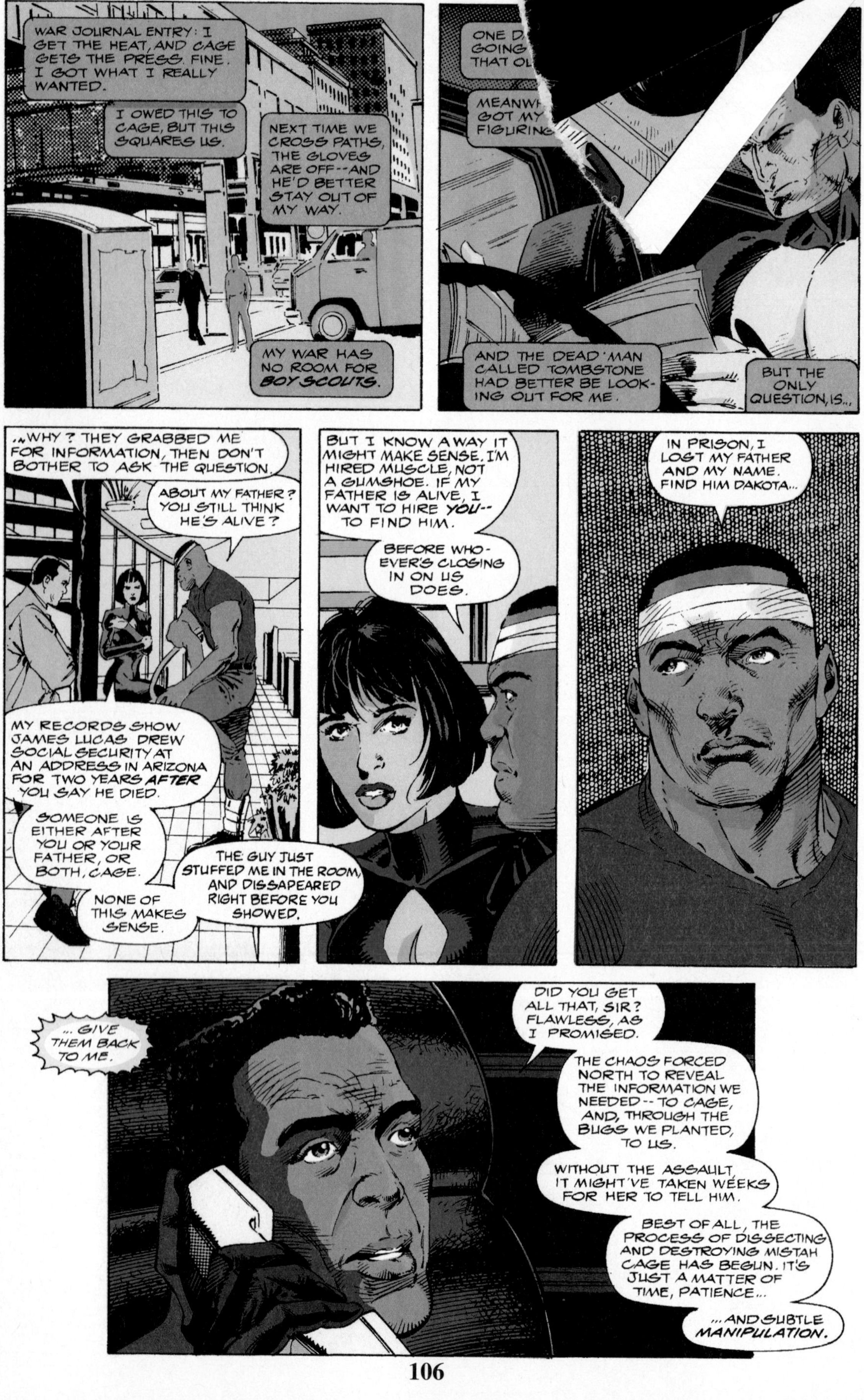

WAR JOURNAL ENTRY: I GET THE HEAT, AND CAGE GETS THE PRESS. FINE. I GOT WHAT I REALLY WANTED.
I OWED THIS TO CAGE, BUT THIS SQUARES US.
NEXT TIME WE CROSS PATHS, THE GLOVES ARE OFF--AND HE'D BETTER STAY OUT OF MY WAY.
MY WAR HAS NO ROOM FOR BOY SCOUTS.
ONE DA
GOING
THAT OL
MEANWH
GOT MY
FIGURING
AND THE DEAD MAN CALLED TOMBSTONE HAD BETTER BE LOOKING OUT FOR ME.
BUT THE ONLY QUESTION, IS...
...WHY? THEY GRABBED ME FOR INFORMATION, THEN DON'T BOTHER TO ASK THE QUESTION.
ABOUT MY FATHER? YOU STILL THINK HE'S ALIVE?
MY RECORDS SHOW JAMES LUCAS DREW SOCIAL SECURITY AT AN ADDRESS IN ARIZONA FOR TWO YEARS AFTER YOU SAY HE DIED.
SOMEONE IS EITHER AFTER YOU OR YOUR FATHER, OR BOTH, CAGE.
NONE OF THIS MAKES SENSE.
THE GUY JUST STUFFED ME IN THE ROOM, AND DISSAPEARED RIGHT BEFORE YOU SHOWED.
BUT I KNOW A WAY IT MIGHT MAKE SENSE. I'M HIRED MUSCLE, NOT A GUMSHOE. IF MY FATHER IS ALIVE, I WANT TO HIRE YOU--TO FIND HIM.
BEFORE WHO-EVER'S CLOSING IN ON US DOES.
IN PRISON, I LOST MY FATHER AND MY NAME. FIND HIM DAKOTA...
...GIVE THEM BACK TO ME.
DID YOU GET ALL THAT, SIR? FLAWLESS, AS I PROMISED.
THE CHAOS FORCED NORTH TO REVEAL THE INFORMATION WE NEEDED--TO CAGE, AND, THROUGH THE BUGS WE PLANTED, TO US.
WITHOUT THE ASSAULT, IT MIGHT'VE TAKEN WEEKS FOR HER TO TELL HIM.
BEST OF ALL, THE PROCESS OF DISSECTING AND DESTROYING MISTAH CAGE HAS BEGUN. IT'S JUST A MATTER OF TIME, PATIENCE...
...AND SUBTLE MANIPULATION.

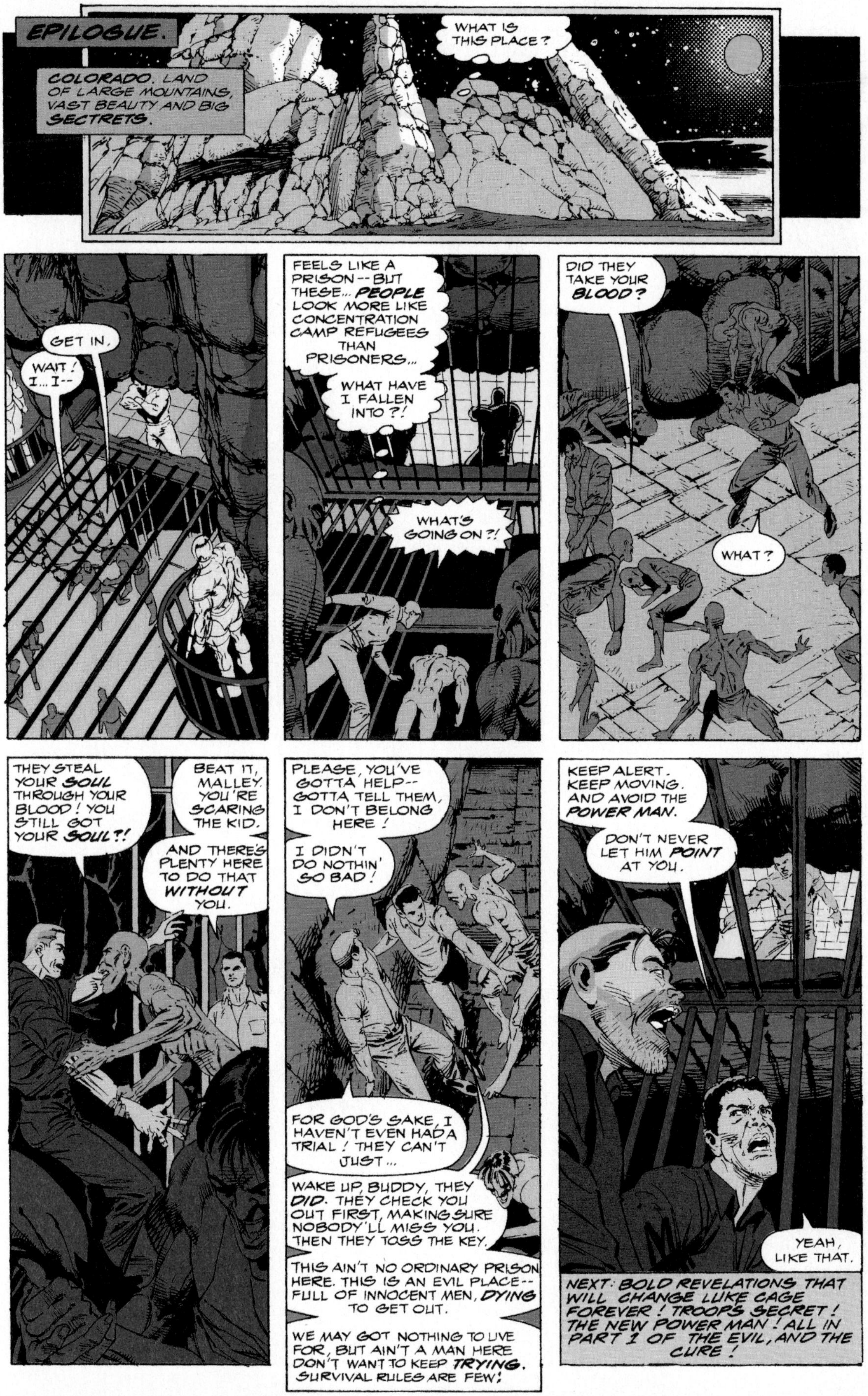
EPILOGUE.
COLORADO. LAND OF LARGE MOUNTAINS, VAST BEAUTY AND BIG SECTRETS.
WHAT IS THIS PLACE?
GET IN.
WAIT! I... I--
FEELS LIKE A PRISON -- BUT THESE... PEOPLE LOOK MORE LIKE CONCENTRATION CAMP REFUGEES THAN PRISONERS...
WHAT HAVE I FALLEN INTO?!
WHAT'S GOING ON?!
DID THEY TAKE YOUR BLOOD?
WHAT?
THEY STEAL YOUR SOUL THROUGH YOUR BLOOD! YOU STILL GOT YOUR SOUL?!
BEAT IT, MALLEY. YOU'RE SCARING THE KID.
AND THERE'S PLENTY HERE TO DO THAT WITHOUT YOU.
PLEASE, YOU'VE GOTTA HELP-- GOTTA TELL THEM, I DON'T BELONG HERE!
I DIDN'T DO NOTHIN' SO BAD!
FOR GOD'S SAKE, I HAVEN'T EVEN HAD A TRIAL! THEY CAN'T JUST...
WAKE UP, BUDDY, THEY DID. THEY CHECK YOU OUT FIRST, MAKING SURE NOBODY'LL MISS YOU. THEN THEY TOSS THE KEY.
THIS AIN'T NO ORDINARY PRISON HERE. THIS IS AN EVIL PLACE-- FULL OF INNOCENT MEN, DYING TO GET OUT.
WE MAY GOT NOTHING TO LIVE FOR, BUT AIN'T A MAN HERE DON'T WANT TO KEEP TRYING. SURVIVAL RULES ARE FEW:
KEEP ALERT. KEEP MOVING. AND AVOID THE POWER MAN.
DON'T NEVER LET HIM POINT AT YOU.
YEAH, LIKE THAT.
NEXT: BOLD REVELATIONS THAT WILL CHANGE LUKE CAGE FOREVER! TROOPS SECRET! THE NEW POWER MAN! ALL IN PART 1 OF THE EVIL, AND THE CURE!

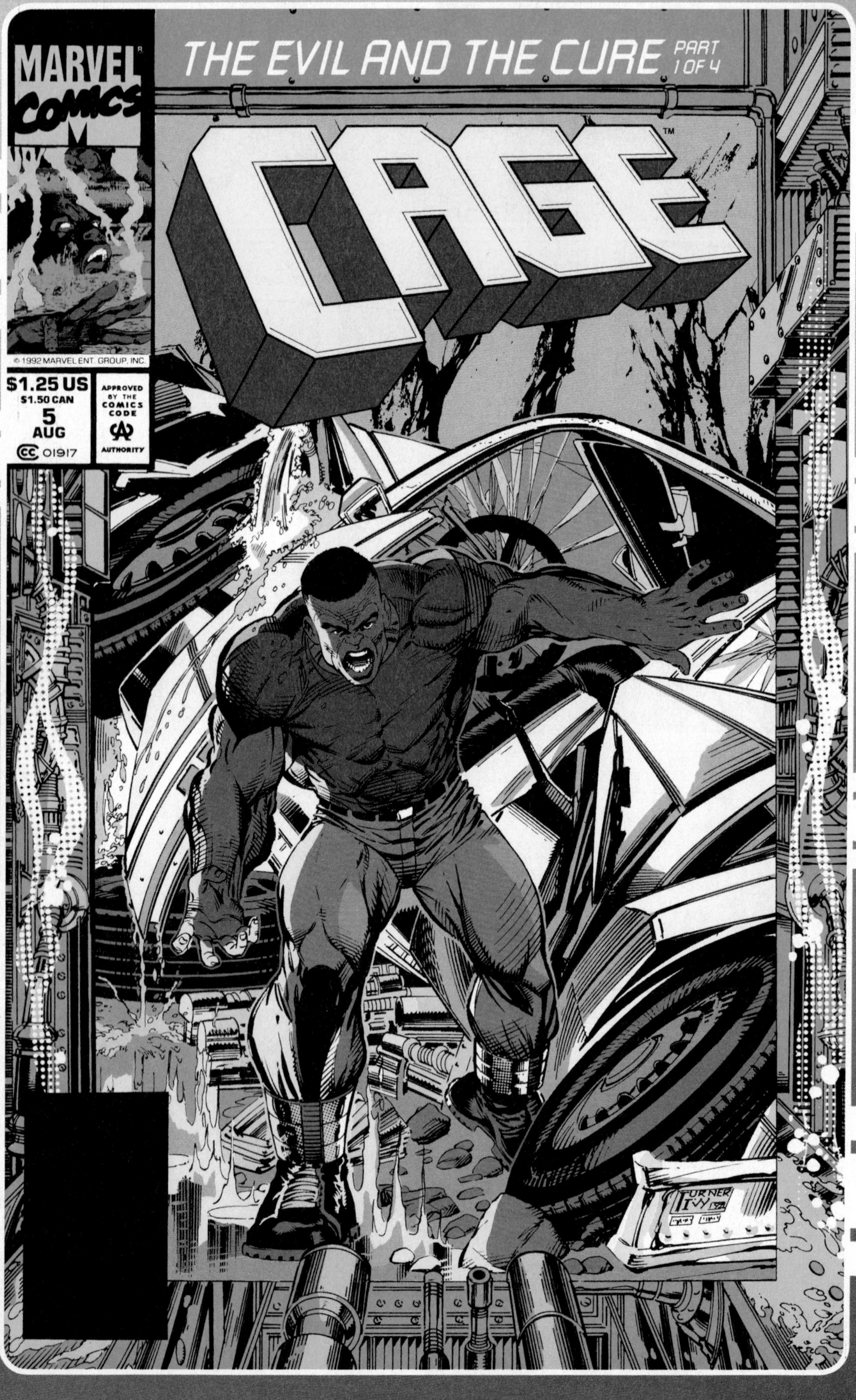
MARVEL COMICS
THE EVIL AND THE CURE PART 1 OF 4
CAGE™
© 1992 MARVEL ENT. GROUP, INC.
$1.25 US
$1.50 CAN
5
AUG
CC 01917
APPROVED BY THE COMICS CODE AUTHORITY
TURNER IVY '92

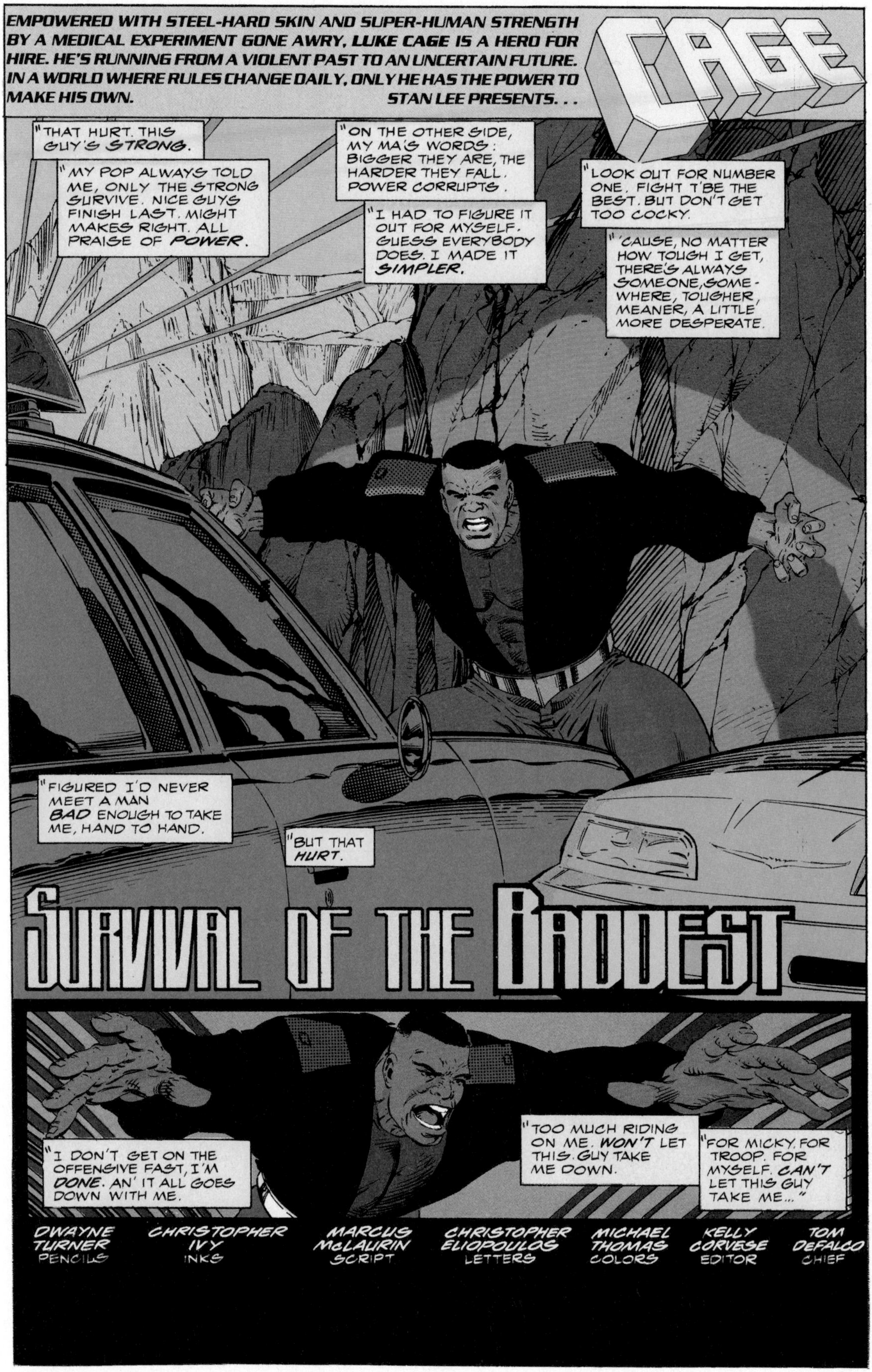

EMPOWERED WITH STEEL-HARD SKIN AND SUPER-HUMAN STRENGTH BY A MEDICAL EXPERIMENT GONE AWRY, LUKE CAGE IS A HERO FOR HIRE. HE'S RUNNING FROM A VIOLENT PAST TO AN UNCERTAIN FUTURE. IN A WORLD WHERE RULES CHANGE DAILY, ONLY HE HAS THE POWER TO MAKE HIS OWN.
STAN LEE PRESENTS. . .
CAGE
"THAT HURT. THIS GUY'S STRONG.
"MY POP ALWAYS TOLD ME, ONLY THE STRONG SURVIVE. NICE GUYS FINISH LAST. MIGHT MAKES RIGHT. ALL PRAISE OF POWER.
"ON THE OTHER SIDE, MY MA'S WORDS: BIGGER THEY ARE, THE HARDER THEY FALL. POWER CORRUPTS.
"I HAD TO FIGURE IT OUT FOR MYSELF. GUESS EVERYBODY DOES. I MADE IT SIMPLER.
"LOOK OUT FOR NUMBER ONE. FIGHT T'BE THE BEST. BUT DON'T GET TOO COCKY.
"'CAUSE, NO MATTER HOW TOUGH I GET, THERE'S ALWAYS SOMEONE, SOMEWHERE, TOUGHER, MEANER, A LITTLE MORE DESPERATE.
"FIGURED I'D NEVER MEET A MAN BAD ENOUGH TO TAKE ME, HAND TO HAND.
"BUT THAT HURT.
SURVIVAL OF THE BADDEST
"I DON'T GET ON THE OFFENSIVE FAST, I'M DONE. AN' IT ALL GOES DOWN WITH ME.
"TOO MUCH RIDING ON ME. WON'T LET THIS GUY TAKE ME DOWN.
"FOR MICKY. FOR TROOP. FOR MYSELF. CAN'T LET THIS GUY TAKE ME..."
DWAYNE TURNER PENCILS
CHRISTOPHER IVY INKS
MARCUS McLAURIN SCRIPT
CHRISTOPHER ELIOPOULOS LETTERS
MICHAEL THOMAS COLORS
KELLY CORVESE EDITOR
TOM DeFALCO CHIEF

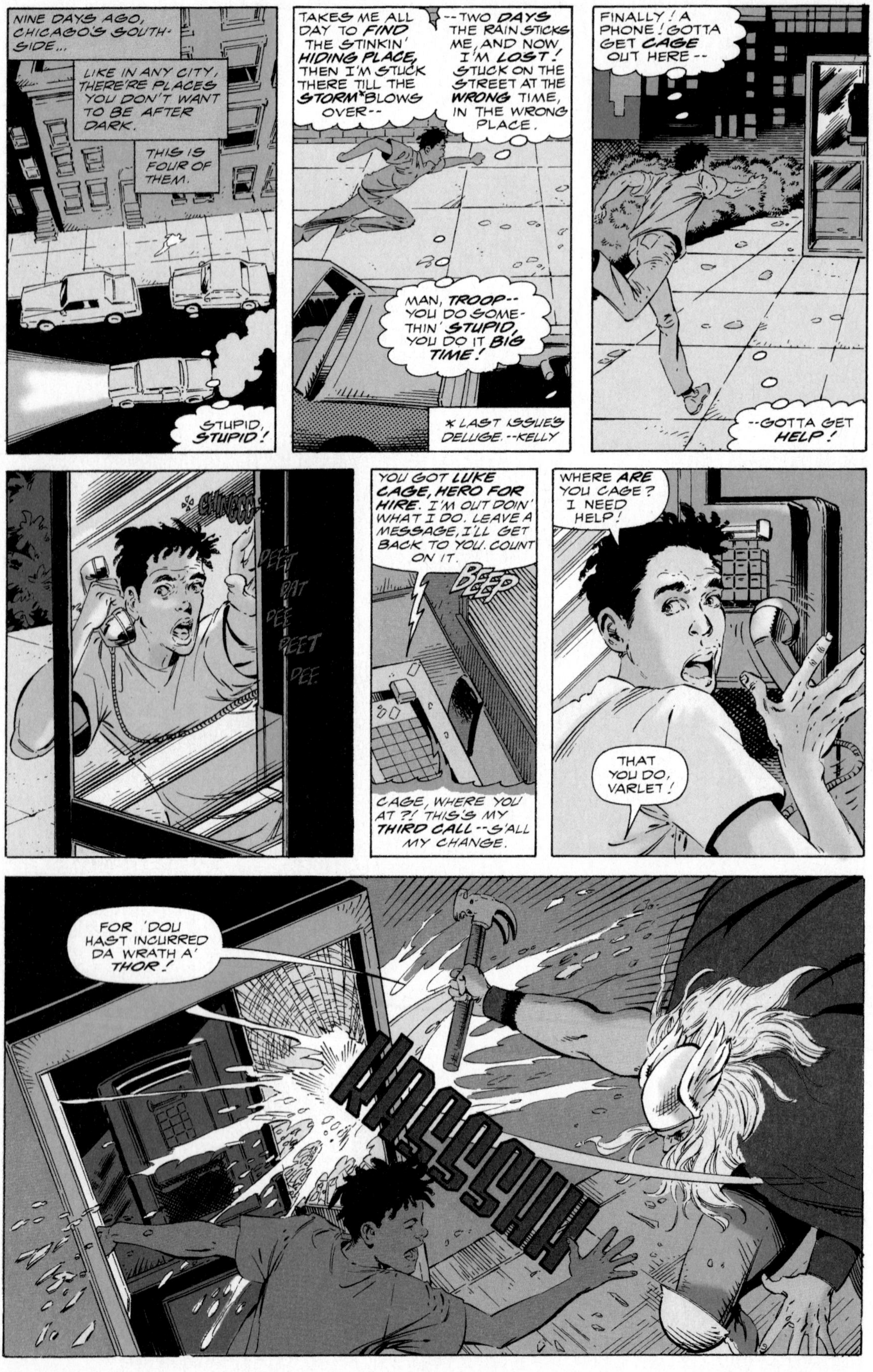
NINE DAYS AGO, CHICAGO'S SOUTH-SIDE...
LIKE IN ANY CITY, THERE'RE PLACES YOU DON'T WANT TO BE AFTER DARK.
THIS IS FOUR OF THEM.
STUPID, STUPID!
TAKES ME ALL DAY TO FIND THE STINKIN' HIDING PLACE, THEN I'M STUCK THERE TILL THE STORM* BLOWS OVER--
--TWO DAYS THE RAIN STICKS ME, AND NOW, I'M LOST! STUCK ON THE STREET AT THE WRONG TIME, IN THE WRONG PLACE.
MAN, TROOP-- YOU DO SOME-THIN' STUPID, YOU DO IT BIG TIME!
* LAST ISSUE'S DELUGE. --KELLY
FINALLY! A PHONE! GOTTA GET CAGE OUT HERE--
--GOTTA GET HELP!
CHINGGG
DEET DAT DEE DEET DEE
YOU GOT LUKE CAGE, HERO FOR HIRE. I'M OUT DOIN' WHAT I DO. LEAVE A MESSAGE, I'LL GET BACK TO YOU. COUNT ON IT.
BEEP
CAGE, WHERE YOU AT?! THIS'S MY THIRD CALL--S'ALL MY CHANGE.
WHERE ARE YOU CAGE? I NEED HELP!
THAT YOU DO, VARLET!
FOR 'DOU HAST INCURRED DA WRATH A' THOR!
KRSSSHH

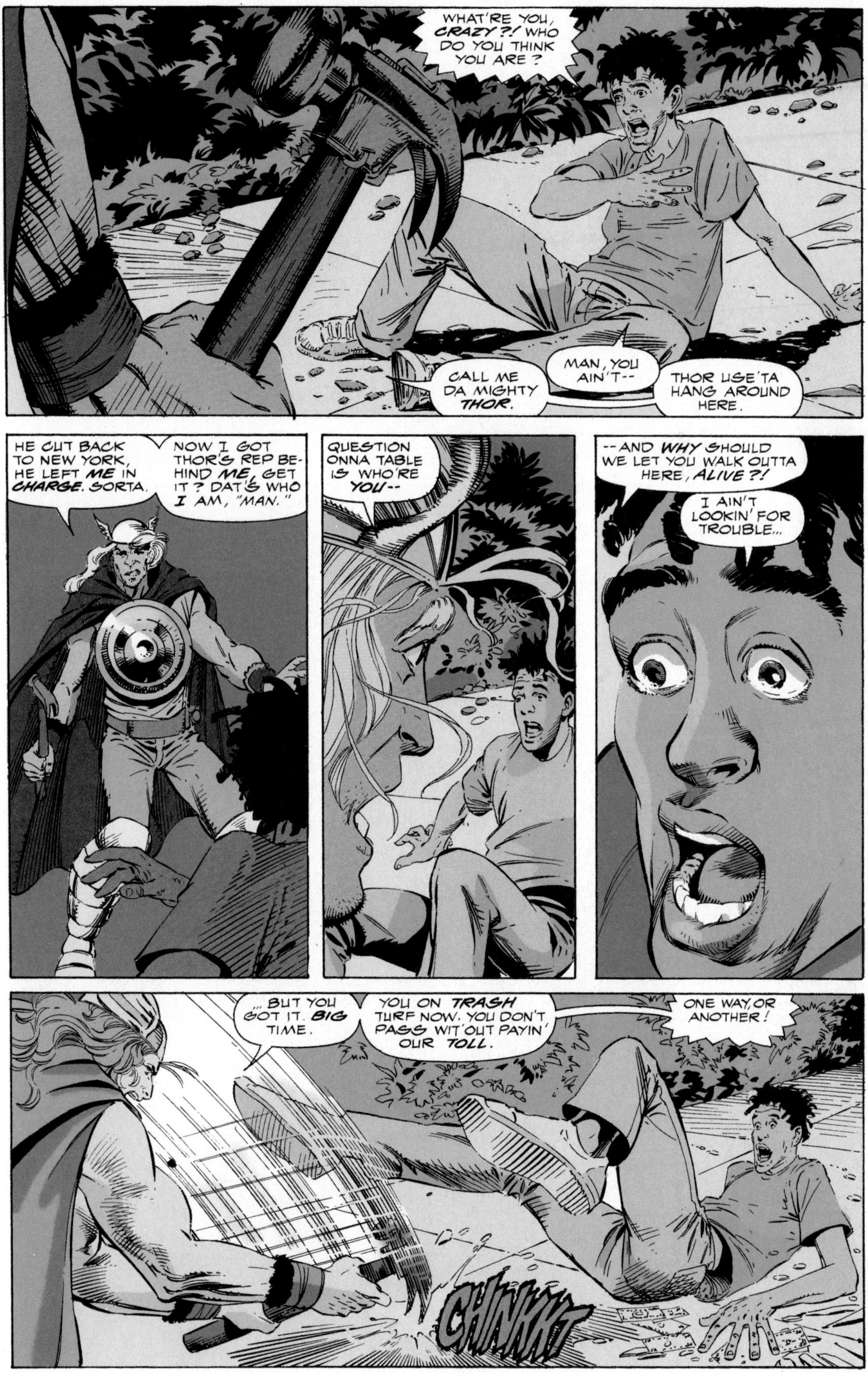
WHAT'RE YOU, CRAZY?! WHO DO YOU THINK YOU ARE?
CALL ME DA MIGHTY THOR.
MAN, YOU AIN'T--
THOR USE'TA HANG AROUND HERE.
HE CUT BACK TO NEW YORK, HE LEFT ME IN CHARGE. SORTA.
NOW I GOT THOR'S REP BE-HIND ME, GET IT? DAT'S WHO I AM, "MAN."
QUESTION ONNA TABLE IS WHO'RE YOU--
--AND WHY SHOULD WE LET YOU WALK OUTTA HERE, ALIVE?!
I AIN'T LOOKIN' FOR TROUBLE...
...BUT YOU GOT IT. BIG TIME.
YOU ON TRASH TURF NOW. YOU DON'T PASS WIT'OUT PAYIN' OUR TOLL.
ONE WAY, OR ANOTHER!
CHINKKT

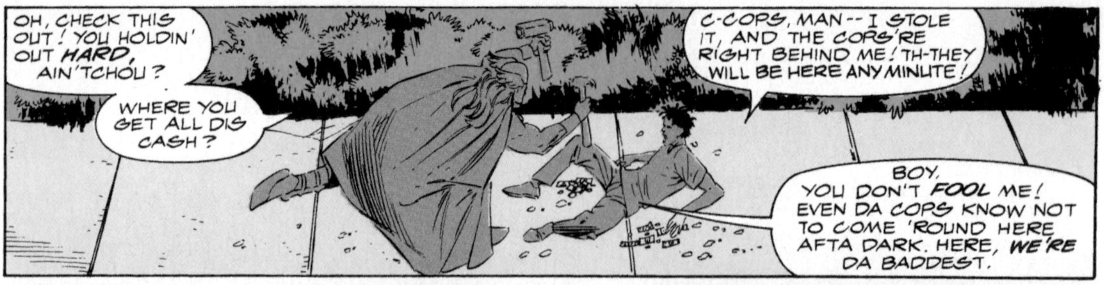
OH, CHECK THIS OUT! YOU HOLDIN' OUT HARD, AIN'TCHOU?
WHERE YOU GET ALL DIS CASH?
C-COPS, MAN-- I STOLE IT, AND THE COPS'RE RIGHT BEHIND ME! TH-THEY WILL BE HERE ANY MINUTE!
BOY, YOU DON'T FOOL ME! EVEN DA COPS KNOW NOT TO COME 'ROUND HERE AFTA DARK. HERE, WE'RE DA BADDEST.

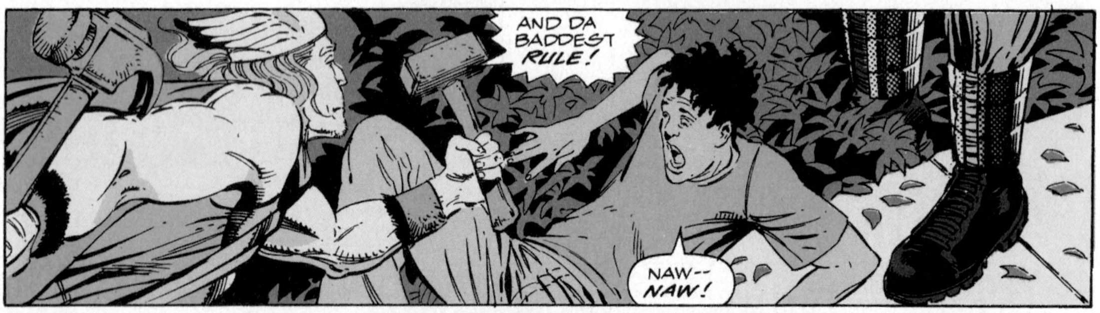
AND DA BADDEST RULE!
NAW-- NAW!

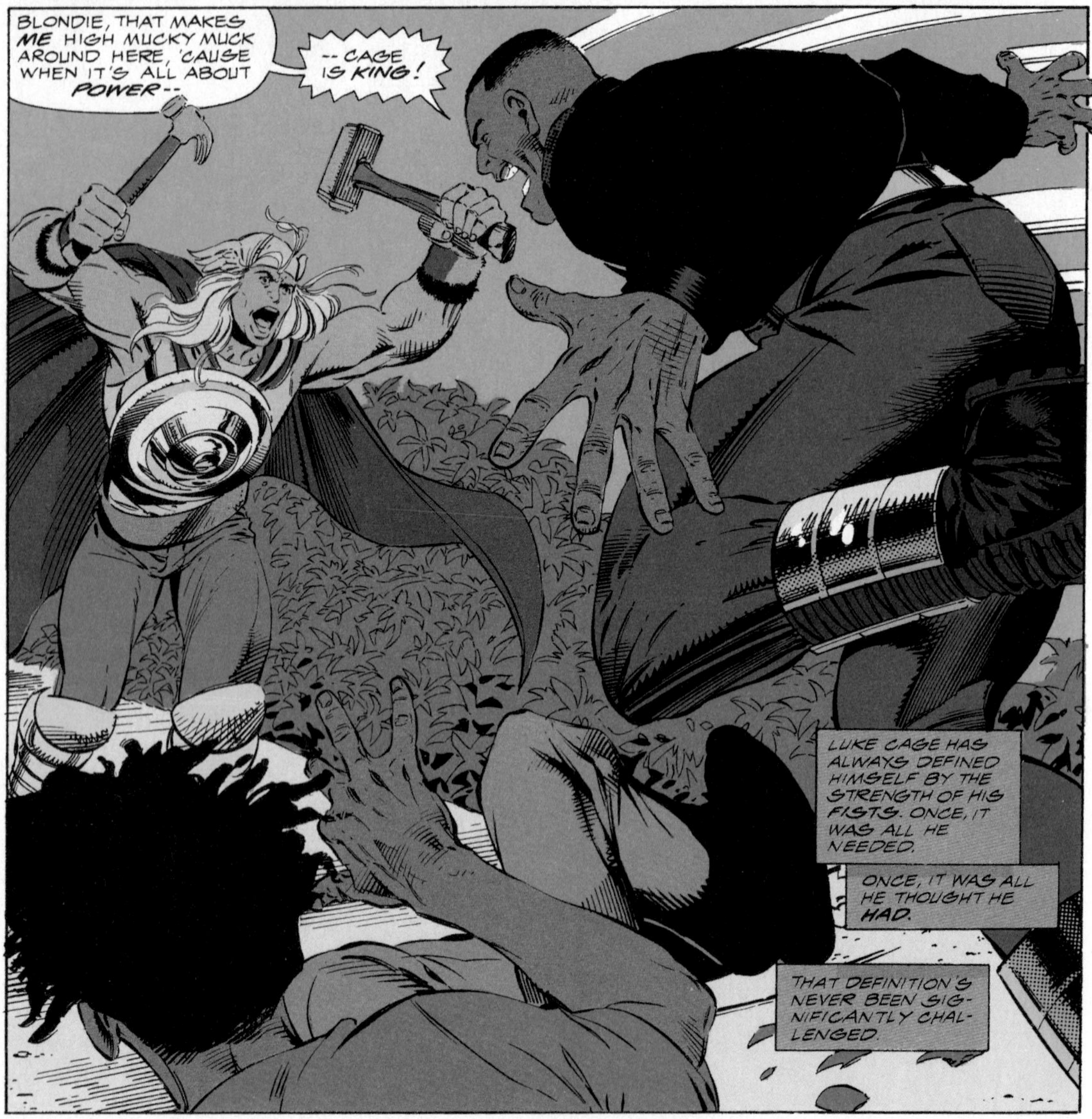
BLONDIE, THAT MAKES ME HIGH MUCKY MUCK AROUND HERE, 'CAUSE WHEN IT'S ALL ABOUT POWER--
--CAGE IS KING!
LUKE CAGE HAS ALWAYS DEFINED HIMSELF BY THE STRENGTH OF HIS FISTS. ONCE, IT WAS ALL HE NEEDED.
ONCE, IT WAS ALL HE THOUGHT HE HAD.
THAT DEFINITION'S NEVER BEEN SIGNIFICANTLY CHALLENGED.

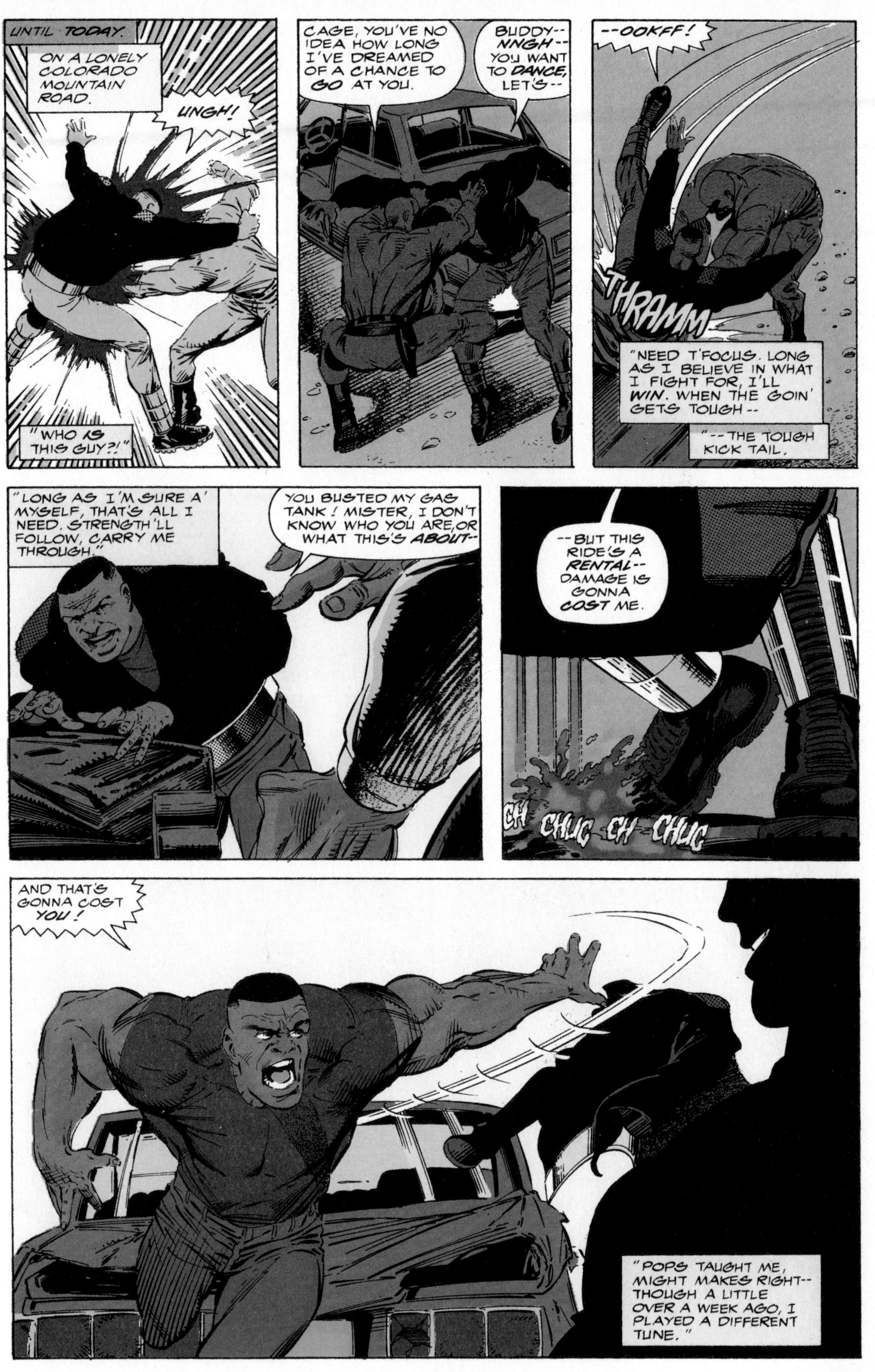
UNTIL TODAY.
ON A LONELY COLORADO MOUNTAIN ROAD.
UNGH!
"WHO IS THIS GUY?!"
CAGE, YOU'VE NO IDEA HOW LONG I'VE DREAMED OF A CHANCE TO GO AT YOU.
BUDDY-- NNGH-- YOU WANT TO DANCE, LET'S--
--OOKFF!
THRAMM
"NEED T'FOCUS. LONG AS I BELIEVE IN WHAT I FIGHT FOR, I'LL WIN. WHEN THE GOIN' GETS TOUGH--
"--THE TOUGH KICK TAIL.
"LONG AS I'M SURE A' MYSELF, THAT'S ALL I NEED. STRENGTH'LL FOLLOW, CARRY ME THROUGH."
YOU BUSTED MY GAS TANK! MISTER, I DON'T KNOW WHO YOU ARE, OR WHAT THIS'S ABOUT--
--BUT THIS RIDE'S A RENTAL-- DAMAGE IS GONNA COST ME.
CH CHUG CH CHUG
AND THAT'S GONNA COST YOU!
"POPS TAUGHT ME, MIGHT MAKES RIGHT-- THOUGH A LITTLE OVER A WEEK AGO, I PLAYED A DIFFERENT TUNE."

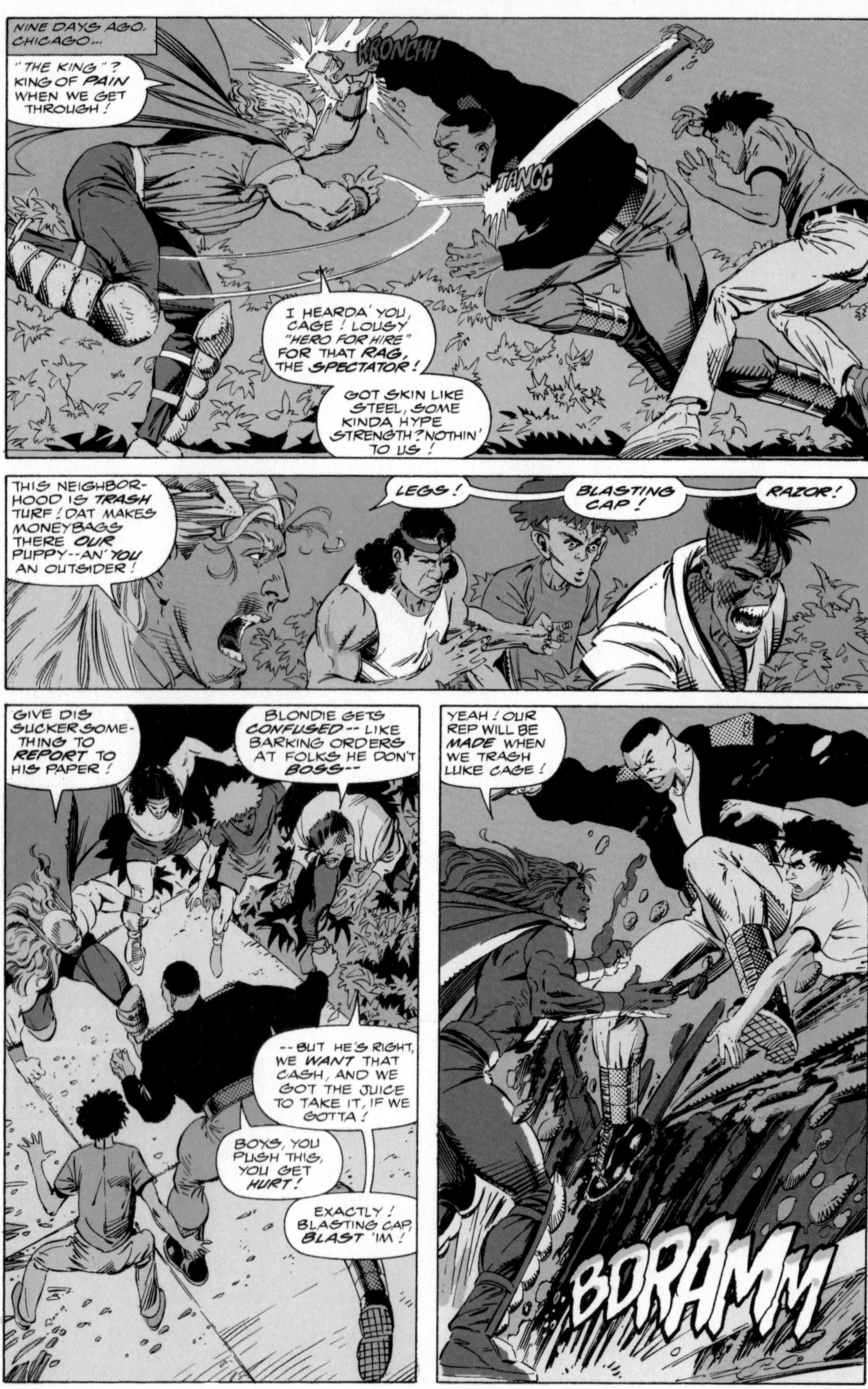
NINE DAYS AGO, CHICAGO...
"THE KING"? KING OF PAIN WHEN WE GET THROUGH!
KRONCHH
TANCC
I HEARDA' YOU, CAGE! LOUSY "HERO FOR HIRE" FOR THAT RAG, THE SPECTATOR!
GOT SKIN LIKE STEEL, SOME KINDA HYPE STRENGTH? NOTHIN' TO US!
THIS NEIGHBOR-HOOD IS TRASH TURF! DAT MAKES MONEYBAGS THERE OUR PUPPY--AN' YOU AN OUTSIDER!
LEGS!
BLASTING CAP!
RAZOR!
GIVE DIS SUCKER SOME-THING TO REPORT TO HIS PAPER!
BLONDIE GETS CONFUSED--LIKE BARKING ORDERS AT FOLKS HE DON'T BOSS--
--BUT HE'S RIGHT, WE WANT THAT CASH, AND WE GOT THE JUICE TO TAKE IT, IF WE GOTTA!
BOYS, YOU PUSH THIS, YOU GET HURT!
EXACTLY! BLASTING CAP, BLAST 'IM!
YEAH! OUR REP WILL BE MADE WHEN WE TRASH LUKE CAGE!
BDRAMM

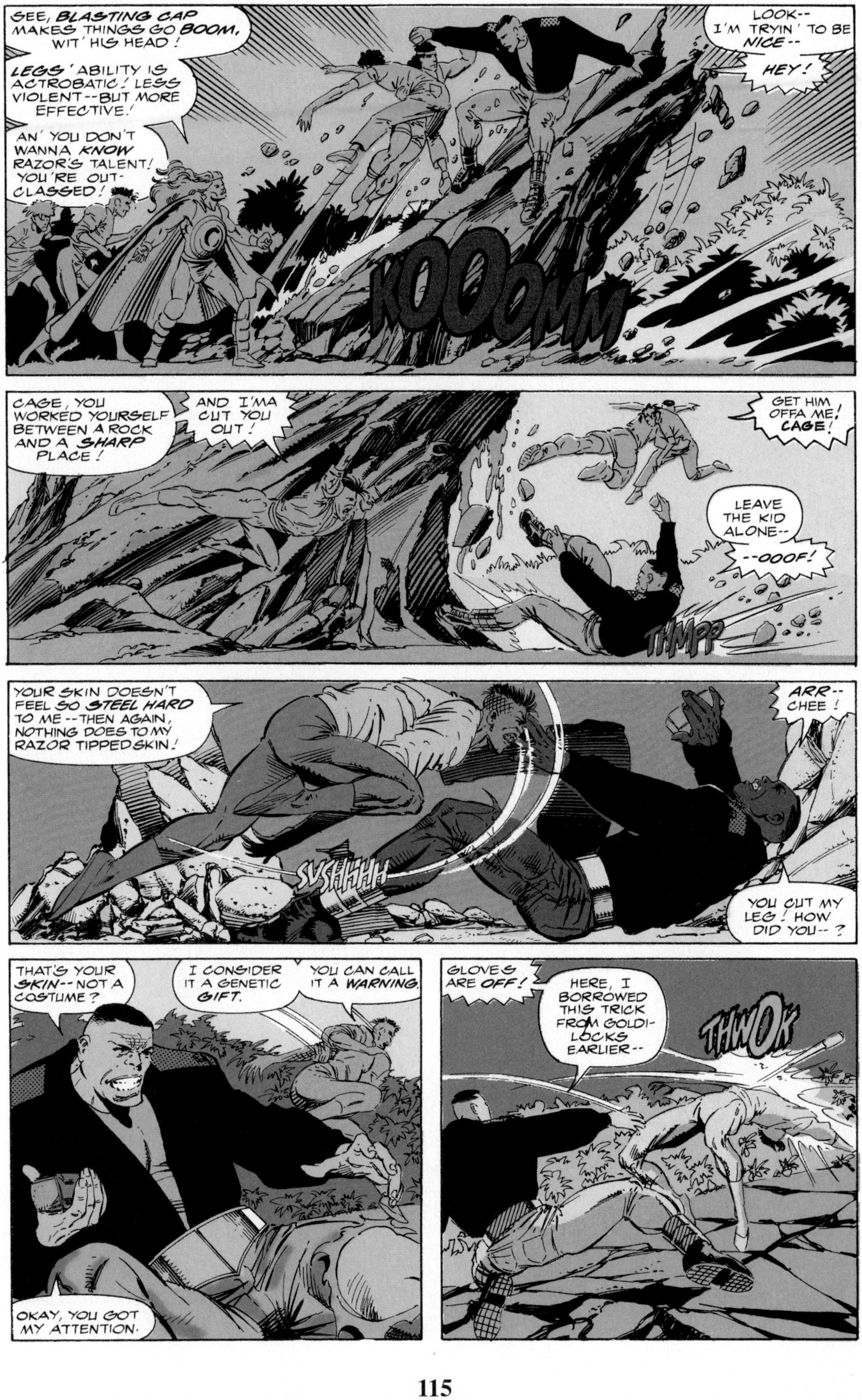
SEE, BLASTING CAP MAKES THINGS GO BOOM, WIT' HIS HEAD!
LEGS' ABILITY IS ACTROBATIC! LESS VIOLENT--BUT MORE EFFECTIVE!
AN' YOU DON'T WANNA KNOW RAZOR'S TALENT! YOU'RE OUT-CLASSED!
LOOK-- I'M TRYIN' TO BE NICE--
HEY!
KOOOMM
CAGE, YOU WORKED YOURSELF BETWEEN A ROCK AND A SHARP PLACE!
AND I'MA CUT YOU OUT!
GET HIM OFFA ME! CAGE!
LEAVE THE KID ALONE--
--OOOF!
THMPP
YOUR SKIN DOESN'T FEEL SO STEEL HARD TO ME--THEN AGAIN, NOTHING DOES TO MY RAZOR TIPPED SKIN!
ARR-- CHEE!
SVSHHHH
YOU CUT MY LEG! HOW DID YOU--?
THAT'S YOUR SKIN--NOT A COSTUME?
I CONSIDER IT A GENETIC GIFT.
YOU CAN CALL IT A WARNING.
OKAY, YOU GOT MY ATTENTION.
GLOVES ARE OFF!
HERE, I BORROWED THIS TRICK FROM GOLDI-LOCKS EARLIER--
THWOK

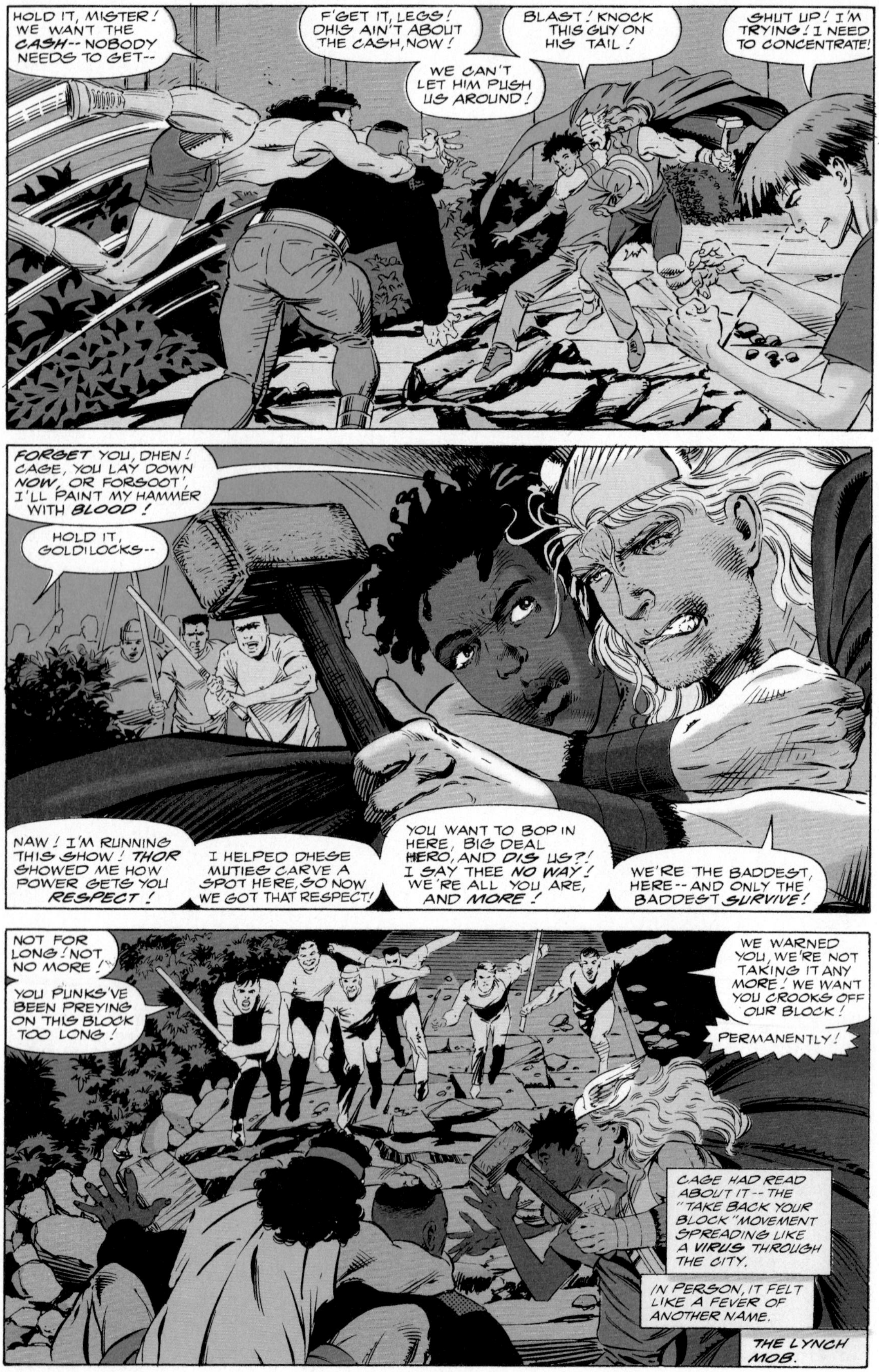
HOLD IT, MISTER! WE WANT THE CASH-- NOBODY NEEDS TO GET--
F'GET IT, LEGS! DHIS AIN'T ABOUT THE CASH, NOW!
WE CAN'T LET HIM PUSH US AROUND!
BLAST! KNOCK THIS GUY ON HIS TAIL!
SHUT UP! I'M TRYING! I NEED TO CONCENTRATE!
FORGET YOU, DHEN! CAGE, YOU LAY DOWN NOW, OR FORSOOT', I'LL PAINT MY HAMMER WITH BLOOD!
HOLD IT, GOLDILOCKS--
NAW! I'M RUNNING THIS SHOW! THOR SHOWED ME HOW POWER GETS YOU RESPECT!
I HELPED DHESE MUTIES CARVE A SPOT HERE, SO NOW WE GOT THAT RESPECT!
YOU WANT TO BOP IN HERE, BIG DEAL HERO, AND DIS US?! I SAY THEE NO WAY! WE'RE ALL YOU ARE, AND MORE!
WE'RE THE BADDEST, HERE-- AND ONLY THE BADDEST SURVIVE!
NOT FOR LONG! NOT NO MORE!
YOU PUNKS'VE BEEN PREYING ON THIS BLOCK TOO LONG!
WE WARNED YOU, WE'RE NOT TAKING IT ANY MORE! WE WANT YOU CROOKS OFF OUR BLOCK!
PERMANENTLY!
CAGE HAD READ ABOUT IT -- THE "TAKE BACK YOUR BLOCK" MOVEMENT SPREADING LIKE A VIRUS THROUGH THE CITY.
IN PERSON, IT FELT LIKE A FEVER OF ANOTHER NAME.
THE LYNCH MOB.

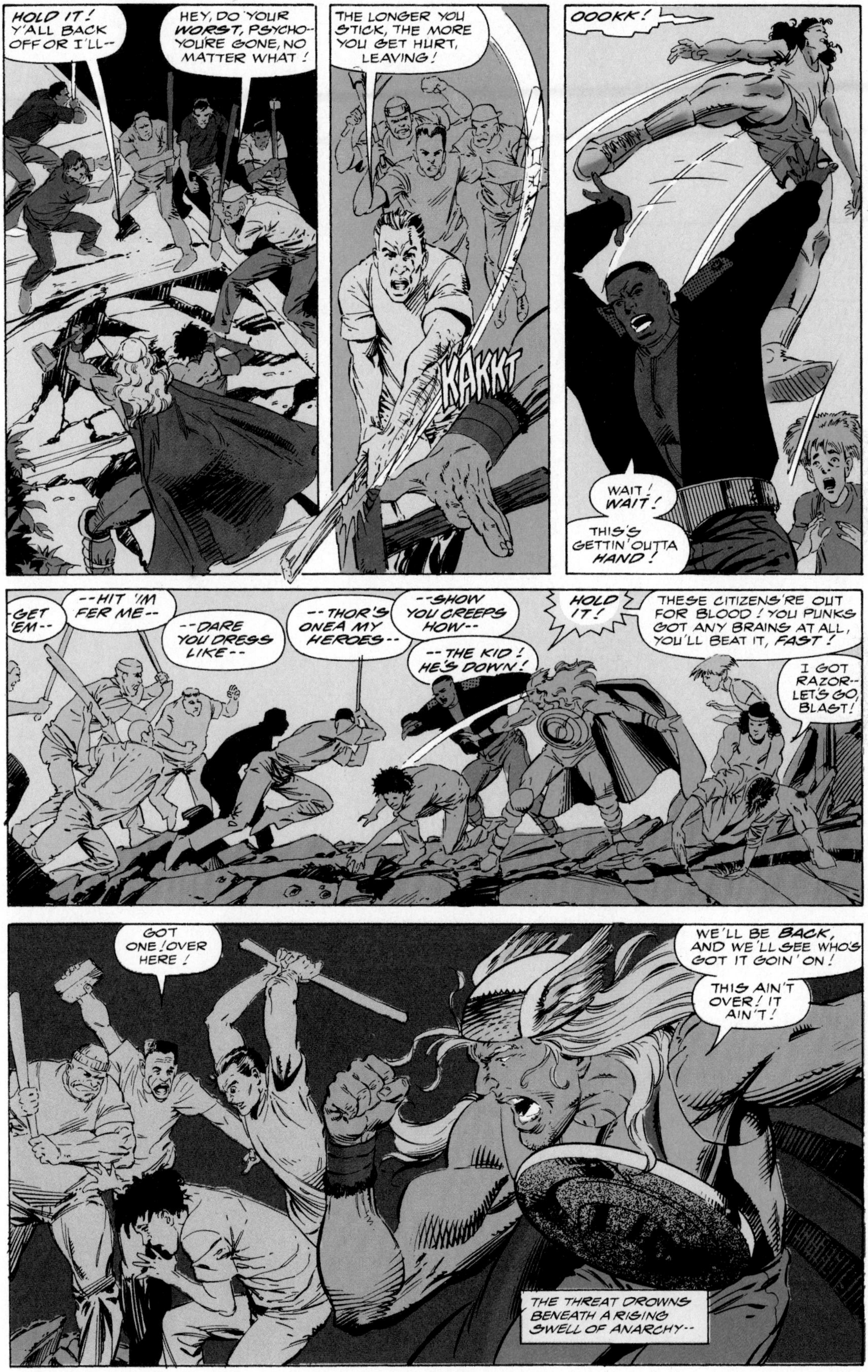
HOLD IT! Y'ALL BACK OFF OR I'LL--
HEY, DO YOUR WORST, PSYCHO-- YOU'RE GONE, NO MATTER WHAT!
THE LONGER YOU STICK, THE MORE YOU GET HURT, LEAVING!
KAKKT
OOOKK!
WAIT! WAIT!
THIS'S GETTIN' OUTTA HAND!
--GET 'EM--
--HIT 'IM FER ME--
--DARE YOU DRESS LIKE--
--THOR'S ONEA MY HEROES--
--SHOW YOU CREEPS HOW--
--THE KID! HE'S DOWN!
HOLD IT!
THESE CITIZENS'RE OUT FOR BLOOD! YOU PUNKS GOT ANY BRAINS AT ALL, YOU'LL BEAT IT, FAST!
I GOT RAZOR-- LET'S GO, BLAST!
GOT ONE! OVER HERE!
WE'LL BE BACK, AND WE'LL SEE WHO'S GOT IT GOIN' ON!
THIS AIN'T OVER! IT AIN'T!
THE THREAT DROWNS BENEATH A RISING SWELL OF ANARCHY--

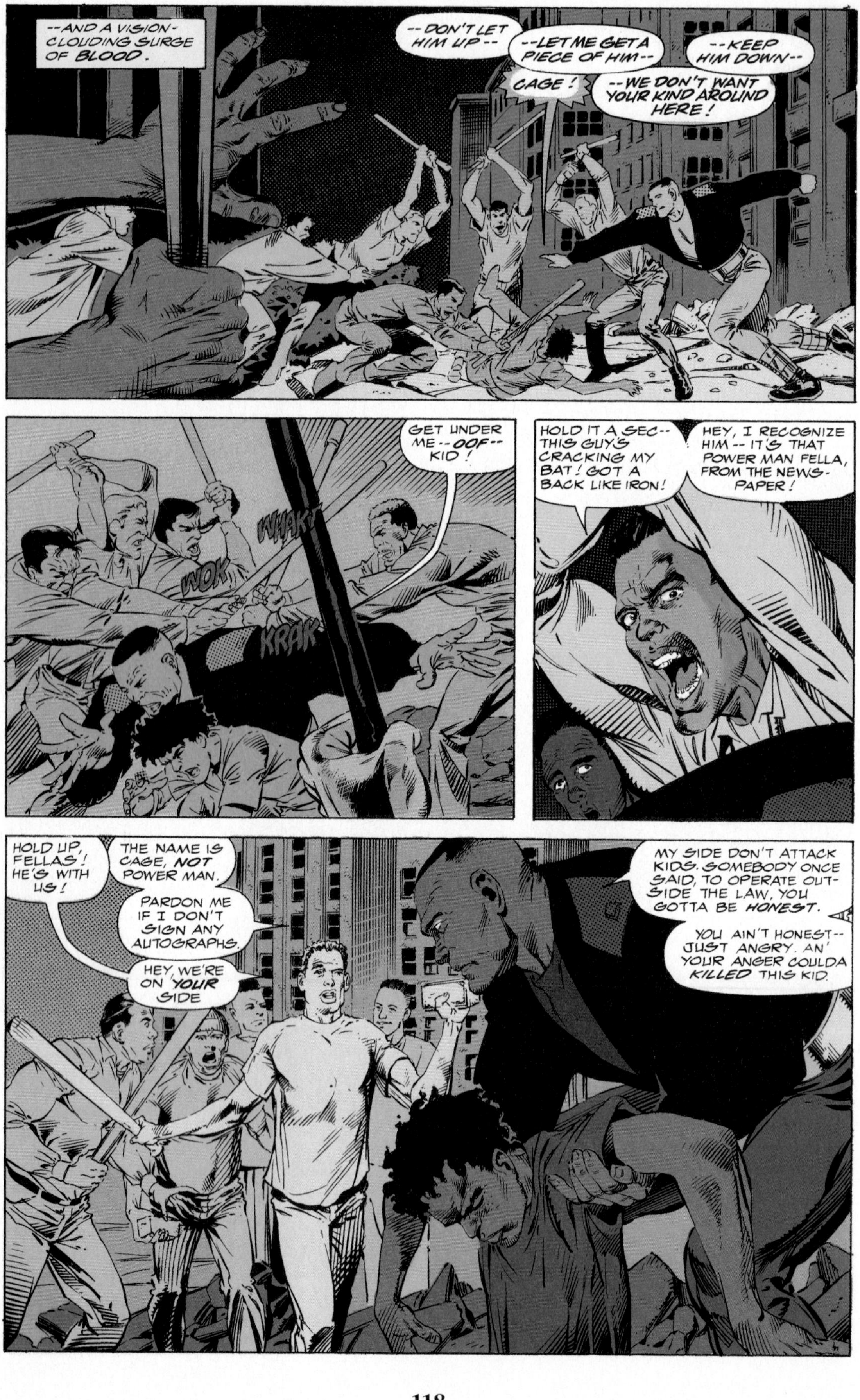
--AND A VISION-CLOUDING SURGE OF BLOOD.
--DON'T LET HIM UP--
--LET ME GET A PIECE OF HIM--
--KEEP HIM DOWN--
CAGE!
--WE DON'T WANT YOUR KIND AROUND HERE!
GET UNDER ME--OOF--KID!
WHAK
WOK
KRAK
HOLD IT A SEC--THIS GUY'S CRACKING MY BAT! GOT A BACK LIKE IRON!
HEY, I RECOGNIZE HIM--IT'S THAT POWER MAN FELLA, FROM THE NEWSPAPER!
HOLD UP, FELLAS! HE'S WITH US!
THE NAME IS CAGE, NOT POWER MAN.
PARDON ME IF I DON'T SIGN ANY AUTOGRAPHS.
HEY, WE'RE ON YOUR SIDE
MY SIDE DON'T ATTACK KIDS. SOMEBODY ONCE SAID, TO OPERATE OUTSIDE THE LAW, YOU GOTTA BE HONEST.
YOU AIN'T HONEST--JUST ANGRY. AN' YOUR ANGER COULDA KILLED THIS KID.

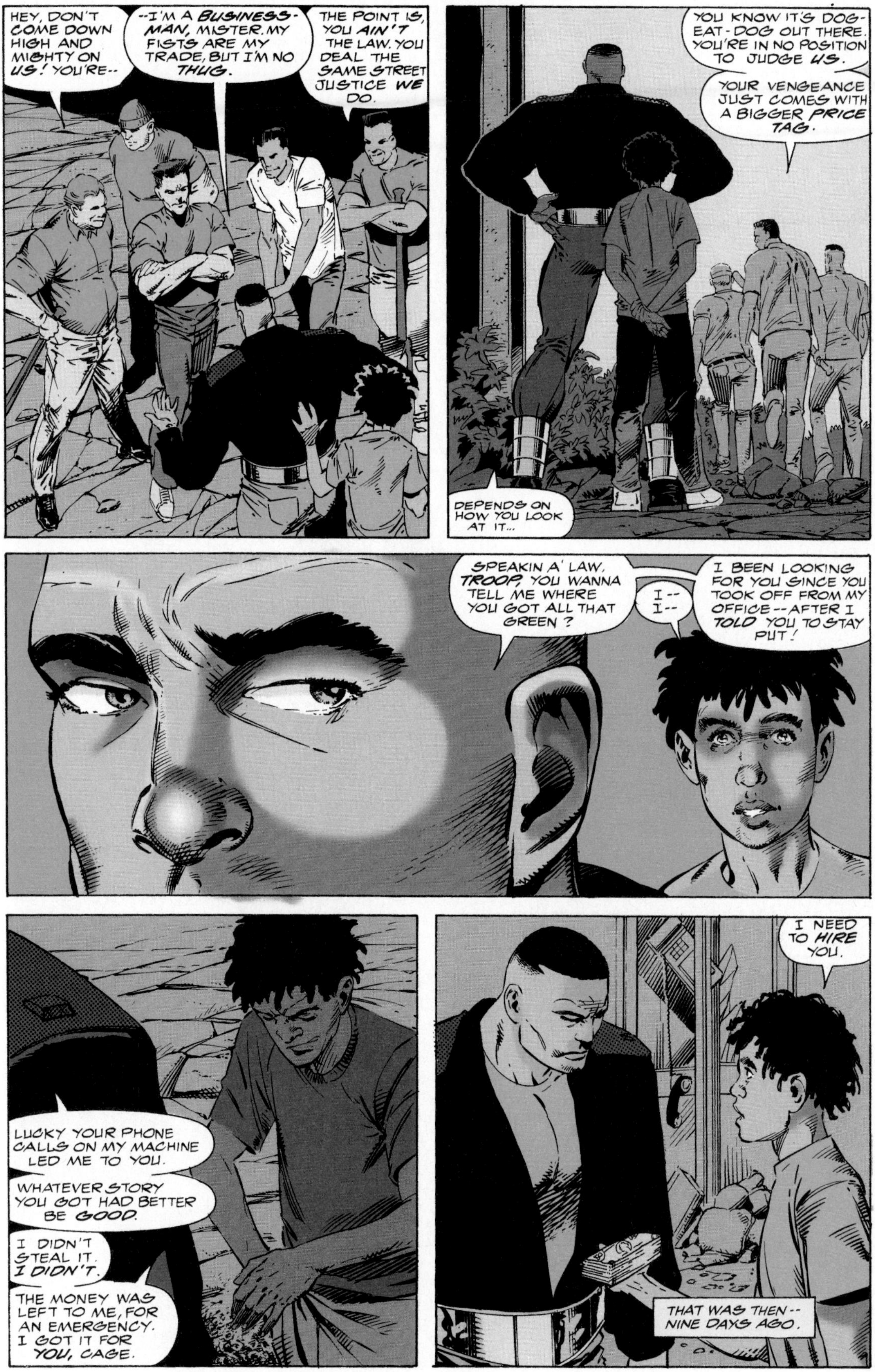
HEY, DON'T COME DOWN HIGH AND MIGHTY ON US! YOU'RE--
--I'M A BUSINESS-MAN, MISTER. MY FISTS ARE MY TRADE, BUT I'M NO THUG.
THE POINT IS, YOU AIN'T THE LAW. YOU DEAL THE SAME STREET JUSTICE WE DO.
YOU KNOW IT'S DOG-EAT-DOG OUT THERE. YOU'RE IN NO POSITION TO JUDGE US.
YOUR VENGEANCE JUST COMES WITH A BIGGER PRICE TAG.
DEPENDS ON HOW YOU LOOK AT IT...
SPEAKIN A' LAW, TROOP, YOU WANNA TELL ME WHERE YOU GOT ALL THAT GREEN?
I-- I--
I BEEN LOOKING FOR YOU SINCE YOU TOOK OFF FROM MY OFFICE--AFTER I TOLD YOU TO STAY PUT!
LUCKY YOUR PHONE CALLS ON MY MACHINE LED ME TO YOU.
WHATEVER STORY YOU GOT HAD BETTER BE GOOD.
I DIDN'T STEAL IT. I DIDN'T.
THE MONEY WAS LEFT TO ME, FOR AN EMERGENCY. I GOT IT FOR YOU, CAGE.
I NEED TO HIRE YOU.
THAT WAS THEN-- NINE DAYS AGO.

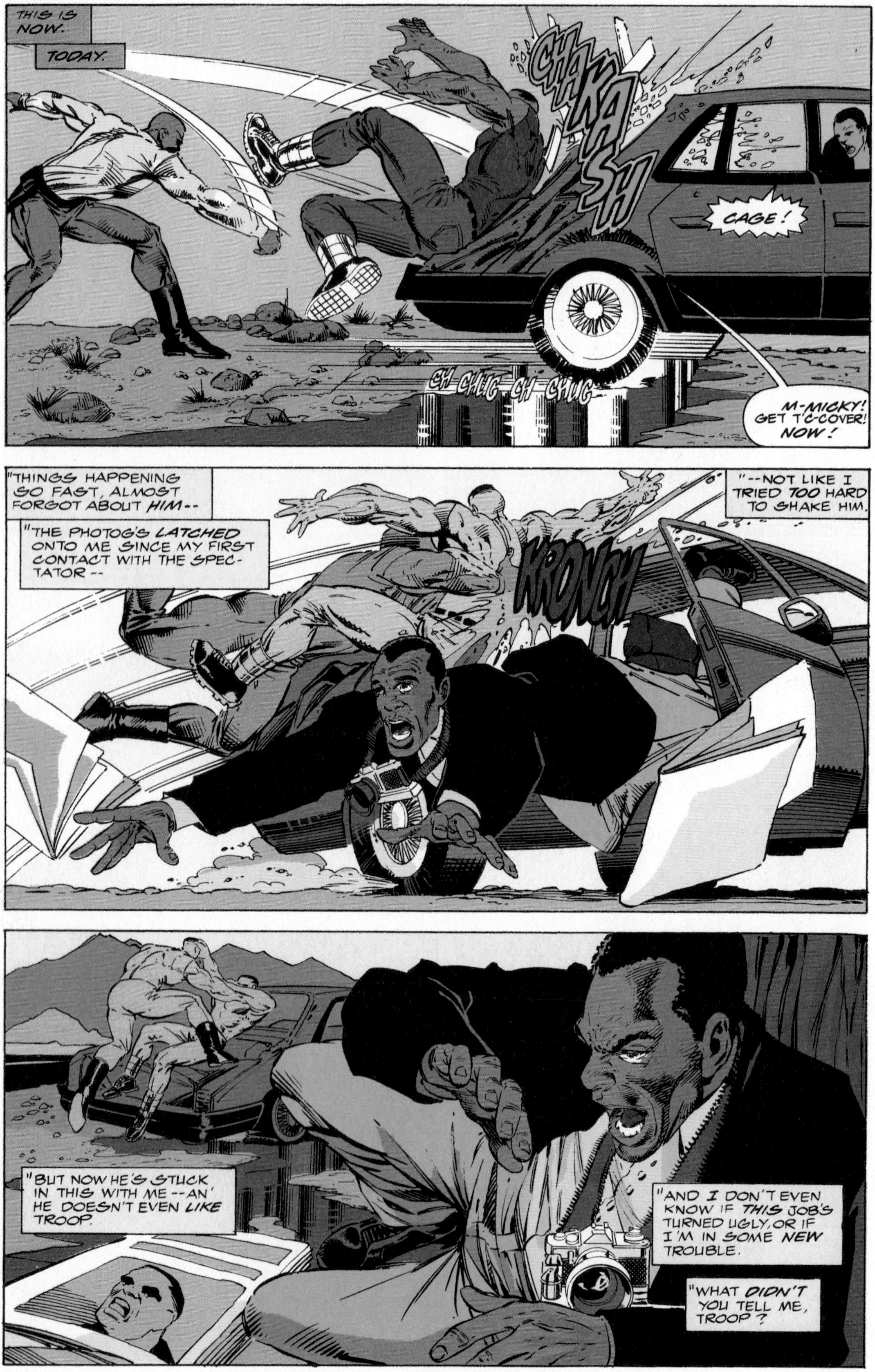
THIS IS NOW.
TODAY.
CHAKASH
CAGE!
CH CHUG CH CHUG
M-MICKY! GET T'C-COVER! NOW!
"THINGS HAPPENING SO FAST, ALMOST FORGOT ABOUT HIM--
"THE PHOTOG'S LATCHED ONTO ME SINCE MY FIRST CONTACT WITH THE SPECTATOR--
"--NOT LIKE I TRIED TOO HARD TO SHAKE HIM.
KRONCH
"BUT NOW HE'S STUCK IN THIS WITH ME--AN' HE DOESN'T EVEN LIKE TROOP.
"AND I DON'T EVEN KNOW IF THIS JOB'S TURNED UGLY, OR IF I'M IN SOME NEW TROUBLE.
"WHAT DIDN'T YOU TELL ME, TROOP?

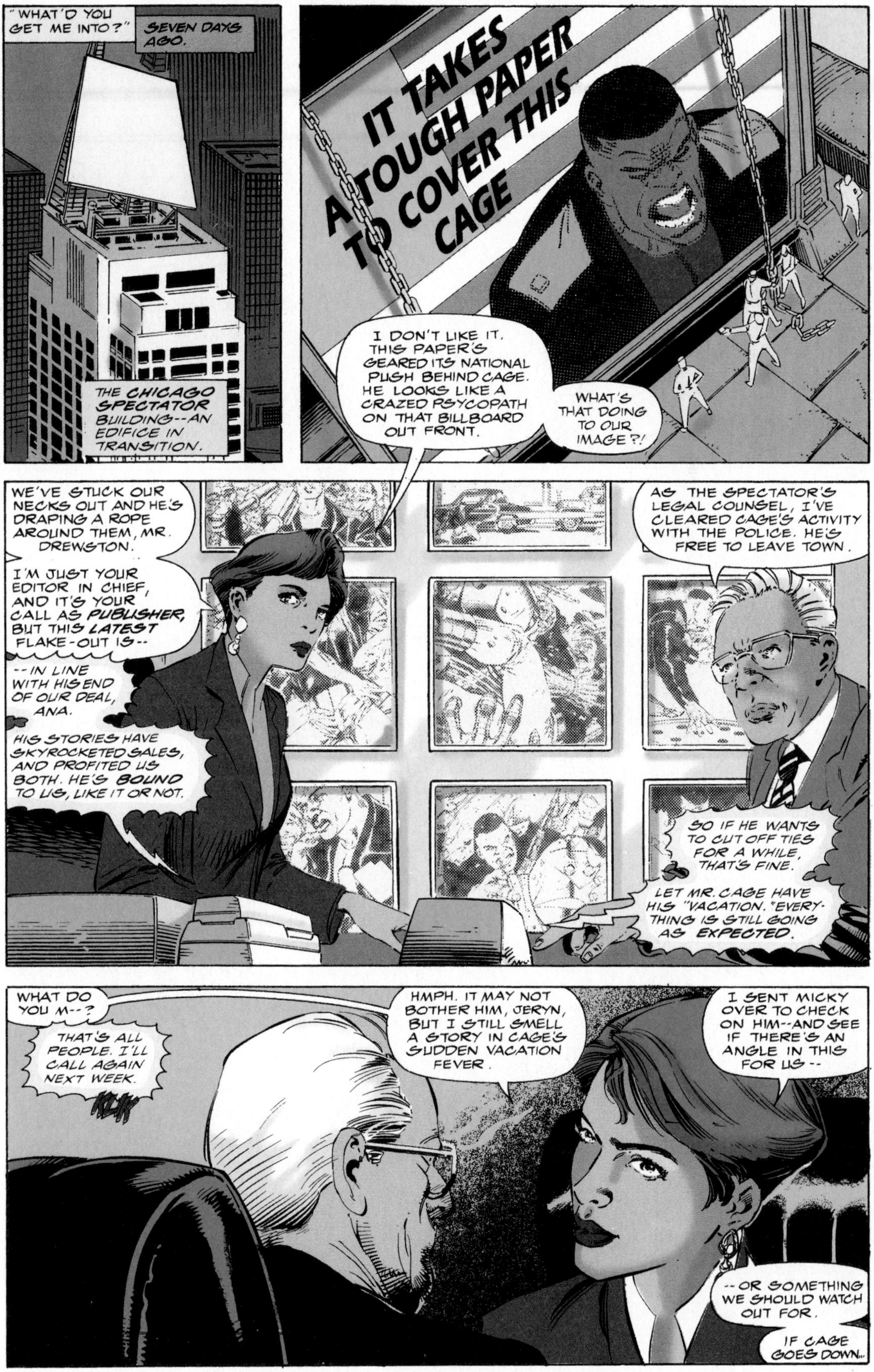
"WHAT'D YOU GET ME INTO?"
SEVEN DAYS AGO.
THE CHICAGO SPECTATOR BUILDING--AN EDIFICE IN TRANSITION.
IT TAKES A TOUGH PAPER TO COVER THIS CAGE
I DON'T LIKE IT. THIS PAPER'S GEARED ITS NATIONAL PUSH BEHIND CAGE. HE LOOKS LIKE A CRAZED PSYCOPATH ON THAT BILLBOARD OUT FRONT.
WHAT'S THAT DOING TO OUR IMAGE?!
WE'VE STUCK OUR NECKS OUT AND HE'S DRAPING A ROPE AROUND THEM, MR. DREWSTON.
I'M JUST YOUR EDITOR IN CHIEF, AND IT'S YOUR CALL AS PUBLISHER, BUT THIS LATEST FLAKE-OUT IS--
--IN LINE WITH HIS END OF OUR DEAL, ANA.
HIS STORIES HAVE SKYROCKETED SALES, AND PROFITED US BOTH. HE'S BOUND TO US, LIKE IT OR NOT.
AS THE SPECTATOR'S LEGAL COUNSEL, I'VE CLEARED CAGE'S ACTIVITY WITH THE POLICE. HE'S FREE TO LEAVE TOWN.
SO IF HE WANTS TO CUT OFF TIES FOR A WHILE, THAT'S FINE.
LET MR. CAGE HAVE HIS "VACATION." EVERYTHING IS STILL GOING AS EXPECTED.
WHAT DO YOU M--?
THAT'S ALL PEOPLE. I'LL CALL AGAIN NEXT WEEK.
KLIK
HMPH. IT MAY NOT BOTHER HIM, JERYN, BUT I STILL SMELL A STORY IN CAGE'S SUDDEN VACATION FEVER.
I SENT MICKY OVER TO CHECK ON HIM--AND SEE IF THERE'S AN ANGLE IN THIS FOR US--
--OR SOMETHING WE SHOULD WATCH OUT FOR.
IF CAGE GOES DOWN...

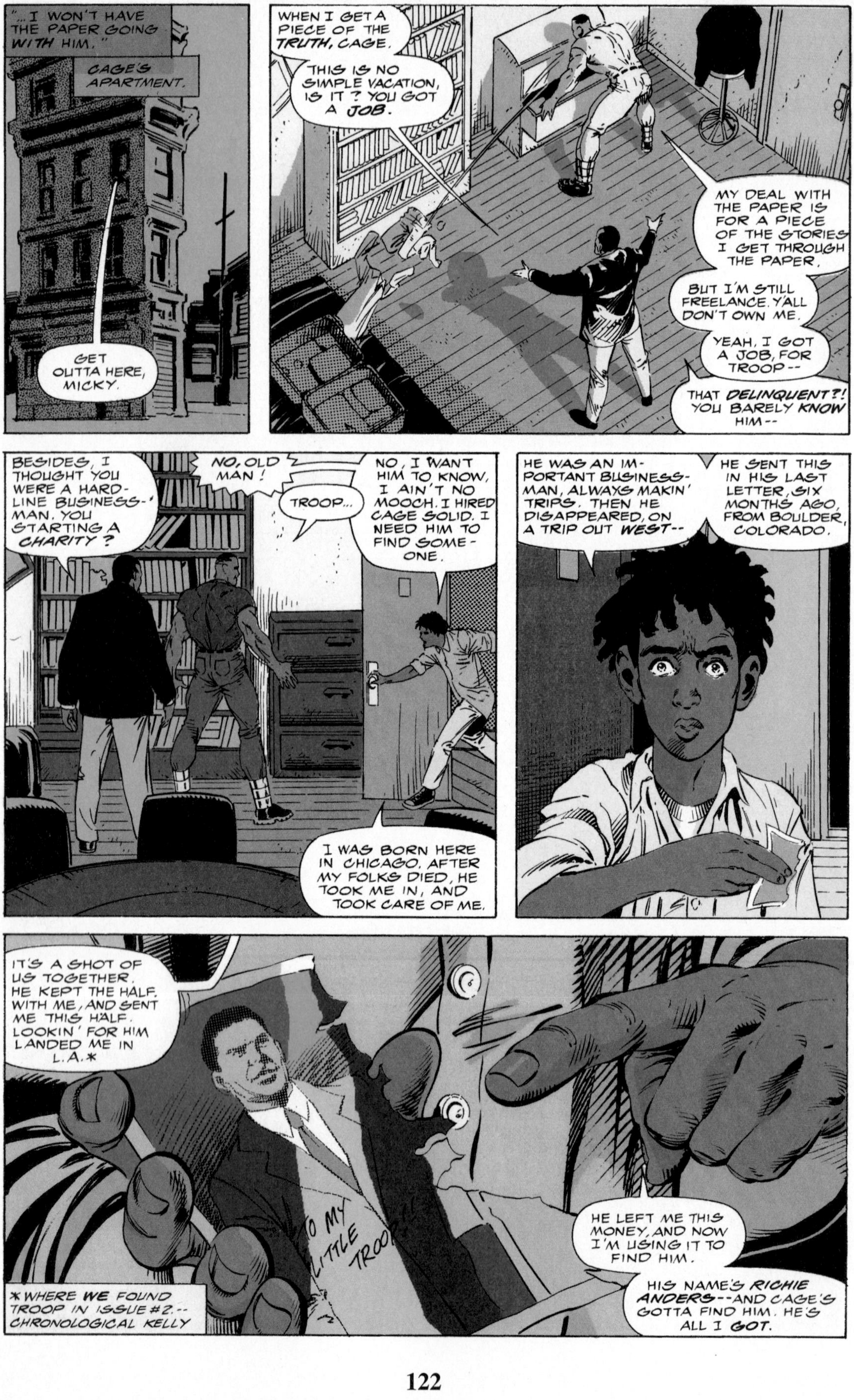

"...I WON'T HAVE THE PAPER GOING WITH HIM."
CAGE'S APARTMENT.
GET OUTTA HERE, MICKY.
WHEN I GET A PIECE OF THE TRUTH, CAGE.
THIS IS NO SIMPLE VACATION, IS IT? YOU GOT A JOB.
MY DEAL WITH THE PAPER IS FOR A PIECE OF THE STORIES I GET THROUGH THE PAPER.
BUT I'M STILL FREELANCE. Y'ALL DON'T OWN ME.
YEAH, I GOT A JOB, FOR TROOP--
THAT DELINQUENT?! YOU BARELY KNOW HIM--
BESIDES, I THOUGHT YOU WERE A HARD-LINE BUSINESS-MAN. YOU STARTING A CHARITY?
NO, OLD MAN!
TROOP...
NO, I WANT HIM TO KNOW, I AIN'T NO MOOCH. I HIRED CAGE SOLID. I NEED HIM TO FIND SOME-ONE.
I WAS BORN HERE IN CHICAGO. AFTER MY FOLKS DIED, HE TOOK ME IN, AND TOOK CARE OF ME.
HE WAS AN IM-PORTANT BUSINESS-MAN, ALWAYS MAKIN' TRIPS. THEN HE DISAPPEARED, ON A TRIP OUT WEST--
HE SENT THIS IN HIS LAST LETTER, SIX MONTHS AGO, FROM BOULDER, COLORADO.
IT'S A SHOT OF US TOGETHER. HE KEPT THE HALF WITH ME, AND SENT ME THIS HALF. LOOKIN' FOR HIM LANDED ME IN L.A.*
TO MY LITTLE TROOP
HE LEFT ME THIS MONEY, AND NOW I'M USING IT TO FIND HIM.
HIS NAME'S RICHIE ANDERS--AND CAGE'S GOTTA FIND HIM. HE'S ALL I GOT.
*WHERE WE FOUND TROOP IN ISSUE #2.--CHRONOLOGICAL KELLY

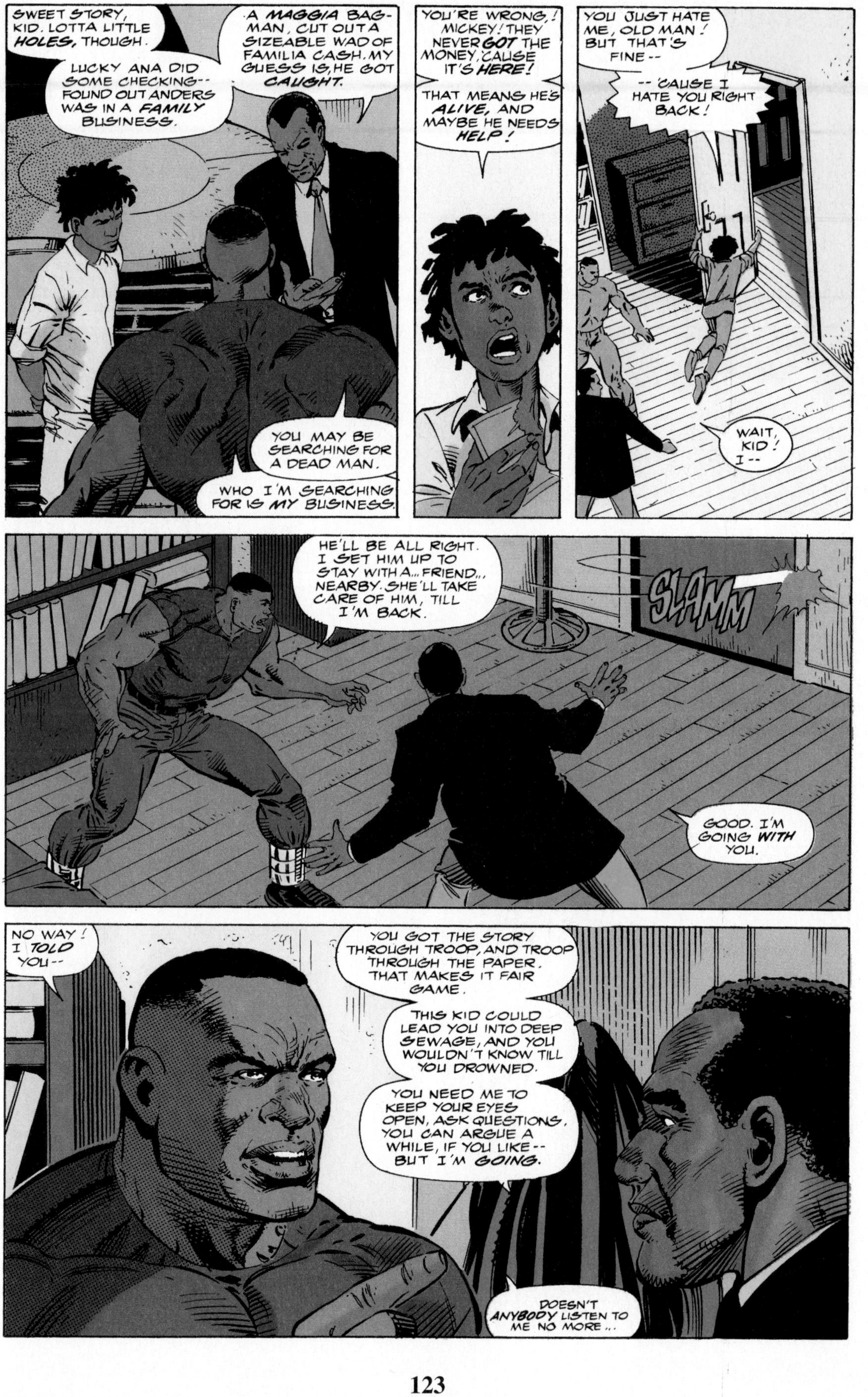
SWEET STORY, KID. LOTTA LITTLE HOLES, THOUGH.
LUCKY ANA DID SOME CHECKING-- FOUND OUT ANDERS WAS IN A FAMILY BUSINESS.
A MAGGIA BAG-MAN, CUT OUT A SIZEABLE WAD OF FAMILIA CASH. MY GUESS IS, HE GOT CAUGHT.
YOU MAY BE SEARCHING FOR A DEAD MAN.
WHO I'M SEARCHING FOR IS MY BUSINESS.
YOU'RE WRONG, MICKEY! THEY NEVER GOT THE MONEY, 'CAUSE IT'S HERE!
THAT MEANS HE'S ALIVE, AND MAYBE HE NEEDS HELP!
YOU JUST HATE ME, OLD MAN! BUT THAT'S FINE --
-- 'CAUSE I HATE YOU RIGHT BACK!
WAIT, KID! I --
HE'LL BE ALL RIGHT. I SET HIM UP TO STAY WITH A... FRIEND... NEARBY. SHE'LL TAKE CARE OF HIM, TILL I'M BACK.
SLAMM
GOOD. I'M GOING WITH YOU.
NO WAY! I TOLD YOU--
YOU GOT THE STORY THROUGH TROOP, AND TROOP THROUGH THE PAPER. THAT MAKES IT FAIR GAME.
THIS KID COULD LEAD YOU INTO DEEP SEWAGE, AND YOU WOULDN'T KNOW TILL YOU DROWNED.
YOU NEED ME TO KEEP YOUR EYES OPEN, ASK QUESTIONS. YOU CAN ARGUE A WHILE, IF YOU LIKE-- BUT I'M GOING.
DOESN'T ANYBODY LISTEN TO ME NO MORE...

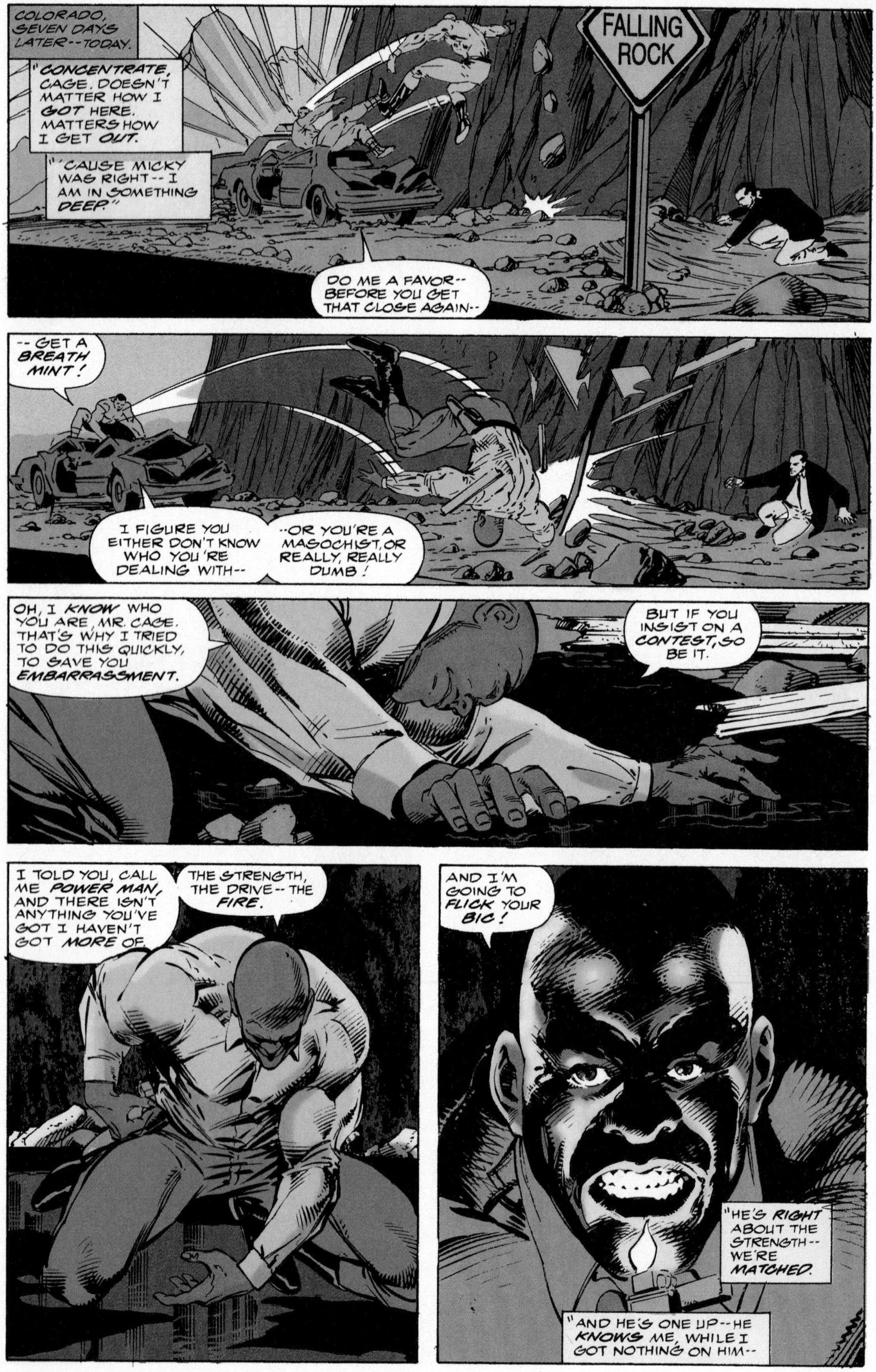

COLORADO, SEVEN DAYS LATER--TODAY.
"CONCENTRATE, CAGE. DOESN'T MATTER HOW I GOT HERE. MATTERS HOW I GET OUT.
"'CAUSE MICKY WAS RIGHT--I AM IN SOMETHING DEEP."
FALLING ROCK
DO ME A FAVOR--BEFORE YOU GET THAT CLOSE AGAIN--
--GET A BREATH MINT!
I FIGURE YOU EITHER DON'T KNOW WHO YOU'RE DEALING WITH--
--OR YOU'RE A MASOCHIST, OR REALLY, REALLY DUMB!
OH, I KNOW WHO YOU ARE, MR. CAGE. THAT'S WHY I TRIED TO DO THIS QUICKLY, TO SAVE YOU EMBARRASSMENT.
BUT IF YOU INSIST ON A CONTEST, SO BE IT.
I TOLD YOU, CALL ME POWER MAN, AND THERE ISN'T ANYTHING YOU'VE GOT I HAVEN'T GOT MORE OF.
THE STRENGTH, THE DRIVE--THE FIRE.
AND I'M GOING TO FLICK YOUR BIC!
"HE'S RIGHT ABOUT THE STRENGTH--WE'RE MATCHED.
"AND HE'S ONE UP--HE KNOWS ME, WHILE I GOT NOTHING ON HIM--

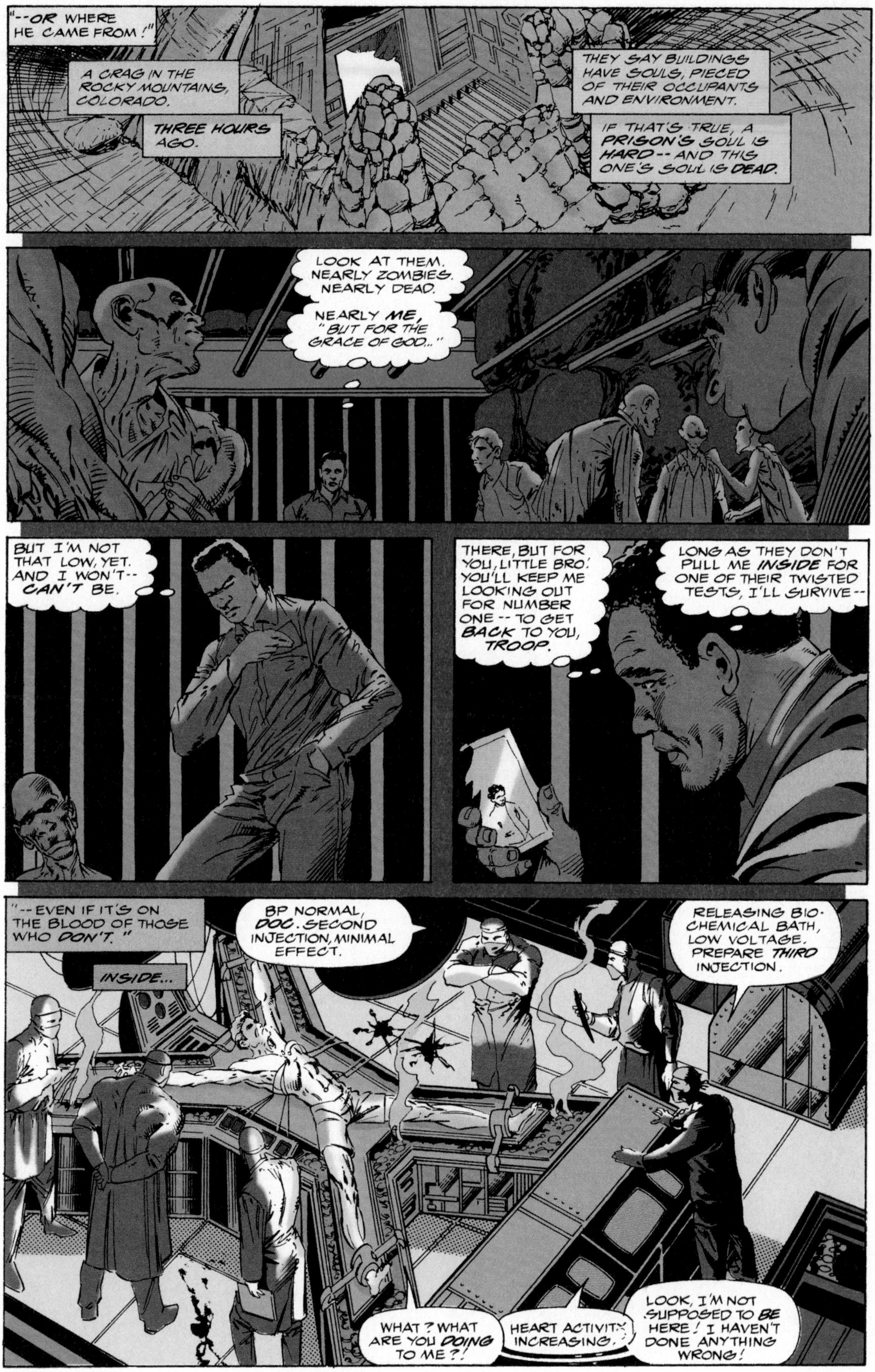
"--OR WHERE HE CAME FROM!"
A CRAG IN THE ROCKY MOUNTAINS, COLORADO.
THREE HOURS AGO.
THEY SAY BUILDINGS HAVE SOULS, PIECED OF THEIR OCCUPANTS AND ENVIRONMENT.
IF THAT'S TRUE, A PRISON'S SOUL IS HARD-- AND THIS ONE'S SOUL IS DEAD.
LOOK AT THEM. NEARLY ZOMBIES. NEARLY DEAD.
NEARLY ME, "BUT FOR THE GRACE OF GOD..."
BUT I'M NOT THAT LOW, YET. AND I WON'T-- CAN'T BE.
THERE, BUT FOR YOU, LITTLE BRO! YOU'LL KEEP ME LOOKING OUT FOR NUMBER ONE -- TO GET BACK TO YOU, TROOP.
LONG AS THEY DON'T PULL ME INSIDE FOR ONE OF THEIR TWISTED TESTS, I'LL SURVIVE--
"--EVEN IF IT'S ON THE BLOOD OF THOSE WHO DON'T."
INSIDE...
BP NORMAL, DOC. SECOND INJECTION, MINIMAL EFFECT.
RELEASING BIO-CHEMICAL BATH, LOW VOLTAGE. PREPARE THIRD INJECTION.
WHAT? WHAT ARE YOU DOING TO ME?!
HEART ACTIVITY INCREASING.
LOOK, I'M NOT SUPPOSED TO BE HERE! I HAVEN'T DONE ANYTHING WRONG!

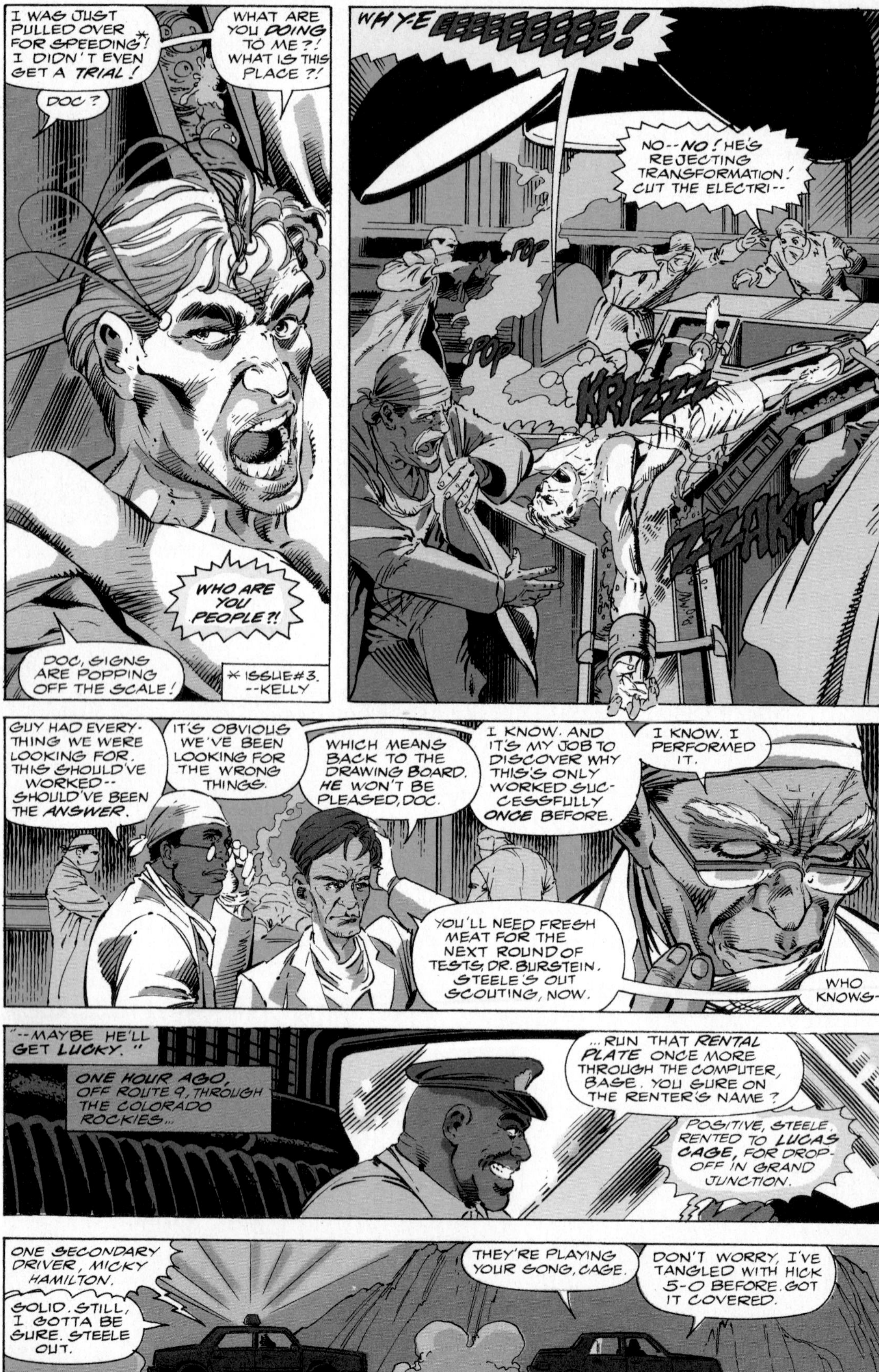

I WAS JUST PULLED OVER FOR SPEEDING!* I DIDN'T EVEN GET A TRIAL!
WHAT ARE YOU DOING TO ME?! WHAT IS THIS PLACE?!
DOC?
WHO ARE YOU PEOPLE?!
DOC, SIGNS ARE POPPING OFF THE SCALE!
* ISSUE #3. --KELLY
WHY-EEEEEEEEEEEEEE!
NO--NO! HE'S REJECTING TRANSFORMATION! CUT THE ELECTRI--
POP
POP
KRIZZZ
ZZAKT
GUY HAD EVERYTHING WE WERE LOOKING FOR. THIS SHOULD'VE WORKED-- SHOULD'VE BEEN THE ANSWER.
IT'S OBVIOUS WE'VE BEEN LOOKING FOR THE WRONG THINGS.
WHICH MEANS BACK TO THE DRAWING BOARD. HE WON'T BE PLEASED, DOC.
I KNOW. AND IT'S MY JOB TO DISCOVER WHY THIS'S ONLY WORKED SUCCESSFULLY ONCE BEFORE.
I KNOW. I PERFORMED IT.
YOU'LL NEED FRESH MEAT FOR THE NEXT ROUND OF TESTS, DR. BURSTEIN. STEELE'S OUT SCOUTING, NOW.
WHO KNOWS--
"--MAYBE HE'LL GET LUCKY."
ONE HOUR AGO, OFF ROUTE 9, THROUGH THE COLORADO ROCKIES...
...RUN THAT RENTAL PLATE ONCE MORE THROUGH THE COMPUTER, BASE. YOU SURE ON THE RENTER'S NAME?
POSITIVE, STEELE. RENTED TO LUCAS CAGE, FOR DROP-OFF IN GRAND JUNCTION.
ONE SECONDARY DRIVER, MICKY HAMILTON.
SOLID. STILL, I GOTTA BE SURE. STEELE OUT.
THEY'RE PLAYING YOUR SONG, CAGE.
DON'T WORRY, I'VE TANGLED WITH HICK 5-O BEFORE. GOT IT COVERED.

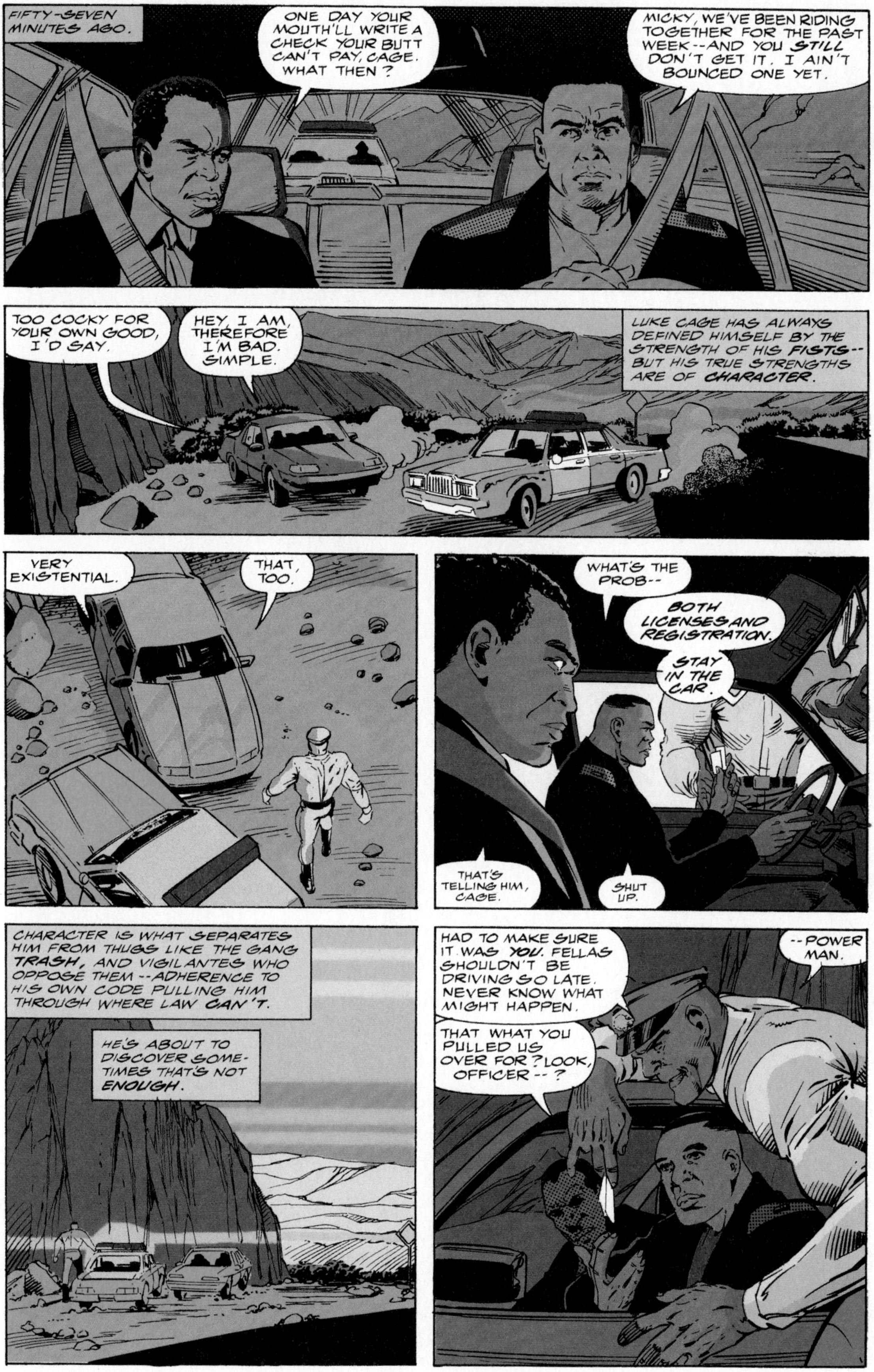

FIFTY-SEVEN MINUTES AGO.
ONE DAY YOUR MOUTH'LL WRITE A CHECK YOUR BUTT CAN'T PAY, CAGE. WHAT THEN?
MICKY, WE'VE BEEN RIDING TOGETHER FOR THE PAST WEEK--AND YOU STILL DON'T GET IT. I AIN'T BOUNCED ONE YET.
TOO COCKY FOR YOUR OWN GOOD, I'D SAY.
HEY, I AM, THEREFORE I'M BAD. SIMPLE.
LUKE CAGE HAS ALWAYS DEFINED HIMSELF BY THE STRENGTH OF HIS FISTS--BUT HIS TRUE STRENGTHS ARE OF CHARACTER.
VERY EXISTENTIAL.
THAT, TOO.
WHAT'S THE PROB--
BOTH LICENSES AND REGISTRATION.
STAY IN THE CAR.
THAT'S TELLING HIM, CAGE.
SHUT UP.
CHARACTER IS WHAT SEPARATES HIM FROM THUGS LIKE THE GANG TRASH, AND VIGILANTES WHO OPPOSE THEM--ADHERENCE TO HIS OWN CODE PULLING HIM THROUGH WHERE LAW CAN'T.
HE'S ABOUT TO DISCOVER SOMETIMES THAT'S NOT ENOUGH.
HAD TO MAKE SURE IT WAS YOU. FELLAS SHOULDN'T BE DRIVING SO LATE. NEVER KNOW WHAT MIGHT HAPPEN.
THAT WHAT YOU PULLED US OVER FOR? LOOK, OFFICER--?
--POWER MAN.

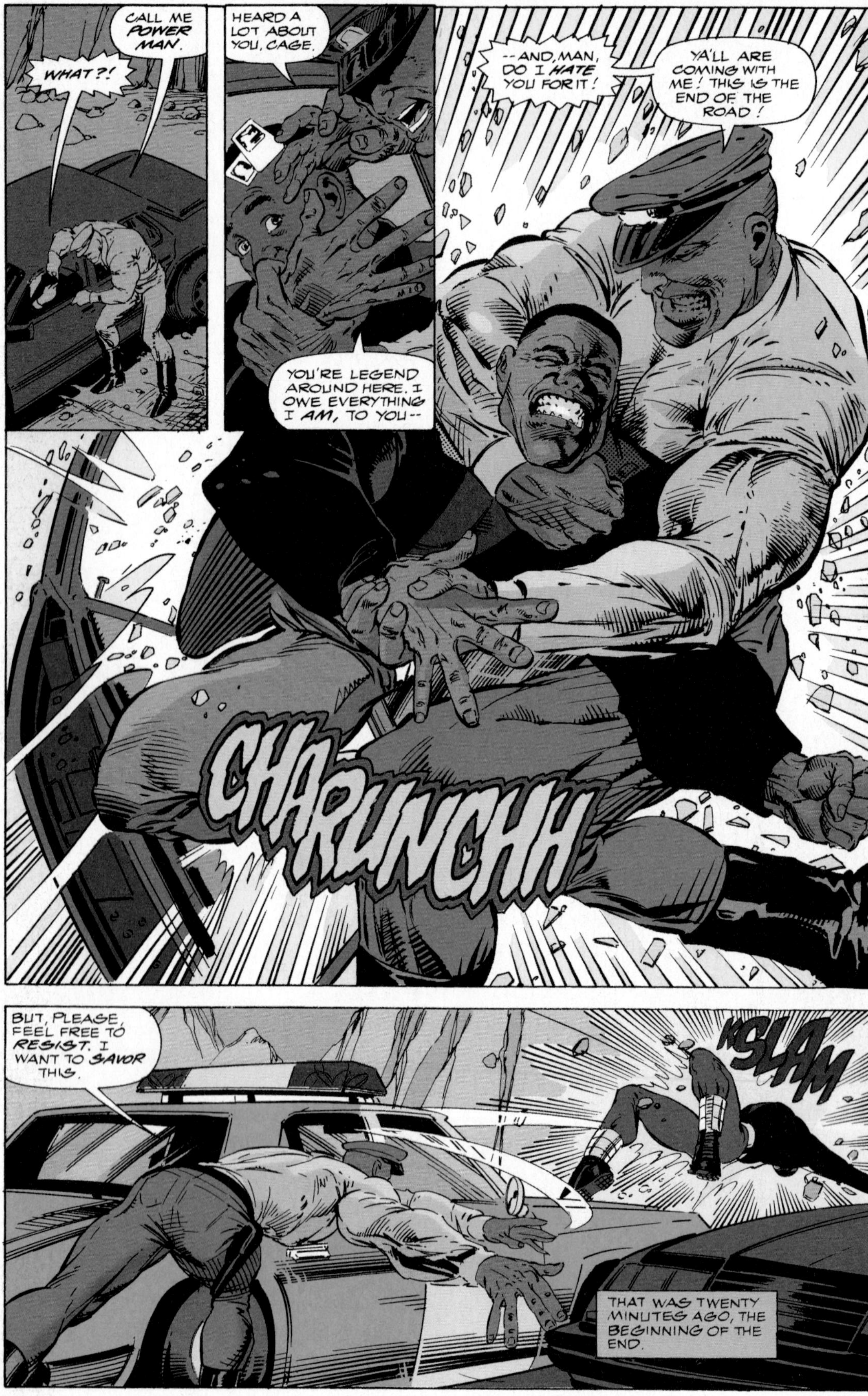
CALL ME POWER MAN.
WHAT?!
HEARD A LOT ABOUT YOU, CAGE.
YOU'RE LEGEND AROUND HERE. I OWE EVERYTHING I AM, TO YOU--
--AND, MAN, DO I HATE YOU FOR IT!
YA'LL ARE COMING WITH ME! THIS IS THE END OF THE ROAD!
CHARUNCHH
BUT, PLEASE, FEEL FREE TO RESIST. I WANT TO SAVOR THIS.
KSLAM
THAT WAS TWENTY MINUTES AGO, THE BEGINNING OF THE END.

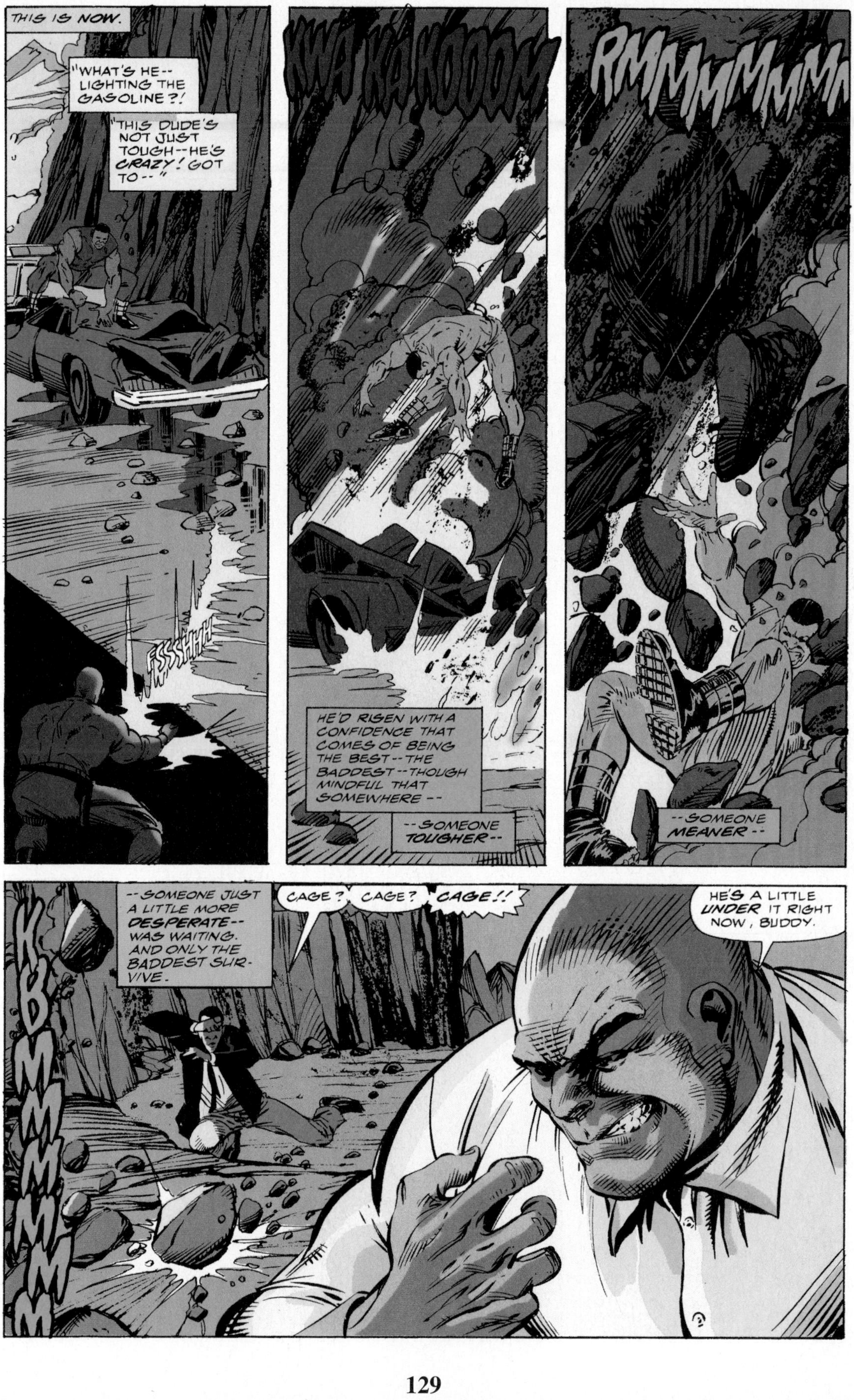
THIS IS NOW.
"WHAT'S HE-- LIGHTING THE GASOLINE?!
"THIS DUDE'S NOT JUST TOUGH--HE'S CRAZY! GOT TO--"
FSSSHHH
KWA KA KOOOM
HE'D RISEN WITH A CONFIDENCE THAT COMES OF BEING THE BEST--THE BADDEST--THOUGH MINDFUL THAT SOMEWHERE--
--SOMEONE TOUGHER--
RMMMMMMM
--SOMEONE MEANER--
KBMMMMMMM
--SOMEONE JUST A LITTLE MORE DESPERATE--WAS WAITING. AND ONLY THE BADDEST SURVIVE.
CAGE? CAGE? CAGE!!
HE'S A LITTLE UNDER IT RIGHT NOW, BUDDY.

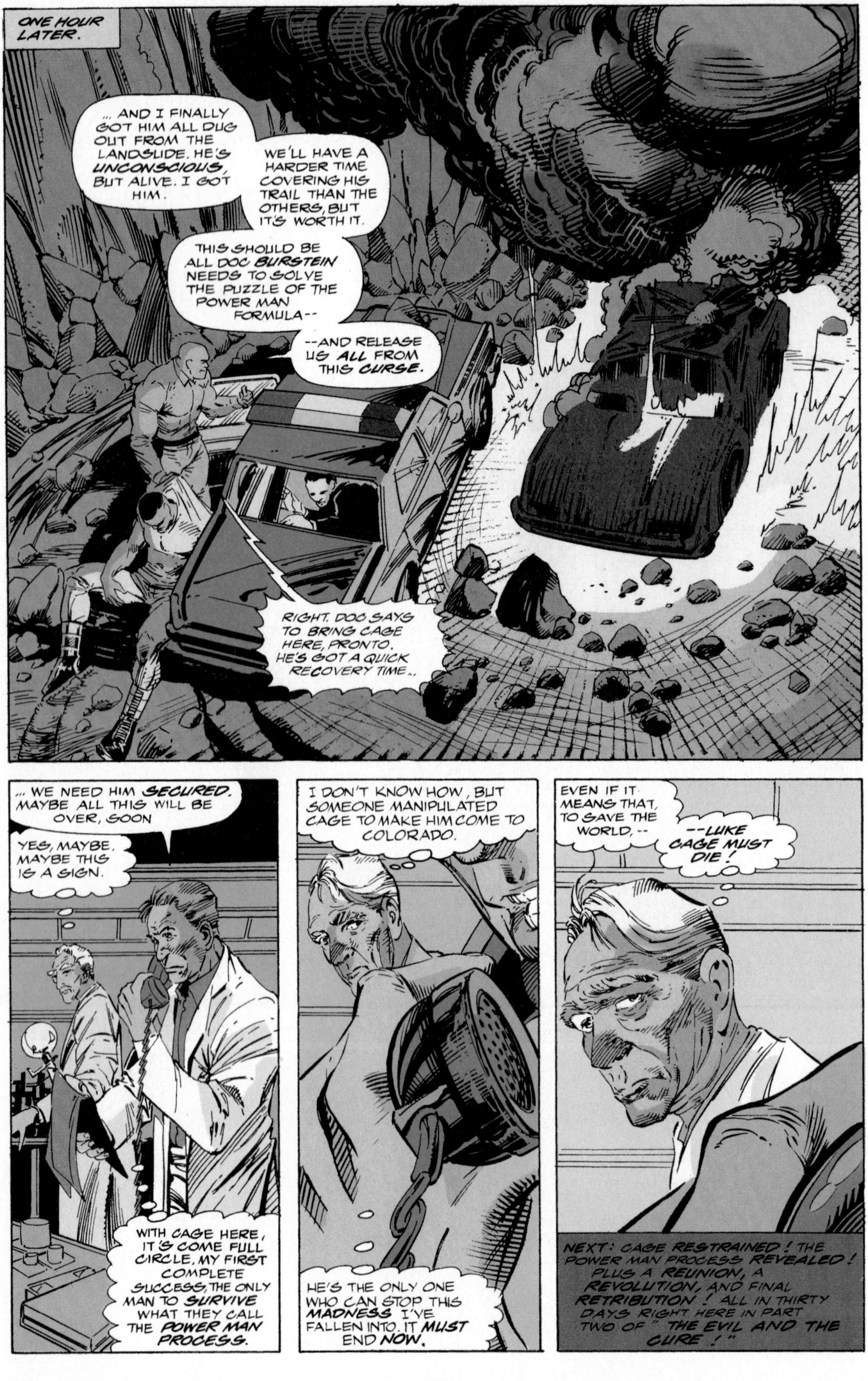
ONE HOUR LATER.
... AND I FINALLY GOT HIM ALL DUG OUT FROM THE LANDSLIDE. HE'S UNCONSCIOUS, BUT ALIVE. I GOT HIM.
WE'LL HAVE A HARDER TIME COVERING HIS TRAIL THAN THE OTHERS, BUT IT'S WORTH IT.
THIS SHOULD BE ALL DOC BURSTEIN NEEDS TO SOLVE THE PUZZLE OF THE POWER MAN FORMULA--
--AND RELEASE US ALL FROM THIS CURSE.
RIGHT. DOC SAYS TO BRING CAGE HERE, PRONTO. HE'S GOT A QUICK RECOVERY TIME...
... WE NEED HIM SECURED. MAYBE ALL THIS WILL BE OVER, SOON
YES, MAYBE. MAYBE THIS IS A SIGN.
WITH CAGE HERE, IT'S COME FULL CIRCLE, MY FIRST COMPLETE SUCCESS, THE ONLY MAN TO SURVIVE WHAT THEY CALL THE POWER MAN PROCESS.
I DON'T KNOW HOW, BUT SOMEONE MANIPULATED CAGE TO MAKE HIM COME TO COLORADO.
HE'S THE ONLY ONE WHO CAN STOP THIS MADNESS I'VE FALLEN INTO. IT MUST END NOW.
EVEN IF IT MEANS THAT, TO SAVE THE WORLD, --
--LUKE CAGE MUST DIE!
NEXT: CAGE RESTRAINED! THE POWER MAN PROCESS REVEALED! PLUS A REUNION, A REVOLUTION, AND FINAL RETRIBUTION! ALL IN THIRTY DAYS RIGHT HERE IN PART TWO OF "THE EVIL AND THE CURE!"

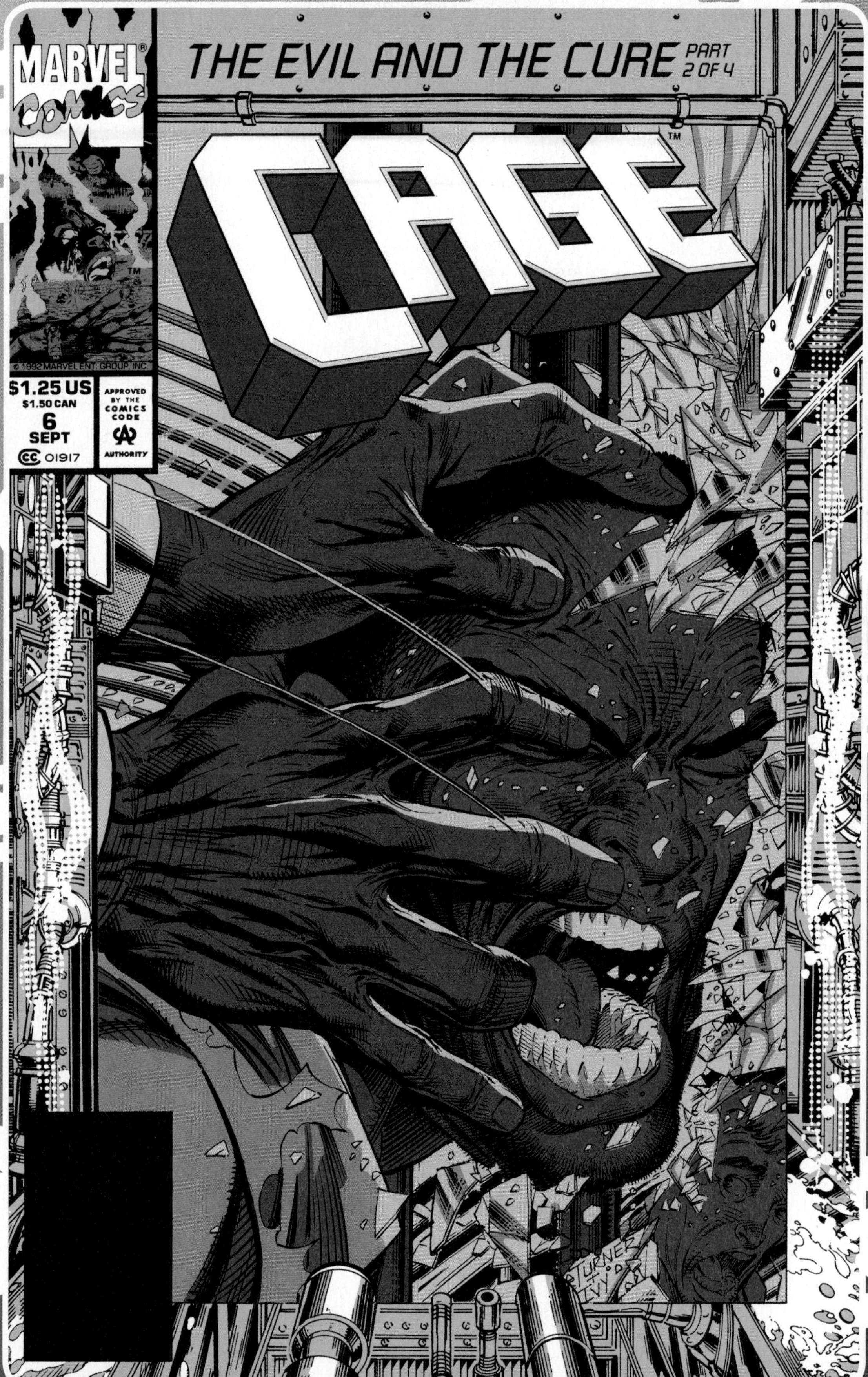
MARVEL COMICS
THE EVIL AND THE CURE PART 2 OF 4
CAGE™
© 1992 MARVEL ENT. GROUP, INC.
$1.25 US
$1.50 CAN
6
SEPT
APPROVED BY THE COMICS CODE AUTHORITY
TURNER
IVY

There needeth not the hell that bigots frame to punish those who err, earth in itself contains at once the evil and the cure.
--SHELLEY Queen Mab, III

HE IS LUKE CAGE, AND HE'S BEEN WRONGLY IMPRISONED. HE'S BEEN THIS WAY BEFORE.

LAST TIME, HE'D BEEN FRAMED. HE FREED HIMSELF THROUGH PARTICIPATION IN AN EXPERIMENT THAT CHANGED HIS LIFE--

-- GIVING HIM SKIN TO MATCH HIS STEELY ATTITUDE, AND STRENGTH TO MATCH HIS IRON WILL.

HE CALLED HIMSELF POWER MAN, BUT THAT WAS A LONG TIME AGO.

THIS TIME, HE'S BEEN CHARGED WITH NO CRIME.

KEEP MOVIN', 'LESS YOU WANT ANOTHER TASTE OF THIS PROD!

ON A DESOLATE STRETCH OF COLORADO ROAD WITH COMPANION MICKY HAMILTON, CAGE CONFRONTED A JUGGERNAUT IN A HIGHWAY PATROLMAN'S UNIFORM*--

--AN IMPOSTOR WHO CALLED HIMSELF THE NEW POWER MAN.

THAT WAS YESTERDAY. SINCE AWAKING IN CHAINS, CAGE HAS SEEN NO SIGN OF HAMILTON. FOR ALL HE KNOWS, MICKY'S DEAD.

CAPTAIN OF DESTINY

THE EVIL AND THE CURE. PART 2

HIS NAME'S LUKE CAGE, AND HE'S ABSOLUTELY ALONE. HE'S BEEN THIS WAY BEFORE.

* LAST ISSUE.-- KELLY

| MARC McLAURIN WRITER | DWAYNE TURNER PENCILER | CHRISTOPHER IVY INKER | CHRIS ELIOPOULOS LETTERER | MIKE THOMAS COLORIST | KELLY CORVESE EDITOR | TOM DeFALCO CHIEF |

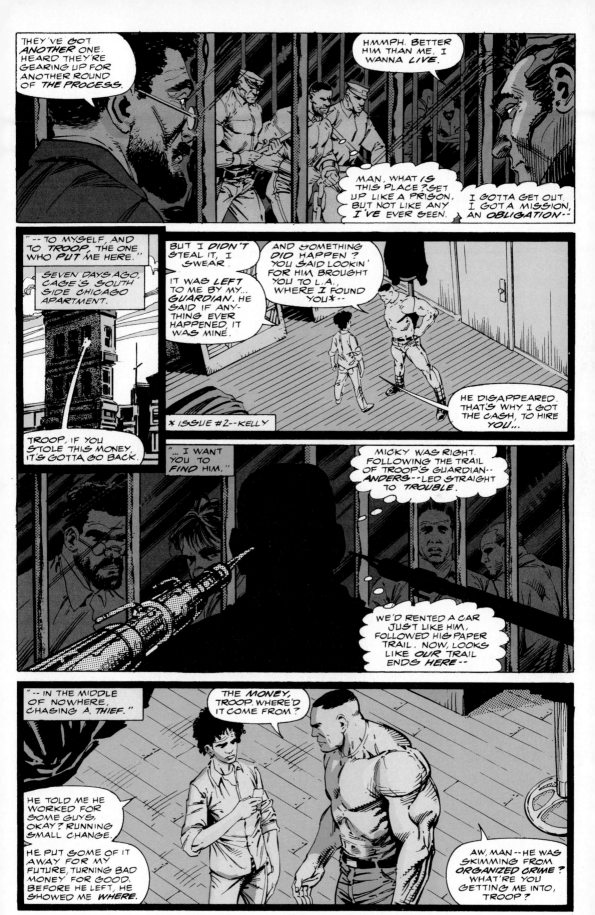

THEY'VE GOT *ANOTHER* ONE. HEARD THEY'RE GEARING UP FOR ANOTHER ROUND OF *THE PROCESS.*

HMMPH. BETTER HIM THAN ME, I WANNA *LIVE.*

MAN, WHAT *IS* THIS PLACE? SET UP LIKE A PRISON, BUT NOT LIKE ANY I'VE EVER SEEN.

I GOTTA GET OUT. I GOTTA MISSION, AN *OBLIGATION*--

"-- TO MYSELF, AND TO *TROOP,* THE ONE WHO *PUT* ME HERE."

SEVEN DAYS AGO, CAGE'S SOUTH SIDE CHICAGO APARTMENT.

BUT I *DIDN'T* STEAL IT, I SWEAR. IT WAS *LEFT* TO ME BY MY... *GUARDIAN.* HE SAID IF ANYTHING EVER HAPPENED, IT WAS MINE.

AND SOMETHING *DID* HAPPEN? YOU SAID LOOKIN' FOR HIM BROUGHT YOU TO L.A., WHERE *I* FOUND YOU*--

HE DISAPPEARED. THAT'S WHY I GOT THE *CASH,* TO HIRE *YOU...*

* ISSUE #2--KELLY

TROOP, IF YOU STOLE THIS MONEY, IT'S GOTTA GO BACK.

"... I WANT YOU TO *FIND* HIM,"

MICKY WAS RIGHT. FOLLOWING THE TRAIL OF TROOP'S GUARDIAN-- ANDERS--LED STRAIGHT TO *TROUBLE.*

WE'D RENTED A CAR JUST LIKE HIM, FOLLOWED HIS PAPER TRAIL. NOW, LOOKS LIKE *OUR* TRAIL ENDS *HERE* --

"-- IN THE MIDDLE OF NOWHERE, CHASING A *THIEF.*"

THE *MONEY,* TROOP. WHERE'D IT COME FROM?

HE TOLD ME HE WORKED FOR SOME GUYS, OKAY? RUNNING SMALL CHANGE.

HE PUT SOME OF IT AWAY FOR MY FUTURE, TURNING BAD MONEY FOR GOOD. BEFORE HE LEFT, HE SHOWED ME *WHERE.*

AW, MAN--HE WAS SKIMMING FROM *ORGANIZED CRIME?* WHAT'RE YOU GETTING ME INTO, TROOP?

133

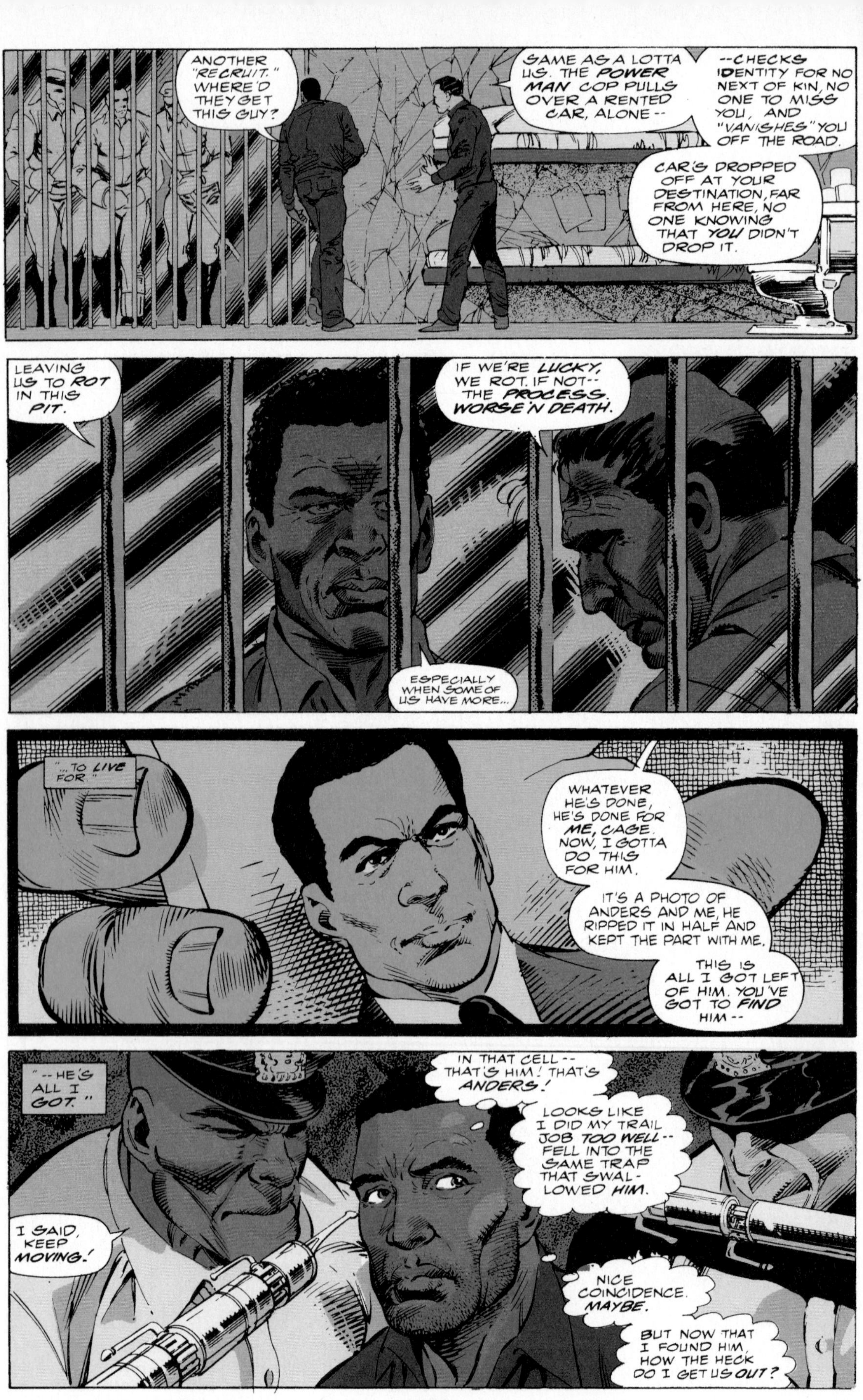
ANOTHER "RECRUIT." WHERE'D THEY GET THIS GUY?
SAME AS A LOTTA US. THE POWER MAN COP PULLS OVER A RENTED CAR, ALONE --
--CHECKS IDENTITY FOR NO NEXT OF KIN, NO ONE TO MISS YOU, AND "VANISHES" YOU OFF THE ROAD.
CAR'S DROPPED OFF AT YOUR DESTINATION, FAR FROM HERE, NO ONE KNOWING THAT YOU DIDN'T DROP IT.
LEAVING US TO ROT IN THIS PIT.
IF WE'RE LUCKY, WE ROT. IF NOT-- THE PROCESS. WORSE'N DEATH.
ESPECIALLY WHEN SOME OF US HAVE MORE...
"...TO LIVE FOR."
WHATEVER HE'S DONE, HE'S DONE FOR ME, CAGE. NOW, I GOTTA DO THIS FOR HIM.
IT'S A PHOTO OF ANDERS AND ME, HE RIPPED IT IN HALF AND KEPT THE PART WITH ME.
THIS IS ALL I GOT LEFT OF HIM. YOU'VE GOT TO FIND HIM --
"--HE'S ALL I GOT."
IN THAT CELL -- THAT'S HIM! THAT'S ANDERS!
LOOKS LIKE I DID MY TRAIL JOB TOO WELL-- FELL INTO THE SAME TRAP THAT SWALLOWED HIM.
I SAID, KEEP MOVING!
NICE COINCIDENCE. MAYBE.
BUT NOW THAT I FOUND HIM, HOW THE HECK DO I GET US OUT?

AAAARRRGH!!

OH NO--
IT'S SIMMS!

REKKTCH

OH-- OH! I'M BURNING UP! IT'S HAPPENING!

I'M POWERING OUT!

TRY TO RELAX! CONTROL YOURSE--

IT HURTS! IT HURTS SO MUCH!!

IT--

CHIK

CHIK

KRAK

KRAK

THAT GUARD JUST--JUST DISINTIGRATED! HE NEVER HAD A CHANCE--

K!-KRROCH

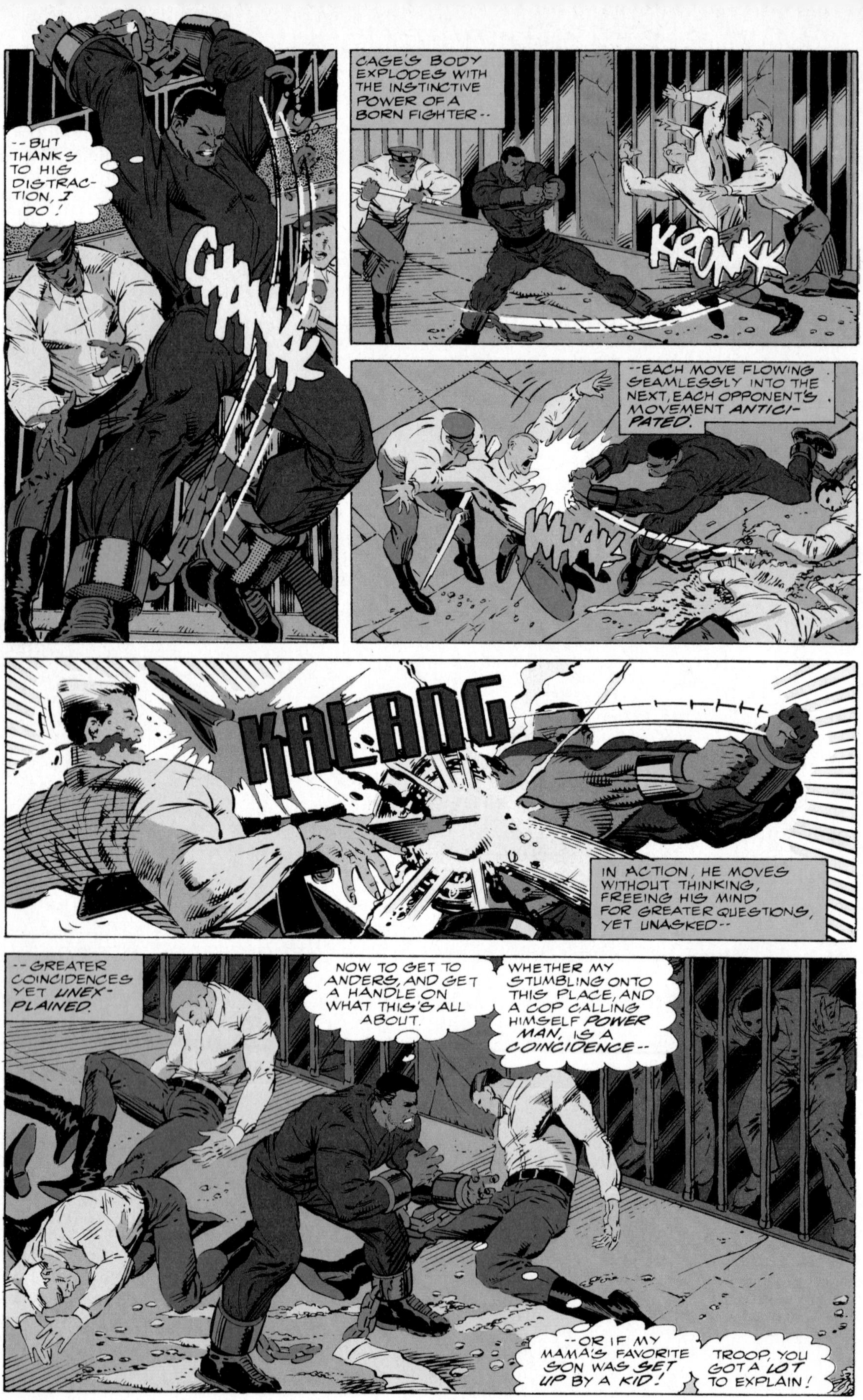
--BUT THANKS TO HIS DISTRACTION, I DO!
CHANKK
CAGE'S BODY EXPLODES WITH THE INSTINCTIVE POWER OF A BORN FIGHTER--
KRONKK
--EACH MOVE FLOWING SEAMLESSLY INTO THE NEXT, EACH OPPONENT'S MOVEMENT ANTICIPATED.
KALANG
IN ACTION, HE MOVES WITHOUT THINKING, FREEING HIS MIND FOR GREATER QUESTIONS, YET UNASKED--
--GREATER COINCIDENCES YET UNEXPLAINED.
NOW TO GET TO ANDERS, AND GET A HANDLE ON WHAT THIS'S ALL ABOUT.
WHETHER MY STUMBLING ONTO THIS PLACE, AND A COP CALLING HIMSELF POWER MAN, IS A COINCIDENCE--
--OR IF MY MAMA'S FAVORITE SON WAS SET UP BY A KID!
TROOP, YOU GOT A LOT TO EXPLAIN!

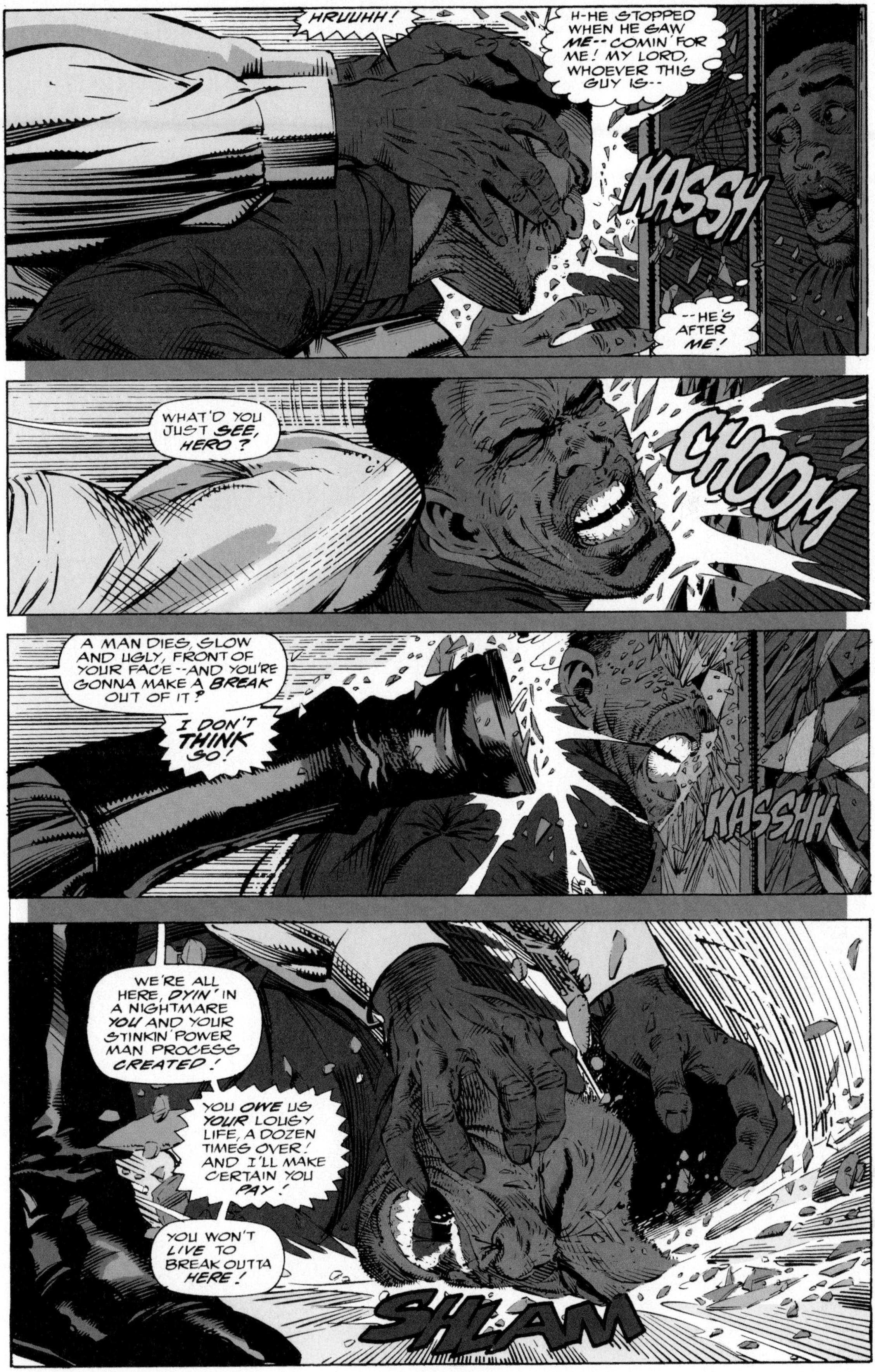
HRUUHH!
H-HE STOPPED WHEN HE SAW ME-- COMIN' FOR ME! MY LORD, WHOEVER THIS GUY IS--
KASSH
--HE'S AFTER ME!
WHAT'D YOU JUST SEE, HERO?
CHOOM
A MAN DIES, SLOW AND UGLY, FRONT OF YOUR FACE--AND YOU'RE GONNA MAKE A BREAK OUT OF IT?
I DON'T THINK SO!
KASSHH
WE'RE ALL HERE, DYIN' IN A NIGHTMARE YOU AND YOUR STINKIN' POWER MAN PROCESS CREATED!
YOU OWE US YOUR LOUSY LIFE, A DOZEN TIMES OVER! AND I'LL MAKE CERTAIN YOU PAY!
YOU WON'T LIVE TO BREAK OUTTA HERE!
SHLAM

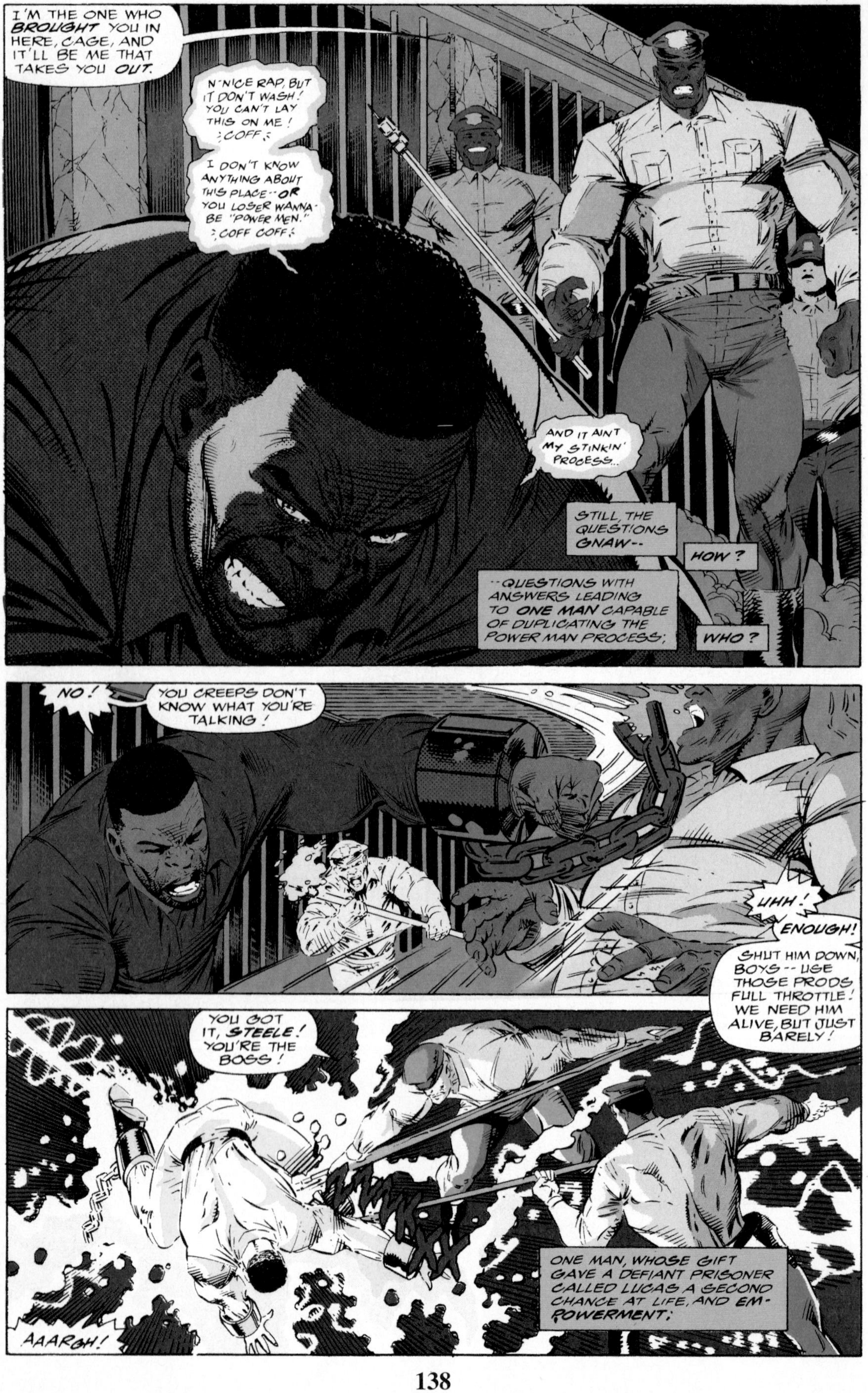
I'M THE ONE WHO BROUGHT YOU IN HERE, CAGE, AND IT'LL BE ME THAT TAKES YOU OUT.
N-NICE RAP, BUT IT DON'T WASH! YOU CAN'T LAY THIS ON ME! ;COFF;
I DON'T KNOW ANYTHING ABOUT THIS PLACE--OR YOU LOSER WANNA-BE "POWER MEN." ;COFF COFF;
AND IT AIN'T MY STINKIN' PROCESS...
STILL, THE QUESTIONS GNAW--
HOW?
--QUESTIONS WITH ANSWERS LEADING TO ONE MAN CAPABLE OF DUPLICATING THE POWER MAN PROCESS;
WHO?
NO!
YOU CREEPS DON'T KNOW WHAT YOU'RE TALKING!
UHH!
ENOUGH!
SHUT HIM DOWN, BOYS--USE THOSE PRODS FULL THROTTLE! WE NEED HIM ALIVE, BUT JUST BARELY!
YOU GOT IT, STEELE! YOU'RE THE BOSS!
ONE MAN, WHOSE GIFT GAVE A DEFIANT PRISONER CALLED LUCAS A SECOND CHANCE AT LIFE, AND EMPOWERMENT;
AAARGH!

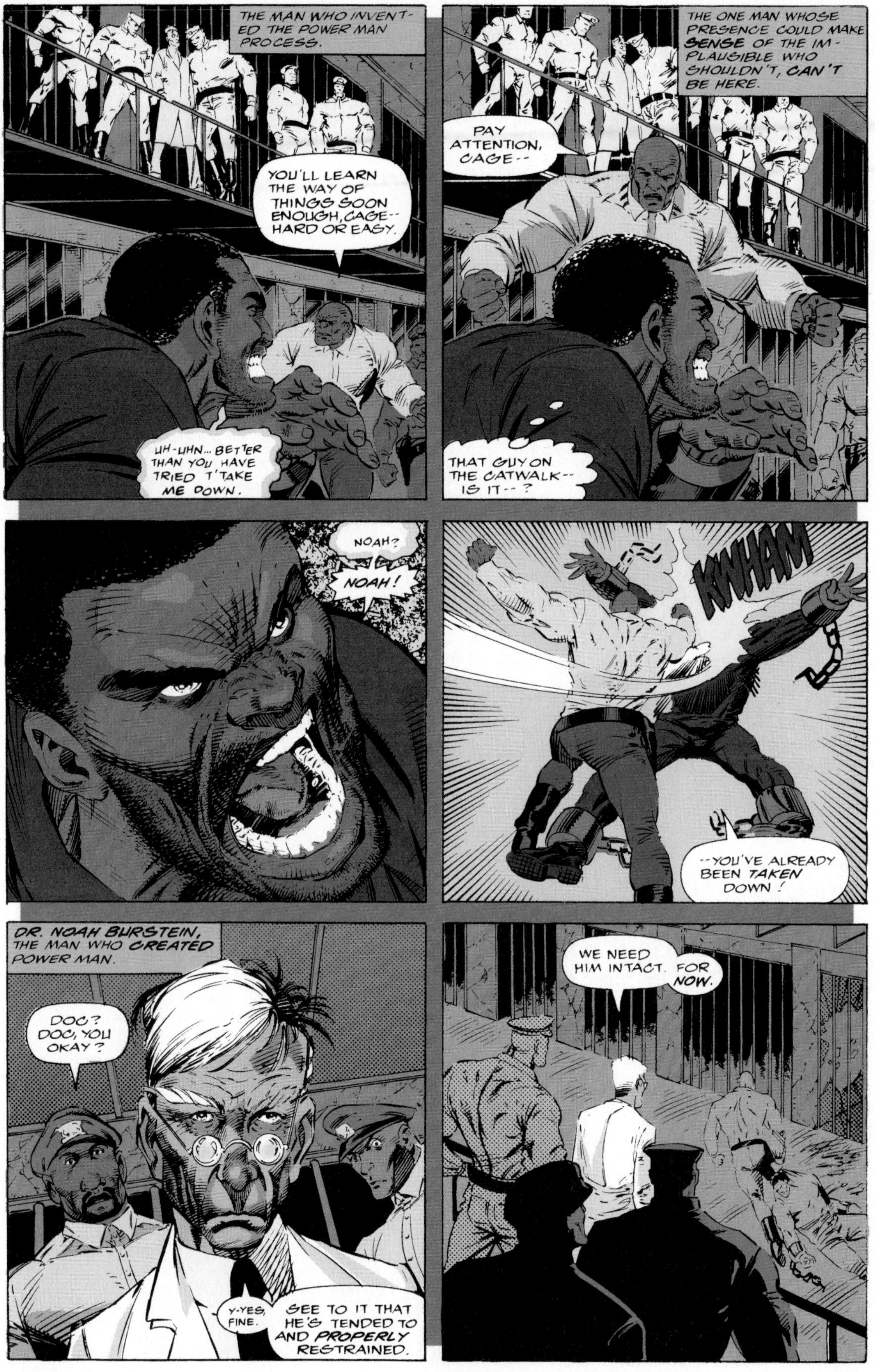
THE MAN WHO INVENTED THE POWER MAN PROCESS.
YOU'LL LEARN THE WAY OF THINGS SOON ENOUGH, CAGE-- HARD OR EASY.
UH-UHN... BETTER THAN YOU HAVE TRIED T'TAKE ME DOWN.
THE ONE MAN WHOSE PRESENCE COULD MAKE SENSE OF THE IMPLAUSIBLE WHO SHOULDN'T, CAN'T BE HERE.
PAY ATTENTION, CAGE--
THAT GUY ON THE CATWALK-- IS IT--?
NOAH?
NOAH!
KWHAM
--YOU'VE ALREADY BEEN TAKEN DOWN!
DR. NOAH BURSTEIN, THE MAN WHO CREATED POWER MAN.
DOC? DOC, YOU OKAY?
Y-YES, FINE.
SEE TO IT THAT HE'S TENDED TO AND PROPERLY RESTRAINED.
WE NEED HIM INTACT. FOR NOW.

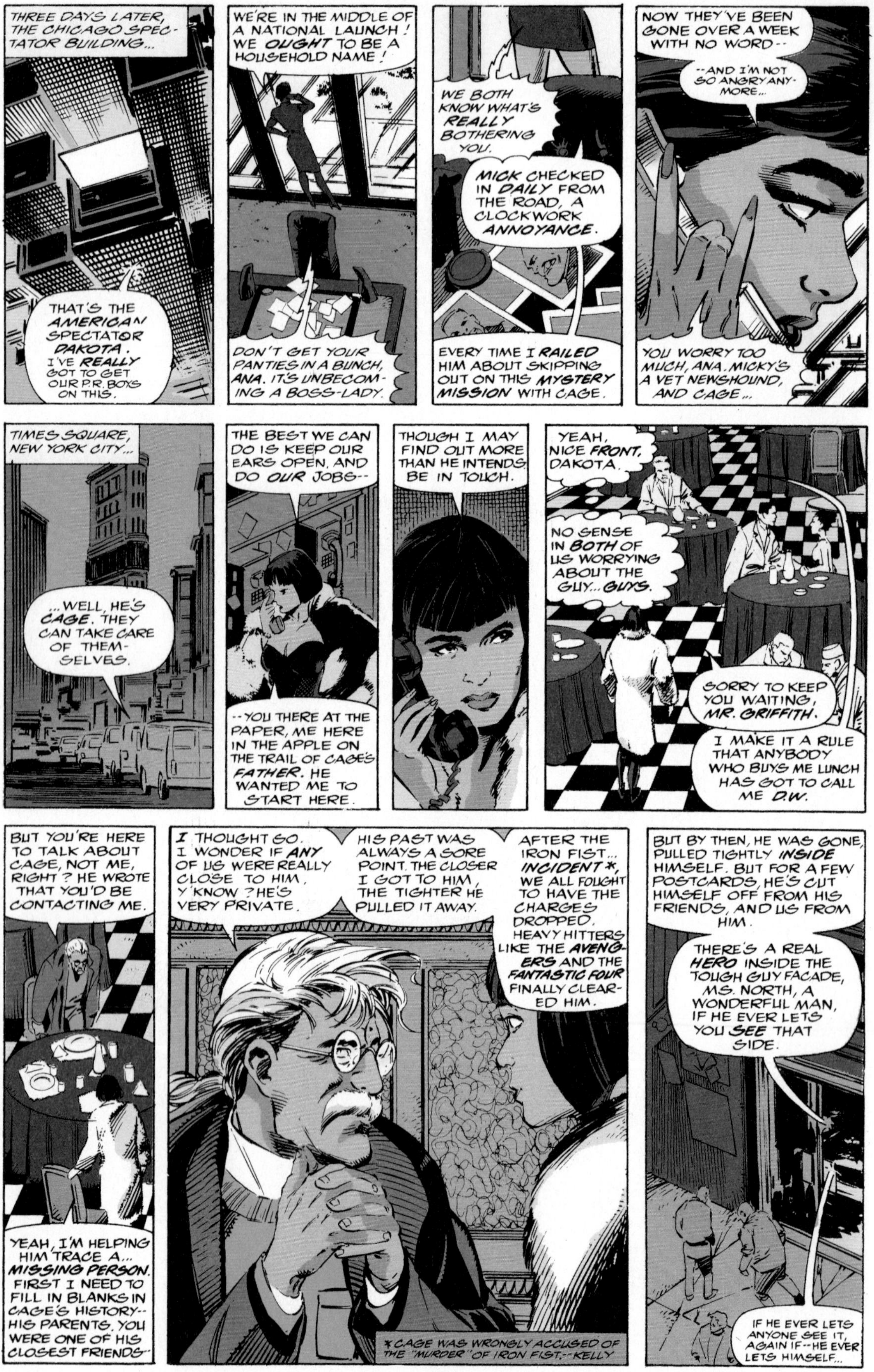
THREE DAYS LATER, THE CHICAGO SPECTATOR BUILDING...
THAT'S THE AMERICAN SPECTATOR DAKOTA. I'VE REALLY GOT TO GET OUR P.R. BOYS ON THIS.
WE'RE IN THE MIDDLE OF A NATIONAL LAUNCH! WE OUGHT TO BE A HOUSEHOLD NAME!
DON'T GET YOUR PANTIES IN A BUNCH, ANA. IT'S UNBECOMING A BOSS-LADY.
WE BOTH KNOW WHAT'S REALLY BOTHERING YOU.
MICK CHECKED IN DAILY FROM THE ROAD, A CLOCKWORK ANNOYANCE.
EVERY TIME I RAILED HIM ABOUT SKIPPING OUT ON THIS MYSTERY MISSION WITH CAGE.
NOW THEY'VE BEEN GONE OVER A WEEK WITH NO WORD--
--AND I'M NOT SO ANGRY ANYMORE...
YOU WORRY TOO MUCH, ANA. MICKY'S A VET NEWSHOUND, AND CAGE...
TIMES SQUARE, NEW YORK CITY...
...WELL, HE'S CAGE. THEY CAN TAKE CARE OF THEMSELVES.
THE BEST WE CAN DO IS KEEP OUR EARS OPEN, AND DO OUR JOBS--
--YOU THERE AT THE PAPER, ME HERE IN THE APPLE ON THE TRAIL OF CAGE'S FATHER. HE WANTED ME TO START HERE.
THOUGH I MAY FIND OUT MORE THAN HE INTENDS. BE IN TOUCH.
YEAH, NICE FRONT, DAKOTA.
NO SENSE IN BOTH OF US WORRYING ABOUT THE GUY... GUYS.
SORRY TO KEEP YOU WAITING, MR. GRIFFITH.
I MAKE IT A RULE THAT ANYBODY WHO BUYS ME LUNCH HAS GOT TO CALL ME D.W.
BUT YOU'RE HERE TO TALK ABOUT CAGE, NOT ME, RIGHT? HE WROTE THAT YOU'D BE CONTACTING ME.
YEAH, I'M HELPING HIM TRACE A... MISSING PERSON. FIRST I NEED TO FILL IN BLANKS IN CAGE'S HISTORY-- HIS PARENTS. YOU WERE ONE OF HIS CLOSEST FRIENDS--
I THOUGHT SO. I WONDER IF ANY OF US WERE REALLY CLOSE TO HIM, Y'KNOW? HE'S VERY PRIVATE.
HIS PAST WAS ALWAYS A SORE POINT. THE CLOSER I GOT TO HIM, THE TIGHTER HE PULLED IT AWAY.
AFTER THE IRON FIST... INCIDENT*, WE ALL FOUGHT TO HAVE THE CHARGES DROPPED. HEAVY HITTERS LIKE THE AVENGERS AND THE FANTASTIC FOUR FINALLY CLEARED HIM.
*CAGE WAS WRONGLY ACCUSED OF THE "MURDER" OF IRON FIST.--KELLY
BUT BY THEN, HE WAS GONE, PULLED TIGHTLY INSIDE HIMSELF. BUT FOR A FEW POSTCARDS, HE'S CUT HIMSELF OFF FROM HIS FRIENDS, AND US FROM HIM.
THERE'S A REAL HERO INSIDE THE TOUGH GUY FACADE, MS. NORTH, A WONDERFUL MAN, IF HE EVER LETS YOU SEE THAT SIDE.
IF HE EVER LETS ANYONE SEE IT, AGAIN IF--HE EVER LETS HIMSELF...

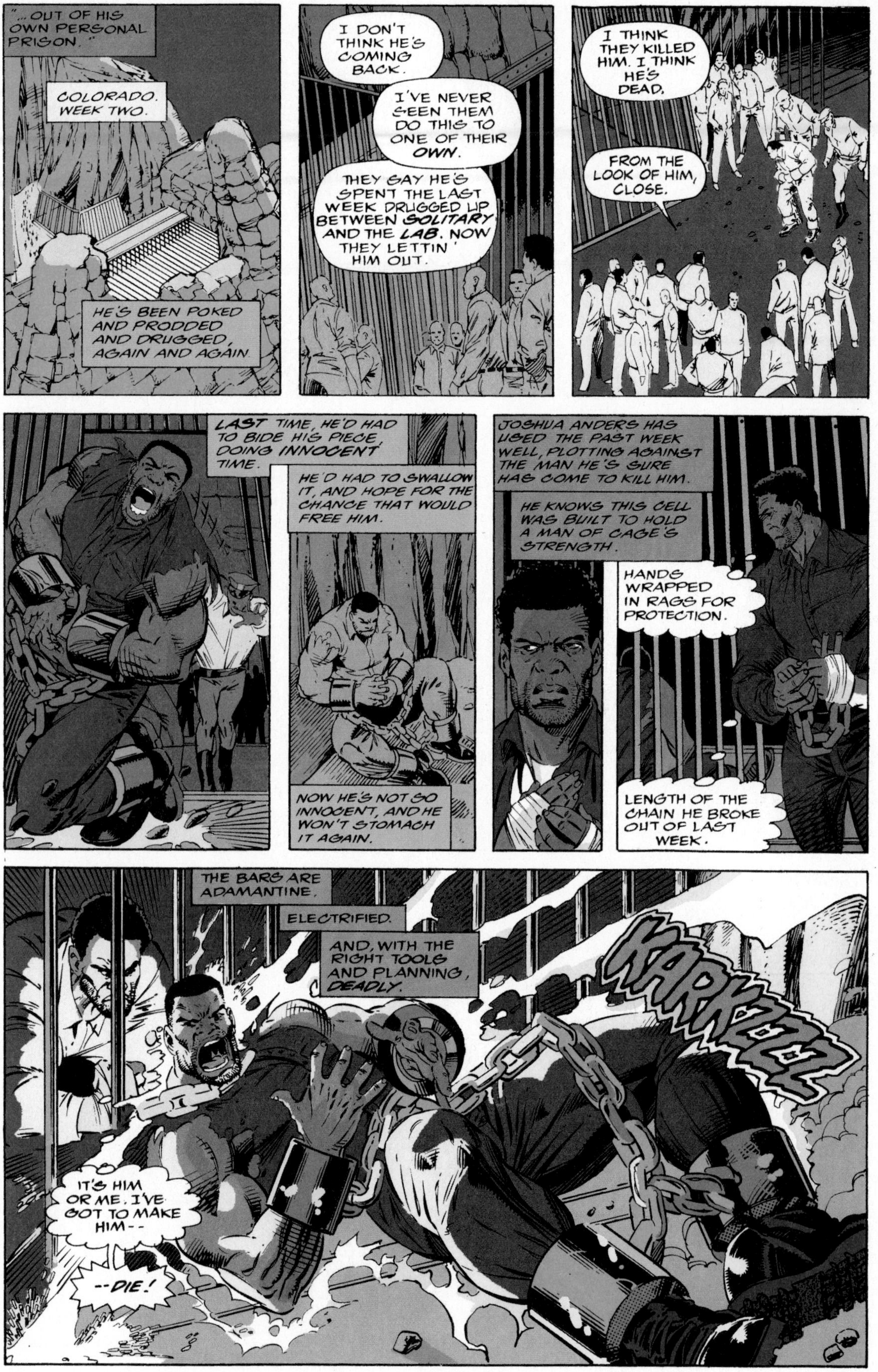
"...OUT OF HIS OWN PERSONAL PRISON."
COLORADO. WEEK TWO.
HE'S BEEN POKED AND PRODDED AND DRUGGED, AGAIN AND AGAIN.
I DON'T THINK HE'S COMING BACK.
I'VE NEVER SEEN THEM DO THIS TO ONE OF THEIR OWN.
THEY SAY HE'S SPENT THE LAST WEEK DRUGGED UP BETWEEN SOLITARY AND THE LAB. NOW THEY LETTIN' HIM OUT.
I THINK THEY KILLED HIM. I THINK HE'S DEAD.
FROM THE LOOK OF HIM, CLOSE.
LAST TIME, HE'D HAD TO BIDE HIS PIECE, DOING INNOCENT TIME.
HE'D HAD TO SWALLOW IT, AND HOPE FOR THE CHANCE THAT WOULD FREE HIM.
NOW HE'S NOT SO INNOCENT, AND HE WON'T STOMACH IT AGAIN.
JOSHUA ANDERS HAS USED THE PAST WEEK WELL, PLOTTING AGAINST THE MAN HE'S SURE HAS COME TO KILL HIM.
HE KNOWS THIS CELL WAS BUILT TO HOLD A MAN OF CAGE'S STRENGTH.
HANDS WRAPPED IN RAGS FOR PROTECTION.
LENGTH OF THE CHAIN HE BROKE OUT OF LAST WEEK.
THE BARS ARE ADAMANTINE.
ELECTRIFIED.
AND, WITH THE RIGHT TOOLS AND PLANNING, DEADLY.
KARKZZT
IT'S HIM OR ME. I'VE GOT TO MAKE HIM--
--DIE!

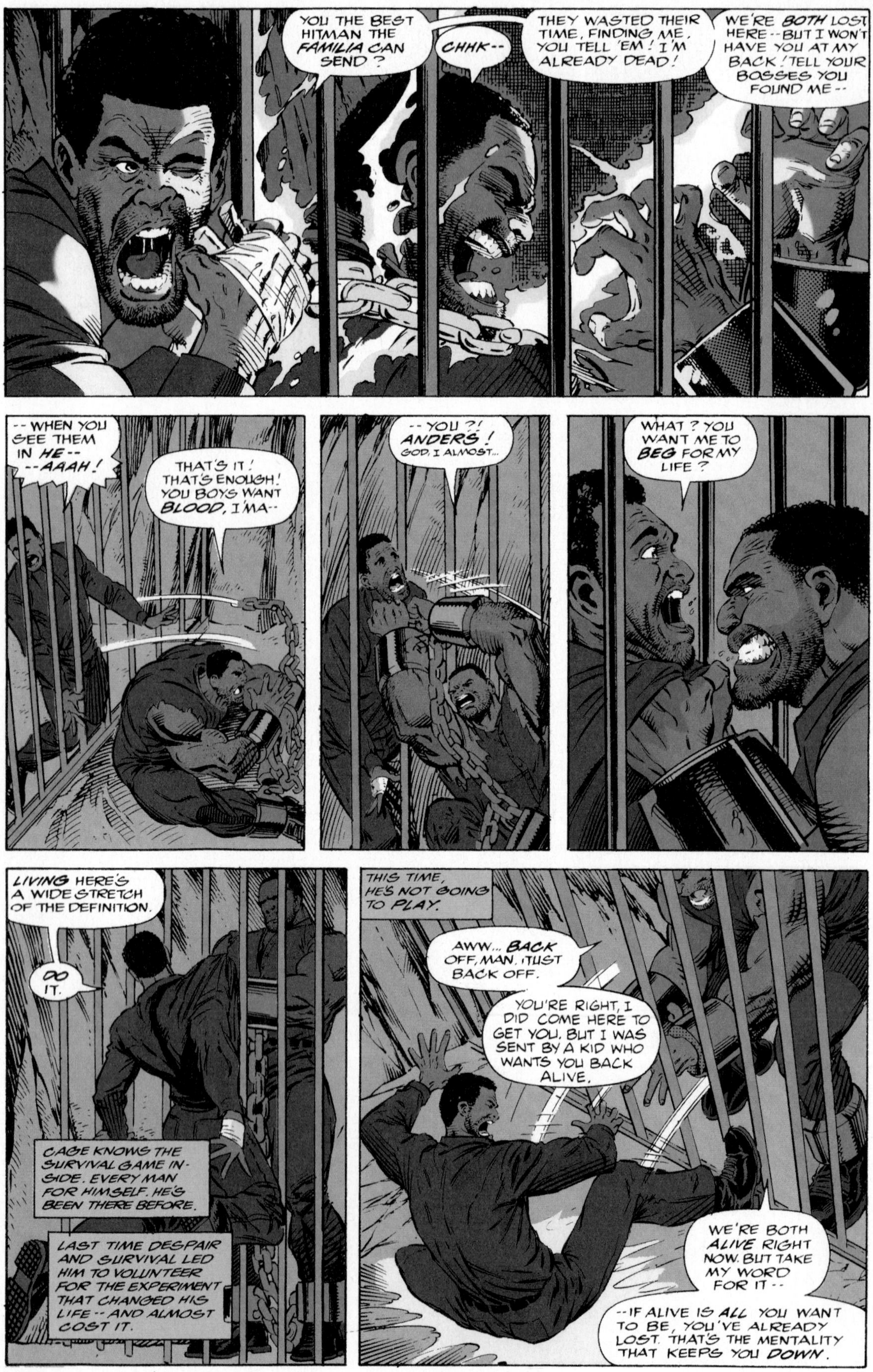

YOU THE BEST HITMAN THE FAMILIA CAN SEND?
CHHK--
THEY WASTED THEIR TIME, FINDING ME. YOU TELL 'EM! I'M ALREADY DEAD!
WE'RE BOTH LOST HERE--BUT I WON'T HAVE YOU AT MY BACK! TELL YOUR BOSSES YOU FOUND ME--
--WHEN YOU SEE THEM IN HE-- --AAAH!
THAT'S IT! THAT'S ENOUGH! YOU BOYS WANT BLOOD, I'MA--
--YOU?! ANDERS! GOD, I ALMOST...
WHAT? YOU WANT ME TO BEG FOR MY LIFE?
LIVING HERE'S A WIDE STRETCH OF THE DEFINITION.
DO IT.
CAGE KNOWS THE SURVIVAL GAME IN-SIDE. EVERY MAN FOR HIMSELF. HE'S BEEN THERE BEFORE.
LAST TIME DESPAIR AND SURVIVAL LED HIM TO VOLUNTEER FOR THE EXPERIMENT THAT CHANGED HIS LIFE--AND ALMOST COST IT.
THIS TIME, HE'S NOT GOING TO PLAY.
AWW... BACK OFF, MAN. JUST BACK OFF.
YOU'RE RIGHT, I DID COME HERE TO GET YOU. BUT I WAS SENT BY A KID WHO WANTS YOU BACK ALIVE.
WE'RE BOTH ALIVE RIGHT NOW. BUT TAKE MY WORD FOR IT--
--IF ALIVE IS ALL YOU WANT TO BE, YOU'VE ALREADY LOST. THAT'S THE MENTALITY THAT KEEPS YOU DOWN.

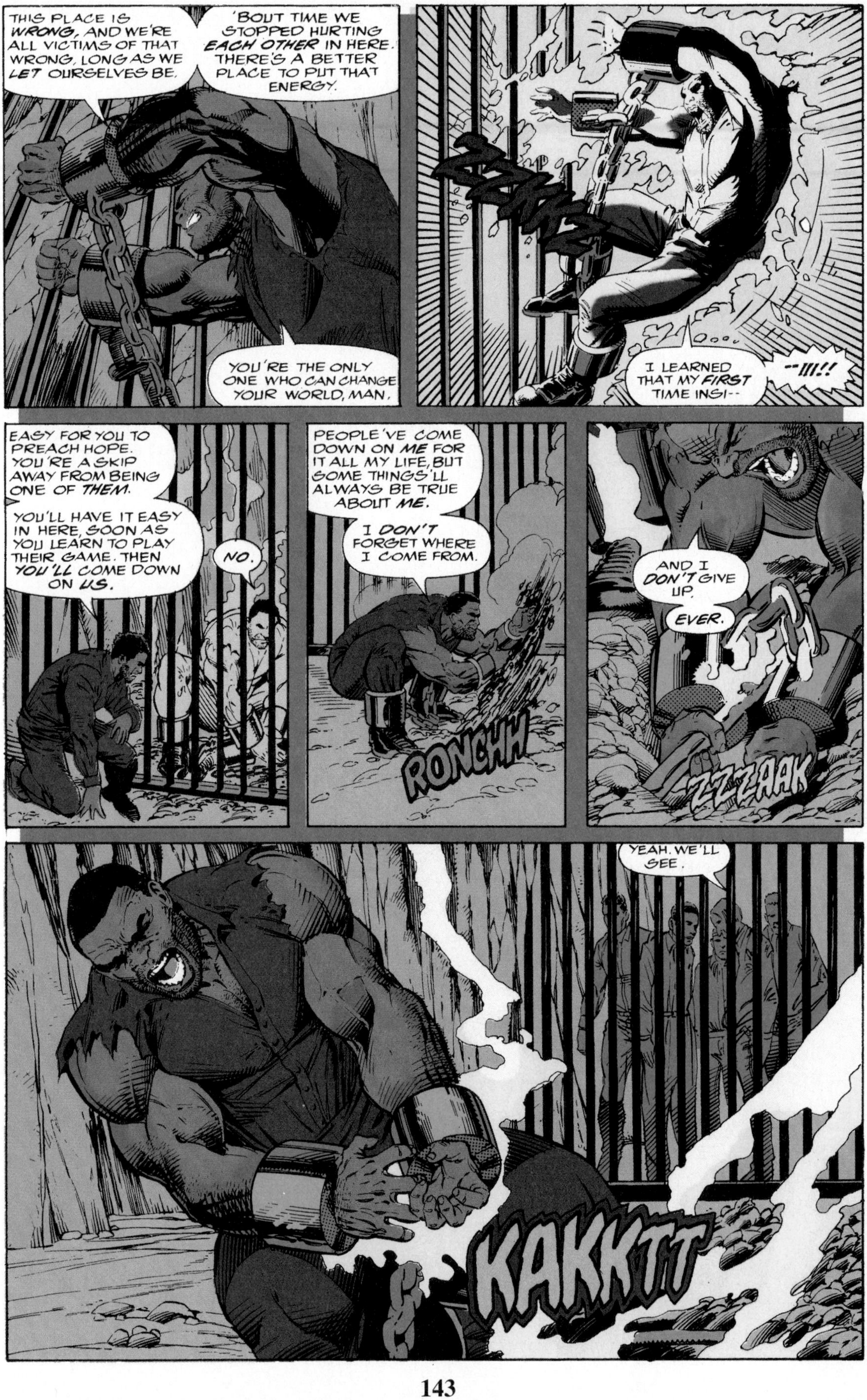
THIS PLACE IS WRONG, AND WE'RE ALL VICTIMS OF THAT WRONG, LONG AS WE LET OURSELVES BE.
'BOUT TIME WE STOPPED HURTING EACH OTHER IN HERE. THERE'S A BETTER PLACE TO PUT THAT ENERGY.
YOU'RE THE ONLY ONE WHO CAN CHANGE YOUR WORLD, MAN.
I LEARNED THAT MY FIRST TIME INSI--
--III!!
EASY FOR YOU TO PREACH HOPE. YOU'RE A SKIP AWAY FROM BEING ONE OF THEM.
YOU'LL HAVE IT EASY IN HERE, SOON AS YOU LEARN TO PLAY THEIR GAME. THEN YOU'LL COME DOWN ON US.
NO.
PEOPLE'VE COME DOWN ON ME FOR IT ALL MY LIFE, BUT SOME THINGS'LL ALWAYS BE TRUE ABOUT ME.
I DON'T FORGET WHERE I COME FROM.
RONCHH
AND I DON'T GIVE UP.
EVER.
ZZZAAK
YEAH. WE'LL SEE.
KAKKTT

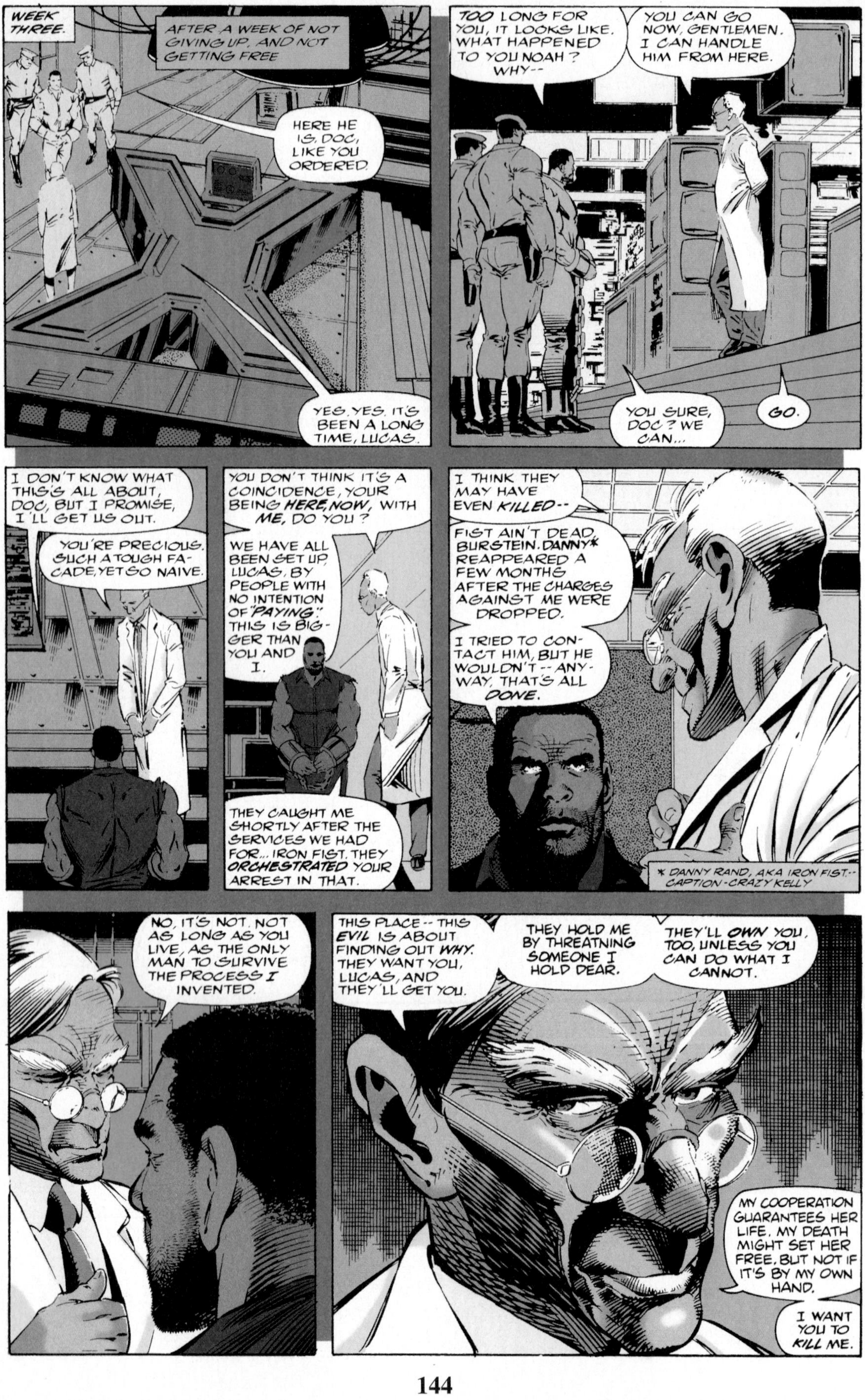
WEEK THREE.
AFTER A WEEK OF NOT GIVING UP, AND NOT GETTING FREE
HERE HE IS, DOC, LIKE YOU ORDERED.
YES. YES. IT'S BEEN A LONG TIME, LUCAS.
TOO LONG FOR YOU, IT LOOKS LIKE. WHAT HAPPENED TO YOU NOAH? WHY--
YOU CAN GO NOW, GENTLEMEN. I CAN HANDLE HIM FROM HERE.
YOU SURE, DOC? WE CAN...
GO.
I DON'T KNOW WHAT THIS'S ALL ABOUT, DOC, BUT I PROMISE, I'LL GET US OUT.
YOU'RE PRECIOUS. SUCH A TOUGH FACADE, YET SO NAIVE.
YOU DON'T THINK IT'S A COINCIDENCE, YOUR BEING HERE, NOW, WITH ME, DO YOU?
WE HAVE ALL BEEN SET UP, LUCAS, BY PEOPLE WITH NO INTENTION OF "PAYING". THIS IS BIGGER THAN YOU AND I.
THEY CAUGHT ME SHORTLY AFTER THE SERVICES WE HAD FOR... IRON FIST. THEY ORCHESTRATED YOUR ARREST IN THAT.
I THINK THEY MAY HAVE EVEN KILLED--
FIST AIN'T DEAD, BURSTEIN. DANNY* REAPPEARED A FEW MONTHS AFTER THE CHARGES AGAINST ME WERE DROPPED.
I TRIED TO CONTACT HIM, BUT HE WOULDN'T -- ANYWAY, THAT'S ALL DONE.
* DANNY RAND, AKA IRON FIST.-- CAPTION-CRAZY KELLY
NO, IT'S NOT. NOT AS LONG AS YOU LIVE, AS THE ONLY MAN TO SURVIVE THE PROCESS I INVENTED.
THIS PLACE -- THIS EVIL IS ABOUT FINDING OUT WHY. THEY WANT YOU, LUCAS, AND THEY'LL GET YOU.
THEY HOLD ME BY THREATNING SOMEONE I HOLD DEAR.
THEY'LL OWN YOU, TOO, UNLESS YOU CAN DO WHAT I CANNOT.
MY COOPERATION GUARANTEES HER LIFE. MY DEATH MIGHT SET HER FREE. BUT NOT IF IT'S BY MY OWN HAND.
I WANT YOU TO KILL ME.

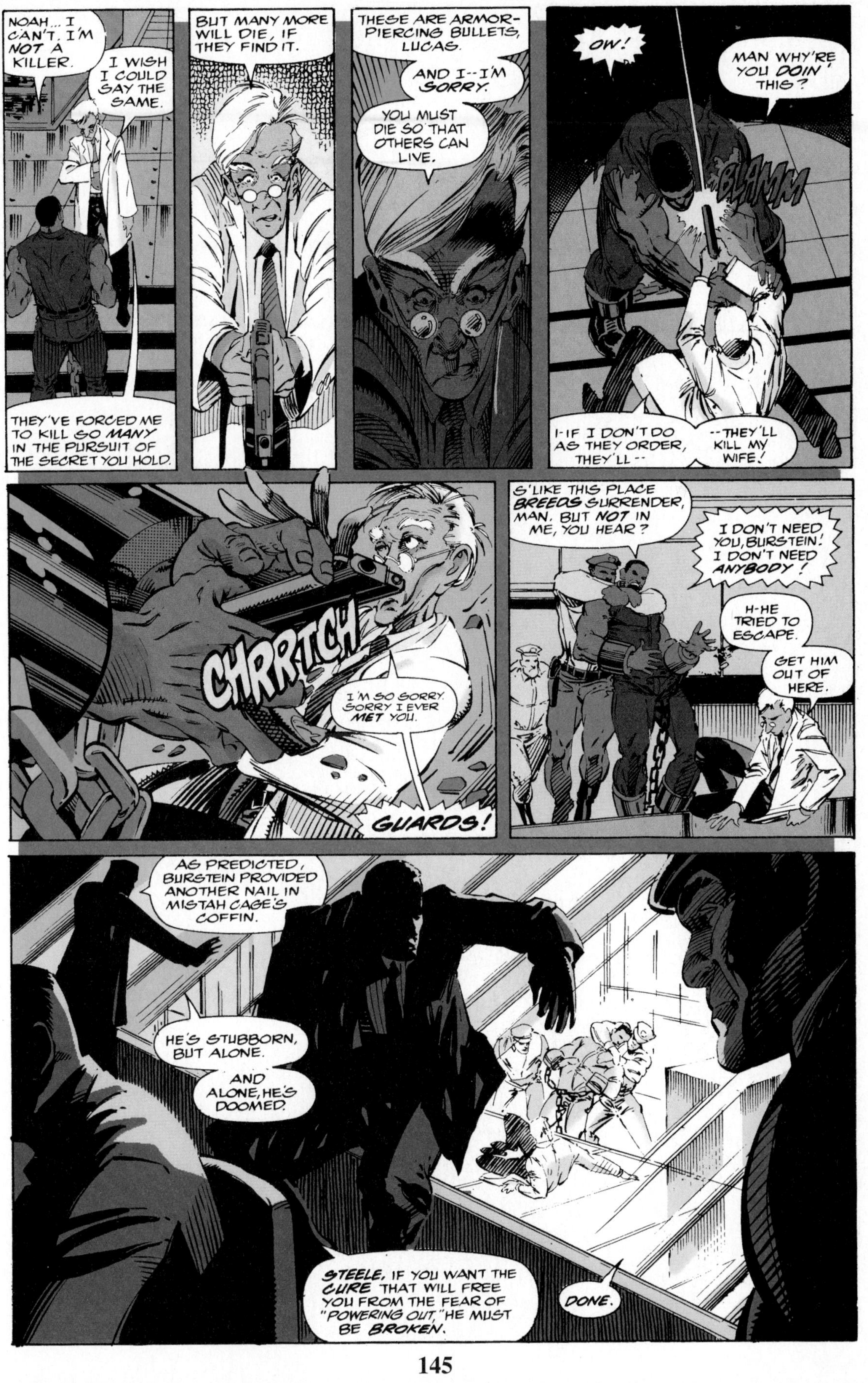
NOAH... I CAN'T. I'M NOT A KILLER.
I WISH I COULD SAY THE SAME.
THEY'VE FORCED ME TO KILL SO MANY IN THE PURSUIT OF THE SECRET YOU HOLD.
BUT MANY MORE WILL DIE, IF THEY FIND IT.
THESE ARE ARMOR-PIERCING BULLETS, LUCAS.
AND I--I'M SORRY.
YOU MUST DIE SO THAT OTHERS CAN LIVE.
OW!
MAN WHY'RE YOU DOIN' THIS?
BLAMM
I-IF I DON'T DO AS THEY ORDER, THEY'LL --
--THEY'LL KILL MY WIFE!
CHRRTCH
I'M SO SORRY. SORRY I EVER MET YOU.
GUARDS!
S'LIKE THIS PLACE BREEDS SURRENDER, MAN. BUT NOT IN ME, YOU HEAR?
I DON'T NEED YOU, BURSTEIN! I DON'T NEED ANYBODY!
H-HE TRIED TO ESCAPE.
GET HIM OUT OF HERE.
AS PREDICTED, BURSTEIN PROVIDED ANOTHER NAIL IN MISTAH CAGE'S COFFIN.
HE'S STUBBORN, BUT ALONE.
AND ALONE, HE'S DOOMED.
STEELE, IF YOU WANT THE CURE THAT WILL FREE YOU FROM THE FEAR OF "POWERING OUT," HE MUST BE BROKEN.
DONE.

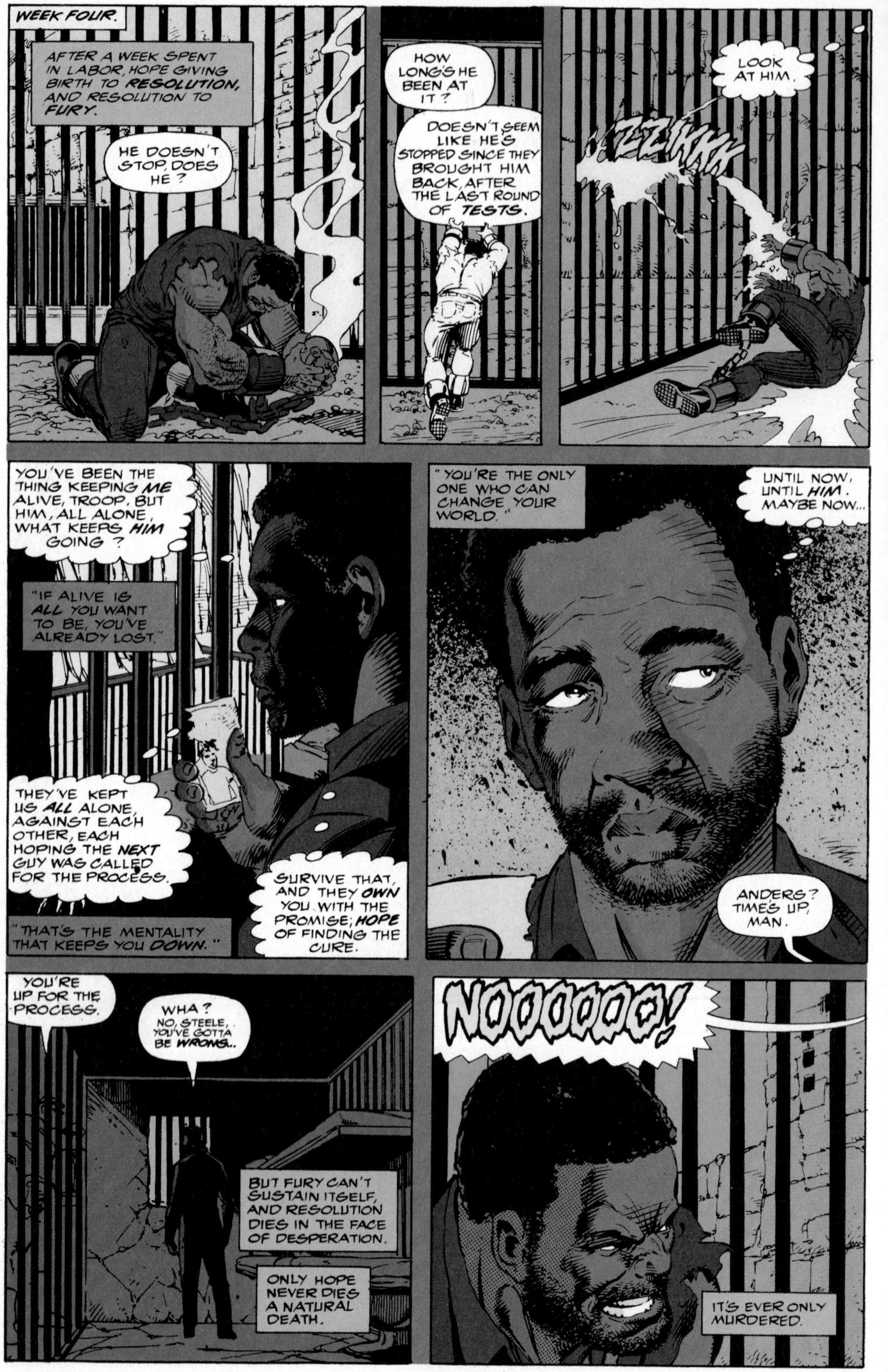
WEEK FOUR.
AFTER A WEEK SPENT IN LABOR, HOPE GIVING BIRTH TO RESOLUTION, AND RESOLUTION TO FURY.
HE DOESN'T STOP, DOES HE?
HOW LONG'S HE BEEN AT IT?
DOESN'T SEEM LIKE HE'S STOPPED SINCE THEY BROUGHT HIM BACK, AFTER THE LAST ROUND OF TESTS.
LOOK AT HIM.
ZZZIKKK
YOU'VE BEEN THE THING KEEPING ME ALIVE, TROOP. BUT HIM, ALL ALONE, WHAT KEEPS HIM GOING?
"IF ALIVE IS ALL YOU WANT TO BE, YOU'VE ALREADY LOST."
THEY'VE KEPT US ALL ALONE, AGAINST EACH OTHER, EACH HOPING THE NEXT GUY WAS CALLED FOR THE PROCESS.
"THAT'S THE MENTALITY THAT KEEPS YOU DOWN."
SURVIVE THAT, AND THEY OWN YOU WITH THE PROMISE; HOPE OF FINDING THE CURE.
"YOU'RE THE ONLY ONE WHO CAN CHANGE YOUR WORLD."
UNTIL NOW, UNTIL HIM. MAYBE NOW...
ANDERS? TIME'S UP, MAN.
YOU'RE UP FOR THE PROCESS.
WHA? NO, STEELE, YOU'VE GOTTA BE WRONG...
BUT FURY CAN'T SUSTAIN ITSELF, AND RESOLUTION DIES IN THE FACE OF DESPERATION.
ONLY HOPE NEVER DIES A NATURAL DEATH.
NOOOOOO!
IT'S EVER ONLY MURDERED.

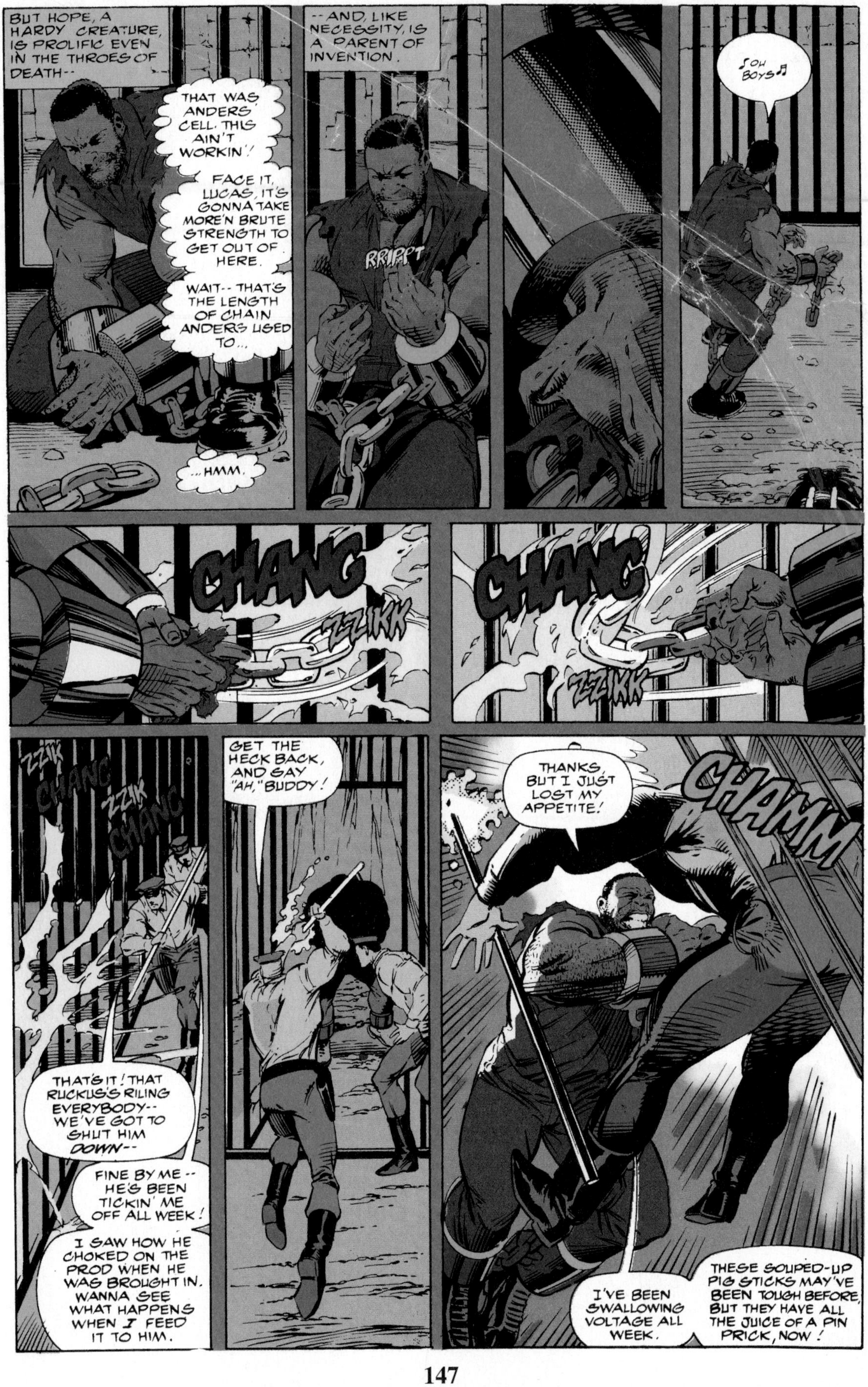
BUT HOPE, A HARDY CREATURE, IS PROLIFIC EVEN IN THE THROES OF DEATH--
THAT WAS ANDERS' CELL. THIS AIN'T WORKIN'!
FACE IT, LUCAS, IT'S GONNA TAKE MORE'N BRUTE STRENGTH TO GET OUT OF HERE.
WAIT-- THAT'S THE LENGTH OF CHAIN ANDERS USED TO...
...HMM.
--AND, LIKE NECESSITY, IS A PARENT OF INVENTION.
RRIPPT
♪OH BOYS♪
CHANG
ZZIKK
CHANG
ZZIKK
ZZIK CHANG ZZIK CHANG
GET THE HECK BACK, AND SAY "AH," BUDDY!
THANKS, BUT I JUST LOST MY APPETITE!
CHAMM
THAT'S IT! THAT RUCKUS'S RILING EVERYBODY-- WE'VE GOT TO SHUT HIM DOWN--
FINE BY ME-- HE'S BEEN TICKIN' ME OFF ALL WEEK!
I SAW HOW HE CHOKED ON THE PROD WHEN HE WAS BROUGHT IN. WANNA SEE WHAT HAPPENS WHEN I FEED IT TO HIM.
I'VE BEEN SWALLOWING VOLTAGE ALL WEEK.
THESE SOUPED-UP PIG STICKS MAY'VE BEEN TOUGH BEFORE, BUT THEY HAVE ALL THE JUICE OF A PIN PRICK, NOW!

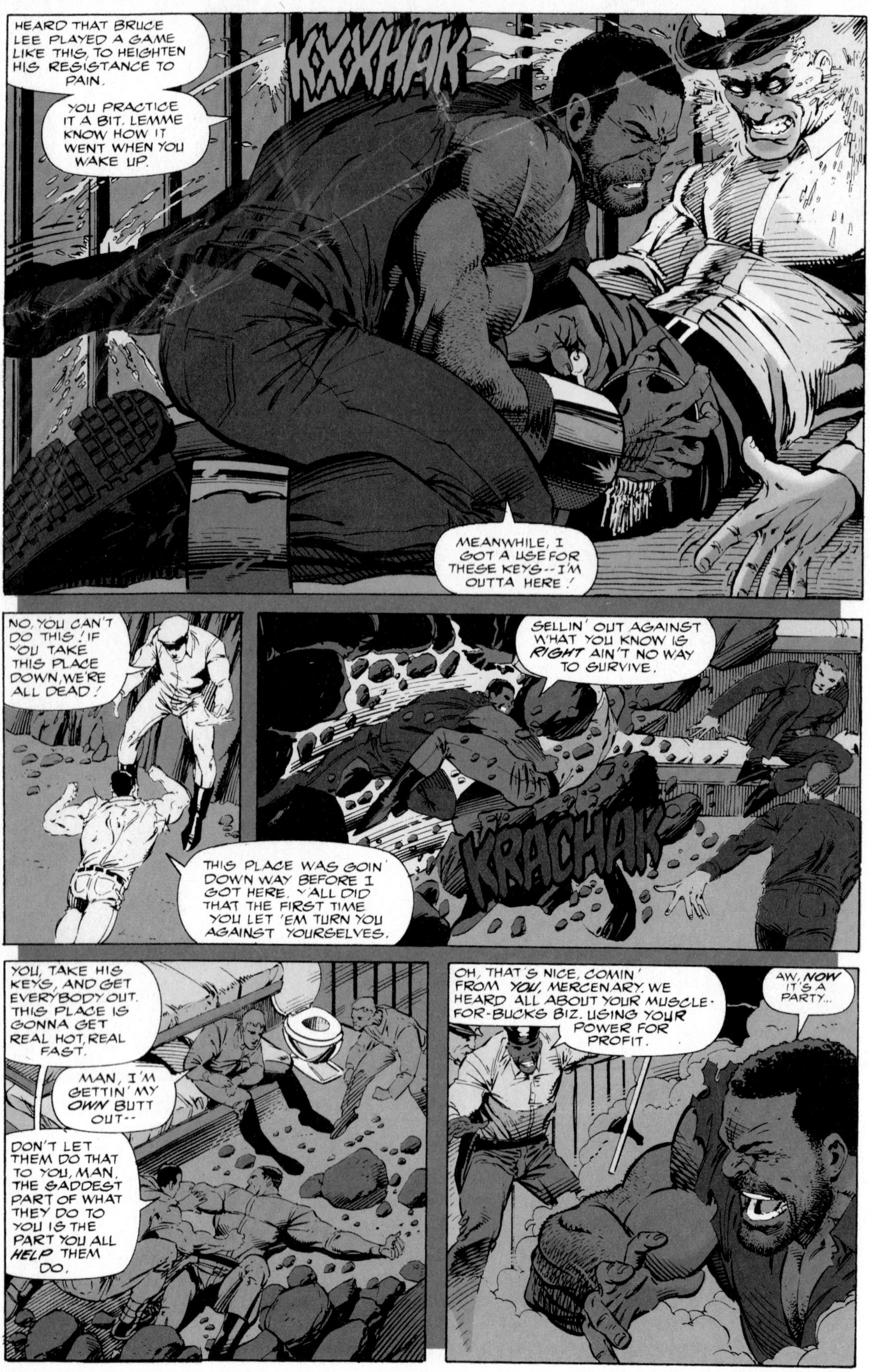
HEARD THAT BRUCE LEE PLAYED A GAME LIKE THIS, TO HEIGHTEN HIS RESISTANCE TO PAIN.
YOU PRACTICE IT A BIT. LEMME KNOW HOW IT WENT WHEN YOU WAKE UP.
KXXHAK
MEANWHILE, I GOT A USE FOR THESE KEYS--I'M OUTTA HERE!
NO, YOU CAN'T DO THIS! IF YOU TAKE THIS PLACE DOWN, WE'RE ALL DEAD!
THIS PLACE WAS GOIN' DOWN WAY BEFORE I GOT HERE. Y'ALL DID THAT THE FIRST TIME YOU LET 'EM TURN YOU AGAINST YOURSELVES.
SELLIN' OUT AGAINST WHAT YOU KNOW IS RIGHT AIN'T NO WAY TO SURVIVE.
KRACHAK
YOU, TAKE HIS KEYS, AND GET EVERYBODY OUT. THIS PLACE IS GONNA GET REAL HOT, REAL FAST.
MAN, I'M GETTIN' MY OWN BUTT OUT--
DON'T LET THEM DO THAT TO YOU, MAN. THE SADDEST PART OF WHAT THEY DO TO YOU IS THE PART YOU ALL HELP THEM DO.
OH, THAT'S NICE, COMIN' FROM YOU, MERCENARY. WE HEARD ALL ABOUT YOUR MUSCLE-FOR-BUCKS BIZ. USING YOUR POWER FOR PROFIT.
AW, NOW IT'S A PARTY...

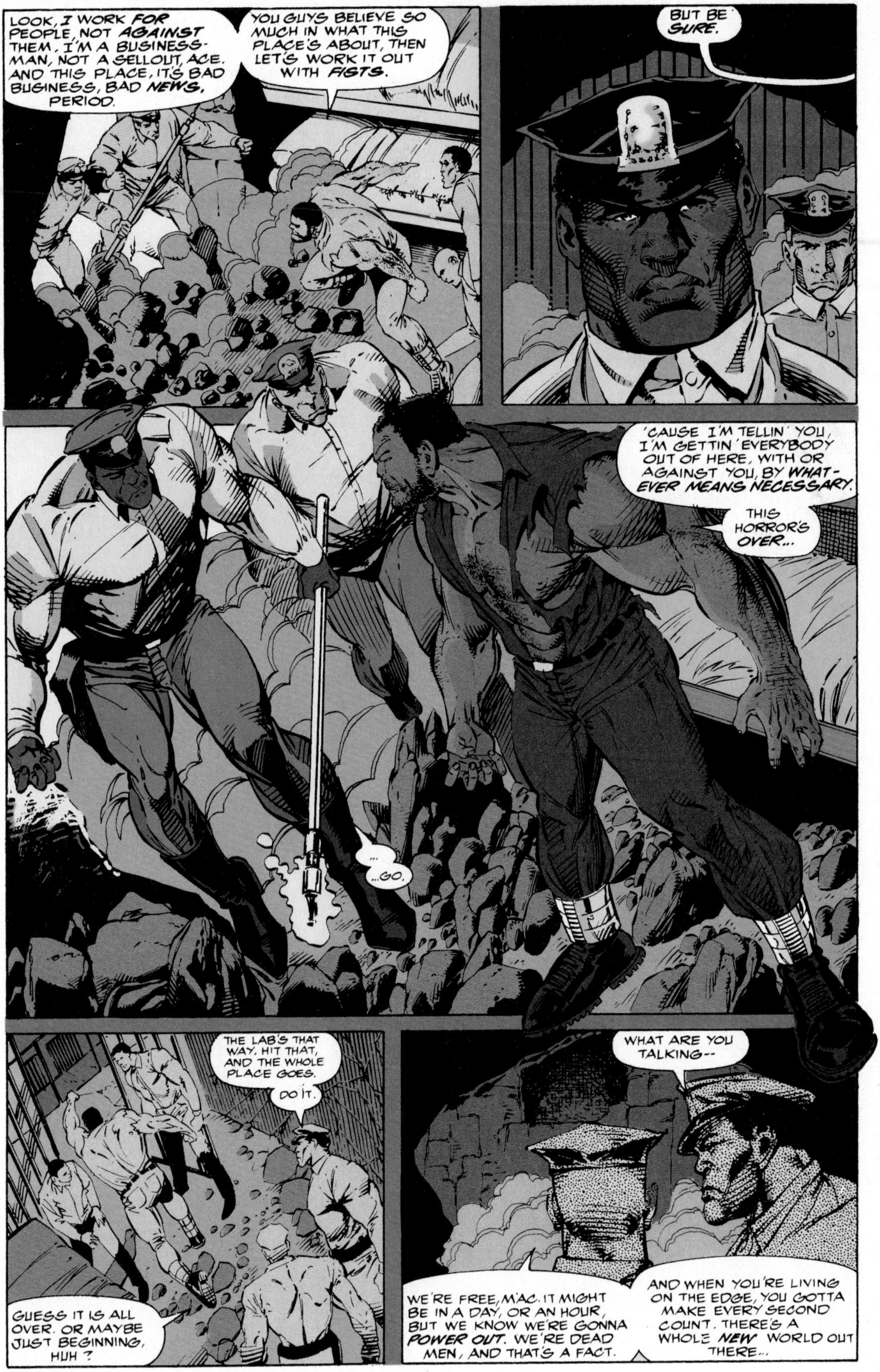
LOOK, I WORK FOR PEOPLE, NOT AGAINST THEM. I'M A BUSINESSMAN, NOT A SELLOUT, ACE. AND THIS PLACE, IT'S BAD BUSINESS, BAD NEWS, PERIOD.
YOU GUYS BELIEVE SO MUCH IN WHAT THIS PLACE'S ABOUT, THEN LET'S WORK IT OUT WITH FISTS.
BUT BE SURE.
'CAUSE I'M TELLIN' YOU, I'M GETTIN' EVERYBODY OUT OF HERE, WITH OR AGAINST YOU, BY WHATEVER MEANS NECESSARY.
THIS HORROR'S OVER...
...
...GO.
THE LAB'S THAT WAY. HIT THAT, AND THE WHOLE PLACE GOES.
DO IT.
GUESS IT IS ALL OVER. OR MAYBE JUST BEGINNING, HUH?
WHAT ARE YOU TALKING--
WE'RE FREE, MAC. IT MIGHT BE IN A DAY, OR AN HOUR, BUT WE KNOW WE'RE GONNA POWER OUT. WE'RE DEAD MEN, AND THAT'S A FACT.
AND WHEN YOU'RE LIVING ON THE EDGE, YOU GOTTA MAKE EVERY SECOND COUNT. THERE'S A WHOLE NEW WORLD OUT THERE...

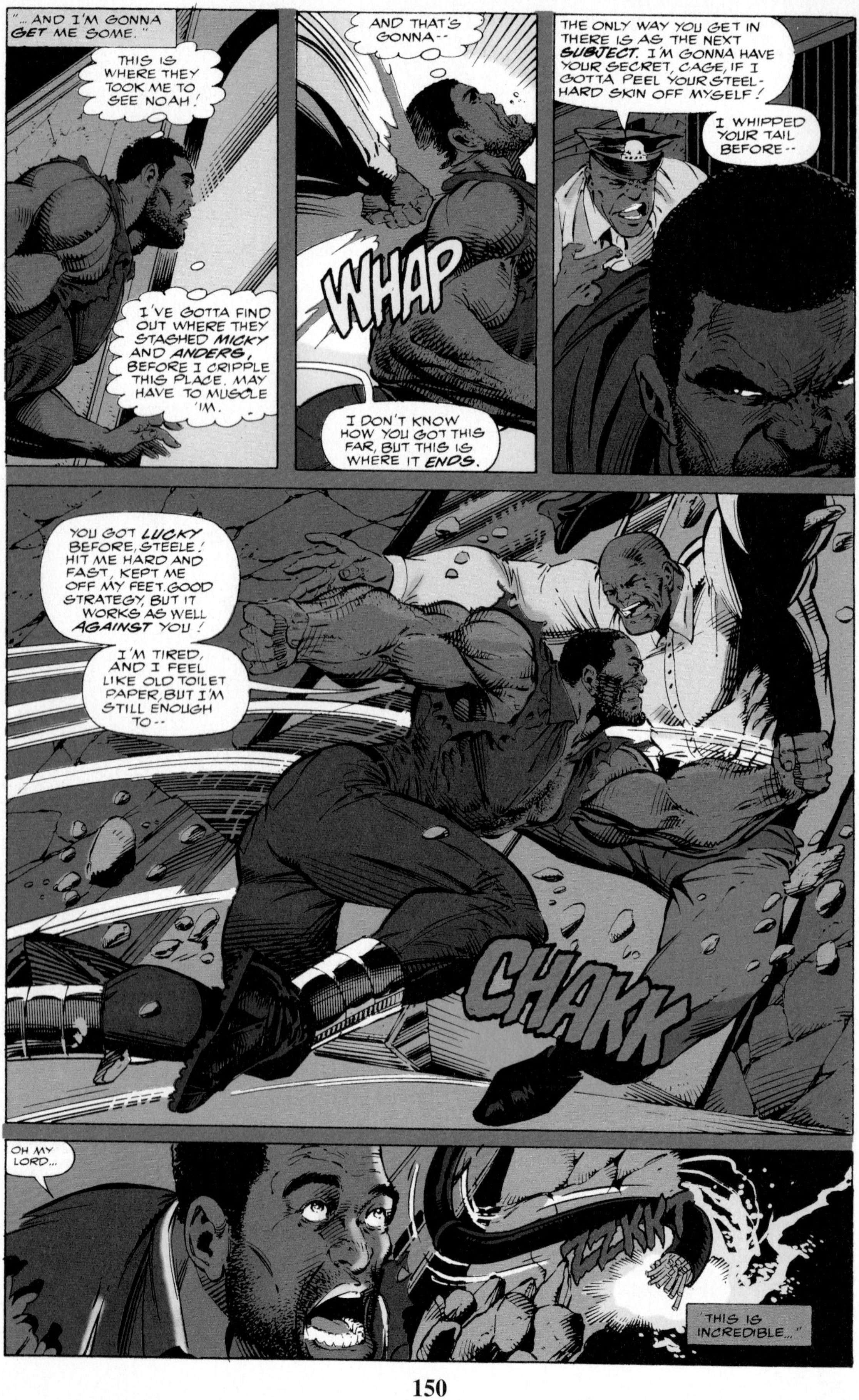
"... AND I'M GONNA GET ME SOME."
THIS IS WHERE THEY TOOK ME TO SEE NOAH!
I'VE GOTTA FIND OUT WHERE THEY STASHED MICKY AND ANDERS, BEFORE I CRIPPLE THIS PLACE. MAY HAVE TO MUSCLE 'IM.
AND THAT'S GONNA--
WHAP
I DON'T KNOW HOW YOU GOT THIS FAR, BUT THIS IS WHERE IT ENDS.
THE ONLY WAY YOU GET IN THERE IS AS THE NEXT SUBJECT. I'M GONNA HAVE YOUR SECRET, CAGE, IF I GOTTA PEEL YOUR STEEL-HARD SKIN OFF MYSELF!
I WHIPPED YOUR TAIL BEFORE--
YOU GOT LUCKY BEFORE, STEELE! HIT ME HARD AND FAST, KEPT ME OFF MY FEET. GOOD STRATEGY, BUT IT WORKS AS WELL AGAINST YOU!
I'M TIRED, AND I FEEL LIKE OLD TOILET PAPER, BUT I'M STILL ENOUGH TO--
CHAKK
OH MY LORD...
ZZKKT
"THIS IS INCREDIBLE..."

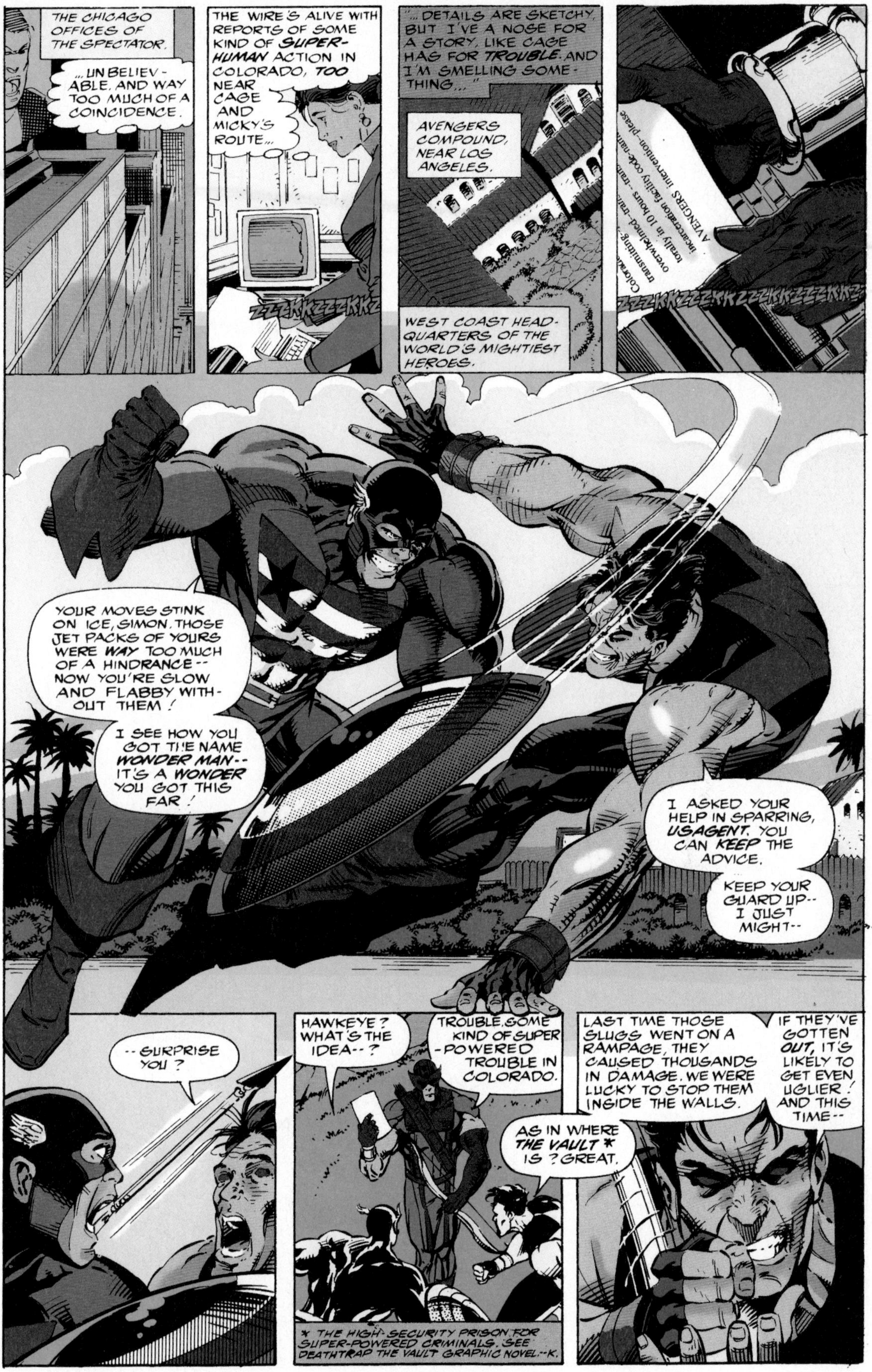

THE CHICAGO OFFICES OF THE SPECTATOR.
...UNBELIEVABLE, AND WAY TOO MUCH OF A COINCIDENCE.
THE WIRE'S ALIVE WITH REPORTS OF SOME KIND OF SUPER-HUMAN ACTION IN COLORADO, TOO NEAR CAGE AND MICKY'S ROUTE...
"...DETAILS ARE SKETCHY, BUT I'VE A NOSE FOR A STORY, LIKE CAGE HAS FOR TROUBLE, AND I'M SMELLING SOMETHING..."
AVENGERS COMPOUND, NEAR LOS ANGELES.
WEST COAST HEADQUARTERS OF THE WORLD'S MIGHTIEST HEROES.
AVENGERS intervention--please
incarceration facility code-
totally in 10 hours--
overwhelmed--
transmitting--
YOUR MOVES STINK ON ICE, SIMON. THOSE JET PACKS OF YOURS WERE WAY TOO MUCH OF A HINDRANCE-- NOW YOU'RE SLOW AND FLABBY WITHOUT THEM!
I SEE HOW YOU GOT THE NAME WONDER MAN-- IT'S A WONDER YOU GOT THIS FAR!
I ASKED YOUR HELP IN SPARRING, USAGENT. YOU CAN KEEP THE ADVICE.
KEEP YOUR GUARD UP-- I JUST MIGHT--
--SURPRISE YOU?
HAWKEYE? WHAT'S THE IDEA--?
TROUBLE. SOME KIND OF SUPER-POWERED TROUBLE IN COLORADO.
AS IN WHERE THE VAULT * IS? GREAT.
* THE HIGH-SECURITY PRISON FOR SUPER-POWERED CRIMINALS. SEE DEATHTRAP THE VAULT GRAPHIC NOVEL.--K.
LAST TIME THOSE SLUGS WENT ON A RAMPAGE, THEY CAUSED THOUSANDS IN DAMAGE. WE WERE LUCKY TO STOP THEM INSIDE THE WALLS.
IF THEY'VE GOTTEN OUT, IT'S LIKELY TO GET EVEN UGLIER! AND THIS TIME--

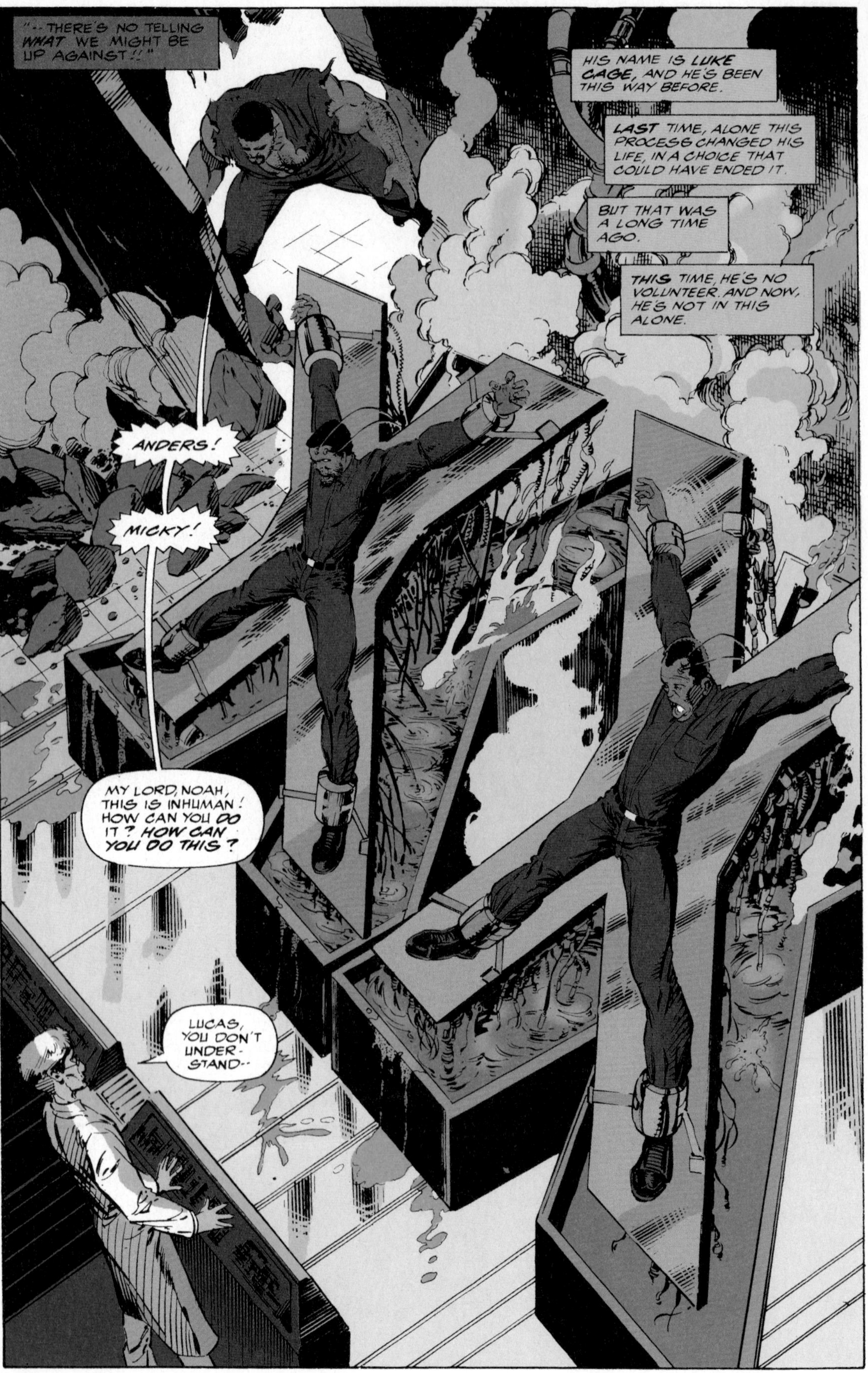
"--THERE'S NO TELLING WHAT WE MIGHT BE UP AGAINST!!"
HIS NAME IS LUKE CAGE, AND HE'S BEEN THIS WAY BEFORE.
LAST TIME, ALONE THIS PROCESS CHANGED HIS LIFE, IN A CHOICE THAT COULD HAVE ENDED IT.
BUT THAT WAS A LONG TIME AGO.
THIS TIME, HE'S NO VOLUNTEER. AND NOW, HE'S NOT IN THIS ALONE.
ANDERS!
MICKY!
MY LORD, NOAH, THIS IS INHUMAN! HOW CAN YOU DO IT? HOW CAN YOU DO THIS?
LUCAS, YOU DON'T UNDER-STAND--

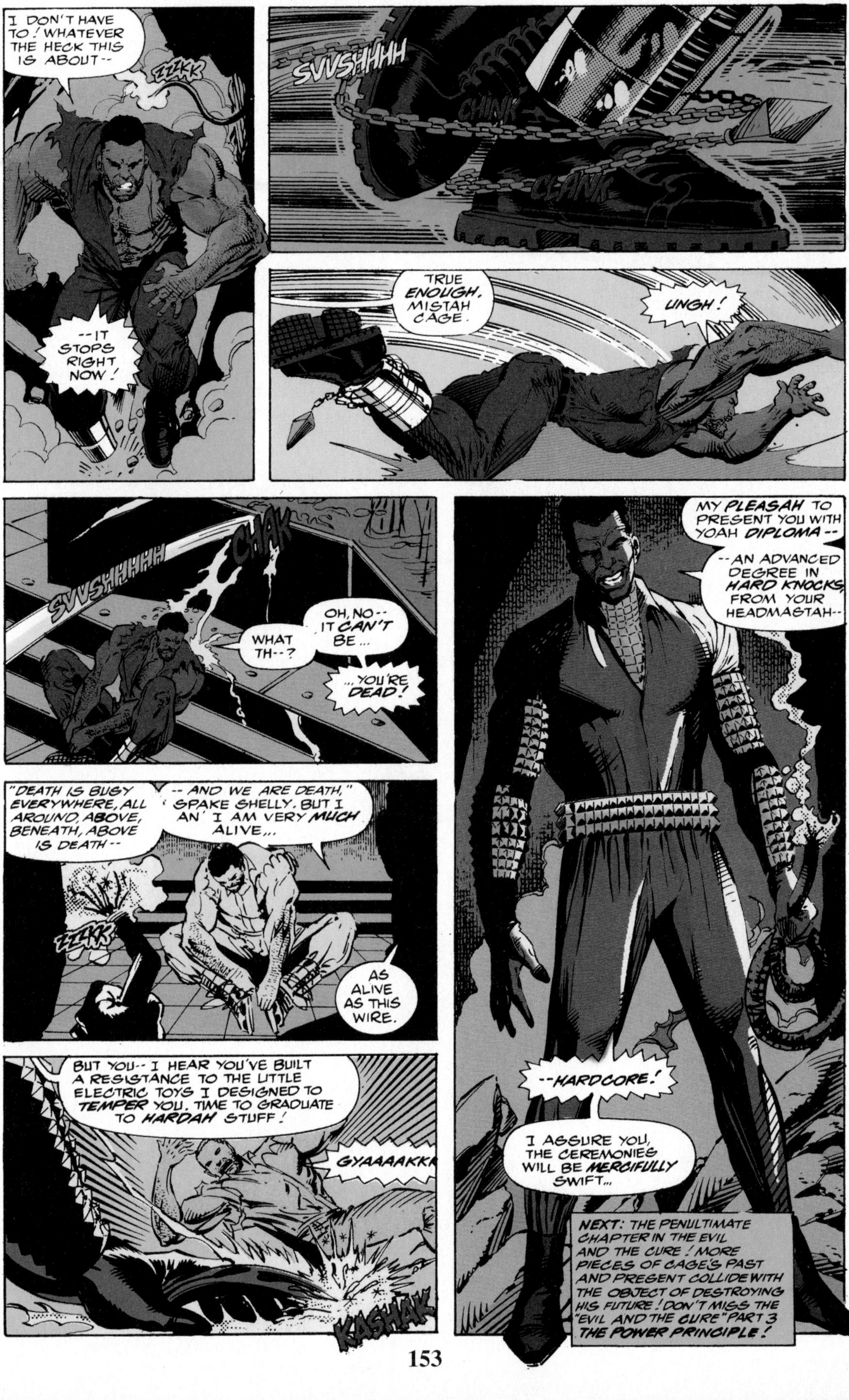

I DON'T HAVE TO! WHATEVER THE HECK THIS IS ABOUT--
ZZZKK
--IT STOPS RIGHT NOW!
SVVSHHHH
CHINK
CLANK
TRUE ENOUGH, MISTAH CAGE.
UNGH!
SVVSHHHH
CHAK
WHAT TH--?
OH, NO-- IT CAN'T BE...
...YOU'RE DEAD!
"DEATH IS BUSY EVERYWHERE, ALL AROUND, ABOVE, BENEATH, ABOVE IS DEATH--
-- AND WE ARE DEATH," SPAKE SHELLY. BUT I AN' I AM VERY MUCH ALIVE...
ZZZKK
AS ALIVE AS THIS WIRE.
BUT YOU-- I HEAR YOU'VE BUILT A RESISTANCE TO THE LITTLE ELECTRIC TOYS I DESIGNED TO TEMPER YOU. TIME TO GRADUATE TO HARDAH STUFF!
GYAAAAKK
KASHAK
MY PLEASAH TO PRESENT YOU WITH YOAH DIPLOMA--
--AN ADVANCED DEGREE IN HARD KNOCKS, FROM YOUR HEADMASTAH--
--HARDCORE!
I ASSURE YOU, THE CEREMONIES WILL BE MERCIFULLY SWIFT...
NEXT: THE PENULTIMATE CHAPTER IN THE EVIL AND THE CURE! MORE PIECES OF CAGE'S PAST AND PRESENT COLLIDE WITH THE OBJECT OF DESTROYING HIS FUTURE! DON'T MISS THE "EVIL AND THE CURE" PART 3 THE POWER PRINCIPLE!

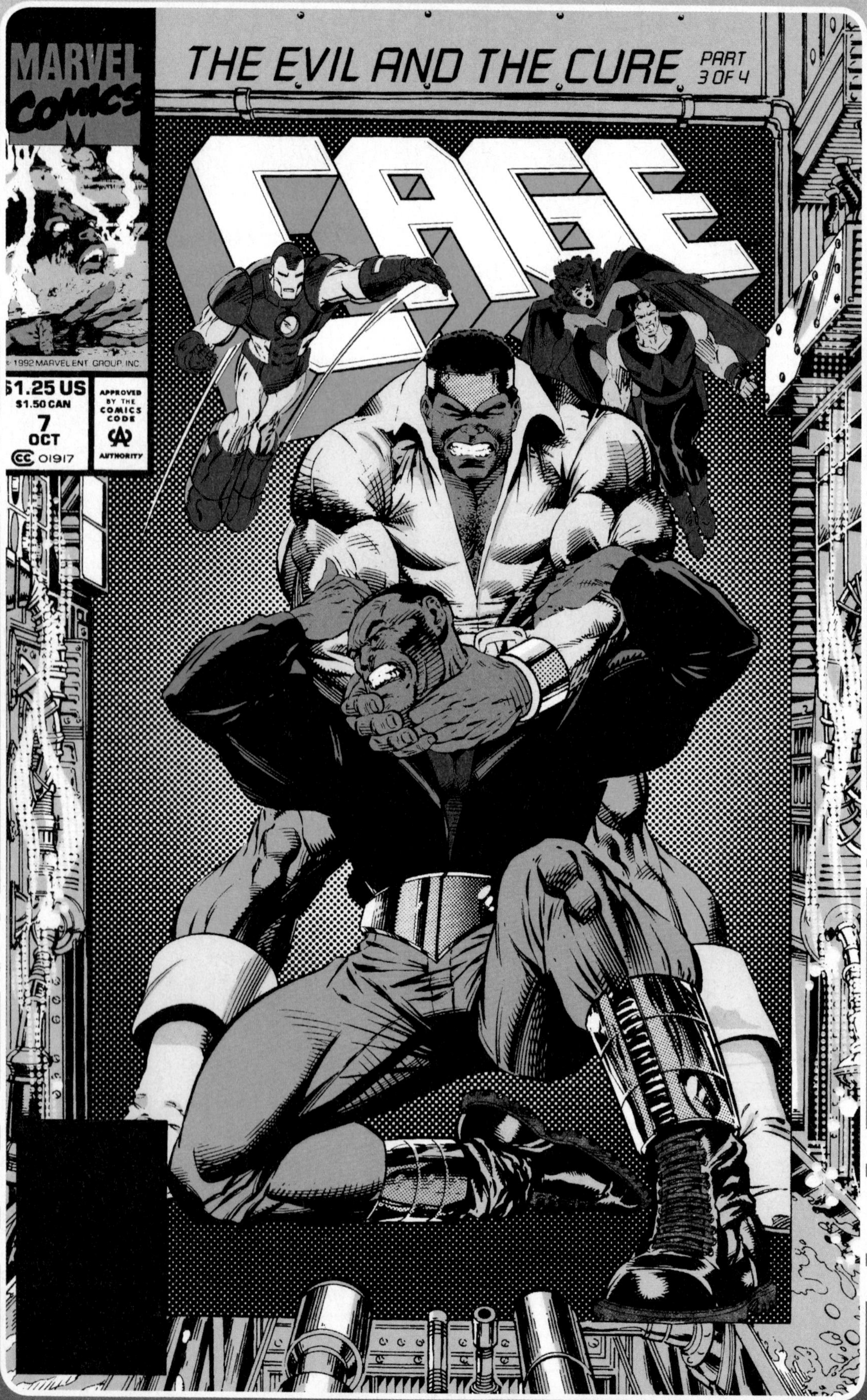
MARVEL COMICS
THE EVIL AND THE CURE
PART 3 OF 4
CAGE
© 1992 MARVEL ENT. GROUP, INC.
$1.25 US
$1.50 CAN
7
OCT
01917
APPROVED BY THE COMICS CODE AUTHORITY

EMPOWERED WITH STEEL-HARD SKIN AND SUPER-HUMAN STRENGTH BY A MEDICAL EXPERIMENT GONE AWRY, LUKE CAGE IS A HERO FOR HIRE. HE'S RUNNING FROM A VIOLENT PAST TO AN UNCERTAIN FUTURE. IN A WORLD WHERE RULES CHANGE DAILY, ONLY HE HAS THE POWER TO MAKE HIS OWN.

STAN LEE PRESENTS. . .

CAGE

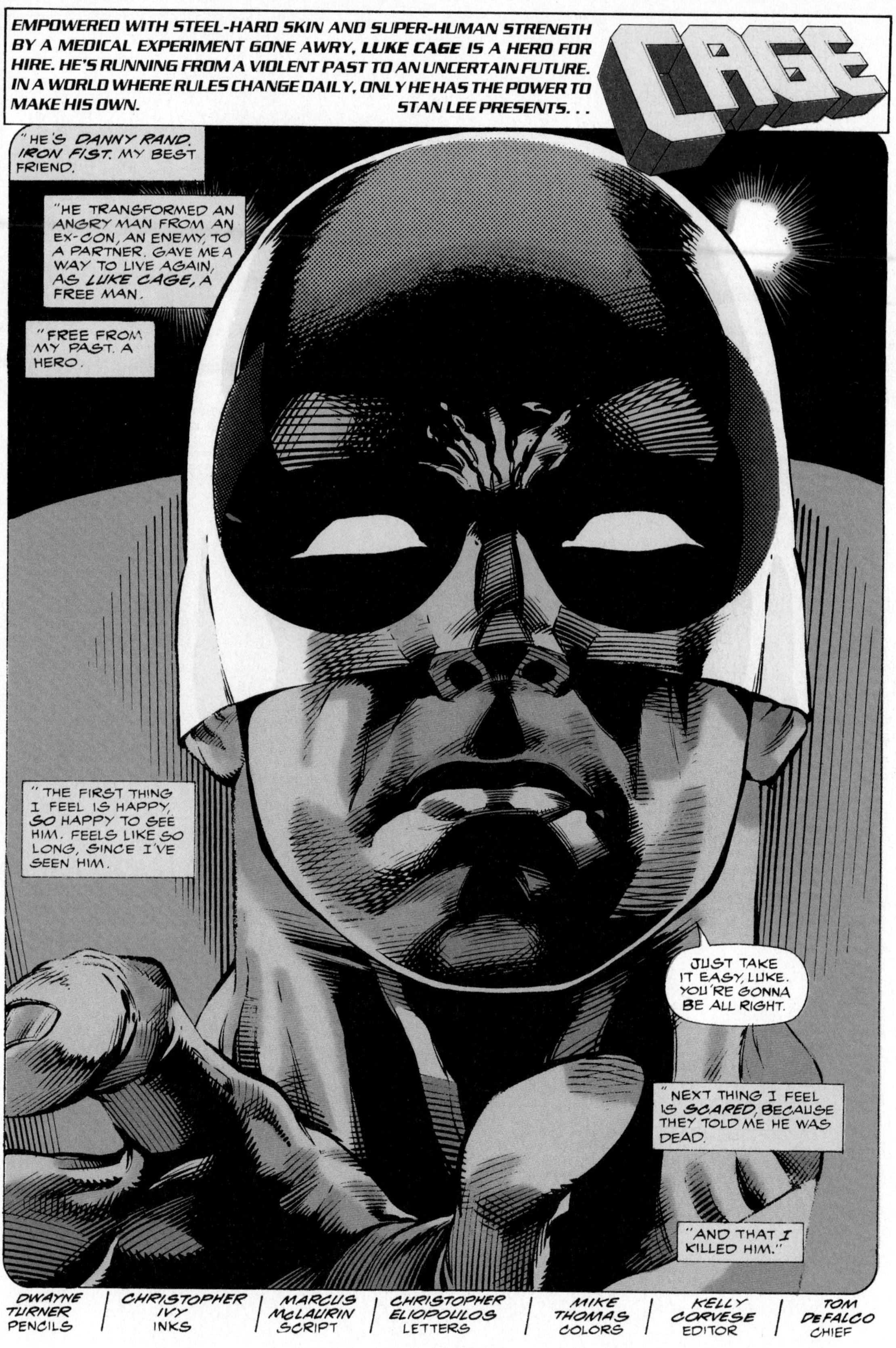

"HE'S DANNY RAND. IRON FIST. MY BEST FRIEND.
"HE TRANSFORMED AN ANGRY MAN FROM AN EX-CON, AN ENEMY, TO A PARTNER. GAVE ME A WAY TO LIVE AGAIN, AS LUKE CAGE, A FREE MAN.
"FREE FROM MY PAST. A HERO.
"THE FIRST THING I FEEL IS HAPPY, SO HAPPY TO SEE HIM. FEELS LIKE SO LONG, SINCE I'VE SEEN HIM.
JUST TAKE IT EASY, LUKE. YOU'RE GONNA BE ALL RIGHT.
"NEXT THING I FEEL IS SCARED, BECAUSE THEY TOLD ME HE WAS DEAD.
"AND THAT I KILLED HIM."

DWAYNE TURNER PENCILS | CHRISTOPHER IVY INKS | MARCUS McLAURIN SCRIPT | CHRISTOPHER ELIOPOULOS LETTERS | MIKE THOMAS COLORS | KELLY CORVESE EDITOR | TOM DeFALCO CHIEF

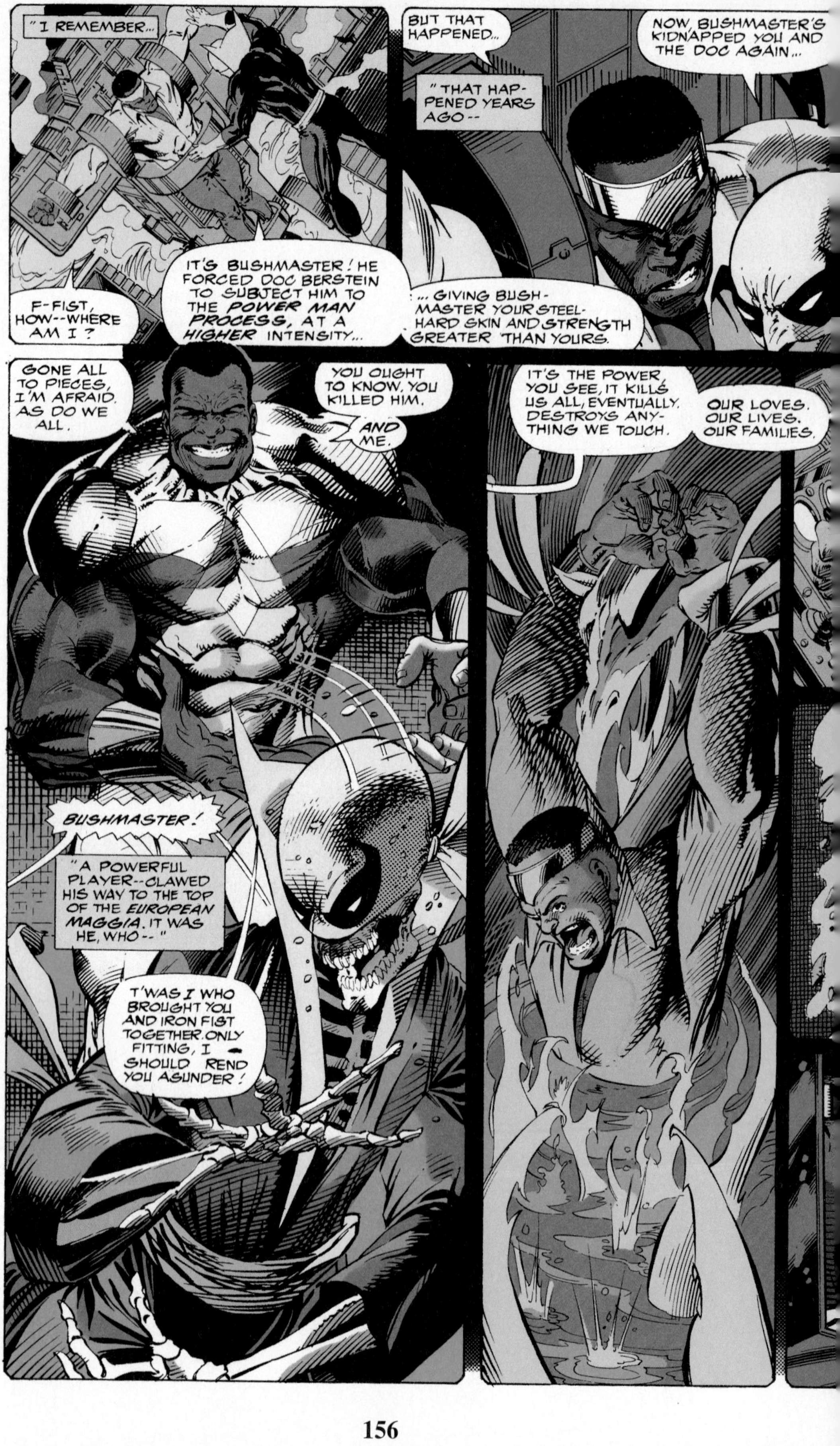
"I REMEMBER...
IT'S BUSHMASTER! HE FORCED DOC BERSTEIN TO SUBJECT HIM TO THE POWER MAN PROCESS, AT A HIGHER INTENSITY...
F-FIST, HOW--WHERE AM I?
BUT THAT HAPPENED...
"THAT HAPPENED YEARS AGO--
NOW, BUSHMASTER'S KIDNAPPED YOU AND THE DOC AGAIN...
...GIVING BUSHMASTER YOUR STEEL-HARD SKIN AND STRENGTH GREATER THAN YOURS.
GONE ALL TO PIECES, I'M AFRAID. AS DO WE ALL.
YOU OUGHT TO KNOW. YOU KILLED HIM.
AND ME.
BUSHMASTER!
"A POWERFUL PLAYER--CLAWED HIS WAY TO THE TOP OF THE EUROPEAN MAGGIA. IT WAS HE, WHO--"
T'WAS I WHO BROUGHT YOU AND IRON FIST TOGETHER. ONLY FITTING, I SHOULD REND YOU ASUNDER!
IT'S THE POWER, YOU SEE. IT KILLS US ALL, EVENTUALLY. DESTROYS ANYTHING WE TOUCH.
OUR LOVES. OUR LIVES. OUR FAMILIES.

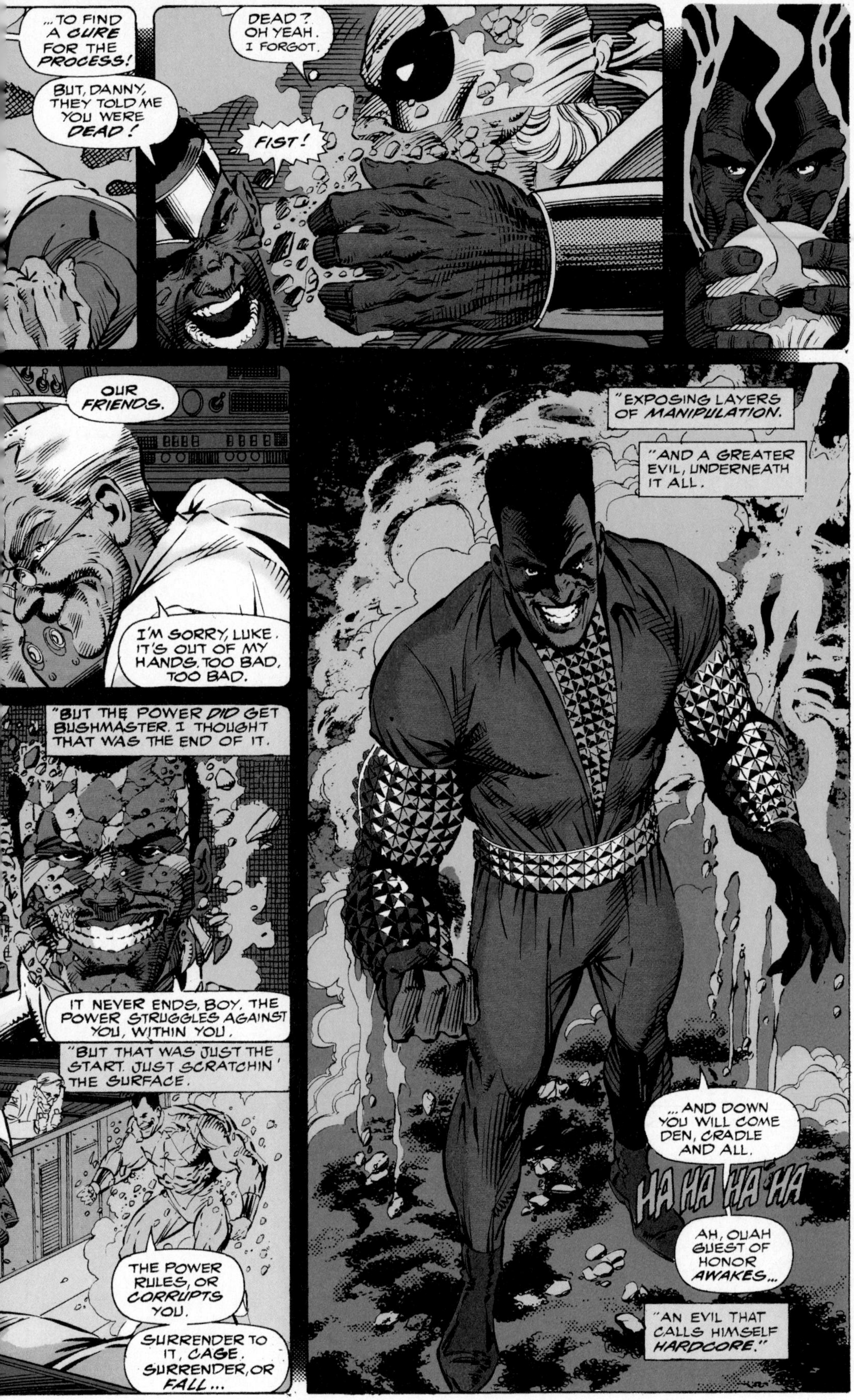
...TO FIND A CURE FOR THE PROCESS!
BUT, DANNY, THEY TOLD ME YOU WERE DEAD!
DEAD? OH YEAH. I FORGOT.
FIST!
OUR FRIENDS.
I'M SORRY, LUKE. IT'S OUT OF MY HANDS. TOO BAD, TOO BAD.
"BUT THE POWER DID GET BUSHMASTER. I THOUGHT THAT WAS THE END OF IT.
IT NEVER ENDS, BOY. THE POWER STRUGGLES AGAINST YOU, WITHIN YOU.
"BUT THAT WAS JUST THE START. JUST SCRATCHIN' THE SURFACE.
THE POWER RULES, OR CORRUPTS YOU.
SURRENDER TO IT, CAGE. SURRENDER, OR FALL...
"EXPOSING LAYERS OF MANIPULATION.
"AND A GREATER EVIL, UNDERNEATH IT ALL.
...AND DOWN YOU WILL COME DEN, CRADLE AND ALL.
HA HA HA HA
AH, OUAH GUEST OF HONOR AWAKES...
"AN EVIL THAT CALLS HIMSELF HARDCORE."

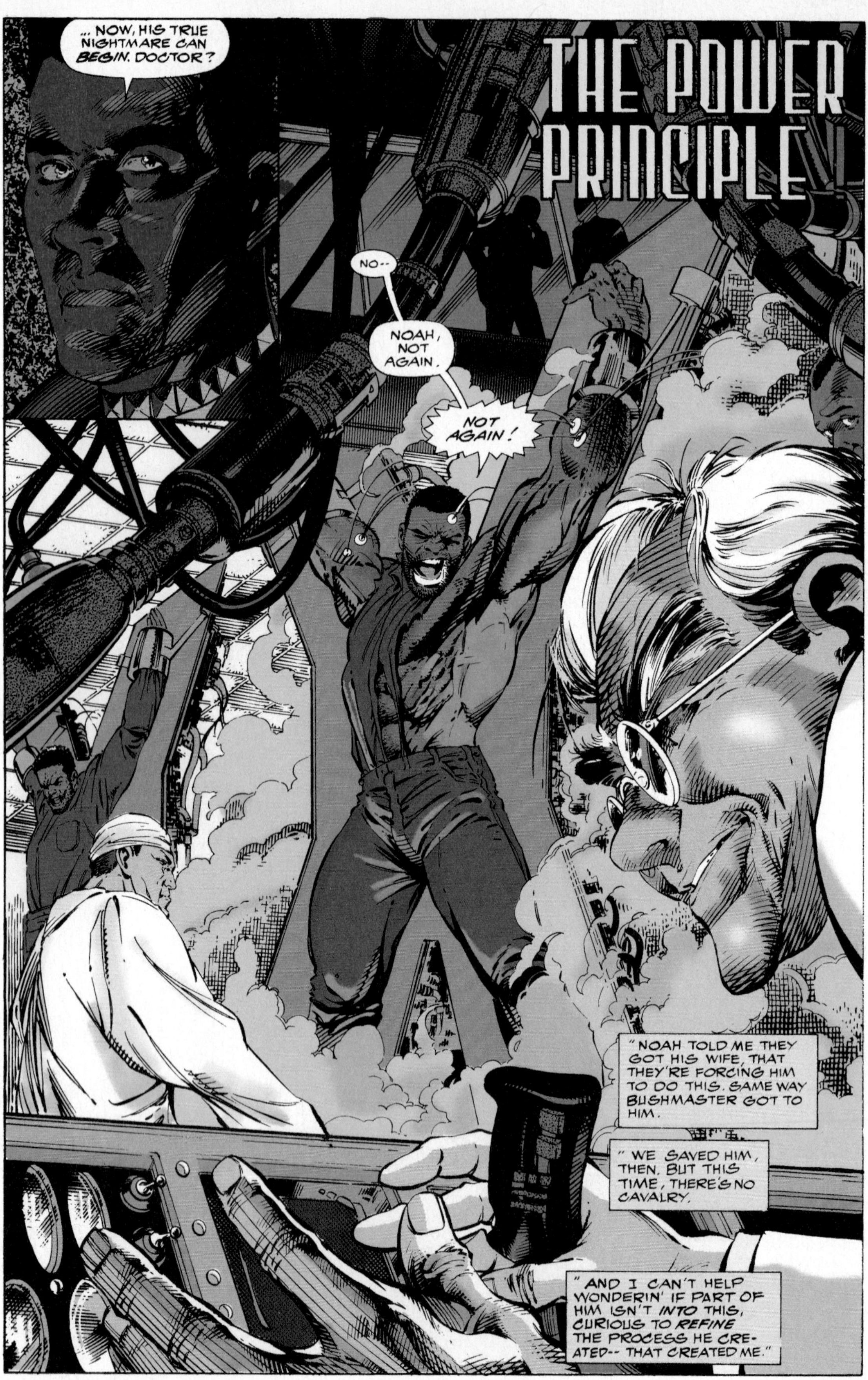

... NOW, HIS TRUE NIGHTMARE CAN BEGIN. DOCTOR?
THE POWER PRINCIPLE!
NO--
NOAH, NOT AGAIN.
NOT AGAIN!
"NOAH TOLD ME THEY GOT HIS WIFE, THAT THEY'RE FORCING HIM TO DO THIS. SAME WAY BUSHMASTER GOT TO HIM.
"WE SAVED HIM, THEN. BUT THIS TIME, THERE'S NO CAVALRY.
"AND I CAN'T HELP WONDERIN' IF PART OF HIM ISN'T INTO THIS, CURIOUS TO REFINE THE PROCESS HE CREATED-- THAT CREATED ME."

"NO MATTER WHO HAS TO DIE."

HELPLESSNESS BECOMES YOU, MISTAH CAGE. BUT, DON'T WORRY. IT WILL BE ALL OVER SOON.

"MEN HAVE DIED AS GUINEA PIGS ALREADY, HERE IN THIS BOGUS ROCKY MOUNTAIN PRISON. TILL I BROUGHT IT ALL DOWN.

"BUT NOW, TRAPPED LIKE THIS BETWEEN MY... MY FRIEND, MICKY HAMILTON, AND RITCHIE ANDERS, THE MAN I WAS SUPPOSED TO FIND--

"-- I CAN'T SHAKE THE FEELIN' THAT MORE'LL DIE BEHIND THIS.

"AND, AIN'T A THING I CAN DO ABOUT IT... "

YOU SEE OUAH EXAMINATION OF YOU HAS GIVEN US THE KEY TO CONVERTING DR. BERSTEIN'S PROCESS DOWN TO A SIMPLE VIRUS-LIKE FORM.

HIGHLY INFECTIOUS, AND TRANSFORMATIVE ON ORGANIC FORMS, SUCH AS YOUR LEATHER JACKET.

MISSED IT, HAVE YOU? IT'S PROVEN AN INTERESTING TROPHY-- BUT A MORE VALUABLE VISUAL AID.

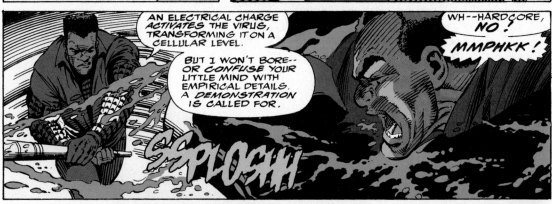

AN ELECTRICAL CHARGE ACTIVATES THE VIRUS, TRANSFORMING IT ON A CELLULAR LEVEL.

BUT I WON'T BORE-- OR CONFUSE YOUR LITTLE MIND WITH EMPIRICAL DETAILS. A DEMONSTRATION IS CALLED FOR.

WH--HARDCORE, NO!

MMPHKK!

SSPLOSHH

RELAX, HAMILTON, THE VIRUS HAS BEEN CLEANSED FROM THE JACKET, EARLIER.

OUR SUPPLY IS TOO LIMITED TO ALLOW SUCH CASUAL WASTE.

BUT IN THE SERVICE OF EDUCATION, SACRIFICES ARE MADE.

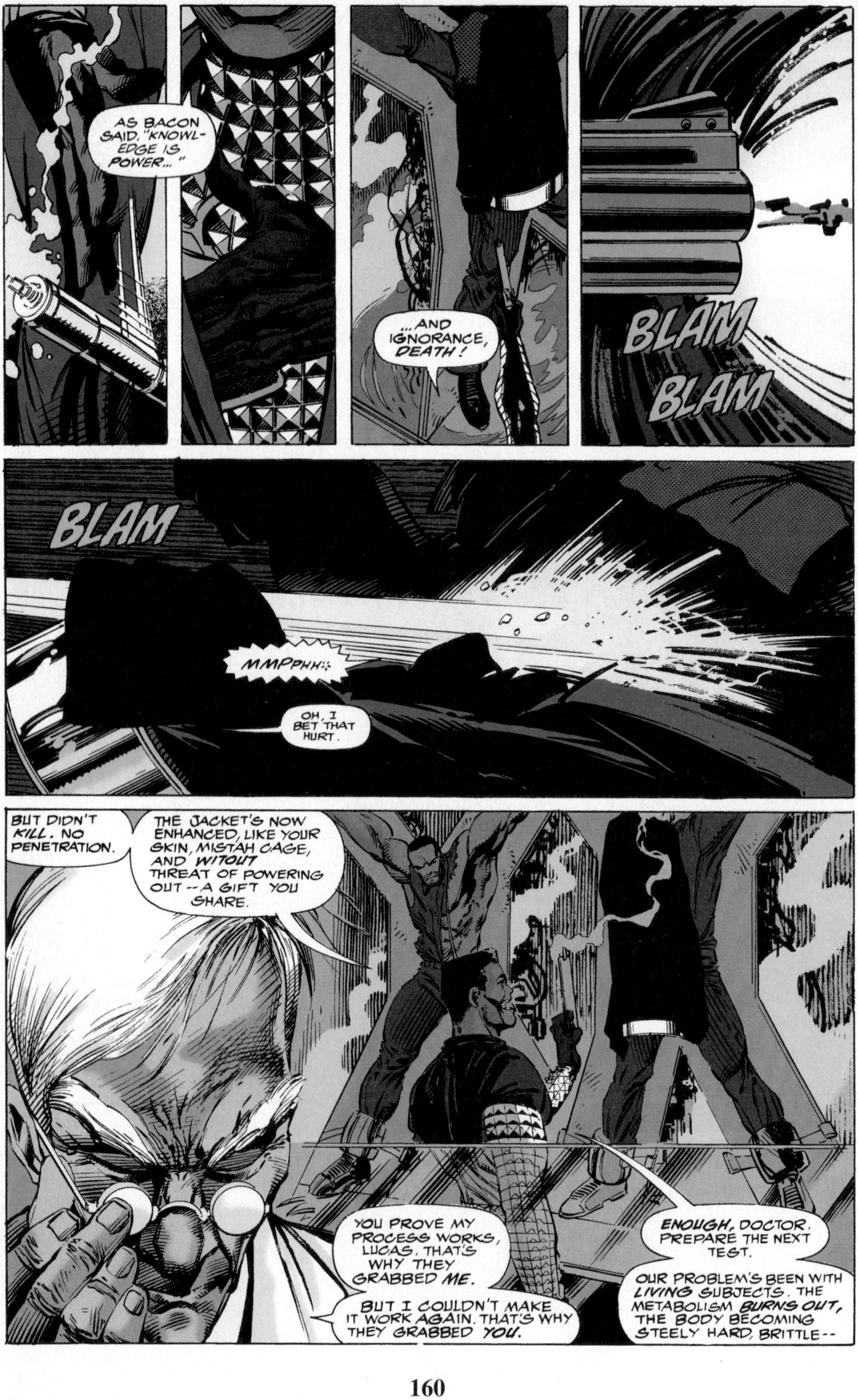

AS BACON SAID, "KNOWLEDGE IS POWER..."
...AND IGNORANCE, DEATH!
BLAM
BLAM
BLAM
MMPPHH!
OH, I BET THAT HURT.
BUT DIDN'T KILL. NO PENETRATION.
THE JACKET'S NOW ENHANCED, LIKE YOUR SKIN, MISTAH CAGE, AND WITOUT THREAT OF POWERING OUT--A GIFT YOU SHARE.
YOU PROVE MY PROCESS WORKS, LUCAS. THAT'S WHY THEY GRABBED ME.
BUT I COULDN'T MAKE IT WORK AGAIN. THAT'S WHY THEY GRABBED YOU.
ENOUGH, DOCTOR. PREPARE THE NEXT TEST.
OUR PROBLEM'S BEEN WITH LIVING SUBJECTS. THE METABOLISM BURNS OUT, THE BODY BECOMING STEELY HARD, BRITTLE--

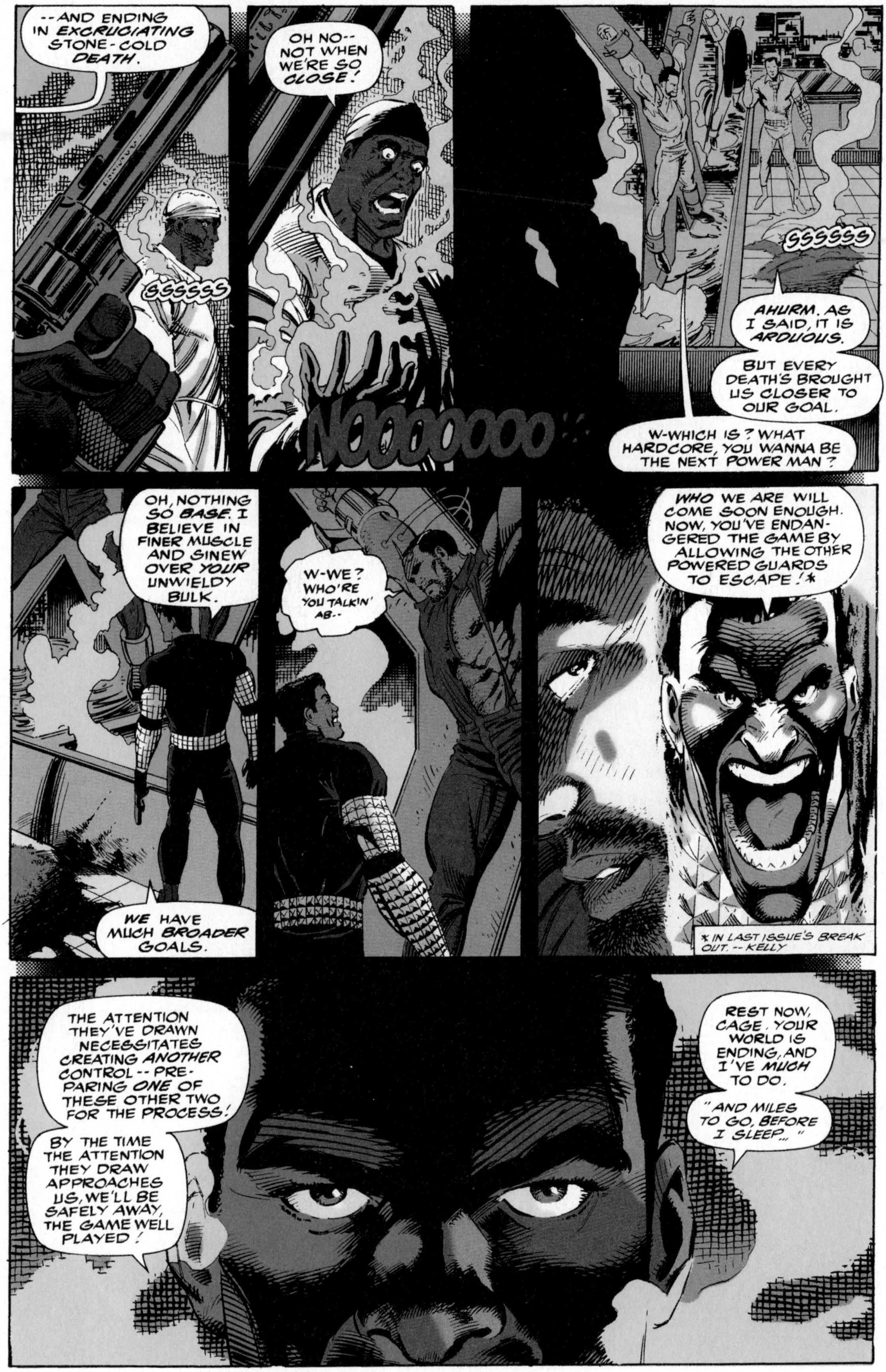
--AND ENDING IN EXCRUCIATING STONE-COLD DEATH.
SSSSSS
OH NO-- NOT WHEN WE'RE SO CLOSE!
NOOOOOOO!!
SSSSSS
AHURM. AS I SAID, IT IS ARDUOUS.
BUT EVERY DEATH'S BROUGHT US CLOSER TO OUR GOAL.
W-WHICH IS? WHAT HARDCORE, YOU WANNA BE THE NEXT POWER MAN?
OH, NOTHING SO BASE. I BELIEVE IN FINER MUSCLE AND SINEW OVER YOUR UNWIELDY BULK.
WE HAVE MUCH BROADER GOALS.
W-WE? WHO'RE YOU TALKIN' AB--
WHO WE ARE WILL COME SOON ENOUGH. NOW, YOU'VE ENDANGERED THE GAME BY ALLOWING THE OTHER POWERED GUARDS TO ESCAPE!*
*IN LAST ISSUE'S BREAK OUT. --KELLY
THE ATTENTION THEY'VE DRAWN NECESSITATES CREATING ANOTHER CONTROL--PREPARING ONE OF THESE OTHER TWO FOR THE PROCESS!
BY THE TIME THE ATTENTION THEY DRAW APPROACHES US, WE'LL BE SAFELY AWAY, THE GAME WELL PLAYED!
REST NOW, CAGE. YOUR WORLD IS ENDING, AND I'VE MUCH TO DO.
"AND MILES TO GO, BEFORE I SLEEP..."

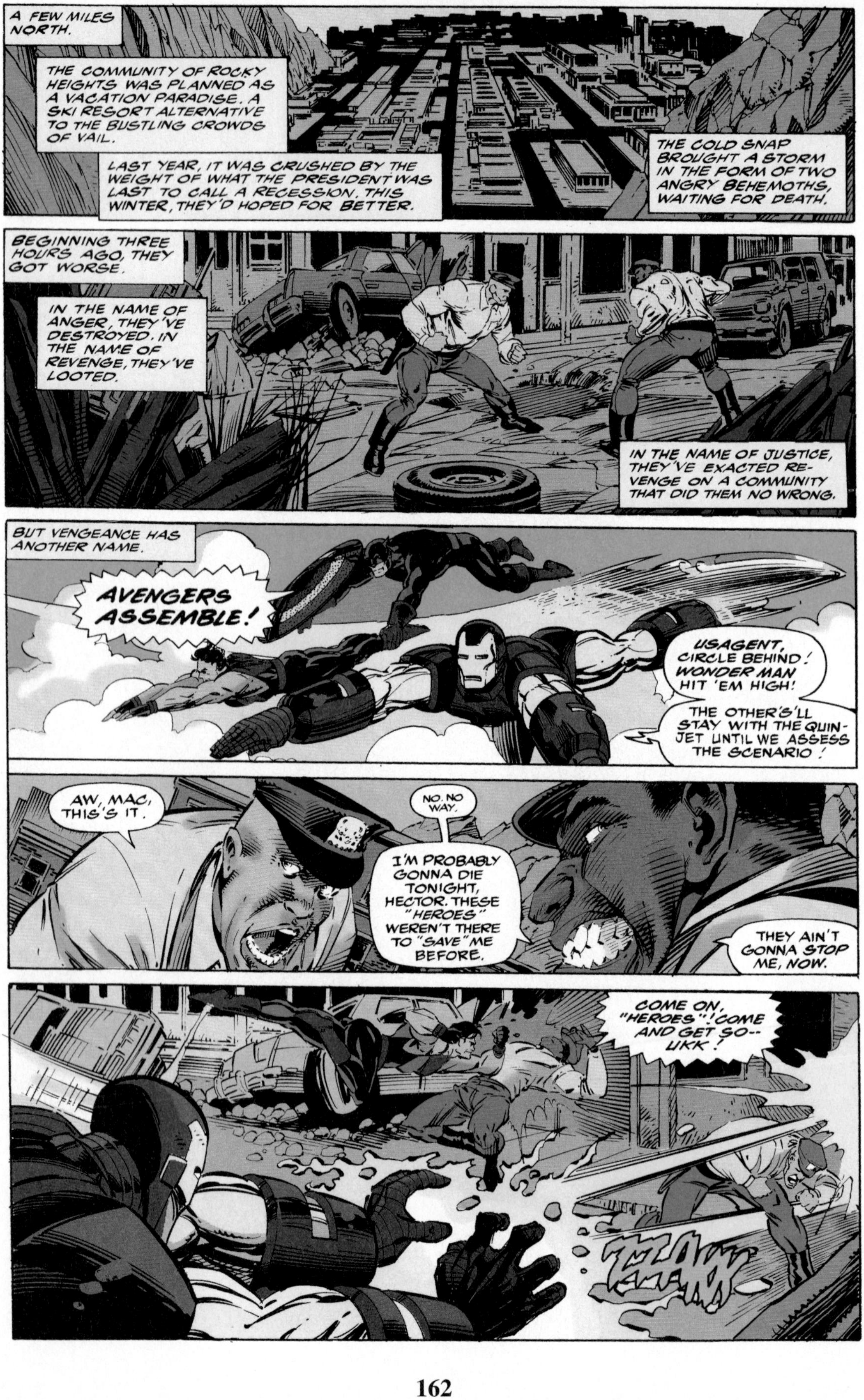
A FEW MILES NORTH.
THE COMMUNITY OF ROCKY HEIGHTS WAS PLANNED AS A VACATION PARADISE. A SKI RESORT ALTERNATIVE TO THE BUSTLING CROWDS OF VAIL.
LAST YEAR, IT WAS CRUSHED BY THE WEIGHT OF WHAT THE PRESIDENT WAS LAST TO CALL A RECESSION. THIS WINTER, THEY'D HOPED FOR BETTER.
THE COLD SNAP BROUGHT A STORM IN THE FORM OF TWO ANGRY BEHEMOTHS, WAITING FOR DEATH.
BEGINNING THREE HOURS AGO, THEY GOT WORSE.
IN THE NAME OF ANGER, THEY'VE DESTROYED. IN THE NAME OF REVENGE, THEY'VE LOOTED.
IN THE NAME OF JUSTICE, THEY'VE EXACTED REVENGE ON A COMMUNITY THAT DID THEM NO WRONG.
BUT VENGEANCE HAS ANOTHER NAME.
AVENGERS ASSEMBLE!
USAGENT, CIRCLE BEHIND! WONDER MAN HIT 'EM HIGH!
THE OTHER'S'LL STAY WITH THE QUINJET UNTIL WE ASSESS THE SCENARIO!
AW, MAC, THIS'S IT.
NO. NO WAY.
I'M PROBABLY GONNA DIE TONIGHT, HECTOR. THESE "HEROES" WEREN'T THERE TO "SAVE" ME BEFORE.
THEY AIN'T GONNA STOP ME, NOW.
COME ON, "HEROES"! COME AND GET SO-- UKK!

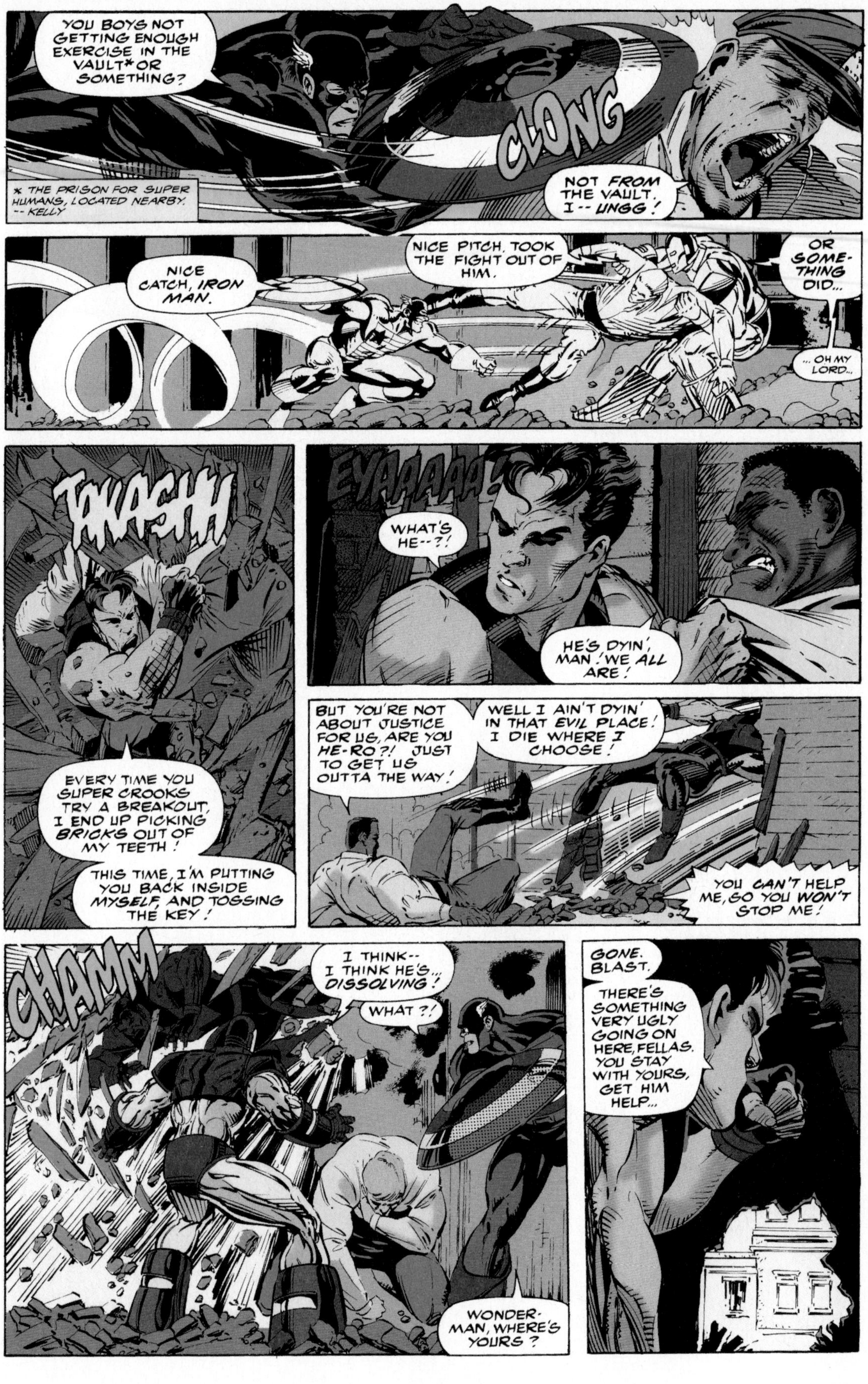
YOU BOYS NOT GETTING ENOUGH EXERCISE IN THE VAULT* OR SOMETHING?
CLONG
NOT FROM THE VAULT. I -- UNGG!
* THE PRISON FOR SUPER HUMANS, LOCATED NEARBY. -- KELLY
NICE CATCH, IRON MAN.
NICE PITCH. TOOK THE FIGHT OUT OF HIM.
OR SOMETHING DID...
...OH MY LORD...
TAKASHH
EVERY TIME YOU SUPER CROOKS TRY A BREAKOUT, I END UP PICKING BRICKS OUT OF MY TEETH!
THIS TIME, I'M PUTTING YOU BACK INSIDE MYSELF, AND TOSSING THE KEY!
EYAAAAAA!
WHAT'S HE--?!
HE'S DYIN', MAN! WE ALL ARE!
BUT YOU'RE NOT ABOUT JUSTICE FOR US, ARE YOU HE-RO?! JUST TO GET US OUTTA THE WAY!
WELL I AIN'T DYIN' IN THAT EVIL PLACE! I DIE WHERE I CHOOSE!
YOU CAN'T HELP ME, SO YOU WON'T STOP ME!
CHAMM
I THINK-- I THINK HE'S... DISSOLVING!
WHAT?!
WONDER-MAN, WHERE'S YOURS?
GONE. BLAST.
THERE'S SOMETHING VERY UGLY GOING ON HERE, FELLAS. YOU STAY WITH YOURS, GET HIM HELP...

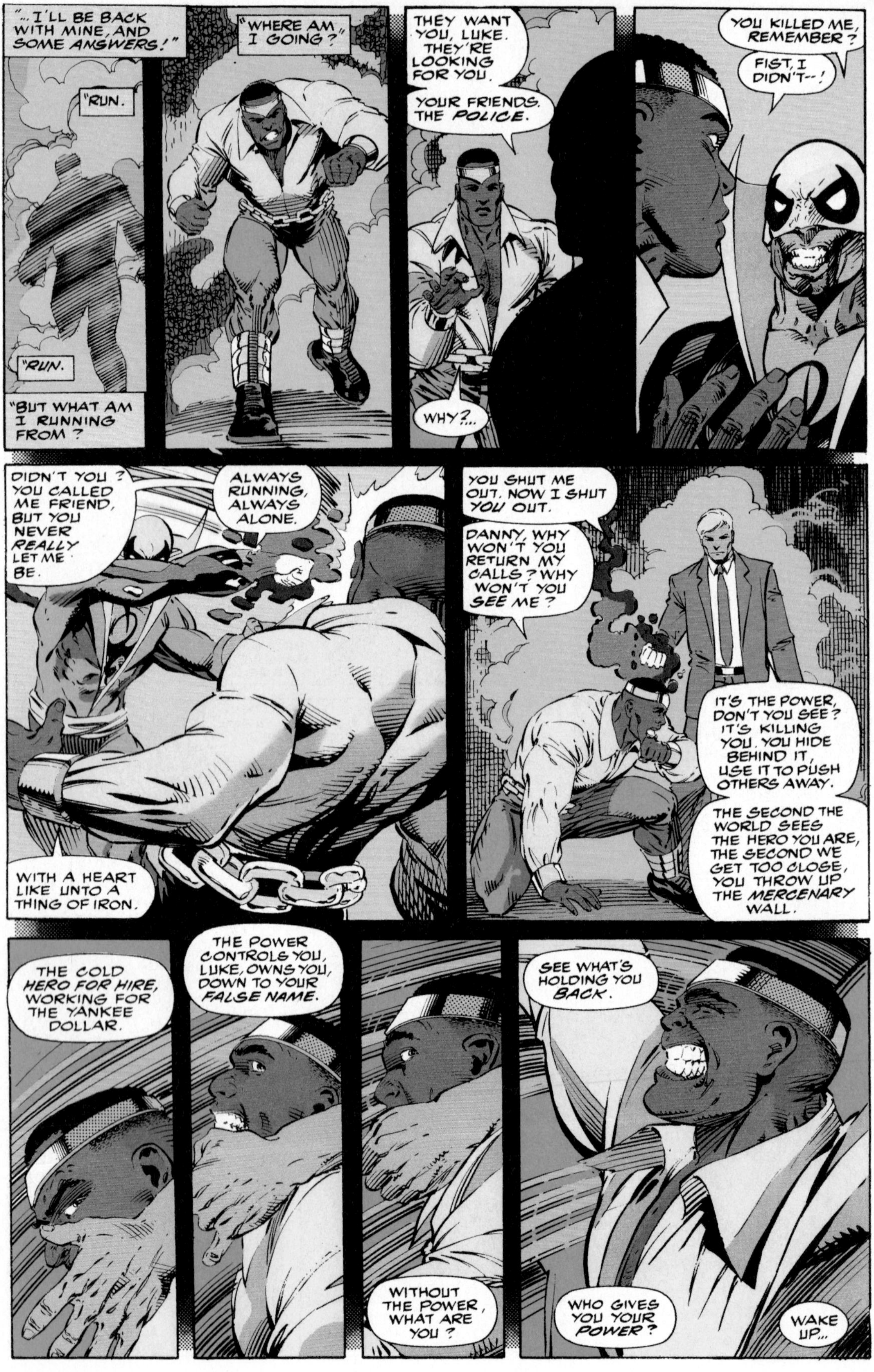
"...I'LL BE BACK WITH MINE, AND SOME ANSWERS!"
"RUN.
"RUN.
"BUT WHAT AM I RUNNING FROM?
"WHERE AM I GOING?"
THEY WANT YOU, LUKE. THEY'RE LOOKING FOR YOU.
YOUR FRIENDS. THE POLICE.
WHY?...
YOU KILLED ME, REMEMBER?
FIST, I DIDN'T--!
DIDN'T YOU? YOU CALLED ME FRIEND, BUT YOU NEVER REALLY LET ME BE.
ALWAYS RUNNING, ALWAYS ALONE.
WITH A HEART LIKE UNTO A THING OF IRON.
YOU SHUT ME OUT. NOW I SHUT YOU OUT.
DANNY, WHY WON'T YOU RETURN MY CALLS? WHY WON'T YOU SEE ME?
IT'S THE POWER, DON'T YOU SEE? IT'S KILLING YOU. YOU HIDE BEHIND IT, USE IT TO PUSH OTHERS AWAY.
THE SECOND THE WORLD SEES THE HERO YOU ARE, THE SECOND WE GET TOO CLOSE, YOU THROW UP THE MERCENARY WALL.
THE COLD HERO FOR HIRE, WORKING FOR THE YANKEE DOLLAR.
THE POWER CONTROLS YOU, LUKE, OWNS YOU, DOWN TO YOUR FALSE NAME.
WITHOUT THE POWER, WHAT ARE YOU?
SEE WHAT'S HOLDING YOU BACK.
WHO GIVES YOU YOUR POWER?
WAKE UP...

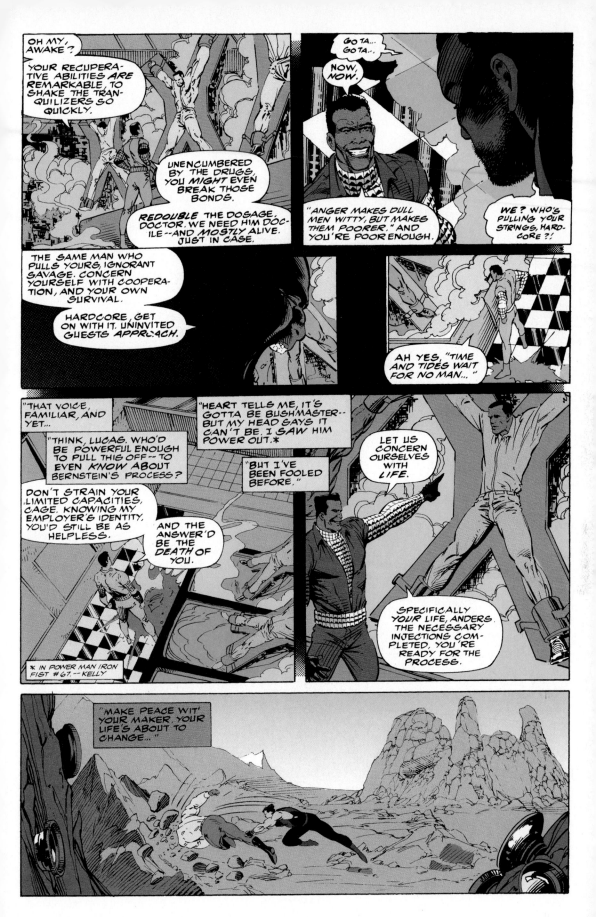

OH MY, AWAKE? YOUR RECUPERATIVE ABILITIES ARE REMARKABLE, TO SHAKE THE TRANQUILIZERS SO QUICKLY.

UNENCUMBERED BY THE DRUGS, YOU MIGHT EVEN BREAK THOSE BONDS.

REDOUBLE THE DOSAGE, DOCTOR. WE NEED HIM DOCILE--AND MOSTLY ALIVE. JUST IN CASE.

GOTA... GOTA...

NOW, NOW.

"ANGER MAKES DULL MEN WITTY, BUT MAKES THEM POORER." AND YOU'RE POOR ENOUGH.

WE? WHO'S PULLING YOUR STRINGS, HARDCORE?!

THE SAME MAN WHO PULLS YOURS, IGNORANT SAVAGE. CONCERN YOURSELF WITH COOPERATION, AND YOUR OWN SURVIVAL.

HARDCORE, GET ON WITH IT. UNINVITED GUESTS APPROACH.

AH YES, "TIME AND TIDES WAIT FOR NO MAN..."

"THAT VOICE, FAMILIAR, AND YET...

"THINK, LUCAS. WHO'D BE POWERFUL ENOUGH TO PULL THIS OFF -- TO EVEN KNOW ABOUT BERNSTEIN'S PROCESS?

"HEART TELLS ME, IT'S GOTTA BE BUSHMASTER-- BUT MY HEAD SAYS IT CAN'T BE. I SAW HIM POWER OUT.*

"BUT I'VE BEEN FOOLED BEFORE."

DON'T STRAIN YOUR LIMITED CAPACITIES, CAGE. KNOWING MY EMPLOYER'S IDENTITY, YOU'D STILL BE AS HELPLESS.

AND THE ANSWER'D BE THE DEATH OF YOU.

LET US CONCERN OURSELVES WITH LIFE.

SPECIFICALLY YOUR LIFE, ANDERS. THE NECESSARY INJECTIONS COMPLETED, YOU'RE READY FOR THE PROCESS.

* IN POWER MAN IRON FIST #67.--KELLY

"MAKE PEACE WIT' YOUR MAKER, YOUR LIFE'S ABOUT TO CHANGE..."

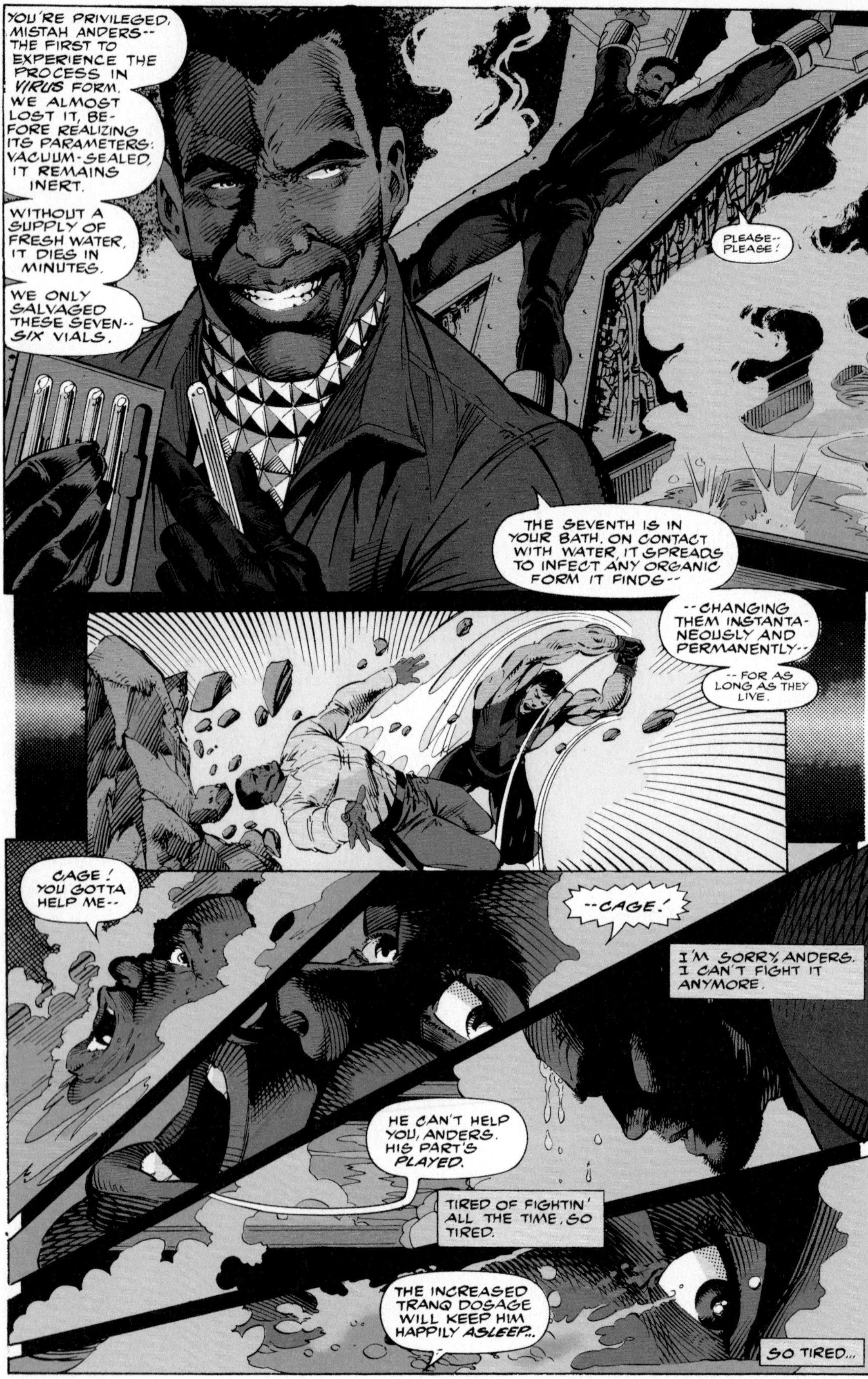
YOU'RE PRIVILEGED, MISTAH ANDERS-- THE FIRST TO EXPERIENCE THE PROCESS IN VIRUS FORM.
WE ALMOST LOST IT, BEFORE REALIZING ITS PARAMETERS: VACUUM-SEALED, IT REMAINS INERT.
WITHOUT A SUPPLY OF FRESH WATER, IT DIES IN MINUTES.
WE ONLY SALVAGED THESE SEVEN-- SIX VIALS.
PLEASE-- PLEASE!
THE SEVENTH IS IN YOUR BATH. ON CONTACT WITH WATER, IT SPREADS TO INFECT ANY ORGANIC FORM IT FINDS--
--CHANGING THEM INSTANTANEOUSLY AND PERMANENTLY--
--FOR AS LONG AS THEY LIVE.
CAGE! YOU GOTTA HELP ME--
--CAGE!
I'M SORRY, ANDERS. I CAN'T FIGHT IT ANYMORE.
HE CAN'T HELP YOU, ANDERS. HIS PART'S PLAYED.
TIRED OF FIGHTIN' ALL THE TIME. SO TIRED.
THE INCREASED TRANQ DOSAGE WILL KEEP HIM HAPPILY ASLEEP...
SO TIRED...

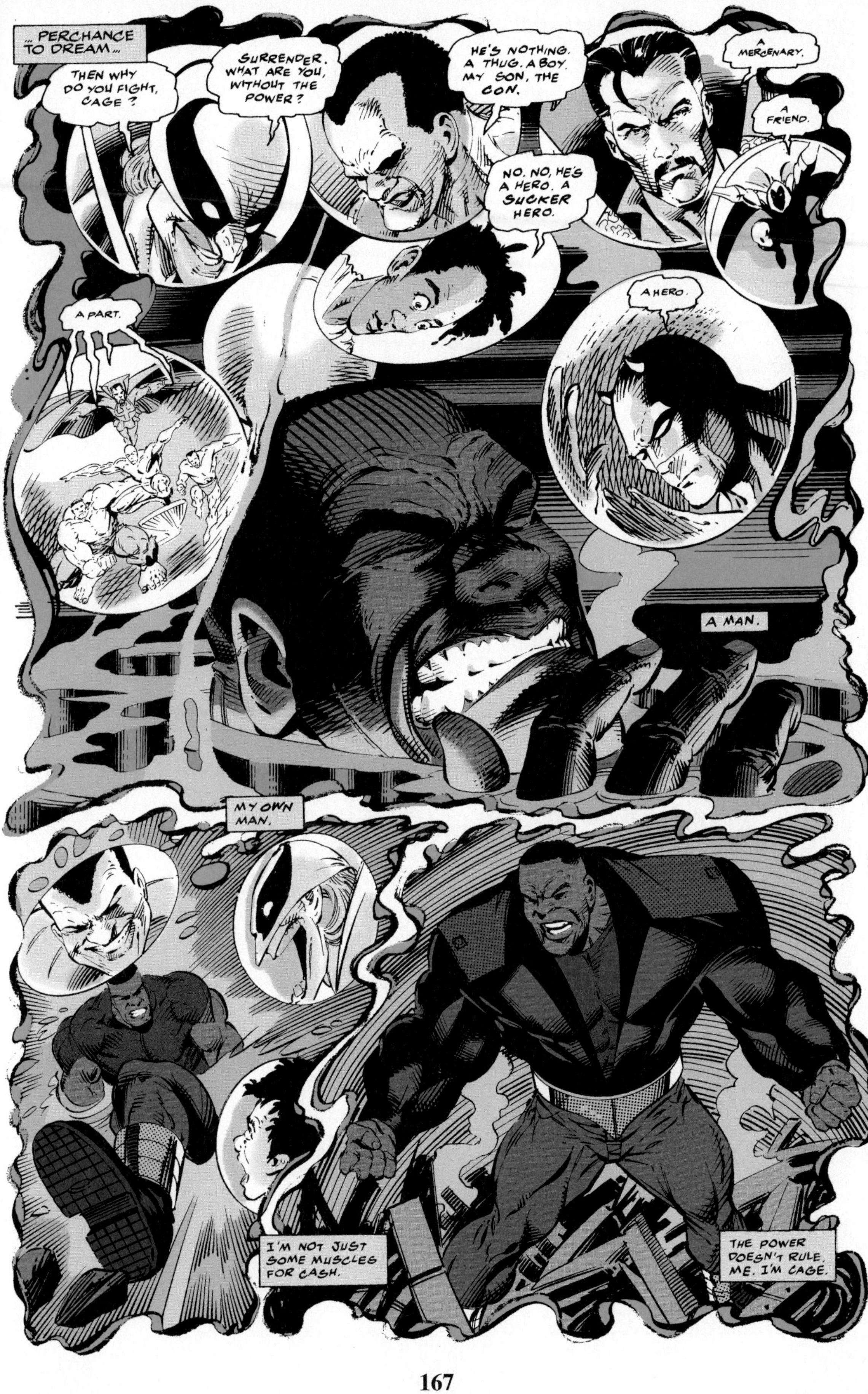
...PERCHANCE TO DREAM...
THEN WHY DO YOU FIGHT, CAGE?
SURRENDER. WHAT ARE YOU, WITHOUT THE POWER?
HE'S NOTHING. A THUG. A BOY. MY SON, THE CON.
NO. NO, HE'S A HERO. A SUCKER HERO.
A MERCENARY.
A FRIEND.
A PART.
A HERO.
A MAN.
MY OWN MAN.
I'M NOT JUST SOME MUSCLES FOR CASH.
THE POWER DOESN'T RULE ME. I'M CAGE.

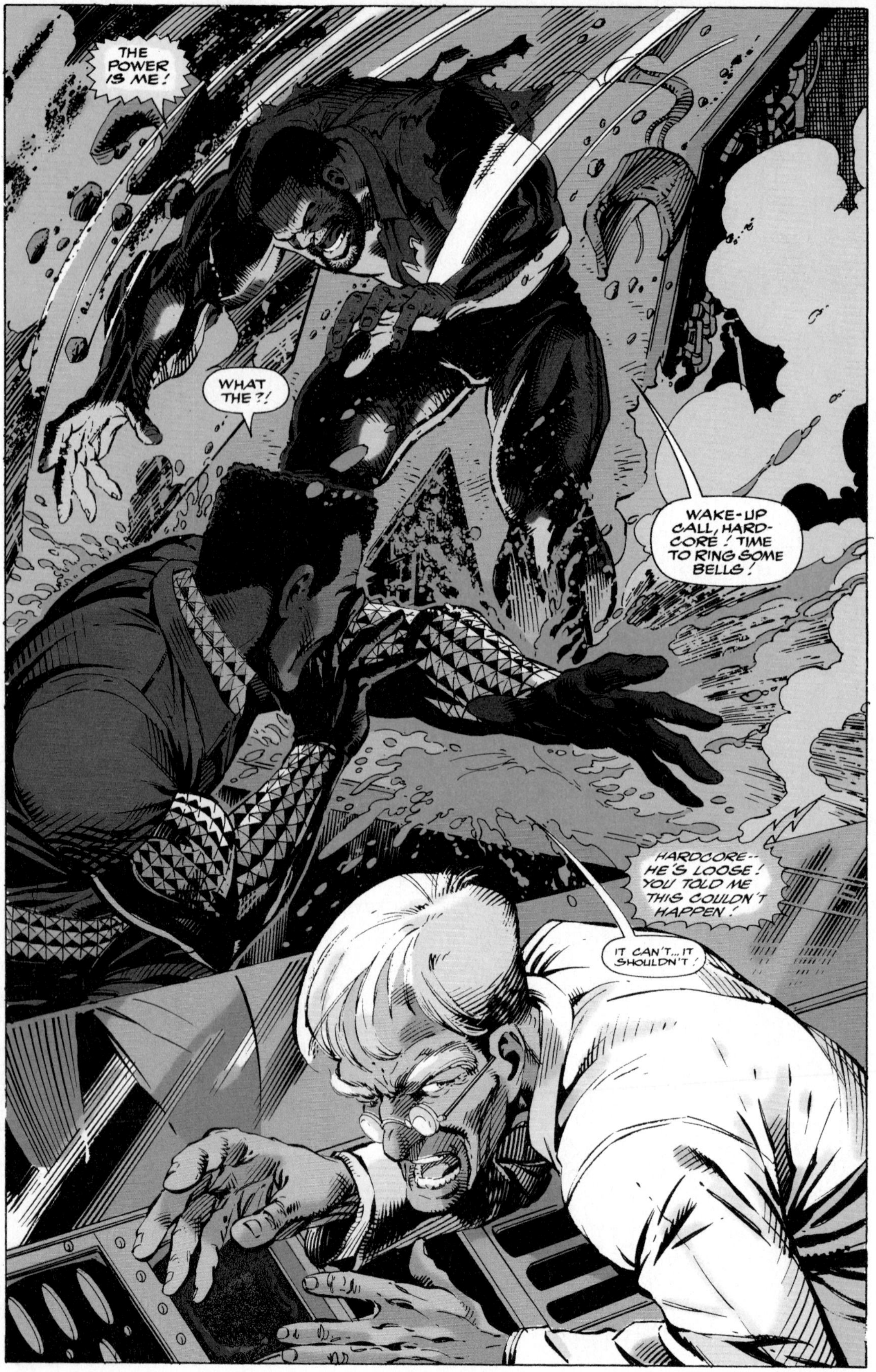
THE POWER IS ME!
WHAT THE?!
WAKE-UP CALL, HARD-CORE! TIME TO RING SOME BELLS!
HARDCORE--HE'S LOOSE! YOU TOLD ME THIS COULDN'T HAPPEN!
IT CAN'T... IT SHOULDN'T!

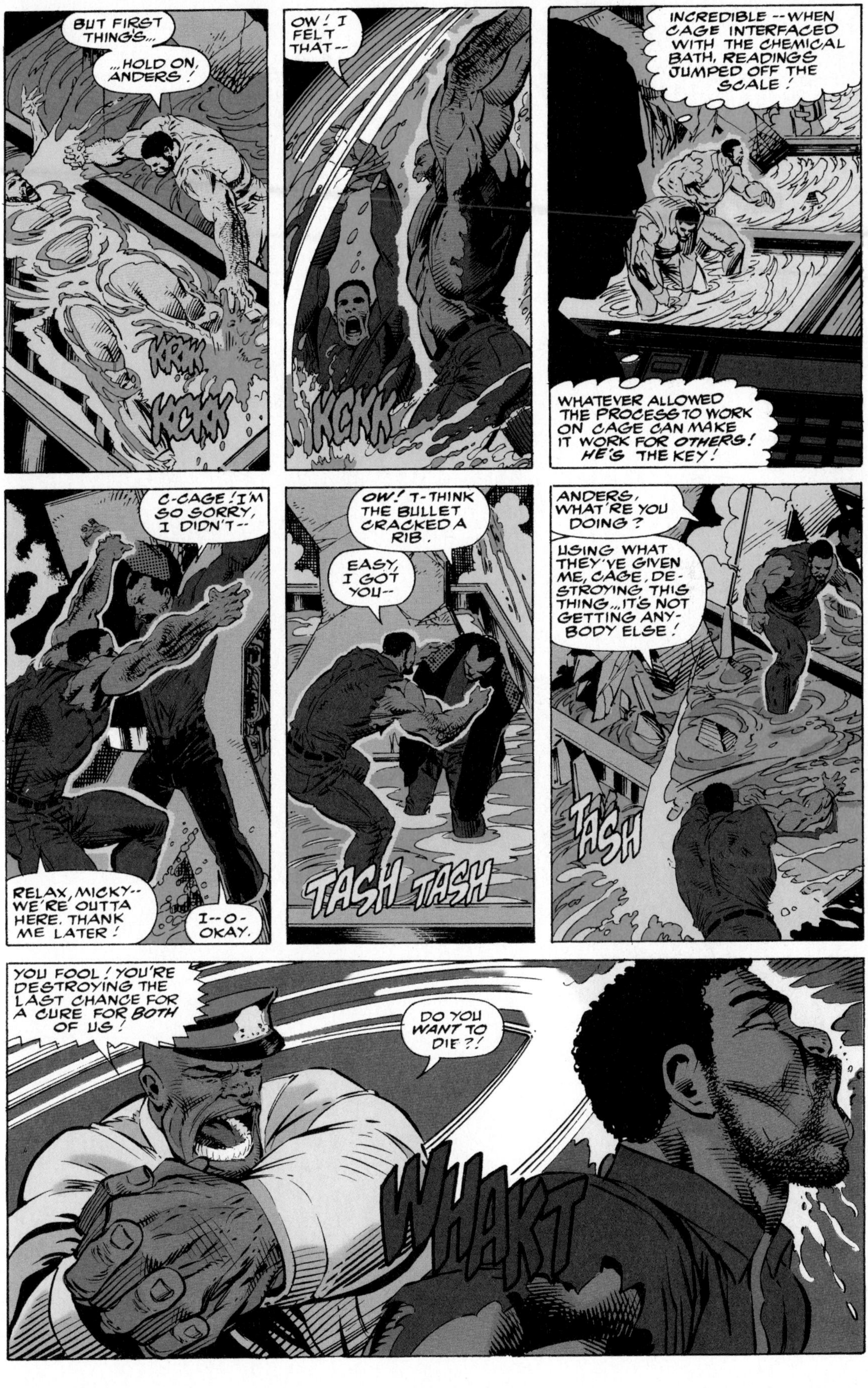
BUT FIRST THING'S...
...HOLD ON, ANDERS!
KRKK
KCKK
OW! I FELT THAT--
KCKK
INCREDIBLE--WHEN CAGE INTERFACED WITH THE CHEMICAL BATH, READINGS JUMPED OFF THE SCALE!
WHATEVER ALLOWED THE PROCESS TO WORK ON CAGE CAN MAKE IT WORK FOR OTHERS! HE'S THE KEY!
C-CAGE! I'M SO SORRY, I DIDN'T--
RELAX, MICKY--WE'RE OUTTA HERE. THANK ME LATER!
I--O-OKAY.
OW! T-THINK THE BULLET CRACKED A RIB.
EASY, I GOT YOU--
TASH TASH
ANDERS, WHAT'RE YOU DOING?
USING WHAT THEY'VE GIVEN ME, CAGE, DESTROYING THIS THING... IT'S NOT GETTING ANYBODY ELSE!
TASH
YOU FOOL! YOU'RE DESTROYING THE LAST CHANCE FOR A CURE FOR BOTH OF US!
DO YOU WANT TO DIE?!
WHAKT

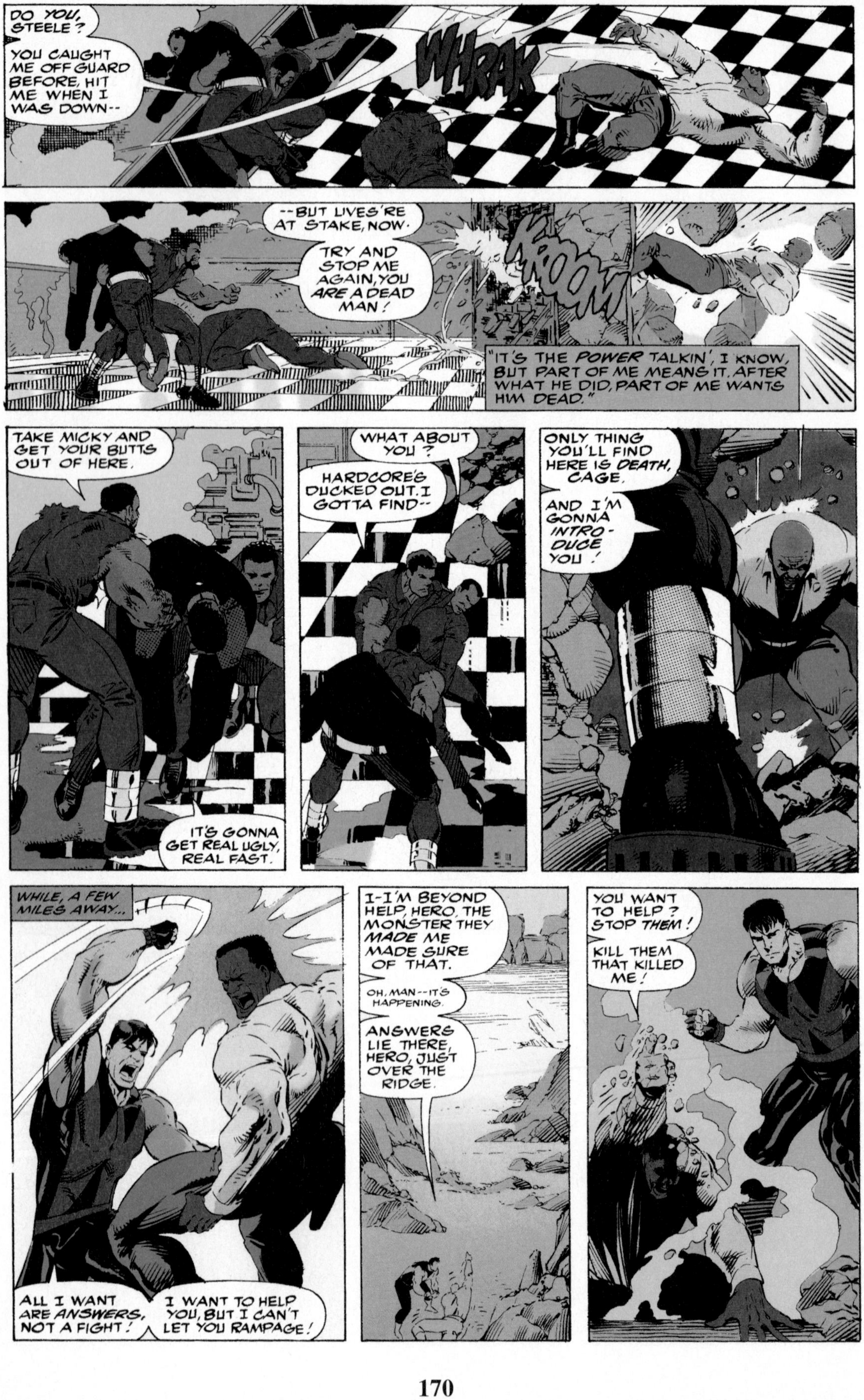
DO YOU, STEELE?
YOU CAUGHT ME OFF GUARD BEFORE, HIT ME WHEN I WAS DOWN--
WHRAK
--BUT LIVES'RE AT STAKE, NOW.
TRY AND STOP ME AGAIN, YOU ARE A DEAD MAN!
KROOOM
"IT'S THE POWER TALKIN', I KNOW, BUT PART OF ME MEANS IT. AFTER WHAT HE DID, PART OF ME WANTS HIM DEAD."
TAKE MICKY AND GET YOUR BUTTS OUT OF HERE.
IT'S GONNA GET REAL UGLY, REAL FAST.
WHAT ABOUT YOU?
HARDCORE'S DUCKED OUT. I GOTTA FIND--
ONLY THING YOU'LL FIND HERE IS DEATH, CAGE.
AND I'M GONNA INTRO-DUCE YOU!
WHILE, A FEW MILES AWAY...
ALL I WANT ARE ANSWERS, NOT A FIGHT!
I WANT TO HELP YOU, BUT I CAN'T LET YOU RAMPAGE!
I-I'M BEYOND HELP, HERO. THE MONSTER THEY MADE ME MADE SURE OF THAT.
OH, MAN--IT'S HAPPENING.
ANSWERS LIE THERE, HERO, JUST OVER THE RIDGE.
YOU WANT TO HELP? STOP THEM!
KILL THEM THAT KILLED ME!

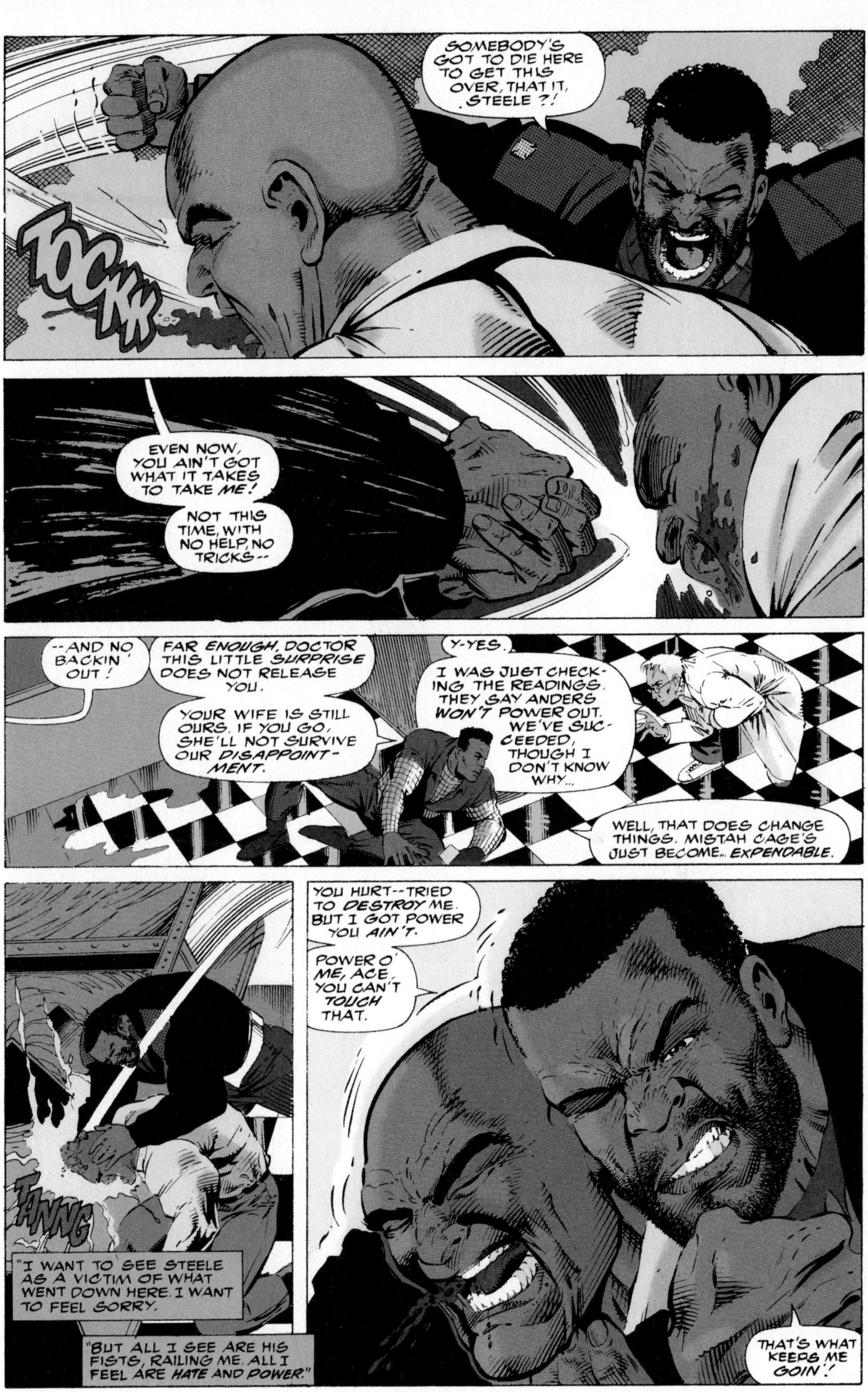
SOMEBODY'S GOT TO DIE HERE TO GET THIS OVER, THAT IT, STEELE ?!
TOCKK
EVEN NOW, YOU AIN'T GOT WHAT IT TAKES TO TAKE ME!
NOT THIS TIME, WITH NO HELP, NO TRICKS--
--AND NO BACKIN' OUT!
FAR ENOUGH, DOCTOR THIS LITTLE SURPRISE DOES NOT RELEASE YOU.
YOUR WIFE IS STILL OURS. IF YOU GO, SHE'LL NOT SURVIVE OUR DISAPPOINT-MENT.
Y-YES.
I WAS JUST CHECK-ING THE READINGS. THEY SAY ANDERS WON'T POWER OUT. WE'VE SUC-CEEDED, THOUGH I DON'T KNOW WHY...
WELL, THAT DOES CHANGE THINGS. MISTAH CAGE'S JUST BECOME... EXPENDABLE.
TANNG
"I WANT TO SEE STEELE AS A VICTIM OF WHAT WENT DOWN HERE. I WANT TO FEEL SORRY.
"BUT ALL I SEE ARE HIS FISTS, RAILING ME. ALL I FEEL ARE HATE AND POWER."
YOU HURT--TRIED TO DESTROY ME. BUT I GOT POWER YOU AIN'T.
POWER O' ME, ACE. YOU CAN'T TOUCH THAT.
THAT'S WHAT KEEPS ME GOIN'!

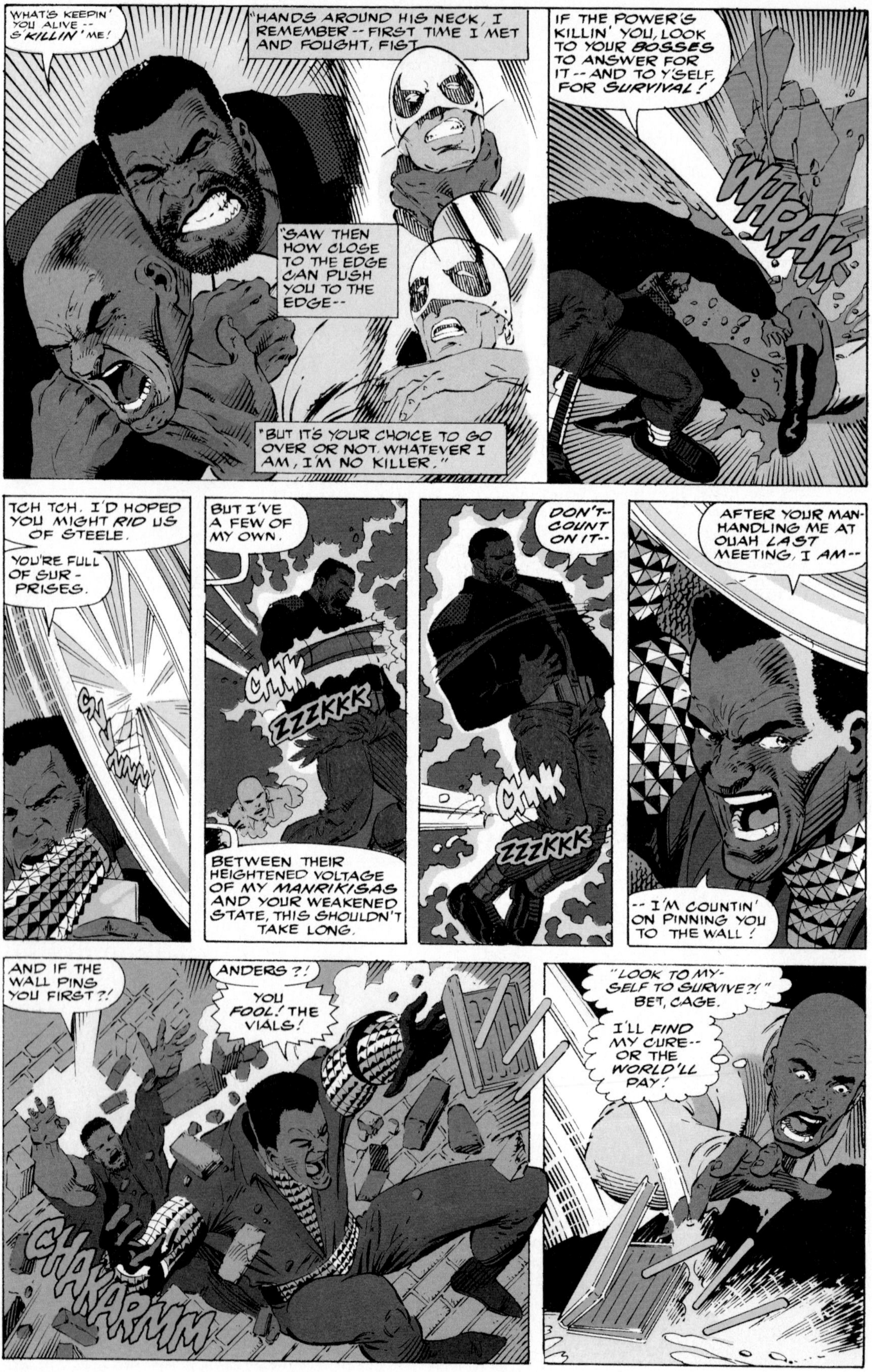

WHAT'S KEEPIN' YOU ALIVE -- S'KILLIN' ME!
"HANDS AROUND HIS NECK, I REMEMBER -- FIRST TIME I MET AND FOUGHT, FIST
"SAW THEN HOW CLOSE TO THE EDGE CAN PUSH YOU TO THE EDGE--
"BUT IT'S YOUR CHOICE TO GO OVER OR NOT. WHATEVER I AM, I'M NO KILLER."
IF THE POWER'S KILLIN' YOU, LOOK TO YOUR BOSSES TO ANSWER FOR IT -- AND TO Y'SELF, FOR SURVIVAL!
WHRAK
TCH TCH. I'D HOPED YOU MIGHT RID US OF STEELE.
YOU'RE FULL OF SUR-PRISES.
BUT I'VE A FEW OF MY OWN.
CHNK
ZZZKKK
BETWEEN THEIR HEIGHTENED VOLTAGE OF MY MANRIKISAS AND YOUR WEAKENED STATE, THIS SHOULDN'T TAKE LONG.
DON'T-- COUNT ON IT--
CHNK
ZZZKKK
AFTER YOUR MAN-HANDLING ME AT OUAH LAST MEETING, I AM--
-- I'M COUNTIN' ON PINNING YOU TO THE WALL!
AND IF THE WALL PINS YOU FIRST?!
ANDERS?!
YOU FOOL! THE VIALS!
CHAKARMM
"LOOK TO MY-SELF TO SURVIVE?!" BET, CAGE.
I'LL FIND MY CURE-- OR THE WORLD'LL PAY!

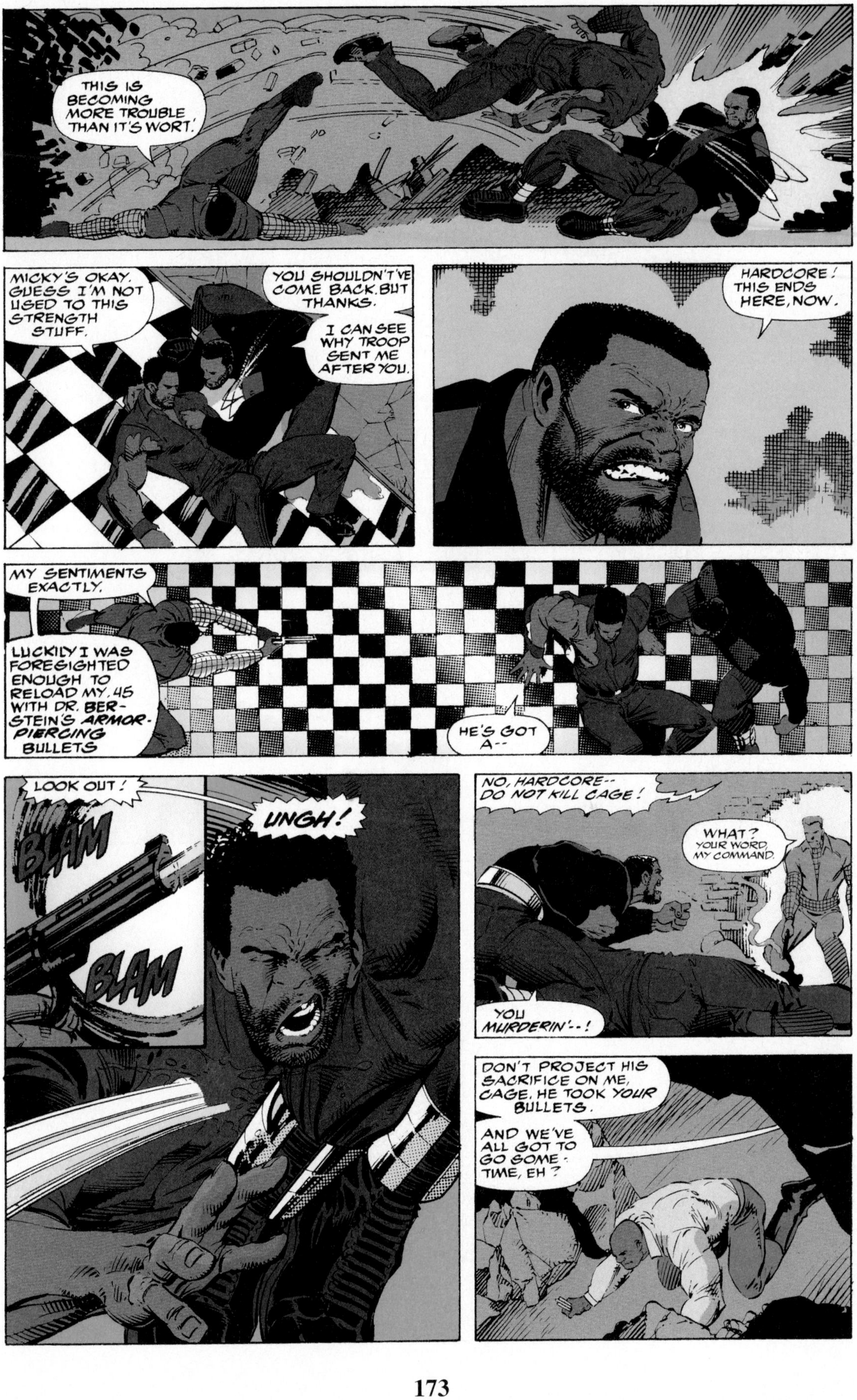

THIS IS BECOMING MORE TROUBLE THAN IT'S WORT'.
MICKY'S OKAY. GUESS I'M NOT USED TO THIS STRENGTH STUFF.
YOU SHOULDN'T'VE COME BACK. BUT THANKS.
I CAN SEE WHY TROOP SENT ME AFTER YOU.
HARDCORE! THIS ENDS HERE, NOW.
MY SENTIMENTS EXACTLY.
LUCKILY I WAS FORESIGHTED ENOUGH TO RELOAD MY .45 WITH DR. BERSTEIN'S ARMOR-PIERCING BULLETS
HE'S GOT A--
LOOK OUT!
BLAM
BLAM
UNGH!
NO, HARDCORE-- DO NOT KILL CAGE!
WHAT? YOUR WORD, MY COMMAND.
YOU MURDERIN'--!
DON'T PROJECT HIS SACRIFICE ON ME, CAGE. HE TOOK YOUR BULLETS.
AND WE'VE ALL GOT TO GO SOMETIME, EH?

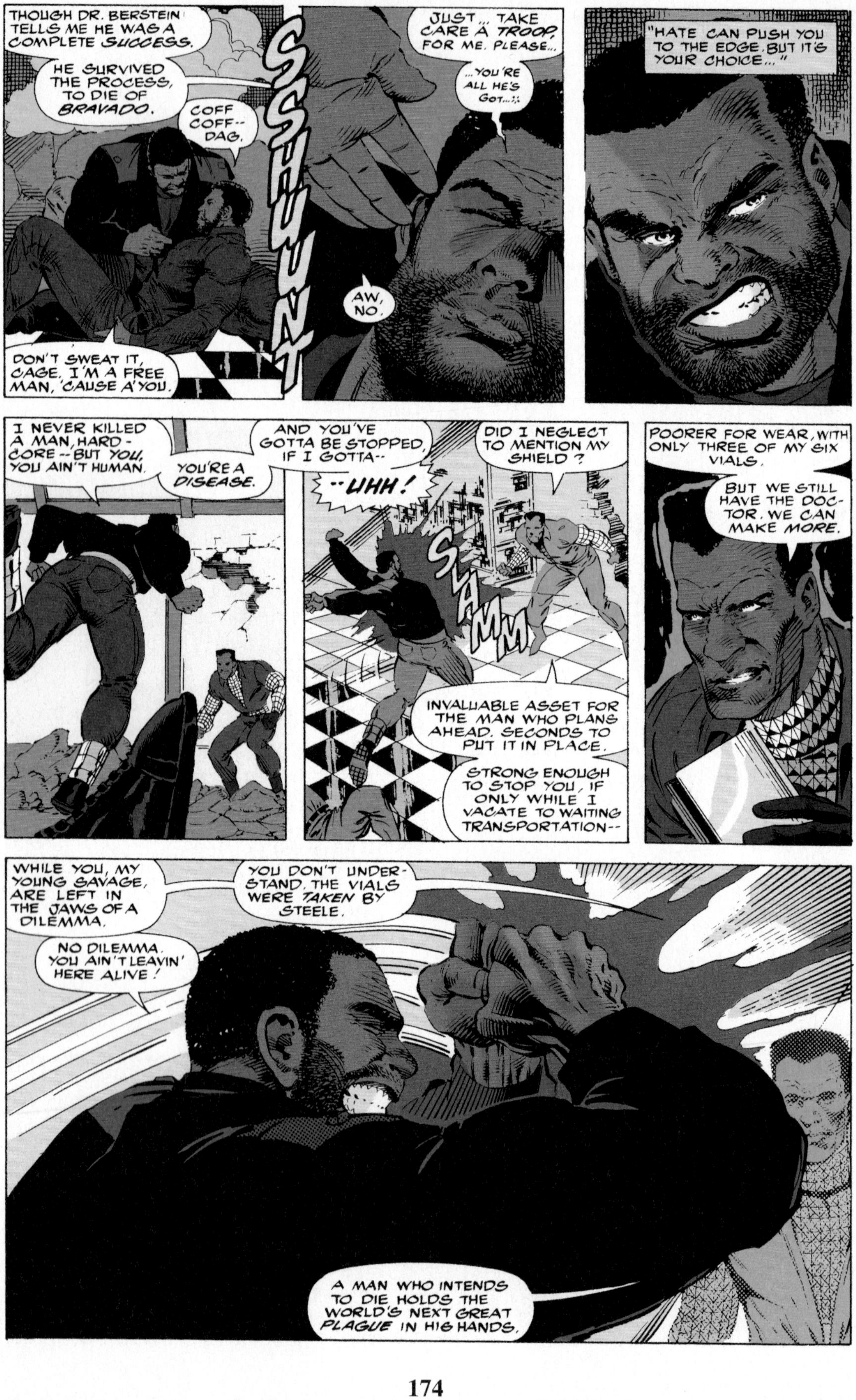
THOUGH DR. BERSTEIN TELLS ME HE WAS A COMPLETE SUCCESS.
HE SURVIVED THE PROCESS, TO DIE OF BRAVADO.
COFF COFF-- DAG.
DON'T SWEAT IT, CAGE. I'M A FREE MAN, 'CAUSE A'YOU.
SSHUUNT
JUST... TAKE CARE A TROOP, FOR ME. PLEASE...
...YOU'RE ALL HE'S GOT...
AW, NO.
"HATE CAN PUSH YOU TO THE EDGE, BUT IT'S YOUR CHOICE..."
I NEVER KILLED A MAN, HARD-CORE--BUT YOU, YOU AIN'T HUMAN.
YOU'RE A DISEASE.
AND YOU'VE GOTTA BE STOPPED, IF I GOTTA--
--UHH!
DID I NEGLECT TO MENTION MY SHIELD?
SLAMM
INVALUABLE ASSET FOR THE MAN WHO PLANS AHEAD. SECONDS TO PUT IT IN PLACE.
STRONG ENOUGH TO STOP YOU, IF ONLY WHILE I VACATE TO WAITING TRANSPORTATION--
POORER FOR WEAR, WITH ONLY THREE OF MY SIX VIALS.
BUT WE STILL HAVE THE DOCTOR. WE CAN MAKE MORE.
WHILE YOU, MY YOUNG SAVAGE, ARE LEFT IN THE JAWS OF A DILEMMA.
NO DILEMMA. YOU AIN'T LEAVIN' HERE ALIVE!
YOU DON'T UNDERSTAND. THE VIALS WERE TAKEN BY STEELE.
A MAN WHO INTENDS TO DIE HOLDS THE WORLD'S NEXT GREAT PLAGUE IN HIS HANDS.

AT THIS MOMENT HE'S MAKING HIS WAY TO A TRIBUTARY OF THE COLORADO RIVER.

MAYHAP, IN SOME VAIN ATTEMPT TO FORCE THE WORLD TO FIND A CURE FOR THE PROCESS.

CHAM CHAM

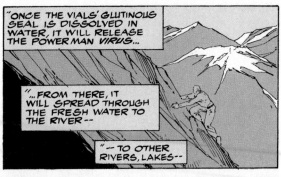

"ONCE THE VIALS' GLUTINOUS SEAL IS DISSOLVED IN WATER, IT WILL RELEASE THE POWER MAN VIRUS...

"...FROM THERE, IT WILL SPREAD THROUGH THE FRESH WATER TO THE RIVER --

" -- TO OTHER RIVERS, LAKES --

" -- THROUGHOUT THE WATER SUPPLY OF THE ENTIRE SOUTH WEST."

YOU'RE NOT LEAVING!

CHAM

YOU MIGHT BREAK THROUGH THE SHIELD EVENTUALLY CAGE -- PERHAPS EVEN HALT OUR ESCAPE.

OR YOU CAN STOP STEELE FROM PERPETRATING ONE OF THE GREAT TRAGEDIES OF THE TWENTIETH CENTURY. YOUR CHOICE.

I TRUST YOU TO FAIL, IN EITHER CASE.

PERHAPS I SHOULD PUT THE DOCTOR TO WORK ON A VACCINE. MIGHT BE QUITE MARKETABLE WORLD-WIDE, SOON.

NO! NO! NO!

175

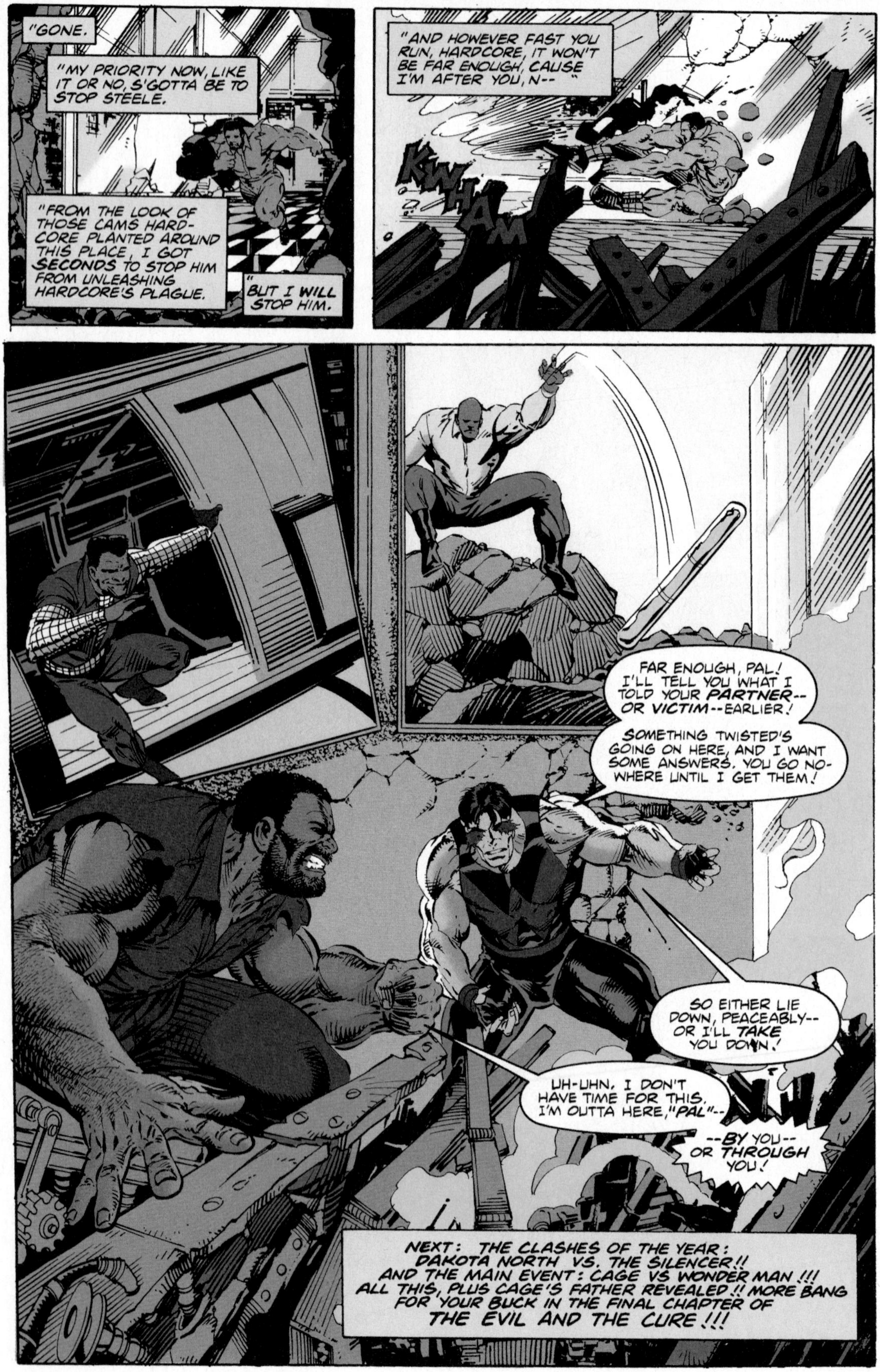
"GONE.
"MY PRIORITY NOW, LIKE IT OR NO, S'GOTTA BE TO STOP STEELE.
"FROM THE LOOK OF THOSE CAMS HARDCORE PLANTED AROUND THIS PLACE, I GOT SECONDS TO STOP HIM FROM UNLEASHING HARDCORE'S PLAGUE.
"BUT I WILL STOP HIM.
"AND HOWEVER FAST YOU RUN, HARDCORE, IT WON'T BE FAR ENOUGH, CAUSE I'M AFTER YOU, N-- "
KWHAM
FAR ENOUGH, PAL! I'LL TELL YOU WHAT I TOLD YOUR PARTNER-- OR VICTIM--EARLIER!
SOMETHING TWISTED'S GOING ON HERE, AND I WANT SOME ANSWERS. YOU GO NOWHERE UNTIL I GET THEM!
SO EITHER LIE DOWN, PEACEABLY-- OR I'LL TAKE YOU DOWN!
UH-UHN. I DON'T HAVE TIME FOR THIS. I'M OUTTA HERE, "PAL"--
--BY YOU-- OR THROUGH YOU!
NEXT: THE CLASHES OF THE YEAR: DAKOTA NORTH VS. THE SILENCER!! AND THE MAIN EVENT: CAGE VS WONDER MAN!!! ALL THIS, PLUS CAGE'S FATHER REVEALED!! MORE BANG FOR YOUR BUCK IN THE FINAL CHAPTER OF THE EVIL AND THE CURE!!!

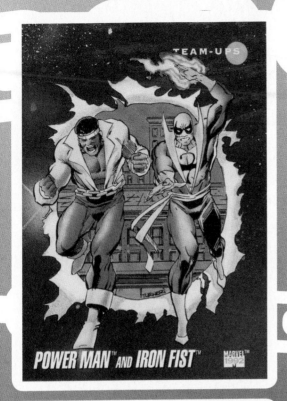

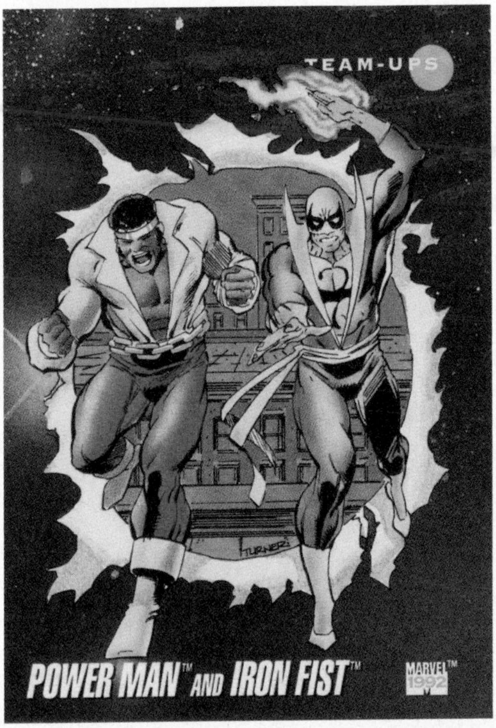
TEAM-UPS
POWER MAN™ AND IRON FIST™
MARVEL™ 1992

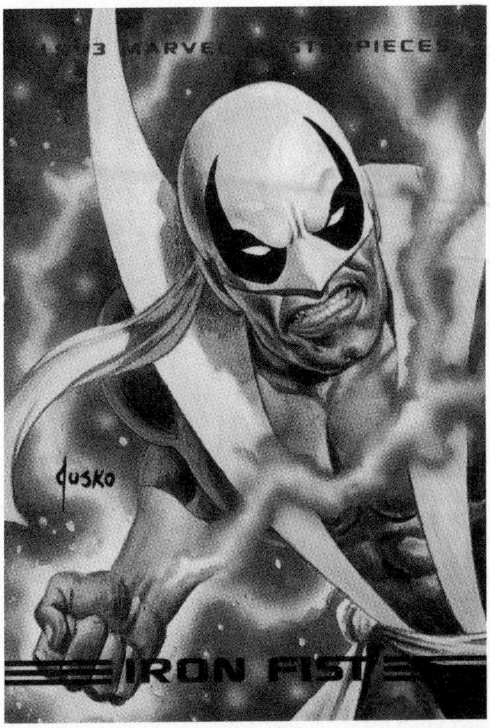
IRON FIST

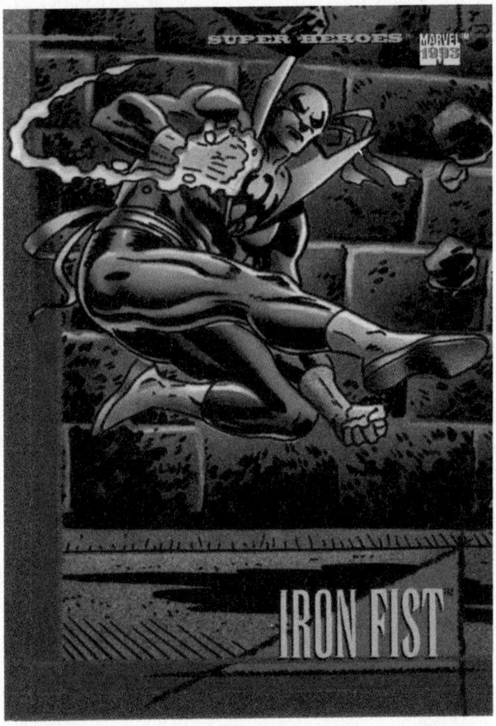
SUPER HEROES
MARVEL™ 1993
IRON FIST™

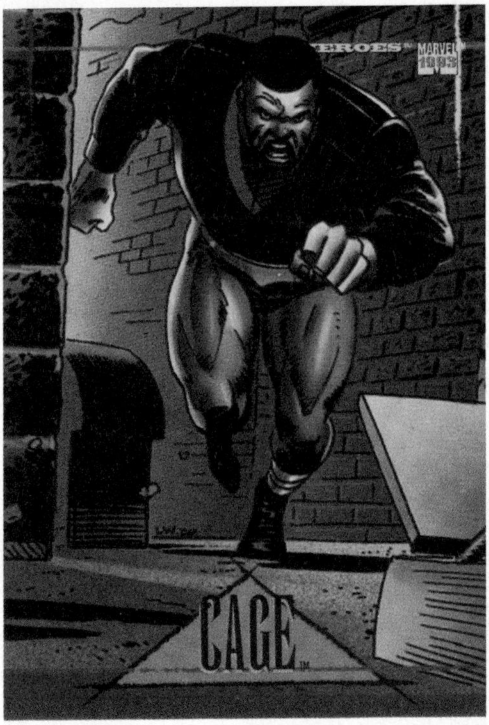
MARVEL™ 1993
CAGE™

1992–1993 TRADING-CARD ART BY DWAYNE TURNER, JOE JUSKO, LEE WEEKS & PAUL MOUNTS

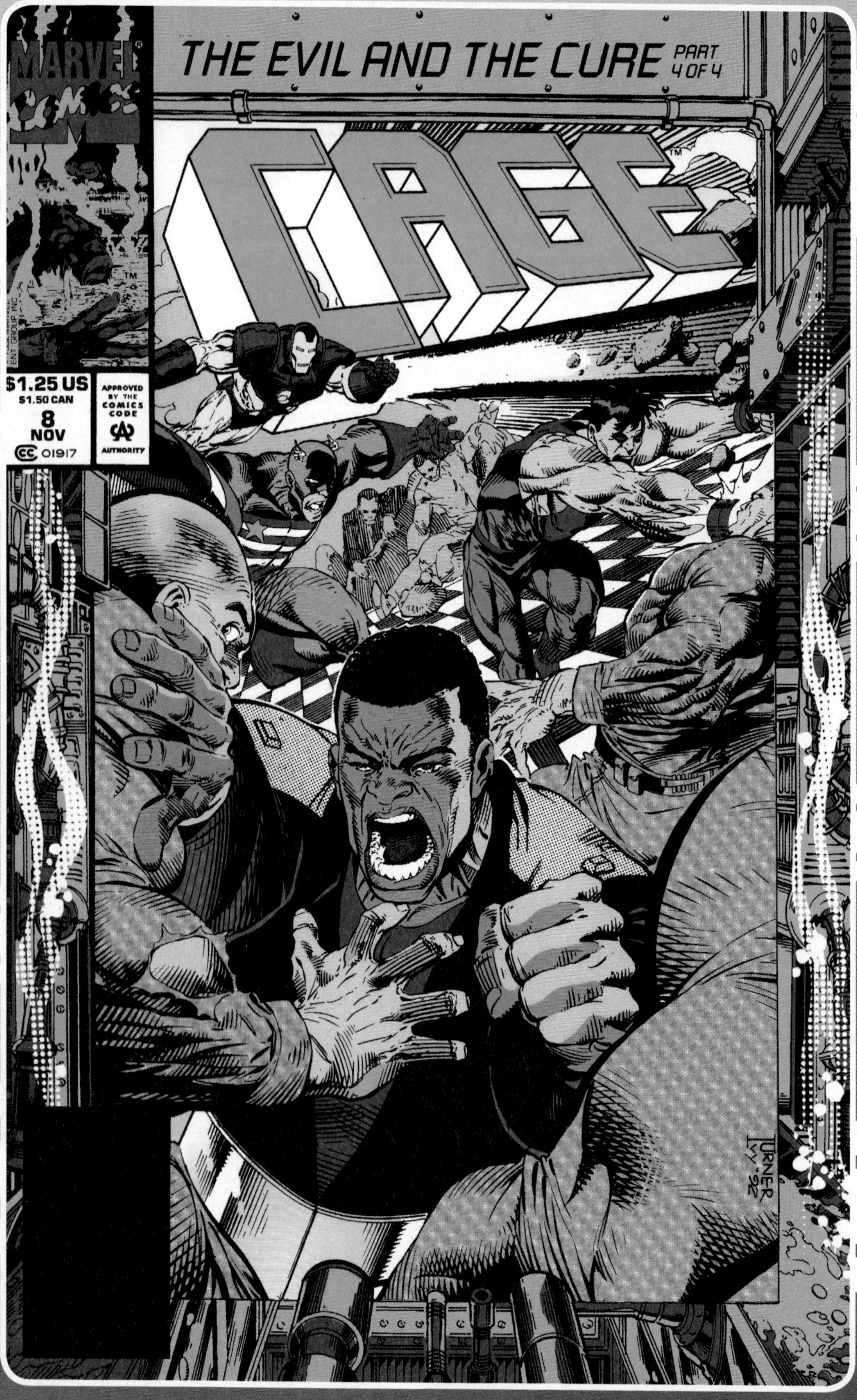
MARVEL COMICS
THE EVIL AND THE CURE PART 4 OF 4
CAGE
$1.25 US
$1.50 CAN
8
NOV
01917
APPROVED BY THE COMICS CODE AUTHORITY
TURNER
IVY '92

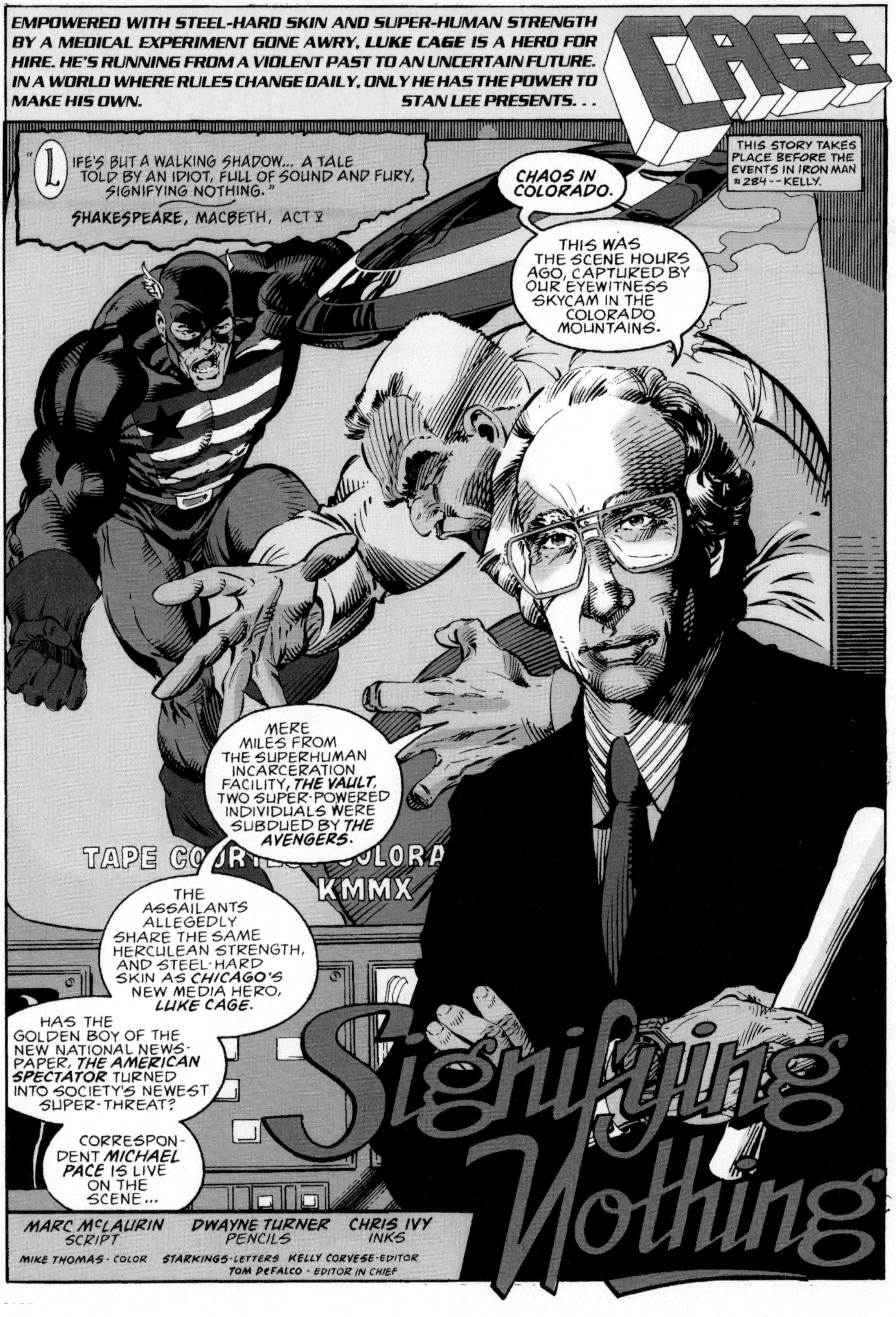

EMPOWERED WITH STEEL-HARD SKIN AND SUPER-HUMAN STRENGTH BY A MEDICAL EXPERIMENT GONE AWRY, LUKE CAGE IS A HERO FOR HIRE. HE'S RUNNING FROM A VIOLENT PAST TO AN UNCERTAIN FUTURE. IN A WORLD WHERE RULES CHANGE DAILY, ONLY HE HAS THE POWER TO MAKE HIS OWN.
STAN LEE PRESENTS. . .
CAGE
"LIFE'S BUT A WALKING SHADOW... A TALE TOLD BY AN IDIOT, FULL OF SOUND AND FURY, SIGNIFYING NOTHING." SHAKESPEARE, MACBETH, ACT V
THIS STORY TAKES PLACE BEFORE THE EVENTS IN IRON MAN #284--KELLY.
CHAOS IN COLORADO.
THIS WAS THE SCENE HOURS AGO, CAPTURED BY OUR EYEWITNESS SKYCAM IN THE COLORADO MOUNTAINS.
MERE MILES FROM THE SUPERHUMAN INCARCERATION FACILITY, THE VAULT, TWO SUPER-POWERED INDIVIDUALS WERE SUBDUED BY THE AVENGERS.
TAPE CO RT COLORA
KMMX
THE ASSAILANTS ALLEGEDLY SHARE THE SAME HERCULEAN STRENGTH, AND STEEL-HARD SKIN AS CHICAGO'S NEW MEDIA HERO, LUKE CAGE.
HAS THE GOLDEN BOY OF THE NEW NATIONAL NEWS-PAPER, THE AMERICAN SPECTATOR TURNED INTO SOCIETY'S NEWEST SUPER-THREAT?
CORRESPON-DENT MICHAEL PACE IS LIVE ON THE SCENE...
Signifying Nothing
MARC McLAURIN SCRIPT
DWAYNE TURNER PENCILS
CHRIS IVY INKS
MIKE THOMAS - COLOR
STARKINGS - LETTERS
KELLY CORVESE - EDITOR
TOM DEFALCO - EDITOR IN CHIEF

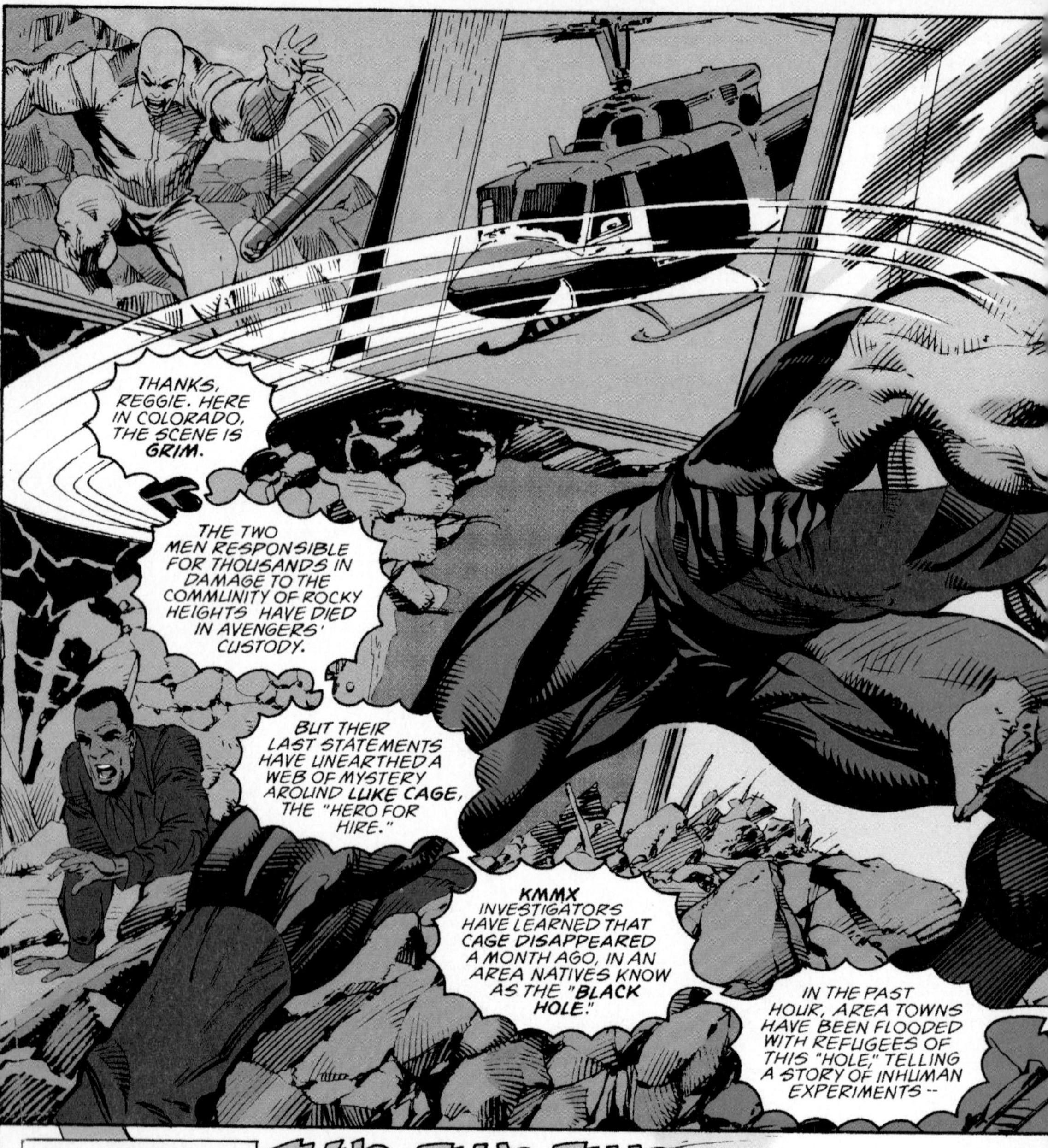
THANKS, REGGIE. HERE IN COLORADO, THE SCENE IS GRIM.
THE TWO MEN RESPONSIBLE FOR THOUSANDS IN DAMAGE TO THE COMMUNITY OF ROCKY HEIGHTS HAVE DIED IN AVENGERS' CUSTODY.
BUT THEIR LAST STATEMENTS HAVE UNEARTHED A WEB OF MYSTERY AROUND LUKE CAGE, THE "HERO FOR HIRE."
KMMX INVESTIGATORS HAVE LEARNED THAT CAGE DISAPPEARED A MONTH AGO, IN AN AREA NATIVES KNOW AS THE "BLACK HOLE."
IN THE PAST HOUR, AREA TOWNS HAVE BEEN FLOODED WITH REFUGEES OF THIS "HOLE," TELLING A STORY OF INHUMAN EXPERIMENTS --

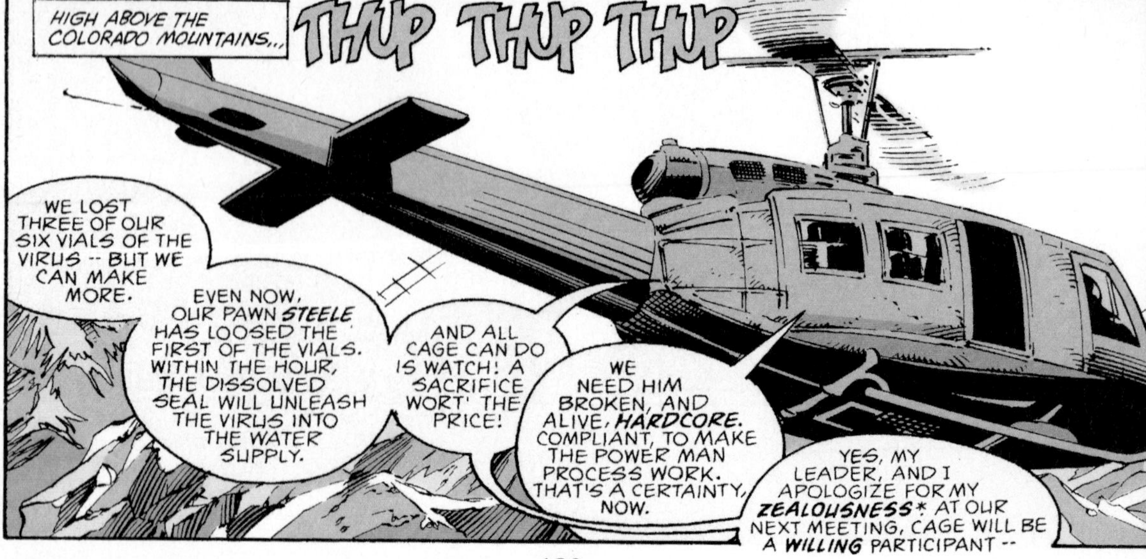
HIGH ABOVE THE COLORADO MOUNTAINS...
THUP THUP THUP
WE LOST THREE OF OUR SIX VIALS OF THE VIRUS -- BUT WE CAN MAKE MORE.
EVEN NOW, OUR PAWN STEELE HAS LOOSED THE FIRST OF THE VIALS. WITHIN THE HOUR, THE DISSOLVED SEAL WILL UNLEASH THE VIRUS INTO THE WATER SUPPLY.
AND ALL CAGE CAN DO IS WATCH! A SACRIFICE WORT' THE PRICE!
WE NEED HIM BROKEN, AND ALIVE, HARDCORE. COMPLIANT, TO MAKE THE POWER MAN PROCESS WORK. THAT'S A CERTAINTY, NOW.
YES, MY LEADER, AND I APOLOGIZE FOR MY ZEALOUSNESS* AT OUR NEXT MEETING, CAGE WILL BE A WILLING PARTICIPANT --

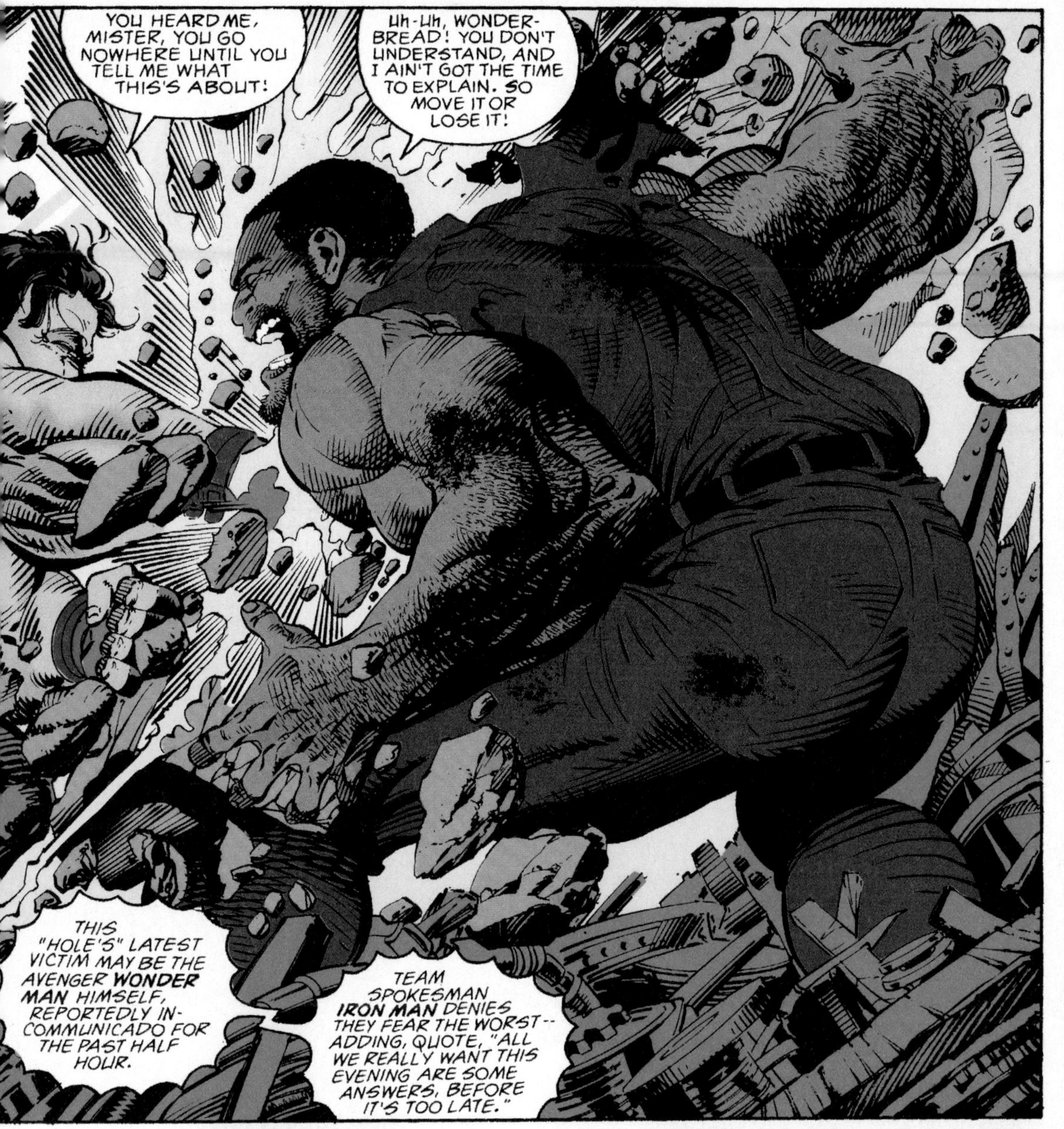
YOU HEARD ME, MISTER, YOU GO NOWHERE UNTIL YOU TELL ME WHAT THIS'S ABOUT!
UH-UH, WONDER-BREAD! YOU DON'T UNDERSTAND, AND I AIN'T GOT THE TIME TO EXPLAIN. SO MOVE IT OR LOSE IT!
THIS "HOLE'S" LATEST VICTIM MAY BE THE AVENGER WONDER MAN HIMSELF, REPORTEDLY IN-COMMUNICADO FOR THE PAST HALF HOUR.
TEAM SPOKESMAN IRON MAN DENIES THEY FEAR THE WORST-- ADDING, QUOTE, "ALL WE REALLY WANT THIS EVENING ARE SOME ANSWERS, BEFORE IT'S TOO LATE."

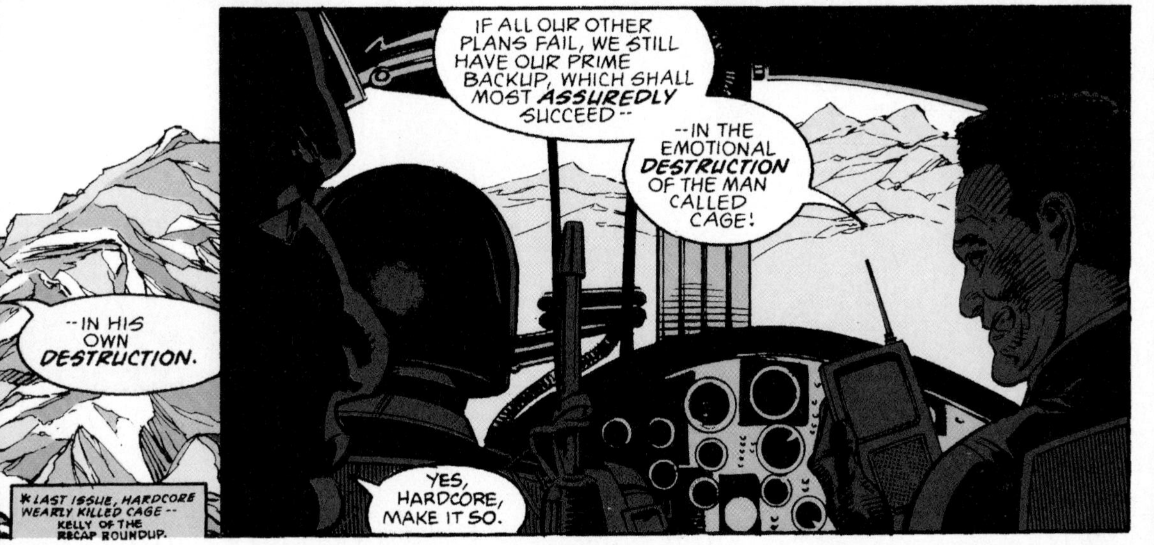
IF ALL OUR OTHER PLANS FAIL, WE STILL HAVE OUR PRIME BACKUP, WHICH SHALL MOST ASSUREDLY SUCCEED--
--IN THE EMOTIONAL DESTRUCTION OF THE MAN CALLED CAGE!
--IN HIS OWN DESTRUCTION.
YES, HARDCORE, MAKE IT SO.
*LAST ISSUE, HARDCORE WEARLY KILLED CAGE -- KELLY OF THE RECAP ROUNDUP.

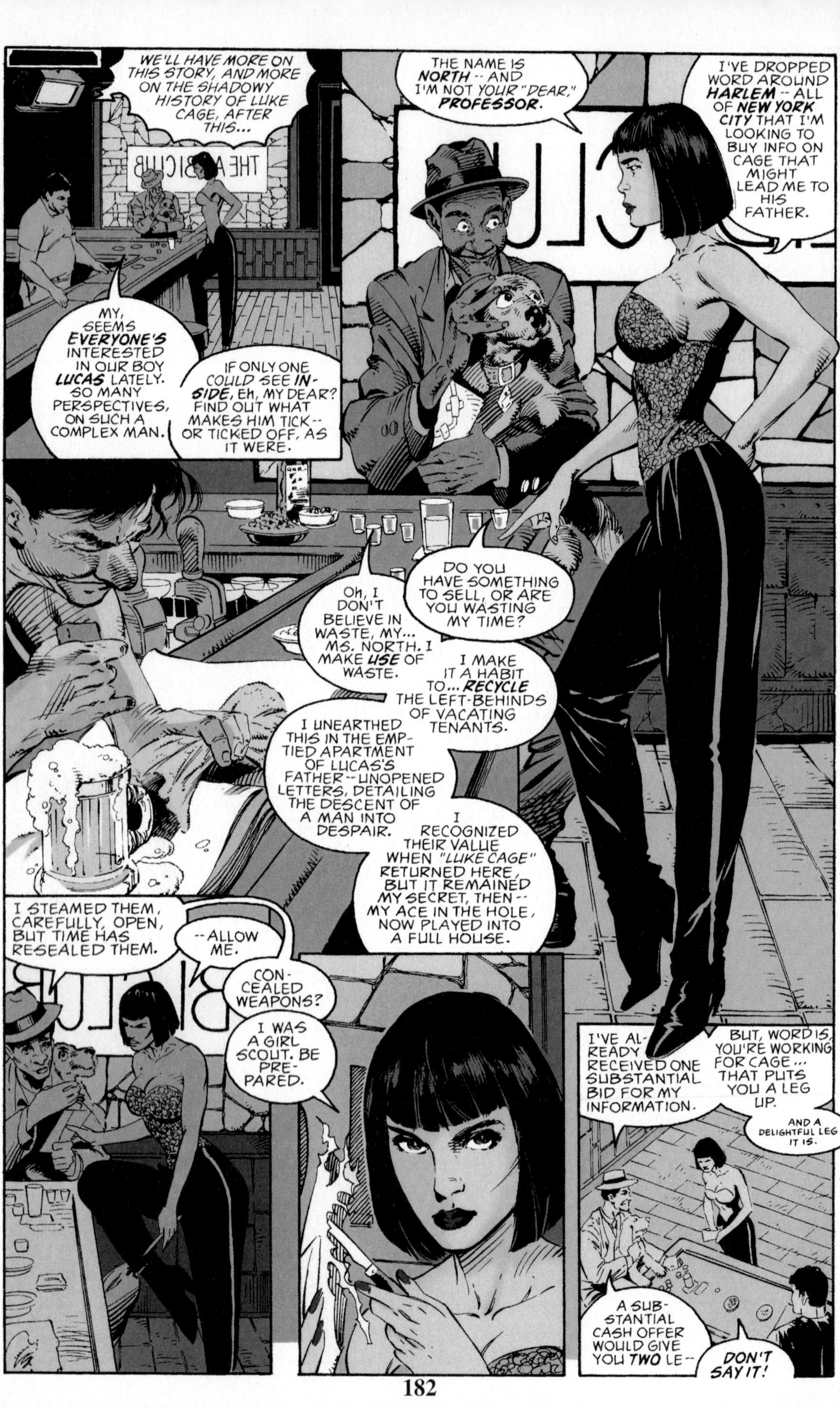
WE'LL HAVE MORE ON THIS STORY, AND MORE ON THE SHADOWY HISTORY OF LUKE CAGE, AFTER THIS...
MY, SEEMS EVERYONE'S INTERESTED IN OUR BOY LUCAS LATELY. SO MANY PERSPECTIVES, ON SUCH A COMPLEX MAN.
IF ONLY ONE COULD SEE INSIDE, EH, MY DEAR? FIND OUT WHAT MAKES HIM TICK-- OR TICKED OFF, AS IT WERE.
THE NAME IS NORTH -- AND I'M NOT YOUR "DEAR," PROFESSOR.
I'VE DROPPED WORD AROUND HARLEM -- ALL OF NEW YORK CITY THAT I'M LOOKING TO BUY INFO ON CAGE THAT MIGHT LEAD ME TO HIS FATHER.
DO YOU HAVE SOMETHING TO SELL, OR ARE YOU WASTING MY TIME?
OH, I DON'T BELIEVE IN WASTE, MY... MS. NORTH. I MAKE USE OF WASTE.
I MAKE IT A HABIT TO... RECYCLE THE LEFT-BEHINDS OF VACATING TENANTS.
I UNEARTHED THIS IN THE EMPTIED APARTMENT OF LUCAS'S FATHER--UNOPENED LETTERS, DETAILING THE DESCENT OF A MAN INTO DESPAIR.
I RECOGNIZED THEIR VALUE WHEN "LUKE CAGE" RETURNED HERE, BUT IT REMAINED MY SECRET, THEN-- MY ACE IN THE HOLE, NOW PLAYED INTO A FULL HOUSE.
I STEAMED THEM, CAREFULLY, OPEN, BUT TIME HAS RESEALED THEM.
--ALLOW ME.
CONCEALED WEAPONS?
I WAS A GIRL SCOUT. BE PREPARED.
I'VE ALREADY RECEIVED ONE SUBSTANTIAL BID FOR MY INFORMATION.
BUT, WORD IS, YOU'RE WORKING FOR CAGE... THAT PUTS YOU A LEG UP.
AND A DELIGHTFUL LEG IT IS.
A SUBSTANTIAL CASH OFFER WOULD GIVE YOU TWO LE--
DON'T SAY IT!

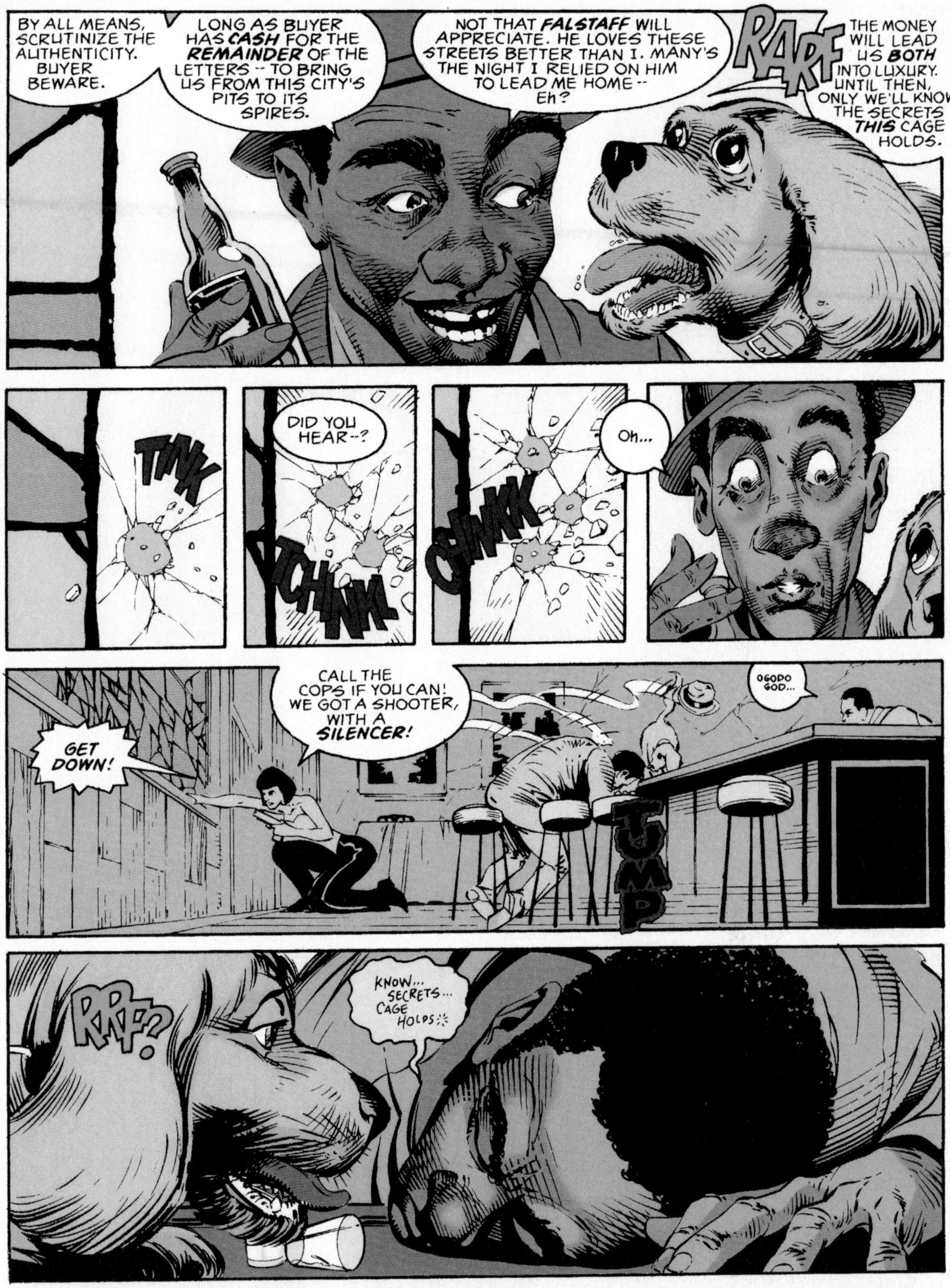
BY ALL MEANS, SCRUTINIZE THE AUTHENTICITY. BUYER BEWARE.
LONG AS BUYER HAS CASH FOR THE REMAINDER OF THE LETTERS -- TO BRING US FROM THIS CITY'S PITS TO ITS SPIRES.
NOT THAT FALSTAFF WILL APPRECIATE. HE LOVES THESE STREETS BETTER THAN I. MANY'S THE NIGHT I RELIED ON HIM TO LEAD ME HOME -- Eh?
RARF
THE MONEY WILL LEAD US BOTH INTO LUXURY. UNTIL THEN, ONLY WE'LL KNOW THE SECRETS THIS CAGE HOLDS.
TINK
DID YOU HEAR--?
TCHINK
CHINKK
Oh...
CALL THE COPS IF YOU CAN! WE GOT A SHOOTER, WITH A SILENCER!
GET DOWN!
OGODO GOD...
JUMP
RARF?
KNOW... SECRETS... CAGE HOLDS

Dear Pop,

I know this all hasn't been easy for you. You're an ex-cop, and everyone's telling you I've been dealing drugs. But you've got to know it's not true. After what happened to Ma, because of ME, I ~~[illegible]~~ I promised I'd clean myself up, and I DID. I got out of the gangs. I know I've been framed. But it's more important to me that YOU know it.

Carl still visits, mostly to rub my nose in something or other. He tells me you're not well, that all this has nearly killed you. I hope that somehow, you can get well enough to visit, to call or something, so that I can get to explain all of this to you face to face.

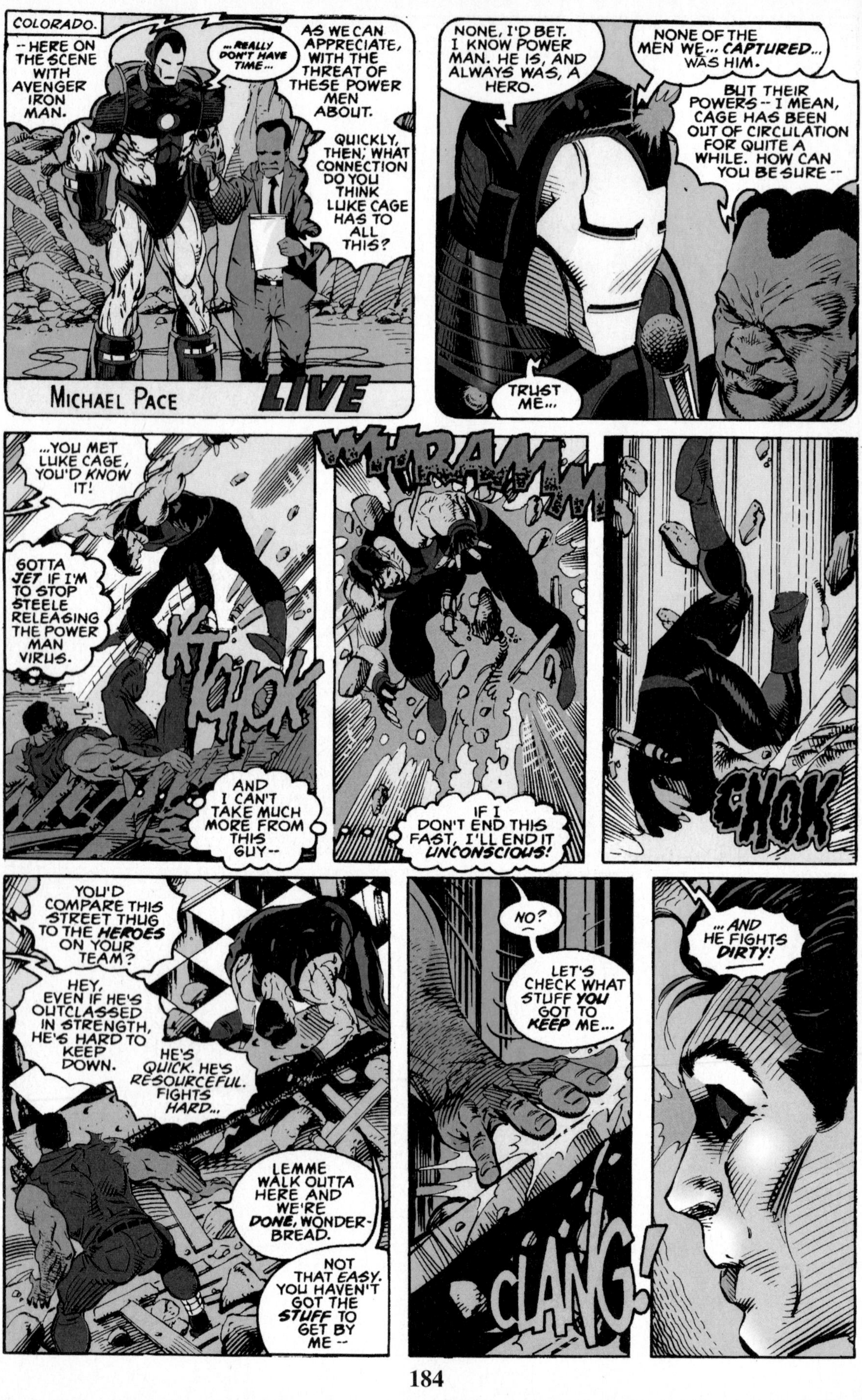
COLORADO.
-- HERE ON THE SCENE WITH AVENGER IRON MAN.
...REALLY DON'T HAVE TIME...
AS WE CAN APPRECIATE, WITH THE THREAT OF THESE POWER MEN ABOUT.
QUICKLY, THEN; WHAT CONNECTION DO YOU THINK LUKE CAGE HAS TO ALL THIS?
MICHAEL PACE
LIVE
NONE, I'D BET. I KNOW POWER MAN. HE IS, AND ALWAYS WAS, A HERO.
NONE OF THE MEN WE... CAPTURED... WAS HIM.
BUT THEIR POWERS -- I MEAN, CAGE HAS BEEN OUT OF CIRCULATION FOR QUITE A WHILE. HOW CAN YOU BE SURE --
TRUST ME...
...YOU MET LUKE CAGE, YOU'D KNOW IT!
GOTTA JET IF I'M TO STOP STEELE RELEASING THE POWER MAN VIRUS.
KTCHOK
AND I CAN'T TAKE MUCH MORE FROM THIS GUY --
WHRAMM
IF I DON'T END THIS FAST, I'LL END IT UNCONSCIOUS!
CHOK
YOU'D COMPARE THIS STREET THUG TO THE HEROES ON YOUR TEAM?
HEY, EVEN IF HE'S OUTCLASSED IN STRENGTH, HE'S HARD TO KEEP DOWN.
HE'S QUICK. HE'S RESOURCEFUL. FIGHTS HARD...
LEMME WALK OUTTA HERE AND WE'RE DONE, WONDER-BREAD.
NOT THAT EASY. YOU HAVEN'T GOT THE STUFF TO GET BY ME --
NO?
LET'S CHECK WHAT STUFF YOU GOT TO KEEP ME...
CLANG!
...AND HE FIGHTS DIRTY!

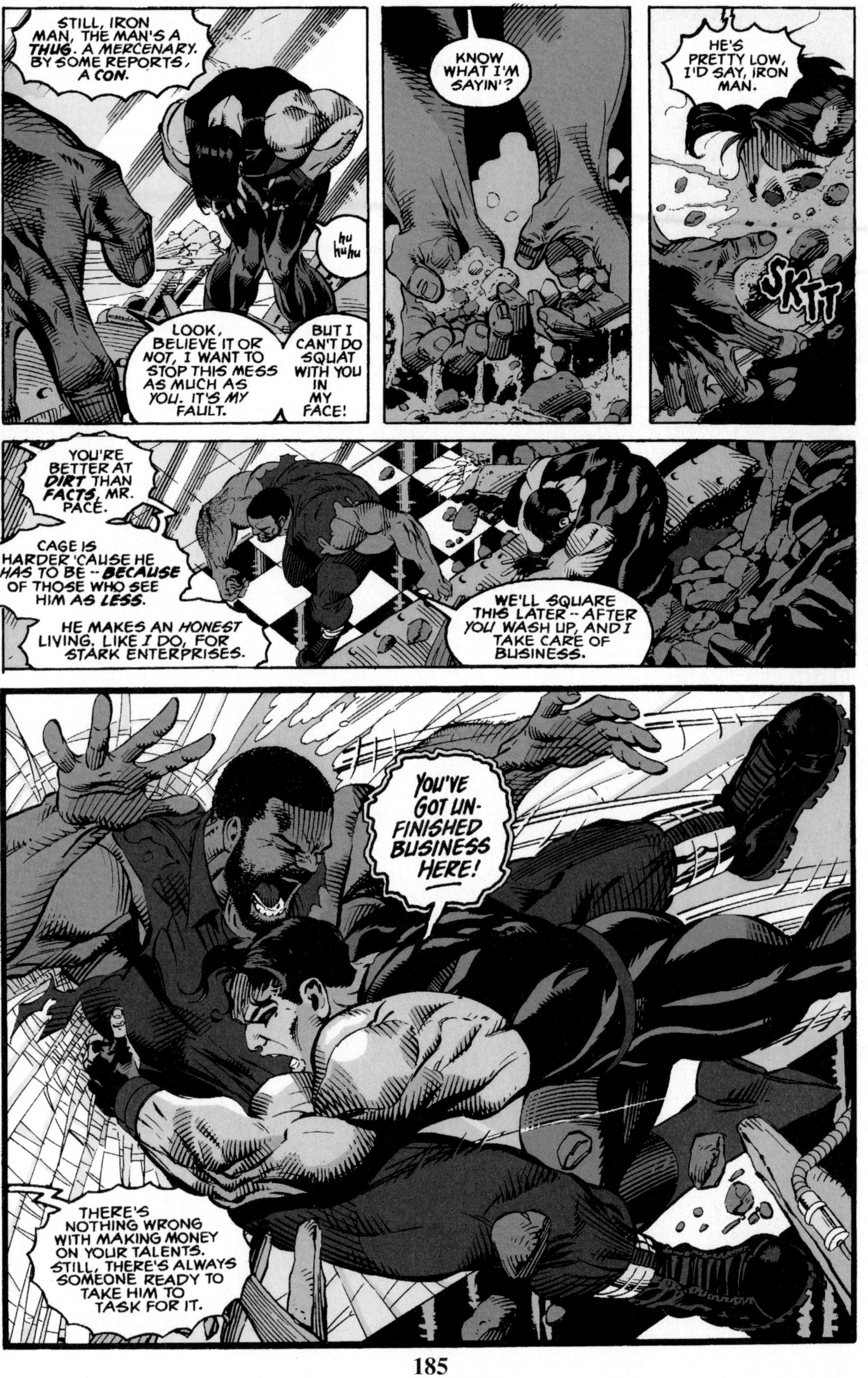

STILL, IRON MAN, THE MAN'S A THUG. A MERCENARY. BY SOME REPORTS, A CON.
hu huhu
LOOK, BELIEVE IT OR NOT, I WANT TO STOP THIS MESS AS MUCH AS YOU. IT'S MY FAULT.
BUT I CAN'T DO SQUAT WITH YOU IN MY FACE!
KNOW WHAT I'M SAYIN'?
HE'S PRETTY LOW, I'D SAY, IRON MAN.
SKTT
YOU'RE BETTER AT DIRT THAN FACTS, MR. PACE.
CAGE IS HARDER 'CAUSE HE HAS TO BE -- BECAUSE OF THOSE WHO SEE HIM AS LESS.
HE MAKES AN HONEST LIVING. LIKE I DO, FOR STARK ENTERPRISES.
WE'LL SQUARE THIS LATER -- AFTER YOU WASH UP, AND I TAKE CARE OF BUSINESS.
YOU'VE GOT UN-FINISHED BUSINESS HERE!
THERE'S NOTHING WRONG WITH MAKING MONEY ON YOUR TALENTS. STILL, THERE'S ALWAYS SOMEONE READY TO TAKE HIM TO TASK FOR IT.

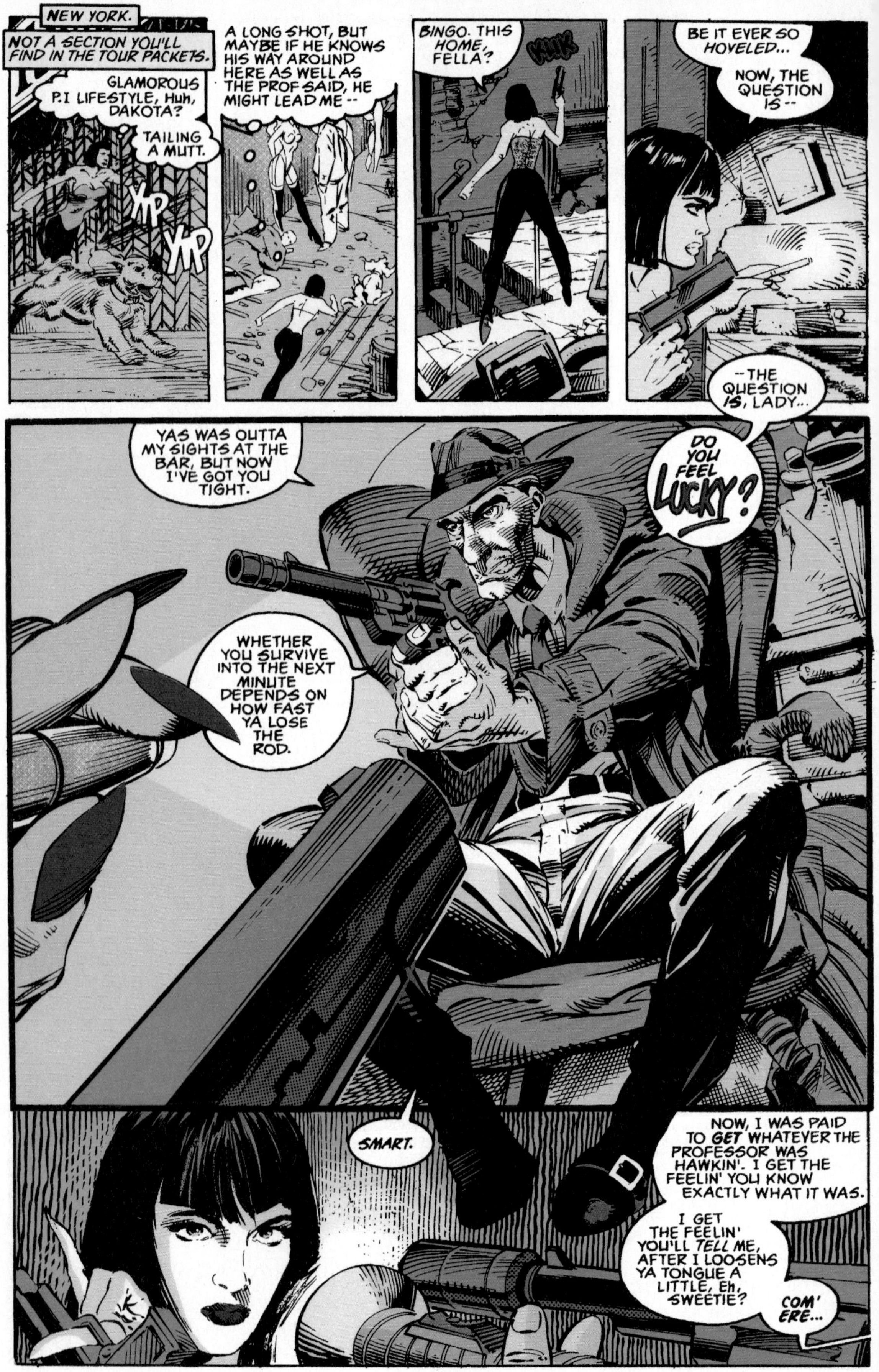

NEW YORK.
NOT A SECTION YOU'LL FIND IN THE TOUR PACKETS.
GLAMOROUS P.I LIFESTYLE, Huh, DAKOTA?
TAILING A MUTT.
YIP
YIP
A LONG SHOT, BUT MAYBE IF HE KNOWS HIS WAY AROUND HERE AS WELL AS THE PROF SAID, HE MIGHT LEAD ME --
BINGO. THIS HOME, FELLA?
KLIK
BE IT EVER SO HOVELED...
NOW, THE QUESTION IS --
-- THE QUESTION IS, LADY...
DO YOU FEEL LUCKY?
YAS WAS OUTTA MY SIGHTS AT THE BAR, BUT NOW I'VE GOT YOU TIGHT.
WHETHER YOU SURVIVE INTO THE NEXT MINUTE DEPENDS ON HOW FAST YA LOSE THE ROD.
SMART.
NOW, I WAS PAID TO GET WHATEVER THE PROFESSOR WAS HAWKIN'. I GET THE FEELIN' YOU KNOW EXACTLY WHAT IT WAS.
I GET THE FEELIN' YOU'LL TELL ME, AFTER I LOOSENS YA TONGUE A LITTLE, Eh, SWEETIE?
COM' ERE...

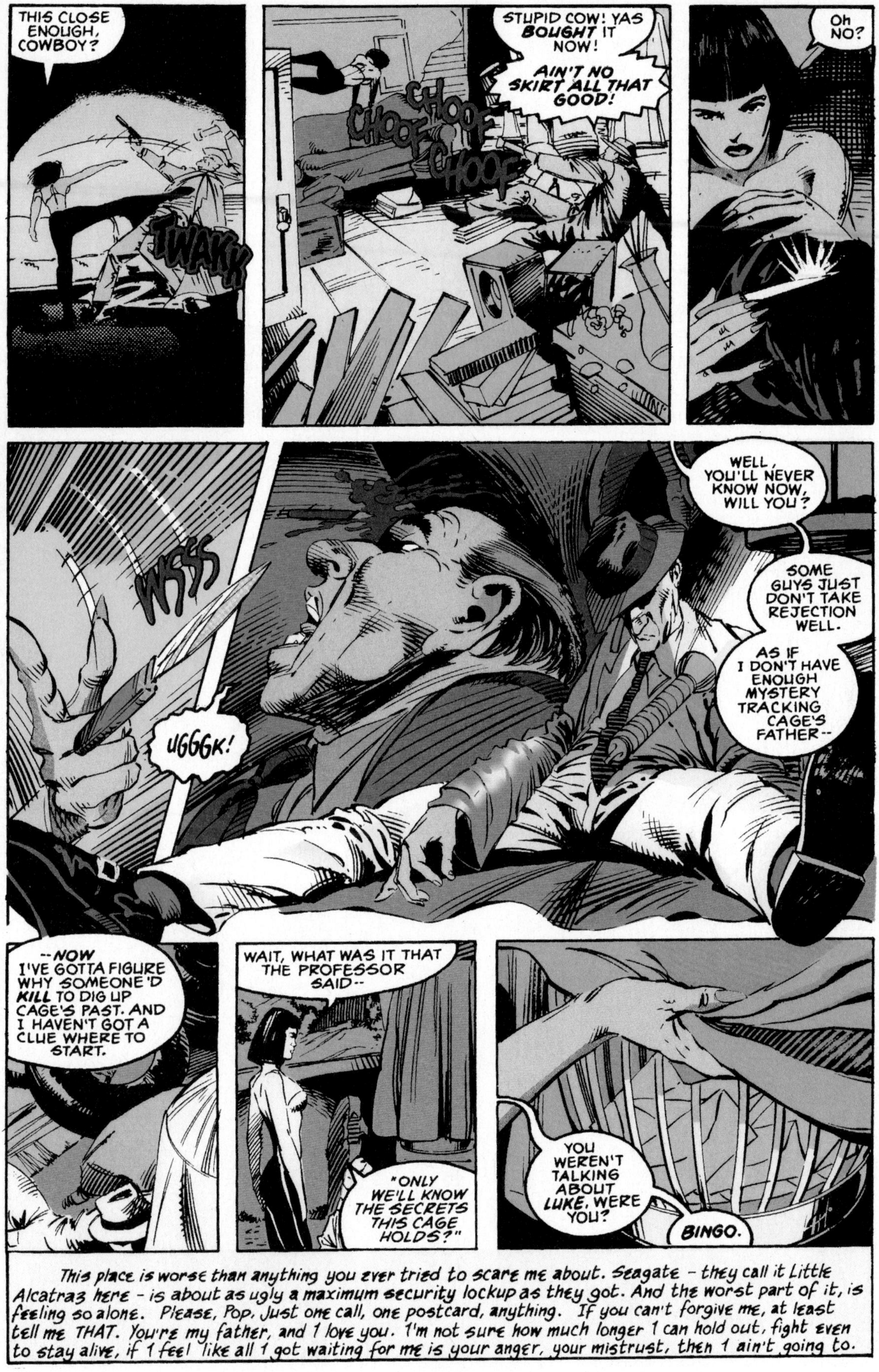
THIS CLOSE ENOUGH, COWBOY?
TWAKK
STUPID COW! YAS BOUGHT IT NOW!
AIN'T NO SKIRT ALL THAT GOOD!
CHOOF CHOOF CHOOF CHOOF
Oh NO?
WSSS
UGGGK!
WELL, YOU'LL NEVER KNOW NOW, WILL YOU?
SOME GUYS JUST DON'T TAKE REJECTION WELL.
AS IF I DON'T HAVE ENOUGH MYSTERY TRACKING CAGE'S FATHER--
--NOW I'VE GOTTA FIGURE WHY SOMEONE'D KILL TO DIG UP CAGE'S PAST. AND I HAVEN'T GOT A CLUE WHERE TO START.
WAIT, WHAT WAS IT THAT THE PROFESSOR SAID--
"ONLY WE'LL KNOW THE SECRETS THIS CAGE HOLDS?"
YOU WEREN'T TALKING ABOUT LUKE, WERE YOU?
BINGO.

This place is worse than anything you ever tried to scare me about. Seagate - they call it Little Alcatraz here - is about as ugly a maximum security lockup as they got. And the worst part of it, is feeling so alone. Please, Pop. Just one call, one postcard, anything. If you can't forgive me, at least tell me THAT. You're my father, and I love you. I'm not sure how much longer I can hold out, fight even to stay alive, if I feel like all I got waiting for me is your anger, your mistrust, then I ain't going to.

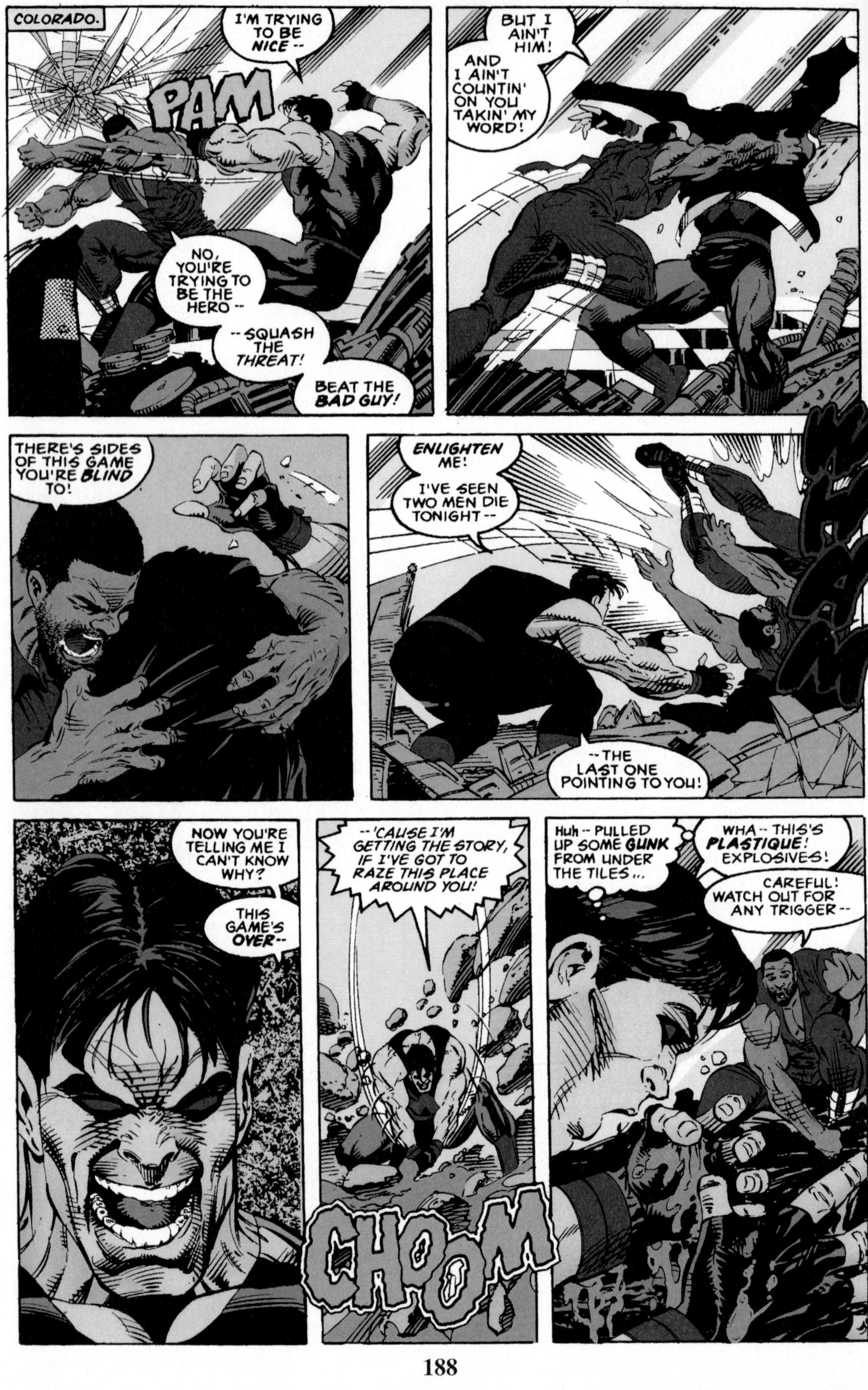
COLORADO.
I'M TRYING TO BE NICE --
PAM
NO, YOU'RE TRYING TO BE THE HERO --
-- SQUASH THE THREAT!
BEAT THE BAD GUY!
BUT I AIN'T HIM!
AND I AIN'T COUNTIN' ON YOU TAKIN' MY WORD!
THERE'S SIDES OF THIS GAME YOU'RE BLIND TO!
ENLIGHTEN ME!
I'VE SEEN TWO MEN DIE TONIGHT --
-- THE LAST ONE POINTING TO YOU!
NOW YOU'RE TELLING ME I CAN'T KNOW WHY?
THIS GAME'S OVER --
-- 'CAUSE I'M GETTING THE STORY, IF I'VE GOT TO RAZE THIS PLACE AROUND YOU!
CHOOM
Huh -- PULLED UP SOME GUNK FROM UNDER THE TILES...
WHA -- THIS'S PLASTIQUE! EXPLOSIVES!
CAREFUL! WATCH OUT FOR ANY TRIGGER --

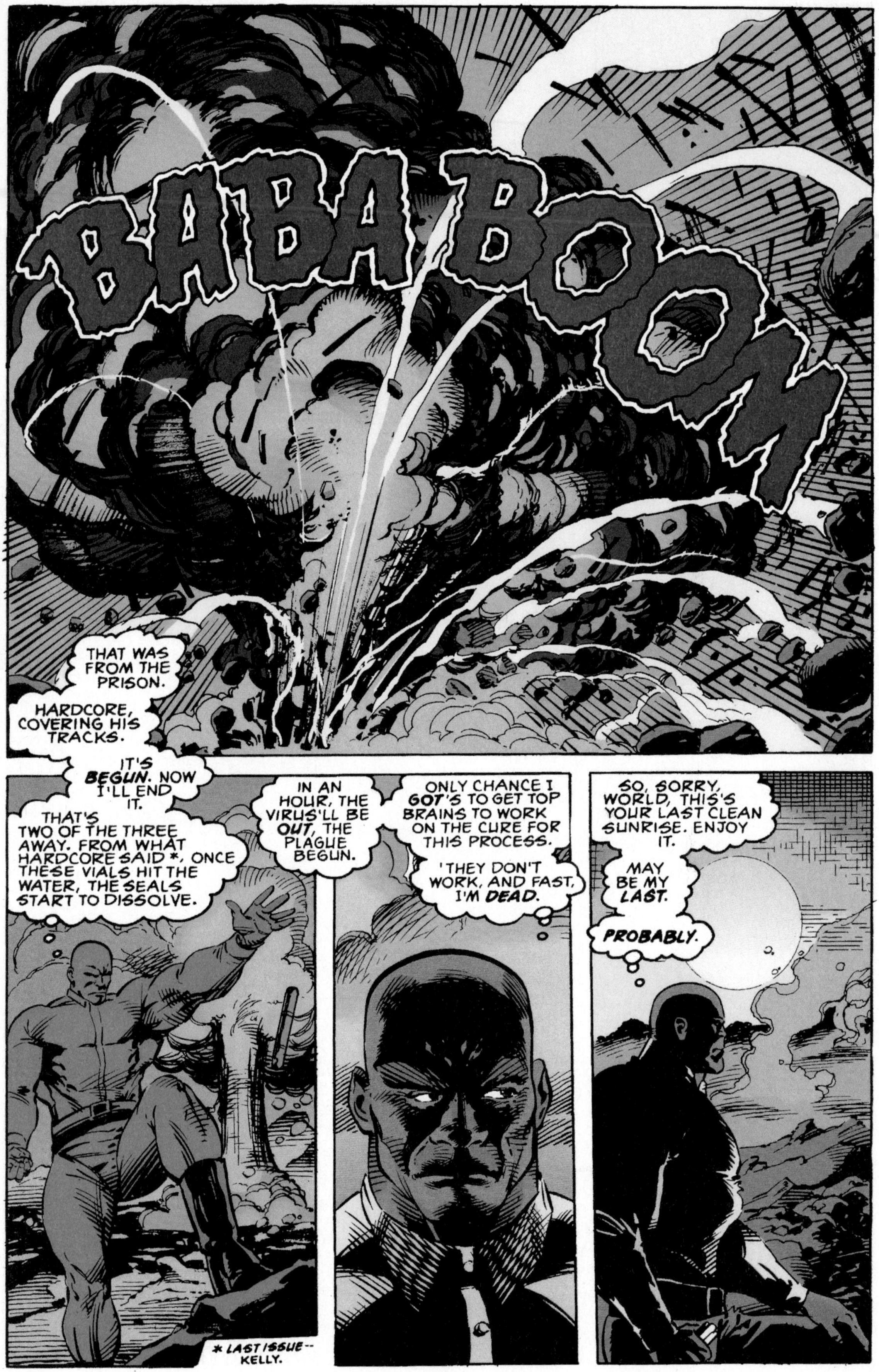
BABABOOOM
THAT WAS FROM THE PRISON.
HARDCORE, COVERING HIS TRACKS.
IT'S BEGUN. NOW I'LL END IT.
THAT'S TWO OF THE THREE AWAY. FROM WHAT HARDCORE SAID *, ONCE THESE VIALS HIT THE WATER, THE SEALS START TO DISSOLVE.
IN AN HOUR, THE VIRUS'LL BE OUT, THE PLAGUE BEGUN.
ONLY CHANCE I GOT'S TO GET TOP BRAINS TO WORK ON THE CURE FOR THIS PROCESS.
'THEY DON'T WORK, AND FAST, I'M DEAD.
SO, SORRY, WORLD, THIS'S YOUR LAST CLEAN SUNRISE. ENJOY IT.
MAY BE MY LAST.
PROBABLY.
* LAST ISSUE-- KELLY.

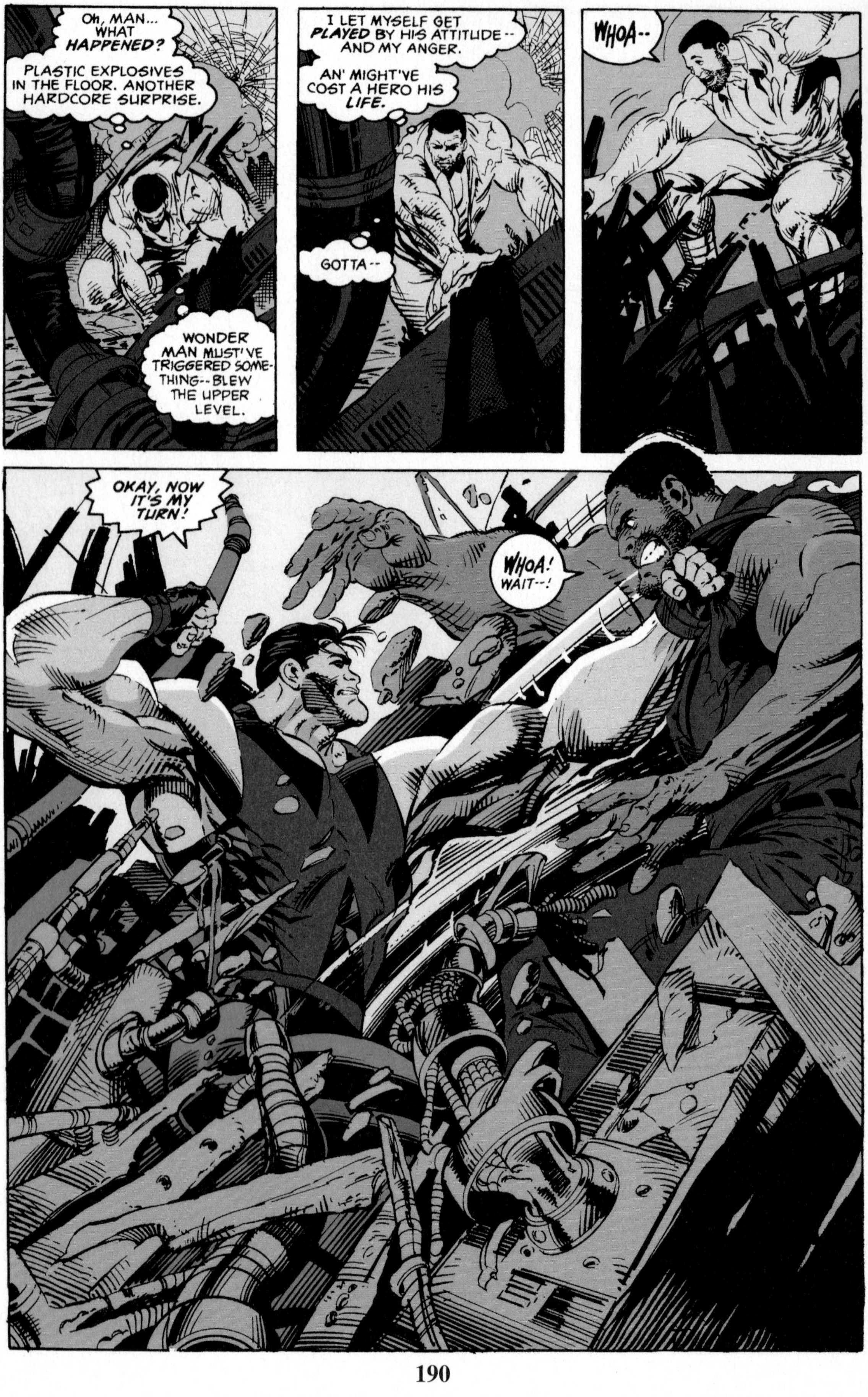
Oh, MAN... WHAT HAPPENED?
PLASTIC EXPLOSIVES IN THE FLOOR. ANOTHER HARDCORE SURPRISE.
WONDER MAN MUST'VE TRIGGERED SOMETHING--BLEW THE UPPER LEVEL.
I LET MYSELF GET PLAYED BY HIS ATTITUDE--AND MY ANGER.
AN' MIGHT'VE COST A HERO HIS LIFE.
GOTTA--
WHOA--
OKAY, NOW IT'S MY TURN!
WHOA! WAIT--!

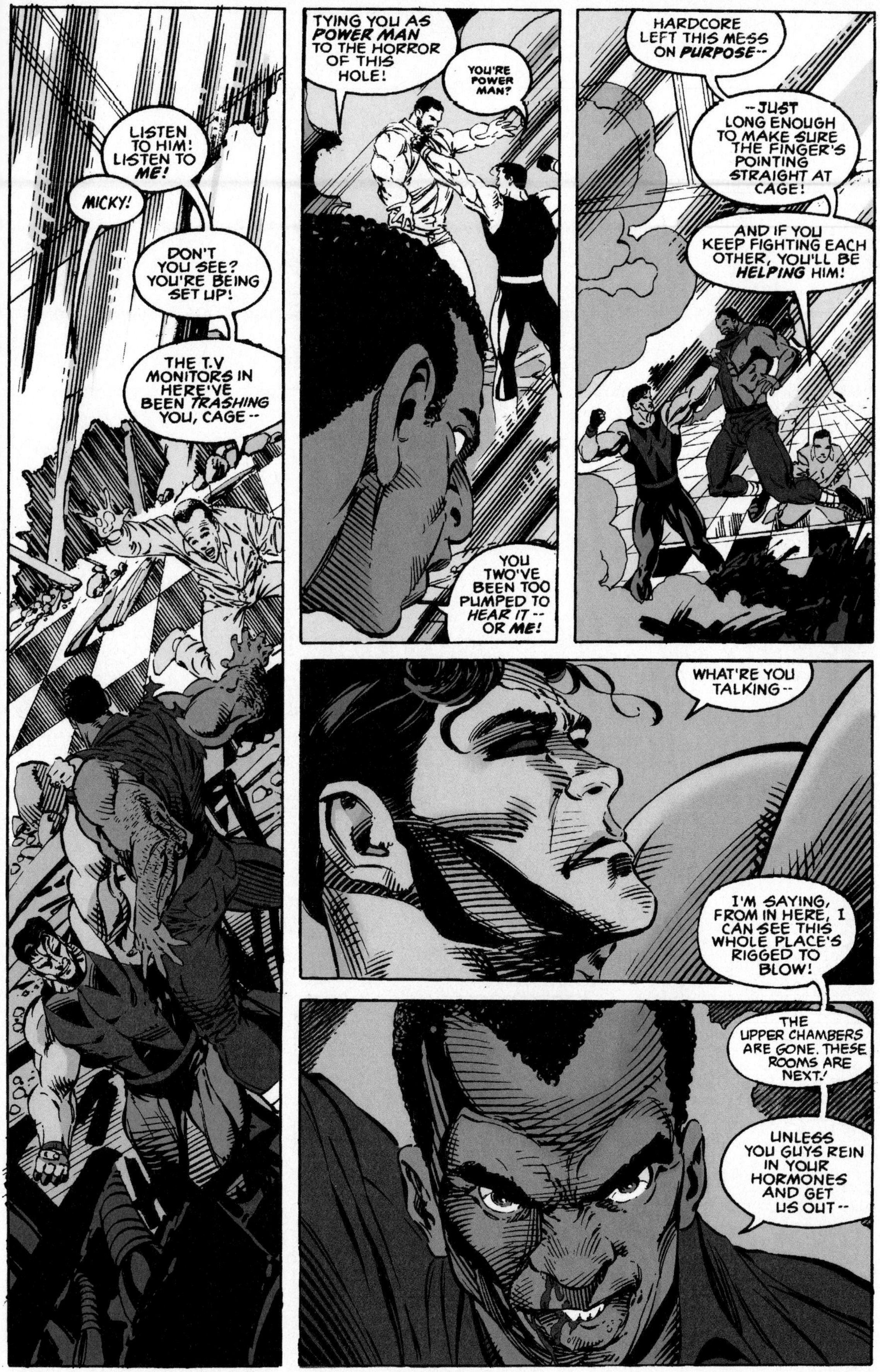
LISTEN TO HIM! LISTEN TO ME!
MICKY!
DON'T YOU SEE? YOU'RE BEING SET UP!
THE T.V MONITORS IN HERE'VE BEEN TRASHING YOU, CAGE --
TYING YOU AS POWER MAN TO THE HORROR OF THIS HOLE!
YOU'RE POWER MAN?
YOU TWO'VE BEEN TOO PUMPED TO HEAR IT -- OR ME!
HARDCORE LEFT THIS MESS ON PURPOSE --
-- JUST LONG ENOUGH TO MAKE SURE THE FINGER'S POINTING STRAIGHT AT CAGE!
AND IF YOU KEEP FIGHTING EACH OTHER, YOU'LL BE HELPING HIM!
WHAT'RE YOU TALKING --
I'M SAYING, FROM IN HERE, I CAN SEE THIS WHOLE PLACE'S RIGGED TO BLOW!
THE UPPER CHAMBERS ARE GONE. THESE ROOMS ARE NEXT!
UNLESS YOU GUYS REIN IN YOUR HORMONES AND GET US OUT --

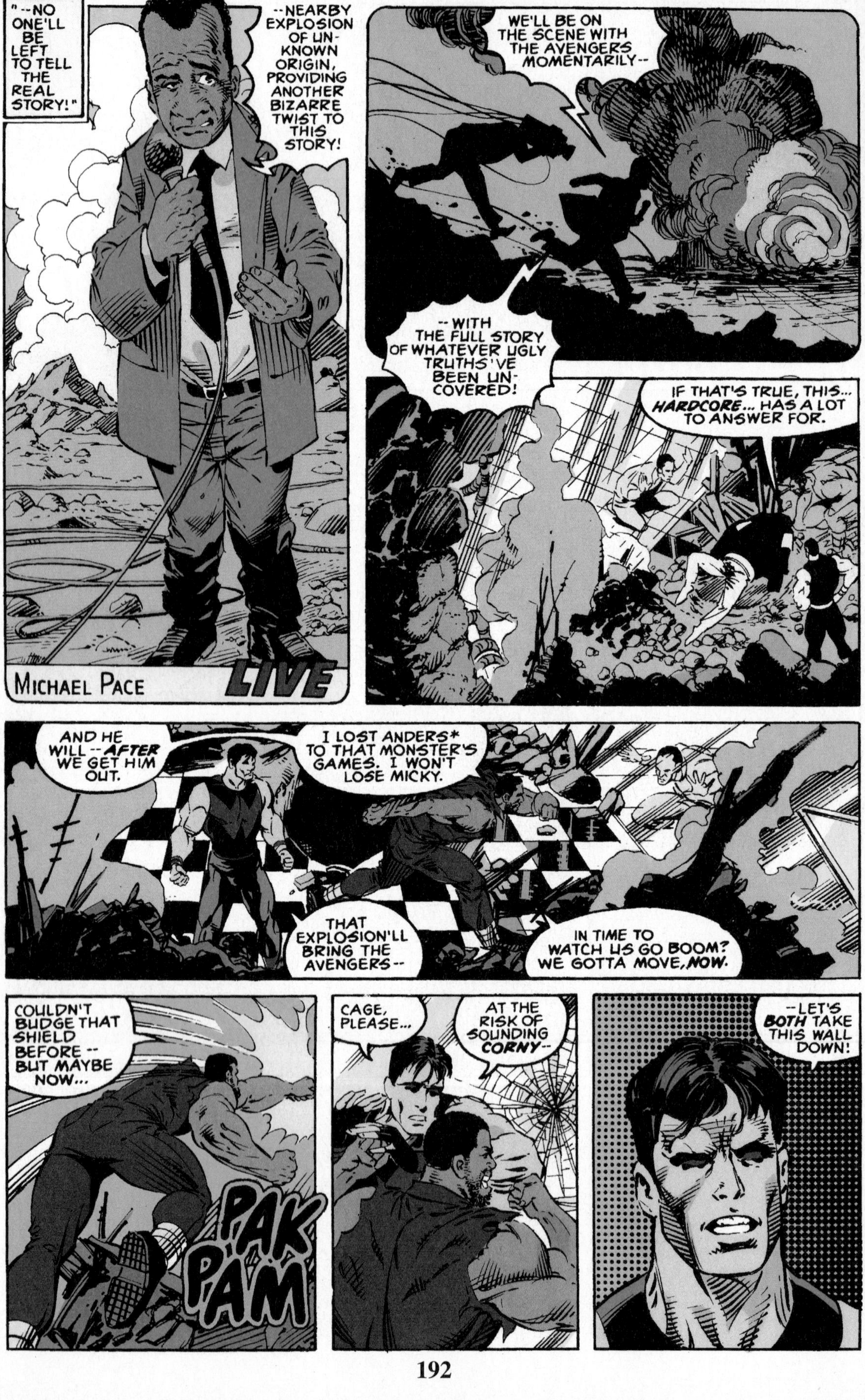
"--NO ONE'LL BE LEFT TO TELL THE REAL STORY!"
--NEARBY EXPLOSION OF UN-KNOWN ORIGIN, PROVIDING ANOTHER BIZARRE TWIST TO THIS STORY!
MICHAEL PACE
LIVE
WE'LL BE ON THE SCENE WITH THE AVENGERS MOMENTARILY--
--WITH THE FULL STORY OF WHATEVER UGLY TRUTHS'VE BEEN UN-COVERED!
IF THAT'S TRUE, THIS... HARDCORE... HAS A LOT TO ANSWER FOR.
AND HE WILL--AFTER WE GET HIM OUT.
I LOST ANDERS* TO THAT MONSTER'S GAMES. I WON'T LOSE MICKY.
THAT EXPLOSION'LL BRING THE AVENGERS--
IN TIME TO WATCH US GO BOOM? WE GOTTA MOVE, NOW.
COULDN'T BUDGE THAT SHIELD BEFORE -- BUT MAYBE NOW...
PAK PAM
CAGE, PLEASE...
AT THE RISK OF SOUNDING CORNY--
--LET'S BOTH TAKE THIS WALL DOWN!

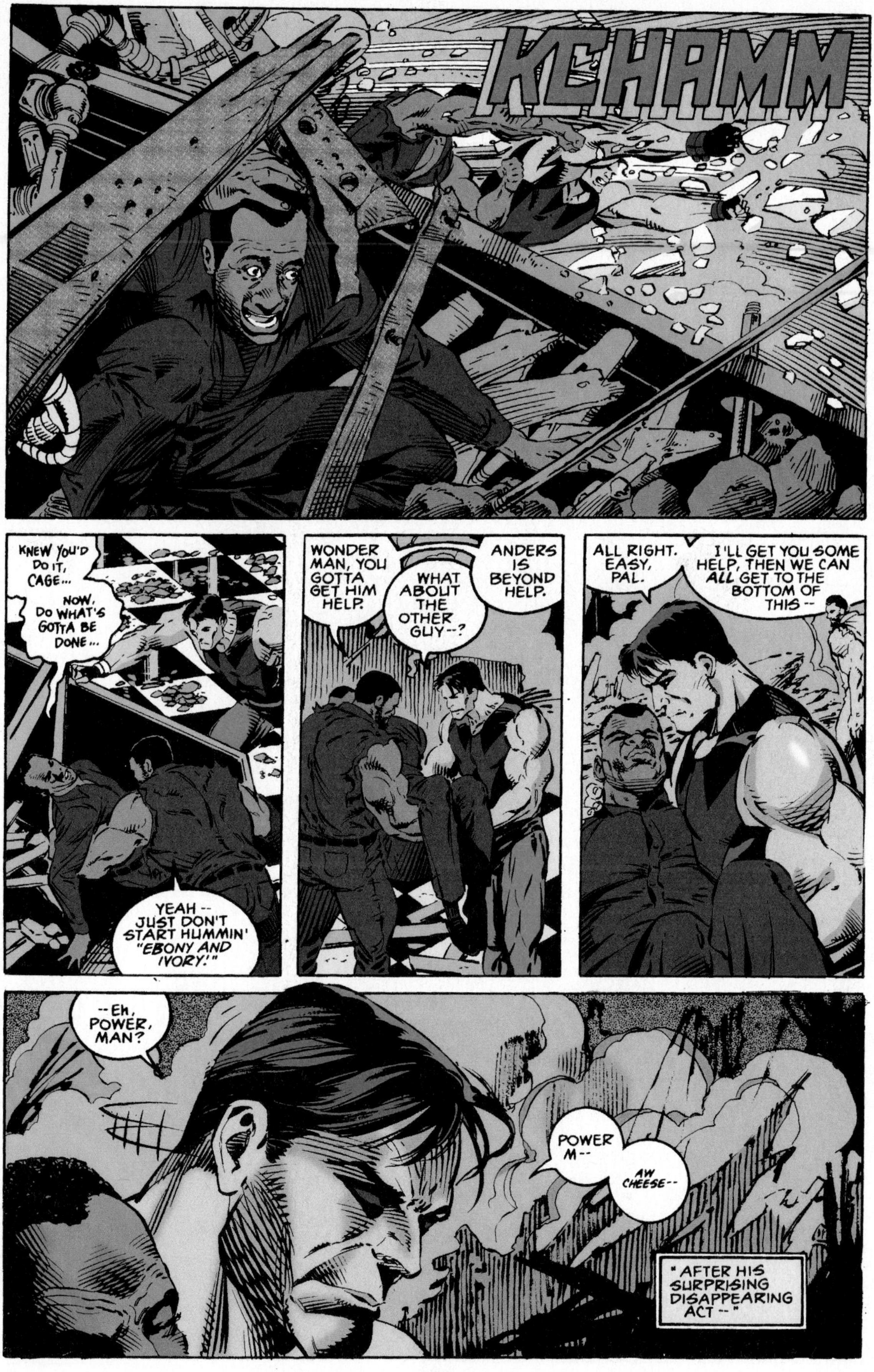
KCHAMM
KNEW YOU'D DO IT, CAGE...
NOW, DO WHAT'S GOTTA BE DONE...
YEAH -- JUST DON'T START HUMMIN' "EBONY AND IVORY!"
WONDER MAN, YOU GOTTA GET HIM HELP.
WHAT ABOUT THE OTHER GUY --?
ANDERS IS BEYOND HELP.
ALL RIGHT. EASY, PAL.
I'LL GET YOU SOME HELP, THEN WE CAN ALL GET TO THE BOTTOM OF THIS --
-- Eh, POWER, MAN?
POWER M --
AW CHEESE --
"AFTER HIS SURPRISING DISAPPEARING ACT -- "

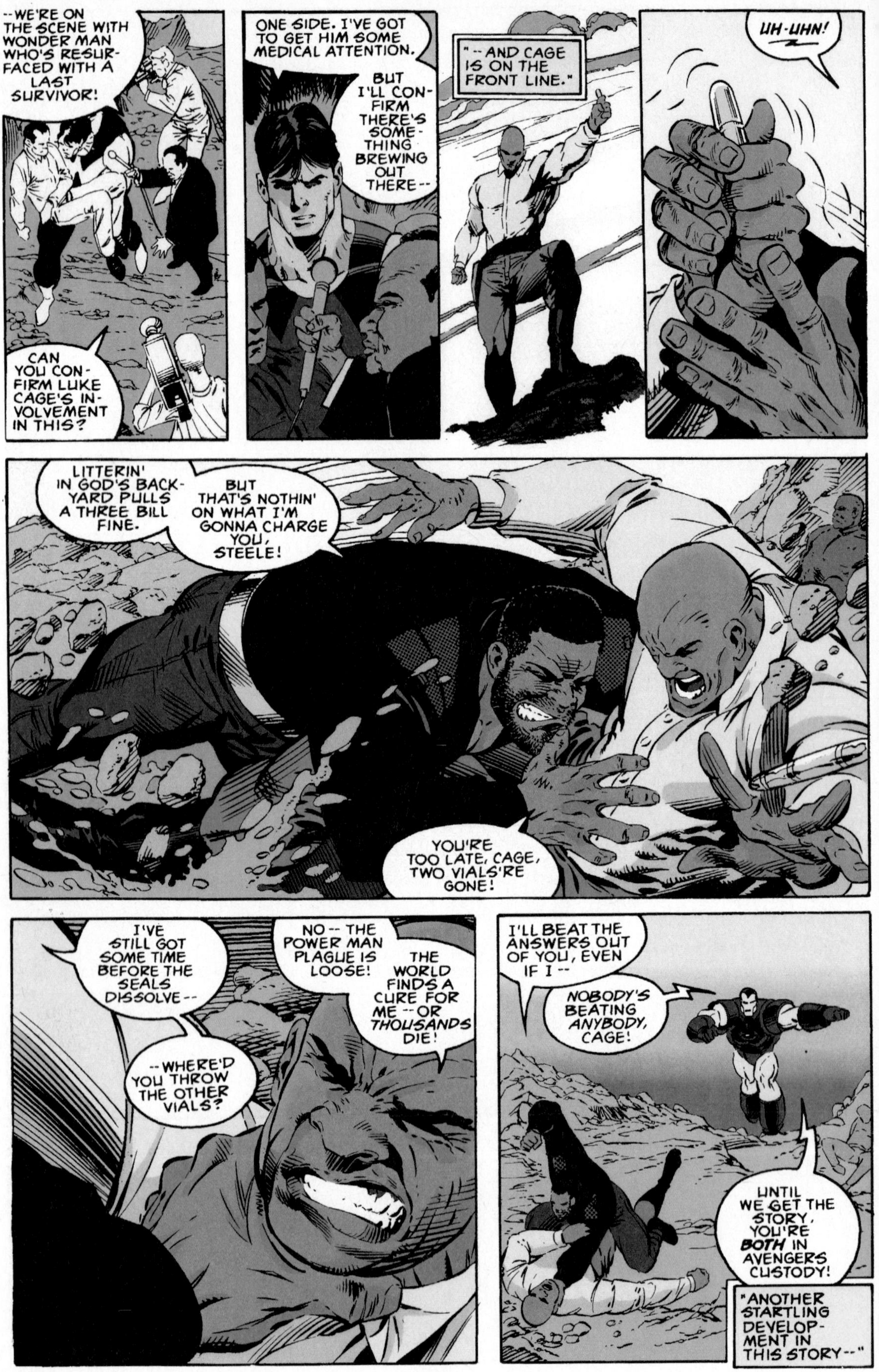
--WE'RE ON THE SCENE WITH WONDER MAN WHO'S RESURFACED WITH A LAST SURVIVOR!
CAN YOU CONFIRM LUKE CAGE'S INVOLVEMENT IN THIS?
ONE SIDE. I'VE GOT TO GET HIM SOME MEDICAL ATTENTION.
BUT I'LL CONFIRM THERE'S SOMETHING BREWING OUT THERE--
"--AND CAGE IS ON THE FRONT LINE."
UH-UHN!
LITTERIN' IN GOD'S BACKYARD PULLS A THREE BILL FINE.
BUT THAT'S NOTHIN' ON WHAT I'M GONNA CHARGE YOU, STEELE!
YOU'RE TOO LATE, CAGE, TWO VIALS'RE GONE!
I'VE STILL GOT SOME TIME BEFORE THE SEALS DISSOLVE--
--WHERE'D YOU THROW THE OTHER VIALS?
NO -- THE POWER MAN PLAGUE IS LOOSE!
THE WORLD FINDS A CURE FOR ME --OR THOUSANDS DIE!
I'LL BEAT THE ANSWERS OUT OF YOU, EVEN IF I --
NOBODY'S BEATING ANYBODY, CAGE!
UNTIL WE GET THE STORY, YOU'RE BOTH IN AVENGERS CUSTODY!
"ANOTHER STARTLING DEVELOPMENT IN THIS STORY--"

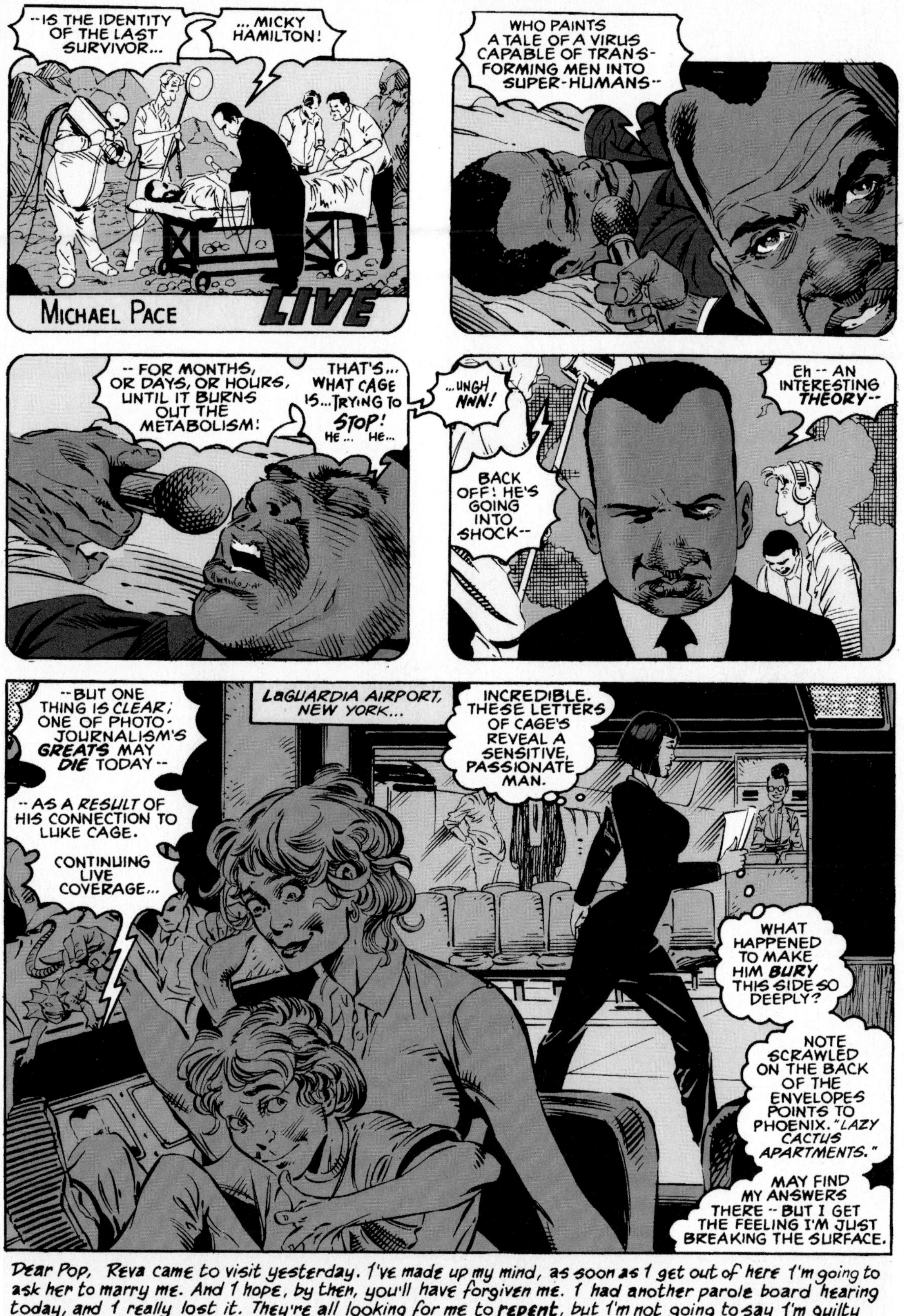
--IS THE IDENTITY OF THE LAST SURVIVOR...
...MICKY HAMILTON!
MICHAEL PACE
LIVE
WHO PAINTS A TALE OF A VIRUS CAPABLE OF TRANS-FORMING MEN INTO SUPER-HUMANS--
--FOR MONTHS, OR DAYS, OR HOURS, UNTIL IT BURNS OUT THE METABOLISM!
THAT'S... WHAT CAGE IS...TRYING TO STOP! HE... HE...
...UNGH NNN!
Eh -- AN INTERESTING THEORY--
BACK OFF! HE'S GOING INTO SHOCK--
--BUT ONE THING IS CLEAR; ONE OF PHOTO-JOURNALISM'S GREATS MAY DIE TODAY--
--AS A RESULT OF HIS CONNECTION TO LUKE CAGE.
CONTINUING LIVE COVERAGE...
LaGUARDIA AIRPORT, NEW YORK...
INCREDIBLE. THESE LETTERS OF CAGE'S REVEAL A SENSITIVE, PASSIONATE MAN.
WHAT HAPPENED TO MAKE HIM BURY THIS SIDE SO DEEPLY?
NOTE SCRAWLED ON THE BACK OF THE ENVELOPES POINTS TO PHOENIX. "LAZY CACTUS APARTMENTS."
MAY FIND MY ANSWERS THERE -- BUT I GET THE FEELING I'M JUST BREAKING THE SURFACE.

Dear Pop, Reva came to visit yesterday. I've made up my mind, as soon as I get out of here I'm going to ask her to marry me. And I hope, by then, you'll have forgiven me. I had another parole board hearing today, and I really lost it. They're all looking for me to **repent**, but I'm not going to say I'm guilty when I know I'm not. That's one thing you taught that stuck --if you know you're right, stick to your guns. And I know I am. I know I'm going to come out of this all right.
I know I'm going to make it up to you.

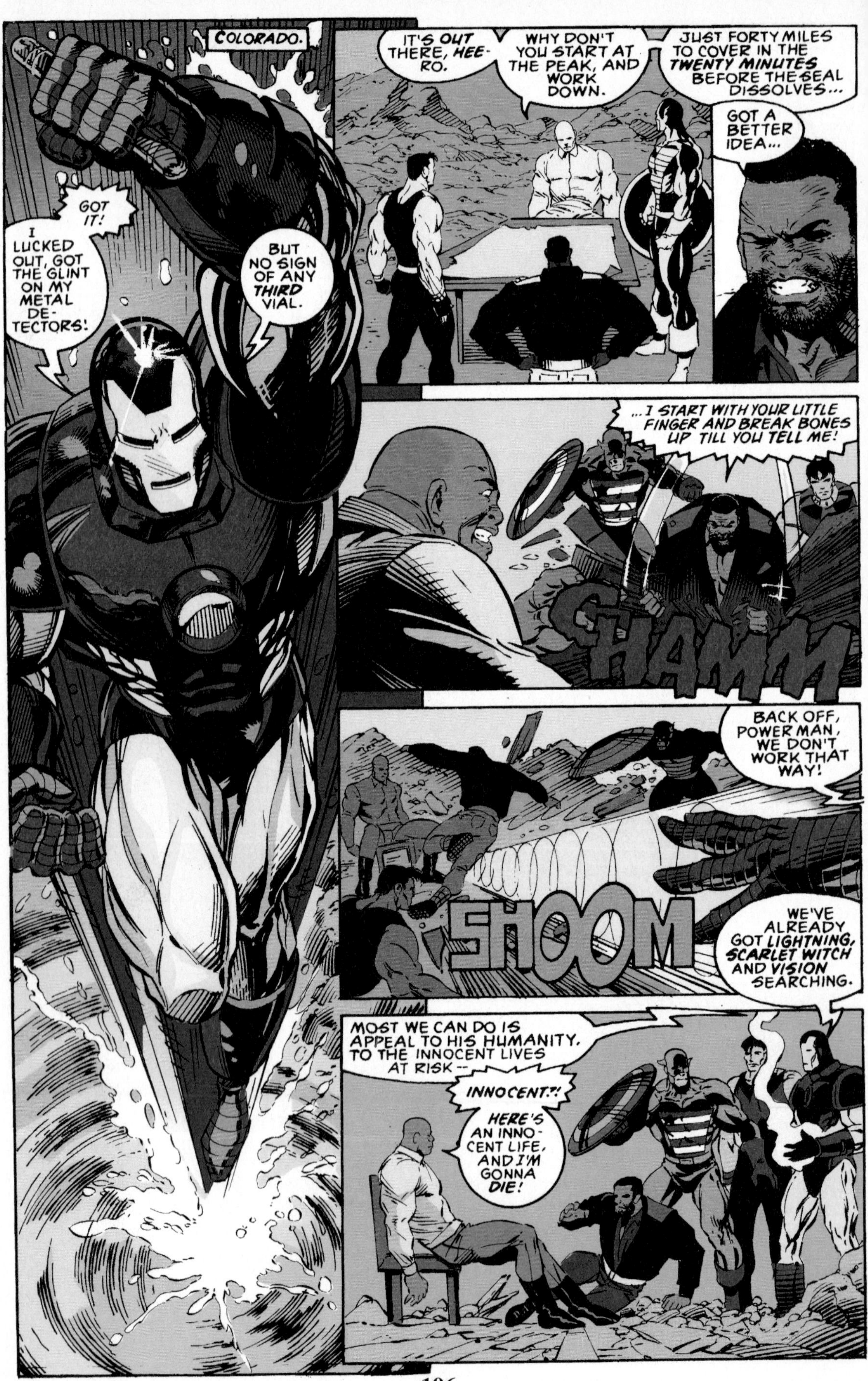
COLORADO.
GOT IT!
I LUCKED OUT, GOT THE GLINT ON MY METAL DE-TECTORS!
BUT NO SIGN OF ANY THIRD VIAL.
IT'S OUT THERE, HEE-RO.
WHY DON'T YOU START AT THE PEAK, AND WORK DOWN.
JUST FORTY MILES TO COVER IN THE TWENTY MINUTES BEFORE THE SEAL DISSOLVES...
GOT A BETTER IDEA...
...I START WITH YOUR LITTLE FINGER AND BREAK BONES UP TILL YOU TELL ME!
CHAMM
BACK OFF, POWER MAN, WE DON'T WORK THAT WAY!
SHOOM
WE'VE ALREADY GOT LIGHTNING, SCARLET WITCH AND VISION SEARCHING.
MOST WE CAN DO IS APPEAL TO HIS HUMANITY. TO THE INNOCENT LIVES AT RISK--
INNOCENT?!
HERE'S AN INNO-CENT LIFE, AND I'M GONNA DIE!

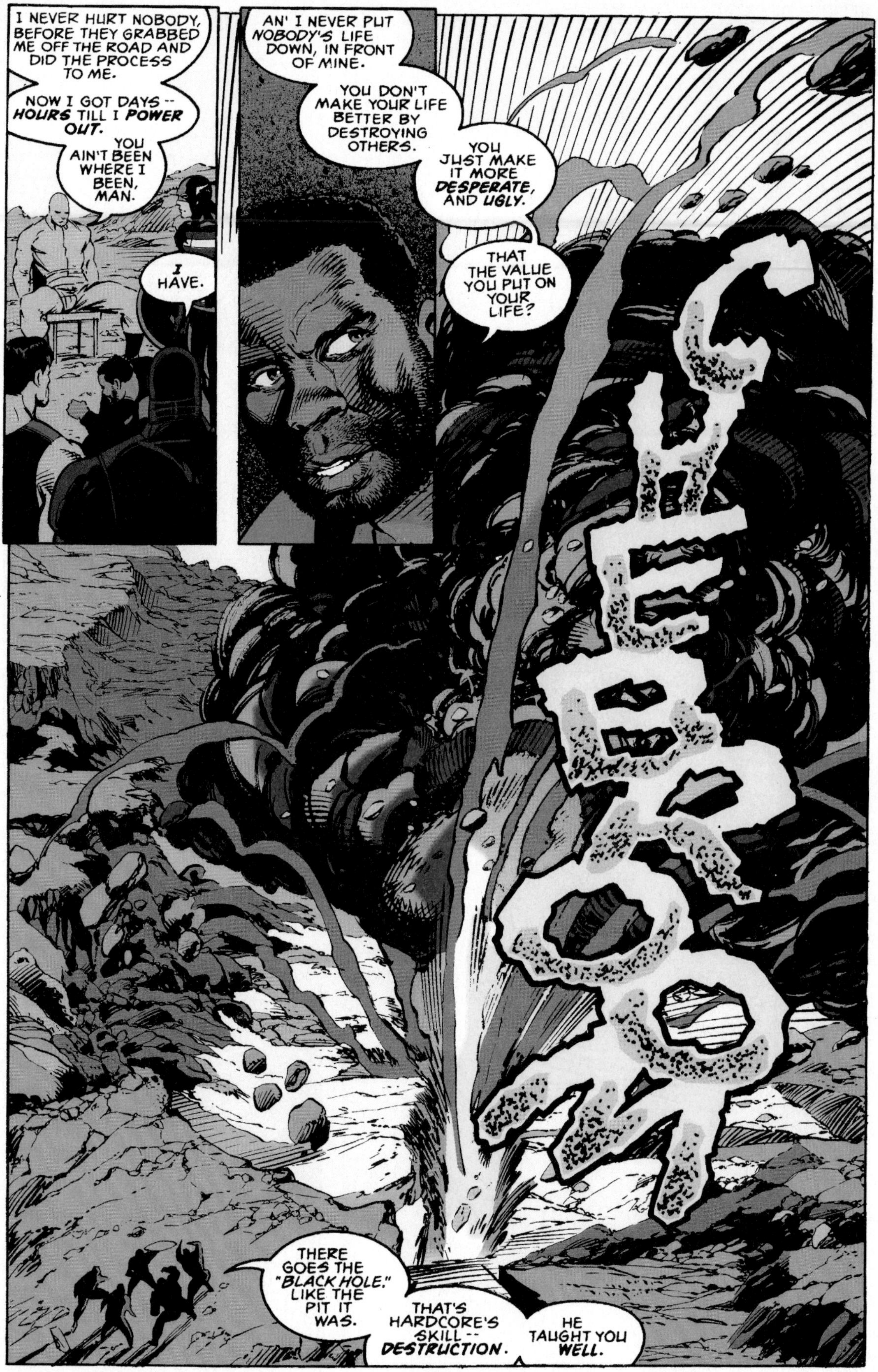

I NEVER HURT NOBODY, BEFORE THEY GRABBED ME OFF THE ROAD AND DID THE PROCESS TO ME.
NOW I GOT DAYS -- HOURS TILL I POWER OUT.
YOU AIN'T BEEN WHERE I BEEN, MAN.
I HAVE.
AN' I NEVER PUT NOBODY'S LIFE DOWN, IN FRONT OF MINE.
YOU DON'T MAKE YOUR LIFE BETTER BY DESTROYING OTHERS.
YOU JUST MAKE IT MORE DESPERATE, AND UGLY.
THAT THE VALUE YOU PUT ON YOUR LIFE?
THERE GOES THE "BLACK HOLE." LIKE THE PIT IT WAS.
THAT'S HARDCORE'S SKILL -- DESTRUCTION.
HE TAUGHT YOU WELL.

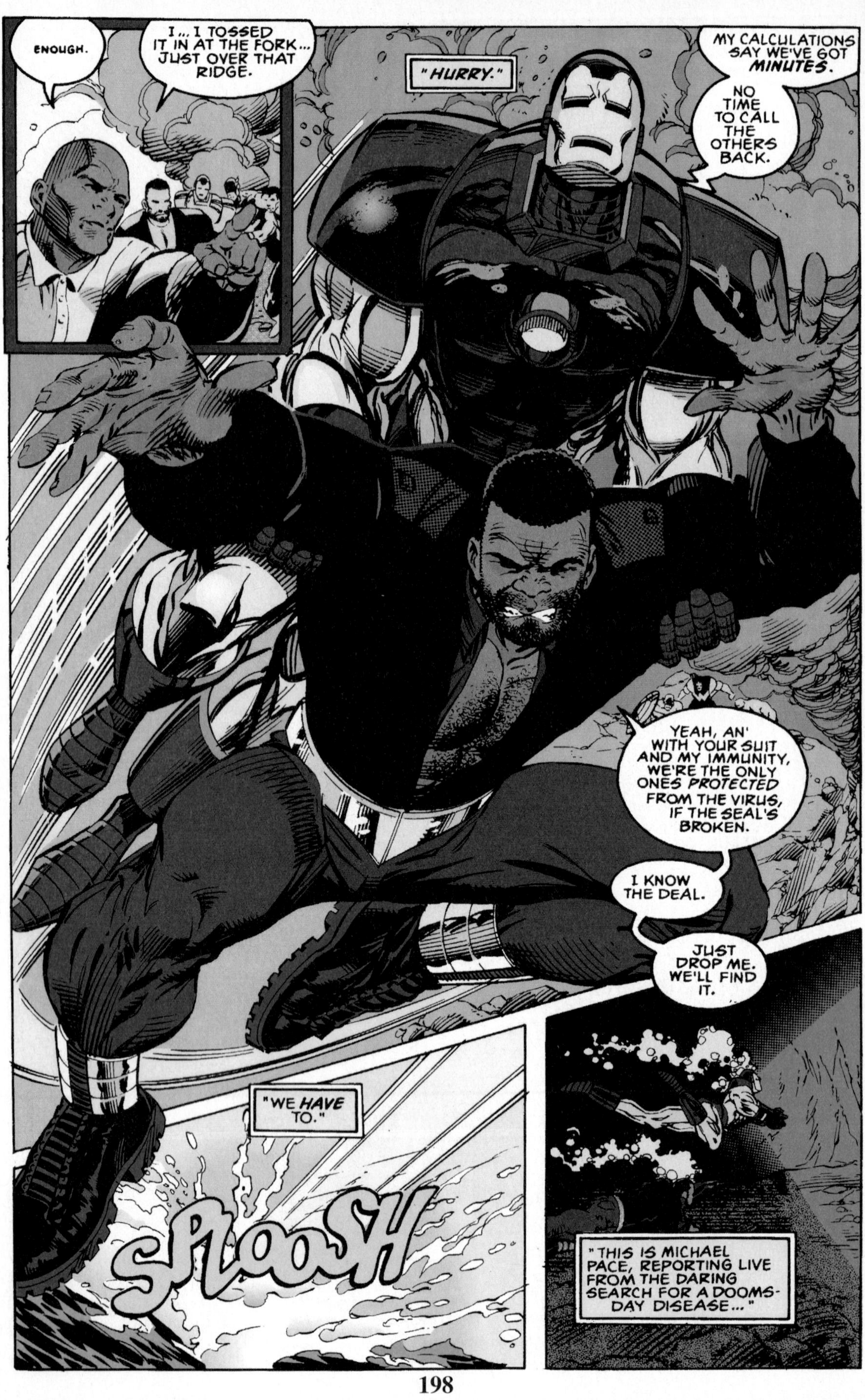
ENOUGH.
I... I TOSSED IT IN AT THE FORK... JUST OVER THAT RIDGE.
"HURRY."
MY CALCULATIONS SAY WE'VE GOT MINUTES.
NO TIME TO CALL THE OTHERS BACK.
YEAH, AN' WITH YOUR SUIT AND MY IMMUNITY, WE'RE THE ONLY ONES PROTECTED FROM THE VIRUS, IF THE SEAL'S BROKEN.
I KNOW THE DEAL.
JUST DROP ME. WE'LL FIND IT.
"WE HAVE TO."
SPLOOSH
"THIS IS MICHAEL PACE, REPORTING LIVE FROM THE DARING SEARCH FOR A DOOMS-DAY DISEASE..."

"A DISEASE WHICH ALLEGEDLY GAVE LUKE CAGE HIS ABILITIES.

"A TRANSFORMATIVE CURSE WHICH HE MAKES HIS LIVING *BY*...

"...AND WHICH HE MIGHT, APPARENTLY, DIE *FOR*...

"..."

RRRAAA!!

IRON MAN!

DO IT!

FZZZH!!

WE DID IT, POWER MAN! IT'S *OVER!*

IRON MAN --

-- THE NAME IS *CAGE.*

OVER. IT'S ALL OVER.

THAT WAS THE SCENE JUST HOURS AGO, AS THE AVENGERS NARROWLY AVERTED DISASTER, HERE IN COLORADO.

ALL CHARGES AGAINST LUKE CAGE HAVE BE--?

WHAT'S WRONG--?

IT'S HAPPENING...

Hrmm... AS IT BEGAN, OUR STORY ENDS WITH DRAMA--

EASY, STEELE!

NO! NO!

THE PERPETRATOR OF CRIMES ON HUMANITY REAPING --

WHAT?

LEMME DROP SOME SCIENCE TO YA, ACE --

-- THERE'RE NO BAD GUYS HERE! ONLY VICTIMS!

STEELE TOOK IT ALL, AND SURVIVED. AND, AT THE LAST, HE WAS THE HERO.

PHOENIX AIRPORT.

LOT OF THINGS START TO MAKE SENSE ABOUT YOU, CAGE.

MAKING ME WANT TO KNOW MORE. IN TIME.

ALL THINGS COME, TO THOSE WHO WAIT...

Dear Pop, I don't know why I'm writing this — knowing you'll never read it. When James told me you died, yesterday, I had to write one last letter. He said you're at rest now. And he said it was my fault.

All my life, that's been true, but the people I care about most are always getting hurt. First, what happened to Ma. A month ago, Reva, dying in that car accident. Now you. I keep wondering how much I'm supposed to take before I go crazy, or just die, inside. I keep wondering — WHY? I swear, Pop, I never meant to hurt you

...HE WAS THE HERO. BUT YOU DON'T WANT TO HEAR THAT, DO YOU?

YOU WANT THE *DIRT* AND *UGLY* INNUENDO, LIKE YOU BEEN SPREADING ABOUT ME!

BUT YOU DON'T KNOW THE *REAL* DEAL ON LUKE CAGE, MISTER. *NOBODY* KNO--

MUTE

HAVEN'T CHANGED A BIT, HAVE YOU, BRO'?

LAZY CACTUS APARTMENTS. PHOENIX, ARIZONA.

JAMES? WHAT'S--

IT'S ALL RIGHT, POP. JUST THE T.V. RUINING MY *SURPRISE!*

WE'RE GOING ON THAT *VACATION* I PROMISED YOU.

AWAY FROM THIS DRY HEAT --

-- AND AWAY FROM *HIM*. HE'S TOO CLOSE.

HE THINKS YOU'RE DEAD, AS YOU THINK *HE* IS. THAT LIE PROTECTS YOU FROM HIM.

AFTER WHAT HE DID TO MA, I MEAN TO *KEEP* THAT PROTECTION.

I WON'T SEE YOU HURT, POP.

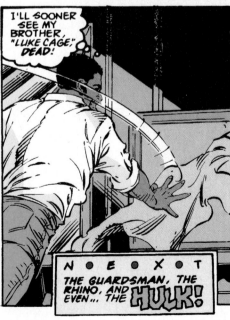

I'LL SOONER SEE MY BROTHER, "LUKE CAGE," DEAD!

N E X T
THE GUARDSMAN, THE RHINO, AND EVEN ... THE HULK!

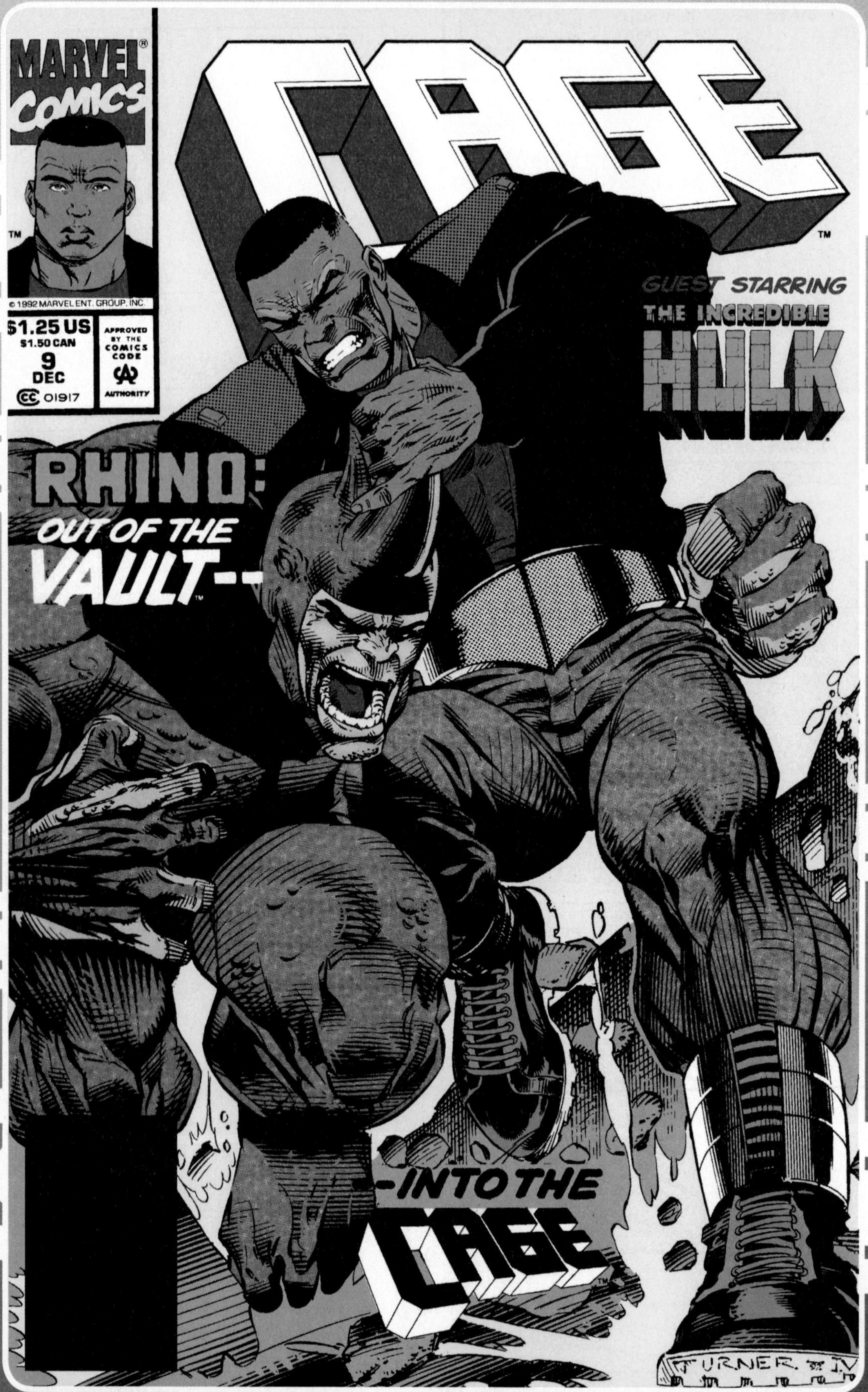
MARVEL COMICS
CAGE
© 1992 MARVEL ENT. GROUP, INC.
$1.25 US
$1.50 CAN
9
DEC
CC 01917
APPROVED BY THE COMICS CODE AUTHORITY
GUEST STARRING
THE INCREDIBLE
HULK
RHINO:
OUT OF THE
VAULT--
-INTO THE
CAGE
TURNER

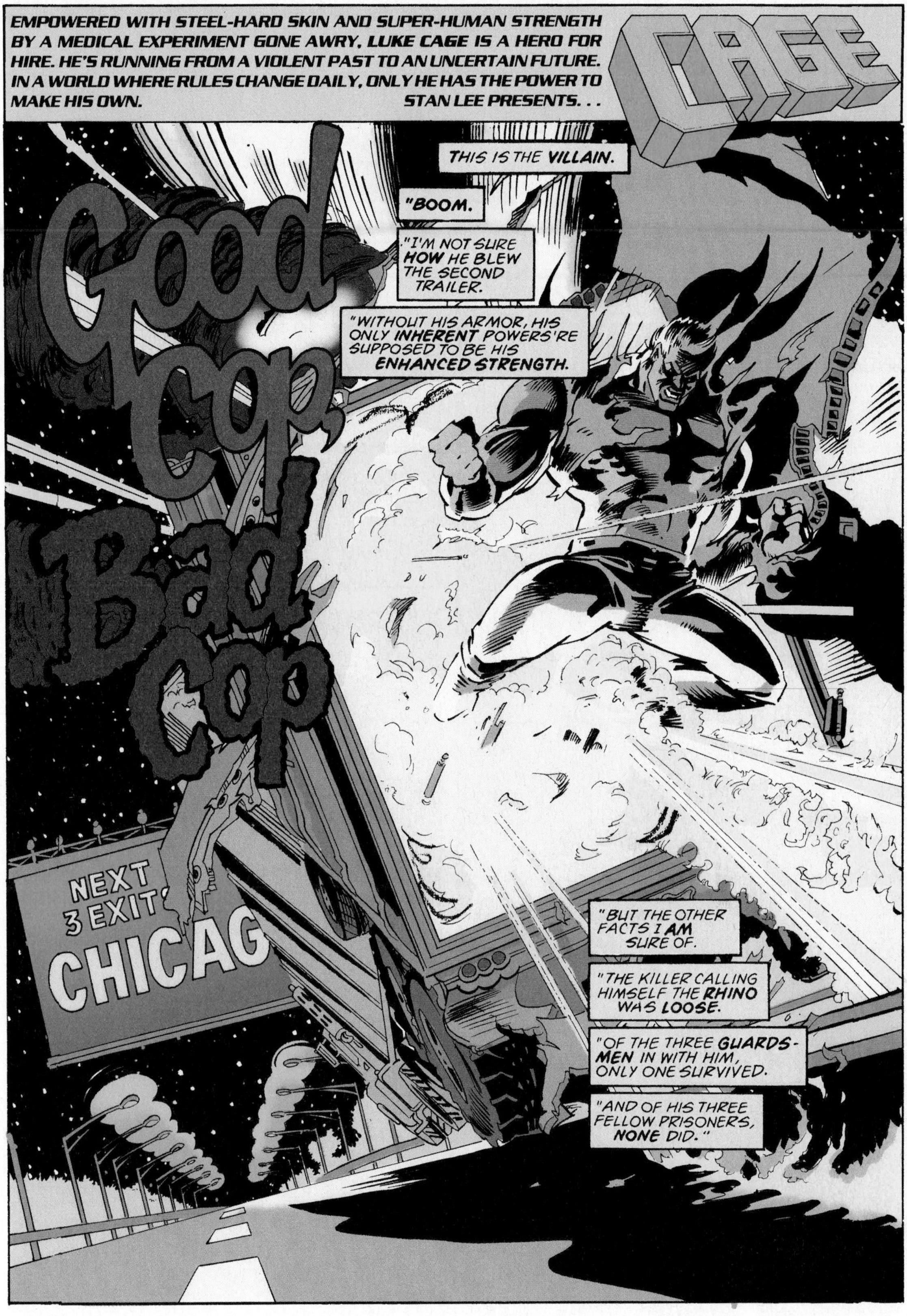
EMPOWERED WITH STEEL-HARD SKIN AND SUPER-HUMAN STRENGTH BY A MEDICAL EXPERIMENT GONE AWRY, LUKE CAGE IS A HERO FOR HIRE. HE'S RUNNING FROM A VIOLENT PAST TO AN UNCERTAIN FUTURE. IN A WORLD WHERE RULES CHANGE DAILY, ONLY HE HAS THE POWER TO MAKE HIS OWN.
STAN LEE PRESENTS. . .
CAGE
Good Cop, Bad Cop
THIS IS THE VILLAIN.
"BOOM.
"I'M NOT SURE HOW HE BLEW THE SECOND TRAILER.
"WITHOUT HIS ARMOR, HIS ONLY INHERENT POWERS'RE SUPPOSED TO BE HIS ENHANCED STRENGTH.
NEXT 3 EXITS CHICAG
"BUT THE OTHER FACTS I AM SURE OF.
"THE KILLER CALLING HIMSELF THE RHINO WAS LOOSE.
"OF THE THREE GUARDS-MEN IN WITH HIM, ONLY ONE SURVIVED.
"AND OF HIS THREE FELLOW PRISONERS, NONE DID."

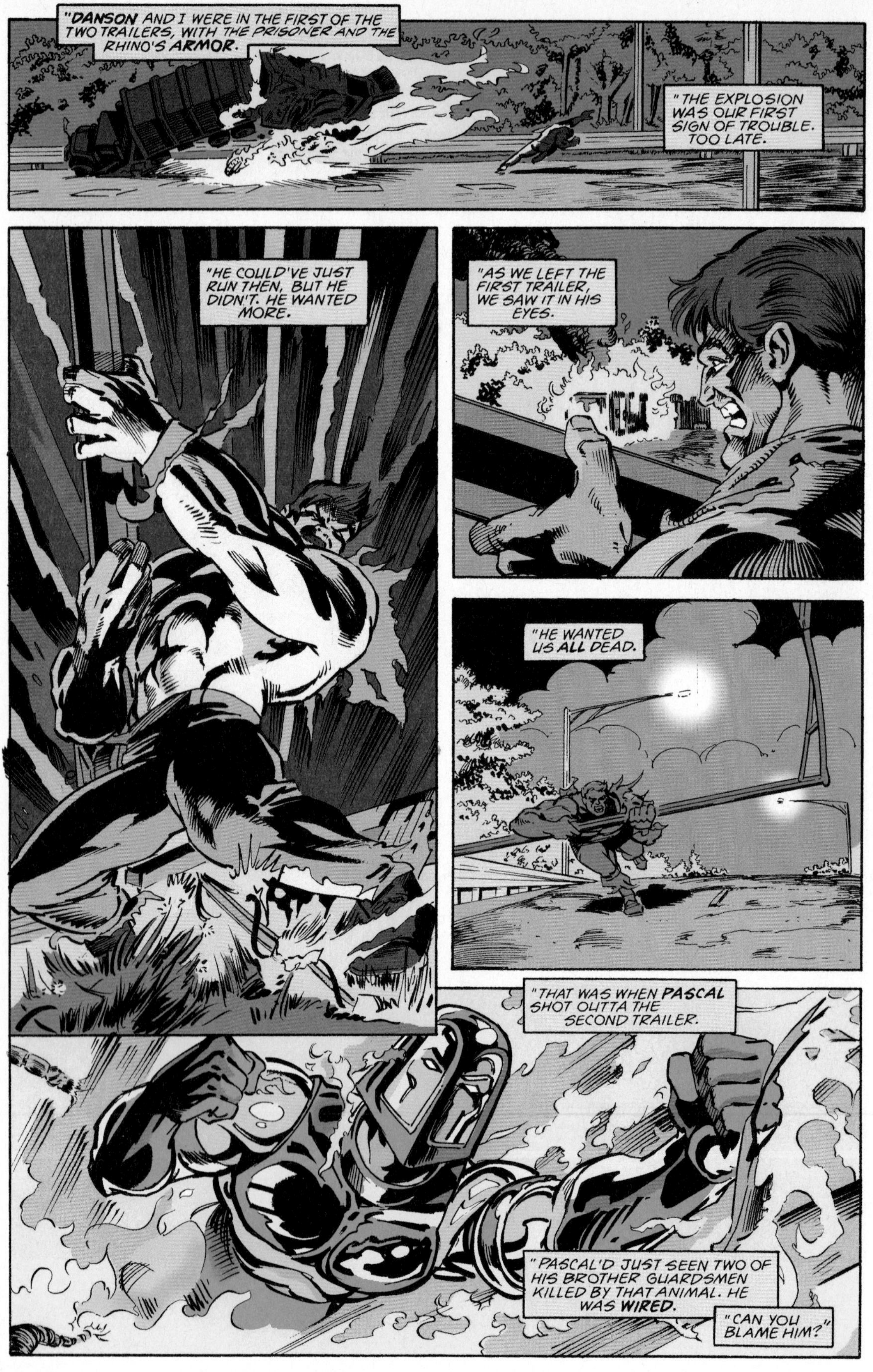
"DANSON AND I WERE IN THE FIRST OF THE TWO TRAILERS, WITH THE PRISONER AND THE RHINO'S ARMOR.
"THE EXPLOSION WAS OUR FIRST SIGN OF TROUBLE. TOO LATE.
"HE COULD'VE JUST RUN THEN, BUT HE DIDN'T. HE WANTED MORE.
"AS WE LEFT THE FIRST TRAILER, WE SAW IT IN HIS EYES.
"HE WANTED US ALL DEAD.
"THAT WAS WHEN PASCAL SHOT OUTTA THE SECOND TRAILER.
"PASCAL'D JUST SEEN TWO OF HIS BROTHER GUARDSMEN KILLED BY THAT ANIMAL. HE WAS WIRED.
"CAN YOU BLAME HIM?"

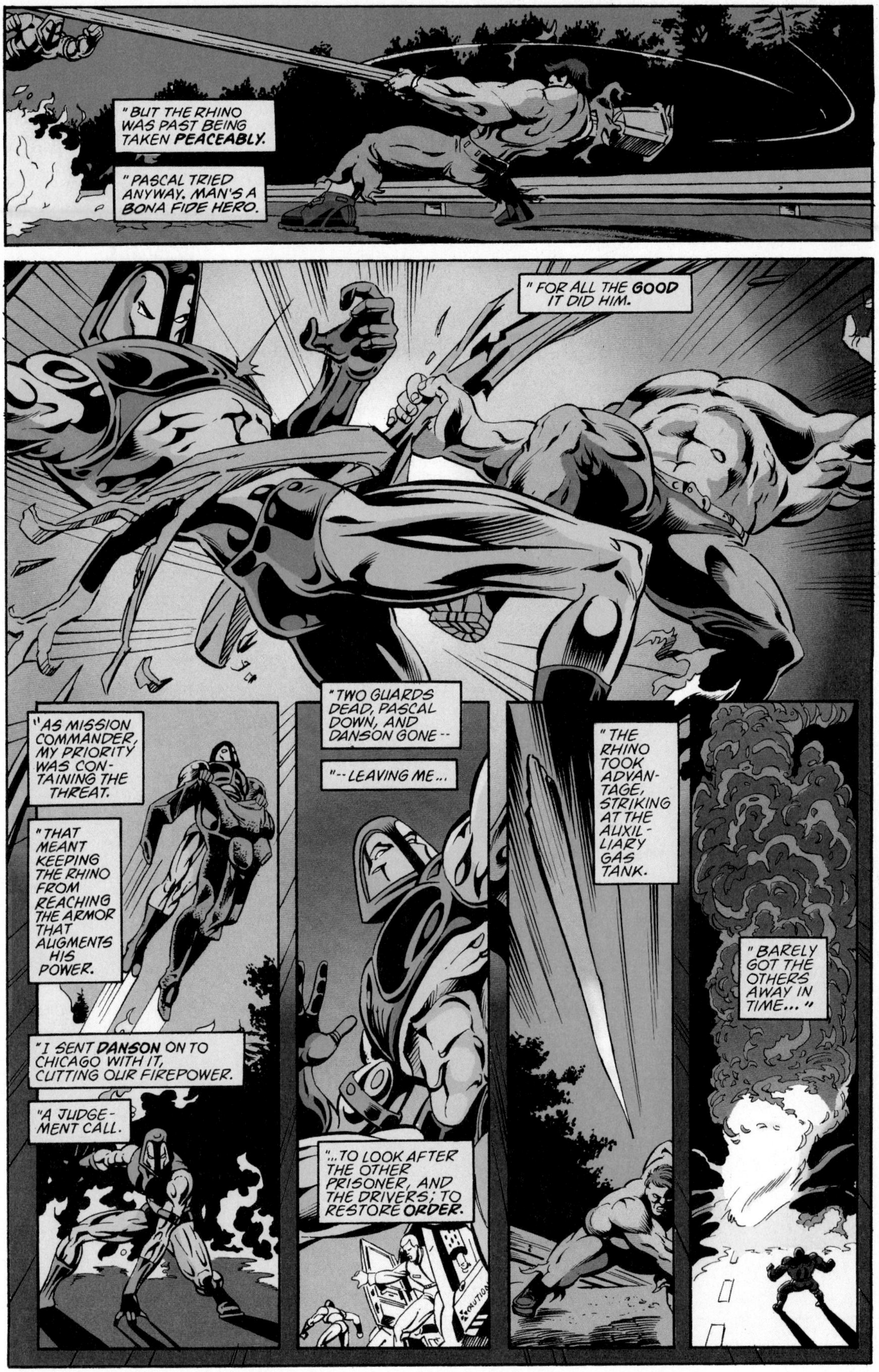
"BUT THE RHINO WAS PAST BEING TAKEN PEACEABLY.
"PASCAL TRIED ANYWAY. MAN'S A BONA FIDE HERO.
"FOR ALL THE GOOD IT DID HIM.
"AS MISSION COMMANDER, MY PRIORITY WAS CONTAINING THE THREAT.
"THAT MEANT KEEPING THE RHINO FROM REACHING THE ARMOR THAT AUGMENTS HIS POWER.
"I SENT DANSON ON TO CHICAGO WITH IT, CUTTING OUR FIREPOWER.
"A JUDGEMENT CALL.
"TWO GUARDS DEAD, PASCAL DOWN, AND DANSON GONE --
"-- LEAVING ME...
"...TO LOOK AFTER THE OTHER PRISONER, AND THE DRIVERS; TO RESTORE ORDER.
"THE RHINO TOOK ADVANTAGE, STRIKING AT THE AUXILIARY GAS TANK.
"BARELY GOT THE OTHERS AWAY IN TIME..."

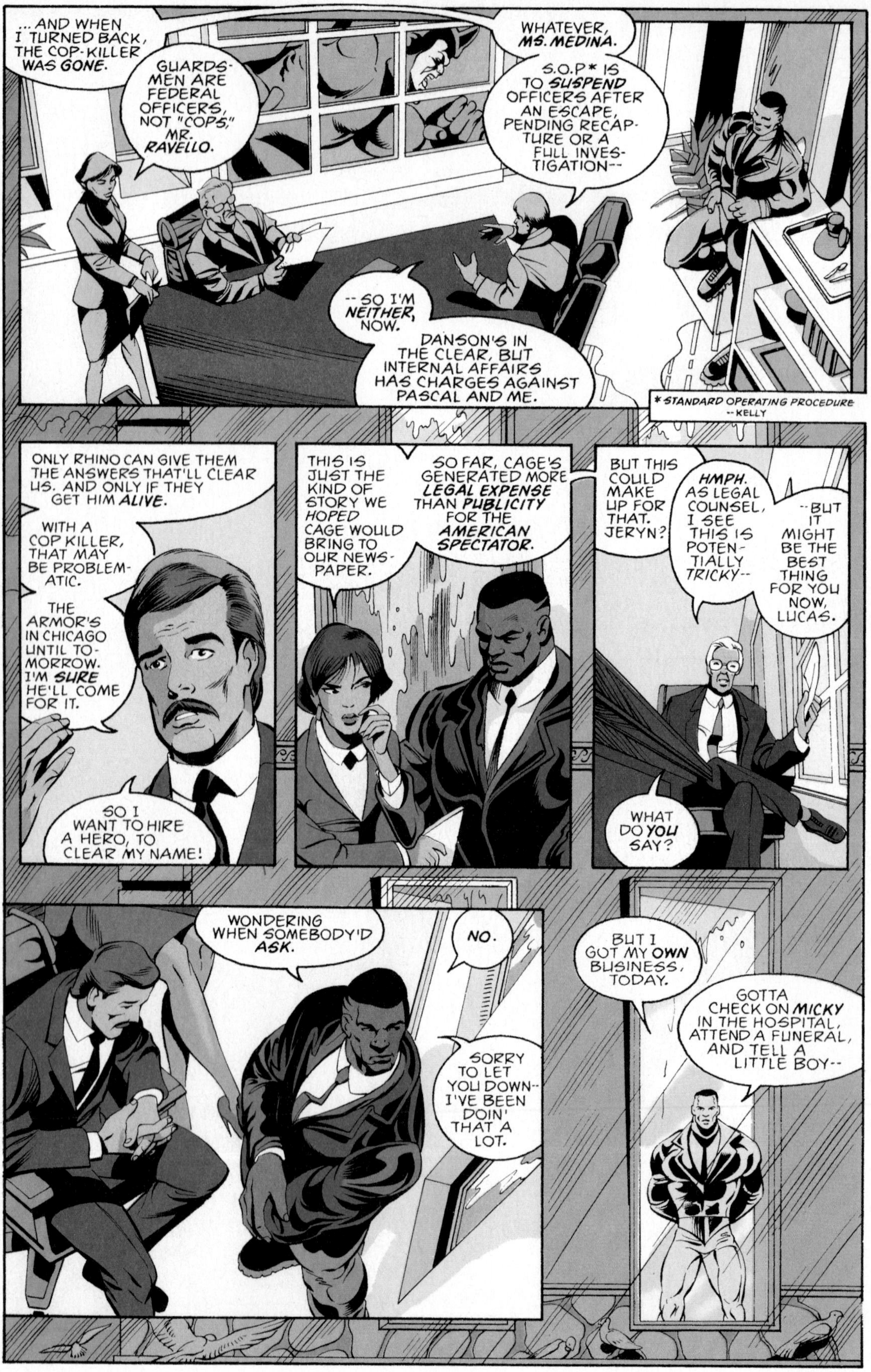
...AND WHEN I TURNED BACK, THE COP-KILLER WAS GONE.
GUARDSMEN ARE FEDERAL OFFICERS, NOT "COPS," MR. RAVELLO.
WHATEVER, MS. MEDINA.
S.O.P* IS TO SUSPEND OFFICERS AFTER AN ESCAPE, PENDING RECAPTURE OR A FULL INVESTIGATION--
--SO I'M NEITHER, NOW.
DANSON'S IN THE CLEAR, BUT INTERNAL AFFAIRS HAS CHARGES AGAINST PASCAL AND ME.
* STANDARD OPERATING PROCEDURE --KELLY
ONLY RHINO CAN GIVE THEM THE ANSWERS THAT'LL CLEAR US. AND ONLY IF THEY GET HIM ALIVE.
WITH A COP KILLER, THAT MAY BE PROBLEMATIC.
THE ARMOR'S IN CHICAGO UNTIL TOMORROW. I'M SURE HE'LL COME FOR IT.
SO I WANT TO HIRE A HERO, TO CLEAR MY NAME!
THIS IS JUST THE KIND OF STORY WE HOPED CAGE WOULD BRING TO OUR NEWSPAPER.
SO FAR, CAGE'S GENERATED MORE LEGAL EXPENSE THAN PUBLICITY FOR THE AMERICAN SPECTATOR.
BUT THIS COULD MAKE UP FOR THAT. JERYN?
HMPH. AS LEGAL COUNSEL, I SEE THIS IS POTENTIALLY TRICKY--
--BUT IT MIGHT BE THE BEST THING FOR YOU NOW, LUCAS.
WHAT DO YOU SAY?
WONDERING WHEN SOMEBODY'D ASK.
NO.
SORRY TO LET YOU DOWN-- I'VE BEEN DOIN' THAT A LOT.
BUT I GOT MY OWN BUSINESS, TODAY.
GOTTA CHECK ON MICKY IN THE HOSPITAL, ATTEND A FUNERAL, AND TELL A LITTLE BOY--

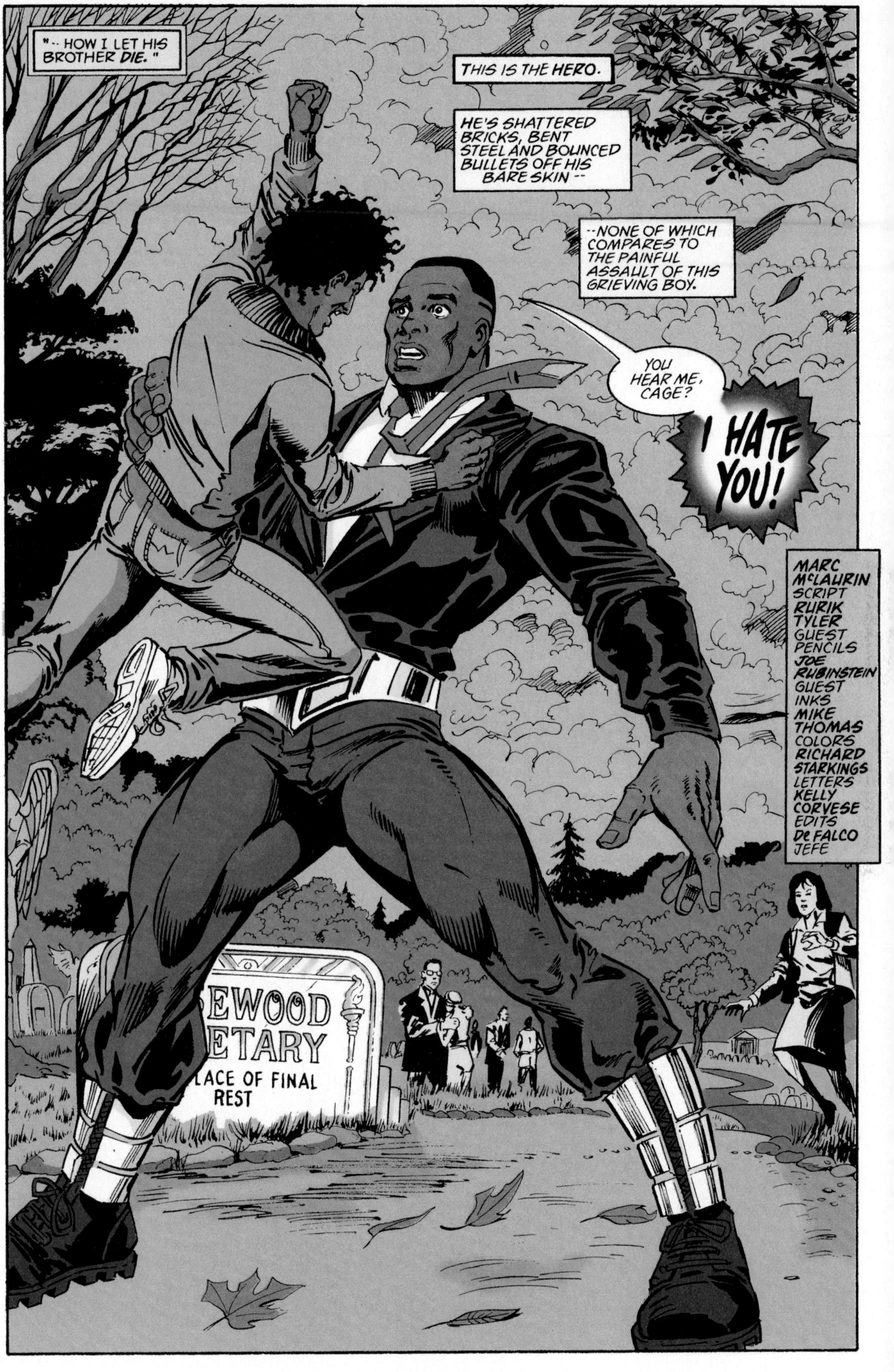
"-- HOW I LET HIS BROTHER DIE."
THIS IS THE HERO.
HE'S SHATTERED BRICKS, BENT STEEL AND BOUNCED BULLETS OFF HIS BARE SKIN --
--NONE OF WHICH COMPARES TO THE PAINFUL ASSAULT OF THIS GRIEVING BOY.
YOU HEAR ME, CAGE?
I HATE YOU!
MARC McLAURIN SCRIPT
RURIK TYLER GUEST PENCILS
JOE RUBINSTEIN GUEST INKS
MIKE THOMAS COLORS
RICHARD STARKINGS LETTERS
KELLY CORVESE EDITS
DeFALCO JEFE
EWOOD
ETARY
LACE OF FINAL
REST

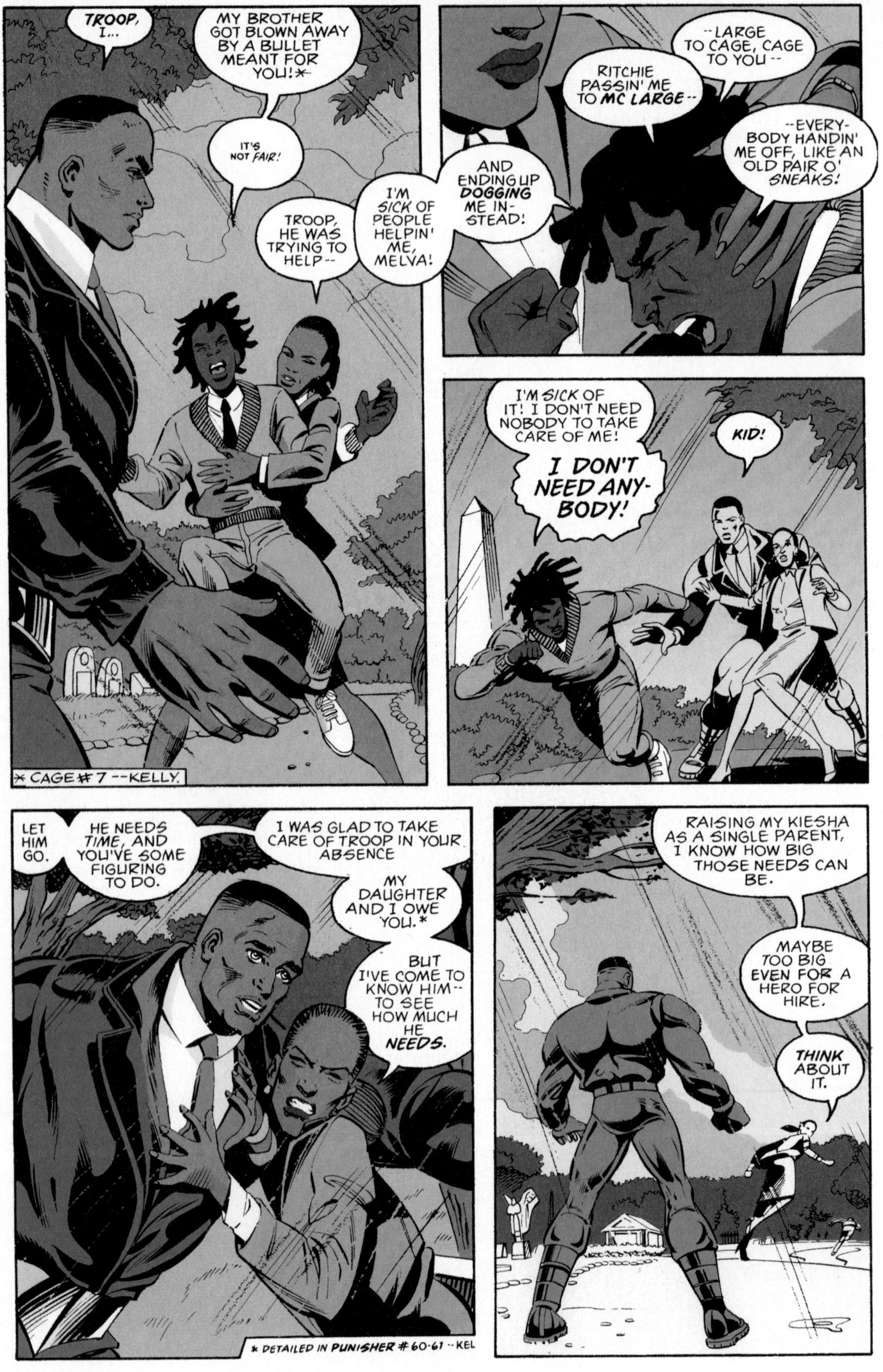
TROOP, I...
MY BROTHER GOT BLOWN AWAY BY A BULLET MEANT FOR YOU!*
IT'S NOT FAIR!
TROOP, HE WAS TRYING TO HELP--
I'M SICK OF PEOPLE HELPIN' ME, MELVA!
AND ENDING UP DOGGING ME INSTEAD!
* CAGE #7 --KELLY.
RITCHIE PASSIN' ME TO MC LARGE--
--LARGE TO CAGE, CAGE TO YOU--
--EVERYBODY HANDIN' ME OFF, LIKE AN OLD PAIR O' SNEAKS!
I'M SICK OF IT! I DON'T NEED NOBODY TO TAKE CARE OF ME!
I DON'T NEED ANYBODY!
KID!
LET HIM GO.
HE NEEDS TIME, AND YOU'VE SOME FIGURING TO DO.
I WAS GLAD TO TAKE CARE OF TROOP IN YOUR ABSENCE
MY DAUGHTER AND I OWE YOU.*
BUT I'VE COME TO KNOW HIM-- TO SEE HOW MUCH HE NEEDS.
* DETAILED IN PUNISHER #60-61 --KEL
RAISING MY KIESHA AS A SINGLE PARENT, I KNOW HOW BIG THOSE NEEDS CAN BE.
MAYBE TOO BIG EVEN FOR A HERO FOR HIRE.
THINK ABOUT IT.

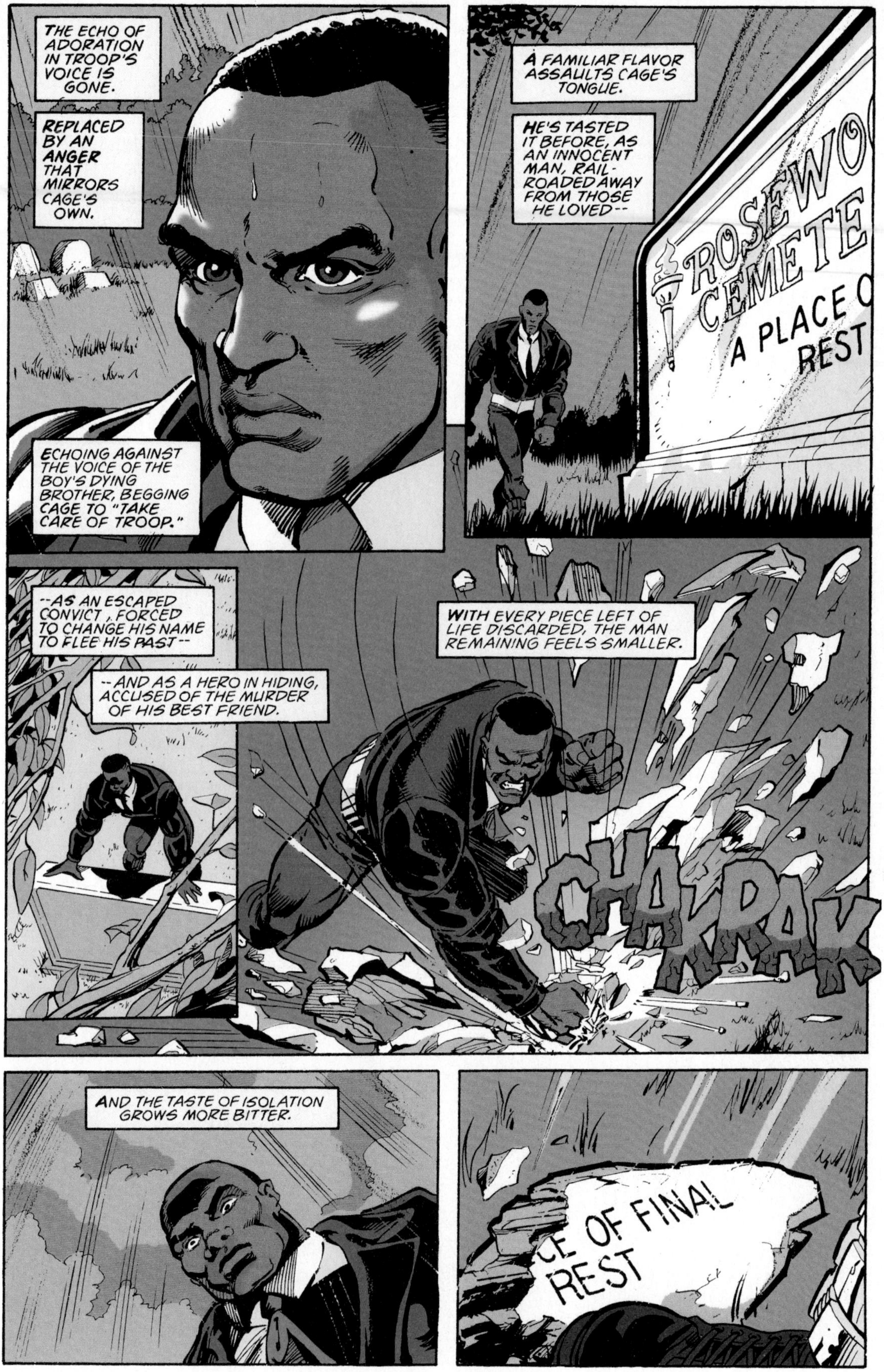

THE ECHO OF ADORATION IN TROOP'S VOICE IS GONE.
REPLACED BY AN ANGER THAT MIRRORS CAGE'S OWN.
ECHOING AGAINST THE VOICE OF THE BOY'S DYING BROTHER, BEGGING CAGE TO "TAKE CARE OF TROOP."
A FAMILIAR FLAVOR ASSAULTS CAGE'S TONGUE.
HE'S TASTED IT BEFORE, AS AN INNOCENT MAN, RAIL-ROADED AWAY FROM THOSE HE LOVED--
ROSEWOO
CEMETE
A PLACE O
REST
--AS AN ESCAPED CONVICT, FORCED TO CHANGE HIS NAME TO FLEE HIS PAST--
--AND AS A HERO IN HIDING, ACCUSED OF THE MURDER OF HIS BEST FRIEND.
WITH EVERY PIECE LEFT OF LIFE DISCARDED, THE MAN REMAINING FEELS SMALLER.
CHAKRAK
AND THE TASTE OF ISOLATION GROWS MORE BITTER.
CE OF FINAL
REST

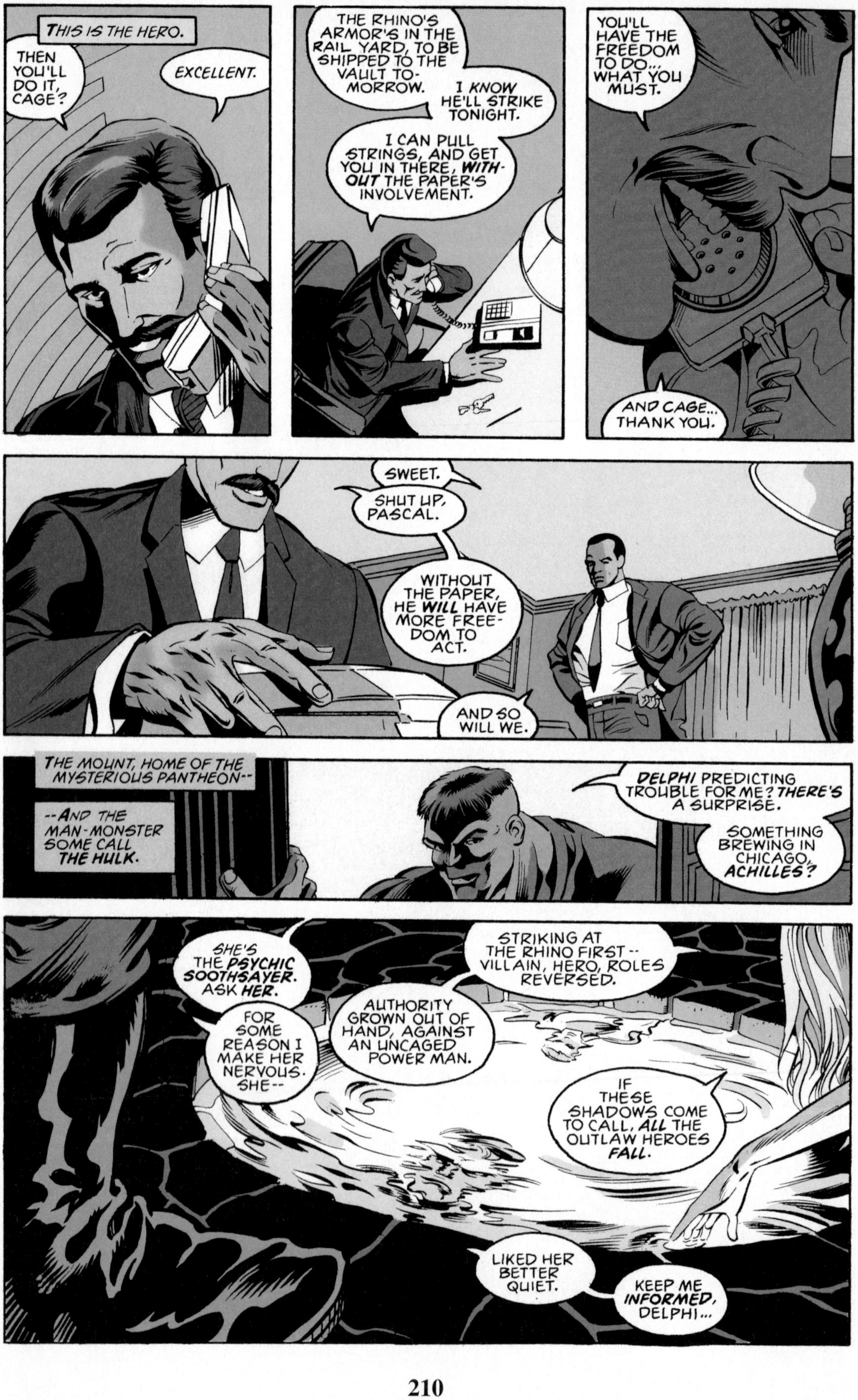

THIS IS THE HERO.
THEN YOU'LL DO IT, CAGE?
EXCELLENT.
THE RHINO'S ARMOR'S IN THE RAIL YARD, TO BE SHIPPED TO THE VAULT TO-MORROW.
I KNOW HE'LL STRIKE TONIGHT.
I CAN PULL STRINGS, AND GET YOU IN THERE, WITH-OUT THE PAPER'S INVOLVEMENT.
YOU'LL HAVE THE FREEDOM TO DO... WHAT YOU MUST.
AND CAGE... THANK YOU.
SWEET.
SHUT UP, PASCAL.
WITHOUT THE PAPER, HE WILL HAVE MORE FREE-DOM TO ACT.
AND SO WILL WE.
THE MOUNT, HOME OF THE MYSTERIOUS PANTHEON--
--AND THE MAN-MONSTER SOME CALL THE HULK.
DELPHI PREDICTING TROUBLE FOR ME? THERE'S A SURPRISE.
SOMETHING BREWING IN CHICAGO, ACHILLES?
SHE'S THE PSYCHIC SOOTHSAYER. ASK HER.
FOR SOME REASON I MAKE HER NERVOUS. SHE--
STRIKING AT THE RHINO FIRST -- VILLAIN, HERO, ROLES REVERSED.
AUTHORITY GROWN OUT OF HAND, AGAINST AN UNCAGED POWER MAN.
IF THESE SHADOWS COME TO CALL, ALL THE OUTLAW HEROES FALL.
LIKED HER BETTER QUIET.
KEEP ME INFORMED, DELPHI...

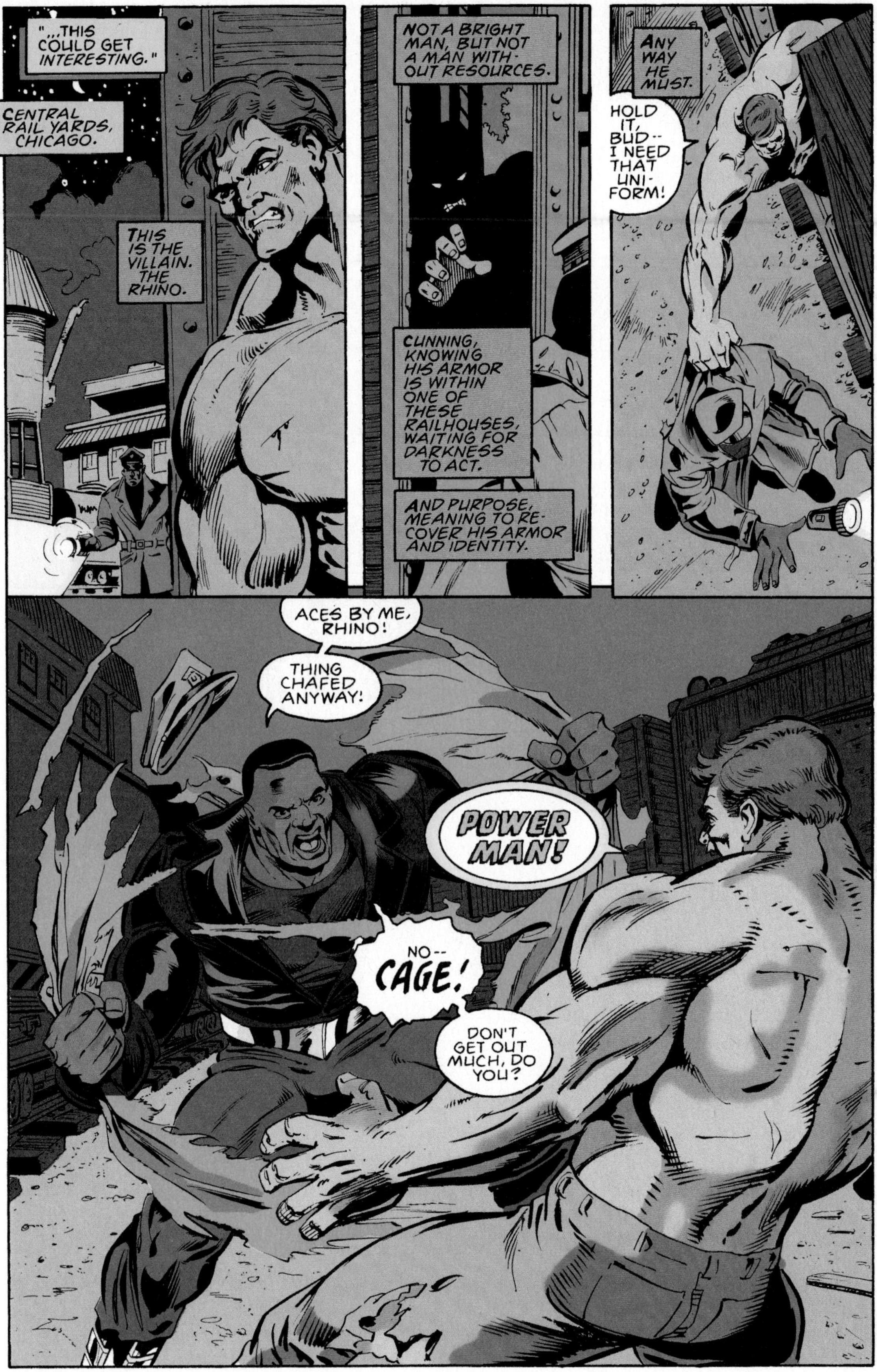
"...THIS COULD GET INTERESTING."
CENTRAL RAIL YARDS, CHICAGO.
THIS IS THE VILLAIN. THE RHINO.
NOT A BRIGHT MAN, BUT NOT A MAN WITH-OUT RESOURCES.
CUNNING, KNOWING HIS ARMOR IS WITHIN ONE OF THESE RAILHOUSES, WAITING FOR DARKNESS TO ACT.
AND PURPOSE, MEANING TO RE-COVER HIS ARMOR AND IDENTITY.
ANY WAY HE MUST.
HOLD IT, BUD-- I NEED THAT UNI-FORM!
ACES BY ME, RHINO!
THING CHAFED ANYWAY!
POWER MAN!
NO-- CAGE!
DON'T GET OUT MUCH, DO YOU?

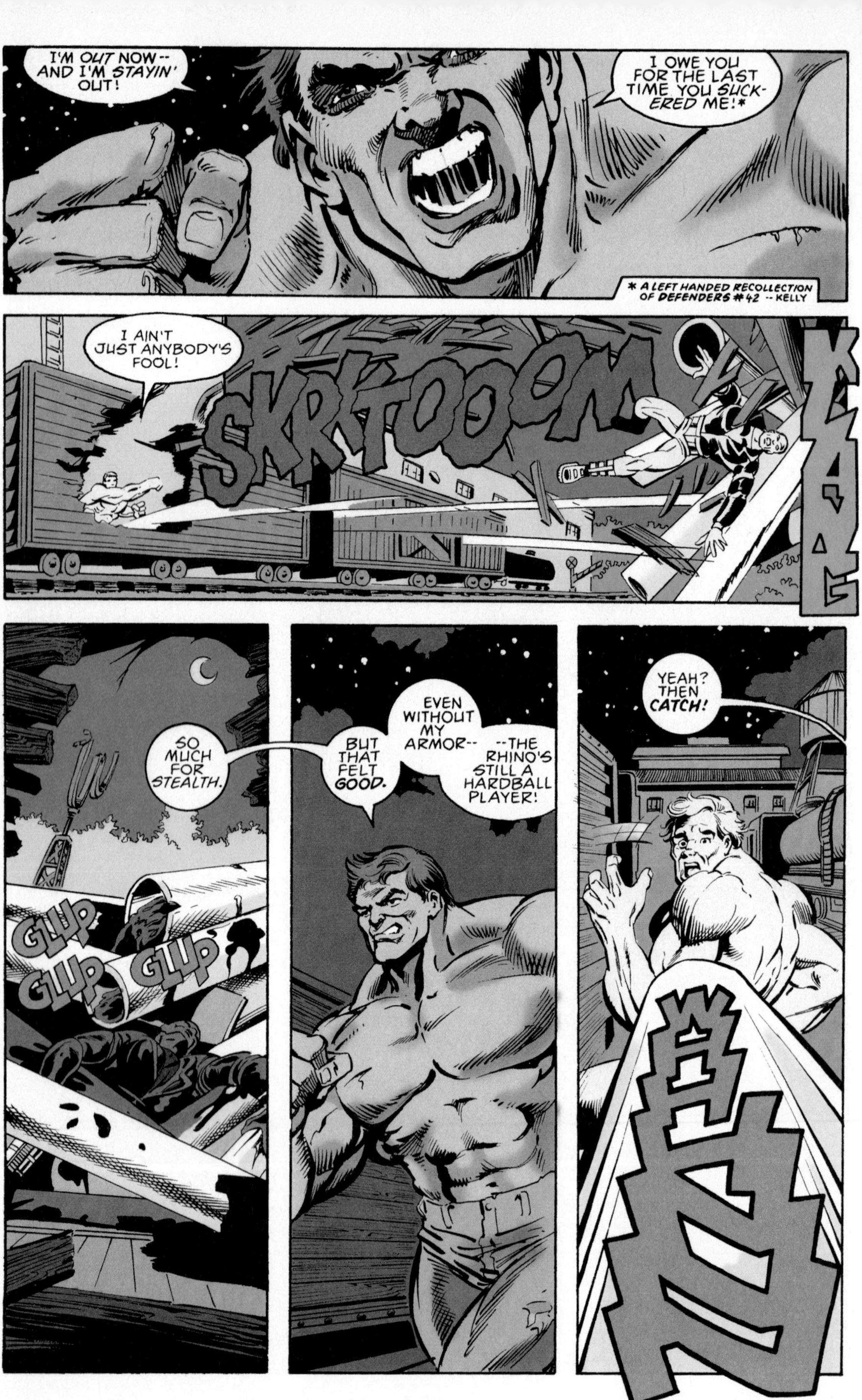

I'M OUT NOW -- AND I'M STAYIN' OUT!
I OWE YOU FOR THE LAST TIME YOU SUCKERED ME!*
* A LEFT HANDED RECOLLECTION OF DEFENDERS #42 -- KELLY
I AIN'T JUST ANYBODY'S FOOL!
SKRKTOOOOM
KLANG
SO MUCH FOR STEALTH.
GLUP GLUP GLUP
EVEN WITHOUT MY ARMOR--
--THE RHINO'S STILL A HARDBALL PLAYER!
BUT THAT FELT GOOD.
YEAH? THEN CATCH!

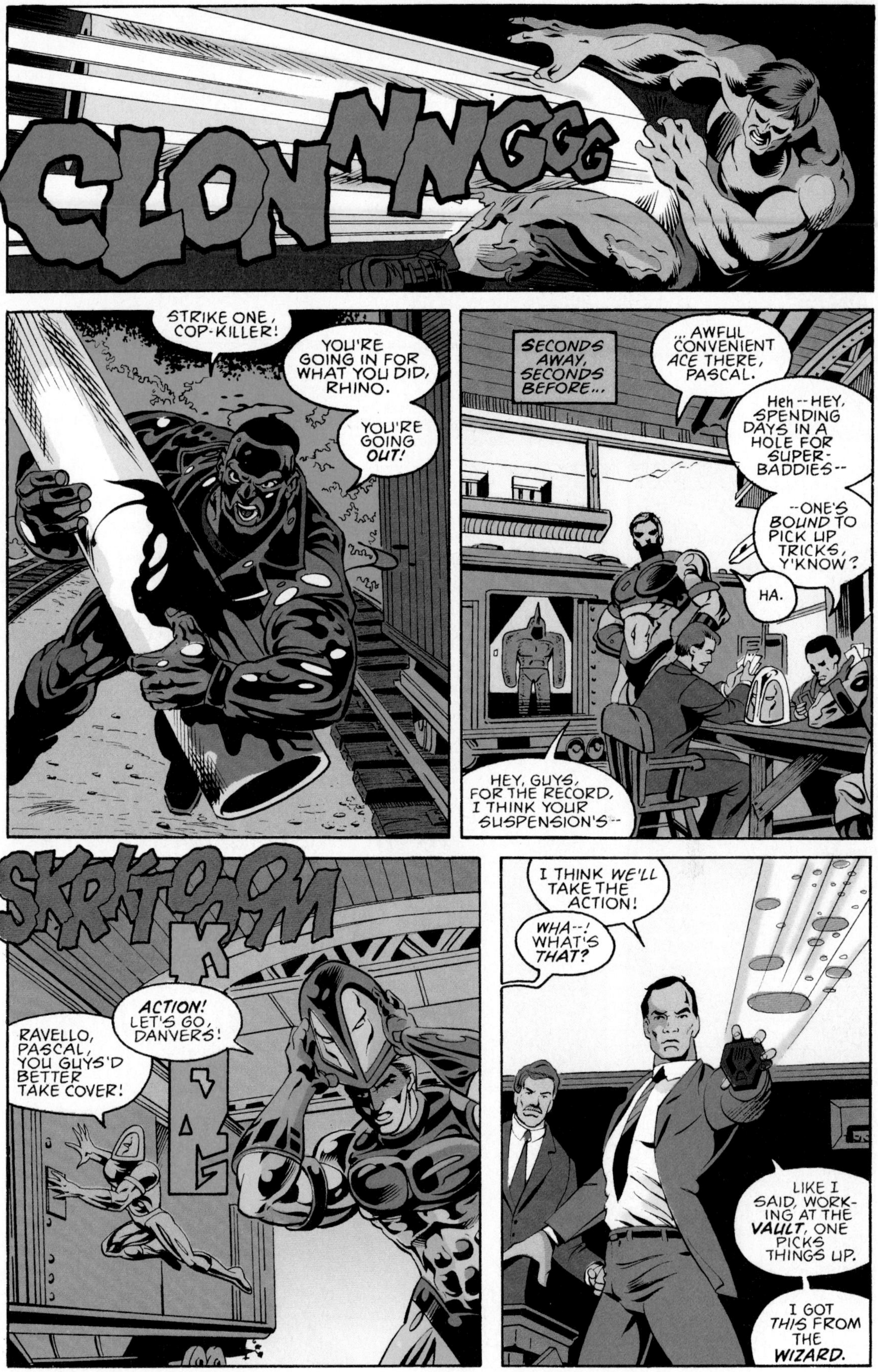
CLONNNGGG
STRIKE ONE, COP-KILLER!
YOU'RE GOING IN FOR WHAT YOU DID, RHINO.
YOU'RE GOING OUT!
SECONDS AWAY, SECONDS BEFORE...
...AWFUL CONVENIENT ACE THERE, PASCAL.
Heh -- HEY, SPENDING DAYS IN A HOLE FOR SUPER-BADDIES--
--ONE'S BOUND TO PICK UP TRICKS, Y'KNOW?
HA.
HEY, GUYS, FOR THE RECORD, I THINK YOUR SUSPENSION'S--
SKRKTOOOM
KRAK
ACTION! LET'S GO, DANVERS!
RAVELLO, PASCAL, YOU GUYS'D BETTER TAKE COVER!
I THINK WE'LL TAKE THE ACTION!
WHA--! WHAT'S THAT?
LIKE I SAID, WORKING AT THE VAULT, ONE PICKS THINGS UP.
I GOT THIS FROM THE WIZARD.

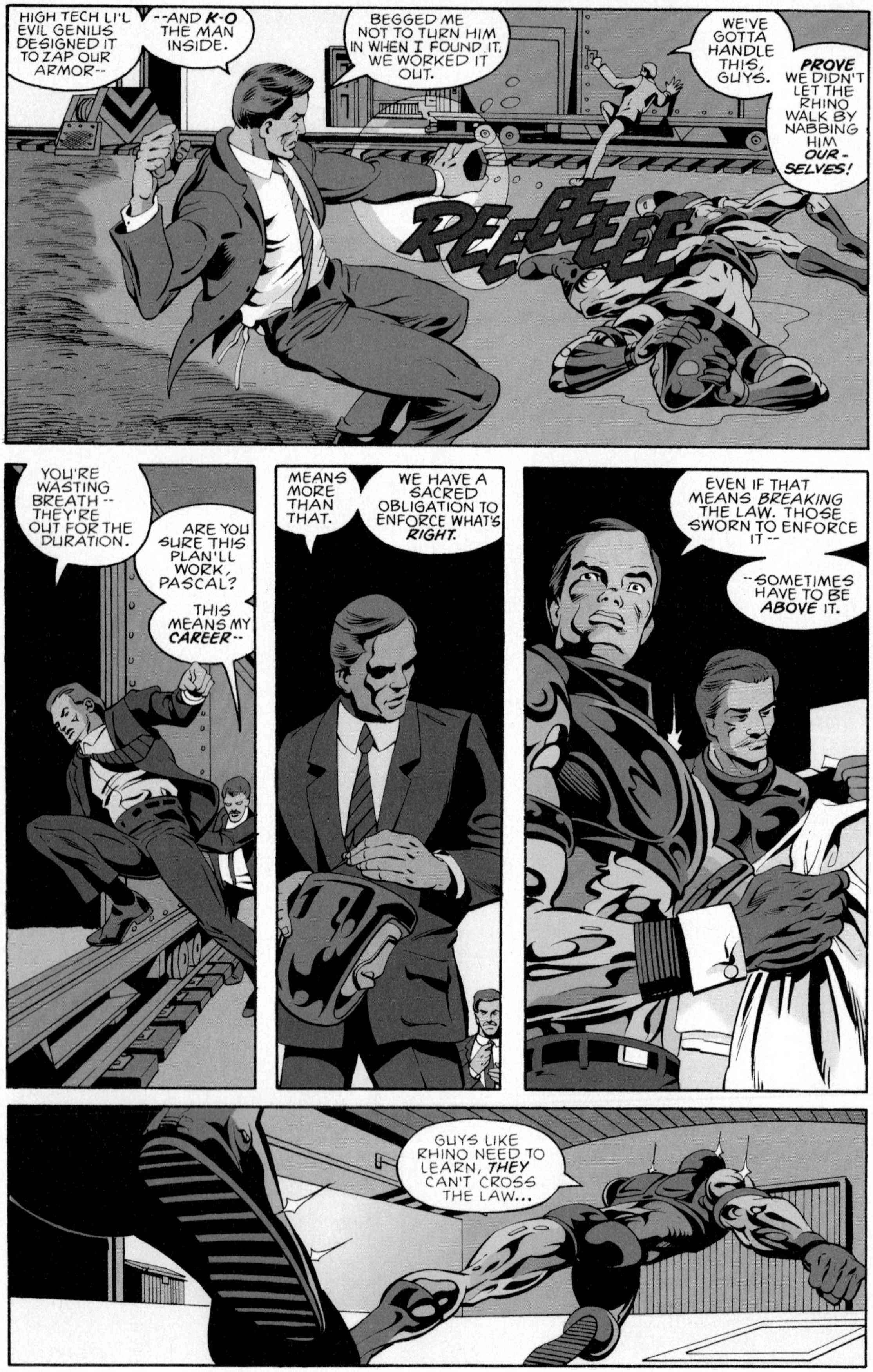
HIGH TECH LI'L EVIL GENIUS DESIGNED IT TO ZAP OUR ARMOR--
--AND K-O THE MAN INSIDE.
BEGGED ME NOT TO TURN HIM IN WHEN I FOUND IT. WE WORKED IT OUT.
WE'VE GOTTA HANDLE THIS, GUYS.
PROVE WE DIDN'T LET THE RHINO WALK BY NABBING HIM OUR-SELVES!
REEEEEEEEE
YOU'RE WASTING BREATH -- THEY'RE OUT FOR THE DURATION.
ARE YOU SURE THIS PLAN'LL WORK, PASCAL?
THIS MEANS MY CAREER--
MEANS MORE THAN THAT.
WE HAVE A SACRED OBLIGATION TO ENFORCE WHAT'S RIGHT.
EVEN IF THAT MEANS BREAKING THE LAW. THOSE SWORN TO ENFORCE IT --
--SOMETIMES HAVE TO BE ABOVE IT.
GUYS LIKE RHINO NEED TO LEARN, THEY CAN'T CROSS THE LAW...

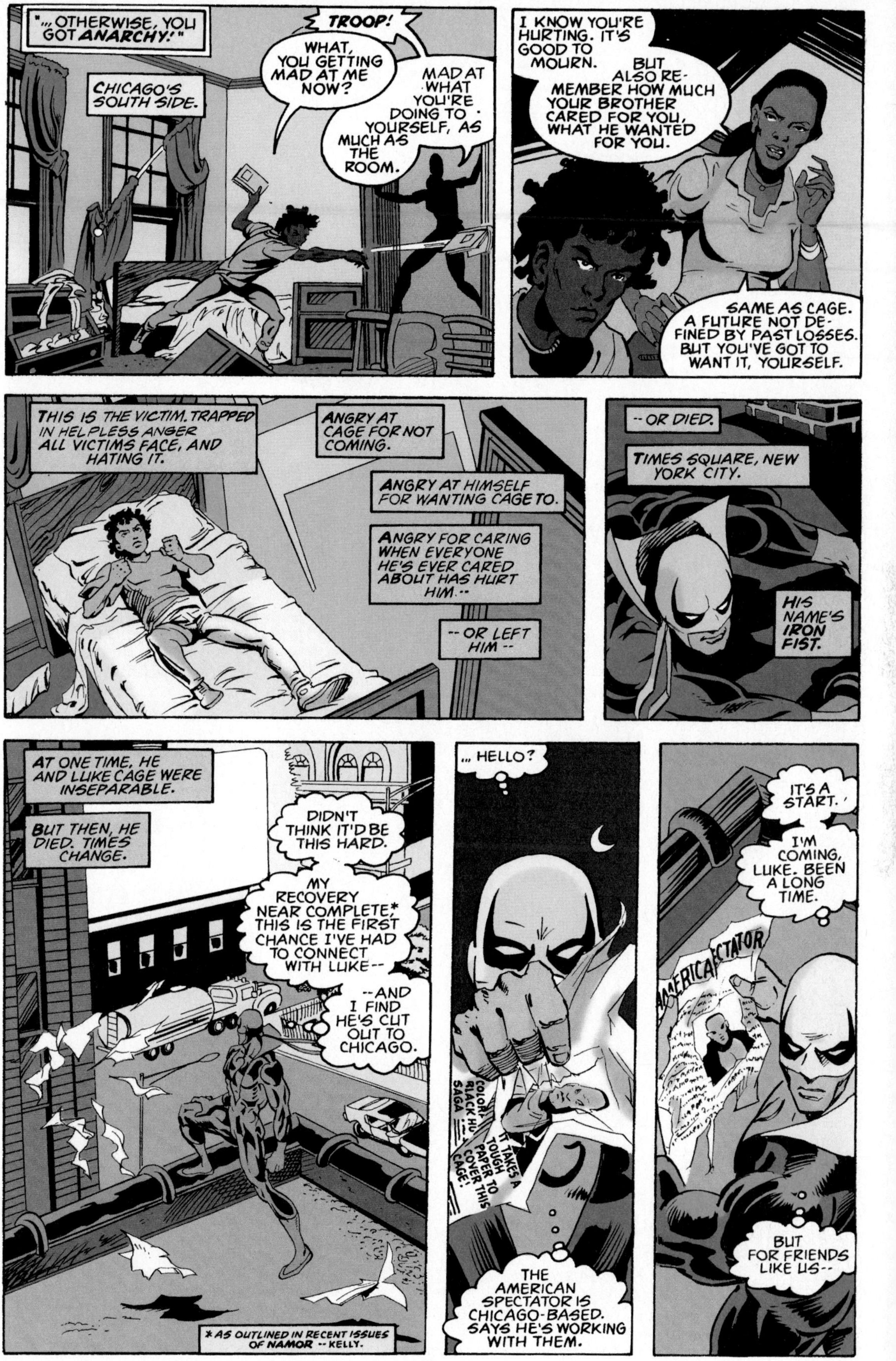
"... OTHERWISE, YOU GOT ANARCHY!"
TROOP!
WHAT, YOU GETTING MAD AT ME NOW?
MAD AT WHAT YOU'RE DOING TO YOURSELF, AS MUCH AS THE ROOM.
CHICAGO'S SOUTH SIDE.
I KNOW YOU'RE HURTING. IT'S GOOD TO MOURN. BUT ALSO REMEMBER HOW MUCH YOUR BROTHER CARED FOR YOU, WHAT HE WANTED FOR YOU.
SAME AS CAGE. A FUTURE NOT DEFINED BY PAST LOSSES. BUT YOU'VE GOT TO WANT IT, YOURSELF.
THIS IS THE VICTIM. TRAPPED IN HELPLESS ANGER ALL VICTIMS FACE, AND HATING IT.
ANGRY AT CAGE FOR NOT COMING.
ANGRY AT HIMSELF FOR WANTING CAGE TO.
ANGRY FOR CARING WHEN EVERYONE HE'S EVER CARED ABOUT HAS HURT HIM --
-- OR LEFT HIM --
-- OR DIED.
TIMES SQUARE, NEW YORK CITY.
HIS NAME'S IRON FIST.
AT ONE TIME, HE AND LUKE CAGE WERE INSEPARABLE.
BUT THEN, HE DIED. TIMES CHANGE.
DIDN'T THINK IT'D BE THIS HARD.
MY RECOVERY NEAR COMPLETE,* THIS IS THE FIRST CHANCE I'VE HAD TO CONNECT WITH LUKE --
-- AND I FIND HE'S CUT OUT TO CHICAGO.
* AS OUTLINED IN RECENT ISSUES OF NAMOR -- KELLY.
... HELLO?
IT TAKES A TOUGH PAPER TO COVER THIS CAGE!
THE AMERICAN SPECTATOR IS CHICAGO-BASED. SAYS HE'S WORKING WITH THEM.
IT'S A START.
I'M COMING, LUKE. BEEN A LONG TIME.
BUT FOR FRIENDS LIKE US --

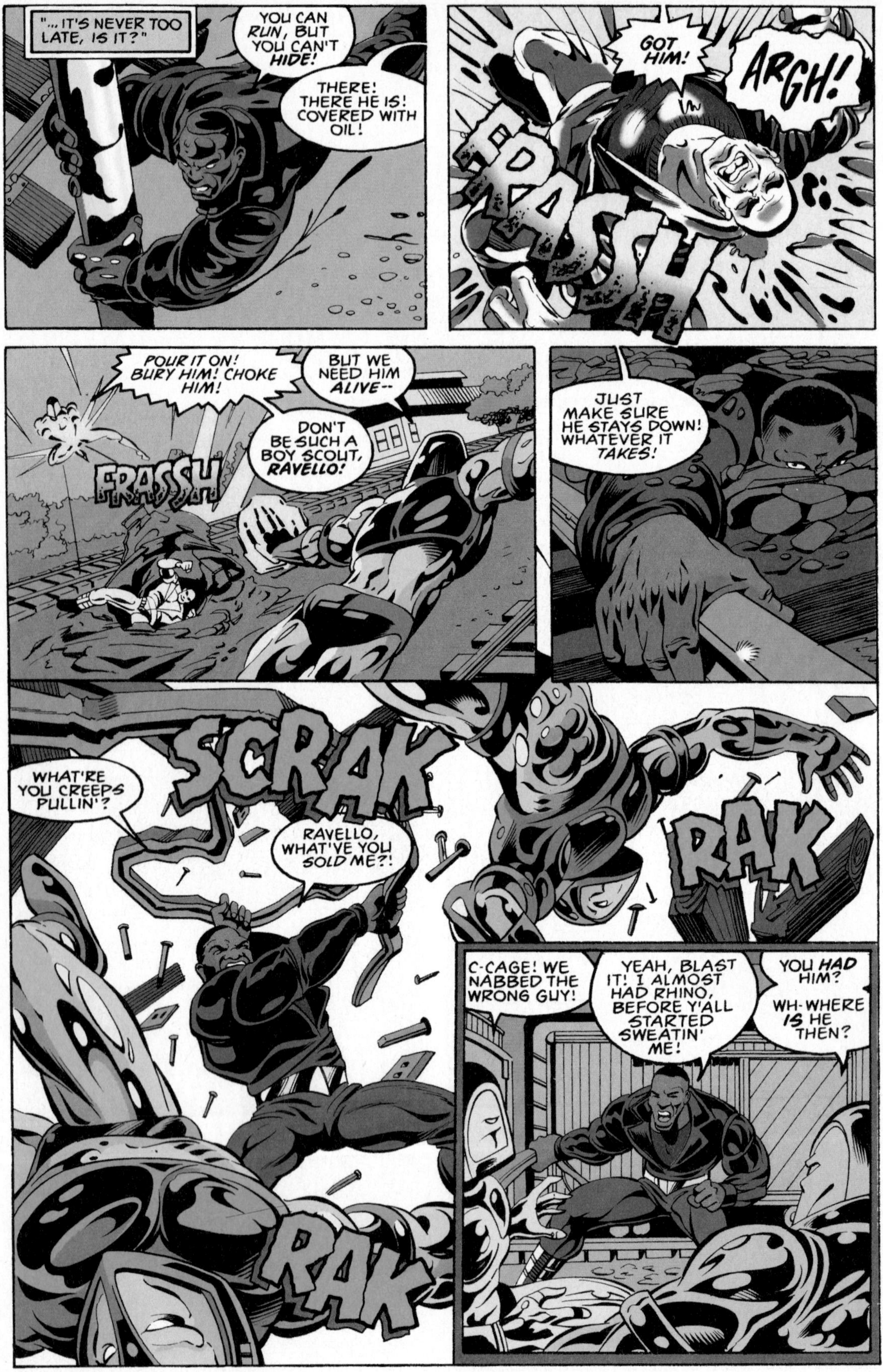
"... IT'S NEVER TOO LATE, IS IT?"
YOU CAN RUN, BUT YOU CAN'T HIDE!
THERE! THERE HE IS! COVERED WITH OIL!
GOT HIM!
ARGH!
FRASSH
POUR IT ON! BURY HIM! CHOKE HIM!
BUT WE NEED HIM ALIVE--
DON'T BE SUCH A BOY SCOUT, RAVELLO!
FRASSH
JUST MAKE SURE HE STAYS DOWN! WHATEVER IT TAKES!
SCRAK
WHAT'RE YOU CREEPS PULLIN'?
RAVELLO, WHAT'VE YOU SOLD ME?!
RAK
C-CAGE! WE NABBED THE WRONG GUY!
YEAH, BLAST IT! I ALMOST HAD RHINO, BEFORE Y'ALL STARTED SWEATIN' ME!
YOU HAD HIM?
WH-WHERE IS HE THEN?
RAK

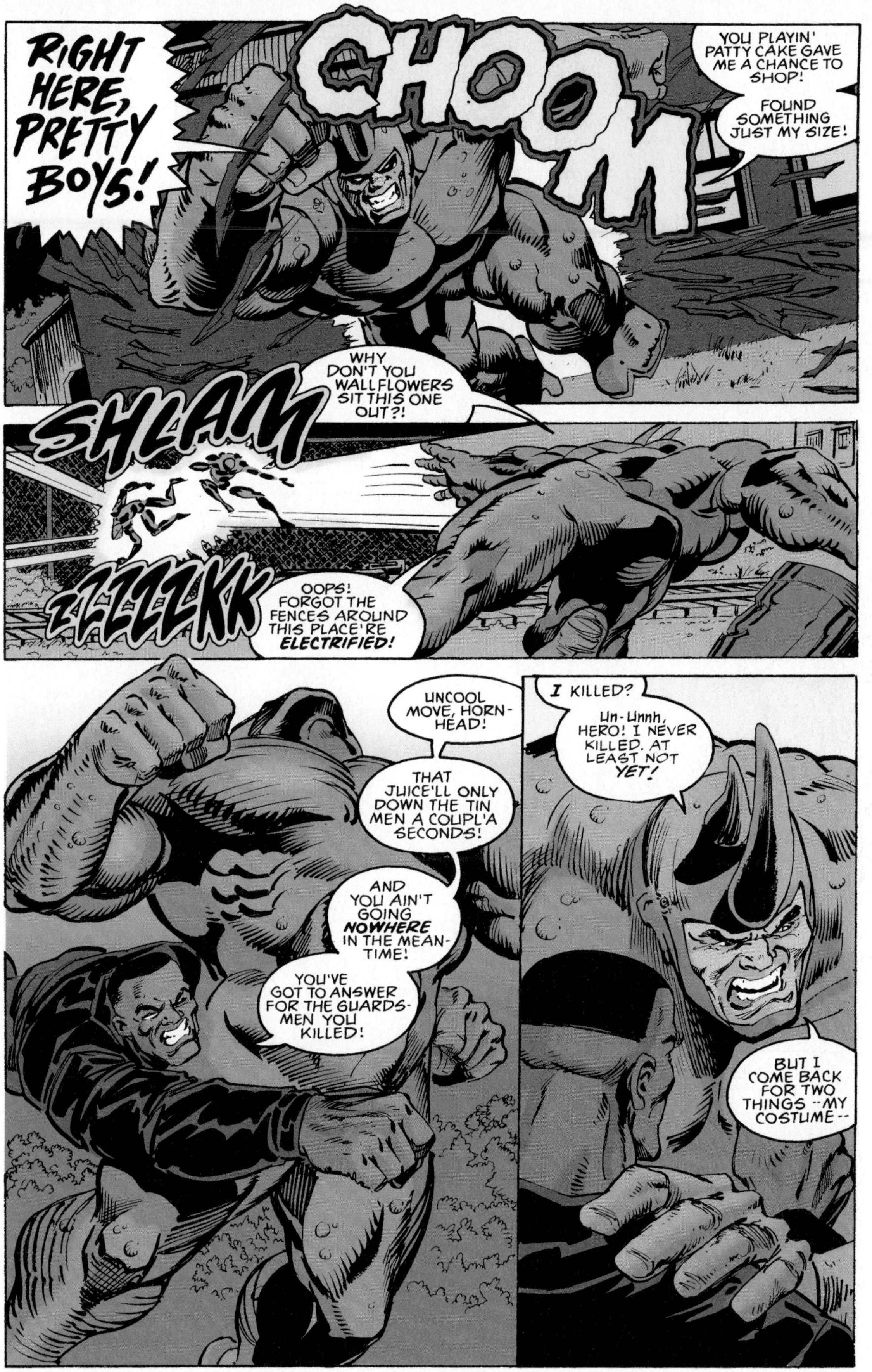
RIGHT HERE, PRETTY BOYS!
CHOOM
YOU PLAYIN' PATTY CAKE GAVE ME A CHANCE TO SHOP!
FOUND SOMETHING JUST MY SIZE!
WHY DON'T YOU WALLFLOWERS SIT THIS ONE OUT?!
SHLAM
ZZZZZZKK
OOPS! FORGOT THE FENCES AROUND THIS PLACE'RE ELECTRIFIED!
UNCOOL MOVE, HORN-HEAD!
THAT JUICE'LL ONLY DOWN THE TIN MEN A COUPL'A SECONDS!
AND YOU AIN'T GOING NOWHERE IN THE MEAN-TIME!
YOU'VE GOT TO ANSWER FOR THE GUARDS-MEN YOU KILLED!
I KILLED?
UN-UNNH, HERO! I NEVER KILLED. AT LEAST NOT YET!
BUT I COME BACK FOR TWO THINGS --MY COSTUME--

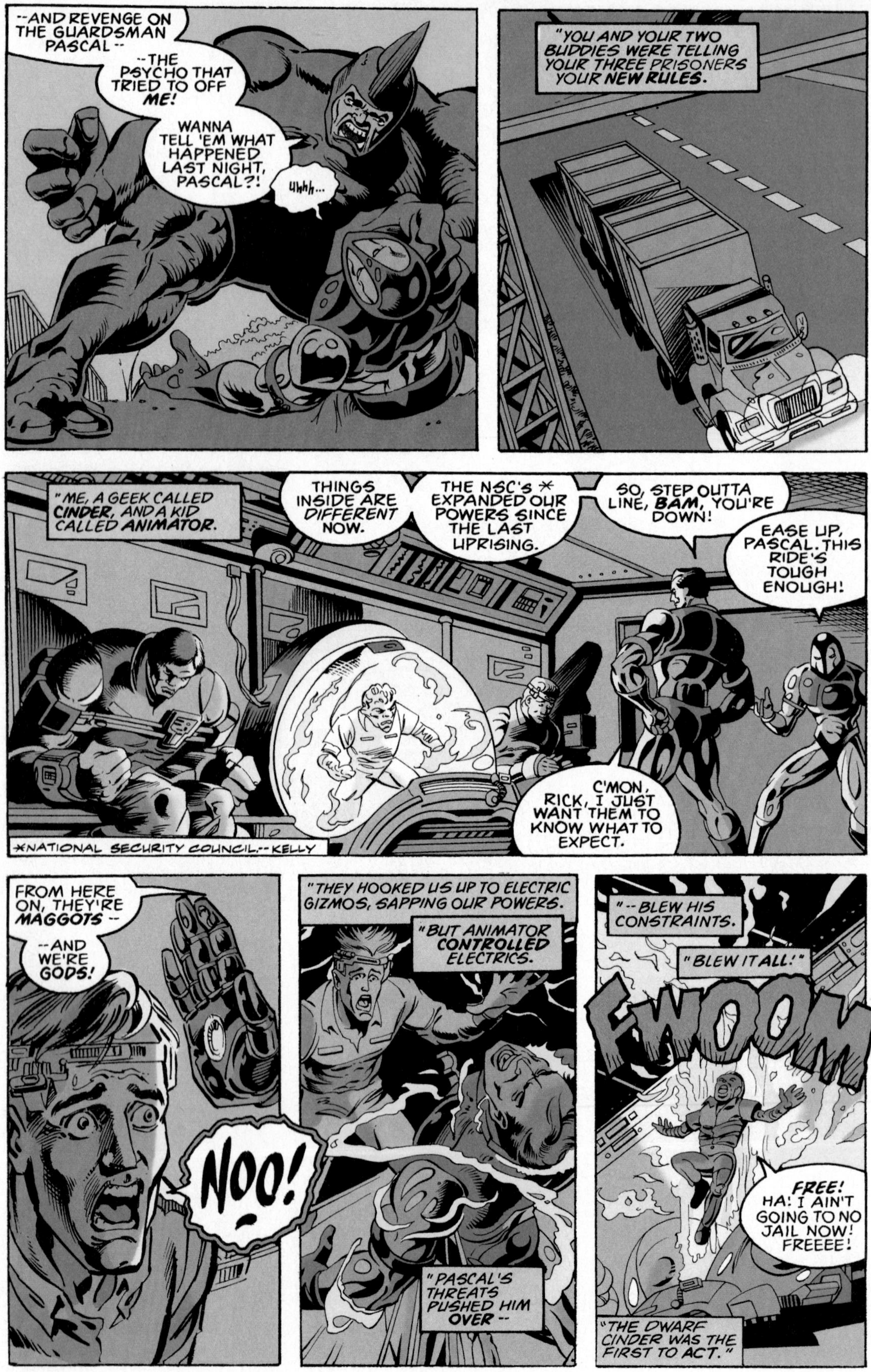
--AND REVENGE ON THE GUARDSMAN PASCAL--
--THE PSYCHO THAT TRIED TO OFF ME!
WANNA TELL 'EM WHAT HAPPENED LAST NIGHT, PASCAL?!
Uhhh...
"YOU AND YOUR TWO BUDDIES WERE TELLING YOUR THREE PRISONERS YOUR NEW RULES.
"ME, A GEEK CALLED CINDER, AND A KID CALLED ANIMATOR.
THINGS INSIDE ARE DIFFERENT NOW.
THE NSC's * EXPANDED OUR POWERS SINCE THE LAST UPRISING.
SO, STEP OUTTA LINE, BAM, YOU'RE DOWN!
EASE UP, PASCAL. THIS RIDE'S TOUGH ENOUGH!
C'MON, RICK, I JUST WANT THEM TO KNOW WHAT TO EXPECT.
*NATIONAL SECURITY COUNCIL.--KELLY
FROM HERE ON, THEY'RE MAGGOTS--
--AND WE'RE GODS!
NOO!
"THEY HOOKED US UP TO ELECTRIC GIZMOS, SAPPING OUR POWERS.
"BUT ANIMATOR CONTROLLED ELECTRICS.
"PASCAL'S THREATS PUSHED HIM OVER--
"--BLEW HIS CONSTRAINTS.
"BLEW IT ALL!"
FWOOM
FREE! HA! I AIN'T GOING TO NO JAIL NOW! FREEEE!
"THE DWARF CINDER WAS THE FIRST TO ACT."

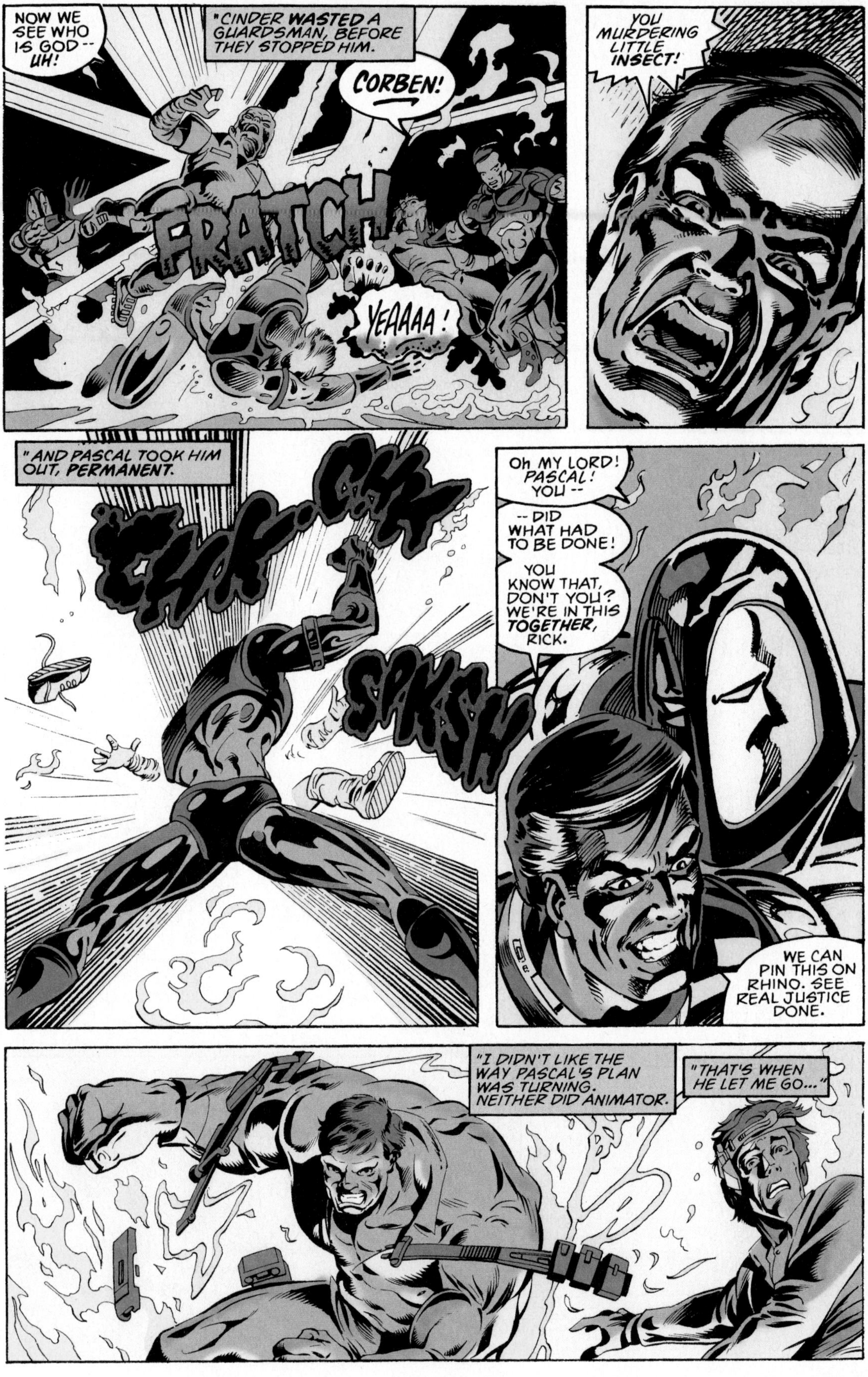

NOW WE SEE WHO IS GOD -- UH!
"CINDER WASTED A GUARDSMAN, BEFORE THEY STOPPED HIM.
CORBEN!
FRATCH
YEAAAA!
YOU MURDERING LITTLE INSECT!
"AND PASCAL TOOK HIM OUT, PERMANENT.
Oh MY LORD! PASCAL! YOU --
-- DID WHAT HAD TO BE DONE!
YOU KNOW THAT, DON'T YOU? WE'RE IN THIS TOGETHER, RICK.
SPKSH
WE CAN PIN THIS ON RHINO. SEE REAL JUSTICE DONE.
"I DIDN'T LIKE THE WAY PASCAL'S PLAN WAS TURNING. NEITHER DID ANIMATOR.
"THAT'S WHEN HE LET ME GO..."

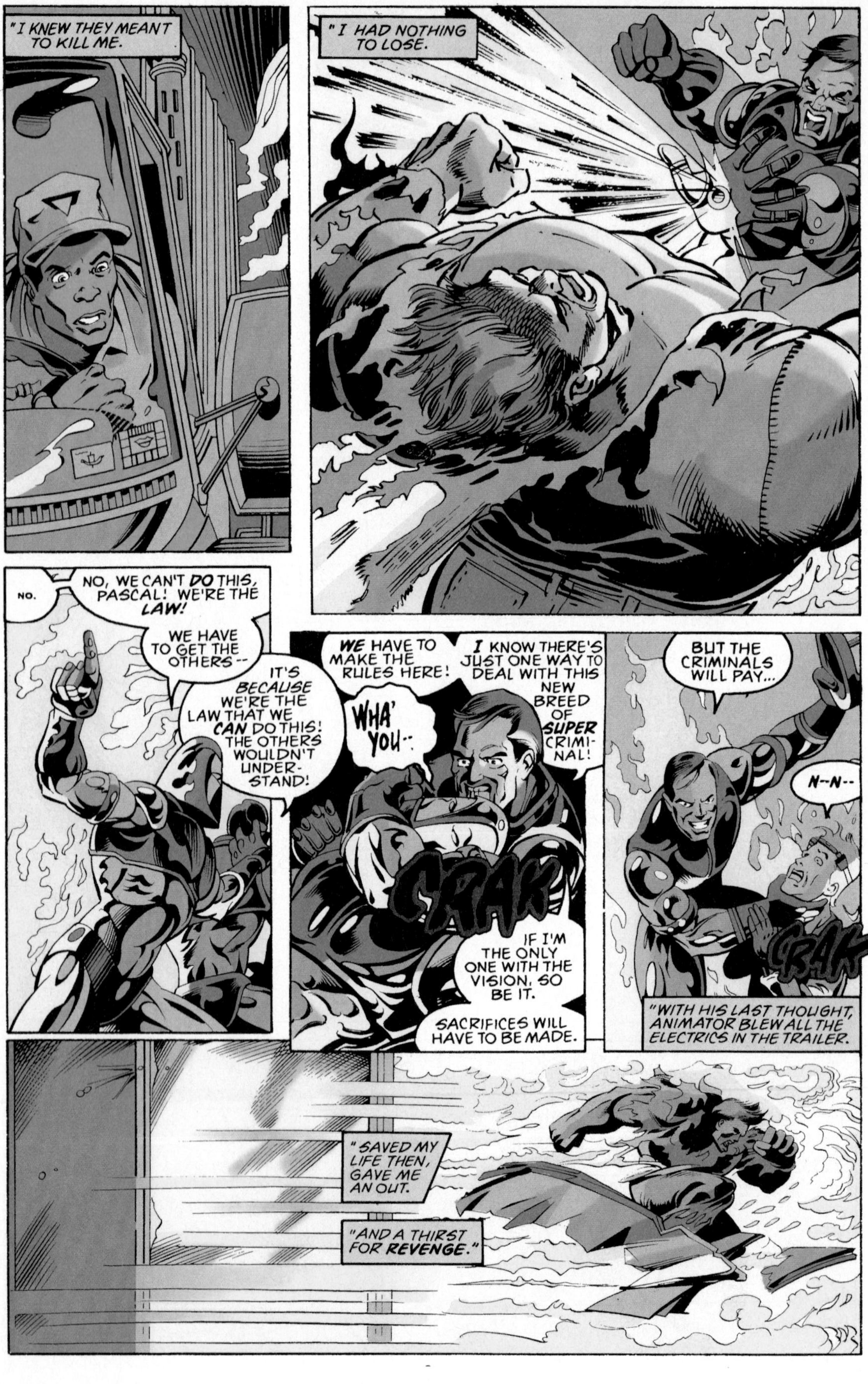
"I KNEW THEY MEANT TO KILL ME.
"I HAD NOTHING TO LOSE.
NO.
NO, WE CAN'T DO THIS, PASCAL! WE'RE THE LAW!
WE HAVE TO GET THE OTHERS --
IT'S BECAUSE WE'RE THE LAW THAT WE CAN DO THIS! THE OTHERS WOULDN'T UNDERSTAND!
WE HAVE TO MAKE THE RULES HERE!
I KNOW THERE'S JUST ONE WAY TO DEAL WITH THIS NEW BREED OF SUPER CRIMINAL!
WHA' YOU--
CRAK
IF I'M THE ONLY ONE WITH THE VISION, SO BE IT.
SACRIFICES WILL HAVE TO BE MADE.
BUT THE CRIMINALS WILL PAY...
N--N--
CRAK
"WITH HIS LAST THOUGHT, ANIMATOR BLEW ALL THE ELECTRICS IN THE TRAILER.
"SAVED MY LIFE THEN, GAVE ME AN OUT.
"AND A THIRST FOR REVENGE."

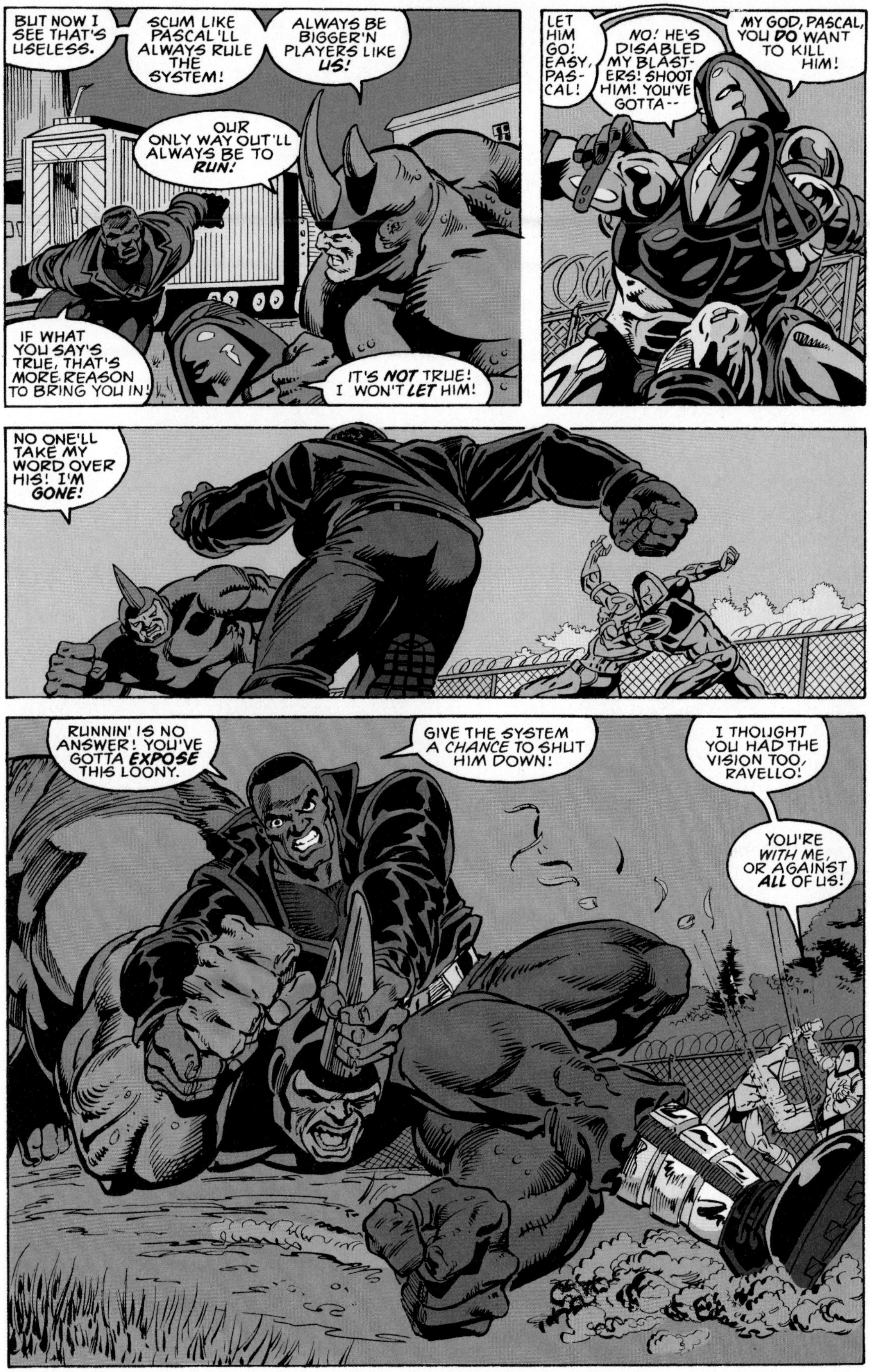
BUT NOW I SEE THAT'S USELESS.
SCUM LIKE PASCAL'LL ALWAYS RULE THE SYSTEM!
ALWAYS BE BIGGER'N PLAYERS LIKE US!
OUR ONLY WAY OUT'LL ALWAYS BE TO RUN!
IF WHAT YOU SAY'S TRUE, THAT'S MORE REASON TO BRING YOU IN!
IT'S NOT TRUE! I WON'T LET HIM!
LET HIM GO! EASY, PASCAL!
NO! HE'S DISABLED MY BLASTERS! SHOOT HIM! YOU'VE GOTTA--
MY GOD, PASCAL, YOU DO WANT TO KILL HIM!
NO ONE'LL TAKE MY WORD OVER HIS! I'M GONE!
RUNNIN' IS NO ANSWER! YOU'VE GOTTA EXPOSE THIS LOONY.
GIVE THE SYSTEM A CHANCE TO SHUT HIM DOWN!
I THOUGHT YOU HAD THE VISION TOO, RAVELLO!
YOU'RE WITH ME, OR AGAINST ALL OF US!

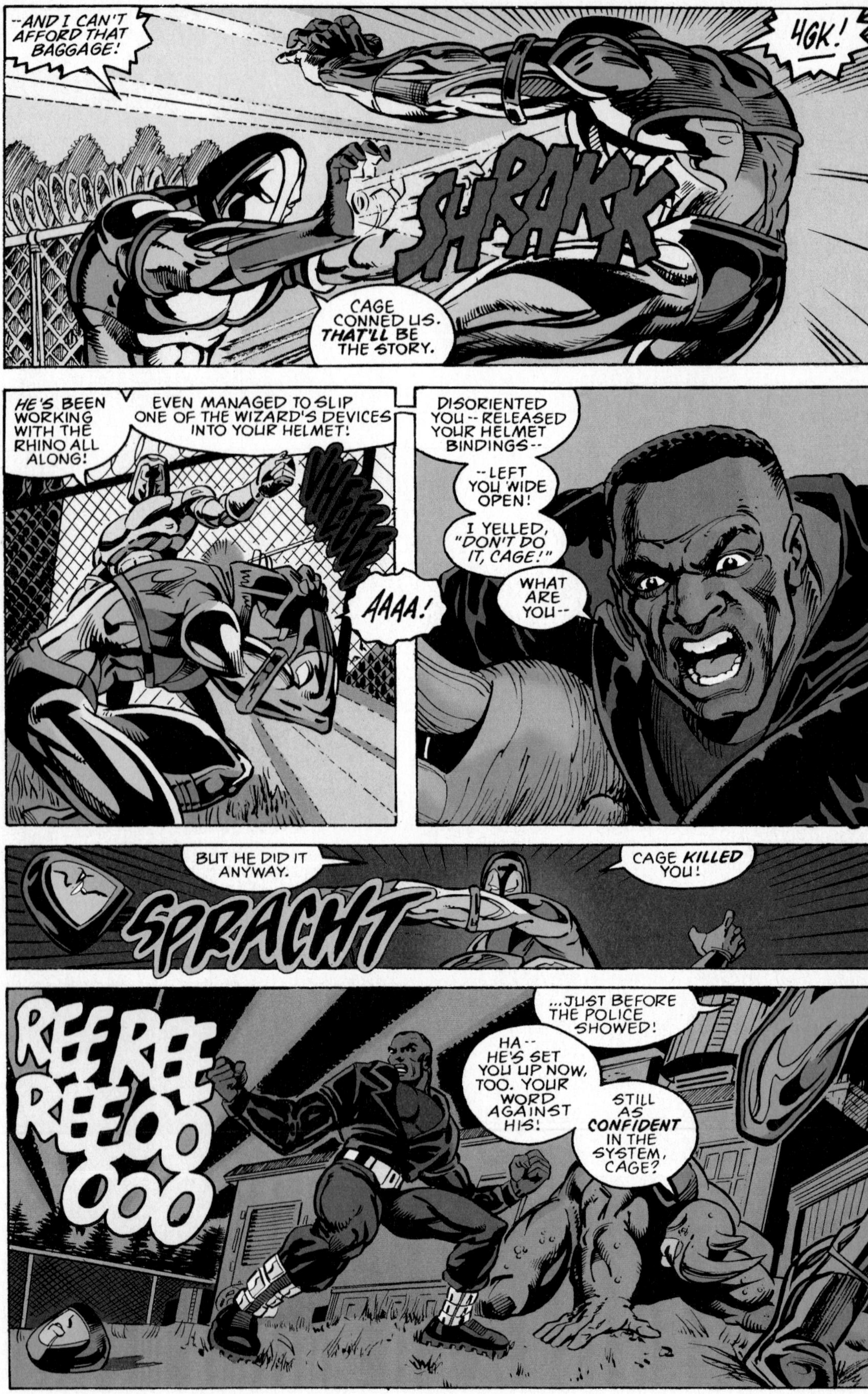
--AND I CAN'T AFFORD THAT BAGGAGE!
UGK!
SHRAKK
CAGE CONNED US. THAT'LL BE THE STORY.
HE'S BEEN WORKING WITH THE RHINO ALL ALONG!
EVEN MANAGED TO SLIP ONE OF THE WIZARD'S DEVICES INTO YOUR HELMET!
AAAA!
DISORIENTED YOU -- RELEASED YOUR HELMET BINDINGS--
--LEFT YOU WIDE OPEN!
I YELLED, "DON'T DO IT, CAGE!"
WHAT ARE YOU--
BUT HE DID IT ANYWAY.
CAGE KILLED YOU!
SPRACHT
REE REE REE OO OOO
...JUST BEFORE THE POLICE SHOWED!
HA-- HE'S SET YOU UP NOW, TOO. YOUR WORD AGAINST HIS!
STILL AS CONFIDENT IN THE SYSTEM, CAGE?

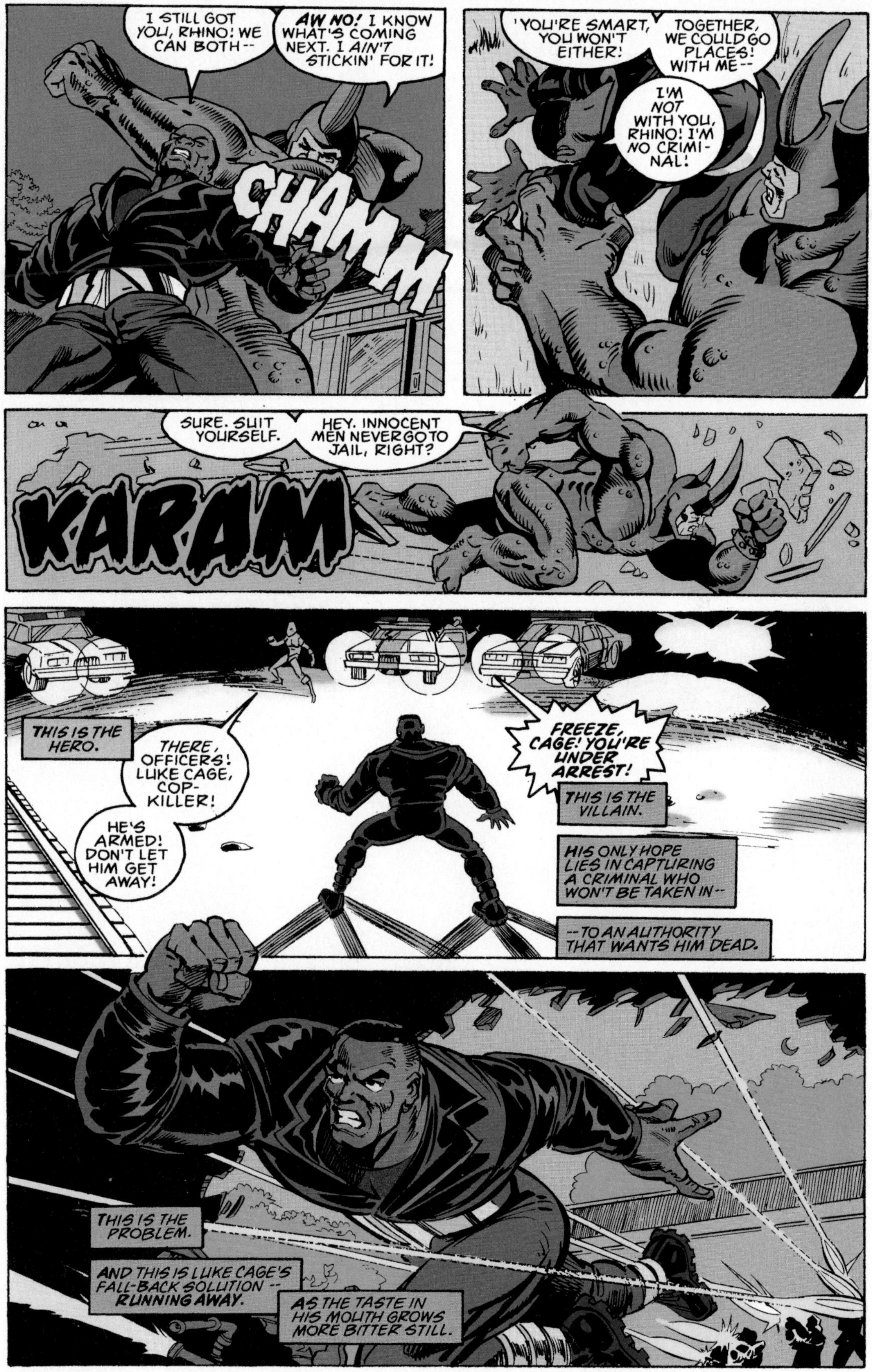
I STILL GOT YOU, RHINO! WE CAN BOTH --
AW NO! I KNOW WHAT'S COMING NEXT. I AIN'T STICKIN' FOR IT!
CHAMM
'YOU'RE SMART, YOU WON'T EITHER!
TOGETHER, WE COULD GO PLACES! WITH ME --
I'M NOT WITH YOU, RHINO! I'M NO CRIMINAL!
SURE. SUIT YOURSELF.
HEY. INNOCENT MEN NEVER GO TO JAIL, RIGHT?
KARAM
THIS IS THE HERO.
THERE, OFFICERS! LUKE CAGE, COP-KILLER!
HE'S ARMED! DON'T LET HIM GET AWAY!
FREEZE, CAGE! YOU'RE UNDER ARREST!
THIS IS THE VILLAIN.
HIS ONLY HOPE LIES IN CAPTURING A CRIMINAL WHO WON'T BE TAKEN IN--
--TO AN AUTHORITY THAT WANTS HIM DEAD.
THIS IS THE PROBLEM.
AND THIS IS LUKE CAGE'S FALL-BACK SOLUTION -- RUNNING AWAY.
AS THE TASTE IN HIS MOUTH GROWS MORE BITTER STILL.

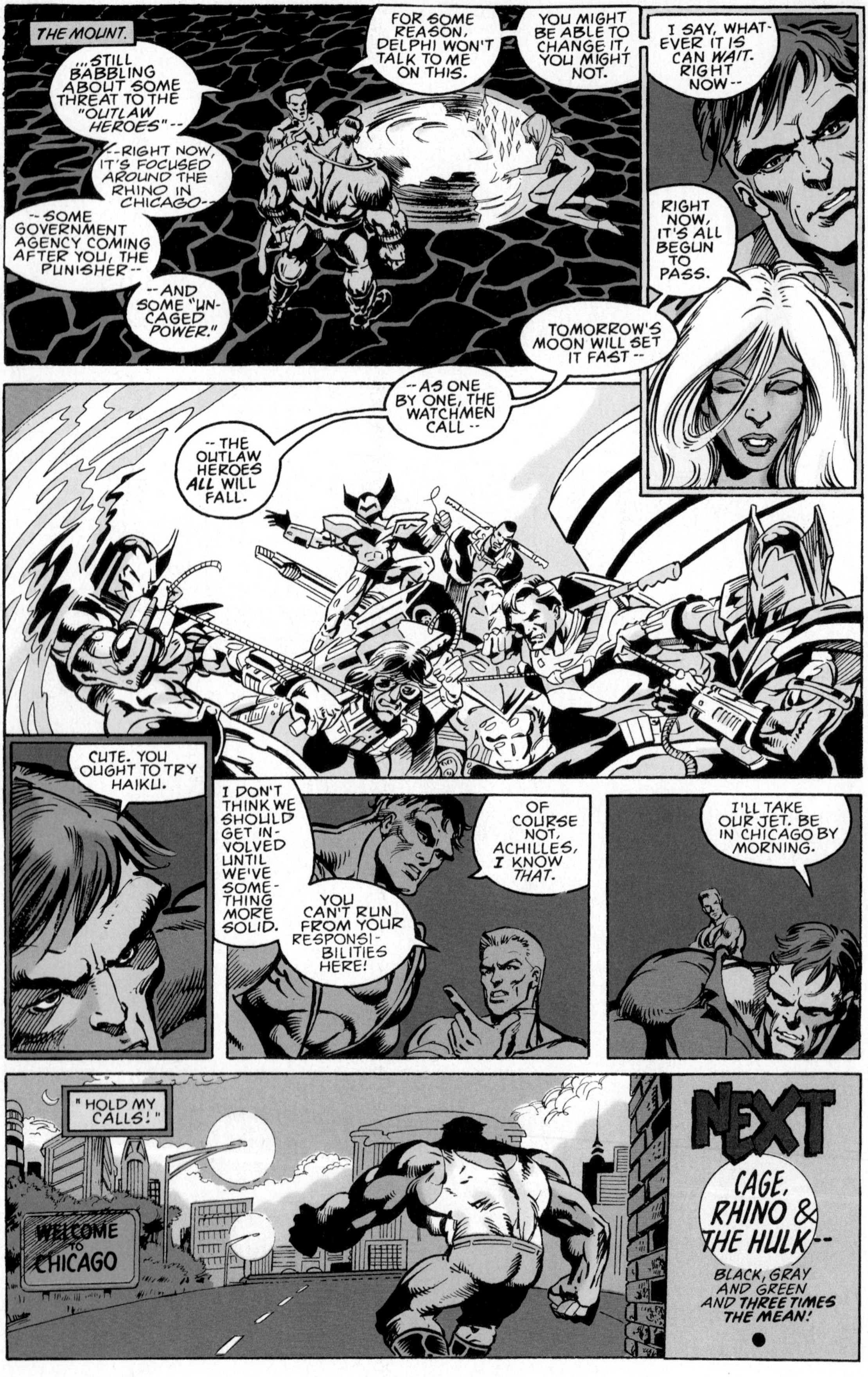
THE MOUNT.
...STILL BABBLING ABOUT SOME THREAT TO THE "OUTLAW HEROES"--
--RIGHT NOW, IT'S FOCUSED AROUND THE RHINO IN CHICAGO--
--SOME GOVERNMENT AGENCY COMING AFTER YOU, THE PUNISHER--
--AND SOME "UNCAGED POWER."
FOR SOME REASON, DELPHI WON'T TALK TO ME ON THIS.
YOU MIGHT BE ABLE TO CHANGE IT, YOU MIGHT NOT.
I SAY, WHATEVER IT IS CAN WAIT. RIGHT NOW--
RIGHT NOW, IT'S ALL BEGUN TO PASS.
TOMORROW'S MOON WILL SET IT FAST--
--AS ONE BY ONE, THE WATCHMEN CALL--
--THE OUTLAW HEROES ALL WILL FALL.
CUTE. YOU OUGHT TO TRY HAIKU.
I DON'T THINK WE SHOULD GET INVOLVED UNTIL WE'VE SOMETHING MORE SOLID.
OF COURSE NOT, ACHILLES, I KNOW THAT.
YOU CAN'T RUN FROM YOUR RESPONSIBILITIES HERE!
I'LL TAKE OUR JET. BE IN CHICAGO BY MORNING.
"HOLD MY CALLS!"
WELCOME TO CHICAGO
NEXT
CAGE, RHINO & THE HULK--
BLACK, GRAY AND GREEN AND THREE TIMES THE MEAN!

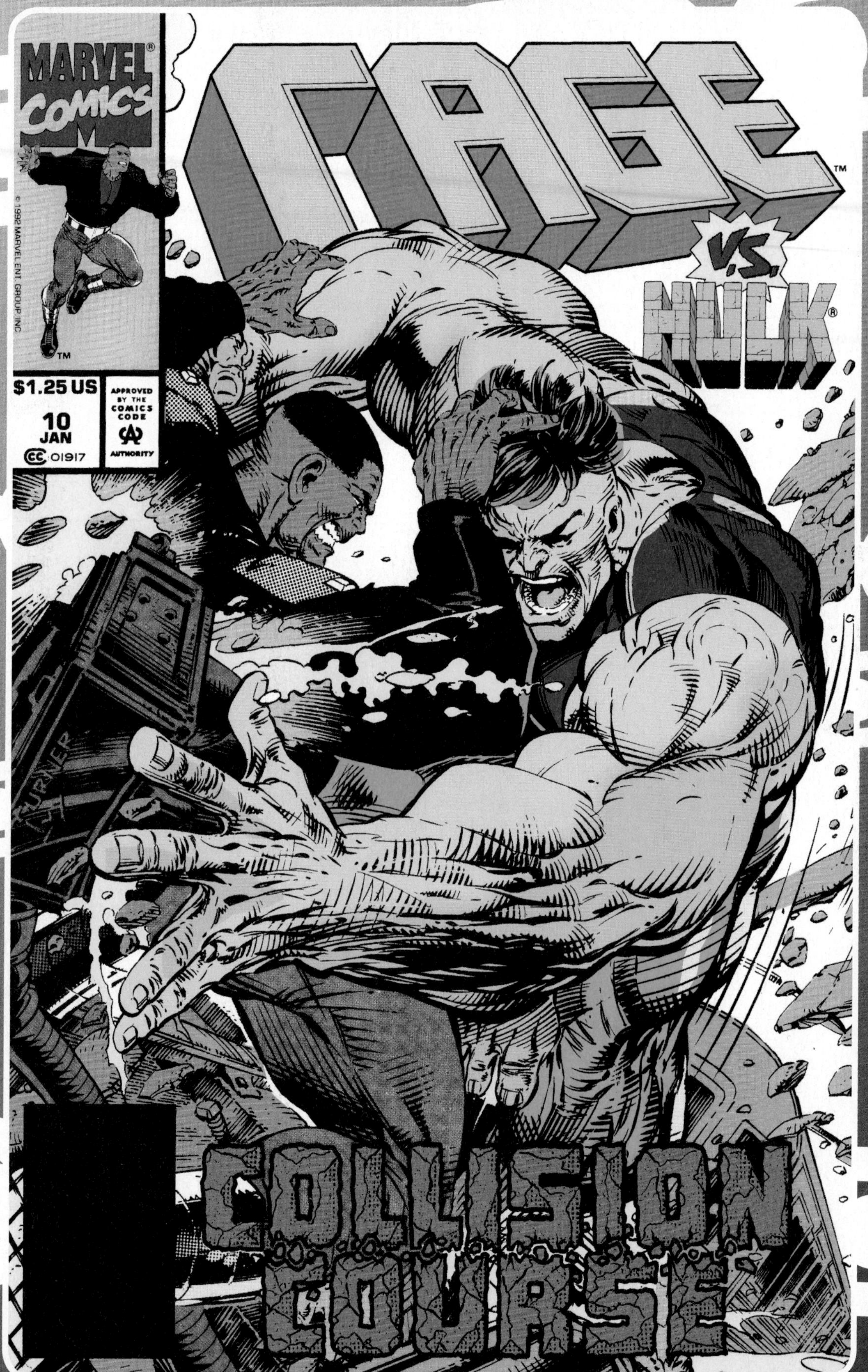
MARVEL® COMICS
© 1992 MARVEL ENT. GROUP, INC.
CAGE™
V.S.
HULK®
$1.25 US
10
JAN
APPROVED BY THE COMICS CODE AUTHORITY
01917
COLLISION COURSE

EMPOWERED WITH STEEL-HARD SKIN AND SUPER-HUMAN STRENGTH BY A MEDICAL EXPERIMENT GONE AWRY, LUKE CAGE IS A HERO FOR HIRE. HE'S RUNNING FROM A VIOLENT PAST TO AN UNCERTAIN FUTURE. IN A WORLD WHERE RULES CHANGE DAILY, ONLY HE HAS THE POWER TO MAKE HIS OWN. STAN LEE PRESENTS...

CAGE

CHICAGO, CALLED BY SOME THE CITY WITH BIG SHOULDERS.

BUT THEY AIN'T SEEN NOTHIN' YET.

THE INCREDIBLE HULK HAS COME TO TOWN.

EXCUSE ME, OFFICER.

I'M LOOKING FOR INFO ON THE RHINO.

HE'S ON THE TRAIL OF A PROPHECY.

IF IT COMES TO PASS, THE WORLD BECOMES A SAFER PLACE--

--WITH THE DESTRUCTION OF ALL THE OUTLAW HEROES IN THE WAKE OF ULTIMATE ORDER. WHICH IS GOOD--

--UNLESS YOU HAPPEN TO BE ONE OF THEM.

COLORS

INKS
CHRIS IVY

MIKE THOMAS

LETTERS
STARKINGS

SCRIPT
MARC McLAURIN

PENCILS
DWAYNE TURNER

EDITOR
KELLY CORVESE

CHIEF
TOM DeFALCO

WANTED

CAGE

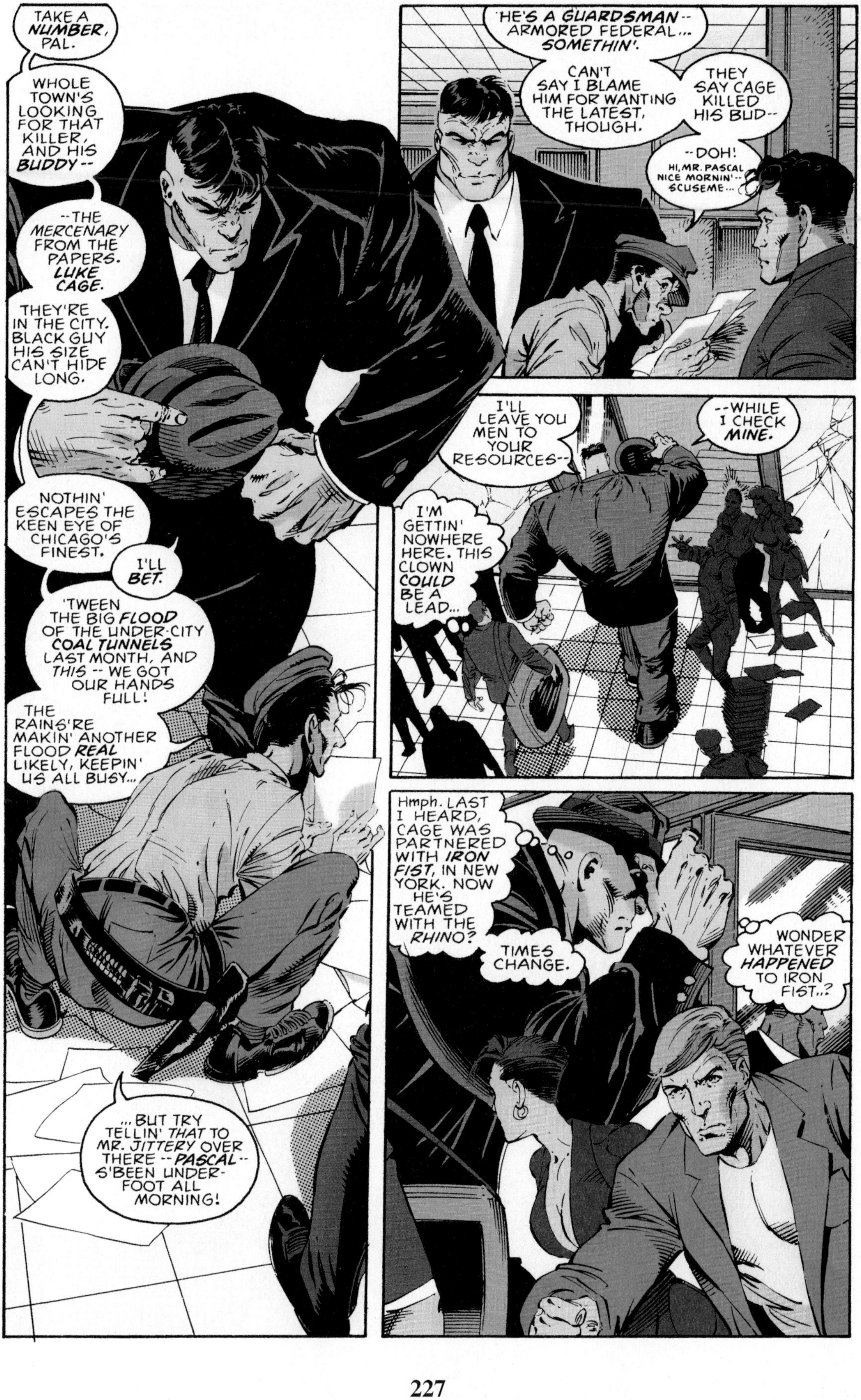
TAKE A NUMBER, PAL.
WHOLE TOWN'S LOOKING FOR THAT KILLER, AND HIS BUDDY--
--THE MERCENARY FROM THE PAPERS. LUKE CAGE.
THEY'RE IN THE CITY. BLACK GUY HIS SIZE CAN'T HIDE LONG.
NOTHIN' ESCAPES THE KEEN EYE OF CHICAGO'S FINEST.
I'LL BET.
'TWEEN THE BIG FLOOD OF THE UNDER-CITY COAL TUNNELS LAST MONTH, AND THIS -- WE GOT OUR HANDS FULL!
THE RAINS'RE MAKIN' ANOTHER FLOOD REAL LIKELY, KEEPIN' US ALL BUSY...
...BUT TRY TELLIN' THAT TO MR. JITTERY OVER THERE --PASCAL-- S'BEEN UNDER-FOOT ALL MORNING!
HE'S A GUARDSMAN-- ARMORED FEDERAL... SOMETHIN'.
CAN'T SAY I BLAME HIM FOR WANTING THE LATEST, THOUGH.
THEY SAY CAGE KILLED HIS BUD--
--DOH! HI, MR. PASCAL NICE MORNIN'-- SCUSEME...
I'LL LEAVE YOU MEN TO YOUR RESOURCES--
--WHILE I CHECK MINE.
I'M GETTIN' NOWHERE HERE. THIS CLOWN COULD BE A LEAD...
Hmph. LAST I HEARD, CAGE WAS PARTNERED WITH IRON FIST, IN NEW YORK. NOW HE'S TEAMED WITH THE RHINO?
TIMES CHANGE.
WONDER WHATEVER HAPPENED TO IRON FIST..?

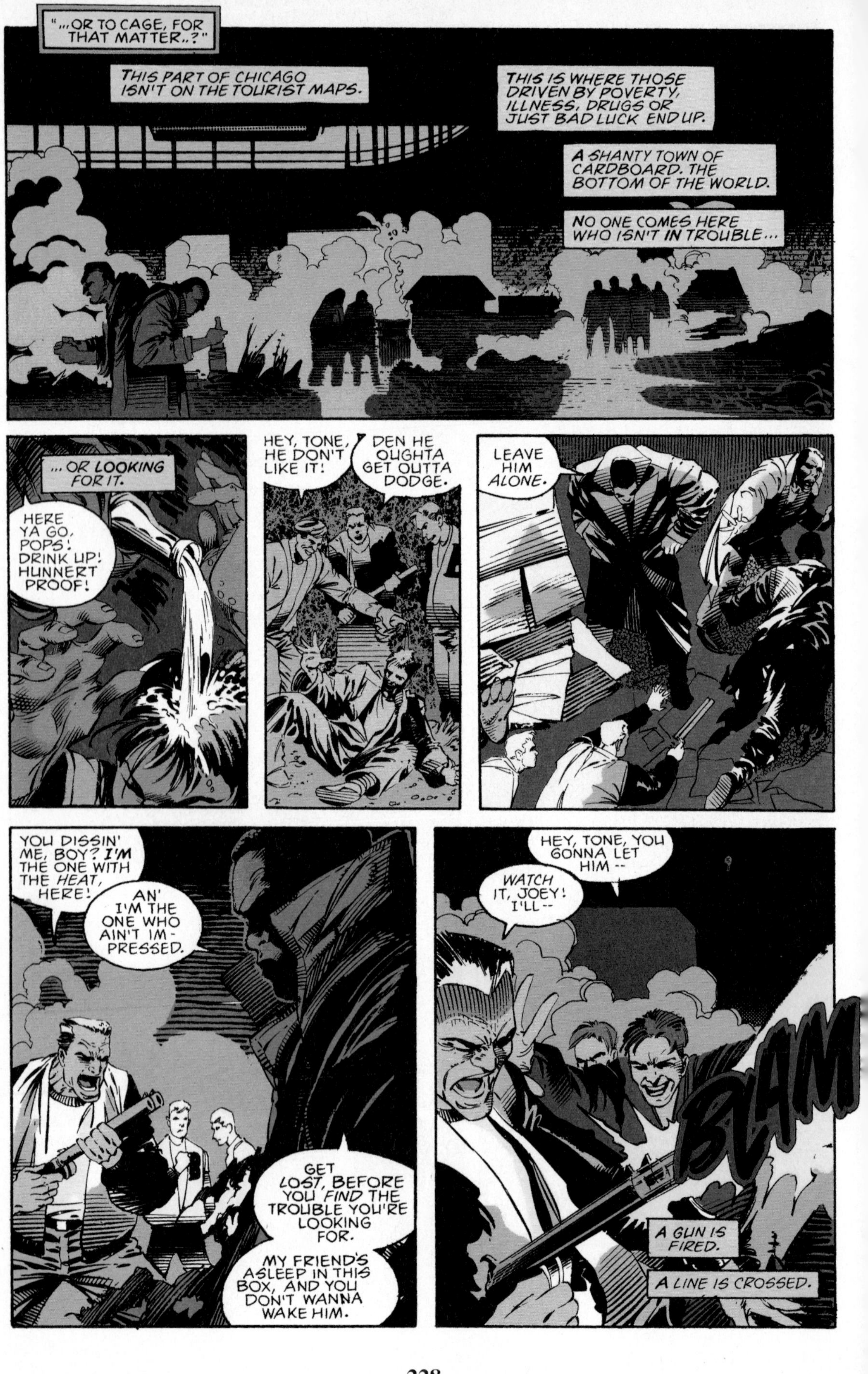
"...OR TO CAGE, FOR THAT MATTER..?"
THIS PART OF CHICAGO ISN'T ON THE TOURIST MAPS.
THIS IS WHERE THOSE DRIVEN BY POVERTY, ILLNESS, DRUGS OR JUST BAD LUCK END UP.
A SHANTY TOWN OF CARDBOARD. THE BOTTOM OF THE WORLD.
NO ONE COMES HERE WHO ISN'T IN TROUBLE...
...OR LOOKING FOR IT.
HERE YA GO, POPS! DRINK UP! HUNNERT PROOF!
HEY, TONE, HE DON'T LIKE IT!
DEN HE OUGHTA GET OUTTA DODGE.
LEAVE HIM ALONE.
YOU DISSIN' ME, BOY? I'M THE ONE WITH THE HEAT, HERE!
AN' I'M THE ONE WHO AIN'T IM-PRESSED.
GET LOST, BEFORE YOU FIND THE TROUBLE YOU'RE LOOKING FOR.
MY FRIEND'S ASLEEP IN THIS BOX, AND YOU DON'T WANNA WAKE HIM.
HEY, TONE, YOU GONNA LET HIM --
WATCH IT, JOEY! I'LL --
BLAM
A GUN IS FIRED.
A LINE IS CROSSED.

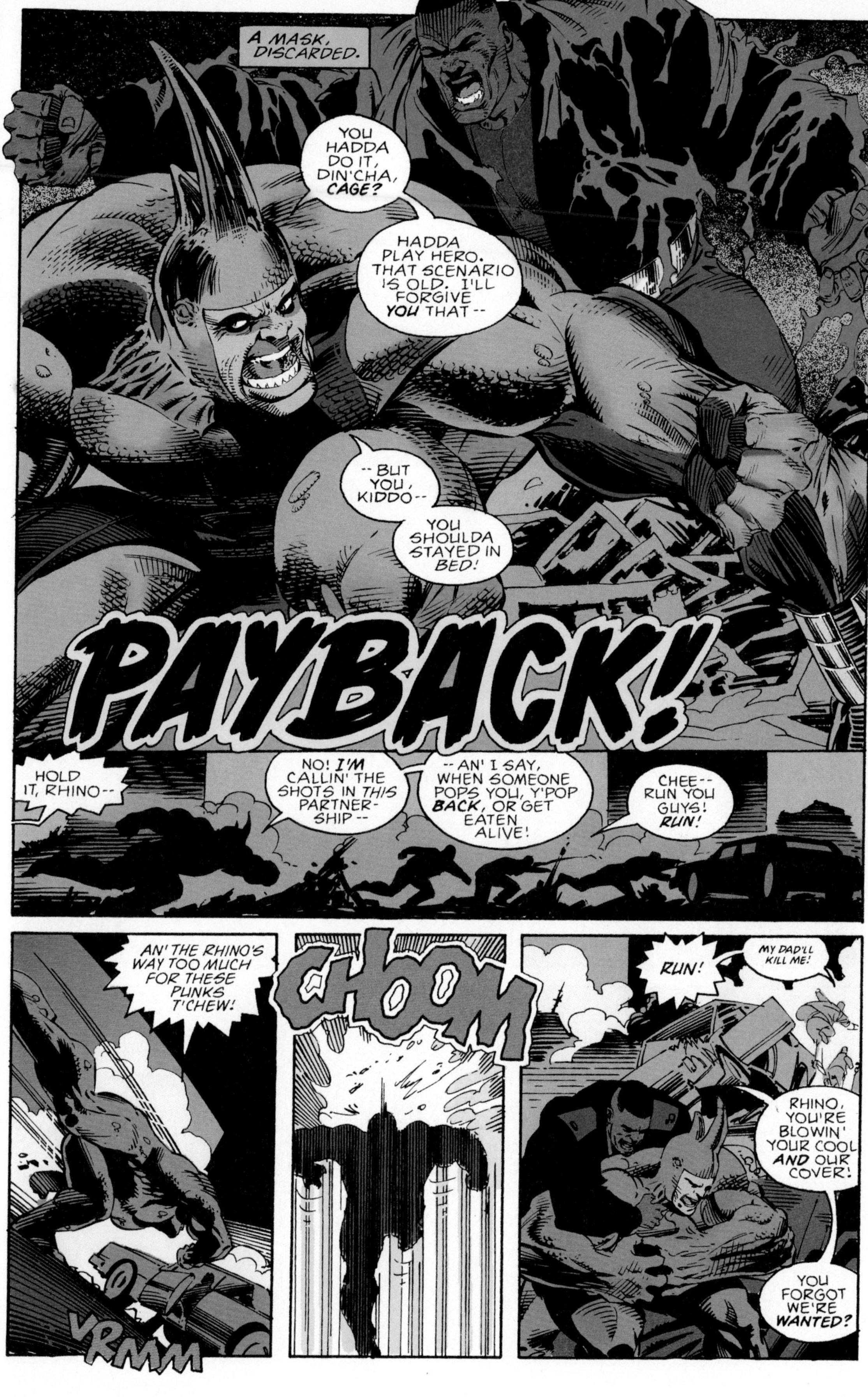
A MASK, DISCARDED.
YOU HADDA DO IT, DIN'CHA, CAGE?
HADDA PLAY HERO. THAT SCENARIO IS OLD. I'LL FORGIVE YOU THAT --
-- BUT YOU, KIDDO --
YOU SHOULDA STAYED IN BED!
PAYBACK!
HOLD IT, RHINO--
NO! I'M CALLIN' THE SHOTS IN THIS PARTNER-SHIP --
-- AN' I SAY, WHEN SOMEONE POPS YOU, Y'POP BACK, OR GET EATEN ALIVE!
CHEE-- RUN YOU GUYS! RUN!
AN' THE RHINO'S WAY TOO MUCH FOR THESE PUNKS T'CHEW!
VRMM
CHOOM
RUN!
MY DAD'LL KILL ME!
RHINO, YOU'RE BLOWIN' YOUR COOL AND OUR COVER!
YOU FORGOT WE'RE WANTED?

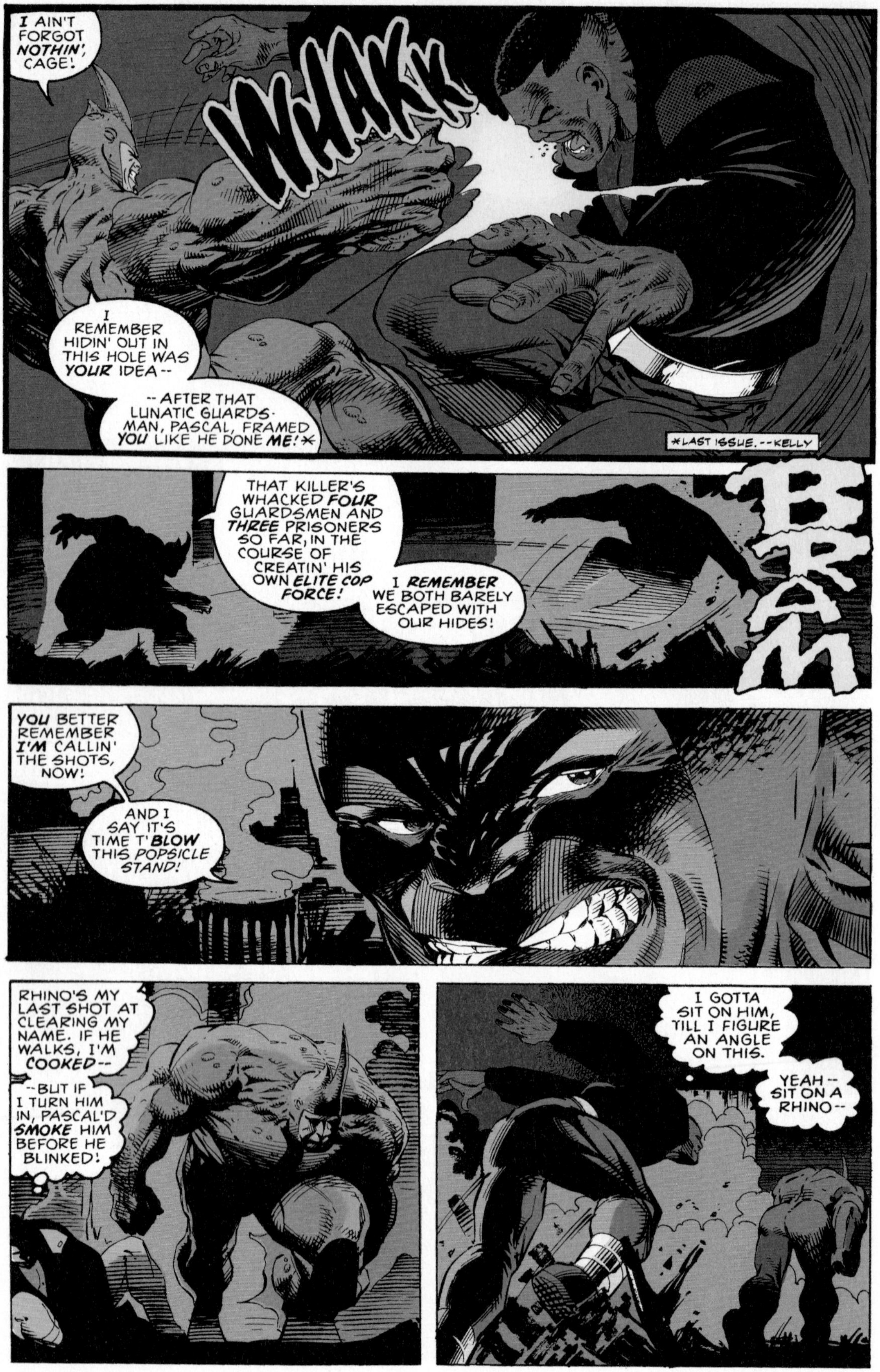
I AIN'T FORGOT NOTHIN', CAGE!
WHAKK
I REMEMBER HIDIN' OUT IN THIS HOLE WAS YOUR IDEA --
-- AFTER THAT LUNATIC GUARDSMAN, PASCAL, FRAMED YOU LIKE HE DONE ME! *
*LAST ISSUE. --KELLY
THAT KILLER'S WHACKED FOUR GUARDSMEN AND THREE PRISONERS SO FAR, IN THE COURSE OF CREATIN' HIS OWN ELITE COP FORCE!
I REMEMBER WE BOTH BARELY ESCAPED WITH OUR HIDES!
BRAM
YOU BETTER REMEMBER I'M CALLIN' THE SHOTS, NOW!
AND I SAY IT'S TIME T' BLOW THIS POPSICLE STAND!
RHINO'S MY LAST SHOT AT CLEARING MY NAME. IF HE WALKS, I'M COOKED--
--BUT IF I TURN HIM IN, PASCAL'D SMOKE HIM BEFORE HE BLINKED!
I GOTTA SIT ON HIM, TILL I FIGURE AN ANGLE ON THIS.
YEAH -- SIT ON A RHINO--

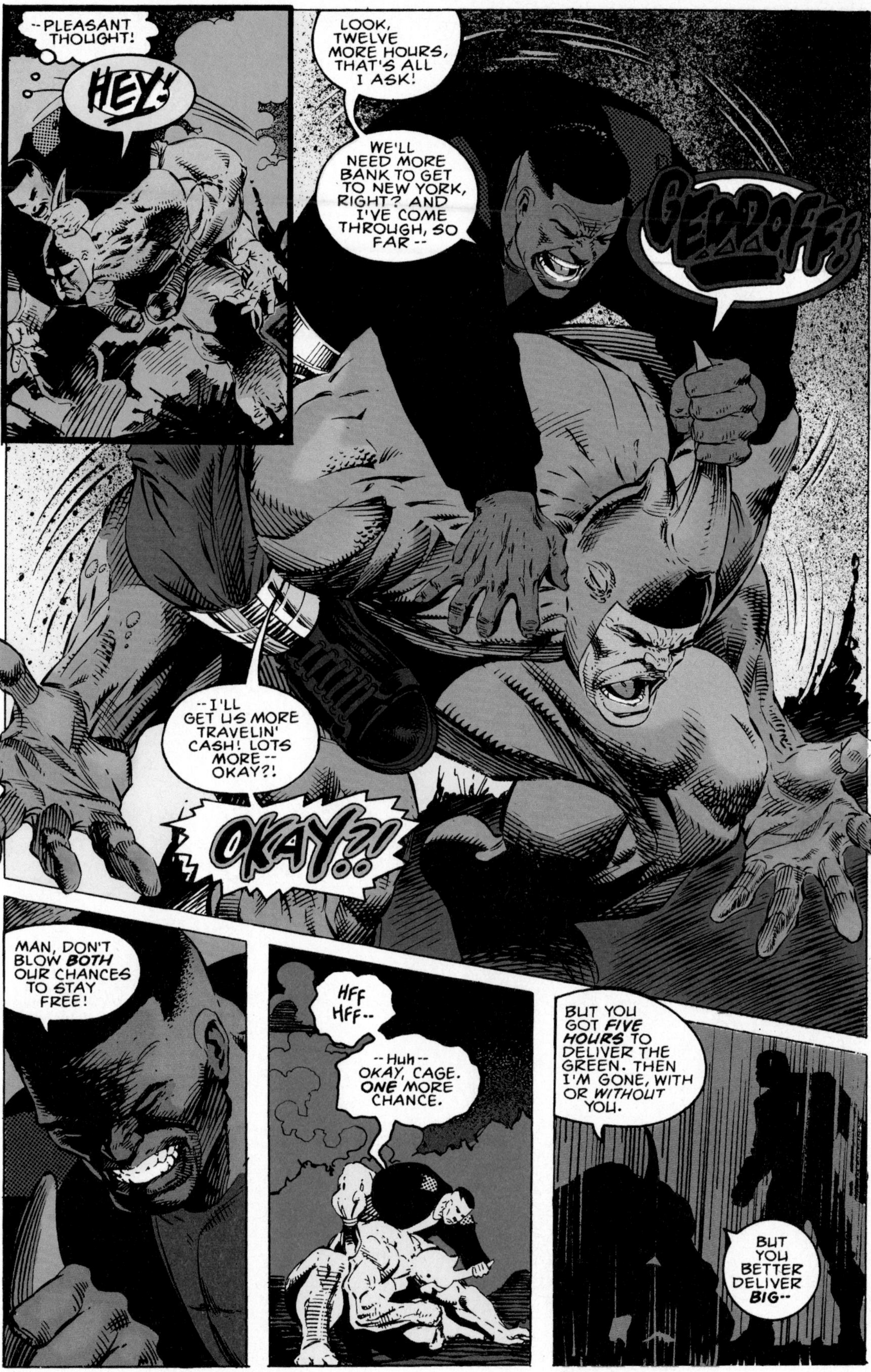
--PLEASANT THOUGHT!
HEY!
LOOK, TWELVE MORE HOURS, THAT'S ALL I ASK!
WE'LL NEED MORE BANK TO GET TO NEW YORK, RIGHT? AND I'VE COME THROUGH, SO FAR--
GEDDOFF!
--I'LL GET US MORE TRAVELIN' CASH! LOTS MORE-- OKAY?!
OKAY?!
MAN, DON'T BLOW BOTH OUR CHANCES TO STAY FREE!
HFF HFF--
--Huh-- OKAY, CAGE. ONE MORE CHANCE.
BUT YOU GOT FIVE HOURS TO DELIVER THE GREEN. THEN I'M GONE, WITH OR WITHOUT YOU.
BUT YOU BETTER DELIVER BIG--

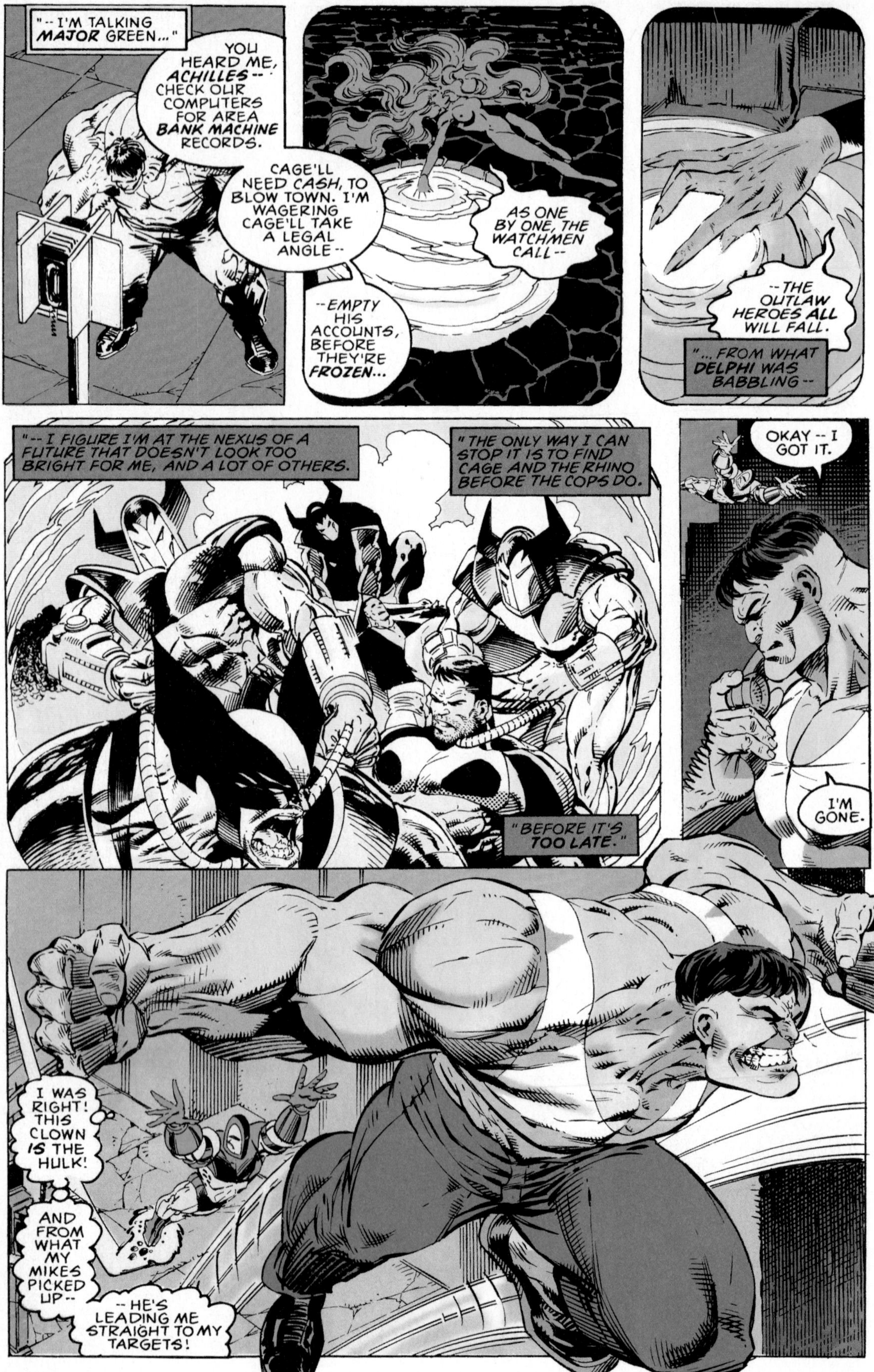
"-- I'M TALKING MAJOR GREEN..."
YOU HEARD ME, ACHILLES -- CHECK OUR COMPUTERS FOR AREA BANK MACHINE RECORDS.
CAGE'LL NEED CASH, TO BLOW TOWN. I'M WAGERING CAGE'LL TAKE A LEGAL ANGLE --
-- EMPTY HIS ACCOUNTS, BEFORE THEY'RE FROZEN...
AS ONE BY ONE, THE WATCHMEN CALL --
-- THE OUTLAW HEROES ALL WILL FALL.
"... FROM WHAT DELPHI WAS BABBLING --
"-- I FIGURE I'M AT THE NEXUS OF A FUTURE THAT DOESN'T LOOK TOO BRIGHT FOR ME, AND A LOT OF OTHERS.
"THE ONLY WAY I CAN STOP IT IS TO FIND CAGE AND THE RHINO BEFORE THE COPS DO.
"BEFORE IT'S TOO LATE."
OKAY -- I GOT IT.
I'M GONE.
I WAS RIGHT! THIS CLOWN IS THE HULK!
AND FROM WHAT MY MIKES PICKED UP --
-- HE'S LEADING ME STRAIGHT TO MY TARGETS!

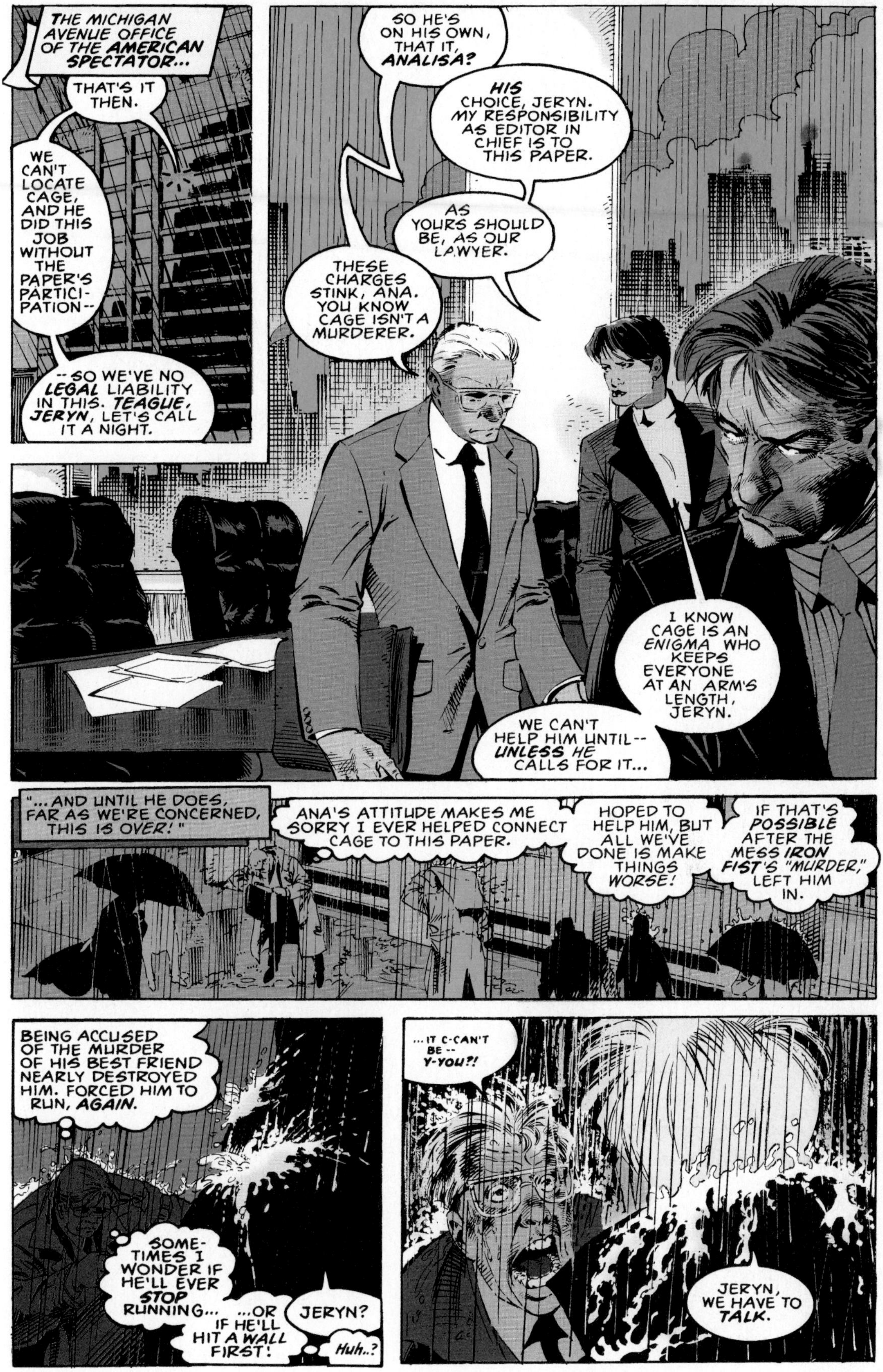
THE MICHIGAN AVENUE OFFICE OF THE AMERICAN SPECTATOR...
THAT'S IT THEN.
WE CAN'T LOCATE CAGE, AND HE DID THIS JOB WITHOUT THE PAPER'S PARTICI-PATION--
--SO WE'VE NO LEGAL LIABILITY IN THIS. TEAGUE, JERYN, LET'S CALL IT A NIGHT.
SO HE'S ON HIS OWN, THAT IT, ANALISA?
HIS CHOICE, JERYN. MY RESPONSIBILITY AS EDITOR IN CHIEF IS TO THIS PAPER.
AS YOURS SHOULD BE, AS OUR LAWYER.
THESE CHARGES STINK, ANA. YOU KNOW CAGE ISN'T A MURDERER.
I KNOW CAGE IS AN ENIGMA WHO KEEPS EVERYONE AT AN ARM'S LENGTH, JERYN.
WE CAN'T HELP HIM UNTIL-- UNLESS HE CALLS FOR IT...
"...AND UNTIL HE DOES, FAR AS WE'RE CONCERNED, THIS IS OVER!"
ANA'S ATTITUDE MAKES ME SORRY I EVER HELPED CONNECT CAGE TO THIS PAPER.
HOPED TO HELP HIM, BUT ALL WE'VE DONE IS MAKE THINGS WORSE!
IF THAT'S POSSIBLE AFTER THE MESS IRON FIST'S "MURDER," LEFT HIM IN.
BEING ACCUSED OF THE MURDER OF HIS BEST FRIEND NEARLY DESTROYED HIM. FORCED HIM TO RUN, AGAIN.
SOME-TIMES I WONDER IF HE'LL EVER STOP RUNNING... ...OR IF HE'LL HIT A WALL FIRST!
JERYN?
Huh..?
...IT C-CAN'T BE -- Y-YOU?!
JERYN, WE HAVE TO TALK.

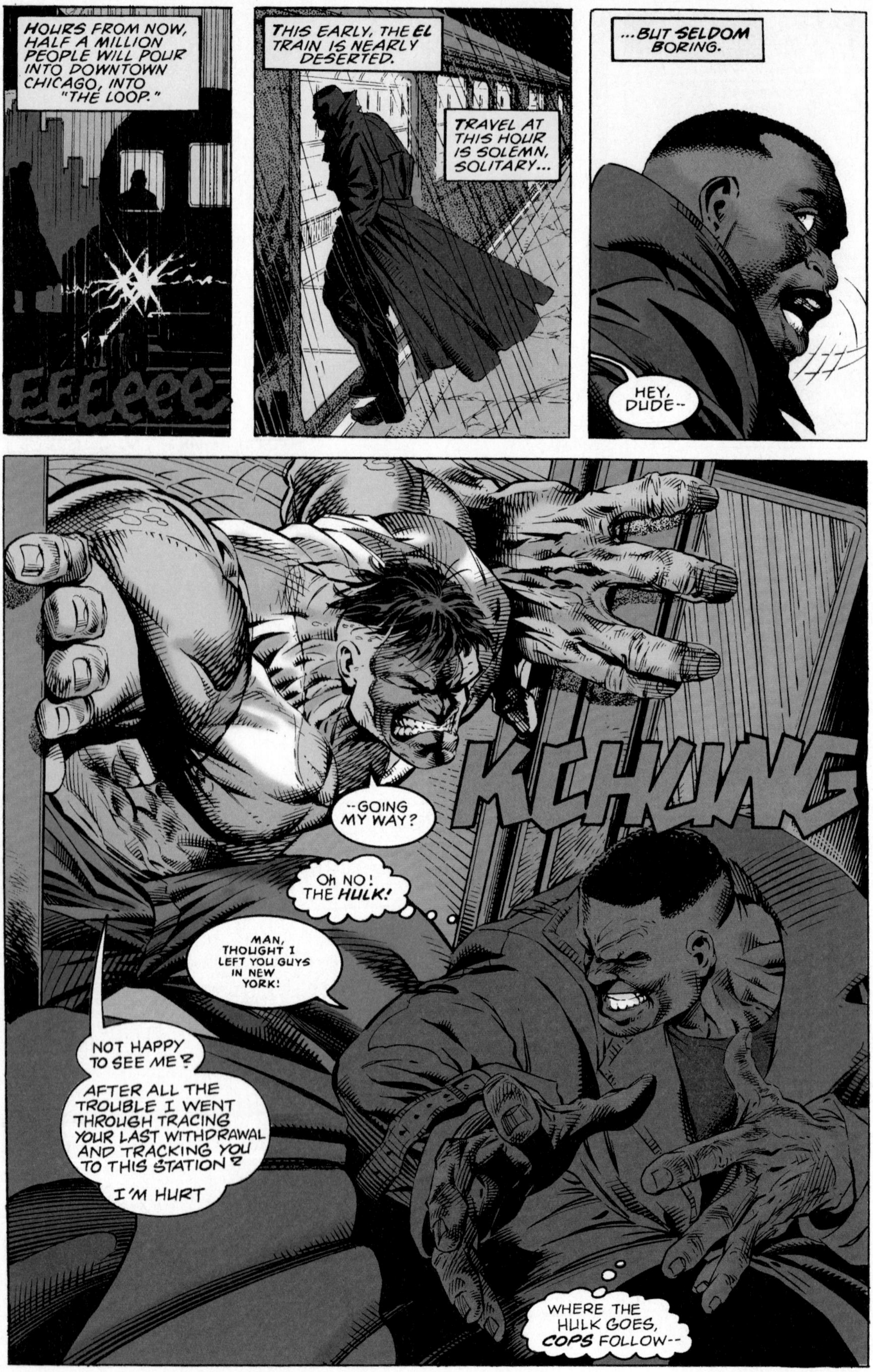
HOURS FROM NOW, HALF A MILLION PEOPLE WILL POUR INTO DOWNTOWN CHICAGO, INTO "THE LOOP."
EEEeee
THIS EARLY, THE EL TRAIN IS NEARLY DESERTED.
TRAVEL AT THIS HOUR IS SOLEMN, SOLITARY...
...BUT SELDOM BORING.
HEY, DUDE--
KCHUNG
--GOING MY WAY?
Oh NO! THE HULK!
MAN, THOUGHT I LEFT YOU GUYS IN NEW YORK!
NOT HAPPY TO SEE ME?
AFTER ALL THE TROUBLE I WENT THROUGH TRACING YOUR LAST WITHDRAWAL AND TRACKING YOU TO THIS STATION?
I'M HURT
WHERE THE HULK GOES, COPS FOLLOW--

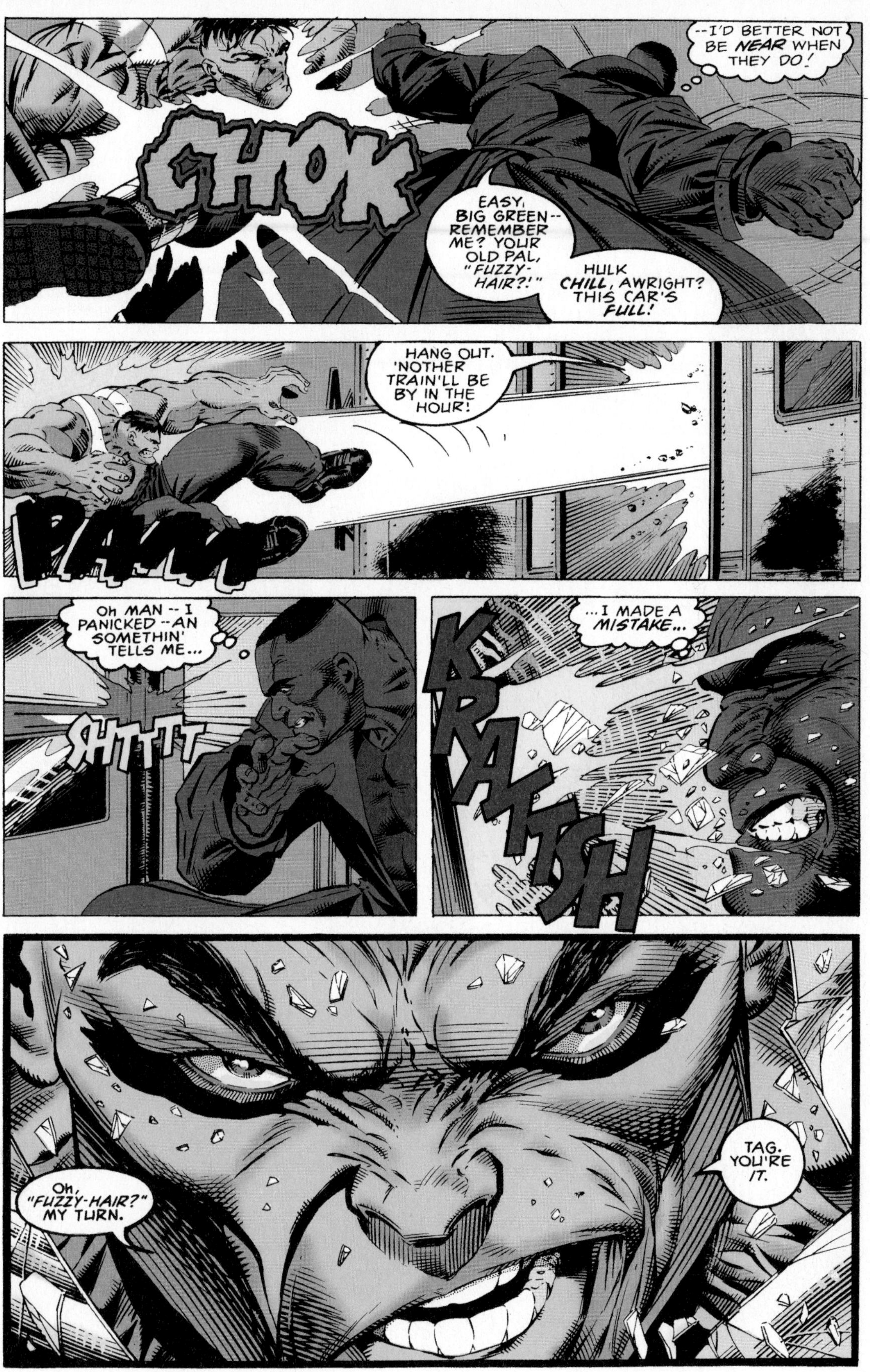
--I'D BETTER NOT BE NEAR WHEN THEY DO!
CHOK
EASY, BIG GREEN-- REMEMBER ME? YOUR OLD PAL, "FUZZY-HAIR?!"
HULK CHILL, AWRIGHT? THIS CAR'S FULL!
HANG OUT. 'NOTHER TRAIN'LL BE BY IN THE HOUR!
Oh MAN -- I PANICKED --AN SOMETHIN' TELLS ME...
SHTTTT
...I MADE A MISTAKE...
KRAKTSH
Oh, "FUZZY-HAIR?" MY TURN.
TAG. YOU'RE IT.

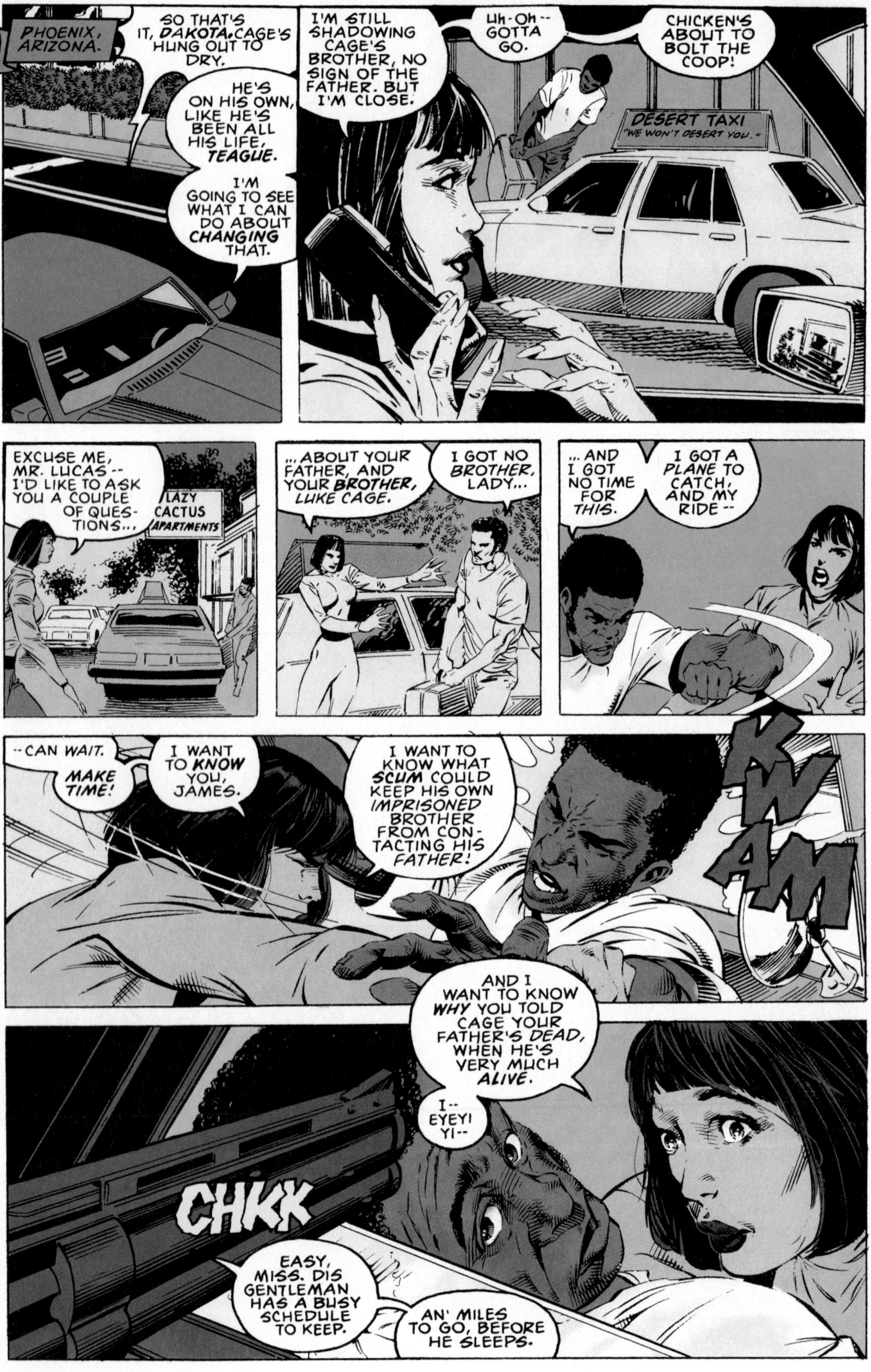
PHOENIX, ARIZONA.
SO THAT'S IT, DAKOTA. CAGE'S HUNG OUT TO DRY.
HE'S ON HIS OWN, LIKE HE'S BEEN ALL HIS LIFE, TEAGUE.
I'M GOING TO SEE WHAT I CAN DO ABOUT CHANGING THAT.
I'M STILL SHADOWING CAGE'S BROTHER, NO SIGN OF THE FATHER. BUT I'M CLOSE.
UH-OH -- GOTTA GO.
CHICKEN'S ABOUT TO BOLT THE COOP!
DESERT TAXI
"WE WON'T DESERT YOU."
EXCUSE ME, MR. LUCAS -- I'D LIKE TO ASK YOU A COUPLE OF QUESTIONS...
LAZY CACTUS APARTMENTS
...ABOUT YOUR FATHER, AND YOUR BROTHER, LUKE CAGE.
I GOT NO BROTHER, LADY...
...AND I GOT NO TIME FOR THIS.
I GOT A PLANE TO CATCH, AND MY RIDE --
-- CAN WAIT.
MAKE TIME!
I WANT TO KNOW YOU, JAMES.
I WANT TO KNOW WHAT SCUM COULD KEEP HIS OWN IMPRISONED BROTHER FROM CONTACTING HIS FATHER!
KWAM
AND I WANT TO KNOW WHY YOU TOLD CAGE YOUR FATHER'S DEAD, WHEN HE'S VERY MUCH ALIVE.
I-- EYEYI YI--
CHKK
EASY, MISS. DIS GENTLEMAN HAS A BUSY SCHEDULE TO KEEP.
AN' MILES TO GO, BEFORE HE SLEEPS.

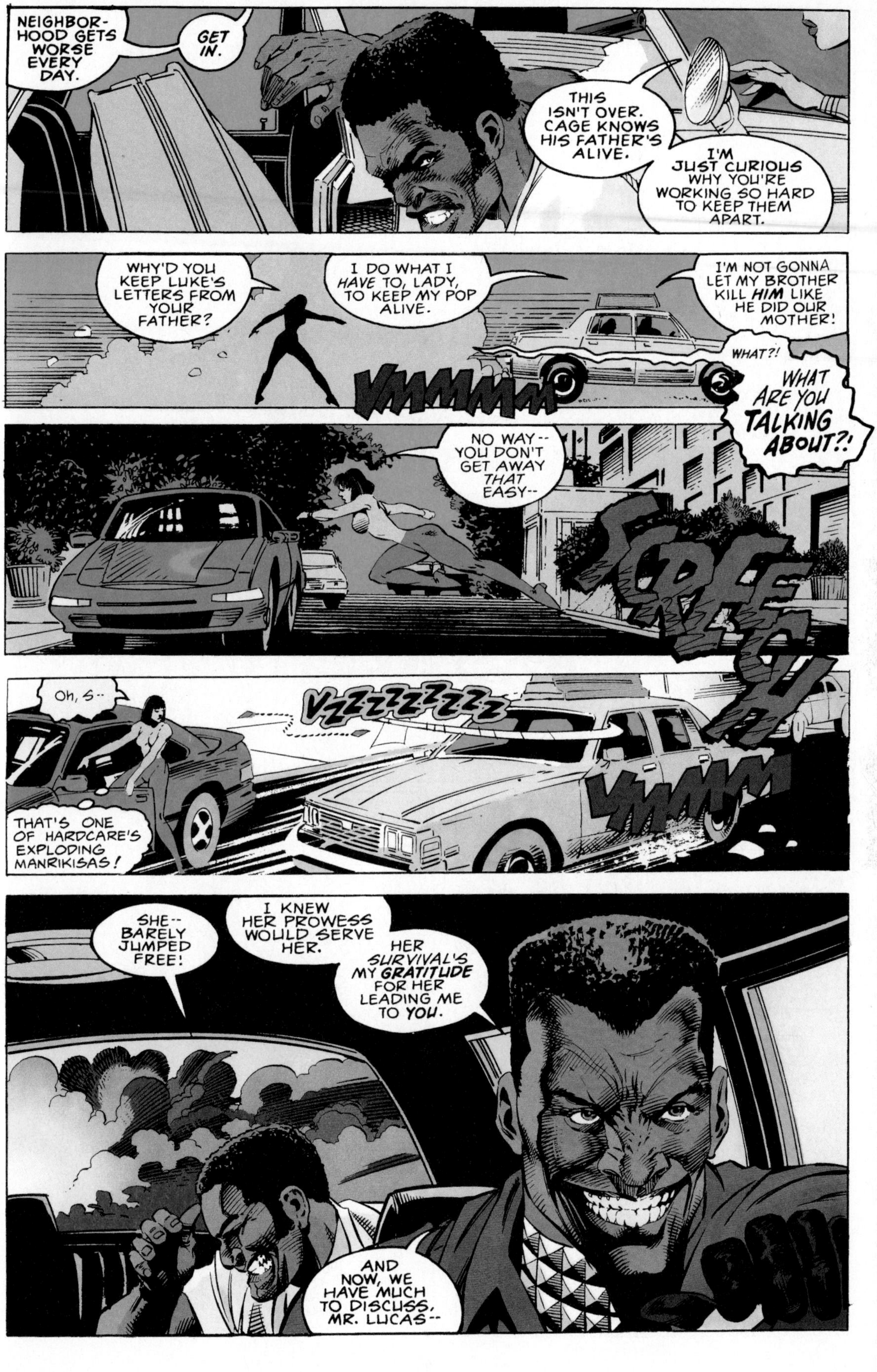

NEIGHBOR-HOOD GETS WORSE EVERY DAY.
GET IN.
THIS ISN'T OVER. CAGE KNOWS HIS FATHER'S ALIVE.
I'M JUST CURIOUS WHY YOU'RE WORKING SO HARD TO KEEP THEM APART.
WHY'D YOU KEEP LUKE'S LETTERS FROM YOUR FATHER?
I DO WHAT I HAVE TO, LADY, TO KEEP MY POP ALIVE.
I'M NOT GONNA LET MY BROTHER KILL HIM LIKE HE DID OUR MOTHER!
VMMMM
WHAT?!
WHAT ARE YOU TALKING ABOUT?!
NO WAY-- YOU DON'T GET AWAY THAT EASY--
SCREEEECH
Oh, S--
VZZZZZZZZZ
VMMM
THAT'S ONE OF HARDCARE'S EXPLODING MANRIKISAS!
SHE-- BARELY JUMPED FREE!
I KNEW HER PROWESS WOULD SERVE HER.
HER SURVIVAL'S MY GRATITUDE FOR HER LEADING ME TO YOU.
AND NOW, WE HAVE MUCH TO DISCUSS, MR. LUCAS--

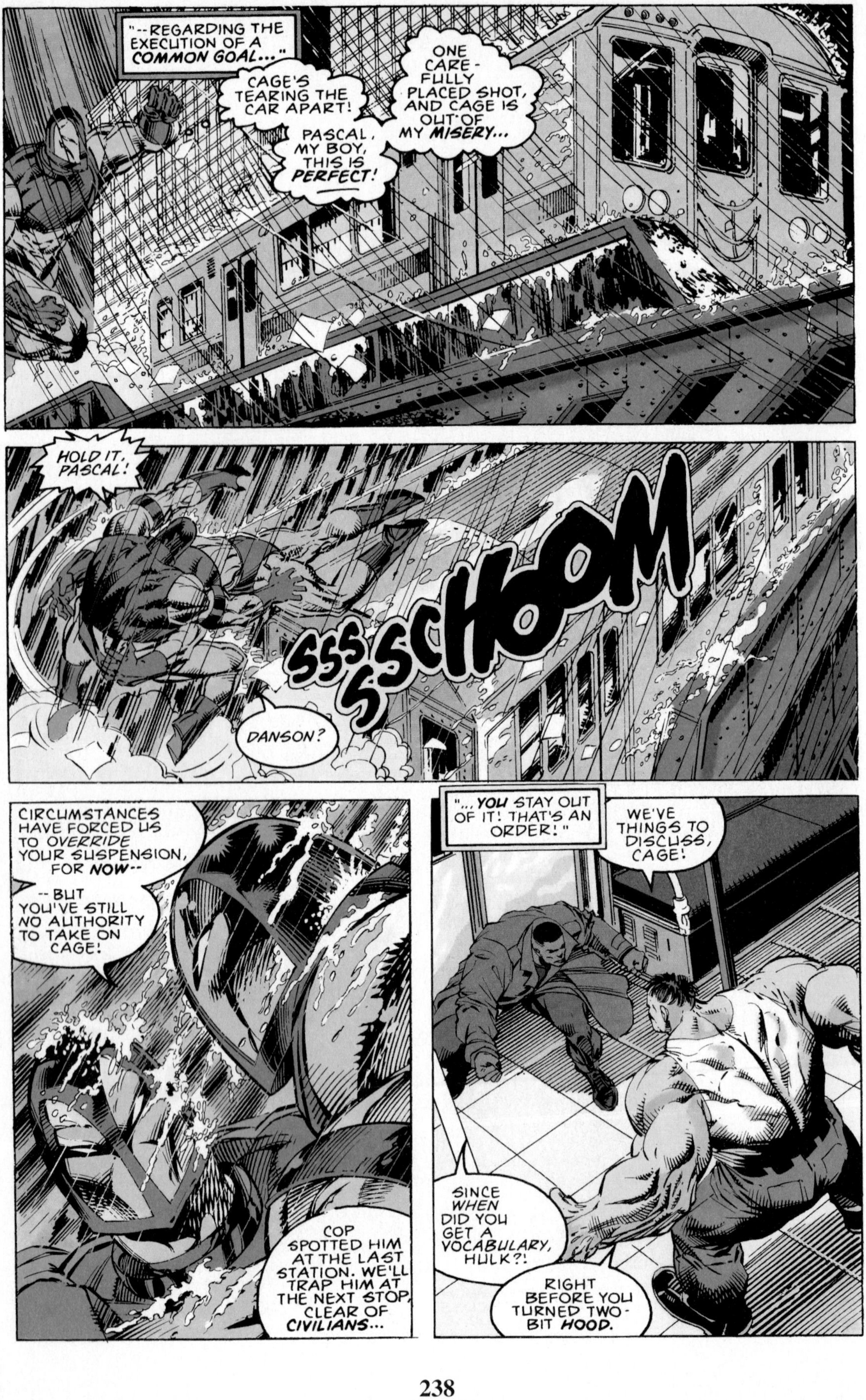
"--REGARDING THE EXECUTION OF A COMMON GOAL..."
CAGE'S TEARING THE CAR APART!
PASCAL, MY BOY, THIS IS PERFECT!
ONE CARE-FULLY PLACED SHOT, AND CAGE IS OUT OF MY MISERY...
HOLD IT, PASCAL!
SSSSSCHOOM
DANSON?
CIRCUMSTANCES HAVE FORCED US TO OVERRIDE YOUR SUSPENSION, FOR NOW--
-- BUT YOU'VE STILL NO AUTHORITY TO TAKE ON CAGE!
COP SPOTTED HIM AT THE LAST STATION. WE'LL TRAP HIM AT THE NEXT STOP, CLEAR OF CIVILIANS...
"... YOU STAY OUT OF IT! THAT'S AN ORDER!"
WE'VE THINGS TO DISCUSS, CAGE!
SINCE WHEN DID YOU GET A VOCABULARY, HULK?!
RIGHT BEFORE YOU TURNED TWO-BIT HOOD.

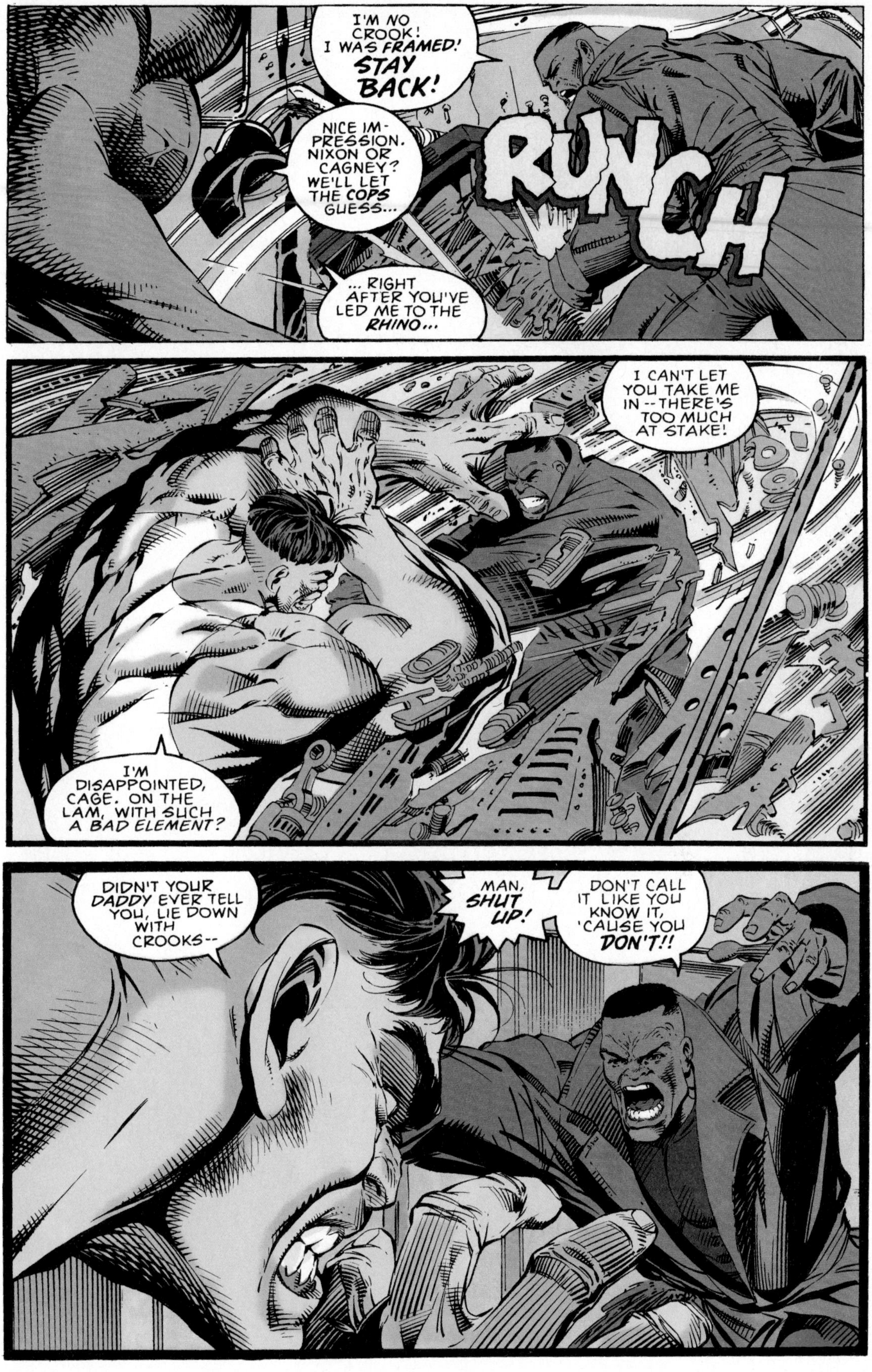
I'M NO CROOK! I WAS FRAMED! STAY BACK!
NICE IM-PRESSION. NIXON OR CAGNEY? WE'LL LET THE COPS GUESS...
RUNCH
...RIGHT AFTER YOU'VE LED ME TO THE RHINO...
I CAN'T LET YOU TAKE ME IN--THERE'S TOO MUCH AT STAKE!
I'M DISAPPOINTED, CAGE. ON THE LAM, WITH SUCH A BAD ELEMENT?
DIDN'T YOUR DADDY EVER TELL YOU, LIE DOWN WITH CROOKS--
MAN, SHUT UP!
DON'T CALL IT LIKE YOU KNOW IT, 'CAUSE YOU DON'T!!

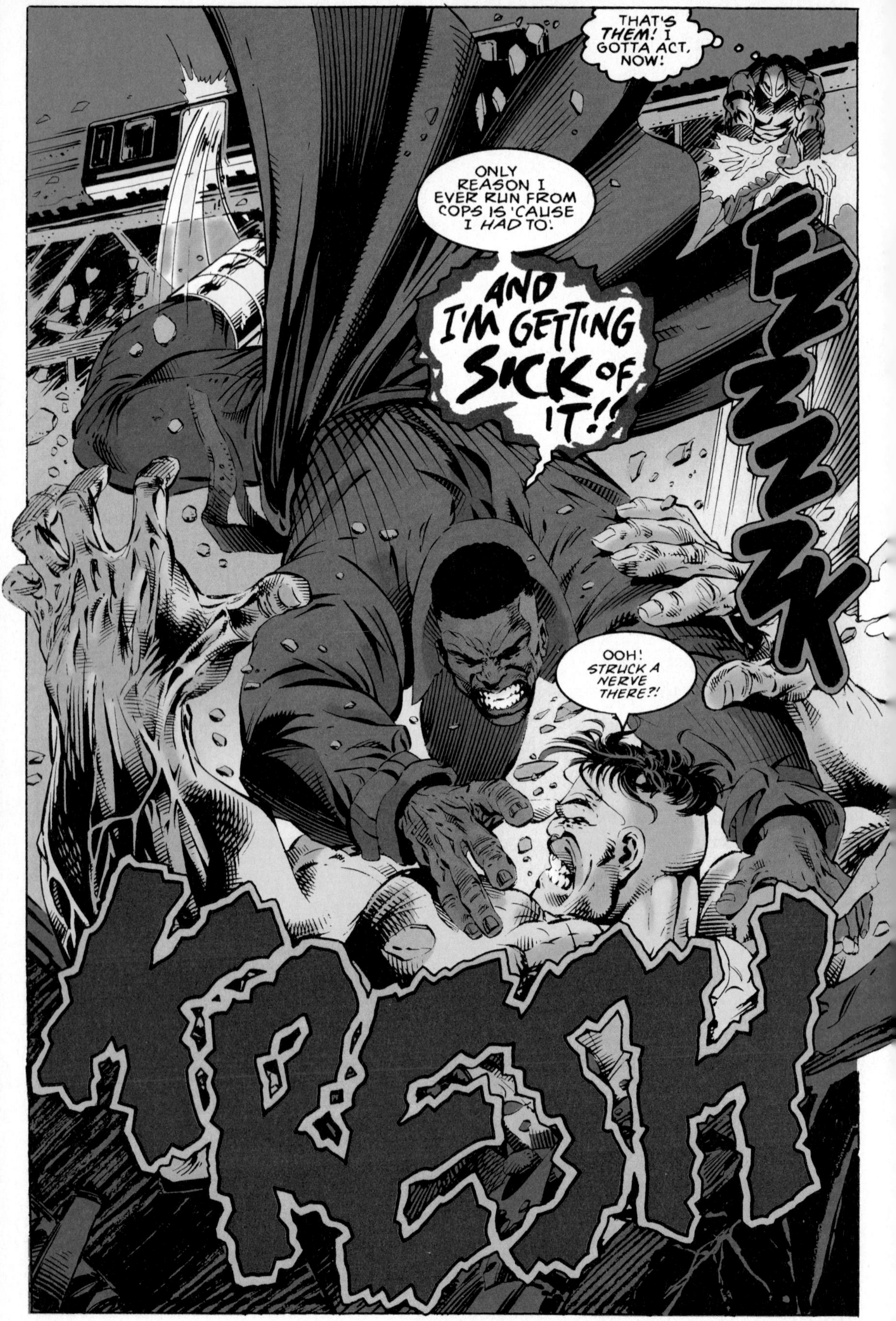

THAT'S *THEM!* I GOTTA ACT, NOW!
ONLY REASON I EVER RUN FROM COPS IS 'CAUSE I *HAD* TO.
AND I'M GETTING SICK OF IT!?
FZZZZK
OOH! STRUCK A NERVE THERE?!
KRASH

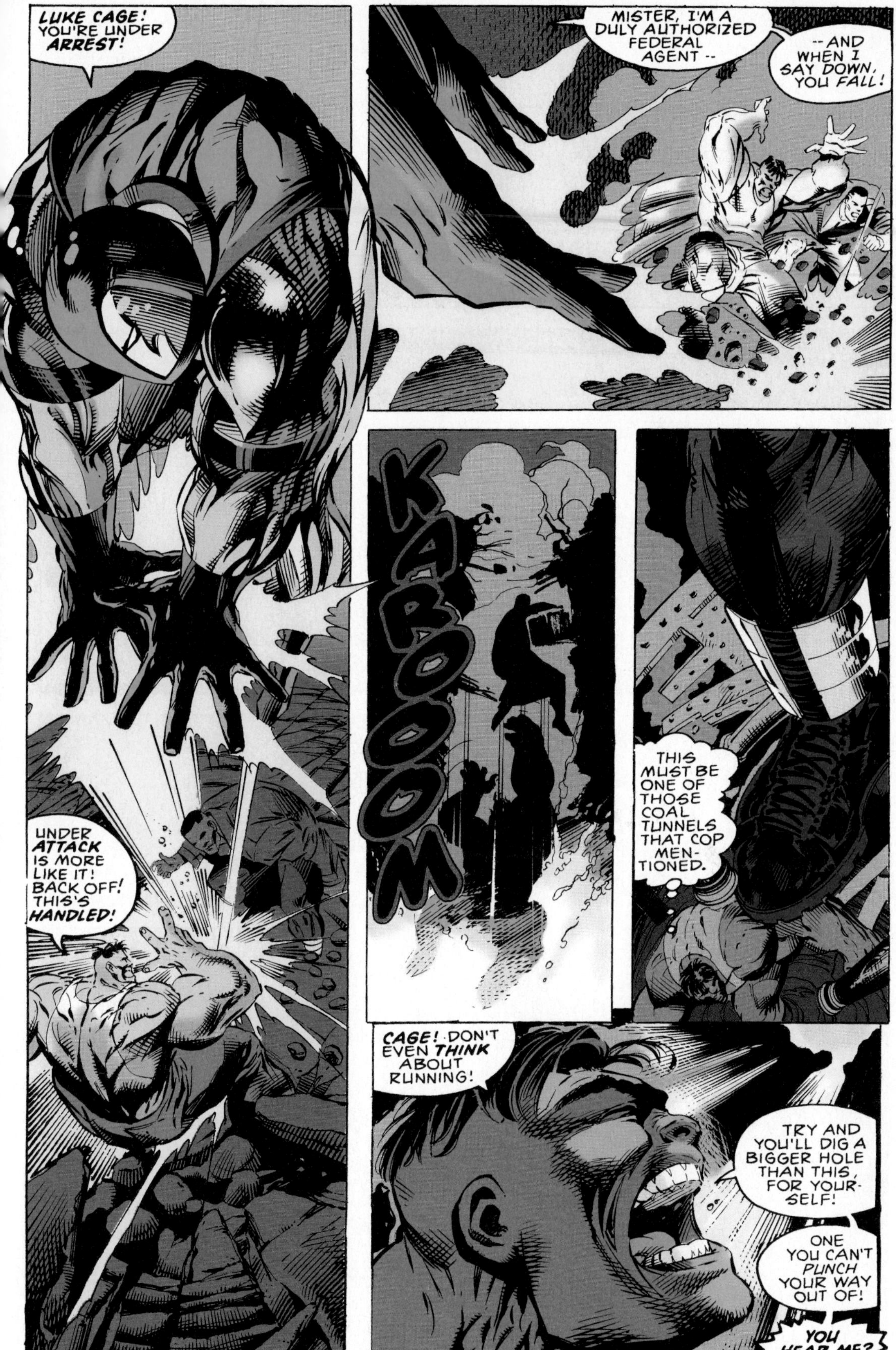
LUKE CAGE! YOU'RE UNDER ARREST!
UNDER ATTACK IS MORE LIKE IT! BACK OFF! THIS'S HANDLED!
MISTER, I'M A DULY AUTHORIZED FEDERAL AGENT --
-- AND WHEN I SAY DOWN, YOU FALL!
KAROOOOM
THIS MUST BE ONE OF THOSE COAL TUNNELS THAT COP MENTIONED.
CAGE! DON'T EVEN THINK ABOUT RUNNING!
TRY AND YOU'LL DIG A BIGGER HOLE THAN THIS, FOR YOURSELF!
ONE YOU CAN'T PUNCH YOUR WAY OUT OF!
YOU HEAR ME?

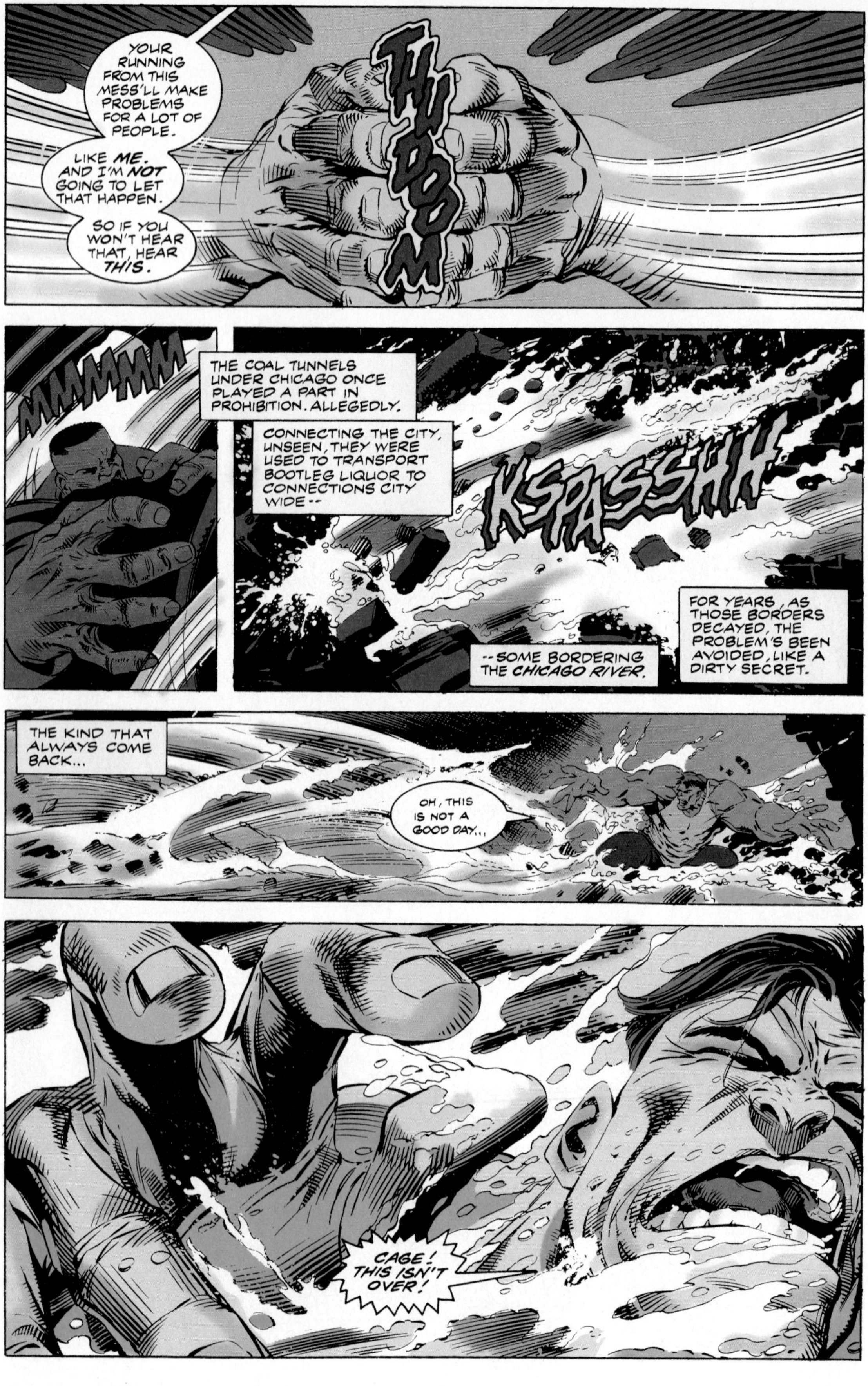

YOUR RUNNING FROM THIS MESS'LL MAKE PROBLEMS FOR A LOT OF PEOPLE.
LIKE ME. AND I'M NOT GOING TO LET THAT HAPPEN.
SO IF YOU WON'T HEAR THAT, HEAR THIS.
THUDOOM
MMMMMM
THE COAL TUNNELS UNDER CHICAGO ONCE PLAYED A PART IN PROHIBITION. ALLEGEDLY.
CONNECTING THE CITY, UNSEEN, THEY WERE USED TO TRANSPORT BOOTLEG LIQUOR TO CONNECTIONS CITY WIDE--
KSPASSHH
--SOME BORDERING THE CHICAGO RIVER.
FOR YEARS, AS THOSE BORDERS DECAYED, THE PROBLEM'S BEEN AVOIDED, LIKE A DIRTY SECRET.
THE KIND THAT ALWAYS COME BACK...
OH, THIS IS NOT A GOOD DAY...
CAGE! THIS ISN'T OVER!

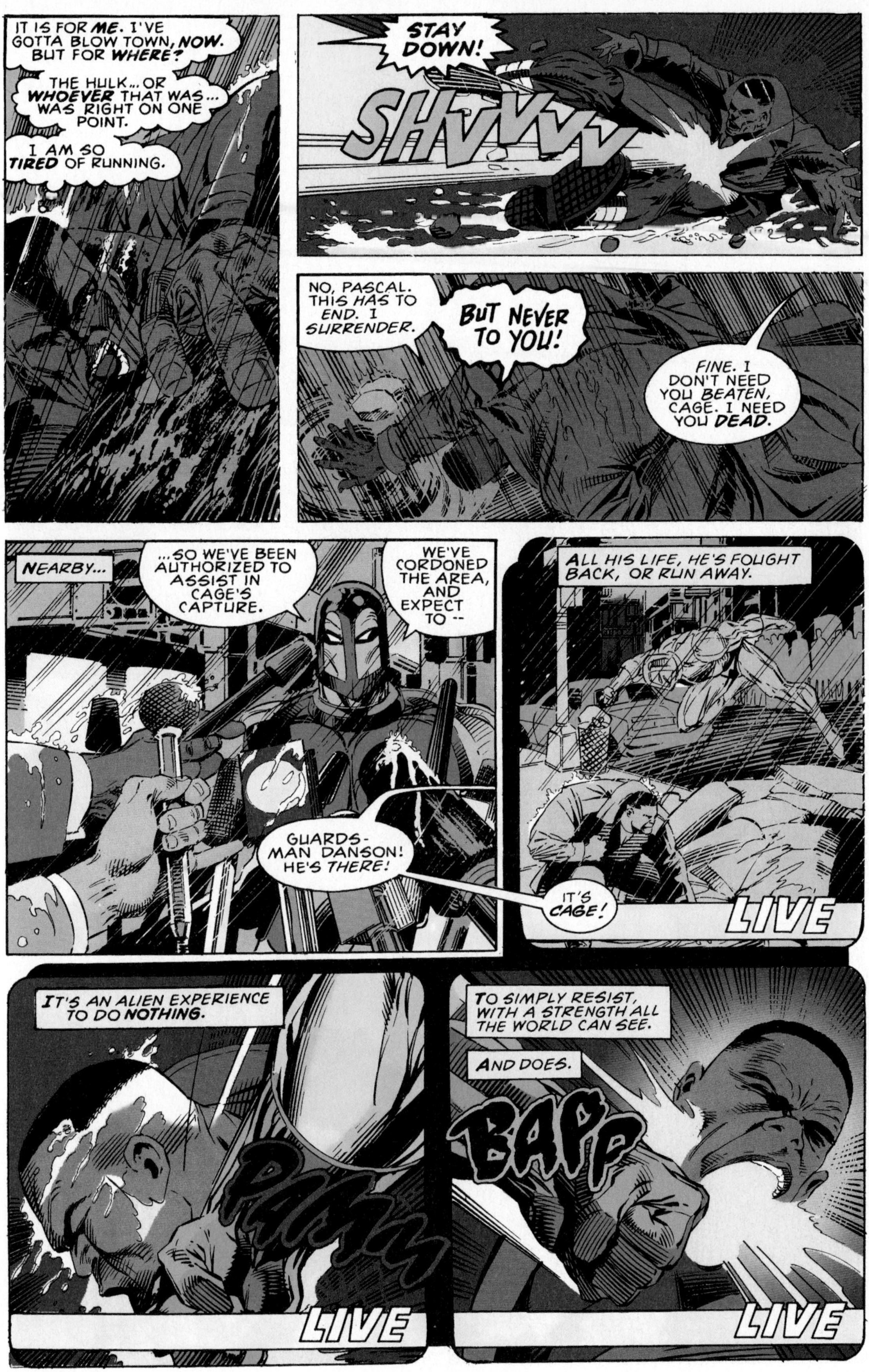
IT IS FOR ME. I'VE GOTTA BLOW TOWN, NOW. BUT FOR WHERE?
THE HULK... OR WHOEVER THAT WAS... WAS RIGHT ON ONE POINT.
I AM SO TIRED OF RUNNING.
STAY DOWN!
SHVVVV
NO, PASCAL. THIS HAS TO END. I SURRENDER.
BUT NEVER TO YOU!
FINE. I DON'T NEED YOU BEATEN, CAGE. I NEED YOU DEAD.
NEARBY...
...SO WE'VE BEEN AUTHORIZED TO ASSIST IN CAGE'S CAPTURE.
WE'VE CORDONED THE AREA, AND EXPECT TO --
GUARDS-MAN DANSON! HE'S THERE!
IT'S CAGE!
ALL HIS LIFE, HE'S FOUGHT BACK, OR RUN AWAY.
LIVE
IT'S AN ALIEN EXPERIENCE TO DO NOTHING.
LIVE
TO SIMPLY RESIST, WITH A STRENGTH ALL THE WORLD CAN SEE.
AND DOES.
BAPP
LIVE

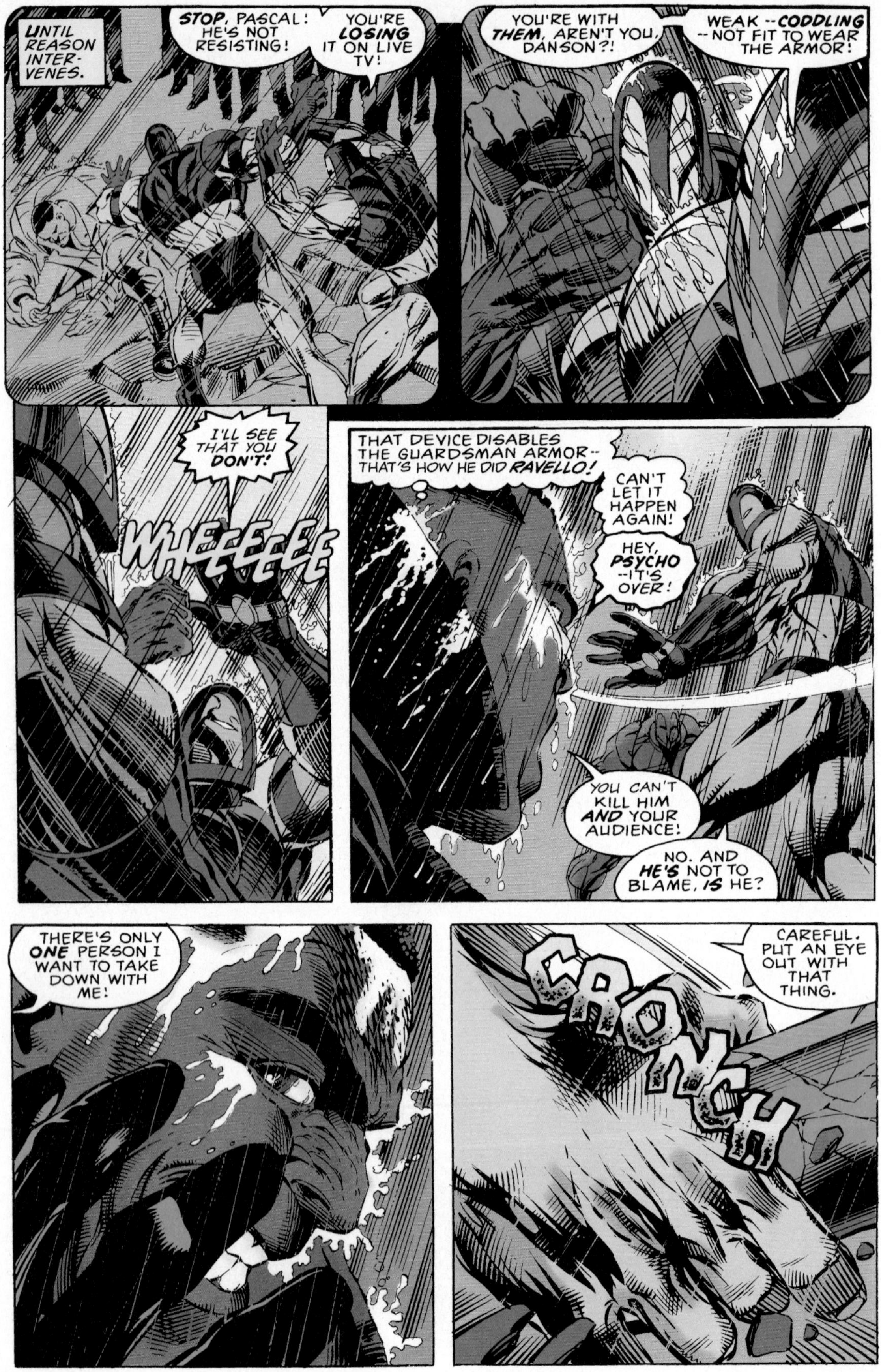
UNTIL REASON INTER-VENES.
STOP, PASCAL: HE'S NOT RESISTING!
YOU'RE LOSING IT ON LIVE TV!
YOU'RE WITH THEM, AREN'T YOU, DANSON?!
WEAK --CODDLING --NOT FIT TO WEAR THE ARMOR!
I'LL SEE THAT YOU DON'T!
WHEEEEEEE
THAT DEVICE DISABLES THE GUARDSMAN ARMOR-- THAT'S HOW HE DID RAVELLO!
CAN'T LET IT HAPPEN AGAIN!
HEY, PSYCHO --IT'S OVER!
YOU CAN'T KILL HIM AND YOUR AUDIENCE!
NO. AND HE'S NOT TO BLAME, IS HE?
THERE'S ONLY ONE PERSON I WANT TO TAKE DOWN WITH ME!
CRONCH
CAREFUL. PUT AN EYE OUT WITH THAT THING.

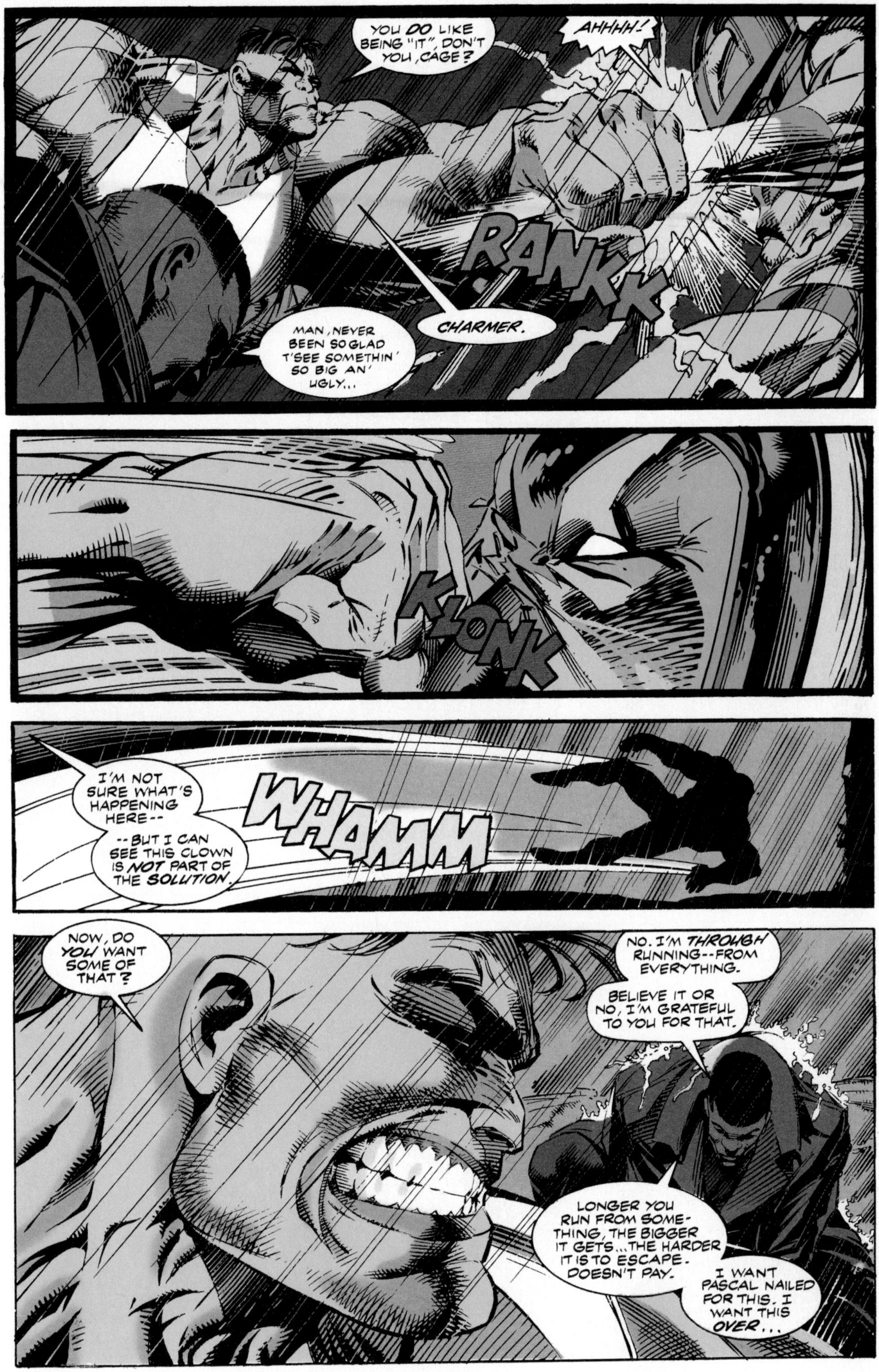
YOU DO LIKE BEING "IT", DON'T YOU, CAGE?
AHHHH!
RANKK
CHARMER.
MAN, NEVER BEEN SO GLAD T'SEE SOMETHIN' SO BIG AN' UGLY...
KLONK
I'M NOT SURE WHAT'S HAPPENING HERE--
--BUT I CAN SEE THIS CLOWN IS NOT PART OF THE SOLUTION.
WHAMM
NOW, DO YOU WANT SOME OF THAT?
NO. I'M THROUGH RUNNING--FROM EVERYTHING.
BELIEVE IT OR NO, I'M GRATEFUL TO YOU FOR THAT.
LONGER YOU RUN FROM SOMETHING, THE BIGGER IT GETS... THE HARDER IT IS TO ESCAPE. DOESN'T PAY.
I WANT PASCAL NAILED FOR THIS. I WANT THIS OVER...

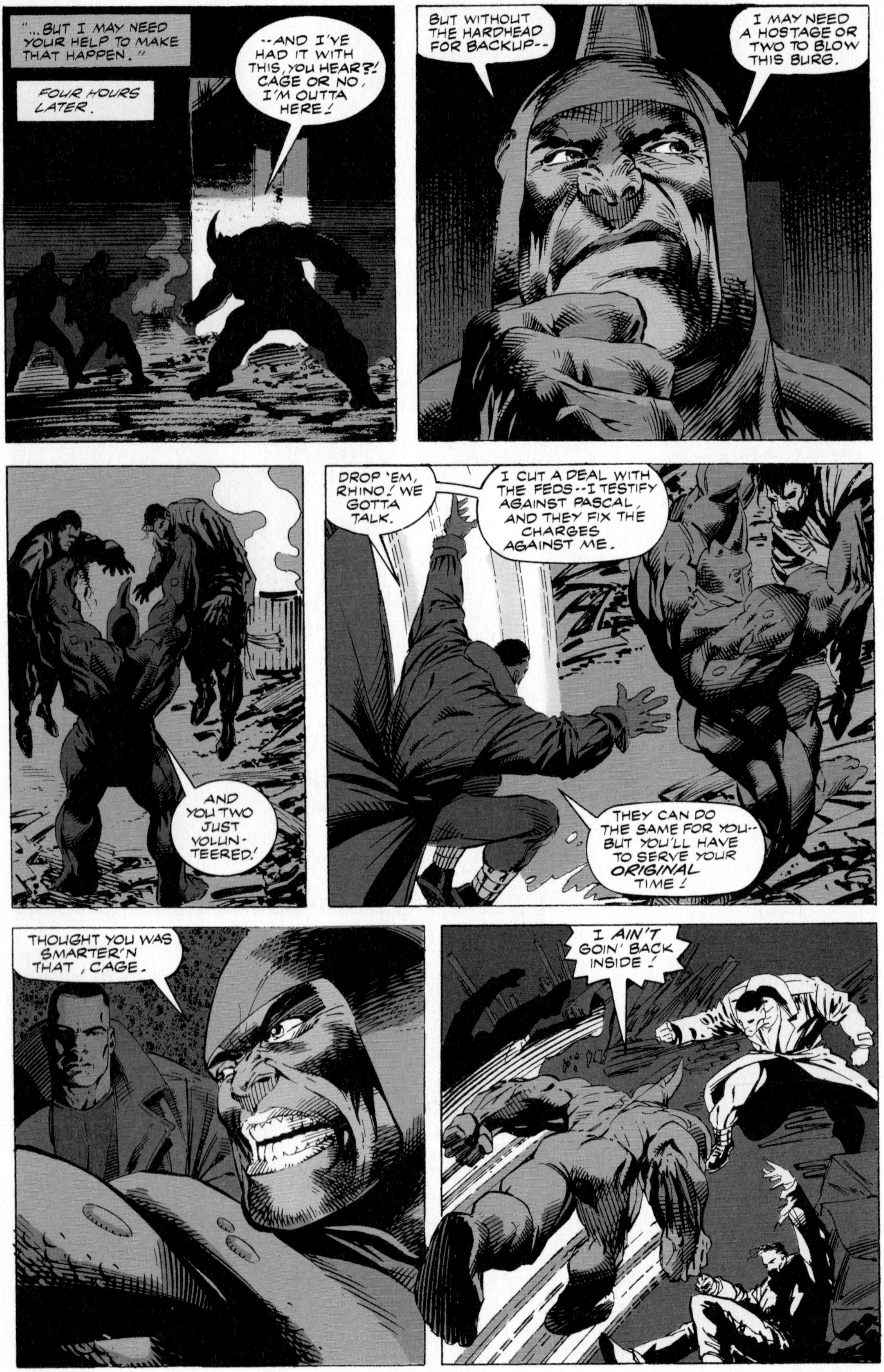
"...BUT I MAY NEED YOUR HELP TO MAKE THAT HAPPEN."
FOUR HOURS LATER.
--AND I'VE HAD IT WITH THIS, YOU HEAR?! CAGE OR NO, I'M OUTTA HERE!
BUT WITHOUT THE HARDHEAD FOR BACKUP--
I MAY NEED A HOSTAGE OR TWO TO BLOW THIS BURG.
AND YOU TWO JUST VOLUNTEERED!
DROP 'EM, RHINO! WE GOTTA TALK.
I CUT A DEAL WITH THE FEDS--I TESTIFY AGAINST PASCAL, AND THEY FIX THE CHARGES AGAINST ME.
THEY CAN DO THE SAME FOR YOU-- BUT YOU'LL HAVE TO SERVE YOUR ORIGINAL TIME!
THOUGHT YOU WAS SMARTER'N THAT, CAGE.
I AIN'T GOIN' BACK INSIDE!

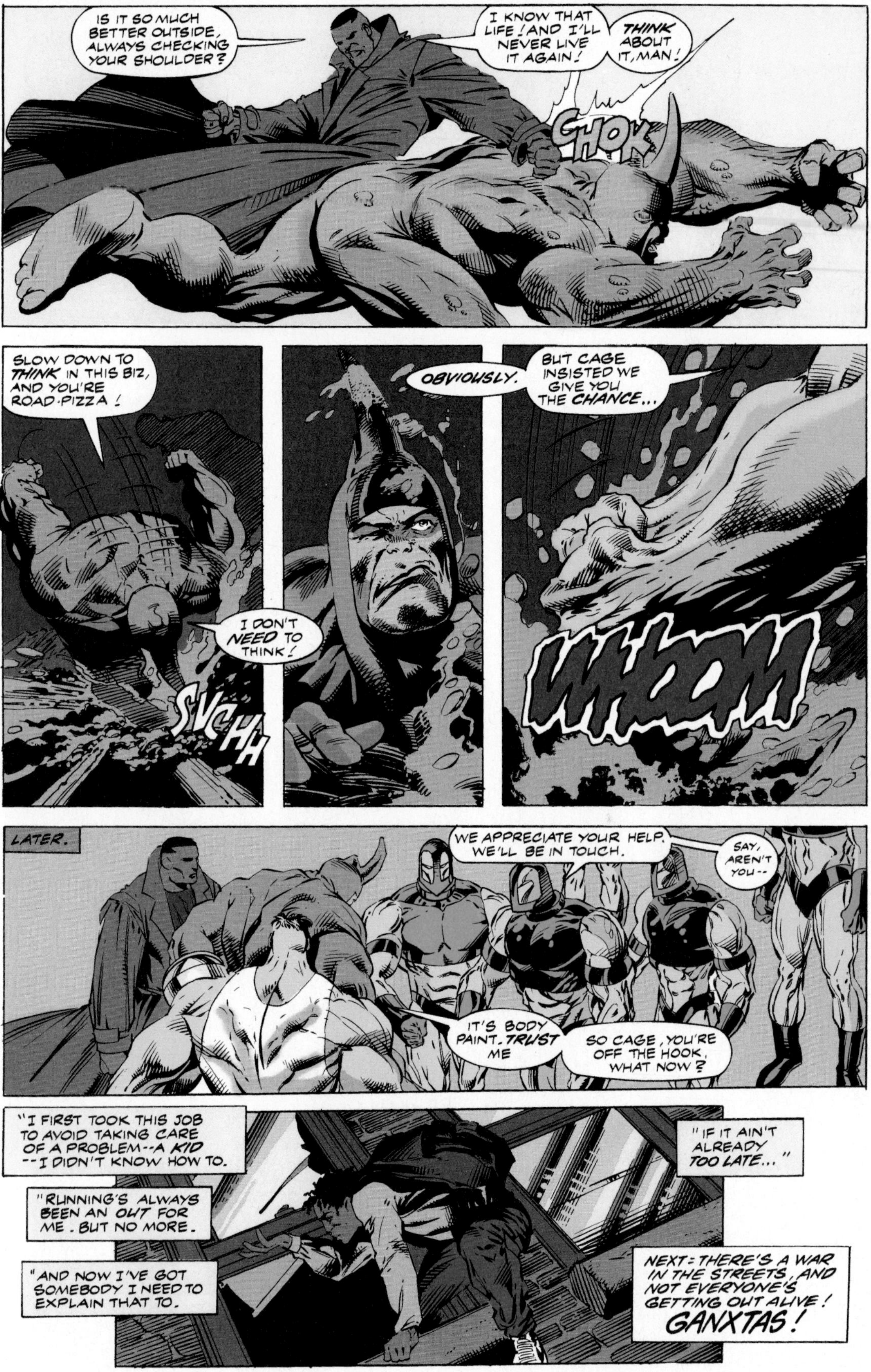
IS IT SO MUCH BETTER OUTSIDE, ALWAYS CHECKING YOUR SHOULDER?
I KNOW THAT LIFE! AND I'LL NEVER LIVE IT AGAIN!
THINK ABOUT IT, MAN!
CHOK
SLOW DOWN TO THINK IN THIS BIZ, AND YOU'RE ROAD-PIZZA!
I DON'T NEED TO THINK!
SVCHH
OBVIOUSLY.
BUT CAGE INSISTED WE GIVE YOU THE CHANCE...
WHOOM
LATER.
WE APPRECIATE YOUR HELP. WE'LL BE IN TOUCH.
SAY, AREN'T YOU--
IT'S BODY PAINT. TRUST ME
SO CAGE, YOU'RE OFF THE HOOK. WHAT NOW?
"I FIRST TOOK THIS JOB TO AVOID TAKING CARE OF A PROBLEM--A KID--I DIDN'T KNOW HOW TO.
"RUNNING'S ALWAYS BEEN AN OUT FOR ME. BUT NO MORE.
"AND NOW I'VE GOT SOMEBODY I NEED TO EXPLAIN THAT TO.
"IF IT AIN'T ALREADY TOO LATE..."
NEXT: THERE'S A WAR IN THE STREETS, AND NOT EVERYONE'S GETTING OUT ALIVE! GANXTAS!

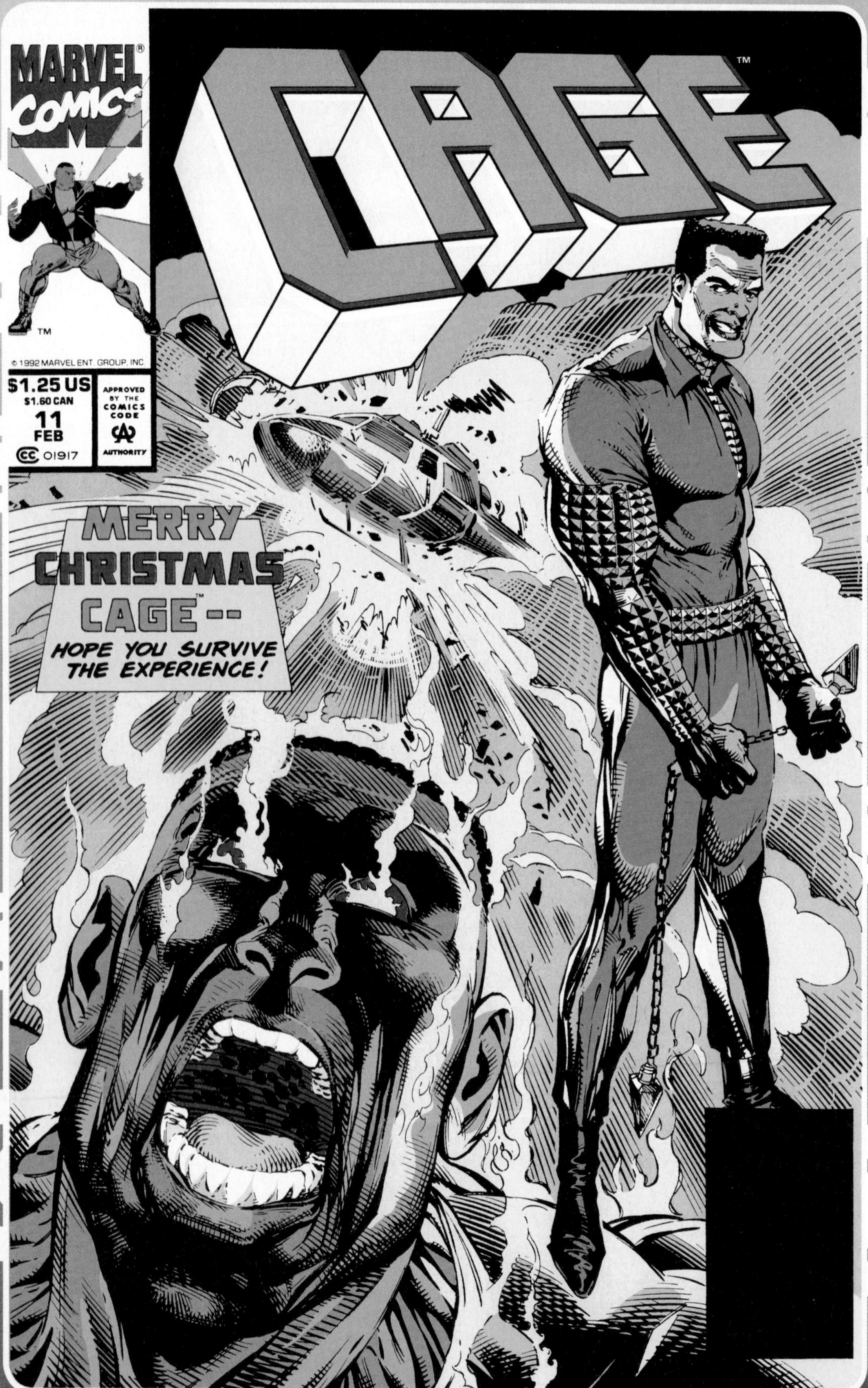
MARVEL®
COMICS
CAGE™
© 1992 MARVEL ENT. GROUP, INC.
$1.25 US
$1.60 CAN
11
FEB
CC 01917
APPROVED BY THE COMICS CODE AUTHORITY
MERRY CHRISTMAS CAGE™--
HOPE YOU SURVIVE THE EXPERIENCE!

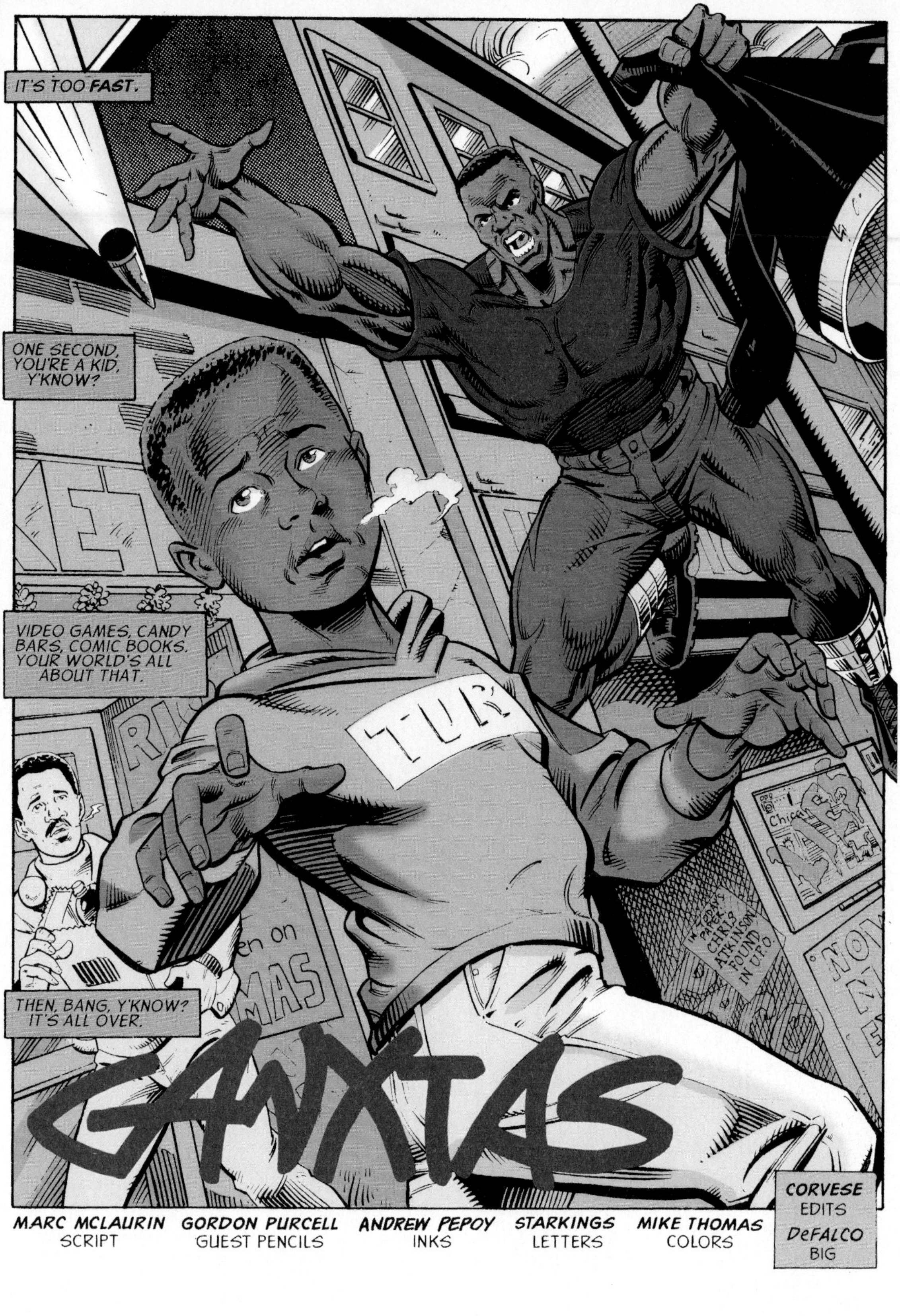
IT'S TOO FAST.
ONE SECOND, YOU'RE A KID, Y'KNOW?
VIDEO GAMES, CANDY BARS, COMIC BOOKS. YOUR WORLD'S ALL ABOUT THAT.
THEN, BANG, Y'KNOW? IT'S ALL OVER.
GANXTAS
MARC MCLAURIN SCRIPT
GORDON PURCELL GUEST PENCILS
ANDREW PEPOY INKS
STARKINGS LETTERS
MIKE THOMAS COLORS
CORVESE EDITS
DeFALCO BIG

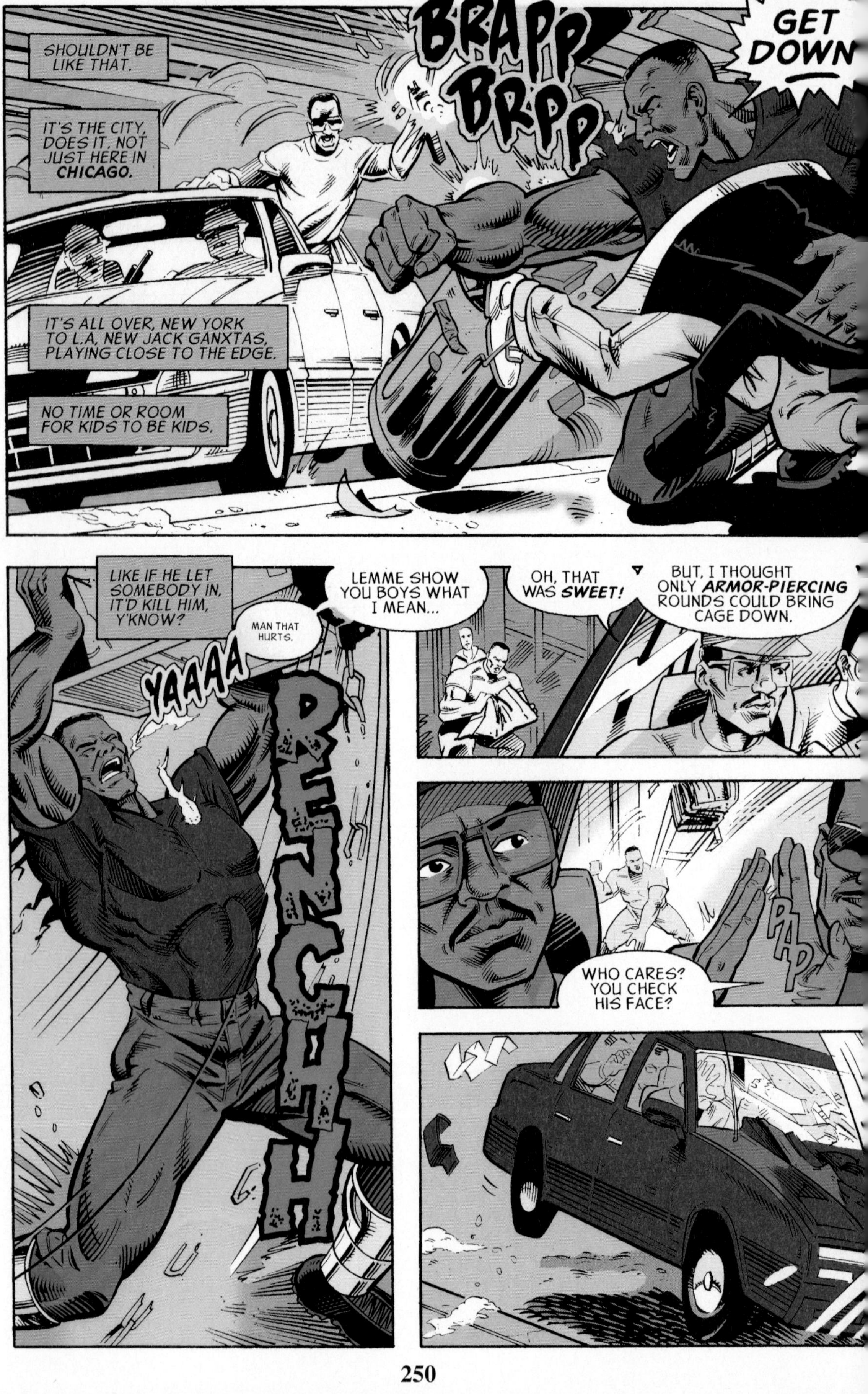
SHOULDN'T BE LIKE THAT.
IT'S THE CITY, DOES IT. NOT JUST HERE IN CHICAGO.
BRAPP BRPP
GET DOWN
IT'S ALL OVER, NEW YORK TO L.A. NEW JACK GANXTAS, PLAYING CLOSE TO THE EDGE.
NO TIME OR ROOM FOR KIDS TO BE KIDS.
LIKE IF HE LET SOMEBODY IN, IT'D KILL HIM, Y'KNOW?
MAN THAT HURTS.
LEMME SHOW YOU BOYS WHAT I MEAN...
YAAAA
RENCHUH
OH, THAT WAS SWEET!
BUT, I THOUGHT ONLY ARMOR-PIERCING ROUNDS COULD BRING CAGE DOWN.
PAP
WHO CARES? YOU CHECK HIS FACE?

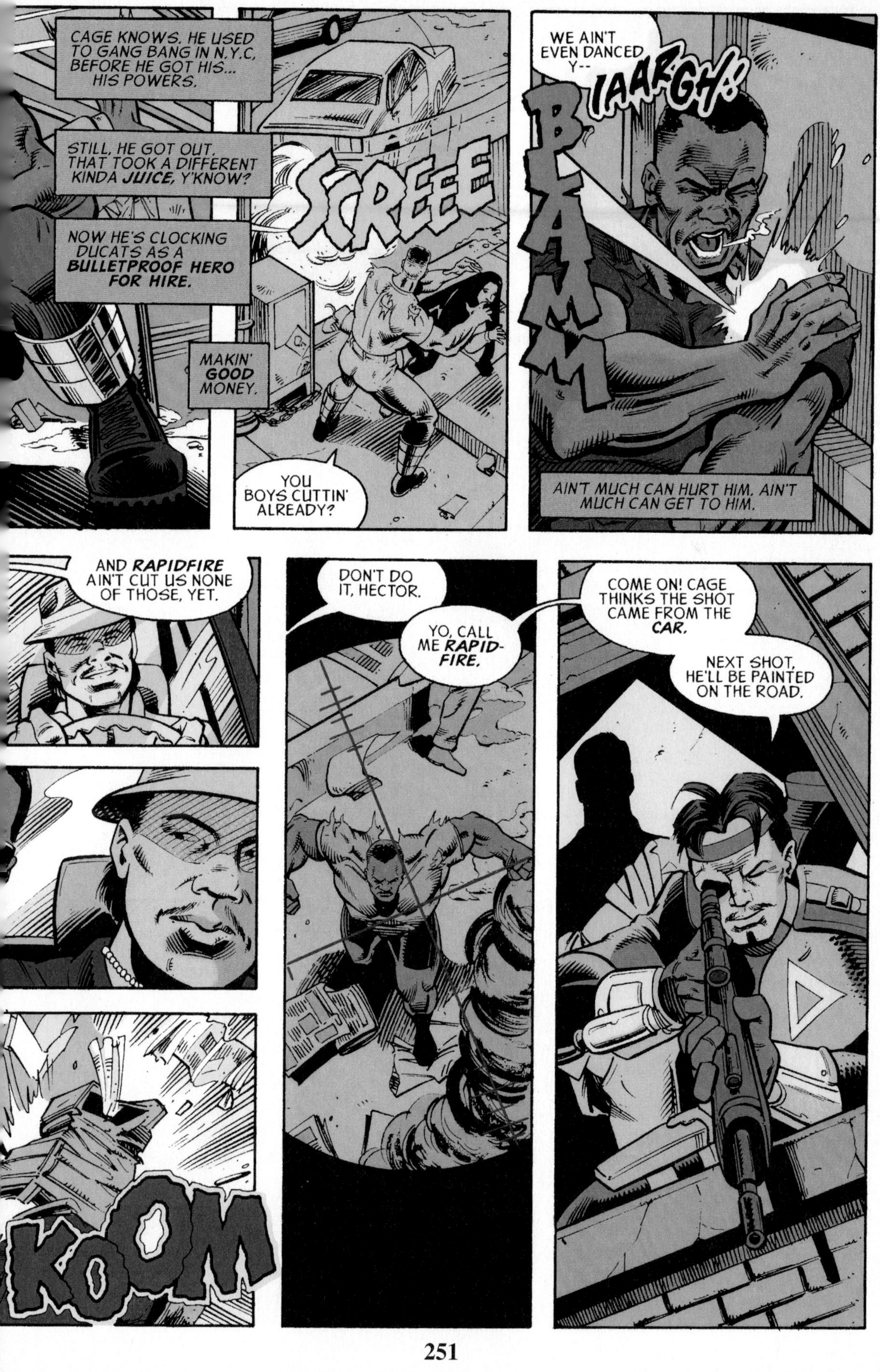
CAGE KNOWS. HE USED TO GANG BANG IN N.Y.C. BEFORE HE GOT HIS... HIS POWERS.
STILL, HE GOT OUT. THAT TOOK A DIFFERENT KINDA **JUICE**, Y'KNOW?
NOW HE'S CLOCKING DUCATS AS A **BULLETPROOF HERO FOR HIRE.**
MAKIN' **GOOD** MONEY.
SCREEE
YOU BOYS CUTTIN' ALREADY?
WE AIN'T EVEN DANCED Y--
BLAMM
IAARGH!
AIN'T MUCH CAN HURT HIM. AIN'T MUCH CAN GET TO HIM.
AND **RAPIDFIRE** AIN'T CUT US NONE OF THOSE, YET.
KOOM
DON'T DO IT, HECTOR.
YO, CALL ME **RAPID-FIRE.**
COME ON! CAGE THINKS THE SHOT CAME FROM THE **CAR.**
NEXT SHOT, HE'LL BE PAINTED ON THE ROAD.

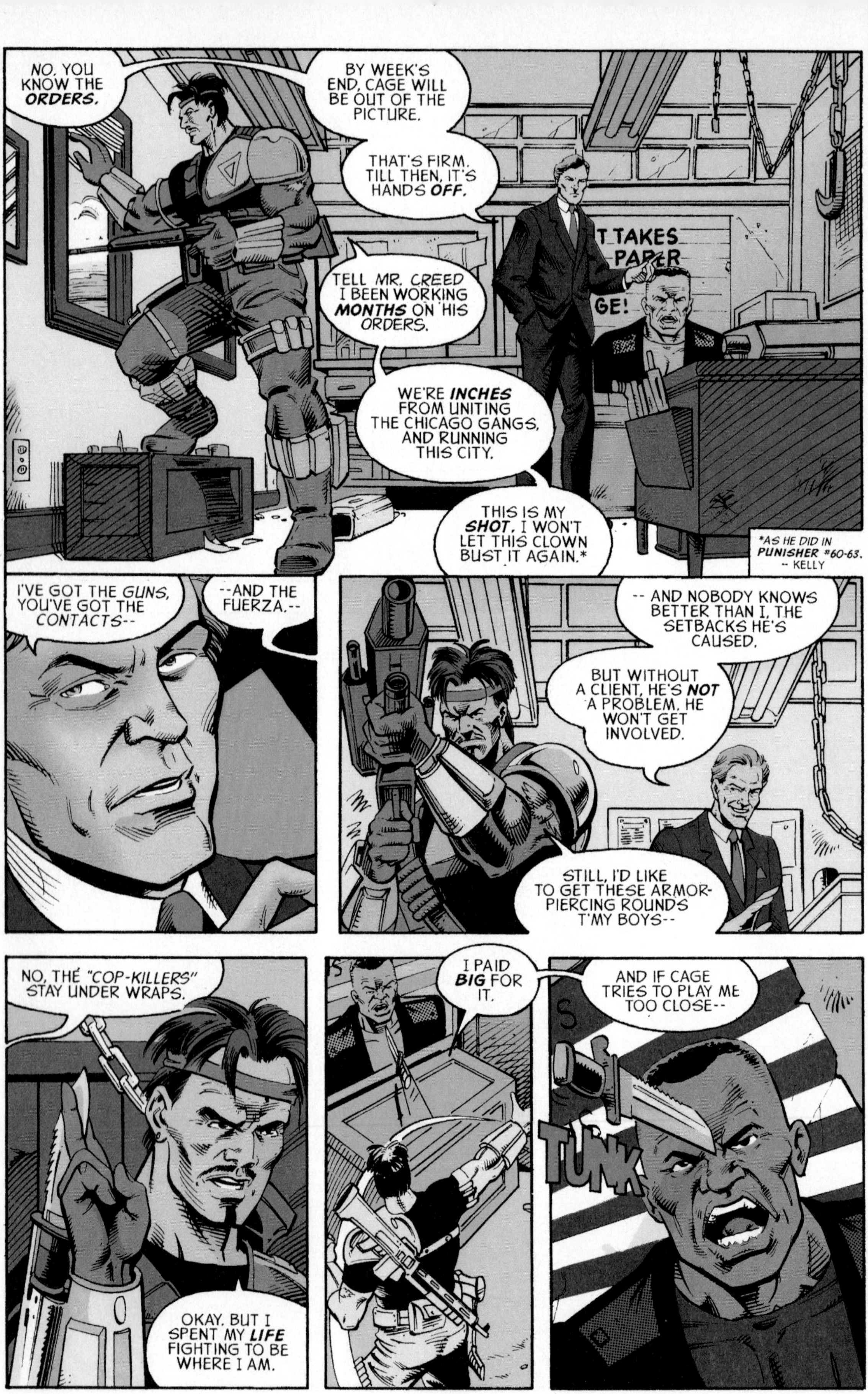
NO. YOU KNOW THE ORDERS.
BY WEEK'S END, CAGE WILL BE OUT OF THE PICTURE.
THAT'S FIRM. TILL THEN, IT'S HANDS OFF.
T TAKES PAPER GE!
TELL MR. CREED I BEEN WORKING MONTHS ON HIS ORDERS.
WE'RE INCHES FROM UNITING THE CHICAGO GANGS, AND RUNNING THIS CITY.
THIS IS MY SHOT. I WON'T LET THIS CLOWN BUST IT AGAIN.*
*AS HE DID IN PUNISHER #60-63. -- KELLY
I'VE GOT THE GUNS, YOU'VE GOT THE CONTACTS--
--AND THE FUERZA.--
-- AND NOBODY KNOWS BETTER THAN I, THE SETBACKS HE'S CAUSED.
BUT WITHOUT A CLIENT, HE'S NOT A PROBLEM. HE WON'T GET INVOLVED.
STILL, I'D LIKE TO GET THESE ARMOR-PIERCING ROUNDS T'MY BOYS--
NO, THE "COP-KILLERS" STAY UNDER WRAPS.
OKAY. BUT I SPENT MY LIFE FIGHTING TO BE WHERE I AM.
I PAID BIG FOR IT.
AND IF CAGE TRIES TO PLAY ME TOO CLOSE--
TUNK

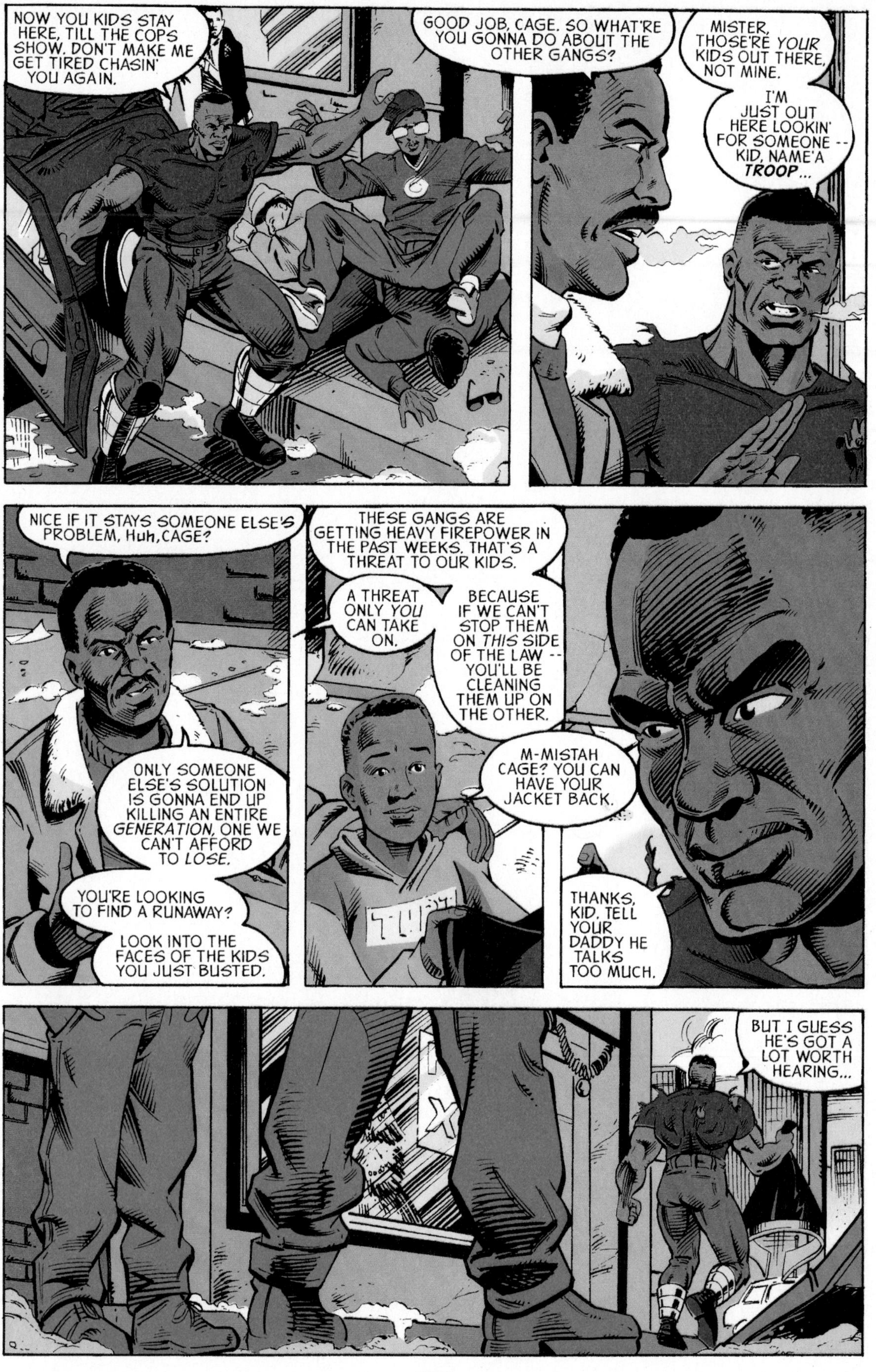
NOW YOU KIDS STAY HERE, TILL THE COPS SHOW. DON'T MAKE ME GET TIRED CHASIN' YOU AGAIN.
GOOD JOB, CAGE. SO WHAT'RE YOU GONNA DO ABOUT THE OTHER GANGS?
MISTER, THOSE'RE *YOUR* KIDS OUT THERE, NOT MINE.
I'M JUST OUT HERE LOOKIN' FOR SOMEONE -- KID, NAME'A ***TROOP***...
NICE IF IT STAYS SOMEONE ELSE'S PROBLEM, Huh, CAGE?
ONLY SOMEONE ELSE'S SOLUTION IS GONNA END UP KILLING AN ENTIRE *GENERATION*, ONE WE CAN'T AFFORD TO *LOSE*.
YOU'RE LOOKING TO FIND A RUNAWAY?
LOOK INTO THE FACES OF THE KIDS YOU JUST BUSTED.
THESE GANGS ARE GETTING HEAVY FIREPOWER IN THE PAST WEEKS. THAT'S A THREAT TO OUR KIDS.
A THREAT ONLY *YOU* CAN TAKE ON.
BECAUSE IF WE CAN'T STOP THEM ON *THIS* SIDE OF THE LAW -- YOU'LL BE CLEANING THEM UP ON THE OTHER.
M-MISTAH CAGE? YOU CAN HAVE YOUR JACKET BACK.
THANKS, KID. TELL YOUR DADDY HE TALKS TOO MUCH.
BUT I GUESS HE'S GOT A LOT WORTH HEARING...

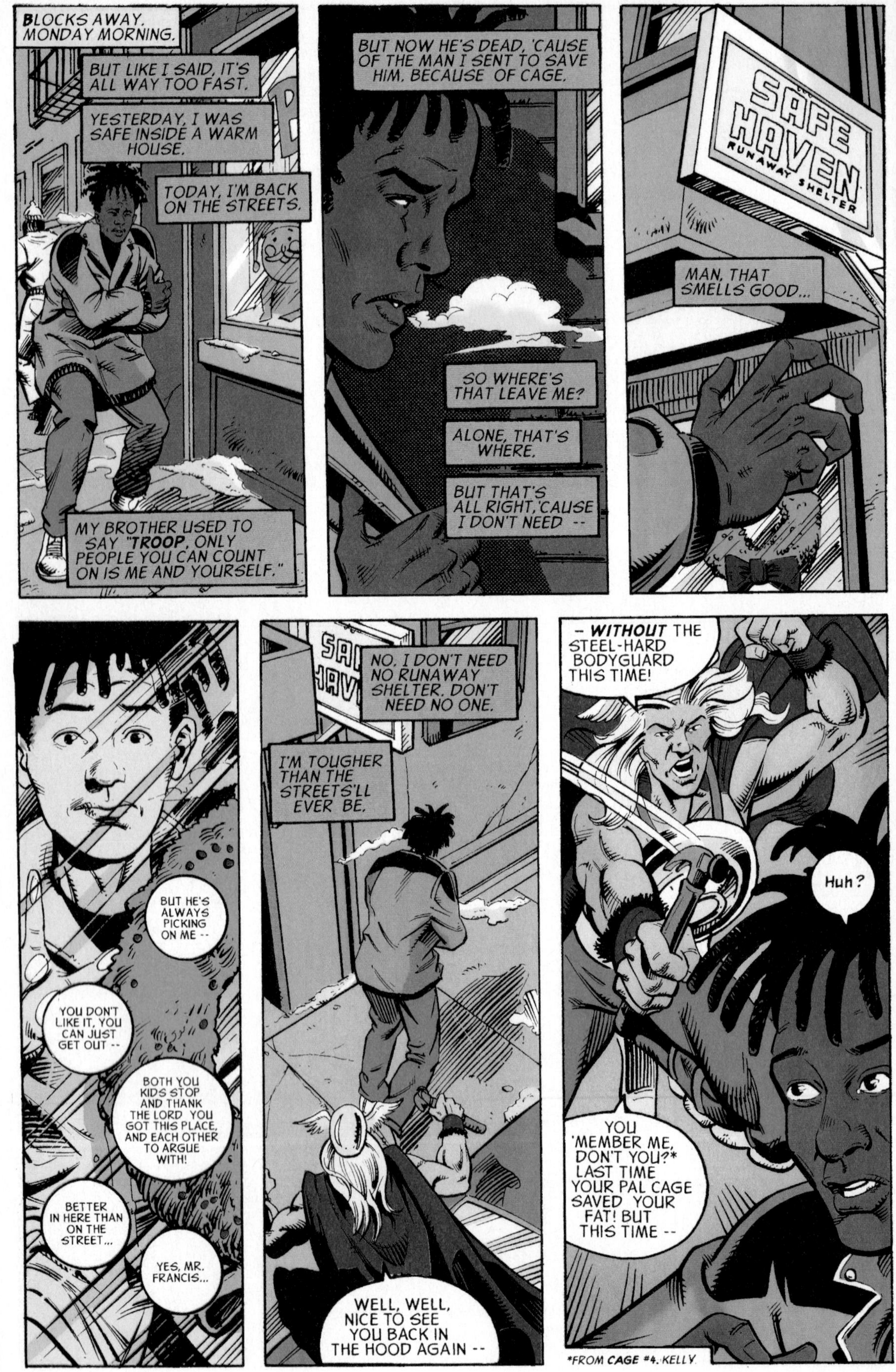
BLOCKS AWAY, MONDAY MORNING.
BUT LIKE I SAID, IT'S ALL WAY TOO FAST.
YESTERDAY, I WAS SAFE INSIDE A WARM HOUSE.
TODAY, I'M BACK ON THE STREETS.
MY BROTHER USED TO SAY "TROOP, ONLY PEOPLE YOU CAN COUNT ON IS ME AND YOURSELF."
BUT NOW HE'S DEAD, 'CAUSE OF THE MAN I SENT TO SAVE HIM, BECAUSE OF CAGE.
SO WHERE'S THAT LEAVE ME?
ALONE, THAT'S WHERE.
BUT THAT'S ALL RIGHT, 'CAUSE I DON'T NEED --
SAFE HAVEN RUNAWAY SHELTER
MAN, THAT SMELLS GOOD...
BUT HE'S ALWAYS PICKING ON ME --
YOU DON'T LIKE IT, YOU CAN JUST GET OUT --
BOTH YOU KIDS STOP AND THANK THE LORD YOU GOT THIS PLACE, AND EACH OTHER TO ARGUE WITH!
BETTER IN HERE THAN ON THE STREET...
YES, MR. FRANCIS...
NO, I DON'T NEED NO RUNAWAY SHELTER. DON'T NEED NO ONE.
I'M TOUGHER THAN THE STREETS'LL EVER BE.
WELL, WELL, NICE TO SEE YOU BACK IN THE HOOD AGAIN --
-- WITHOUT THE STEEL-HARD BODYGUARD THIS TIME!
Huh?
YOU 'MEMBER ME, DON'T YOU?* LAST TIME YOUR PAL CAGE SAVED YOUR FAT! BUT THIS TIME --
*FROM CAGE #4. KELLY.

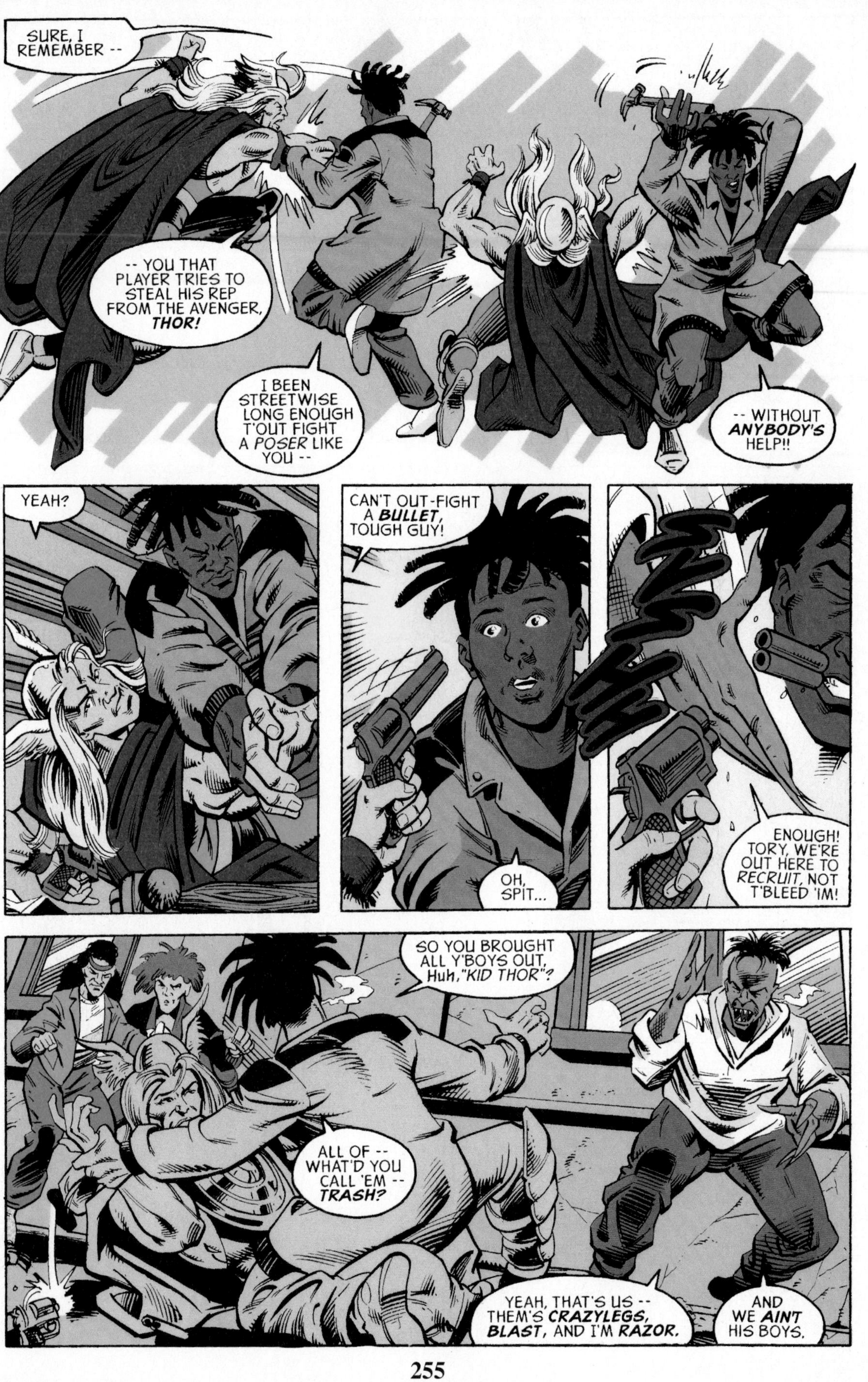
SURE, I REMEMBER --
-- YOU THAT PLAYER TRIES TO STEAL HIS REP FROM THE AVENGER, **THOR!**
I BEEN STREETWISE LONG ENOUGH T'OUT FIGHT A *POSER* LIKE YOU --
-- WITHOUT **ANYBODY'S** HELP!!
YEAH?
CAN'T OUT-FIGHT A **BULLET**, TOUGH GUY!
OH, SPIT...
ENOUGH! TORY, WE'RE OUT HERE TO *RECRUIT*, NOT T'BLEED 'IM!
SO YOU BROUGHT ALL Y'BOYS OUT, Huh, "KID THOR"?
ALL OF -- WHAT'D YOU CALL 'EM -- **TRASH?**
YEAH, THAT'S US -- THEM'S **CRAZYLEGS, BLAST**, AND I'M **RAZOR.**
AND WE **AIN'T** HIS BOYS.

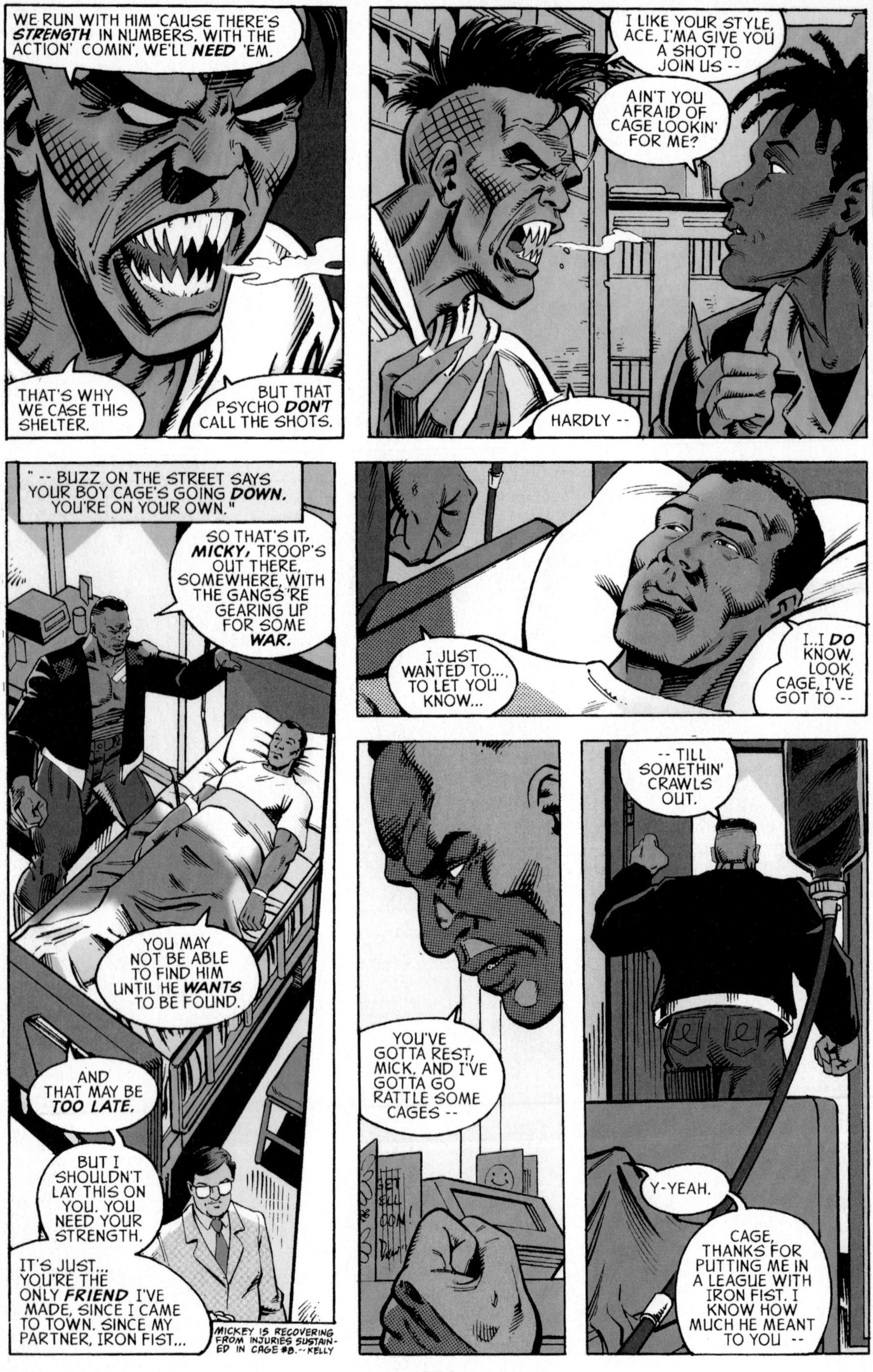
WE RUN WITH HIM 'CAUSE THERE'S STRENGTH IN NUMBERS. WITH THE ACTION' COMIN', WE'LL NEED 'EM.
THAT'S WHY WE CASE THIS SHELTER.
BUT THAT PSYCHO DON'T CALL THE SHOTS.
I LIKE YOUR STYLE, ACE. I'MA GIVE YOU A SHOT TO JOIN US --
AIN'T YOU AFRAID OF CAGE LOOKIN' FOR ME?
HARDLY --
" -- BUZZ ON THE STREET SAYS YOUR BOY CAGE'S GOING DOWN. YOU'RE ON YOUR OWN."
SO THAT'S IT, MICKY, TROOP'S OUT THERE, SOMEWHERE, WITH THE GANGS'RE GEARING UP FOR SOME WAR.
YOU MAY NOT BE ABLE TO FIND HIM UNTIL HE WANTS TO BE FOUND.
AND THAT MAY BE TOO LATE.
BUT I SHOULDN'T LAY THIS ON YOU. YOU NEED YOUR STRENGTH.
IT'S JUST... YOU'RE THE ONLY FRIEND I'VE MADE, SINCE I CAME TO TOWN. SINCE MY PARTNER, IRON FIST...
MICKEY IS RECOVERING FROM INJURIES SUSTAINED IN CAGE #8. --KELLY
I JUST WANTED TO..., TO LET YOU KNOW...
I..I DO KNOW. LOOK, CAGE, I'VE GOT TO --
YOU'VE GOTTA REST, MICK, AND I'VE GOTTA GO RATTLE SOME CAGES --
-- TILL SOMETHIN' CRAWLS OUT.
Y-YEAH.
CAGE, THANKS FOR PUTTING ME IN A LEAGUE WITH IRON FIST. I KNOW HOW MUCH HE MEANT TO YOU --

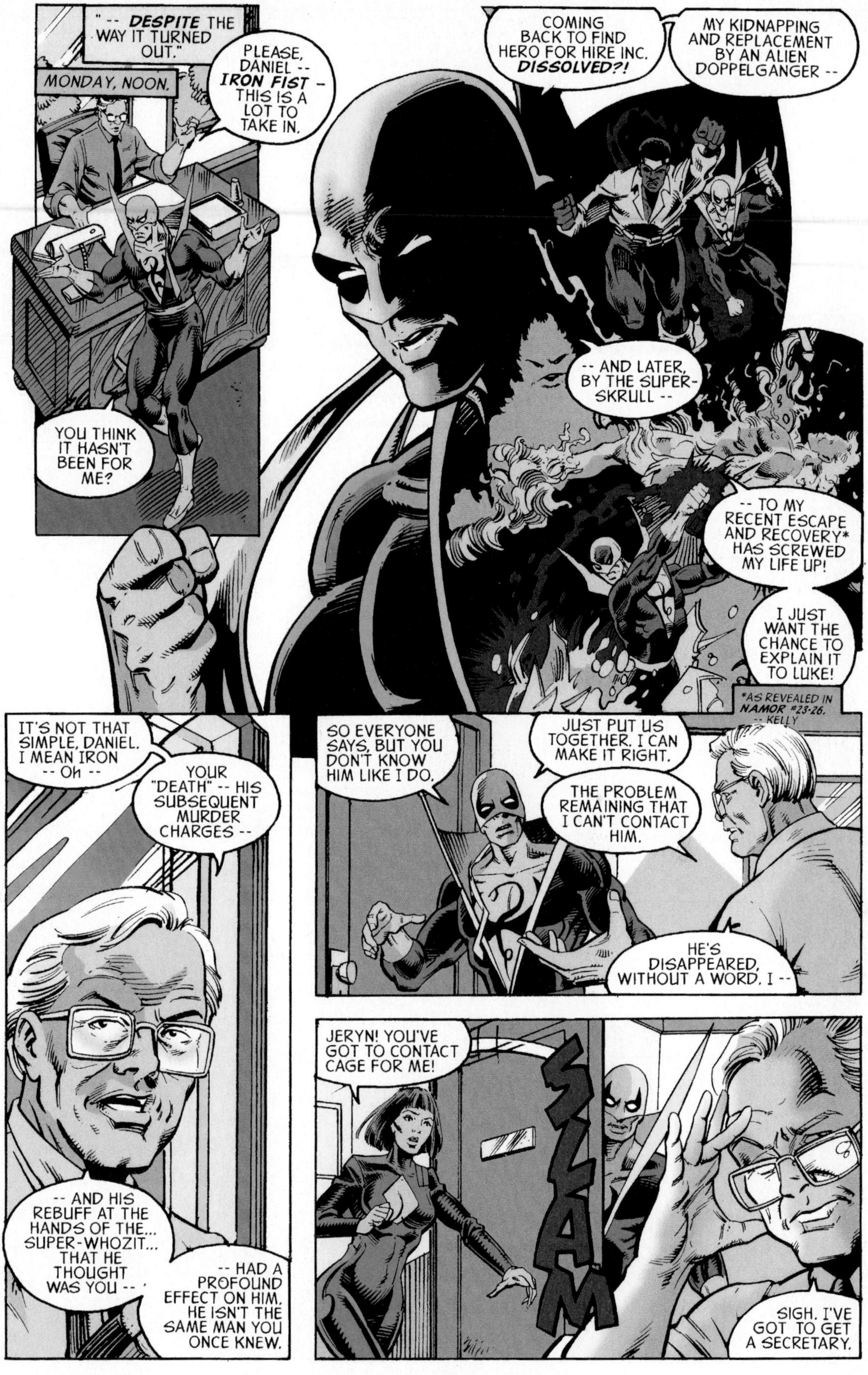
"-- DESPITE THE WAY IT TURNED OUT."
MONDAY, NOON.
PLEASE, DANIEL -- IRON FIST -- THIS IS A LOT TO TAKE IN.
YOU THINK IT HASN'T BEEN FOR ME?
COMING BACK TO FIND HERO FOR HIRE INC. DISSOLVED?!
MY KIDNAPPING AND REPLACEMENT BY AN ALIEN DOPPELGANGER --
-- AND LATER, BY THE SUPER-SKRULL --
-- TO MY RECENT ESCAPE AND RECOVERY* HAS SCREWED MY LIFE UP!
I JUST WANT THE CHANCE TO EXPLAIN IT TO LUKE!
*AS REVEALED IN NAMOR #23-26. -- KELLY
IT'S NOT THAT SIMPLE, DANIEL. I MEAN IRON -- Oh --
YOUR "DEATH" -- HIS SUBSEQUENT MURDER CHARGES --
-- AND HIS REBUFF AT THE HANDS OF THE... SUPER-WHOZIT... THAT HE THOUGHT WAS YOU --
-- HAD A PROFOUND EFFECT ON HIM. HE ISN'T THE SAME MAN YOU ONCE KNEW.
SO EVERYONE SAYS, BUT YOU DON'T KNOW HIM LIKE I DO.
JUST PUT US TOGETHER. I CAN MAKE IT RIGHT.
THE PROBLEM REMAINING THAT I CAN'T CONTACT HIM.
HE'S DISAPPEARED, WITHOUT A WORD. I --
JERYN! YOU'VE GOT TO CONTACT CAGE FOR ME!
SLAM
SIGH. I'VE GOT TO GET A SECRETARY.

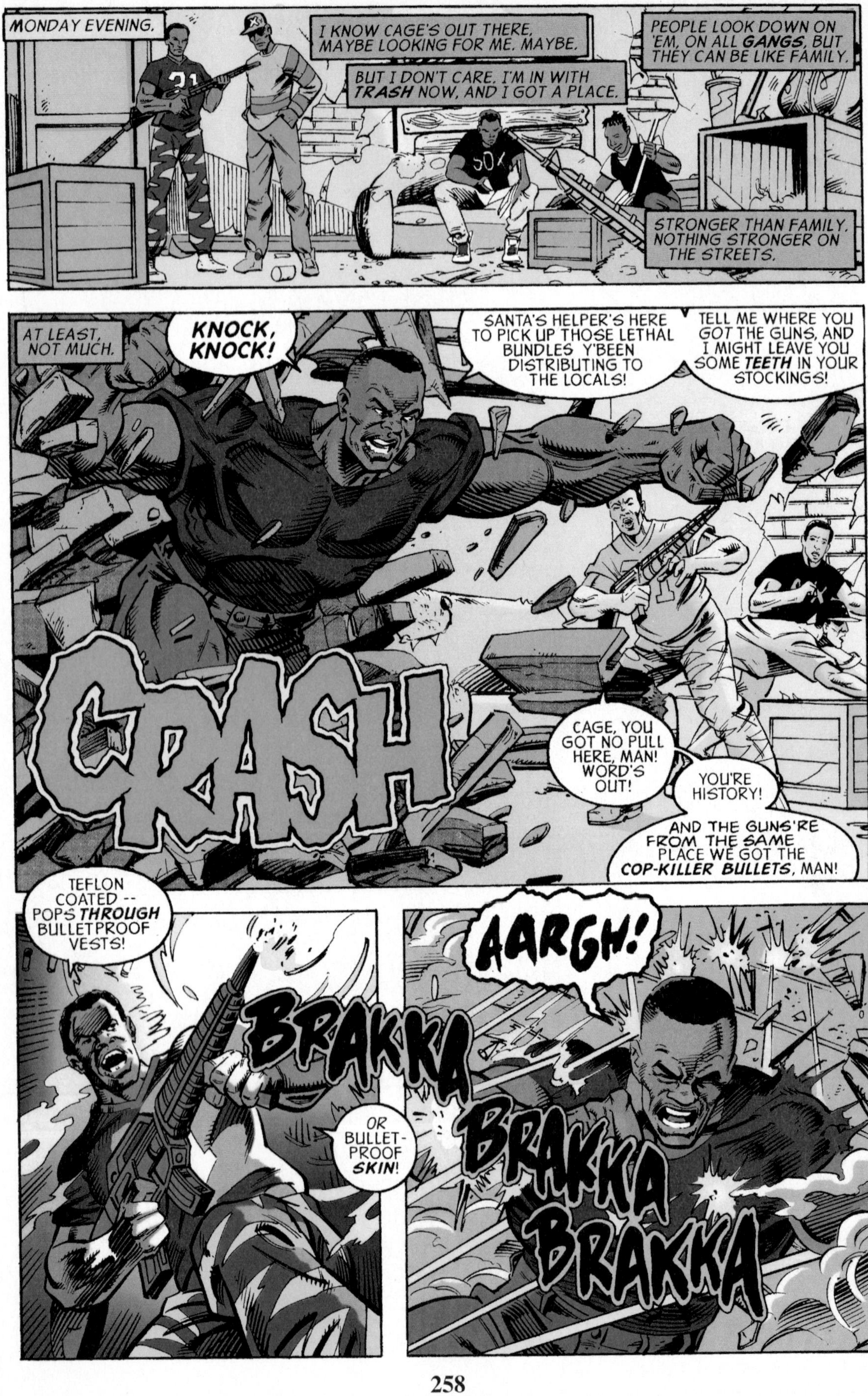

MONDAY EVENING.
I KNOW CAGE'S OUT THERE, MAYBE LOOKING FOR ME. MAYBE.
BUT I DON'T CARE. I'M IN WITH TRASH NOW, AND I GOT A PLACE.
PEOPLE LOOK DOWN ON 'EM, ON ALL GANGS, BUT THEY CAN BE LIKE FAMILY.
STRONGER THAN FAMILY. NOTHING STRONGER ON THE STREETS.
AT LEAST, NOT MUCH.
KNOCK, KNOCK!
SANTA'S HELPER'S HERE TO PICK UP THOSE LETHAL BUNDLES Y'BEEN DISTRIBUTING TO THE LOCALS!
TELL ME WHERE YOU GOT THE GUNS, AND I MIGHT LEAVE YOU SOME TEETH IN YOUR STOCKINGS!
CRASH
CAGE, YOU GOT NO PULL HERE, MAN! WORD'S OUT!
YOU'RE HISTORY!
AND THE GUNS'RE FROM THE SAME PLACE WE GOT THE COP-KILLER BULLETS, MAN!
TEFLON COATED -- POPS THROUGH BULLETPROOF VESTS!
BRAKKA
OR BULLET-PROOF SKIN!
AARGH!
BRAKKA
BRAKKA

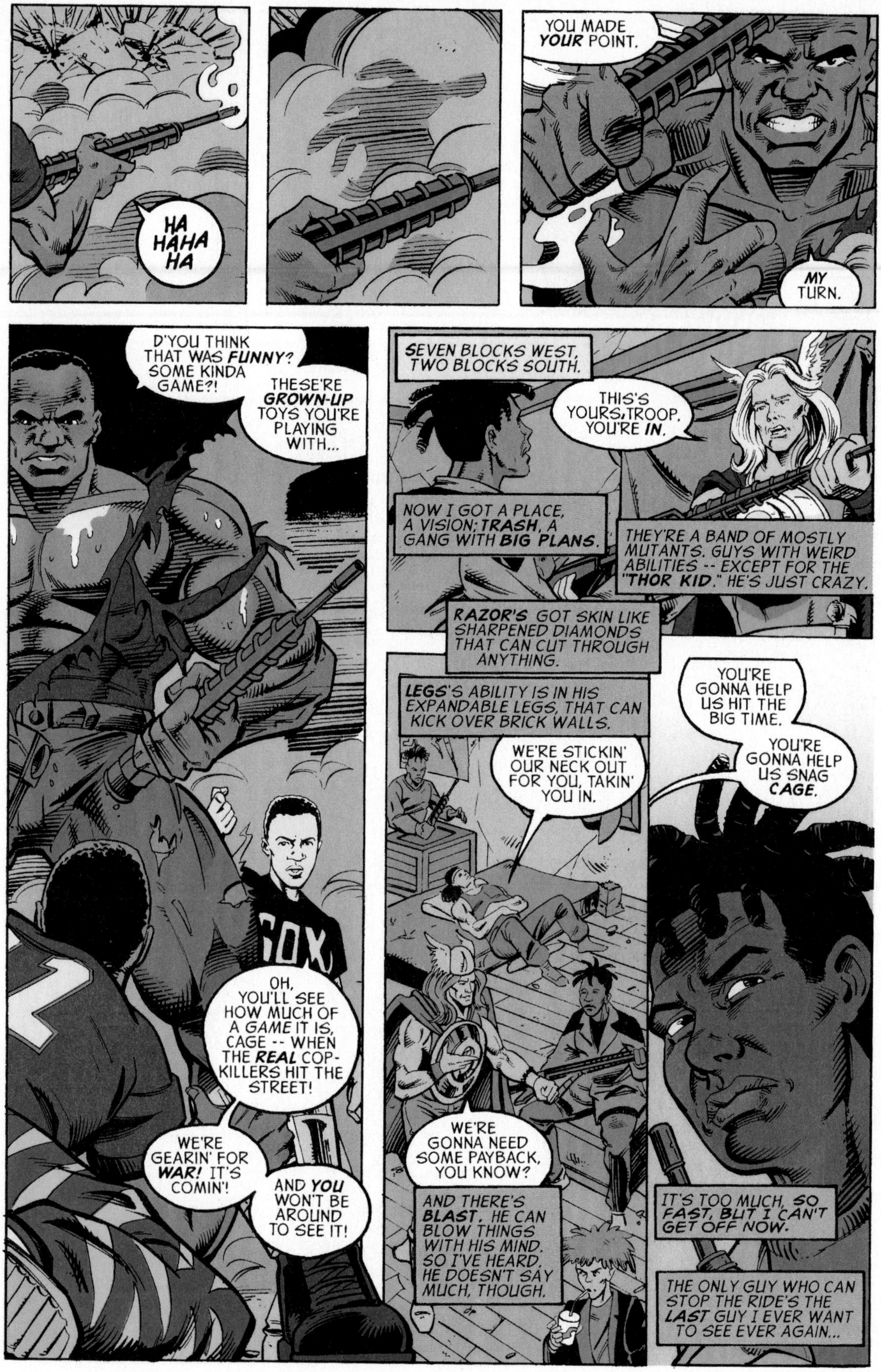
HA HAHAHA HA
YOU MADE YOUR POINT.
MY TURN.
D'YOU THINK THAT WAS FUNNY? SOME KINDA GAME?!
THESE'RE GROWN-UP TOYS YOU'RE PLAYING WITH...
OH, YOU'LL SEE HOW MUCH OF A GAME IT IS, CAGE -- WHEN THE REAL COP-KILLERS HIT THE STREET!
WE'RE GEARIN' FOR WAR! IT'S COMIN'!
AND YOU WON'T BE AROUND TO SEE IT!
SEVEN BLOCKS WEST, TWO BLOCKS SOUTH.
THIS'S YOURS, TROOP. YOU'RE IN.
NOW I GOT A PLACE, A VISION; TRASH, A GANG WITH BIG PLANS.
THEY'RE A BAND OF MOSTLY MUTANTS. GUYS WITH WEIRD ABILITIES -- EXCEPT FOR THE "THOR KID." HE'S JUST CRAZY.
RAZOR'S GOT SKIN LIKE SHARPENED DIAMONDS THAT CAN CUT THROUGH ANYTHING.
LEGS'S ABILITY IS IN HIS EXPANDABLE LEGS, THAT CAN KICK OVER BRICK WALLS.
WE'RE STICKIN' OUR NECK OUT FOR YOU, TAKIN' YOU IN.
WE'RE GONNA NEED SOME PAYBACK, YOU KNOW?
AND THERE'S BLAST. HE CAN BLOW THINGS WITH HIS MIND. SO I'VE HEARD. HE DOESN'T SAY MUCH, THOUGH.
YOU'RE GONNA HELP US HIT THE BIG TIME.
YOU'RE GONNA HELP US SNAG CAGE.
IT'S TOO MUCH, SO FAST, BUT I CAN'T GET OFF NOW.
THE ONLY GUY WHO CAN STOP THE RIDE'S THE LAST GUY I EVER WANT TO SEE EVER AGAIN...

TUESDAY MORNING.

THEY'RE GETTIN' *LOST*, MICK. AN ENTIRE GENERATION

LOST IN THE SAME MEAN STREETS AND ATTITUDES THAT NEARLY SWALLOWED ME.

AND TROOP'S OUT THERE SOMEWHERE, WITH 'EM.

THIS ISN'T A PROBLEM YOU CAN TACKLE *ALONE*, CAGE.

MAYBE NOT, OR MAYBE -- I'M THE ONLY ONE WHO *CAN*.

TUESDAY AFTERNOON.

WE HEAR RUMORS THAT CAGE'S BEEN BUSY AROUND HERE.

HE'S BUSTED THREE MAJOR DISTRIBUTION POINTS, BAGGED A LOT OF HARDWARE.

HE'S MAKIN' PEOPLE UNCOMFORTABLE. AND HE'S LOOKIN' FOR *ME*.

THE KID'S CALLED *TROOP*. YOU GIVE HIM UP, I LET YOU GO HOME.

WITHOUT THE HARDWARE.

AW, PLAY BAD WHILE YOU *CAN*, HOMES. WORD'S OUT -- YOU AIN'T GONNA LAST.

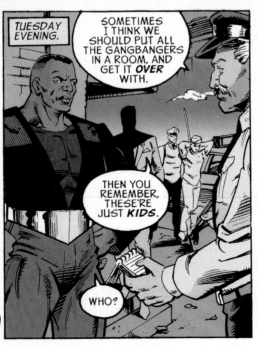

TUESDAY EVENING.

SOMETIMES I THINK WE SHOULD PUT ALL THE GANGBANGERS IN A ROOM, AND GET IT *OVER* WITH.

THEN YOU REMEMBER, THESE'RE JUST *KIDS*.

WHO?

COUNCILMAN *RANDOLPH CREED*, MR. CAGE. I'VE HEARD MUCH ABOUT YOU.

TRAGIC, WHAT ARE KIDS TODAY COMING TO, HMM?

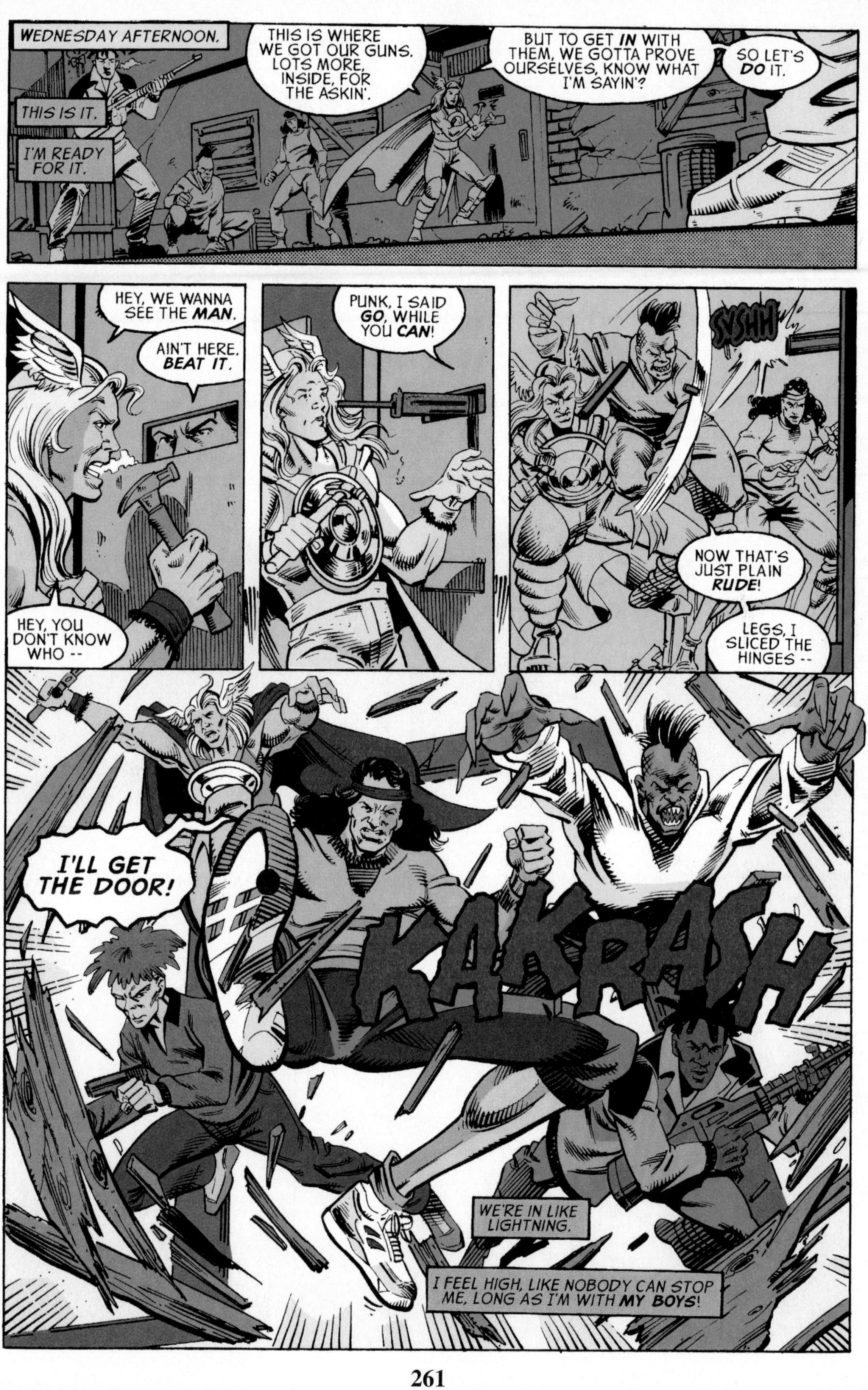
WEDNESDAY AFTERNOON.
THIS IS IT.
I'M READY FOR IT.
THIS IS WHERE WE GOT OUR GUNS. LOTS MORE, INSIDE, FOR THE ASKIN'.
BUT TO GET IN WITH THEM, WE GOTTA PROVE OURSELVES, KNOW WHAT I'M SAYIN'?
SO LET'S DO IT.
HEY, WE WANNA SEE THE MAN.
AIN'T HERE. BEAT IT.
HEY, YOU DON'T KNOW WHO --
PUNK, I SAID GO, WHILE YOU CAN!
SYSHH
NOW THAT'S JUST PLAIN RUDE!
LEGS, I SLICED THE HINGES --
I'LL GET THE DOOR!
KAKRASH
WE'RE IN LIKE LIGHTNING.
I FEEL HIGH, LIKE NOBODY CAN STOP ME, LONG AS I'M WITH MY BOYS!

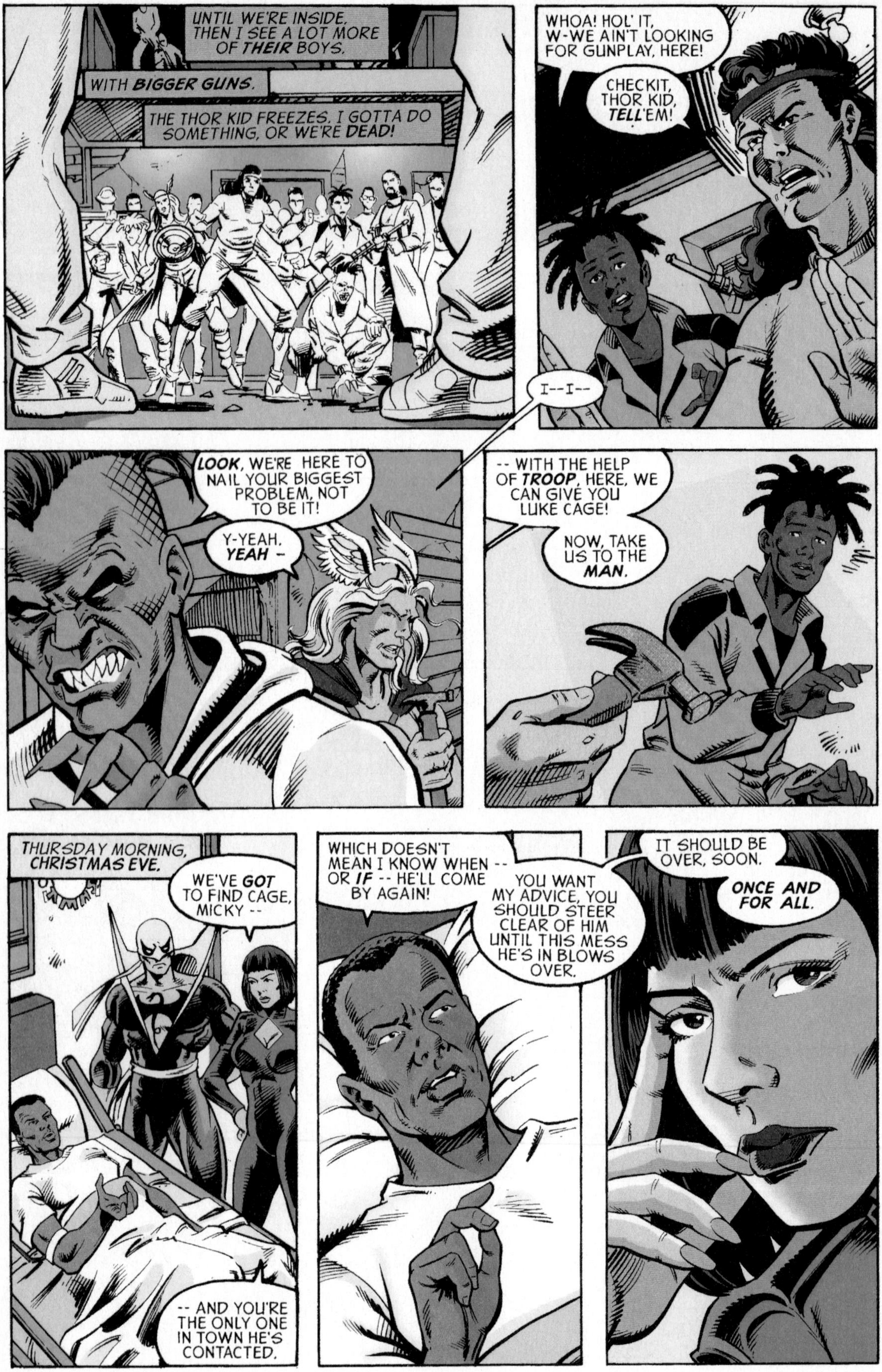
UNTIL WE'RE INSIDE, THEN I SEE A LOT MORE OF THEIR BOYS.
WITH BIGGER GUNS.
THE THOR KID FREEZES. I GOTTA DO SOMETHING, OR WE'RE DEAD!
WHOA! HOL' IT, W-WE AIN'T LOOKING FOR GUNPLAY, HERE!
CHECKIT, THOR KID, TELL'EM!
I--I--
LOOK, WE'RE HERE TO NAIL YOUR BIGGEST PROBLEM, NOT TO BE IT!
Y-YEAH. YEAH --
-- WITH THE HELP OF TROOP, HERE, WE CAN GIVE YOU LUKE CAGE!
NOW, TAKE US TO THE MAN.
THURSDAY MORNING, CHRISTMAS EVE.
WE'VE GOT TO FIND CAGE, MICKY --
-- AND YOU'RE THE ONLY ONE IN TOWN HE'S CONTACTED.
WHICH DOESN'T MEAN I KNOW WHEN -- OR IF -- HE'LL COME BY AGAIN!
YOU WANT MY ADVICE, YOU SHOULD STEER CLEAR OF HIM UNTIL THIS MESS HE'S IN BLOWS OVER.
IT SHOULD BE OVER, SOON.
ONCE AND FOR ALL.

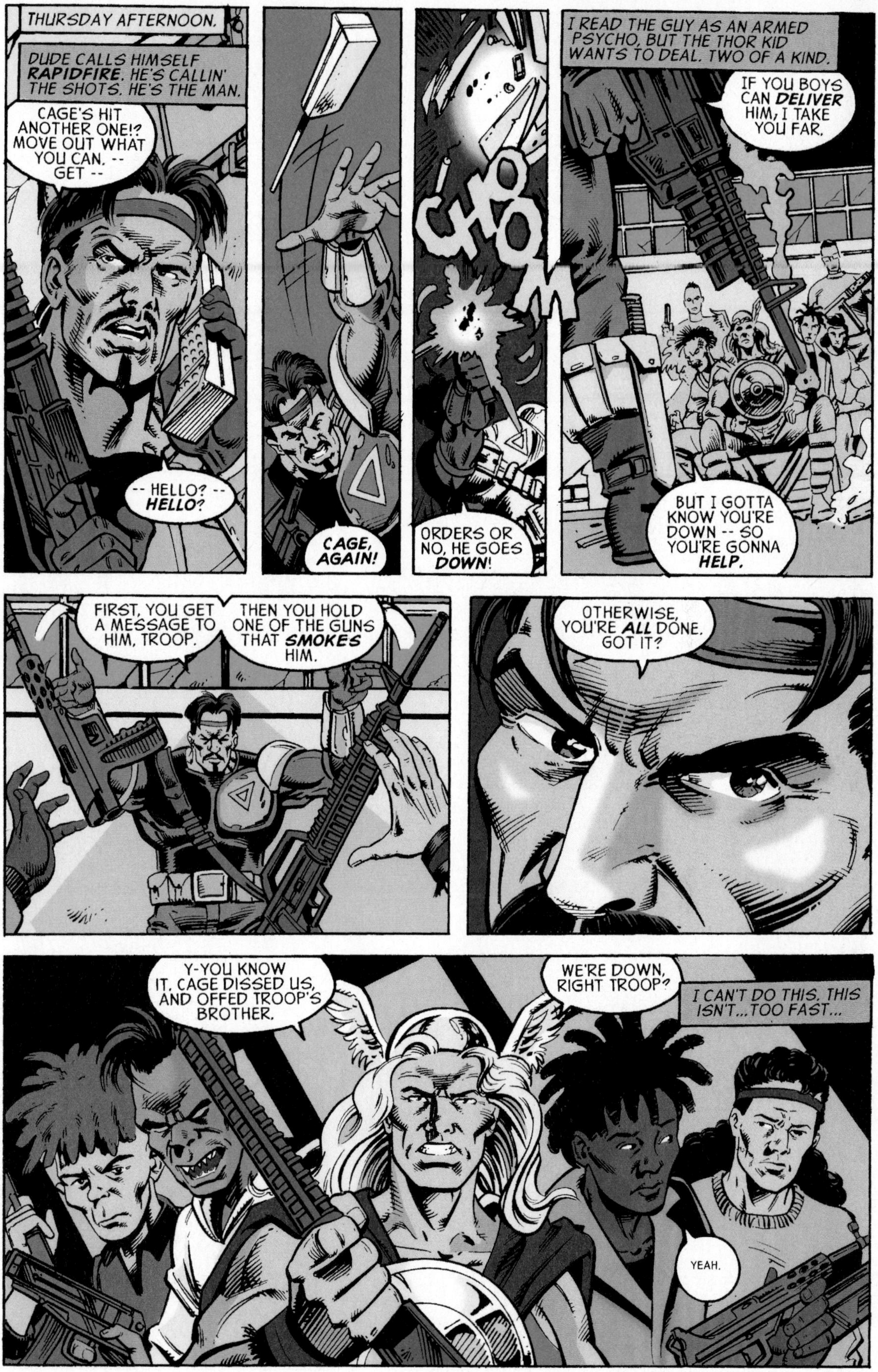
THURSDAY AFTERNOON.
DUDE CALLS HIMSELF RAPIDFIRE. HE'S CALLIN' THE SHOTS. HE'S THE MAN.
CAGE'S HIT ANOTHER ONE!? MOVE OUT WHAT YOU CAN. -- GET --
-- HELLO? -- HELLO?
CAGE, AGAIN!
CHOOM
ORDERS OR NO, HE GOES DOWN!
I READ THE GUY AS AN ARMED PSYCHO, BUT THE THOR KID WANTS TO DEAL. TWO OF A KIND.
IF YOU BOYS CAN DELIVER HIM, I TAKE YOU FAR.
BUT I GOTTA KNOW YOU'RE DOWN -- SO YOU'RE GONNA HELP.
FIRST, YOU GET A MESSAGE TO HIM, TROOP.
THEN YOU HOLD ONE OF THE GUNS THAT SMOKES HIM.
OTHERWISE, YOU'RE ALL DONE. GOT IT?
Y-YOU KNOW IT. CAGE DISSED US, AND OFFED TROOP'S BROTHER.
WE'RE DOWN, RIGHT TROOP?
I CAN'T DO THIS. THIS ISN'T...TOO FAST...
YEAH.

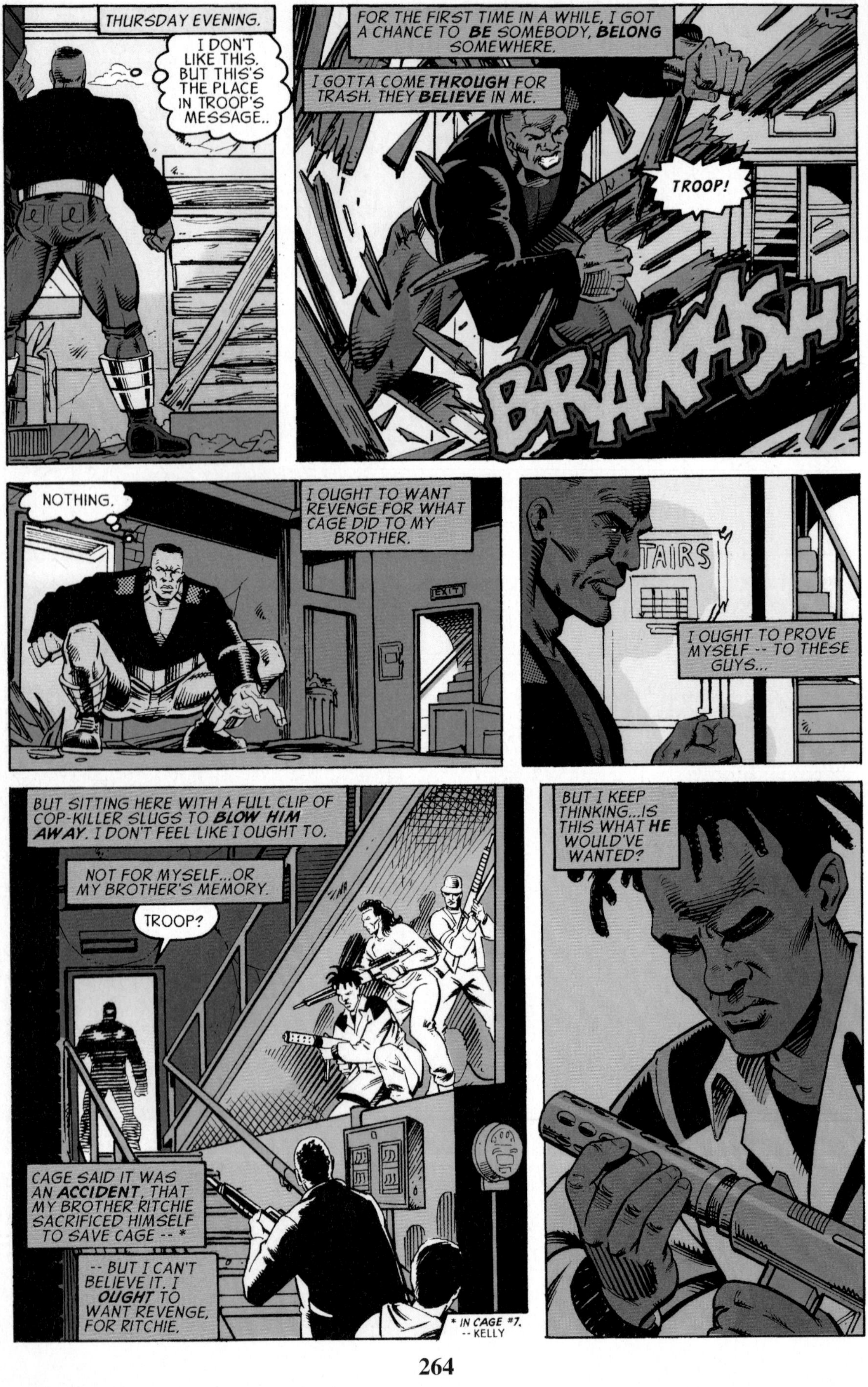
THURSDAY EVENING.
I DON'T LIKE THIS. BUT THIS'S THE PLACE IN TROOP'S MESSAGE..
FOR THE FIRST TIME IN A WHILE, I GOT A CHANCE TO BE SOMEBODY, BELONG SOMEWHERE.
I GOTTA COME THROUGH FOR TRASH. THEY BELIEVE IN ME.
TROOP!
BRAKASH
NOTHING.
I OUGHT TO WANT REVENGE FOR WHAT CAGE DID TO MY BROTHER.
EXIT
TAIRS
I OUGHT TO PROVE MYSELF -- TO THESE GUYS...
BUT SITTING HERE WITH A FULL CLIP OF COP-KILLER SLUGS TO BLOW HIM AWAY, I DON'T FEEL LIKE I OUGHT TO.
NOT FOR MYSELF...OR MY BROTHER'S MEMORY.
TROOP?
CAGE SAID IT WAS AN ACCIDENT, THAT MY BROTHER RITCHIE SACRIFICED HIMSELF TO SAVE CAGE -- *
-- BUT I CAN'T BELIEVE IT. I OUGHT TO WANT REVENGE, FOR RITCHIE.
* IN CAGE #7. -- KELLY
BUT I KEEP THINKING...IS THIS WHAT HE WOULD'VE WANTED?

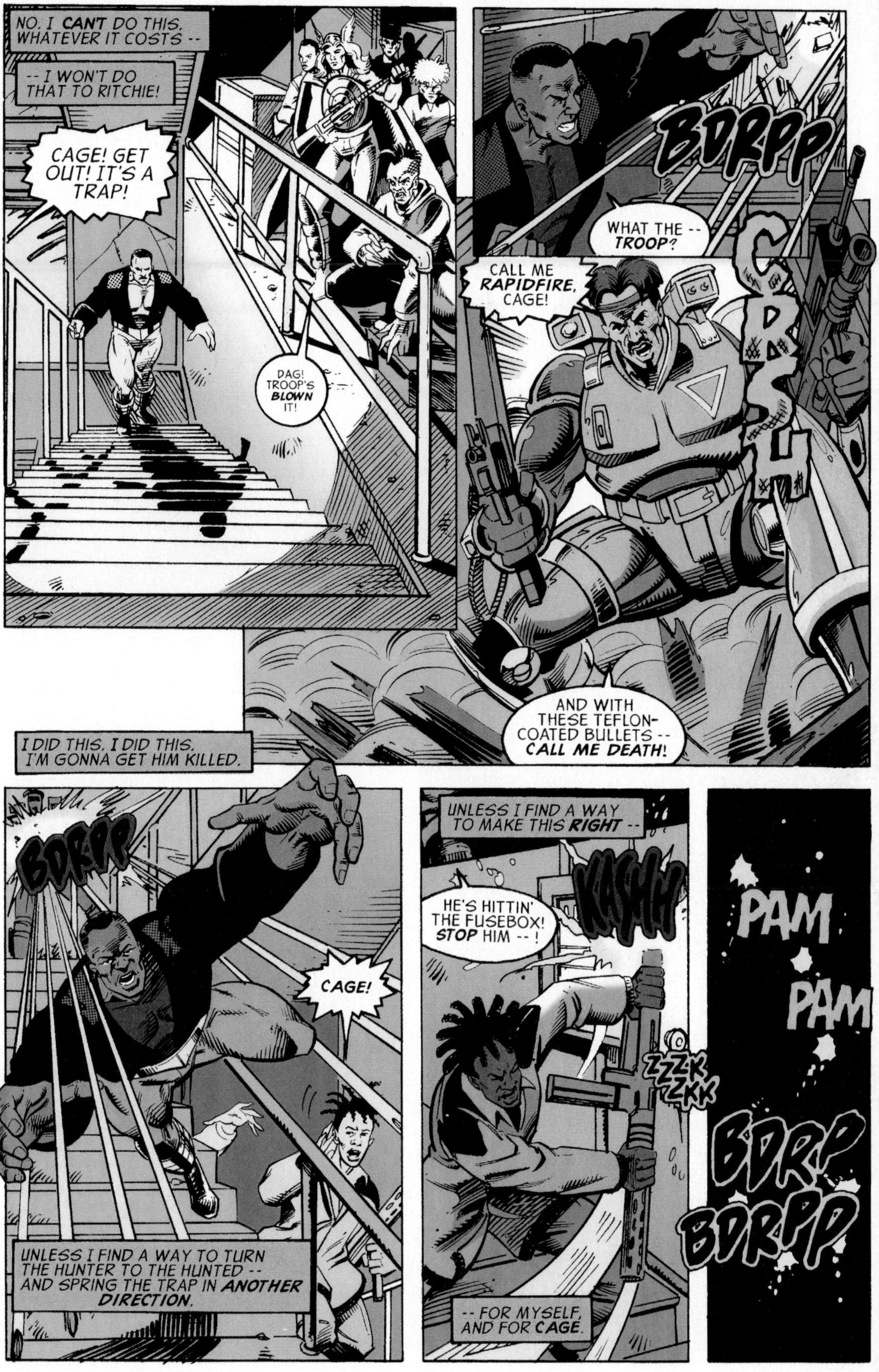
NO. I CAN'T DO THIS. WHATEVER IT COSTS --
-- I WON'T DO THAT TO RITCHIE!
CAGE! GET OUT! IT'S A TRAP!
DAG! TROOP'S BLOWN IT!
BDRPP
WHAT THE -- TROOP?
CRSSH
CALL ME RAPIDFIRE, CAGE!
AND WITH THESE TEFLON-COATED BULLETS -- CALL ME DEATH!
I DID THIS. I DID THIS. I'M GONNA GET HIM KILLED.
BDRPP
CAGE!
UNLESS I FIND A WAY TO TURN THE HUNTER TO THE HUNTED -- AND SPRING THE TRAP IN ANOTHER DIRECTION.
UNLESS I FIND A WAY TO MAKE THIS RIGHT --
KASHH
HE'S HITTIN' THE FUSEBOX! STOP HIM -- !
ZZZK ZKK
-- FOR MYSELF, AND FOR CAGE.
PAM
PAM
BDRP
BDRPP

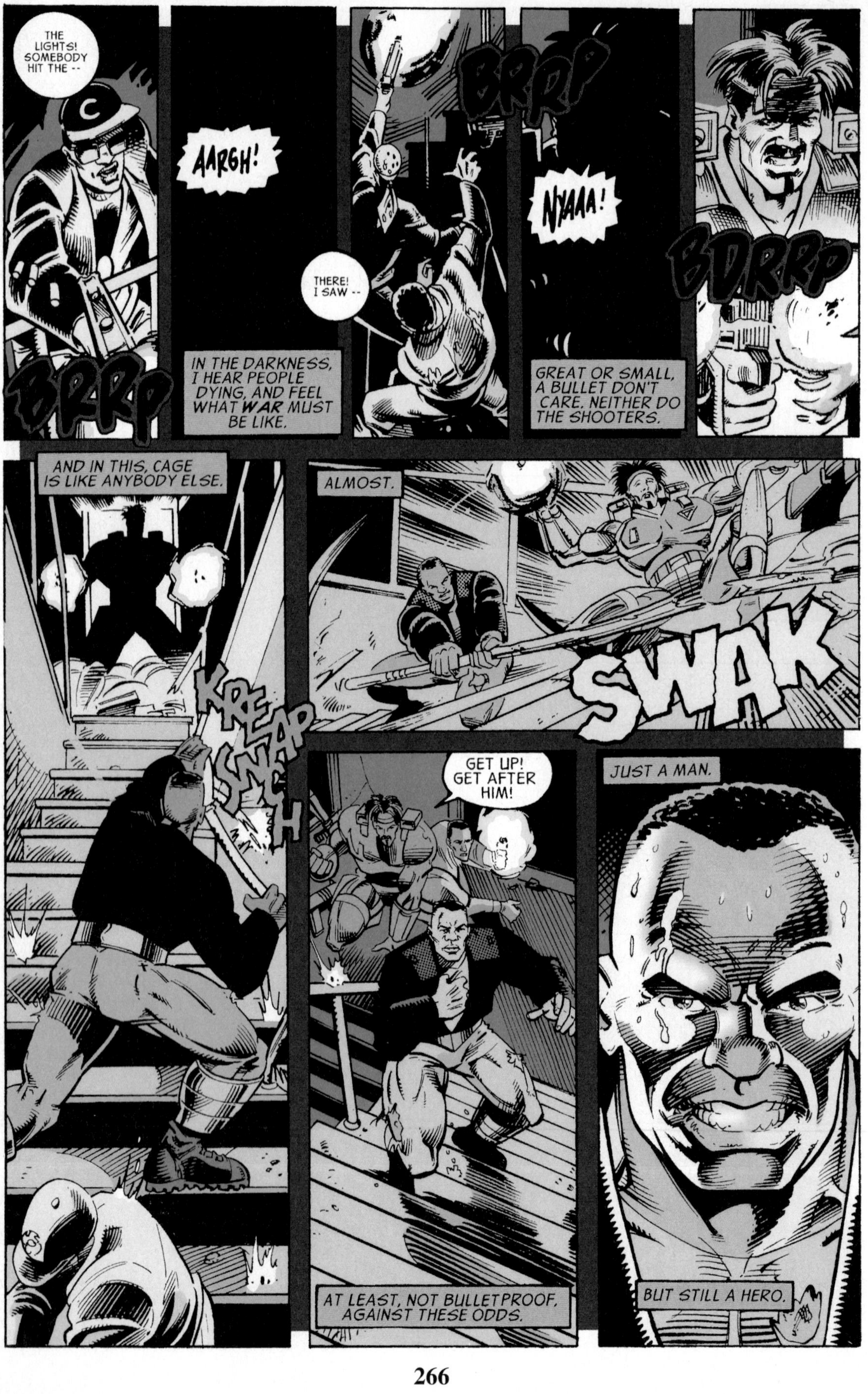
THE LIGHTS! SOMEBODY HIT THE --
BRRP
AARGH!
IN THE DARKNESS, I HEAR PEOPLE DYING, AND FEEL WHAT WAR MUST BE LIKE.
THERE! I SAW --
BRRP
NYAAA!
GREAT OR SMALL, A BULLET DON'T CARE. NEITHER DO THE SHOOTERS.
BDRRP
AND IN THIS, CAGE IS LIKE ANYBODY ELSE.
ALMOST.
SWAK
KREEAP
SMASH
GET UP! GET AFTER HIM!
AT LEAST, NOT BULLETPROOF, AGAINST THESE ODDS.
JUST A MAN.
BUT STILL A HERO.

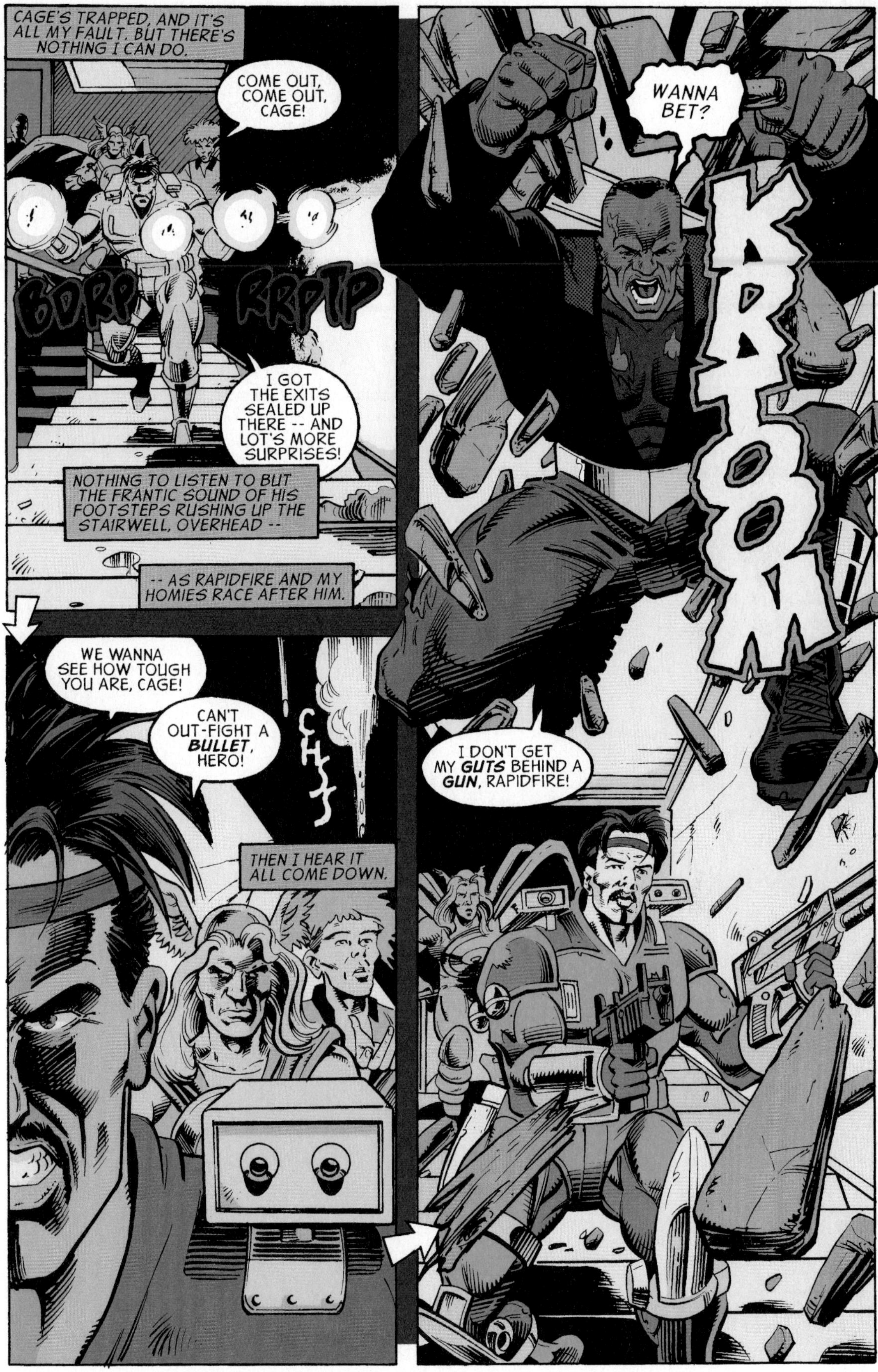
CAGE'S TRAPPED, AND IT'S ALL MY FAULT. BUT THERE'S NOTHING I CAN DO.
COME OUT, COME OUT, CAGE!
BDRP
RRPTP
I GOT THE EXITS SEALED UP THERE -- AND LOT'S MORE SURPRISES!
NOTHING TO LISTEN TO BUT THE FRANTIC SOUND OF HIS FOOTSTEPS RUSHING UP THE STAIRWELL, OVERHEAD --
-- AS RAPIDFIRE AND MY HOMIES RACE AFTER HIM.
WE WANNA SEE HOW TOUGH YOU ARE, CAGE!
CAN'T OUT-FIGHT A BULLET, HERO!
CHTT
THEN I HEAR IT ALL COME DOWN.
WANNA BET?
KRAOOM
I DON'T GET MY GUTS BEHIND A GUN, RAPIDFIRE!

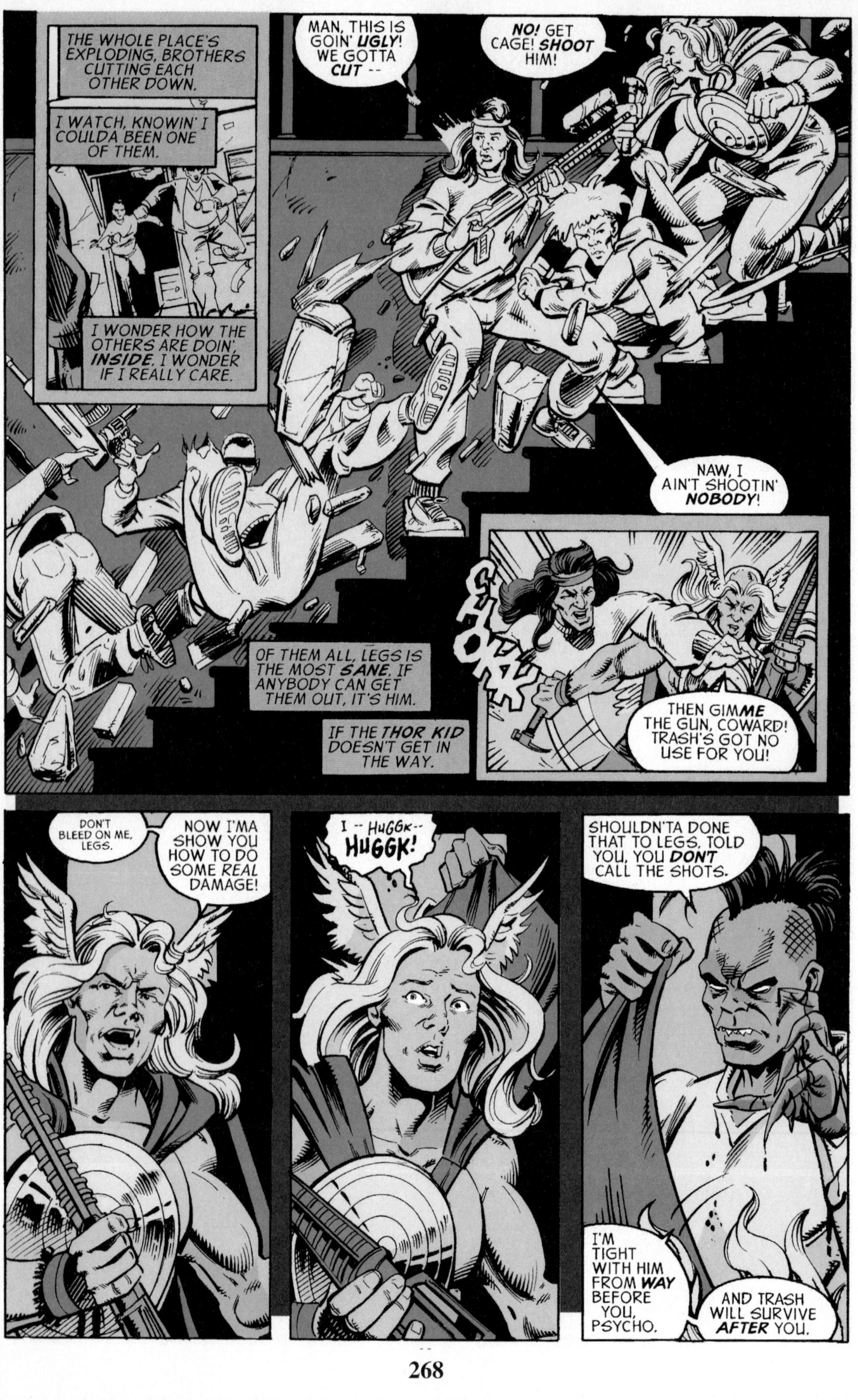

THE WHOLE PLACE'S EXPLODING, BROTHERS CUTTING EACH OTHER DOWN.
I WATCH, KNOWIN' I COULDA BEEN ONE OF THEM.
I WONDER HOW THE OTHERS ARE DOIN' INSIDE. I WONDER IF I REALLY CARE.
MAN, THIS IS GOIN' UGLY! WE GOTTA CUT --
NO! GET CAGE! SHOOT HIM!
NAW, I AIN'T SHOOTIN' NOBODY!
OF THEM ALL, LEGS IS THE MOST SANE. IF ANYBODY CAN GET THEM OUT, IT'S HIM.
IF THE THOR KID DOESN'T GET IN THE WAY.
THEN GIMME THE GUN, COWARD! TRASH'S GOT NO USE FOR YOU!
DON'T BLEED ON ME, LEGS.
NOW I'MA SHOW YOU HOW TO DO SOME REAL DAMAGE!
I -- HUGGK -- HUGGK!
SHOULDN'TA DONE THAT TO LEGS. TOLD YOU, YOU DON'T CALL THE SHOTS.
I'M TIGHT WITH HIM FROM WAY BEFORE YOU, PSYCHO.
AND TRASH WILL SURVIVE AFTER YOU.

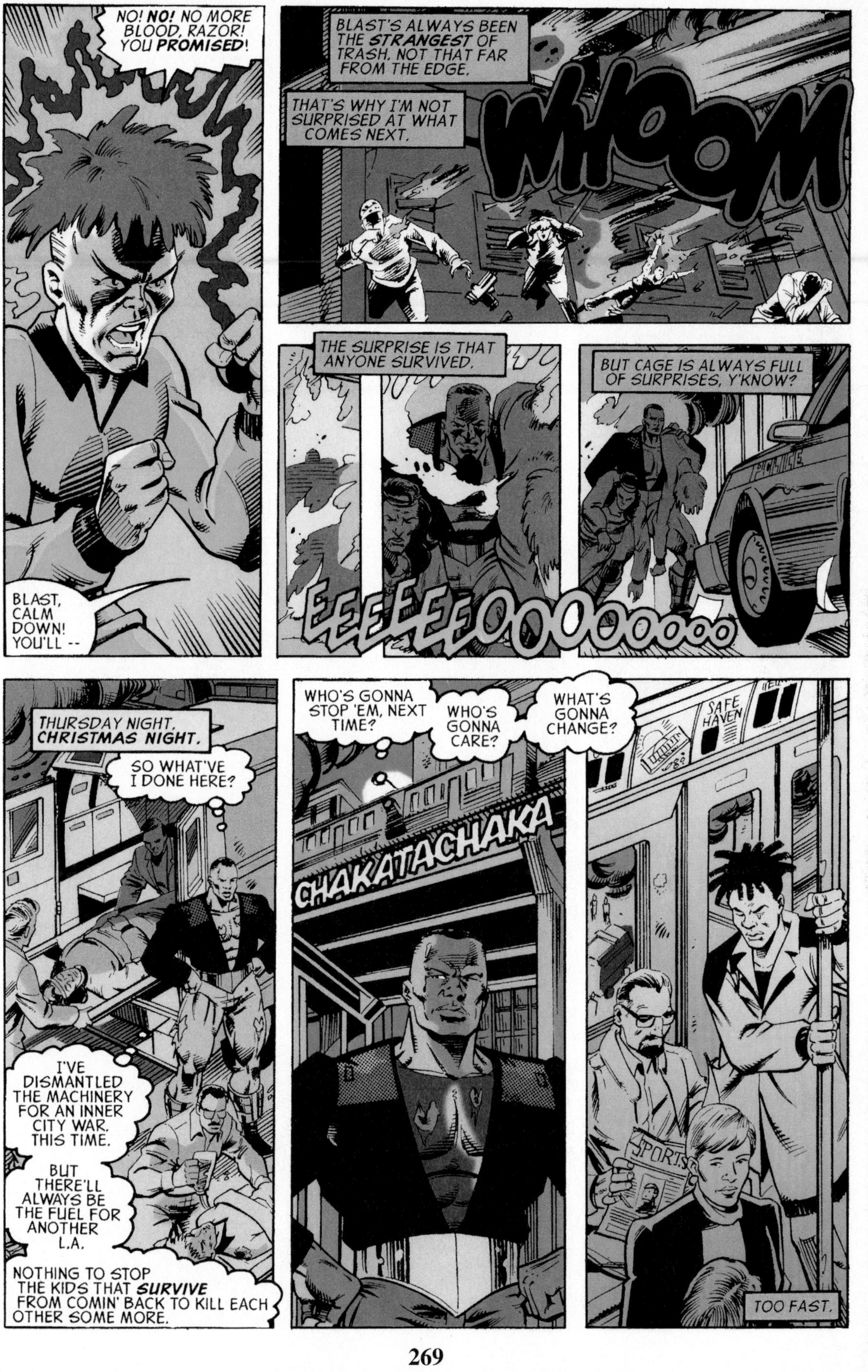

NO! NO! NO MORE BLOOD, RAZOR! YOU PROMISED!
BLAST, CALM DOWN! YOU'LL --
BLAST'S ALWAYS BEEN THE STRANGEST OF TRASH. NOT THAT FAR FROM THE EDGE.
THAT'S WHY I'M NOT SURPRISED AT WHAT COMES NEXT.
WHOOM
THE SURPRISE IS THAT ANYONE SURVIVED.
BUT CAGE IS ALWAYS FULL OF SURPRISES, Y'KNOW?
POLICE
EEEEEEOOOOOooo
THURSDAY NIGHT, CHRISTMAS NIGHT.
SO WHAT'VE I DONE HERE?
I'VE DISMANTLED THE MACHINERY FOR AN INNER CITY WAR, THIS TIME.
BUT THERE'LL ALWAYS BE THE FUEL FOR ANOTHER L.A.
NOTHING TO STOP THE KIDS THAT SURVIVE FROM COMIN' BACK TO KILL EACH OTHER SOME MORE.
WHO'S GONNA STOP 'EM, NEXT TIME?
WHO'S GONNA CARE?
WHAT'S GONNA CHANGE?
SAFE HAVEN
CHAKATACHAKA
SPORTS
TOO FAST.

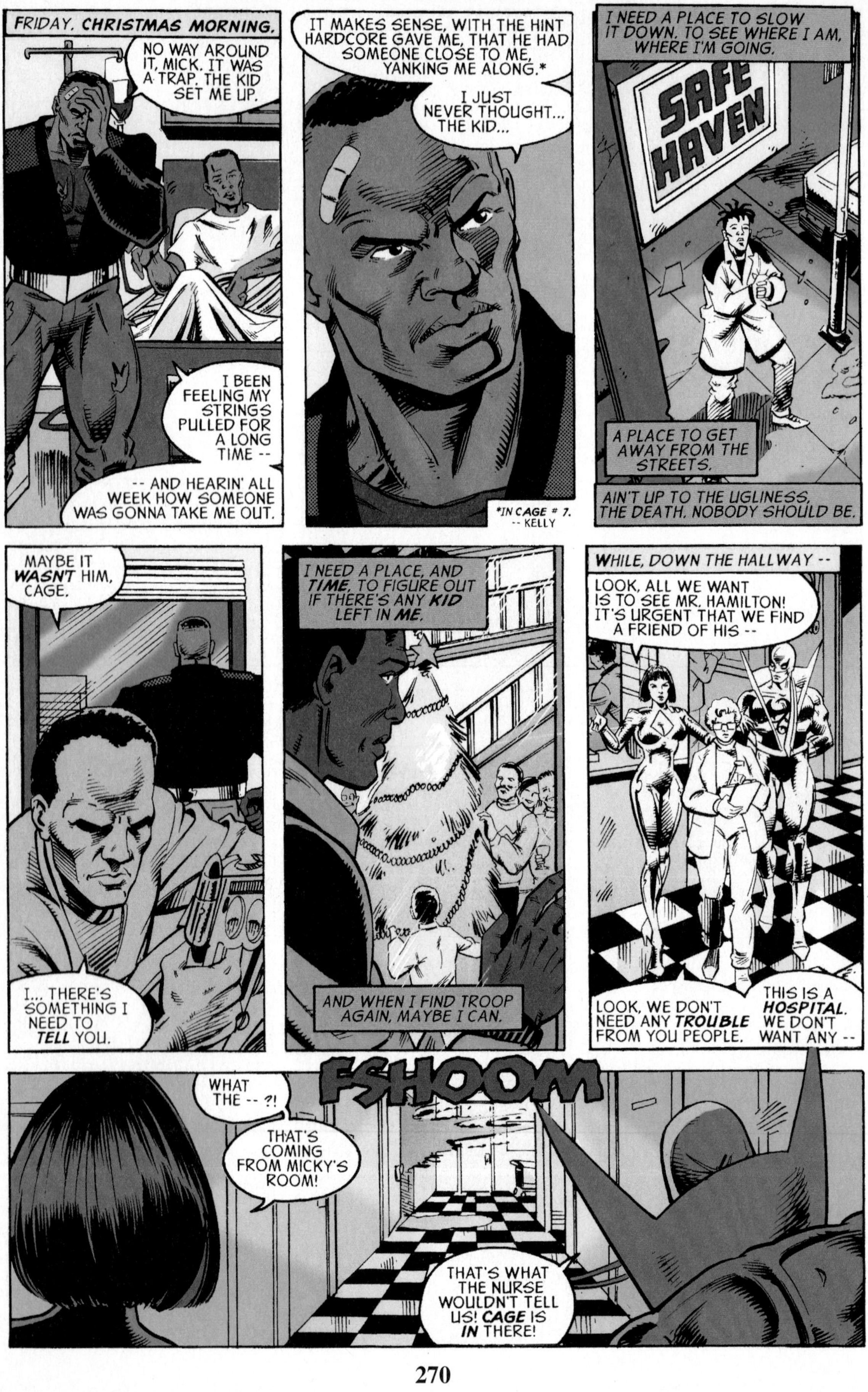
FRIDAY, CHRISTMAS MORNING.
NO WAY AROUND IT, MICK. IT WAS A TRAP. THE KID SET ME UP.
I BEEN FEELING MY STRINGS PULLED FOR A LONG TIME --
-- AND HEARIN' ALL WEEK HOW SOMEONE WAS GONNA TAKE ME OUT.
IT MAKES SENSE, WITH THE HINT HARDCORE GAVE ME, THAT HE HAD SOMEONE CLOSE TO ME, YANKING ME ALONG.*
I JUST NEVER THOUGHT... THE KID...
*IN CAGE # 7. -- KELLY
I NEED A PLACE TO SLOW IT DOWN. TO SEE WHERE I AM, WHERE I'M GOING.
SAFE HAVEN
A PLACE TO GET AWAY FROM THE STREETS.
AIN'T UP TO THE UGLINESS, THE DEATH. NOBODY SHOULD BE.
MAYBE IT WASN'T HIM, CAGE.
I... THERE'S SOMETHING I NEED TO TELL YOU.
I NEED A PLACE, AND TIME, TO FIGURE OUT IF THERE'S ANY KID LEFT IN ME.
AND WHEN I FIND TROOP AGAIN, MAYBE I CAN.
WHILE, DOWN THE HALLWAY --
LOOK, ALL WE WANT IS TO SEE MR. HAMILTON! IT'S URGENT THAT WE FIND A FRIEND OF HIS --
LOOK, WE DON'T NEED ANY TROUBLE FROM YOU PEOPLE.
THIS IS A HOSPITAL. WE DON'T WANT ANY --
FSHOOM
WHAT THE -- ?!
THAT'S COMING FROM MICKY'S ROOM!
THAT'S WHAT THE NURSE WOULDN'T TELL US! CAGE IS IN THERE!

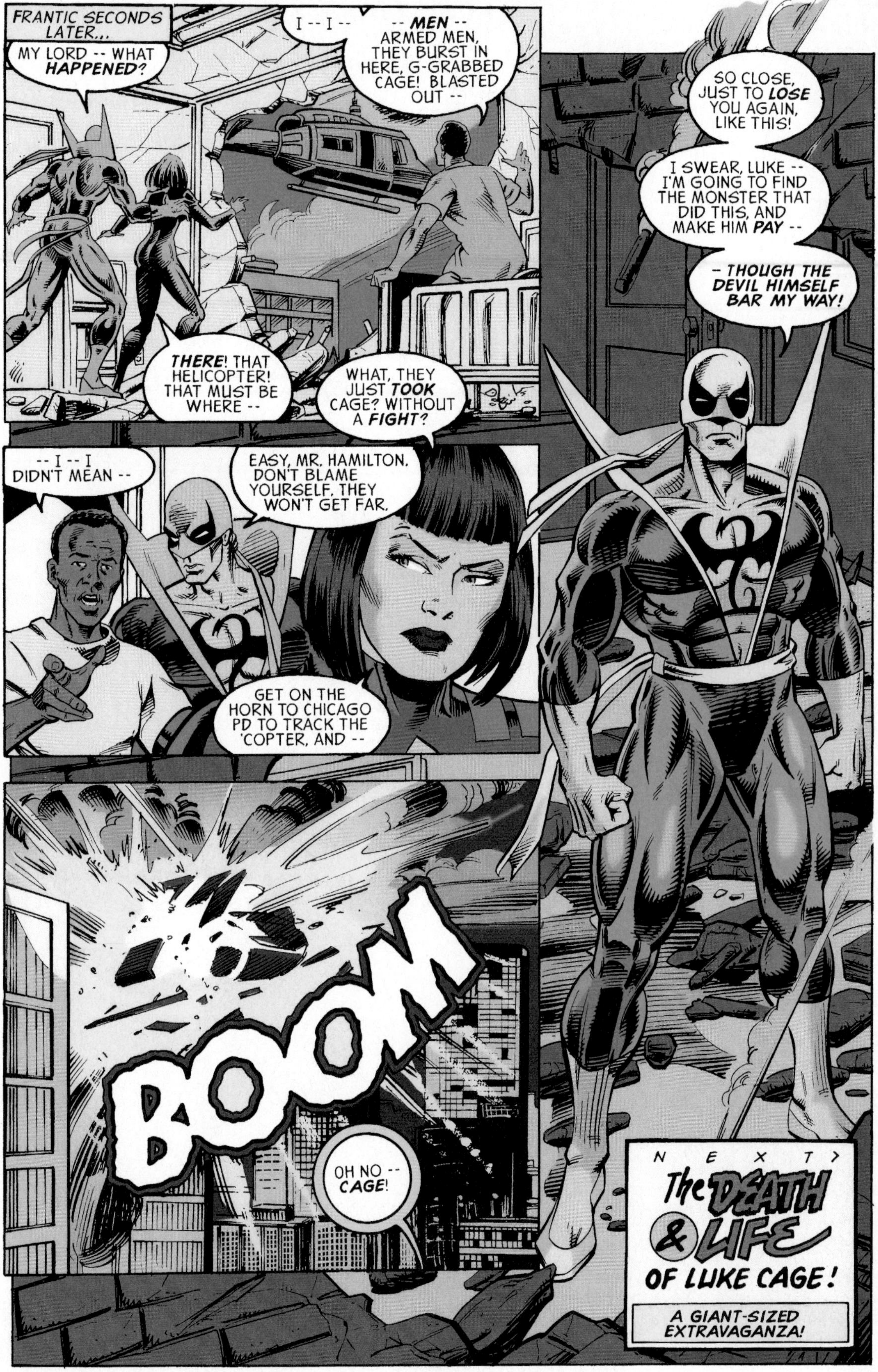

FRANTIC SECONDS LATER...
MY LORD -- WHAT HAPPENED?
I -- I --
-- MEN -- ARMED MEN, THEY BURST IN HERE, G-GRABBED CAGE! BLASTED OUT --
THERE! THAT HELICOPTER! THAT MUST BE WHERE --
WHAT, THEY JUST TOOK CAGE? WITHOUT A FIGHT?
-- I -- I DIDN'T MEAN --
EASY, MR. HAMILTON. DON'T BLAME YOURSELF. THEY WON'T GET FAR.
GET ON THE HORN TO CHICAGO PD TO TRACK THE 'COPTER, AND --
BOOM
OH NO -- CAGE!
SO CLOSE, JUST TO LOSE YOU AGAIN, LIKE THIS!
I SWEAR, LUKE -- I'M GOING TO FIND THE MONSTER THAT DID THIS, AND MAKE HIM PAY --
-- THOUGH THE DEVIL HIMSELF BAR MY WAY!
NEXT
The DEATH & LIFE OF LUKE CAGE!
A GIANT-SIZED EXTRAVAGANZA!

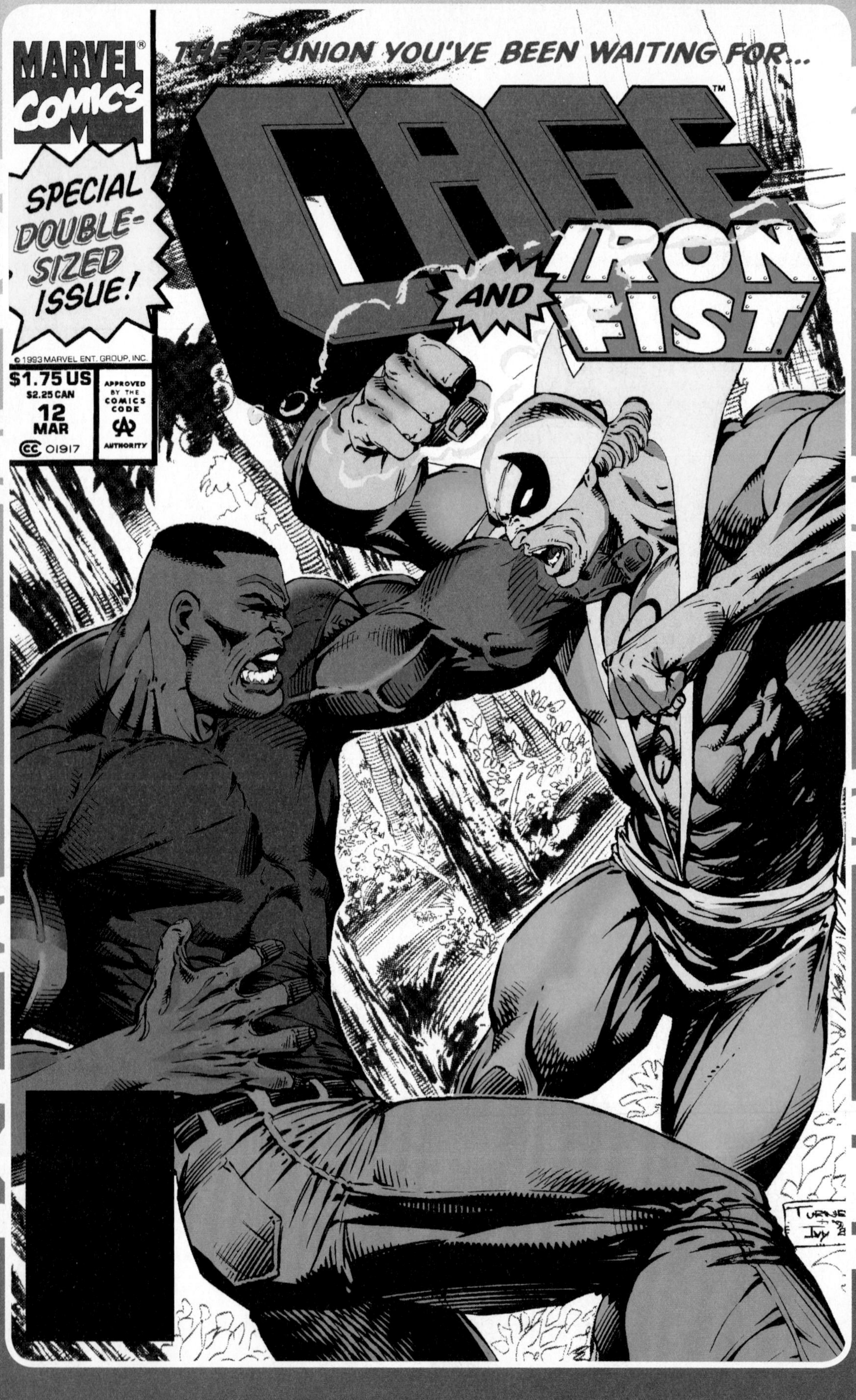
MARVEL COMICS
THE REUNION YOU'VE BEEN WAITING FOR...
CAGE
AND
IRON FIST
SPECIAL DOUBLE-SIZED ISSUE!
© 1993 MARVEL ENT. GROUP, INC.
$1.75 US
$2.25 CAN
12
MAR
01917
APPROVED BY THE COMICS CODE AUTHORITY

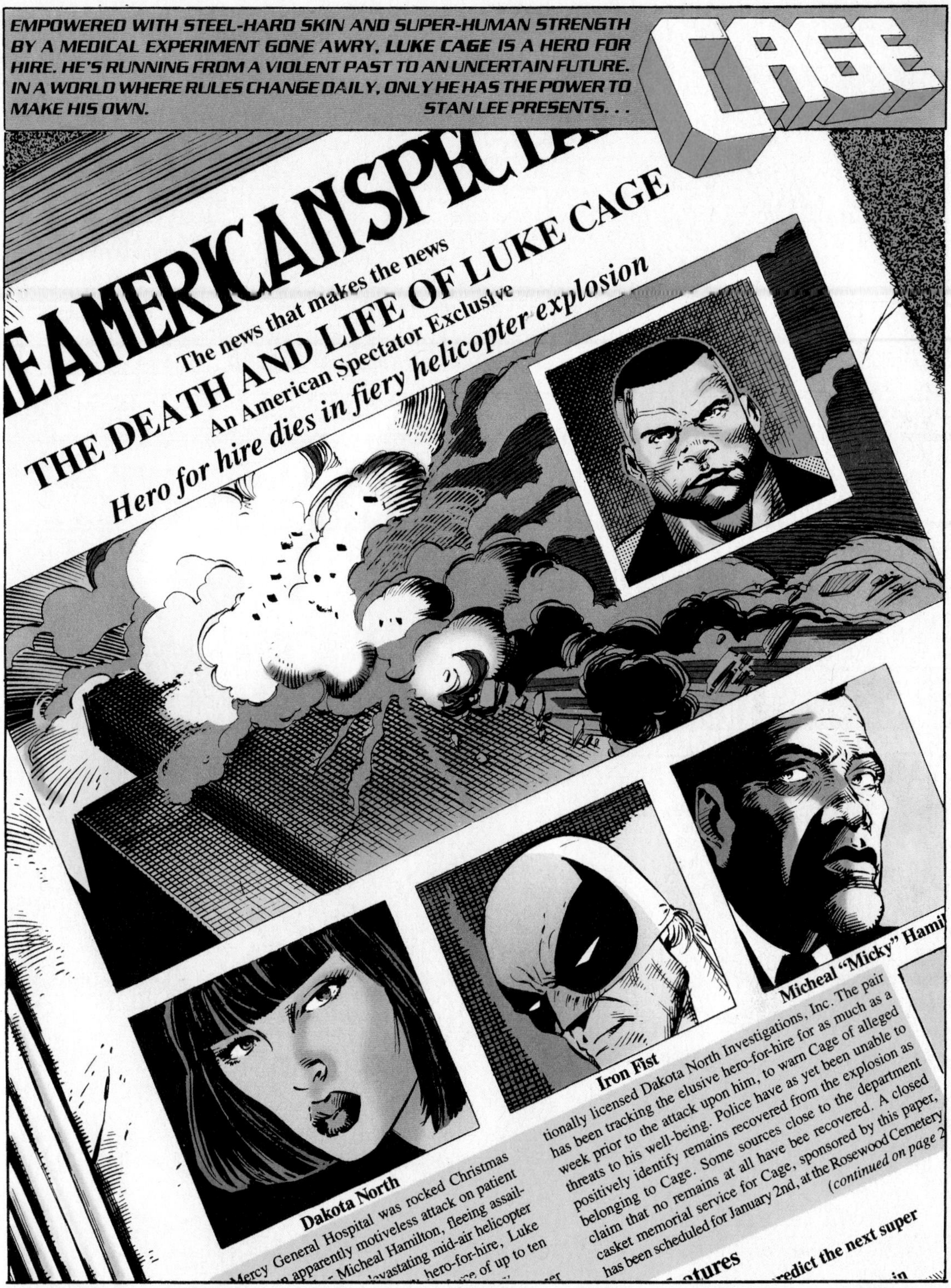

EMPOWERED WITH STEEL-HARD SKIN AND SUPER-HUMAN STRENGTH BY A MEDICAL EXPERIMENT GONE AWRY, LUKE CAGE IS A HERO FOR HIRE. HE'S RUNNING FROM A VIOLENT PAST TO AN UNCERTAIN FUTURE. IN A WORLD WHERE RULES CHANGE DAILY, ONLY HE HAS THE POWER TO MAKE HIS OWN.
STAN LEE PRESENTS. . .
CAGE
EAMERICANSPECTA
The news that makes the news
THE DEATH AND LIFE OF LUKE CAGE
An American Spectator Exclusive
Hero for hire dies in fiery helicopter explosion
Dakota North
Iron Fist
Micheal “Micky” Hamil
Mercy General Hospital was rocked Christmas
apparently motiveless attack on patient
Micheal Hamilton, fleeing assail-
devastating mid-air helicopter
hero-for-hire, Luke
of up to ten
tionally licensed Dakota North Investigations, Inc. The pair has been tracking the elusive hero-for-hire for as much as a week prior to the attack upon him, to warn Cage of alleged threats to his well-being. Police have as yet been unable to positively identify remains recovered from the explosion as belonging to Cage. Some sources close to the department claim that no remains at all have bee recovered. A closed casket memorial service for Cage, sponsored by this paper, has been scheduled for January 2nd, at the Rosewood Cemetery.
(continued on page 2

MARC McLAURIN STORY • DWAYNE TURNER PENCILS • CHRISTOPHER IVY INKS • JANICE CHIANG LETTERS • KRIS RENKEWITZ COLORS • KELLY CORVESE EDITS • TOM DeFALCO EDITOR IN CHIEF

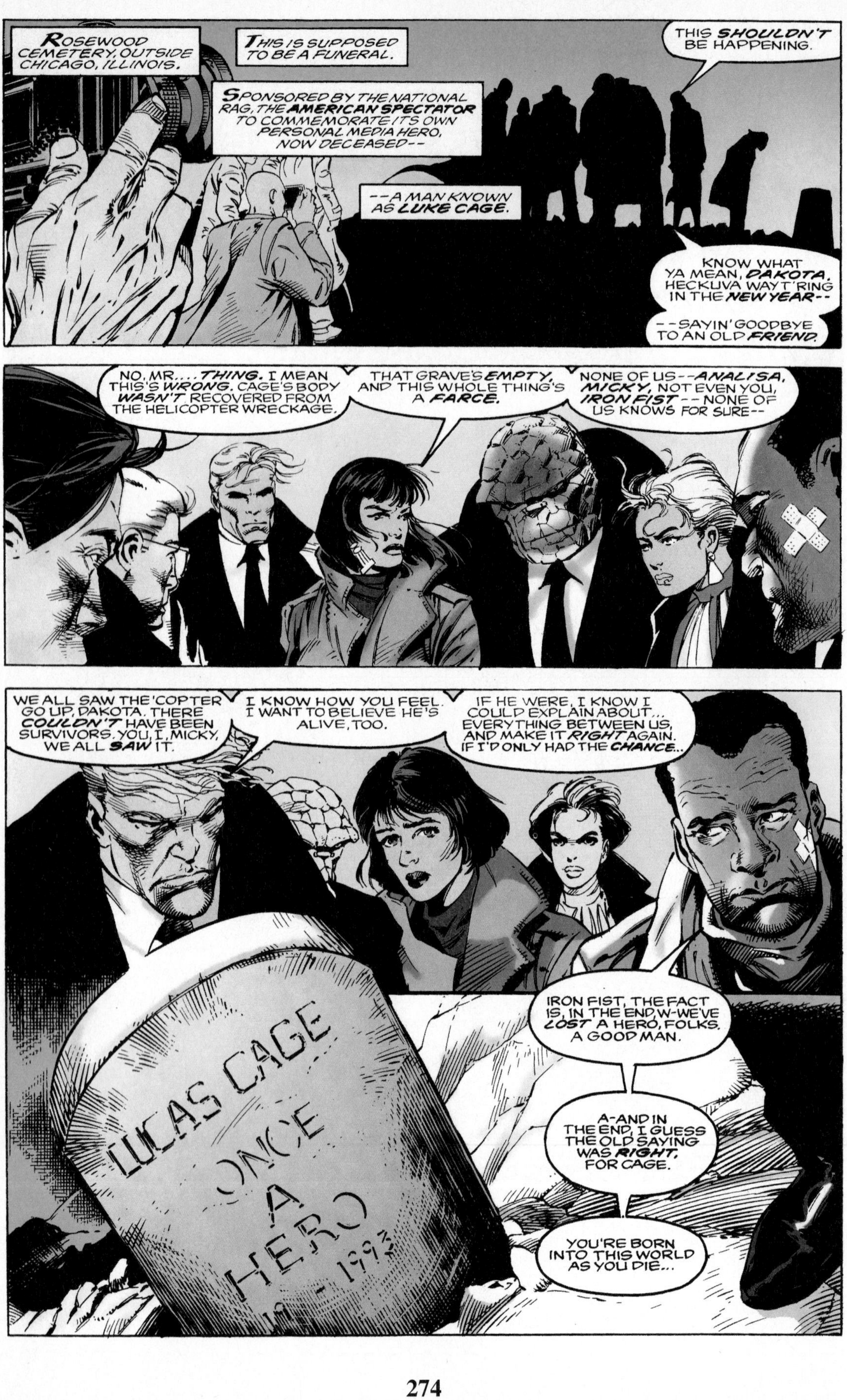
ROSEWOOD CEMETERY, OUTSIDE CHICAGO, ILLINOIS.
THIS IS SUPPOSED TO BE A FUNERAL.
SPONSORED BY THE NATIONAL RAG, THE AMERICAN SPECTATOR TO COMMEMORATE ITS OWN PERSONAL MEDIA HERO, NOW DECEASED--
--A MAN KNOWN AS LUKE CAGE.
THIS SHOULDN'T BE HAPPENING.
KNOW WHAT YA MEAN, DAKOTA. HECKUVA WAY T'RING IN THE NEW YEAR--
--SAYIN' GOODBYE TO AN OLD FRIEND.
NO, MR.... THING. I MEAN THIS'S WRONG. CAGE'S BODY WASN'T RECOVERED FROM THE HELICOPTER WRECKAGE.
THAT GRAVE'S EMPTY, AND THIS WHOLE THING'S A FARCE.
NONE OF US--ANALISA, MICKY, NOT EVEN YOU, IRON FIST--NONE OF US KNOWS FOR SURE--
WE ALL SAW THE 'COPTER GO UP, DAKOTA. THERE COULDN'T HAVE BEEN SURVIVORS. YOU, I, MICKY, WE ALL SAW IT.
I KNOW HOW YOU FEEL. I WANT TO BELIEVE HE'S ALIVE, TOO.
IF HE WERE, I KNOW I COULD EXPLAIN ABOUT... EVERYTHING BETWEEN US, AND MAKE IT RIGHT AGAIN. IF I'D ONLY HAD THE CHANCE...
LUCAS CAGE
ONCE A HERO
IRON FIST, THE FACT IS, IN THE END, W-WE'VE LOST A HERO, FOLKS. A GOOD MAN.
A-AND IN THE END, I GUESS THE OLD SAYING WAS RIGHT, FOR CAGE.
YOU'RE BORN INTO THIS WORLD AS YOU DIE...

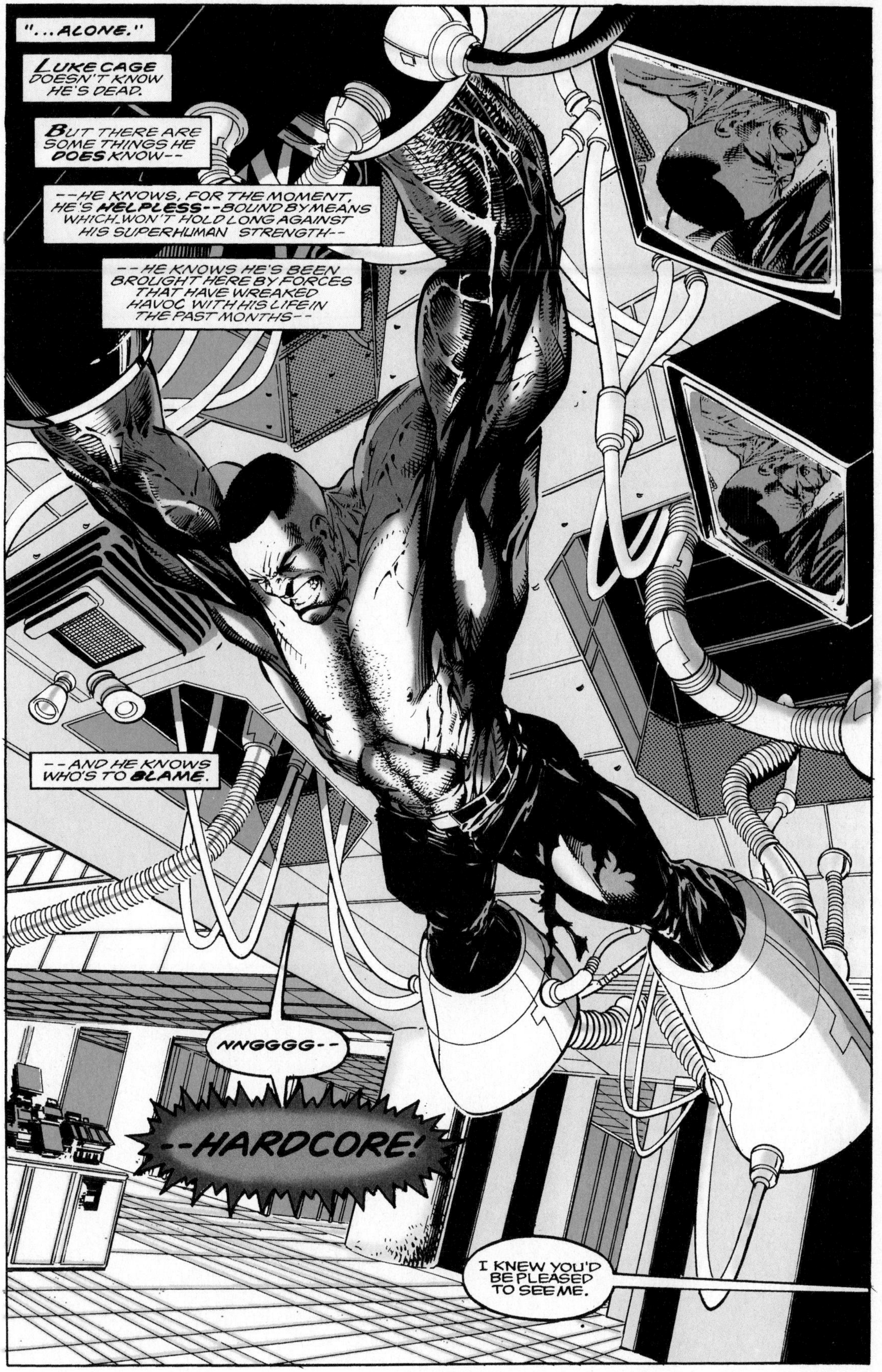
"...ALONE."
LUKE CAGE DOESN'T KNOW HE'S DEAD.
BUT THERE ARE SOME THINGS HE DOES KNOW--
--HE KNOWS, FOR THE MOMENT, HE'S HELPLESS--BOUND BY MEANS WHICH WON'T HOLD LONG AGAINST HIS SUPERHUMAN STRENGTH--
--HE KNOWS HE'S BEEN BROUGHT HERE BY FORCES THAT HAVE WREAKED HAVOC WITH HIS LIFE IN THE PAST MONTHS--
--AND HE KNOWS WHO'S TO BLAME.
NNGGGG--
--HARDCORE!
I KNEW YOU'D BE PLEASED TO SEE ME.

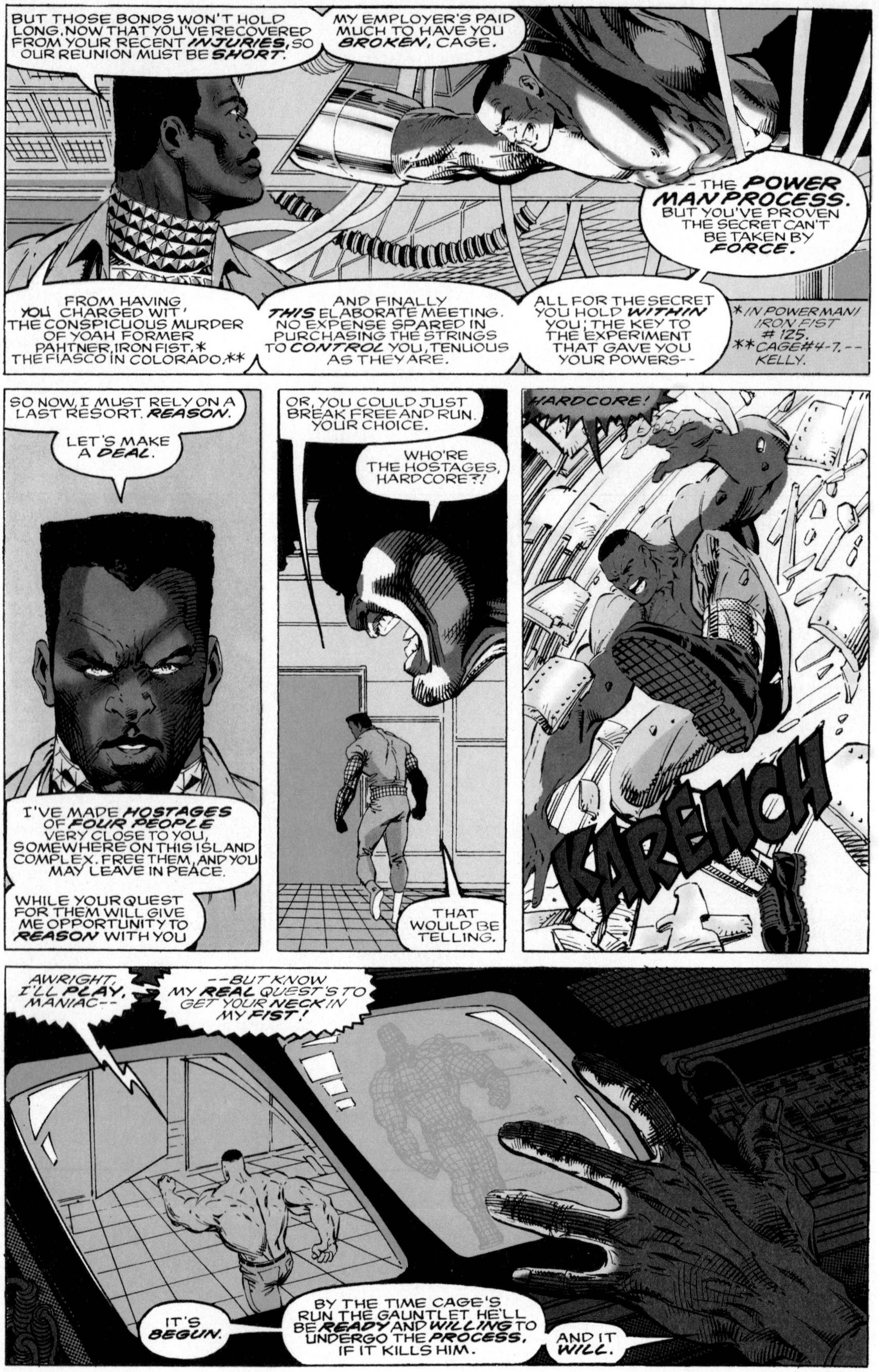
BUT THOSE BONDS WON'T HOLD LONG, NOW THAT YOU'VE RECOVERED FROM YOUR RECENT INJURIES, SO OUR REUNION MUST BE SHORT.
MY EMPLOYER'S PAID MUCH TO HAVE YOU BROKEN, CAGE.
FROM HAVING YOU CHARGED WIT' THE CONSPICUOUS MURDER OF YOAH FORMER PAHTNER, IRON FIST,* THE FIASCO IN COLORADO,**
AND FINALLY THIS ELABORATE MEETING. NO EXPENSE SPARED IN PURCHASING THE STRINGS TO CONTROL YOU, TENUOUS AS THEY ARE.
ALL FOR THE SECRET YOU HOLD WITHIN YOU; THE KEY TO THE EXPERIMENT THAT GAVE YOU YOUR POWERS--
--THE POWER MAN PROCESS. BUT YOU'VE PROVEN THE SECRET CAN'T BE TAKEN BY FORCE.
*IN POWER MAN/IRON FIST #125. **CAGE #4-7. --KELLY.
SO NOW, I MUST RELY ON A LAST RESORT. REASON.
LET'S MAKE A DEAL.
I'VE MADE HOSTAGES OF FOUR PEOPLE VERY CLOSE TO YOU, SOMEWHERE ON THIS ISLAND COMPLEX. FREE THEM, AND YOU MAY LEAVE IN PEACE.
WHILE YOUR QUEST FOR THEM WILL GIVE ME OPPORTUNITY TO REASON WITH YOU
OR, YOU COULD JUST BREAK FREE AND RUN. YOUR CHOICE.
WHO'RE THE HOSTAGES, HARDCORE?!
THAT WOULD BE TELLING.
HARDCORE!
KARENCH
AWRIGHT. I'LL PLAY, MANIAC--
--BUT KNOW MY REAL QUEST'S TO GET YOUR NECK IN MY FIST!
IT'S BEGUN.
BY THE TIME CAGE'S RUN THE GAUNTLET HE'LL BE READY AND WILLING TO UNDERGO THE PROCESS, IF IT KILLS HIM.
AND IT WILL.

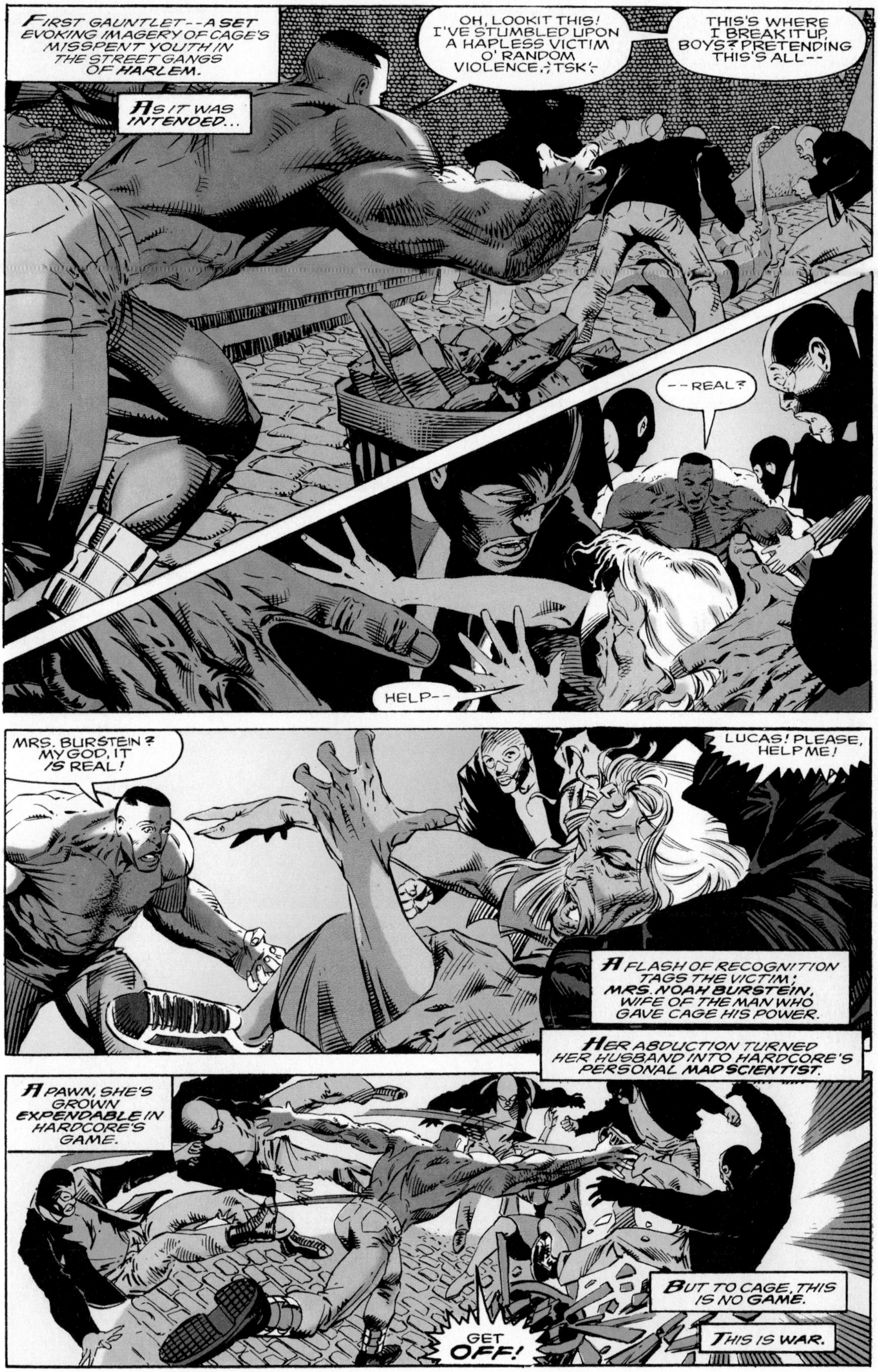
FIRST GAUNTLET--A SET EVOKING IMAGERY OF CAGE'S MISSPENT YOUTH IN THE STREET GANGS OF HARLEM.
AS IT WAS INTENDED...
OH, LOOKIT THIS! I'VE STUMBLED UPON A HAPLESS VICTIM O' RANDOM VIOLENCE. TSK!
THIS'S WHERE I BREAK IT UP, BOYS? PRETENDING THIS'S ALL--
--REAL?
HELP--
MRS. BURSTEIN? MY GOD, IT IS REAL!
LUCAS! PLEASE, HELP ME!
A FLASH OF RECOGNITION TAGS THE VICTIM: MRS. NOAH BURSTEIN, WIFE OF THE MAN WHO GAVE CAGE HIS POWER.
HER ABDUCTION TURNED HER HUSBAND INTO HARDCORE'S PERSONAL MAD SCIENTIST.
A PAWN, SHE'S GROWN EXPENDABLE IN HARDCORE'S GAME.
BUT TO CAGE, THIS IS NO GAME.
THIS IS WAR.
GET OFF!

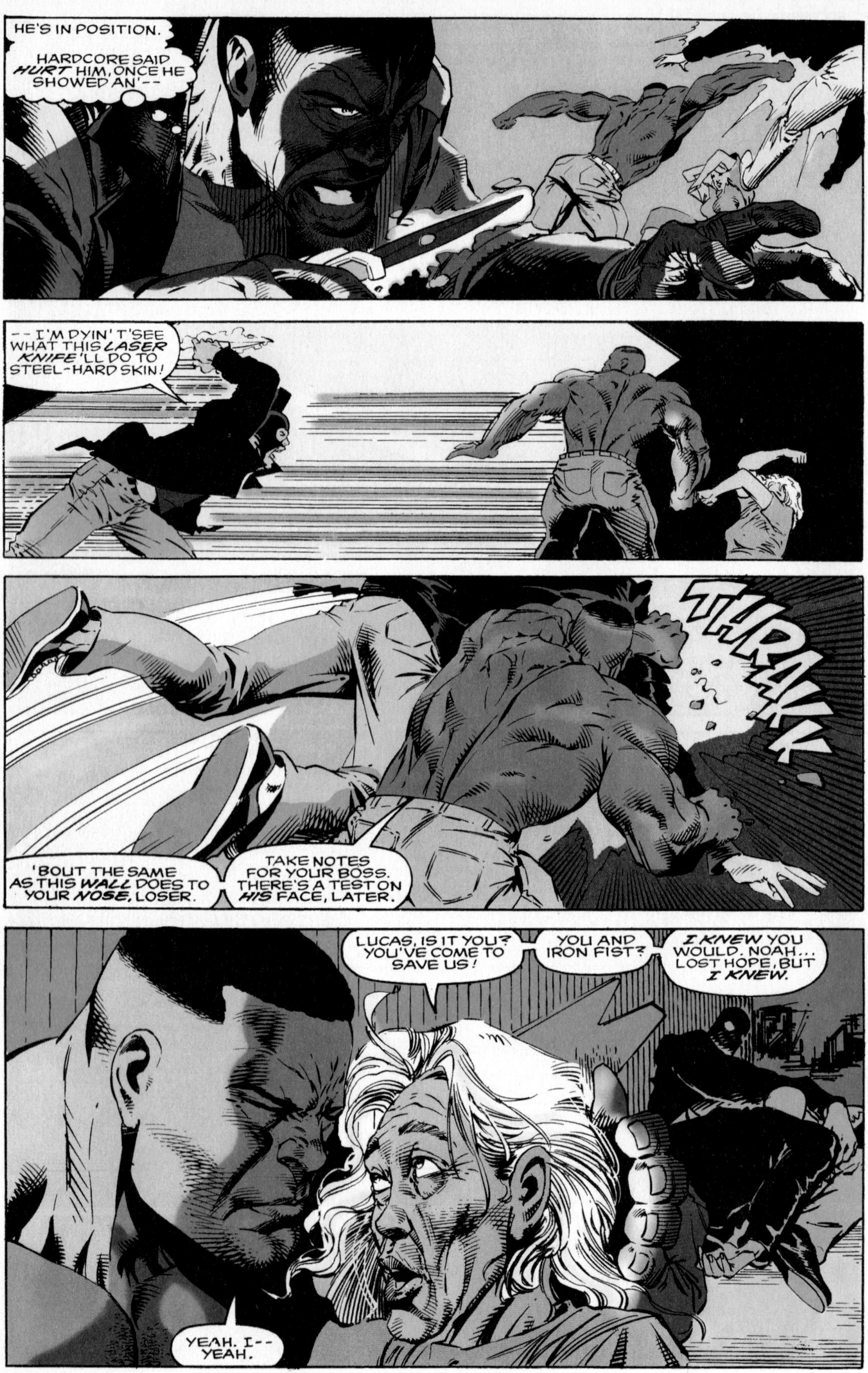
HE'S IN POSITION.
HARDCORE SAID HURT HIM, ONCE HE SHOWED AN'--
-- I'M DYIN' T'SEE WHAT THIS LASER KNIFE'LL DO TO STEEL-HARD SKIN!
THRAKK
'BOUT THE SAME AS THIS WALL DOES TO YOUR NOSE, LOSER.
TAKE NOTES FOR YOUR BOSS. THERE'S A TEST ON HIS FACE, LATER.
LUCAS, IS IT YOU? YOU'VE COME TO SAVE US!
YOU AND IRON FIST?
I KNEW YOU WOULD. NOAH... LOST HOPE, BUT I KNEW.
YEAH. I-- YEAH.

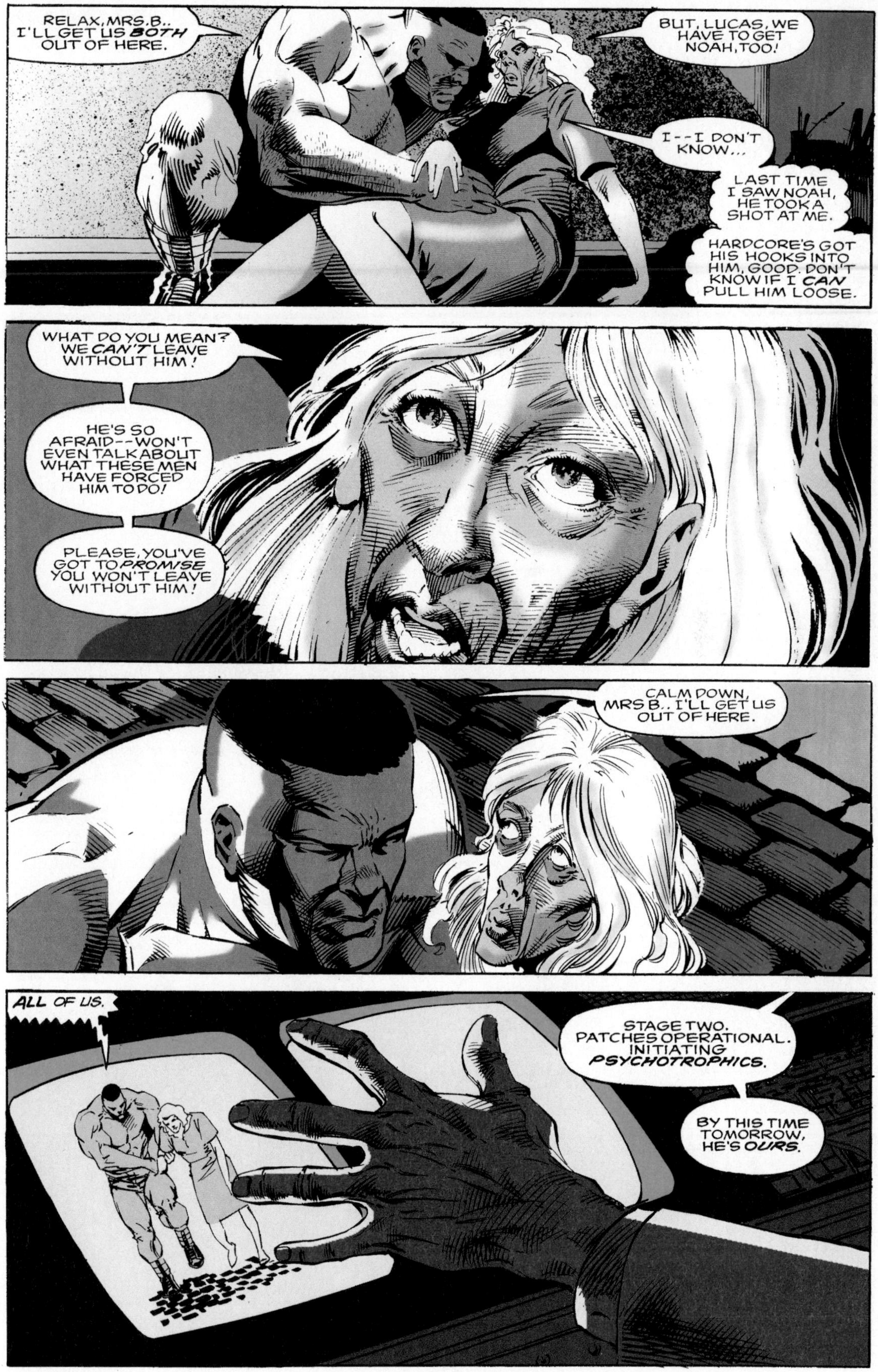
RELAX, MRS. B.. I'LL GET US BOTH OUT OF HERE.
BUT, LUCAS, WE HAVE TO GET NOAH, TOO!
I--I DON'T KNOW...
LAST TIME I SAW NOAH, HE TOOK A SHOT AT ME.
HARDCORE'S GOT HIS HOOKS INTO HIM, GOOD. DON'T KNOW IF I CAN PULL HIM LOOSE.
WHAT DO YOU MEAN? WE CAN'T LEAVE WITHOUT HIM!
HE'S SO AFRAID--WON'T EVEN TALK ABOUT WHAT THESE MEN HAVE FORCED HIM TO DO!
PLEASE, YOU'VE GOT TO PROMISE YOU WON'T LEAVE WITHOUT HIM!
CALM DOWN, MRS B.. I'LL GET US OUT OF HERE.
ALL OF US.
STAGE TWO. PATCHES OPERATIONAL. INITIATING PSYCHOTROPHICS.
BY THIS TIME TOMORROW, HE'S OURS.

NIGHT, ON CHICAGO'S GOLD COAST, WHERE CENTURIES OLD MANSIONS RUB SHOULDERS WITH HIGH-RISES.

WHERE THOSE WHO CAN AFFORD, REST THEIR HEADS, WEARILY--

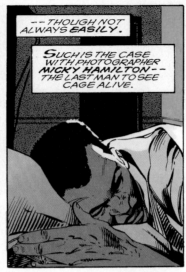

--THOUGH NOT ALWAYS EASILY.

SUCH IS THE CASE WITH PHOTOGRAPHER MICKY HAMILTON-- THE LAST MAN TO SEE CAGE ALIVE.

A DISTINCTION THAT WEIGHS HEAVILY, BRINGING A MAN TO THE EDGE--

--WAITING FOR SOMEONE TO PUSH HIM OVER.

THAT'S IT, HAMILTON. YOU'RE DEAD.

LET ME GUESS, A CHANNELER, COMMUNING WITH SPIRITS?

OR JUST SOME WACKY NEIGHBOR?

WHA?

BUD, YOU PICKED THE WRONG NIGHT FOR A MUGGING!

SKEE SKEE

YEAH, WELL, WEDNESDAYS I HAVE MY HAIR DONE--

--AND FRIDAY'S TARGET PRACTICE!

AND I AIN'T YOUR "BUD".

hukk

Skiraf

BUT ALL THINGS CONSIDERED, AN UNEASY SLEEP IS A PLEASANT ALTERNATIVE--

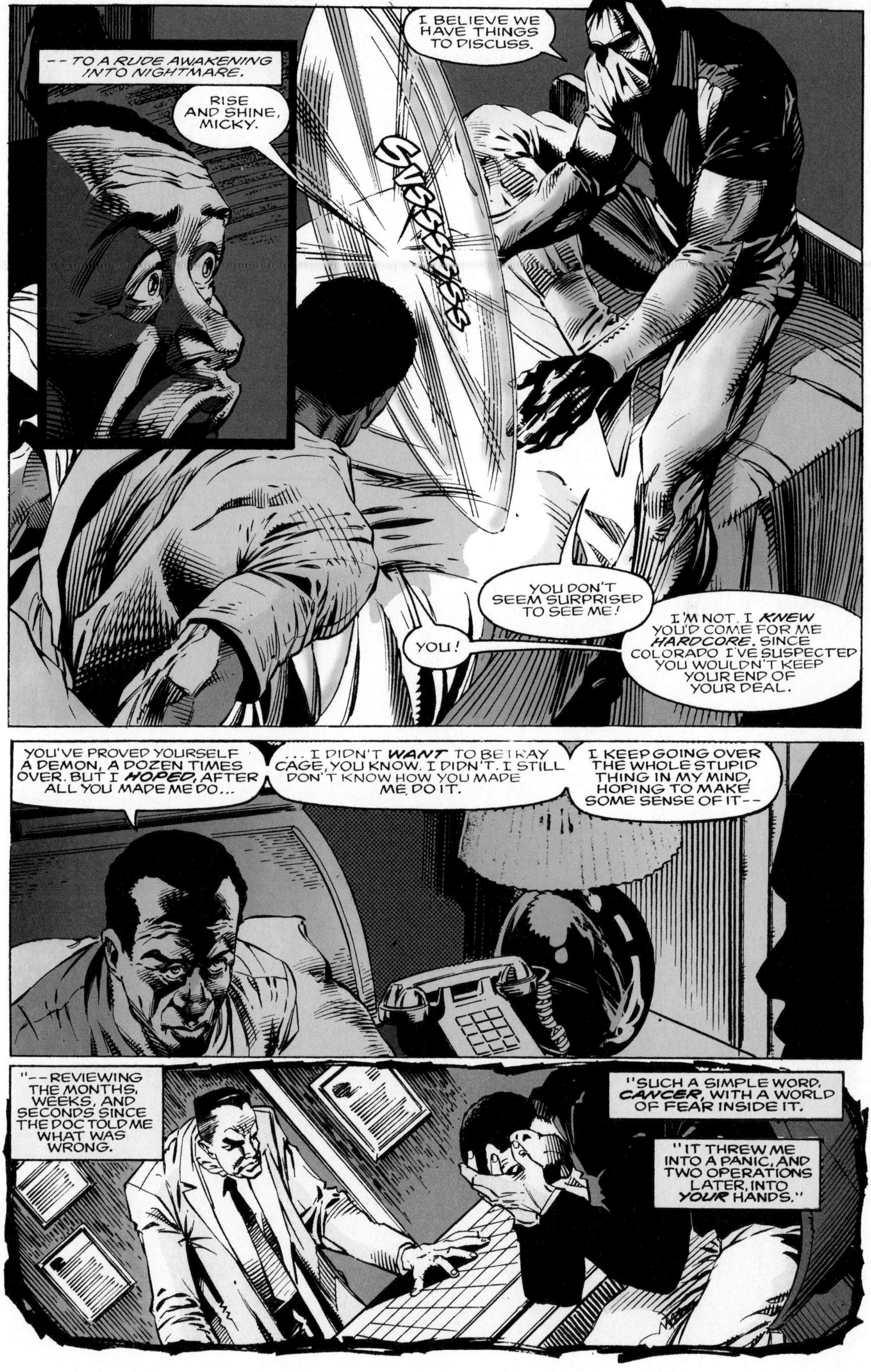

--TO A RUDE AWAKENING INTO NIGHTMARE.
RISE AND SHINE, MICKY.
I BELIEVE WE HAVE THINGS TO DISCUSS.
SVSSSSSSS
YOU DON'T SEEM SURPRISED TO SEE ME!
YOU!
I'M NOT. I KNEW YOU'D COME FOR ME HARDCORE. SINCE COLORADO I'VE SUSPECTED YOU WOULDN'T KEEP YOUR END OF YOUR DEAL.
YOU'VE PROVED YOURSELF A DEMON, A DOZEN TIMES OVER. BUT I HOPED, AFTER ALL YOU MADE ME DO...
...I DIDN'T WANT TO BETRAY CAGE, YOU KNOW. I DIDN'T. I STILL DON'T KNOW HOW YOU MADE ME DO IT.
I KEEP GOING OVER THE WHOLE STUPID THING IN MY MIND, HOPING TO MAKE SOME SENSE OF IT--
"--REVIEWING THE MONTHS, WEEKS, AND SECONDS SINCE THE DOC TOLD ME WHAT WAS WRONG.
"SUCH A SIMPLE WORD, CANCER, WITH A WORLD OF FEAR INSIDE IT.
"IT THREW ME INTO A PANIC, AND TWO OPERATIONS LATER, INTO YOUR HANDS."

"WHERE I MADE A DEAL WITH A DEVIL, OFFERING THE ONE THING SCIENCE COULDN'T *PROMISE.*

A *CURE,* MISTAH HAMILTON. MY *EMPLOYAH* HAS BEEN DOING CERTAIN *RESEARCH* INVOLVING MISTAH CAGE.

RESEARCH WHICH CAN... *WILL* LEAD TO A CURE FOR SEVERAL FORMS OF CANCER AND YOU WOULD BE AMONG THE FIRST BENEFICIARIES.

ALL WE ASK IS YOUR COOPERATION IN A SUBTLE GAME OF... *INFLUENCE* OVER CAGE, AND YOUR LIFE IS YOURS AGAIN.

"I BELIEVED YOU BECAUSE I *WANTED* TO.

"I WAS A FOOL.

"BUT I FOLLOWED INSTRUCTIONS, BRINGING CAGE TOGETHER WITH THE KID, *TROOP,* IN L.A.*...

**CAGE #2.--* KELLY

"... NOT KNOWING THE BIGGER TROUBLE IT'D LEAD TO IN YOUR HIDDEN 'RESEARCH CENTER', A PIT IN THE HEART OF COLORADO.**

***CAGE #5-8.--* KELLY AGAIN

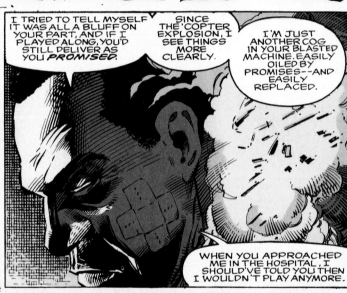

I TRIED TO TELL MYSELF IT WAS ALL A BLUFF ON YOUR PART, AND IF I PLAYED ALONG, YOU'D STILL DELIVER AS YOU *PROMISED.*

SINCE THE 'COPTER EXPLOSION, I SEE THINGS MORE CLEARLY.

I'M JUST ANOTHER COG IN YOUR BLASTED MACHINE. EASILY OILED BY PROMISES--AND EASILY REPLACED.

WHEN YOU APPROACHED ME IN THE HOSPITAL, I SHOULD'VE TOLD YOU THEN I WOULDN'T PLAY ANYMORE.

IT WAS TEARING ME APART TO WORK AGAINST A MAN WHO'D BECOME AS A SON TO ME.

FINALLY, I DECIDED TO TELL CAGE EVERYTHING. TOO LATE.

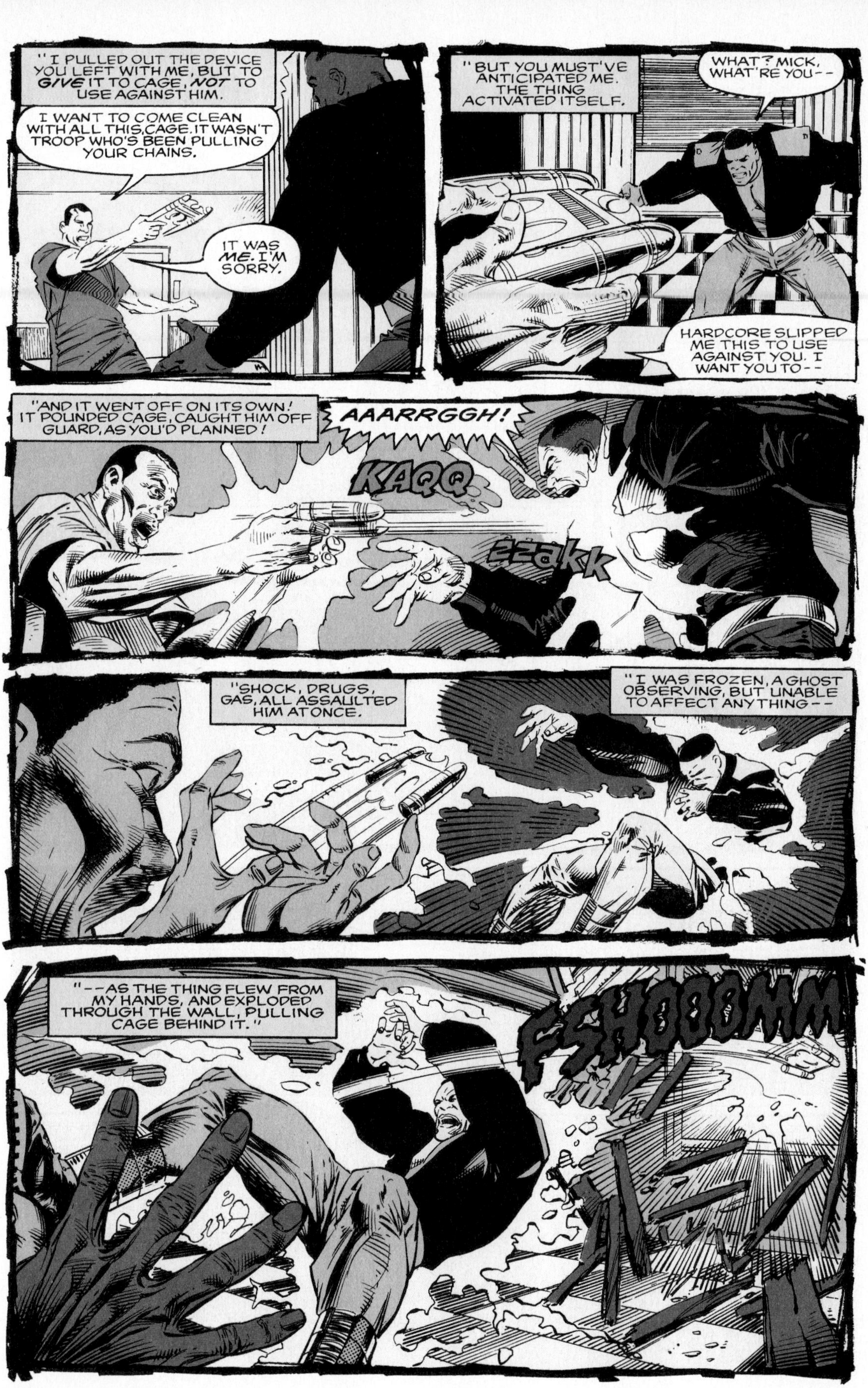
"I PULLED OUT THE DEVICE YOU LEFT WITH ME, BUT TO GIVE IT TO CAGE, NOT TO USE AGAINST HIM.
I WANT TO COME CLEAN WITH ALL THIS, CAGE. IT WASN'T TROOP WHO'S BEEN PULLING YOUR CHAINS.
IT WAS ME. I'M SORRY.
"BUT YOU MUST'VE ANTICIPATED ME. THE THING ACTIVATED ITSELF.
WHAT? MICK, WHAT'RE YOU--
HARDCORE SLIPPED ME THIS TO USE AGAINST YOU. I WANT YOU TO--
"AND IT WENT OFF ON ITS OWN! IT POUNDED CAGE, CAUGHT HIM OFF GUARD, AS YOU'D PLANNED!
AAARRGGH!
KAQQ
ZZAKK
"SHOCK, DRUGS, GAS, ALL ASSAULTED HIM AT ONCE.
"I WAS FROZEN, A GHOST OBSERVING, BUT UNABLE TO AFFECT ANYTHING--
"--AS THE THING FLEW FROM MY HANDS, AND EXPLODED THROUGH THE WALL, PULLING CAGE BEHIND IT."
FSHOOOMM

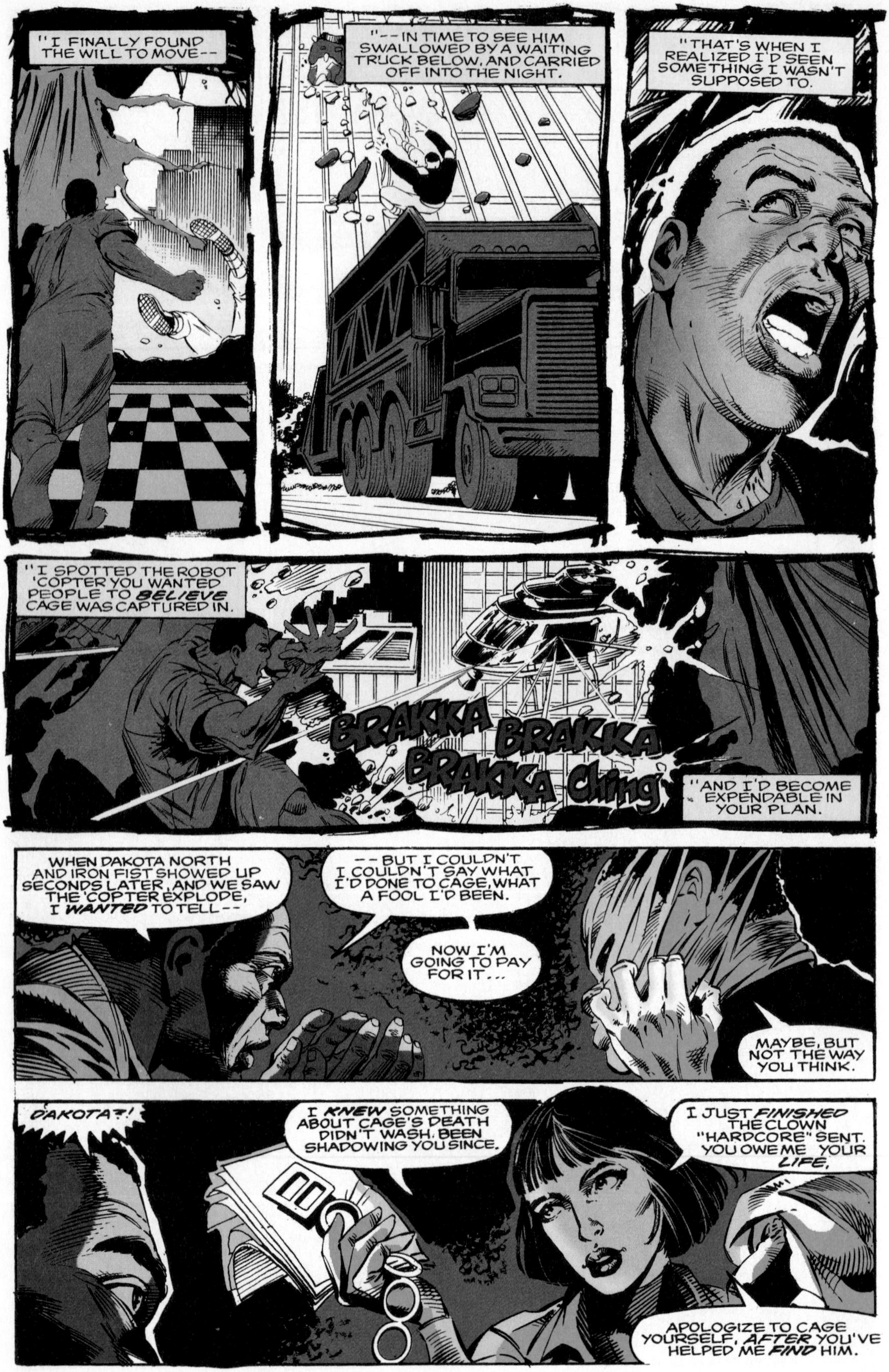
"I FINALLY FOUND THE WILL TO MOVE--
"--IN TIME TO SEE HIM SWALLOWED BY A WAITING TRUCK BELOW, AND CARRIED OFF INTO THE NIGHT.
"THAT'S WHEN I REALIZED I'D SEEN SOMETHING I WASN'T SUPPOSED TO.
"I SPOTTED THE ROBOT 'COPTER YOU WANTED PEOPLE TO BELIEVE CAGE WAS CAPTURED IN.
BRAKKA BRAKKA BRAKKA Ching
"AND I'D BECOME EXPENDABLE IN YOUR PLAN.
WHEN DAKOTA NORTH AND IRON FIST SHOWED UP SECONDS LATER, AND WE SAW THE 'COPTER EXPLODE, I WANTED TO TELL--
--BUT I COULDN'T I COULDN'T SAY WHAT I'D DONE TO CAGE, WHAT A FOOL I'D BEEN.
NOW I'M GOING TO PAY FOR IT...
MAYBE, BUT NOT THE WAY YOU THINK.
DAKOTA?!
I KNEW SOMETHING ABOUT CAGE'S DEATH DIDN'T WASH. BEEN SHADOWING YOU SINCE.
I JUST FINISHED THE CLOWN "HARDCORE" SENT. YOU OWE ME YOUR LIFE.
APOLOGIZE TO CAGE YOURSELF, AFTER YOU'VE HELPED ME FIND HIM.

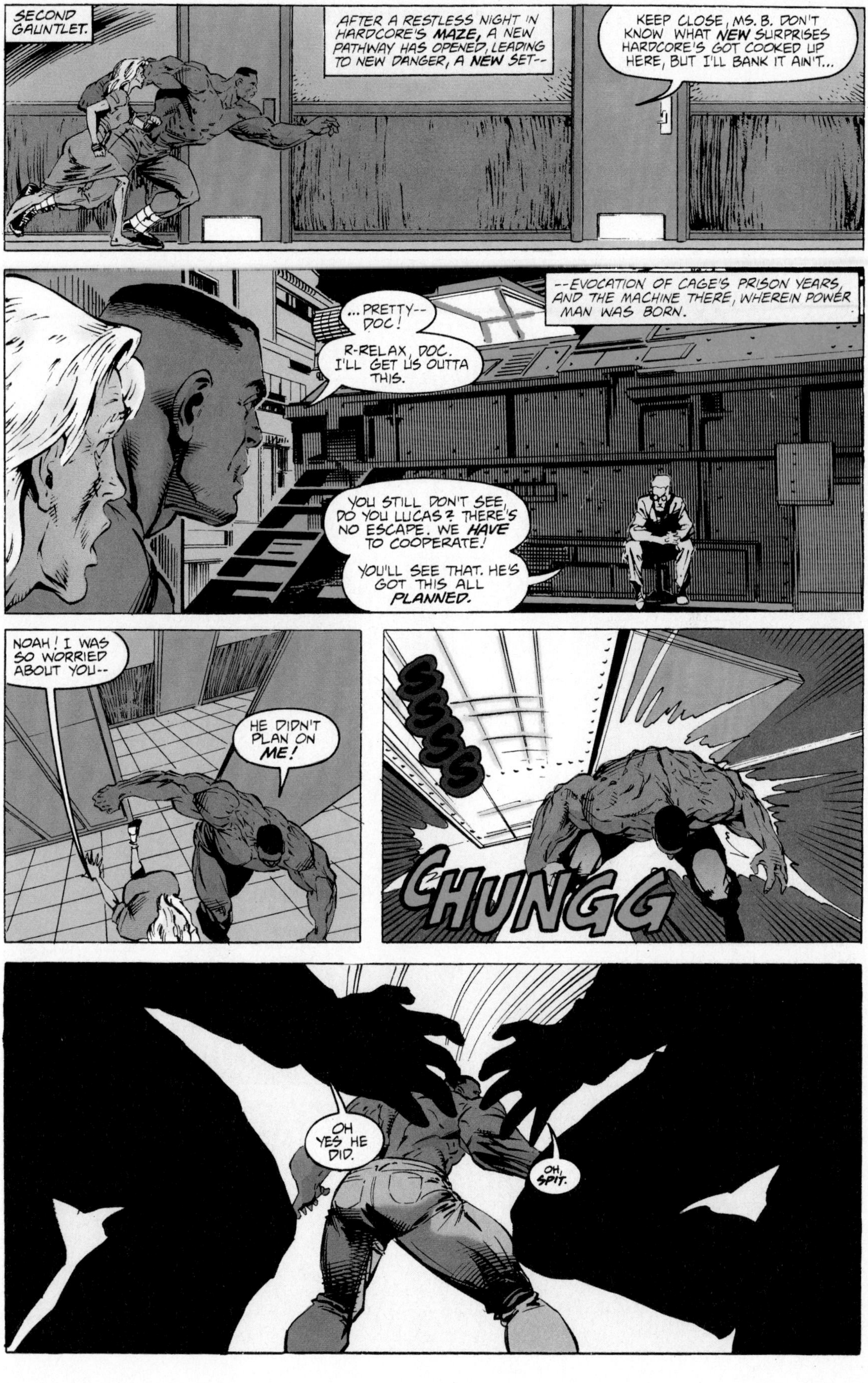
SECOND GAUNTLET.
AFTER A RESTLESS NIGHT IN HARDCORE'S MAZE, A NEW PATHWAY HAS OPENED, LEADING TO NEW DANGER, A NEW SET--
KEEP CLOSE, MS. B. DON'T KNOW WHAT NEW SURPRISES HARDCORE'S GOT COOKED UP HERE, BUT I'LL BANK IT AIN'T...
--EVOCATION OF CAGE'S PRISON YEARS, AND THE MACHINE THERE, WHEREIN POWER MAN WAS BORN.
...PRETTY-- DOC!
R-RELAX, DOC. I'LL GET US OUTTA THIS.
YOU STILL DON'T SEE, DO YOU LUCAS? THERE'S NO ESCAPE. WE HAVE TO COOPERATE!
YOU'LL SEE THAT. HE'S GOT THIS ALL PLANNED.
NOAH! I WAS SO WORRIED ABOUT YOU--
HE DIDN'T PLAN ON ME!
SSSS
CHUNGG
OH YES HE DID.
OH, SPIT.

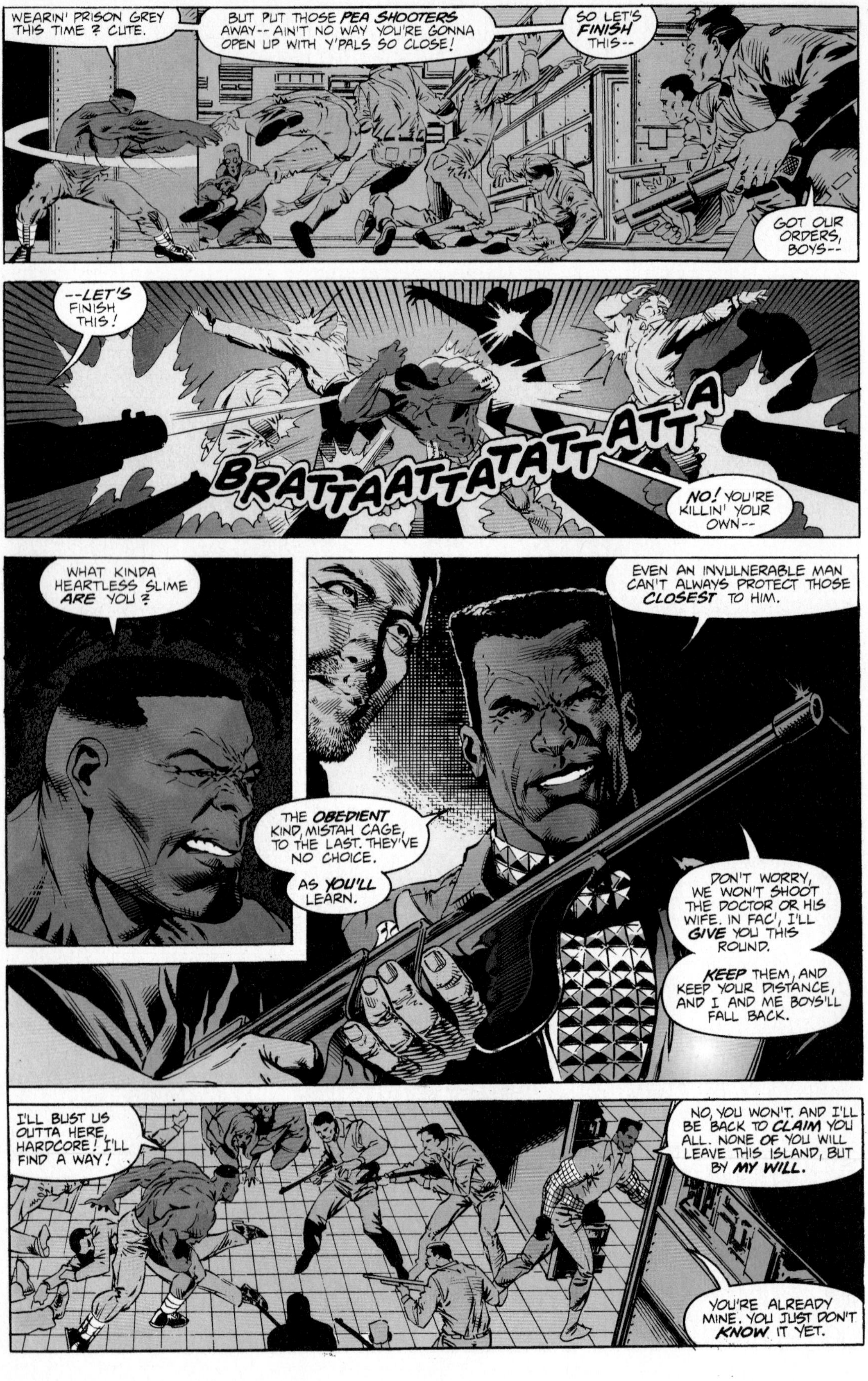
WEARIN' PRISON GREY THIS TIME ? CUTE.
BUT PUT THOSE PEA SHOOTERS AWAY-- AIN'T NO WAY YOU'RE GONNA OPEN UP WITH Y'PALS SO CLOSE!
SO LET'S FINISH THIS--
GOT OUR ORDERS, BOYS--
--LET'S FINISH THIS!
BRATTAATTATATTATTA
NO! YOU'RE KILLIN' YOUR OWN--
WHAT KINDA HEARTLESS SLIME ARE YOU ?
EVEN AN INVULNERABLE MAN CAN'T ALWAYS PROTECT THOSE CLOSEST TO HIM.
THE OBEDIENT KIND, MISTAH CAGE, TO THE LAST. THEY'VE NO CHOICE.
AS YOU'LL LEARN.
DON'T WORRY, WE WON'T SHOOT THE DOCTOR OR HIS WIFE. IN FAC', I'LL GIVE YOU THIS ROUND.
KEEP THEM, AND KEEP YOUR DISTANCE, AND I AND ME BOYS'LL FALL BACK.
I'LL BUST US OUTTA HERE, HARDCORE! I'LL FIND A WAY!
NO, YOU WON'T. AND I'LL BE BACK TO CLAIM YOU ALL. NONE OF YOU WILL LEAVE THIS ISLAND, BUT BY MY WILL.
YOU'RE ALREADY MINE. YOU JUST DON'T KNOW IT YET.

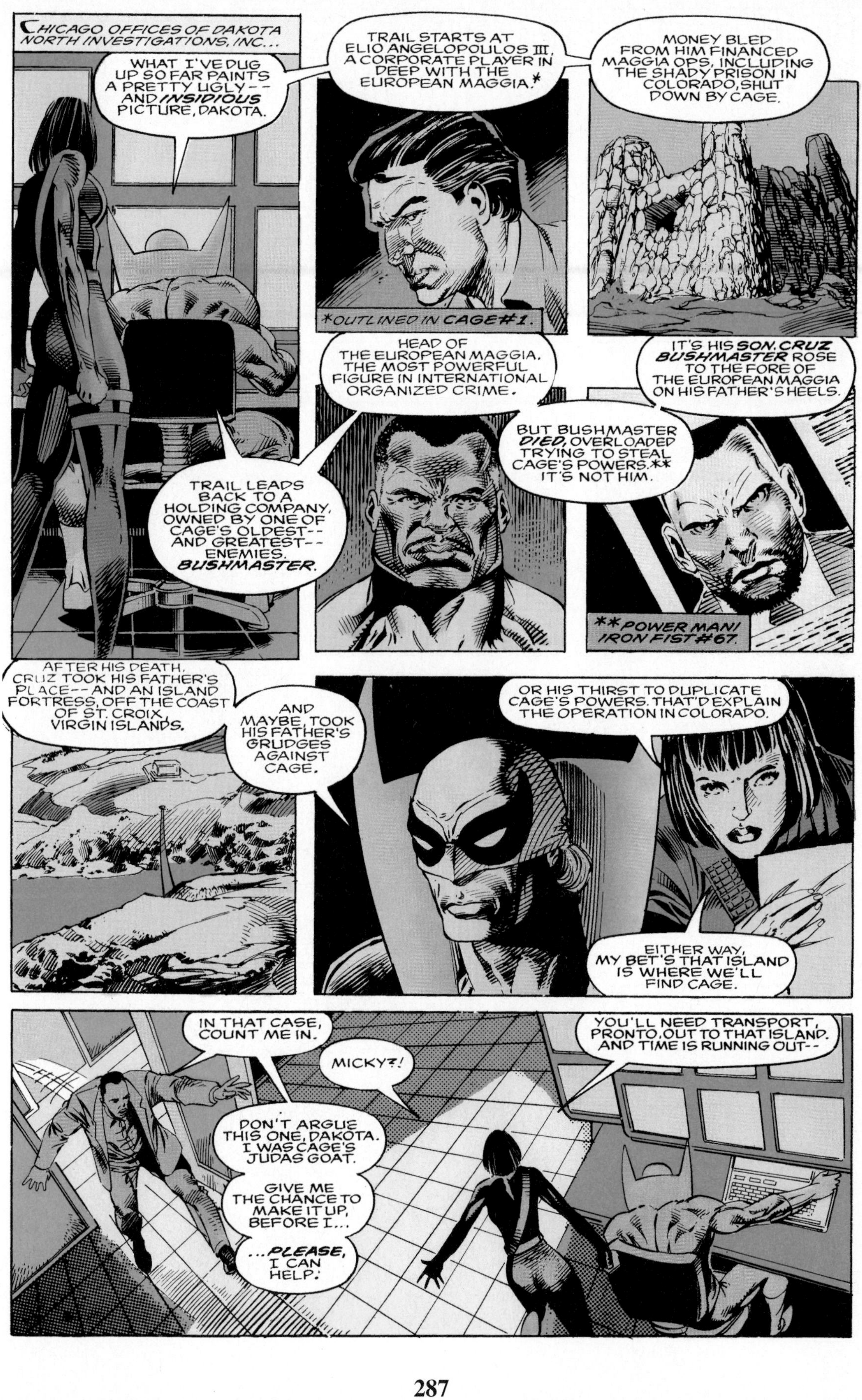
CHICAGO OFFICES OF DAKOTA NORTH INVESTIGATIONS, INC...
WHAT I'VE DUG UP SO FAR PAINTS A PRETTY UGLY-- AND INSIDIOUS PICTURE, DAKOTA.
TRAIL STARTS AT ELIO ANGELOPOULOS III, A CORPORATE PLAYER IN DEEP WITH THE EUROPEAN MAGGIA.*
*OUTLINED IN CAGE #1.
MONEY BLED FROM HIM FINANCED MAGGIA OPS, INCLUDING THE SHADY PRISON IN COLORADO, SHUT DOWN BY CAGE.
TRAIL LEADS BACK TO A HOLDING COMPANY, OWNED BY ONE OF CAGE'S OLDEST-- AND GREATEST-- ENEMIES. BUSHMASTER.
HEAD OF THE EUROPEAN MAGGIA. THE MOST POWERFUL FIGURE IN INTERNATIONAL ORGANIZED CRIME.
BUT BUSHMASTER DIED, OVERLOADED TRYING TO STEAL CAGE'S POWERS.** IT'S NOT HIM.
IT'S HIS SON. CRUZ BUSHMASTER ROSE TO THE FORE OF THE EUROPEAN MAGGIA ON HIS FATHER'S HEELS.
**POWER MAN/ IRON FIST #67.
AFTER HIS DEATH, CRUZ TOOK HIS FATHER'S PLACE-- AND AN ISLAND FORTRESS, OFF THE COAST OF ST. CROIX, VIRGIN ISLANDS.
AND MAYBE, TOOK HIS FATHER'S GRUDGES AGAINST CAGE.
OR HIS THIRST TO DUPLICATE CAGE'S POWERS. THAT'D EXPLAIN THE OPERATION IN COLORADO.
EITHER WAY, MY BET'S THAT ISLAND IS WHERE WE'LL FIND CAGE.
IN THAT CASE, COUNT ME IN.
MICKY?!
YOU'LL NEED TRANSPORT, PRONTO, OUT TO THAT ISLAND. AND TIME IS RUNNING OUT--
DON'T ARGUE THIS ONE, DAKOTA. I WAS CAGE'S JUDAS GOAT.
GIVE ME THE CHANCE TO MAKE IT UP, BEFORE I...
...PLEASE, I CAN HELP.

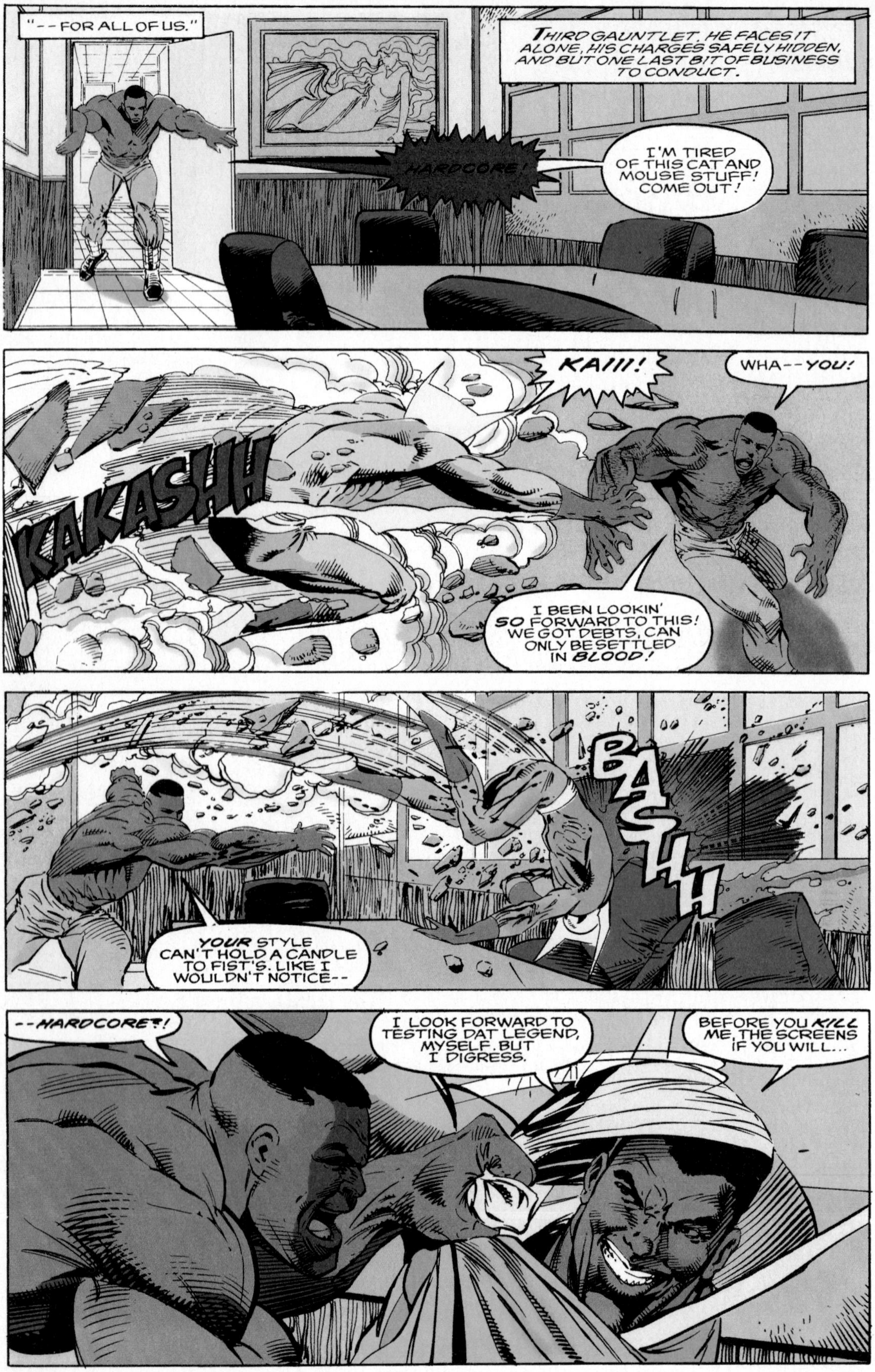
"--FOR ALL OF US."
THIRD GAUNTLET, HE FACES IT ALONE, HIS CHARGES SAFELY HIDDEN, AND BUT ONE LAST BIT OF BUSINESS TO CONDUCT.
HARDCORE!
I'M TIRED OF THIS CAT AND MOUSE STUFF! COME OUT!
KAIII!
WHA--YOU!
KAKASHH
I BEEN LOOKIN' SO FORWARD TO THIS! WE GOT DEBTS, CAN ONLY BE SETTLED IN BLOOD!
BASHH
YOUR STYLE CAN'T HOLD A CANDLE TO FIST'S. LIKE I WOULDN'T NOTICE--
--HARDCORE?!
I LOOK FORWARD TO TESTING DAT LEGEND, MYSELF. BUT I DIGRESS.
BEFORE YOU KILL ME, THE SCREENS IF YOU WILL...

--JUST WANTED TO TELL YOU HOW MUCH WE APPRECIATE YOUR HOSPITALITY, MR....."HARDCORE."

THE PLEASURE'S MINE, MR. LUCAS.

POPS?! YOUR LAST TWO HOSTAGES--

--ARE YOUR FATHER AND BROTHER, CAGE. BUT IS IT LIVE, OR--?

LET ME SHOW YOU A LITTLE TRICK, GENTLEMEN.

THIS TOY'S A MANRIKISA.

ANCIENT EASTERN FIGHTIN' TOOL.

SWIZZZ

SUHH!

THAT THING'S DEADLY! WHAT DID YOU DO TO THEM?!

A T'OUSAND USES-- NOT MANY OF DEM PLEASANT.

SUHH!

--BUT WE'VE ALL HABITS THAT DOOM US, EH?

SUHH!

CHOK

AND "EACH MAN KILLS THE TING HE LOVES," OSCAR WILDE.

HAHAHAHAHAHAAAHA

WHERE-ARE- THEY-HARDCORE!! HOW ARE THEY?

NO LONGER ON THE ISLAND, I ASSURE YOU, AND IN GOOD HEALT'.

THEIR REMAINING SO DEPENDS ON YOAUH ANSWER; WILL YOU SUBMIT?

YOU WIN, YOU #%*@.

"THE RACE IS NOT TO THE SWIFT, NOR THE BATTLE, TO THE STRONG." CHECK AND MATE, CAGE.

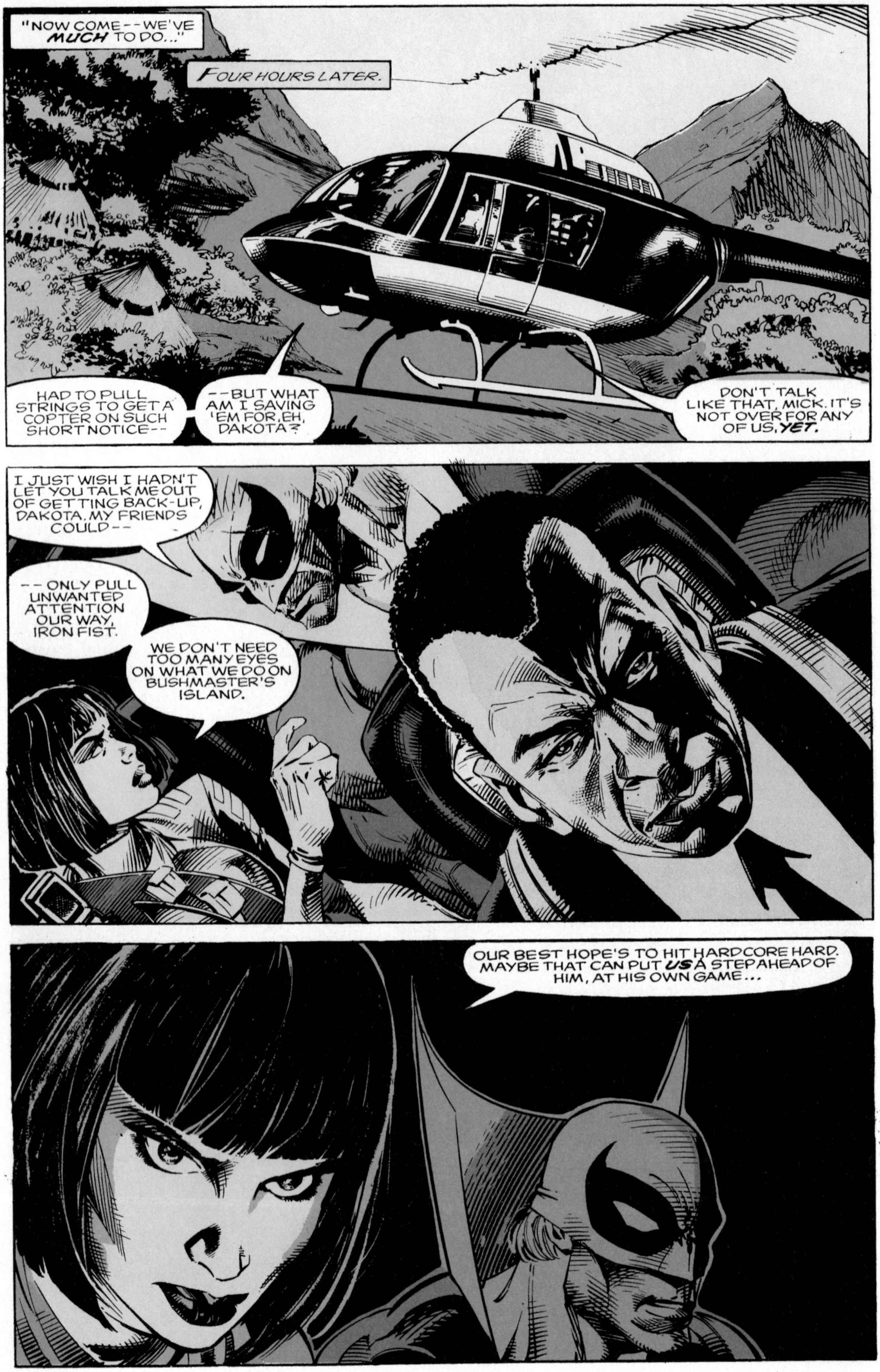
"NOW COME--WE'VE MUCH TO DO..."
FOUR HOURS LATER.
HAD TO PULL STRINGS TO GET A COPTER ON SUCH SHORT NOTICE--
--BUT WHAT AM I SAVING 'EM FOR, EH, DAKOTA?
DON'T TALK LIKE THAT, MICK. IT'S NOT OVER FOR ANY OF US, YET.
I JUST WISH I HADN'T LET YOU TALK ME OUT OF GETTING BACK-UP, DAKOTA. MY FRIENDS COULD--
--ONLY PULL UNWANTED ATTENTION OUR WAY, IRON FIST.
WE DON'T NEED TOO MANY EYES ON WHAT WE DO ON BUSHMASTER'S ISLAND.
OUR BEST HOPE'S TO HIT HARDCORE HARD. MAYBE THAT CAN PUT US A STEP AHEAD OF HIM, AT HIS OWN GAME...

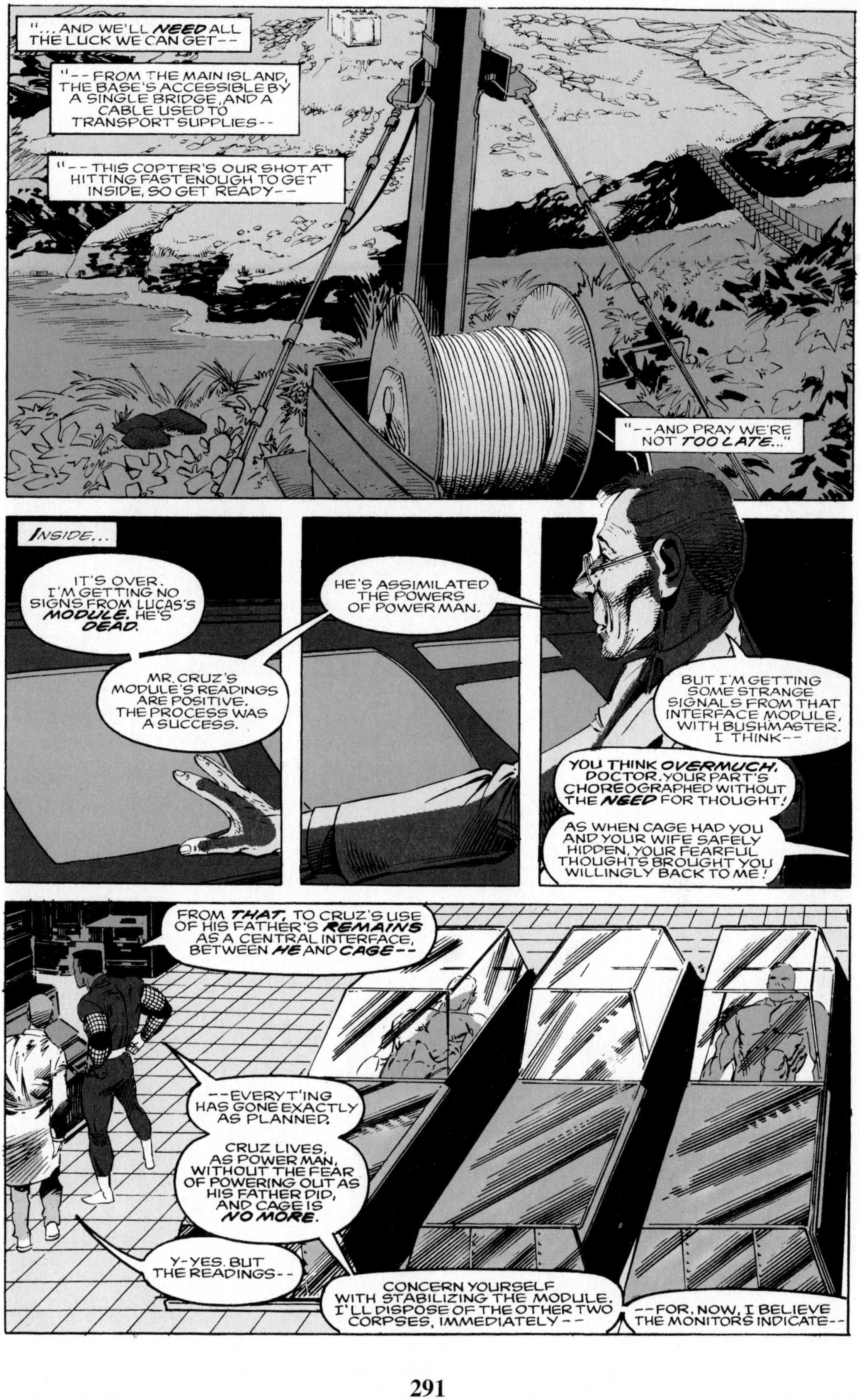
"...AND WE'LL NEED ALL THE LUCK WE CAN GET--
"--FROM THE MAIN ISLAND, THE BASE'S ACCESSIBLE BY A SINGLE BRIDGE, AND A CABLE USED TO TRANSPORT SUPPLIES--
"--THIS COPTER'S OUR SHOT AT HITTING FAST ENOUGH TO GET INSIDE, SO GET READY--
"--AND PRAY WE'RE NOT TOO LATE..."
INSIDE...
IT'S OVER. I'M GETTING NO SIGNS FROM LUCAS'S MODULE. HE'S DEAD.
MR. CRUZ'S MODULE'S READINGS ARE POSITIVE. THE PROCESS WAS A SUCCESS.
HE'S ASSIMILATED THE POWERS OF POWER MAN.
BUT I'M GETTING SOME STRANGE SIGNALS FROM THAT INTERFACE MODULE, WITH BUSHMASTER. I THINK--
YOU THINK OVERMUCH, DOCTOR. YOUR PART'S CHOREOGRAPHED WITHOUT THE NEED FOR THOUGHT!
AS WHEN CAGE HAD YOU AND YOUR WIFE SAFELY HIDDEN, YOUR FEARFUL THOUGHTS BROUGHT YOU WILLINGLY BACK TO ME!
FROM THAT, TO CRUZ'S USE OF HIS FATHER'S REMAINS AS A CENTRAL INTERFACE, BETWEEN HE AND CAGE--
--EVERYT'ING HAS GONE EXACTLY AS PLANNED.
CRUZ LIVES, AS POWER MAN, WITHOUT THE FEAR OF POWERING OUT AS HIS FATHER DID, AND CAGE IS NO MORE.
Y-YES. BUT THE READINGS--
CONCERN YOURSELF WITH STABILIZING THE MODULE. I'LL DISPOSE OF THE OTHER TWO CORPSES, IMMEDIATELY--
--FOR, NOW, I BELIEVE THE MONITORS INDICATE--

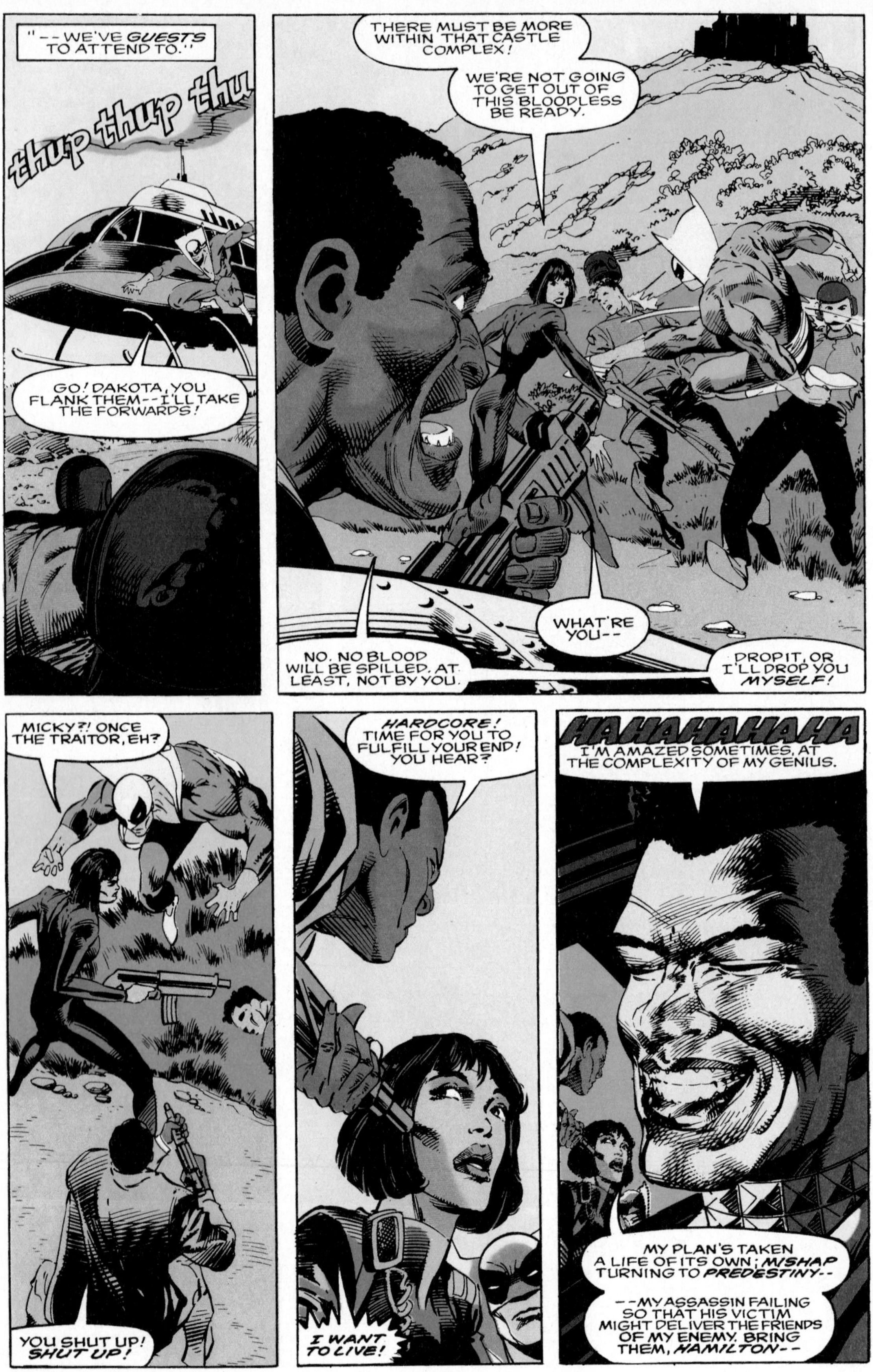
"--WE'VE GUESTS TO ATTEND TO."
thup thup thu
GO! DAKOTA, YOU FLANK THEM--I'LL TAKE THE FORWARDS!
THERE MUST BE MORE WITHIN THAT CASTLE COMPLEX!
WE'RE NOT GOING TO GET OUT OF THIS BLOODLESS BE READY.
WHAT'RE YOU--
NO. NO BLOOD WILL BE SPILLED. AT LEAST, NOT BY YOU.
DROP IT, OR I'LL DROP YOU MYSELF!
MICKY?! ONCE THE TRAITOR, EH?
YOU SHUT UP! SHUT UP!
HARDCORE! TIME FOR YOU TO FULFILL YOUR END! YOU HEAR?
I WANT TO LIVE!
HAHAHAHAHAHA
I'M AMAZED SOMETIMES, AT THE COMPLEXITY OF MY GENIUS.
MY PLAN'S TAKEN A LIFE OF ITS OWN; MISHAP TURNING TO PREDESTINY--
--MY ASSASSIN FAILING SO THAT HIS VICTIM MIGHT DELIVER THE FRIENDS OF MY ENEMY. BRING THEM, HAMILTON--

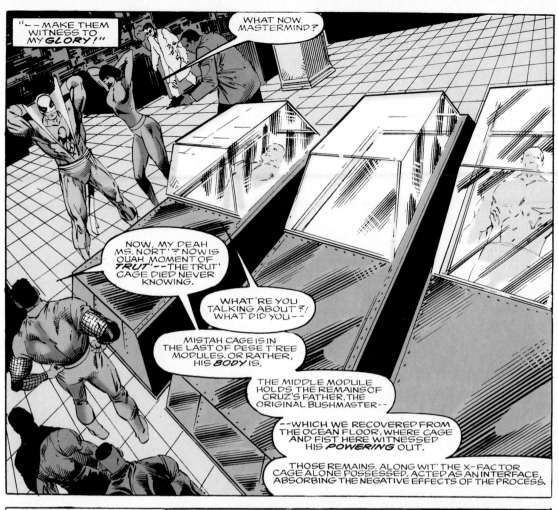

"— MAKE THEM WITNESS TO MY *GLORY!*"

WHAT NOW, MASTERMIND?

NOW, MY DEAH MS. NORT'? NOW IS OUAH MOMENT OF *TRUT*'--THE TRUT' CAGE DIED NEVER KNOWING.

WHAT'RE YOU TALKING ABOUT?! WHAT DID YOU--

MISTAH CAGE IS IN THE LAST OF DESE T'REE MODULES. OR RATHER, HIS *BODY* IS.

THE MIDDLE MODULE HOLDS THE REMAINS OF CRUZ'S FATHER, THE ORIGINAL BUSHMASTER--

--WHICH WE RECOVERED FROM THE OCEAN FLOOR, WHERE CAGE AND FIST HERE WITNESSED HIS *POWERING* OUT.

THOSE REMAINS, ALONG WIT' THE X-FACTOR CAGE ALONE POSSESSED, ACTED AS AN INTERFACE, ABSORBING THE NEGATIVE EFFECTS OF THE PROCESS.

THE KEY WAS MAKING CAGE A WILLING VOLUNTEER. AND WE SUCCEEDED.

THOUGH IN THE END, "SPIRIT WAS WILLING, BUT THE FLESH WAS WEAK."

AND I'M SURE, MR. HAMILTON, THAT WHAT WE'VE LEARNED FROM THIS PROCESS *CAN* BE APPLIED TO YOUR OWN MALADIES--

--AFTER YOU'VE PROVEN YOUR GOOD FAIT' BY ELIMINATING THESE TWO *FOOLS?!*

MICKY, *NOW!*

YOU'RE THE SUCKER, HARDCORE, THINKING ME THE STILL WEAK LOSER YOU ONCE CONTROLLED!

YOU CAN'T SAVE ME BUT THERE'RE SOME THINGS WORTH DYING *FOR!*

click

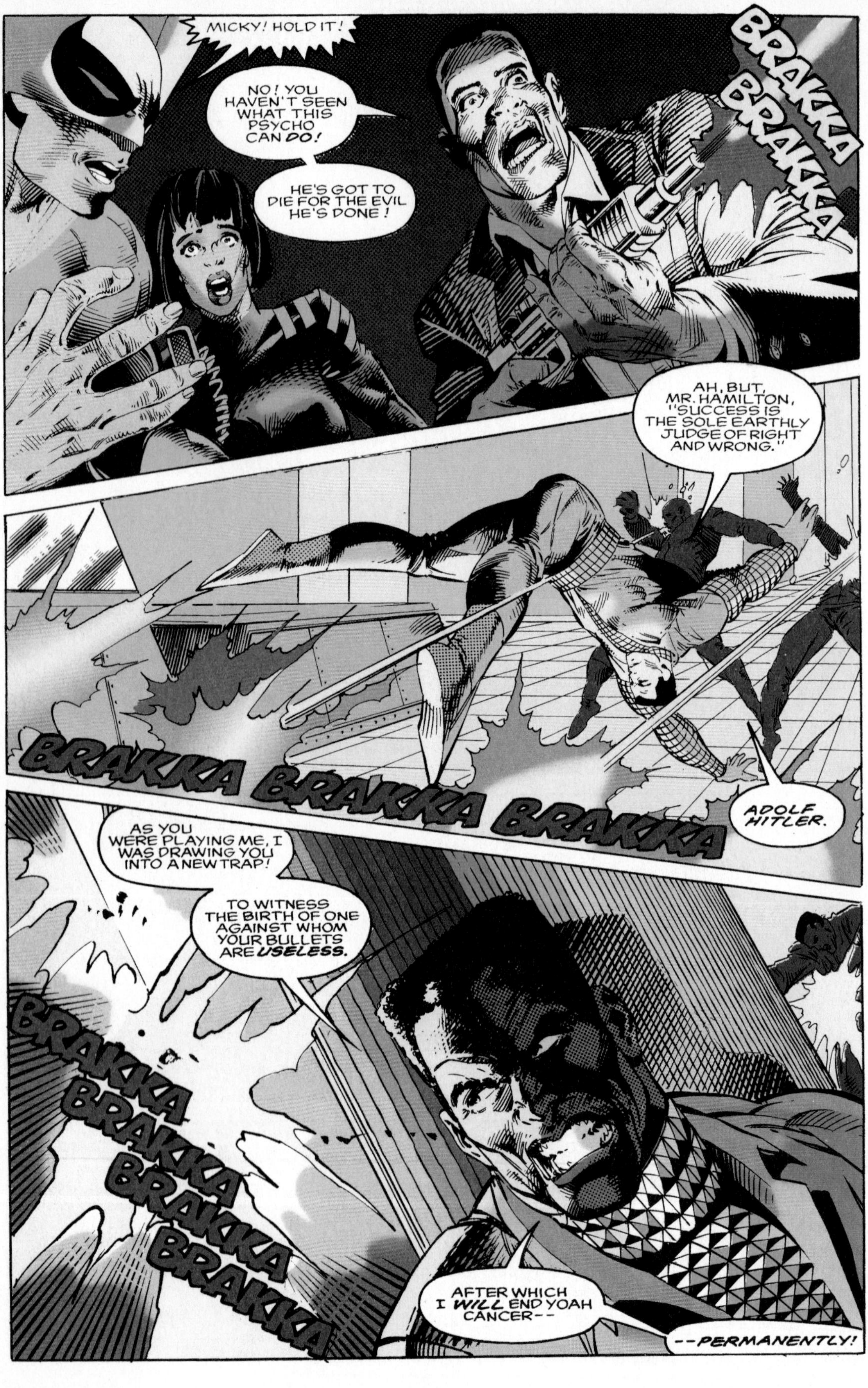
MICKY! HOLD IT!
NO! YOU HAVEN'T SEEN WHAT THIS PSYCHO CAN DO!
HE'S GOT TO DIE FOR THE EVIL HE'S DONE!
BRAKKA BRAKKA BRAKKA
AH, BUT, MR. HAMILTON, "SUCCESS IS THE SOLE EARTHLY JUDGE OF RIGHT AND WRONG."
BRAKKA BRAKKA BRAKKA
ADOLF HITLER.
AS YOU WERE PLAYING ME, I WAS DRAWING YOU INTO A NEW TRAP!
TO WITNESS THE BIRTH OF ONE AGAINST WHOM YOUR BULLETS ARE USELESS.
BRAKKA BRAKKA BRAKKA BRAKKA BRAKKA
AFTER WHICH I WILL END YOAH CANCER--
--PERMANENTLY!

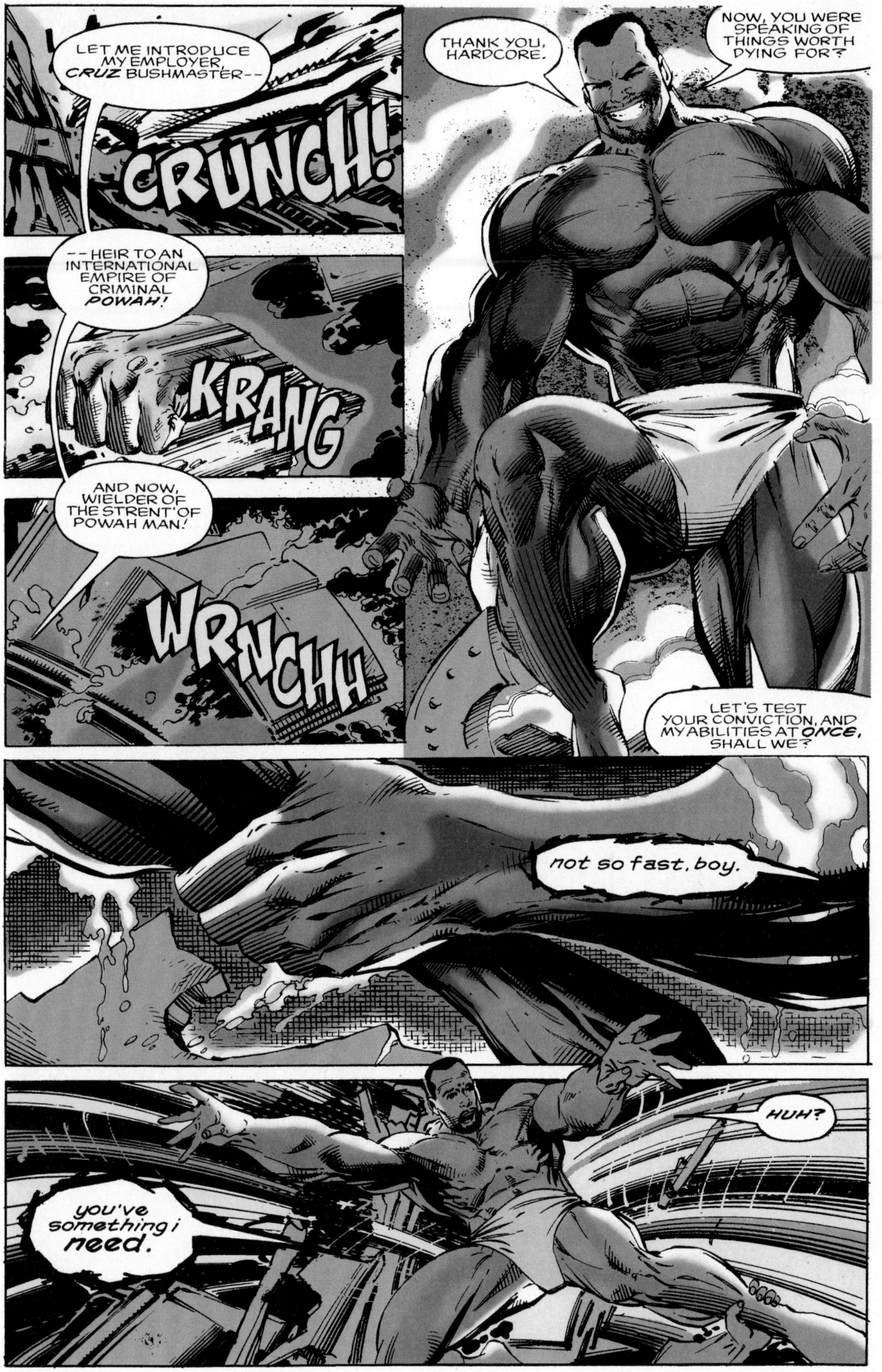
LET ME INTRODUCE MY EMPLOYER, CRUZ BUSHMASTER--
CRUNCH!
--HEIR TO AN INTERNATIONAL EMPIRE OF CRIMINAL POWAH!
KRANG
AND NOW, WIELDER OF THE STRENT'OF POWAH MAN!
WRNCHH
THANK YOU, HARDCORE.
NOW, YOU WERE SPEAKING OF THINGS WORTH DYING FOR?
LET'S TEST YOUR CONVICTION, AND MY ABILITIES AT ONCE, SHALL WE?
not so fast, boy.
HUH?
you've something i need.

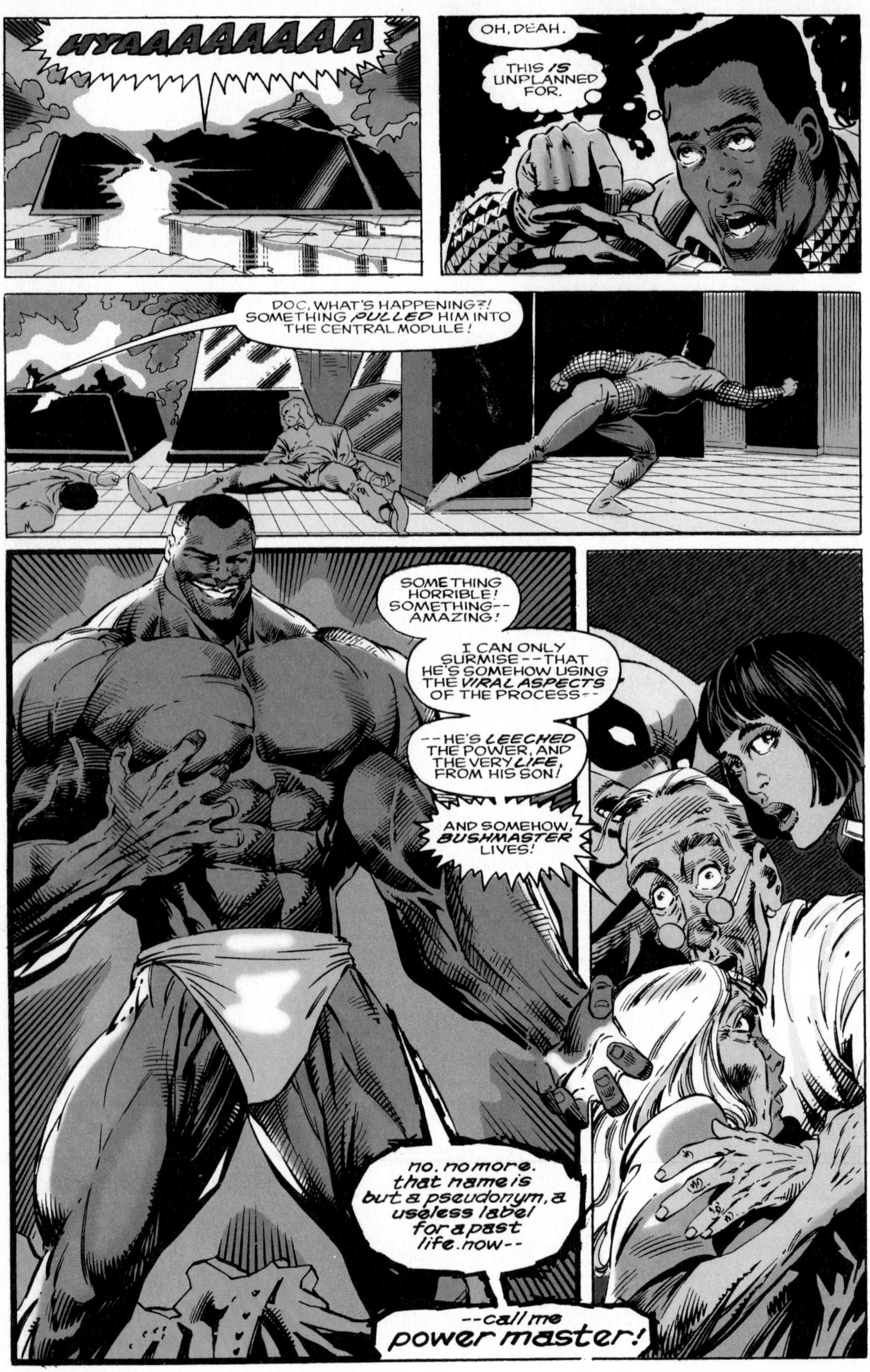
HYAAAAAAAAA
OH, DEAH.
THIS IS UNPLANNED FOR.
DOC, WHAT'S HAPPENING?! SOMETHING PULLED HIM INTO THE CENTRAL MODULE!
SOMETHING HORRIBLE! SOMETHING-- AMAZING!
I CAN ONLY SURMISE--THAT HE'S SOMEHOW USING THE VIRAL ASPECTS OF THE PROCESS--
--HE'S LEECHED THE POWER, AND THE VERY LIFE, FROM HIS SON!
AND SOMEHOW, BUSHMASTER LIVES!
no. no more. that name is but a pseudonym, a useless label for a past life. now--
--call me power master!

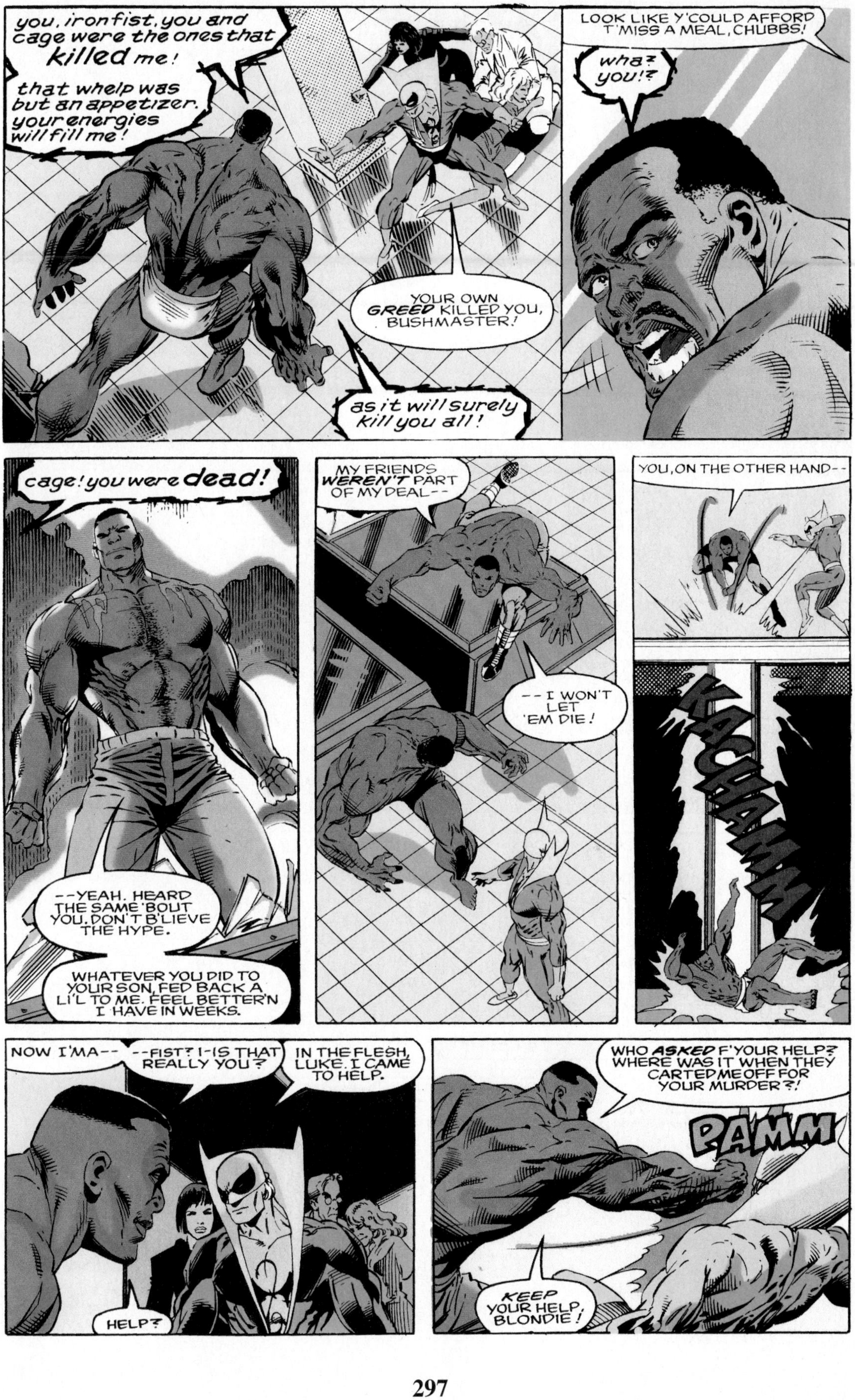
you, iron fist, you and cage were the ones that killed me!
that whelp was but an appetizer. your energies will fill me!
YOUR OWN GREED KILLED YOU, BUSHMASTER!
as it will surely kill you all!
LOOK LIKE Y'COULD AFFORD T'MISS A MEAL, CHUBBS!
wha? you!?
cage! you were dead!
--YEAH. HEARD THE SAME 'BOUT YOU. DON'T B'LIEVE THE HYPE.
WHATEVER YOU DID TO YOUR SON, FED BACK A LI'L TO ME. FEEL BETTER'N I HAVE IN WEEKS.
MY FRIENDS WEREN'T PART OF MY DEAL--
--I WON'T LET 'EM DIE!
YOU, ON THE OTHER HAND--
KACHAMM
NOW I'MA--
--FIST? I-IS THAT REALLY YOU?
IN THE FLESH, LUKE. I CAME TO HELP.
HELP?
WHO ASKED F'YOUR HELP? WHERE WAS IT WHEN THEY CARTED ME OFF FOR YOUR MURDER?!
PAMM
KEEP YOUR HELP, BLONDIE!

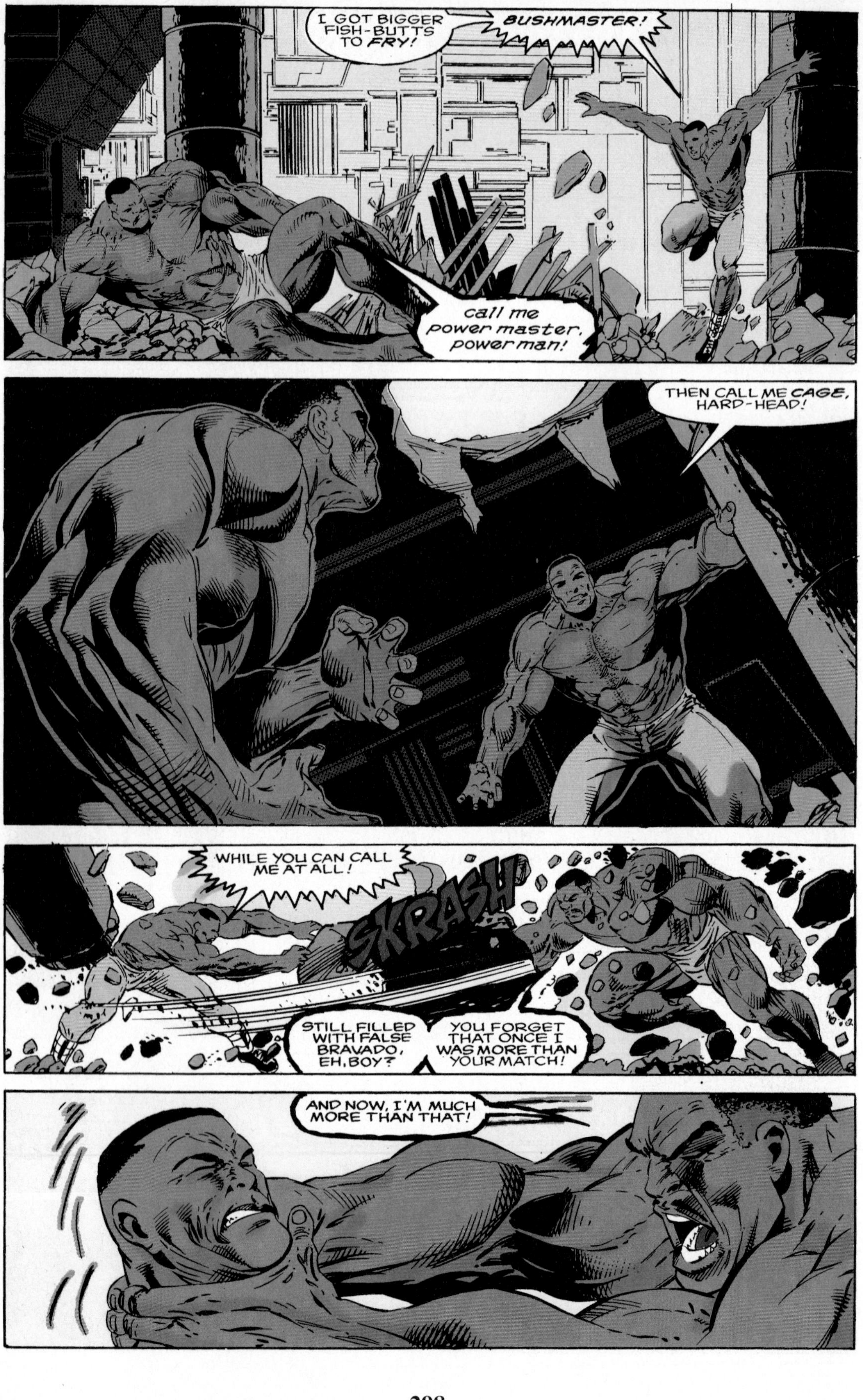
I GOT BIGGER FISH-BUTTS TO FRY!
BUSHMASTER!
call me power master, power man!
THEN CALL ME CAGE, HARD-HEAD!
WHILE YOU CAN CALL ME AT ALL!
SKRASH
STILL FILLED WITH FALSE BRAVADO, EH, BOY?
YOU FORGET THAT ONCE I WAS MORE THAN YOUR MATCH!
AND NOW, I'M MUCH MORE THAN THAT!

CAGE, DAKOTA IS TAKING THE BURNSTIEIN'S OUT THE MAIN GATE. IT'S ONLY *YOU* AND *ME* NOW...

...JUST LIKE OLD TIMES!

F-FIST--GET THE H--OUT!

NO!

arrrgh!

TAMM

fine. you want it first, i'll oblige.

WHHHH

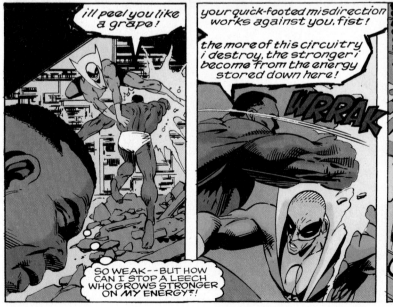

i'll peel you like a grape!

SO WEAK--BUT HOW CAN I STOP A LEECH WHO GROWS STRONGER ON *MY* ENERGY?!

your quick-footed misdirection works against you, fist!

the more of this circuitry i destroy, the stronger i become from the energy stored down here!

WRRAK

sooner or later, you'll be mine!

ENERGY. THAT'S IT.

CHKZZZAKK

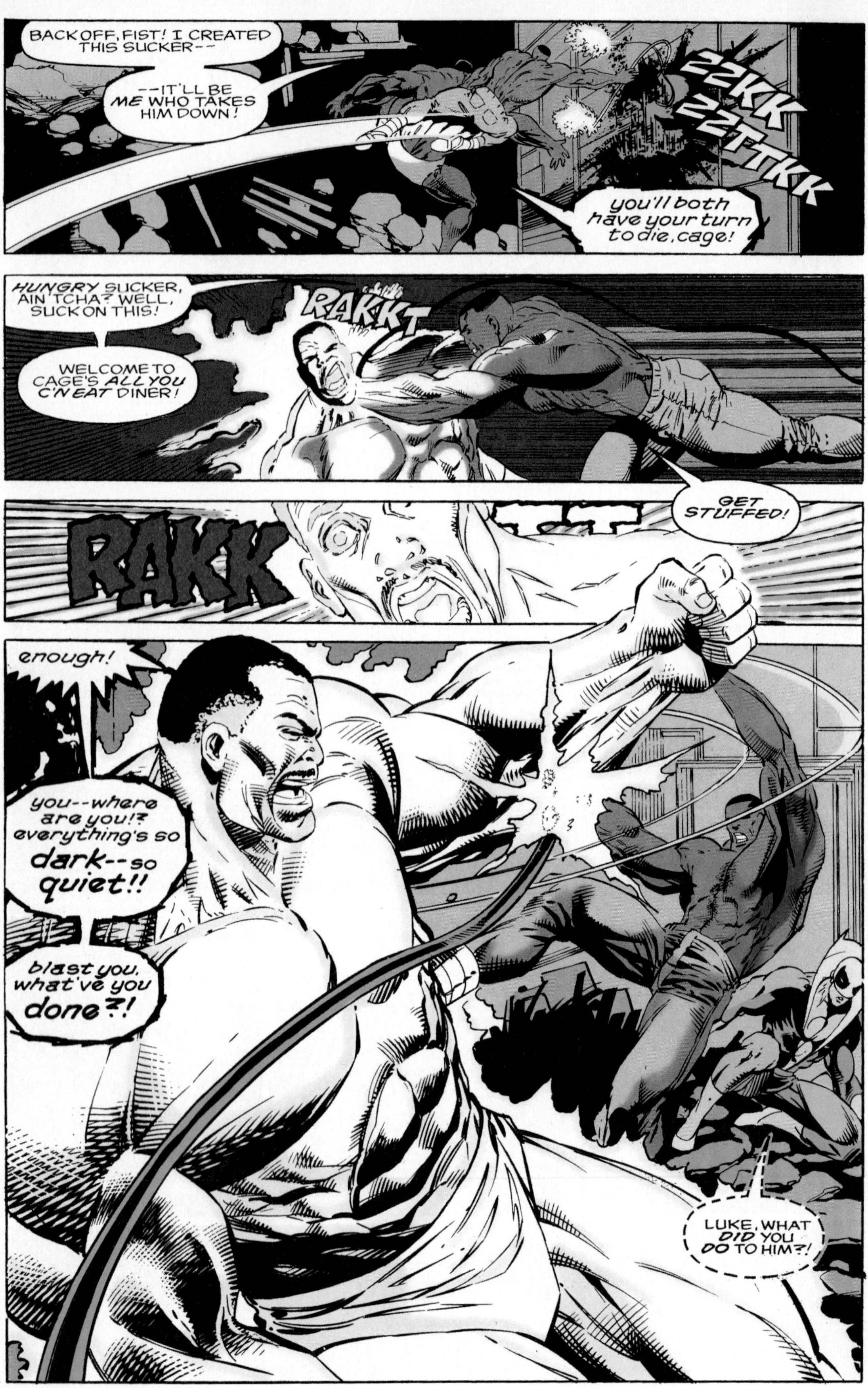
BACK OFF, FIST! I CREATED THIS SUCKER--
--IT'LL BE ME WHO TAKES HIM DOWN!
ZZKK ZZTTKK
you'll both have your turn to die, cage!
HUNGRY SUCKER, AIN'TCHA? WELL, SUCK ON THIS!
RAKKT
WELCOME TO CAGE'S ALL YOU C'N EAT DINER!
RAKK
GET STUFFED!
enough!
you--where are you!? everything's so dark--so quiet!!
blast you. what've you done?!
LUKE, WHAT DID YOU DO TO HIM?!

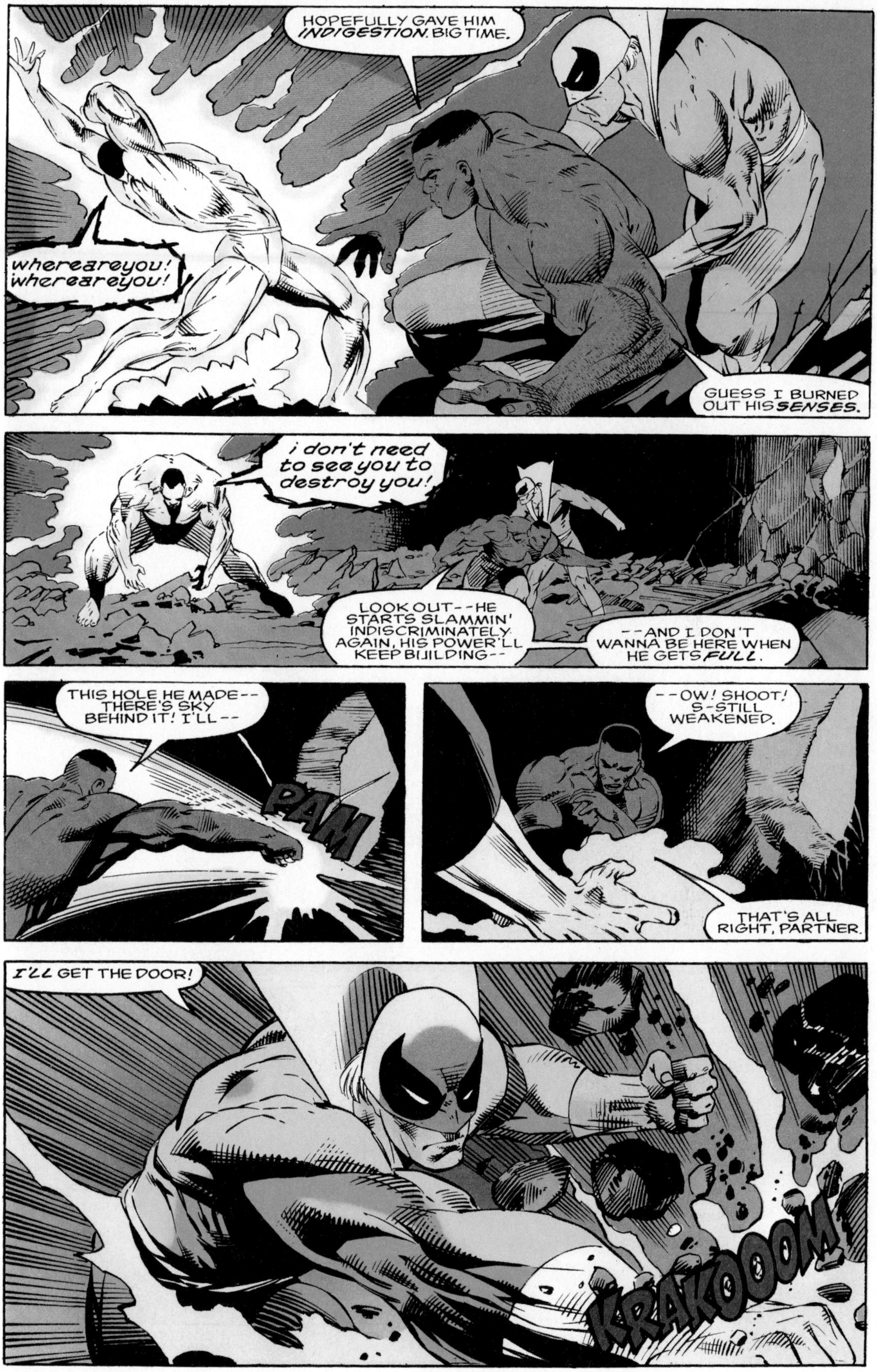
HOPEFULLY GAVE HIM INDIGESTION. BIG TIME.
whereareyou! whereareyou!
GUESS I BURNED OUT HIS SENSES.
i don't need to see you to destroy you!
LOOK OUT--HE STARTS SLAMMIN' INDISCRIMINATELY AGAIN, HIS POWER'LL KEEP BIJILDING--
--AND I DON'T WANNA BE HERE WHEN HE GETS FULL.
THIS HOLE HE MADE--THERE'S SKY BEHIND IT! I'LL--
PAM
--OW! SHOOT! S-STILL WEAKENED.
THAT'S ALL RIGHT, PARTNER.
I'LL GET THE DOOR!
KRAKOOOM

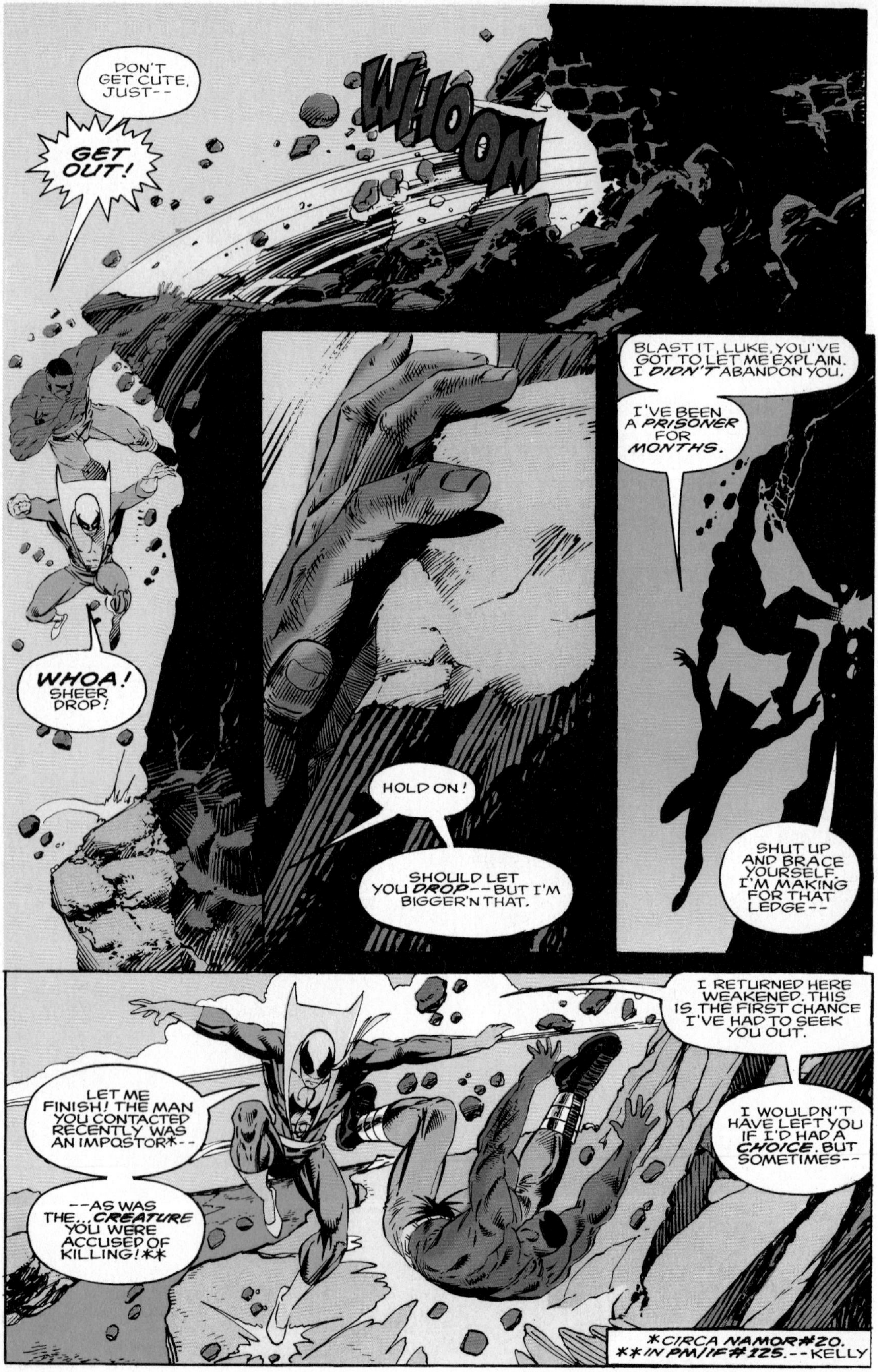
DON'T GET CUTE, JUST--
GET OUT!
WHOOM
WHOA! SHEER DROP!
BLAST IT, LUKE, YOU'VE GOT TO LET ME EXPLAIN. I DIDN'T ABANDON YOU.
I'VE BEEN A PRISONER FOR MONTHS.
HOLD ON!
SHOULD LET YOU DROP--BUT I'M BIGGER'N THAT.
SHUT UP AND BRACE YOURSELF. I'M MAKING FOR THAT LEDGE--
I RETURNED HERE WEAKENED. THIS IS THE FIRST CHANCE I'VE HAD TO SEEK YOU OUT.
I WOULDN'T HAVE LEFT YOU IF I'D HAD A CHOICE. BUT SOMETIMES--
LET ME FINISH! THE MAN YOU CONTACTED RECENTLY WAS AN IMPOSTOR*--
--AS WAS THE... CREATURE YOU WERE ACCUSED OF KILLING!**
*CIRCA NAMOR #20.
**IN PM/IF #125.--KELLY

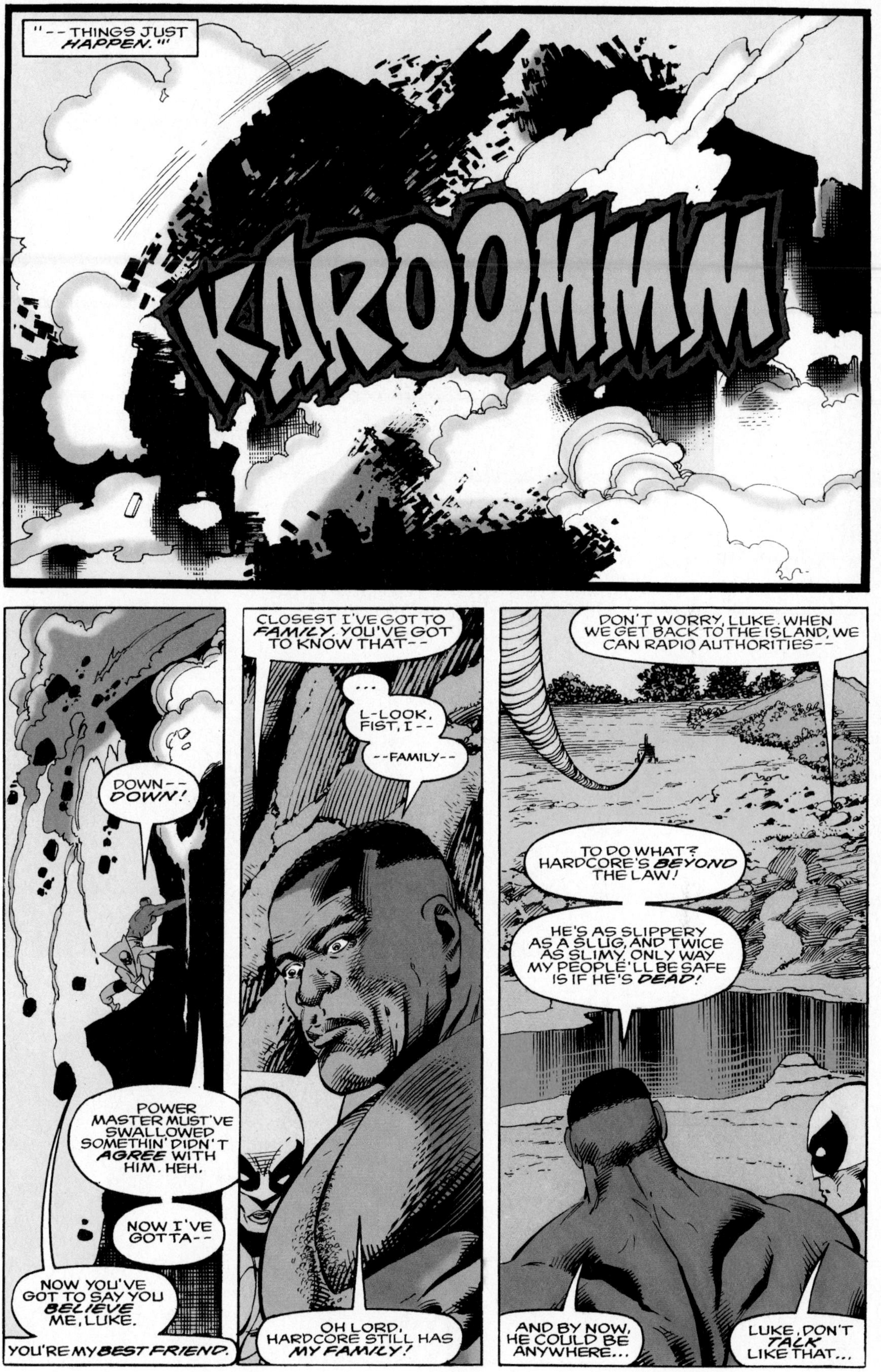
"--THINGS JUST HAPPEN.'"
KAROOMMM
DOWN-- DOWN!
POWER MASTER MUST'VE SWALLOWED SOMETHIN' DIDN'T AGREE WITH HIM. HEH.
NOW I'VE GOTTA--
NOW YOU'VE GOT TO SAY YOU BELIEVE ME, LUKE.
YOU'RE MY BEST FRIEND.
CLOSEST I'VE GOT TO FAMILY. YOU'VE GOT TO KNOW THAT--
...
L-LOOK, FIST, I--
--FAMILY--
OH LORD, HARDCORE STILL HAS MY FAMILY!
DON'T WORRY, LUKE. WHEN WE GET BACK TO THE ISLAND, WE CAN RADIO AUTHORITIES--
TO DO WHAT? HARDCORE'S BEYOND THE LAW!
HE'S AS SLIPPERY AS A SLUG, AND TWICE AS SLIMY. ONLY WAY MY PEOPLE'LL BE SAFE IS IF HE'S DEAD!
AND BY NOW, HE COULD BE ANYWHERE...
LUKE, DON'T TALK LIKE THAT...

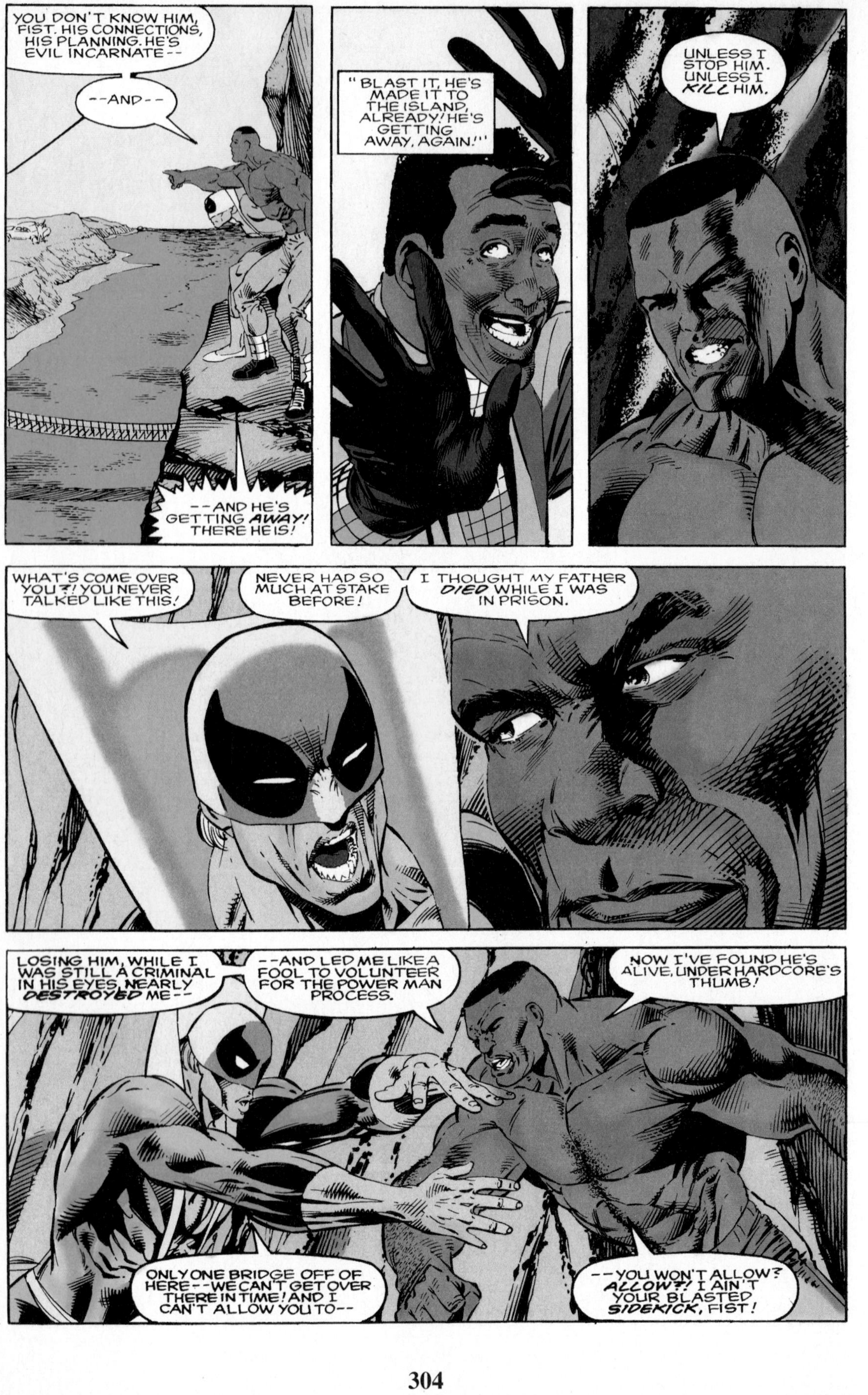
YOU DON'T KNOW HIM, FIST. HIS CONNECTIONS, HIS PLANNING. HE'S EVIL INCARNATE--
--AND--
--AND HE'S GETTING AWAY! THERE HE IS!
"BLAST IT, HE'S MADE IT TO THE ISLAND, ALREADY! HE'S GETTING AWAY, AGAIN!"
UNLESS I STOP HIM. UNLESS I KILL HIM.
WHAT'S COME OVER YOU?! YOU NEVER TALKED LIKE THIS!
NEVER HAD SO MUCH AT STAKE BEFORE!
I THOUGHT MY FATHER DIED WHILE I WAS IN PRISON.
LOSING HIM, WHILE I WAS STILL A CRIMINAL IN HIS EYES, NEARLY DESTROYED ME--
--AND LED ME LIKE A FOOL TO VOLUNTEER FOR THE POWER MAN PROCESS.
NOW I'VE FOUND HE'S ALIVE, UNDER HARDCORE'S THUMB!
ONLY ONE BRIDGE OFF OF HERE--WE CAN'T GET OVER THERE IN TIME! AND I CAN'T ALLOW YOU TO--
--YOU WON'T ALLOW? ALLOW?! I AIN'T YOUR BLASTED SIDEKICK, FIST!

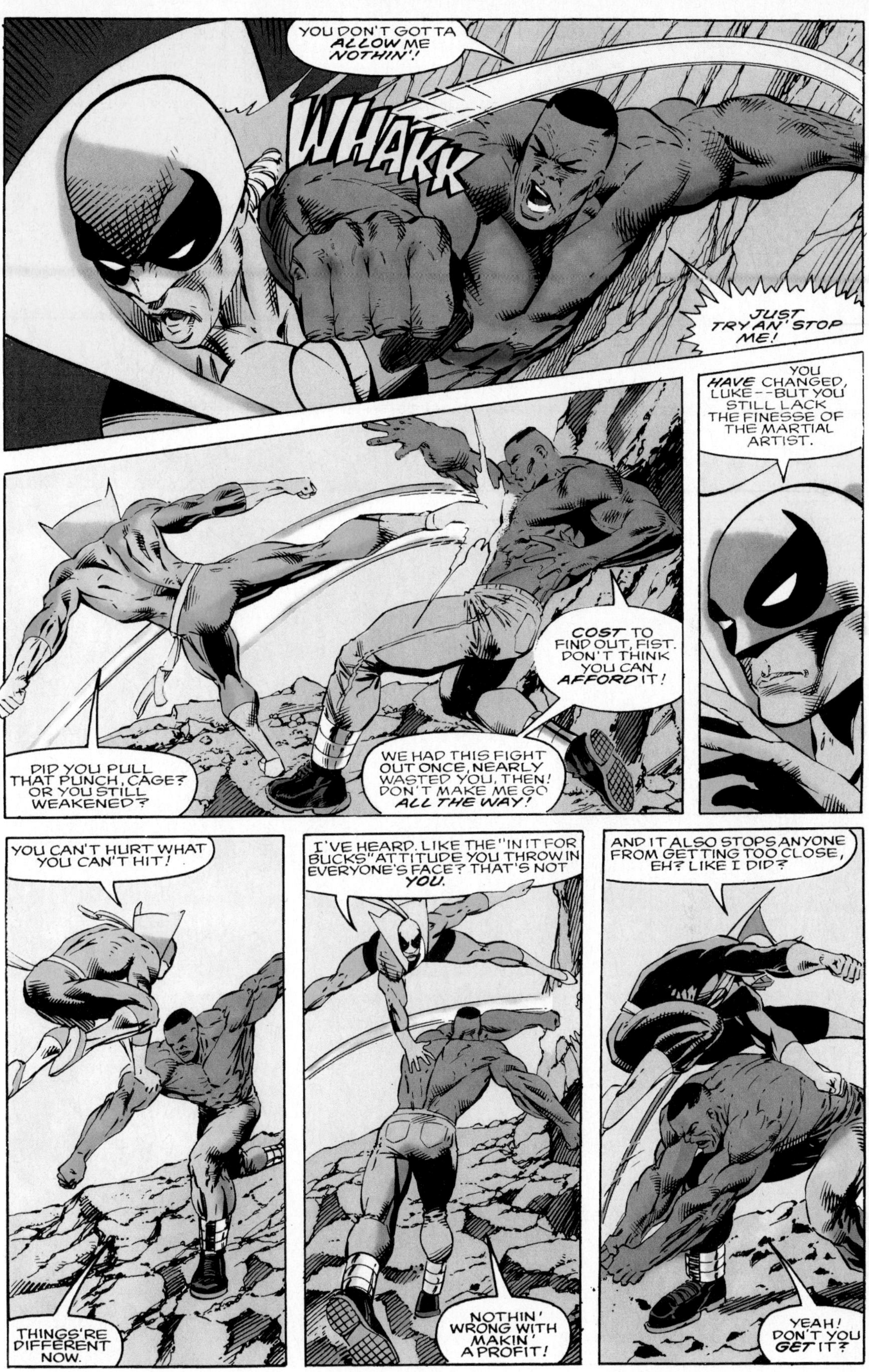
YOU DON'T GOTTA ALLOW ME NOTHIN'!
WHAKK
JUST TRY AN' STOP ME!
DID YOU PULL THAT PUNCH, CAGE? OR YOU STILL WEAKENED?
WE HAD THIS FIGHT OUT ONCE, NEARLY WASTED YOU, THEN! DON'T MAKE ME GO ALL THE WAY!
COST TO FIND OUT, FIST. DON'T THINK YOU CAN AFFORD IT!
YOU HAVE CHANGED, LUKE--BUT YOU STILL LACK THE FINESSE OF THE MARTIAL ARTIST.
YOU CAN'T HURT WHAT YOU CAN'T HIT!
THINGS'RE DIFFERENT NOW.
I'VE HEARD. LIKE THE "IN IT FOR BUCKS" ATTITUDE YOU THROW IN EVERYONE'S FACE? THAT'S NOT YOU.
NOTHIN' WRONG WITH MAKIN' A PROFIT!
AND IT ALSO STOPS ANYONE FROM GETTING TOO CLOSE, EH? LIKE I DID?
YEAH! DON'T YOU GET IT?

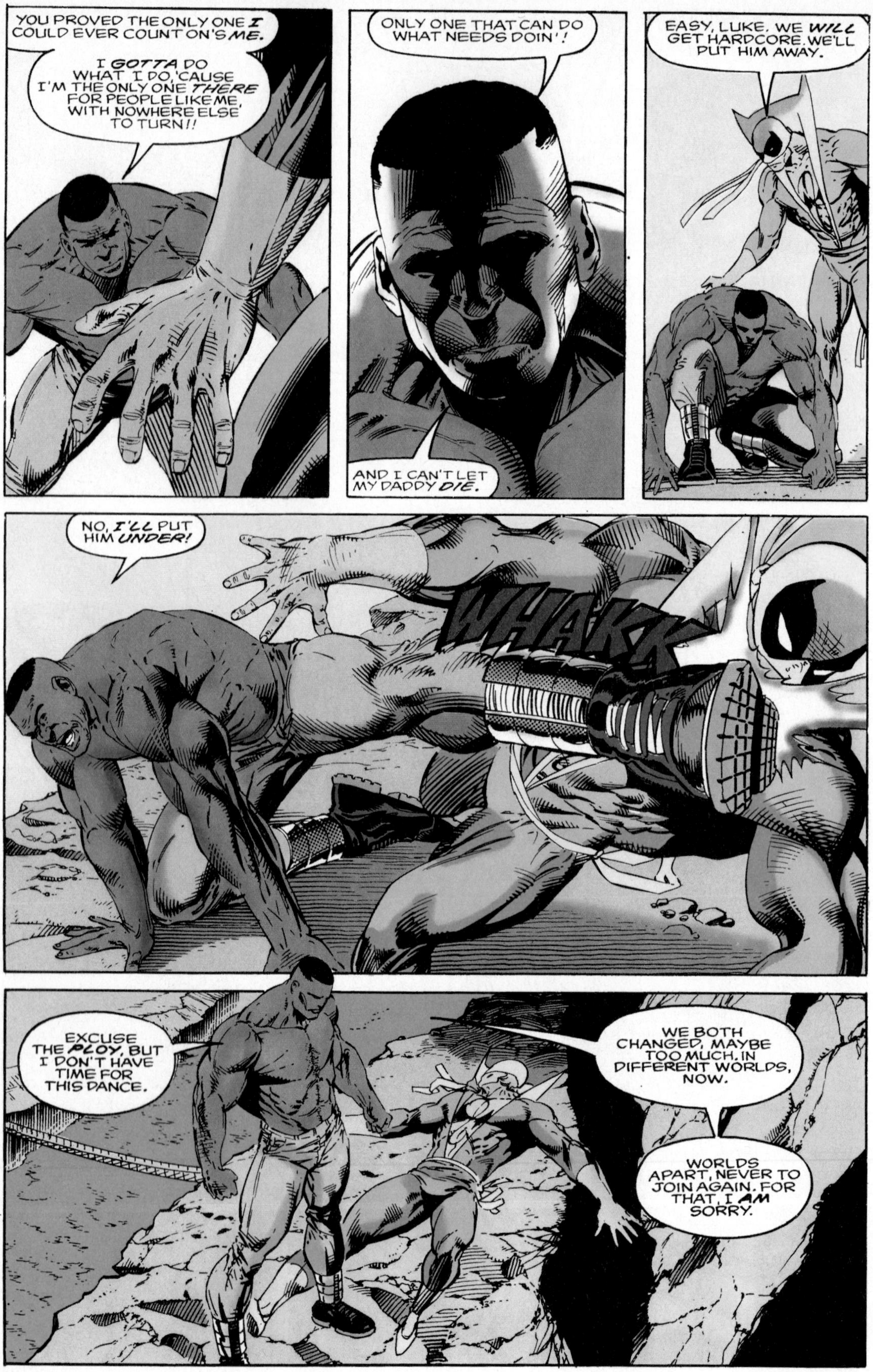
YOU PROVED THE ONLY ONE I COULD EVER COUNT ON'S ME.
I GOTTA DO WHAT I DO, 'CAUSE I'M THE ONLY ONE THERE FOR PEOPLE LIKE ME, WITH NOWHERE ELSE TO TURN!!
ONLY ONE THAT CAN DO WHAT NEEDS DOIN'!
AND I CAN'T LET MY DADDY DIE.
EASY, LUKE. WE WILL GET HARDCORE. WE'LL PUT HIM AWAY.
NO, I'LL PUT HIM UNDER!
WHAKK
EXCUSE THE PLOY, BUT I DON'T HAVE TIME FOR THIS DANCE.
WE BOTH CHANGED, MAYBE TOO MUCH. IN DIFFERENT WORLDS, NOW.
WORLDS APART, NEVER TO JOIN AGAIN. FOR THAT, I AM SORRY.

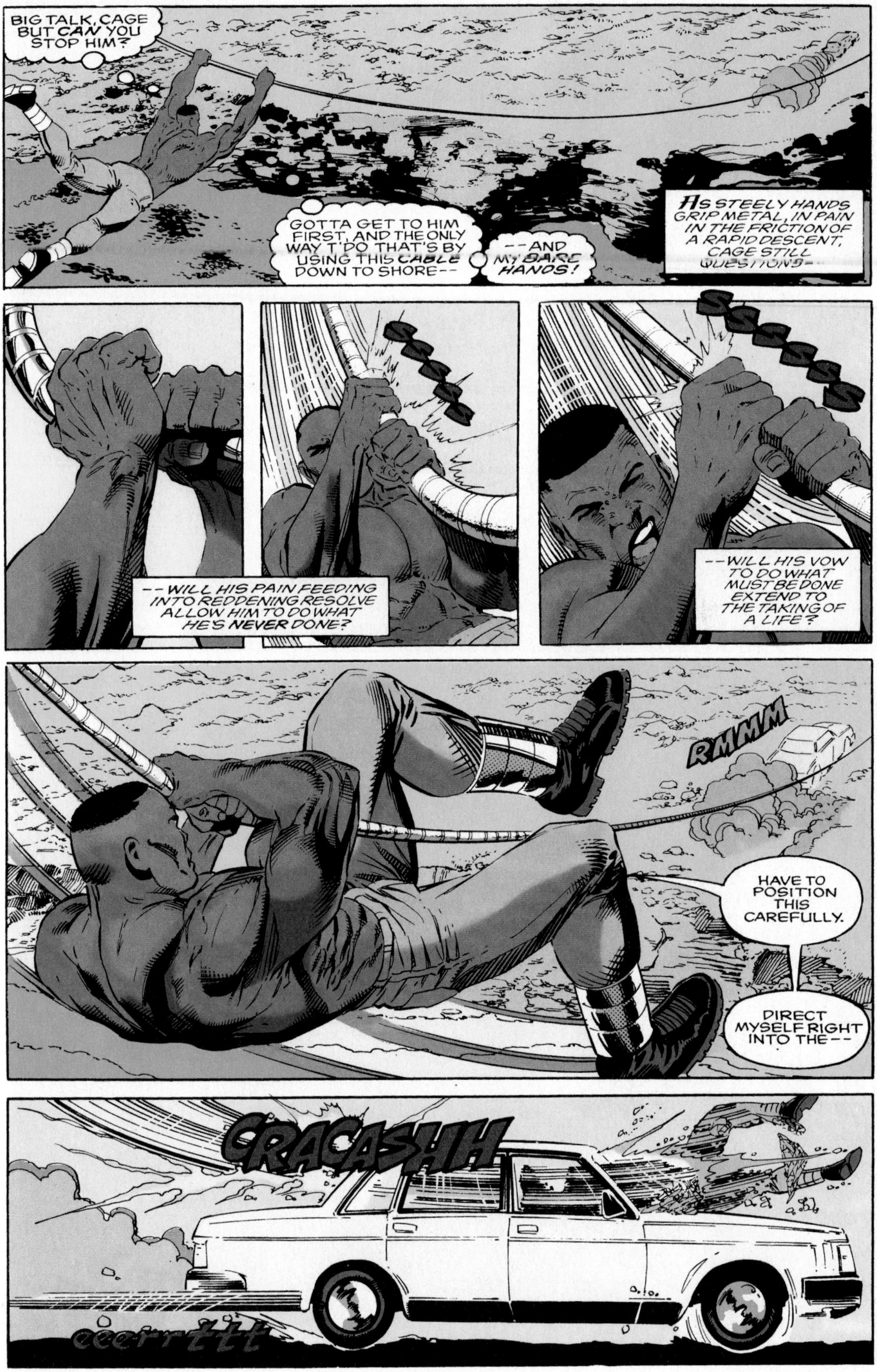
BIG TALK, CAGE BUT CAN YOU STOP HIM?
GOTTA GET TO HIM FIRST, AND THE ONLY WAY T'DO THAT'S BY USING THIS CABLE DOWN TO SHORE--
--AND MY BARE HANDS!
AS STEELY HANDS GRIP METAL, IN PAIN IN THE FRICTION OF A RAPID DESCENT, CAGE STILL QUESTIONS--
SSSSS
--WILL HIS PAIN FEEDING INTO REDDENING RESOLVE ALLOW HIM TO DO WHAT HE'S NEVER DONE?
SSSSSS
--WILL HIS VOW TO DO WHAT MUST BE DONE EXTEND TO THE TAKING OF A LIFE?
RMMM
HAVE TO POSITION THIS CAREFULLY.
DIRECT MYSELF RIGHT INTO THE--
CRACASHH
eeerrrttt

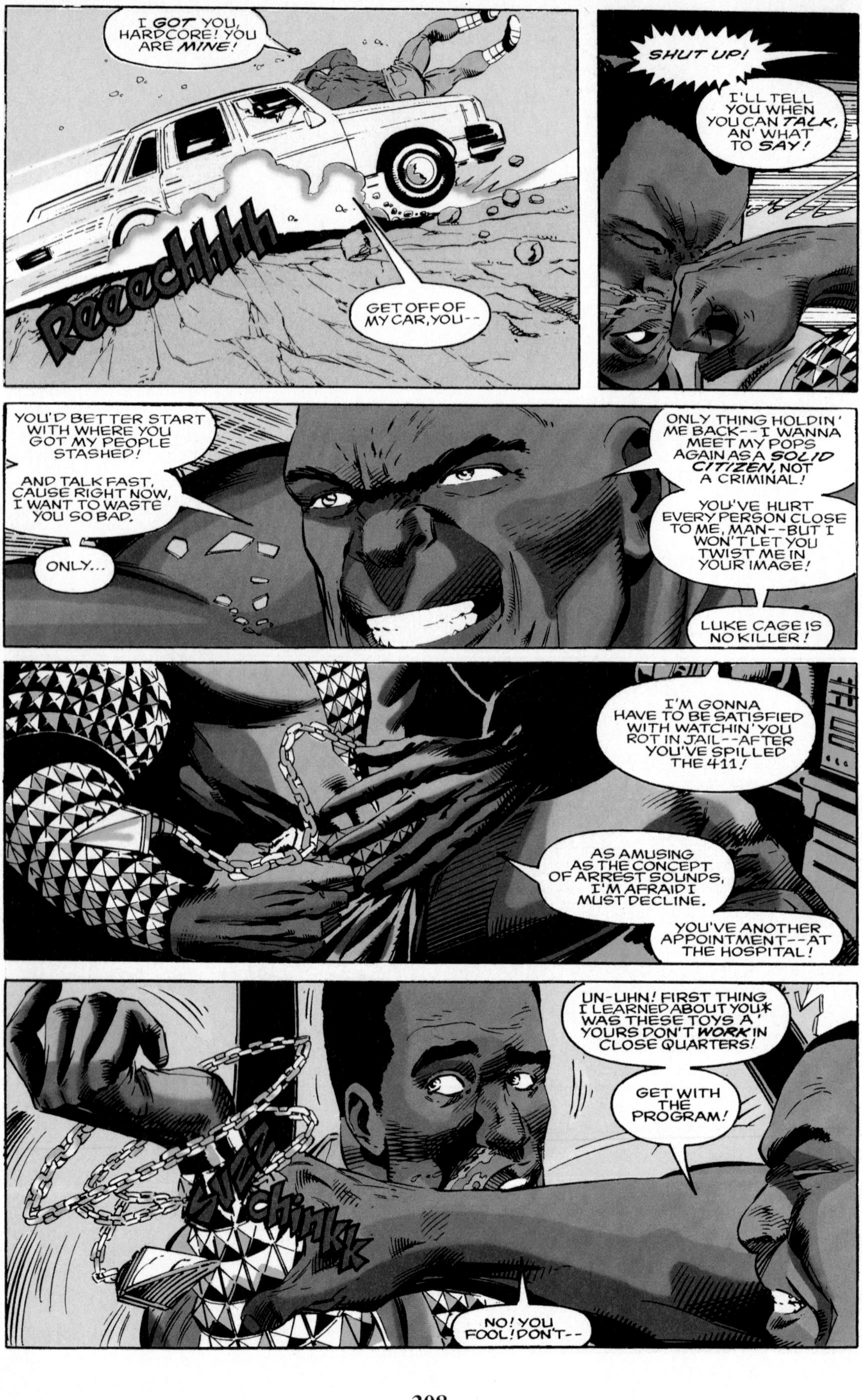
I GOT YOU, HARDCORE! YOU ARE MINE!
Reeechhhhh
GET OFF OF MY CAR, YOU--
SHUT UP!
I'LL TELL YOU WHEN YOU CAN TALK, AN' WHAT TO SAY!
YOU'D BETTER START WITH WHERE YOU GOT MY PEOPLE STASHED!
AND TALK FAST, CAUSE RIGHT NOW, I WANT TO WASTE YOU SO BAD.
ONLY...
ONLY THING HOLDIN' ME BACK--I WANNA MEET MY POPS AGAIN AS A SOLID CITIZEN, NOT A CRIMINAL!
YOU'VE HURT EVERY PERSON CLOSE TO ME, MAN--BUT I WON'T LET YOU TWIST ME IN YOUR IMAGE!
LUKE CAGE IS NO KILLER!
I'M GONNA HAVE TO BE SATISFIED WITH WATCHIN' YOU ROT IN JAIL--AFTER YOU'VE SPILLED THE 411!
AS AMUSING AS THE CONCEPT OF ARREST SOUNDS, I'M AFRAID I MUST DECLINE.
YOU'VE ANOTHER APPOINTMENT--AT THE HOSPITAL!
UN-UHN! FIRST THING I LEARNED ABOUT YOU* WAS THESE TOYS A' YOURS DON'T WORK IN CLOSE QUARTERS!
GET WITH THE PROGRAM!
chinkk
NO! YOU FOOL! DON'T--

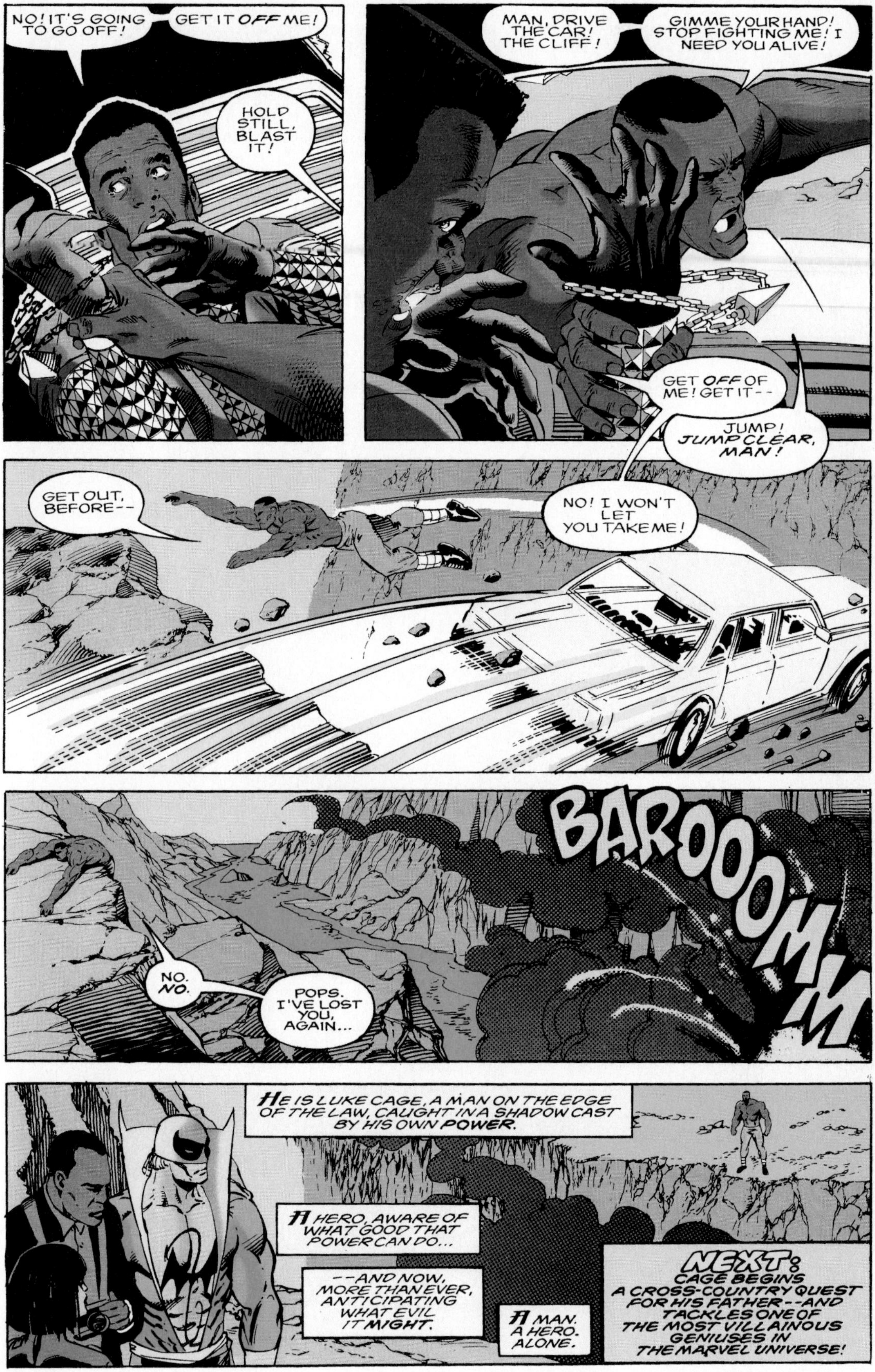
NO! IT'S GOING TO GO OFF!
GET IT OFF ME!
HOLD STILL, BLAST IT!
MAN, DRIVE THE CAR! THE CLIFF!
GIMME YOUR HAND! STOP FIGHTING ME! I NEED YOU ALIVE!
GET OFF OF ME! GET IT--
JUMP! JUMP CLEAR, MAN!
GET OUT, BEFORE--
NO! I WON'T LET YOU TAKE ME!
BAROOOOMMM
NO. NO.
POPS. I'VE LOST YOU, AGAIN...
HE IS LUKE CAGE, A MAN ON THE EDGE OF THE LAW, CAUGHT IN A SHADOW CAST BY HIS OWN POWER.
A HERO, AWARE OF WHAT GOOD THAT POWER CAN DO...
--AND NOW, MORE THAN EVER, ANTICIPATING WHAT EVIL IT MIGHT.
A MAN. A HERO. ALONE.
NEXT: CAGE BEGINS A CROSS-COUNTRY QUEST FOR HIS FATHER--AND TACKLES ONE OF THE MOST VILLAINOUS GENIUSES IN THE MARVEL UNIVERSE!

MARVEL COMICS
TM
© 1992 MARVEL ENT. GROUP, INC.
$1.00 US
$1.25 CAN
110
MAR
UK 65p
APPROVED BY THE COMICS CODE AUTHORITY
WORLD'S BEST-SELLING FAN MAGAZINE!
MARVEL AGE
CATCH OUR EXCLUSIVE PREVIEW OF THE NEW AND IMPROVED
CAGE™
WRESTLE WITH THE NEW
WCW™
WRESTLING COMIC!
MARCH IN THE MACY'S THANKSGIVING PARADE WITH
SPIDER-MAN

? MARVEL® TRIVIA QUIZ ?

One of the great things about being young and reading Luke Cage was deciphering the dialogue codes — what did it mean when Luke yelled "Spit!" or "Christmas!" But that aside, Luke Cage was one of the most exciting Marvel characters of the 70s, first as HERO FOR HIRE, then as POWER MAN, then teamed in POWER MAN AND IRON FIST. Now in the 90s his time is coming again, and so we look back on his long and varied career in the twelve trivia teasers below! Answers on page 31.

— Brian Nelson

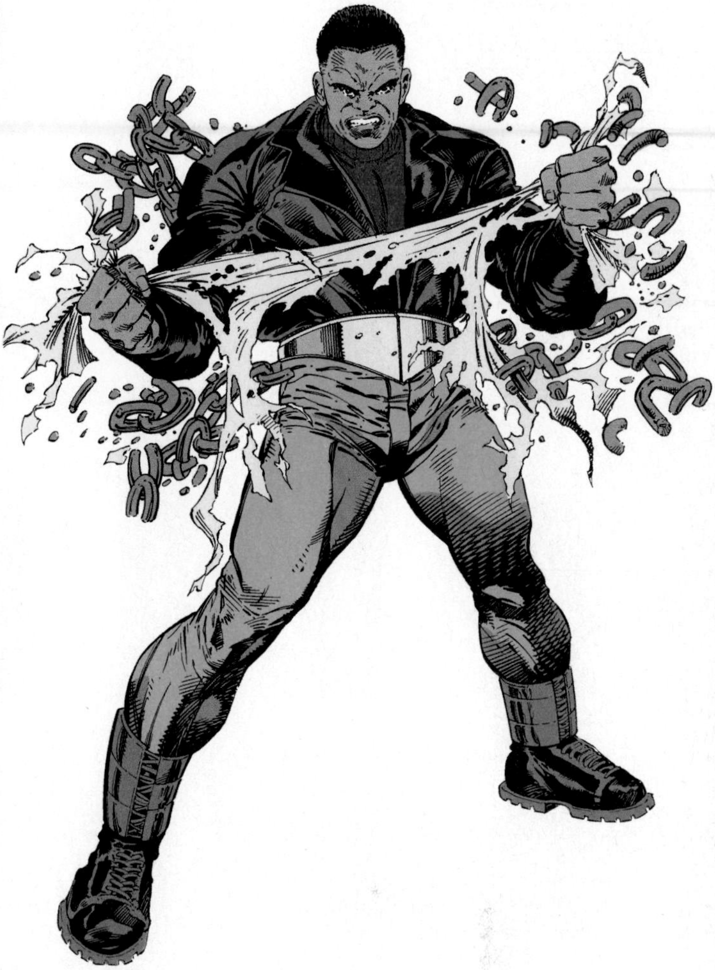

1) On the lam from charges that he killed Danny Rand, Luke has hidden in which city that dubbed him the "South Side Savior?"
A) Chicago
B) St. Louis
C) Detroit
D) Santiago

2) Which hero did Power Man and Iron Fist rescue from being baked alive in an abandoned water tower?
A) El Aguila
B) Moon Knight
C) Daredevil, the Man Without Fear
D) Sassafras, the Dog Filled With Fear

3) The Heroes for Hire teamed with the X-Men to combat:
A) Sabretooth and Constrictor
B) the Living Monolith
C) Unus the Untouchable
D) ring-around-the-collar

4) The battle against which criminal warlord first brought Luke Cage and Danny Rand together as a team?
A) Bushmaster
B) Cottonmouth
C) Sidewinder
D) Princess Python

5) And speaking of serpents, which super-team defeated the Sons of the Serpent with Luke's aid?
A) the Outlaws
B) the Rangers
C) the Defenders
D) the Sons of the Mongoose

6) Reed Richards hired Luke Cage to replace a powerless Ben Grimm in the Fantastic Four because:
A) he was legally required to do so by the EEOC
B) legal contracts require him to maintain four members in the FF
C) Luke had saved Johnny Storm's life
D) Reed thought unstable molecules could stop Luke's shirts from always getting shredded

7) LUKE CAGE, POWER MAN repeatedly brought Luke into conflict with which nefarious mechanical enemy?
A) Ultron-5
B) Tess-One
C) the Adaptoid
D) his office vending machine

8) Luke's first serious romance was with Claire Temple, a successful:
A) reporter
B) doctor
C) tennis player
D) mutant bounty hunter

9) But that relationship was complicated by the return of Claire's first husband, now the super-powered:
A) Falcon
B) Black Goliath
C) Black Talon
D) Ex-Man

10) Which Acts of Vengeance figure premiered in the pages of HERO FOR HIRE fighting our own Luke?
A) the Wizard
B) Chemistro
C) the Grey Gargoyle
D) Robin Chapel of Damage Control

11) At Luke's offices above the Gem Theatre, his best friend was a young film student named:
A) Frank Capra
B) D.W. Griffith
C) Howard Hawks
D) Cecil B. De Mille

12) Dr. Noah Burstein conducted the experiments that gave Luke his powers in a lab constructed at:
A) Ryker's Island Prison
B) Seagate Prison
C) the Vault
D) the studio set for "GERALDO"

QUIZ ANSWERS: 1:A 2:B 3:B 4:A 5:C 6:B 7:D 8:B 9:B 10:B 11:B 12:B

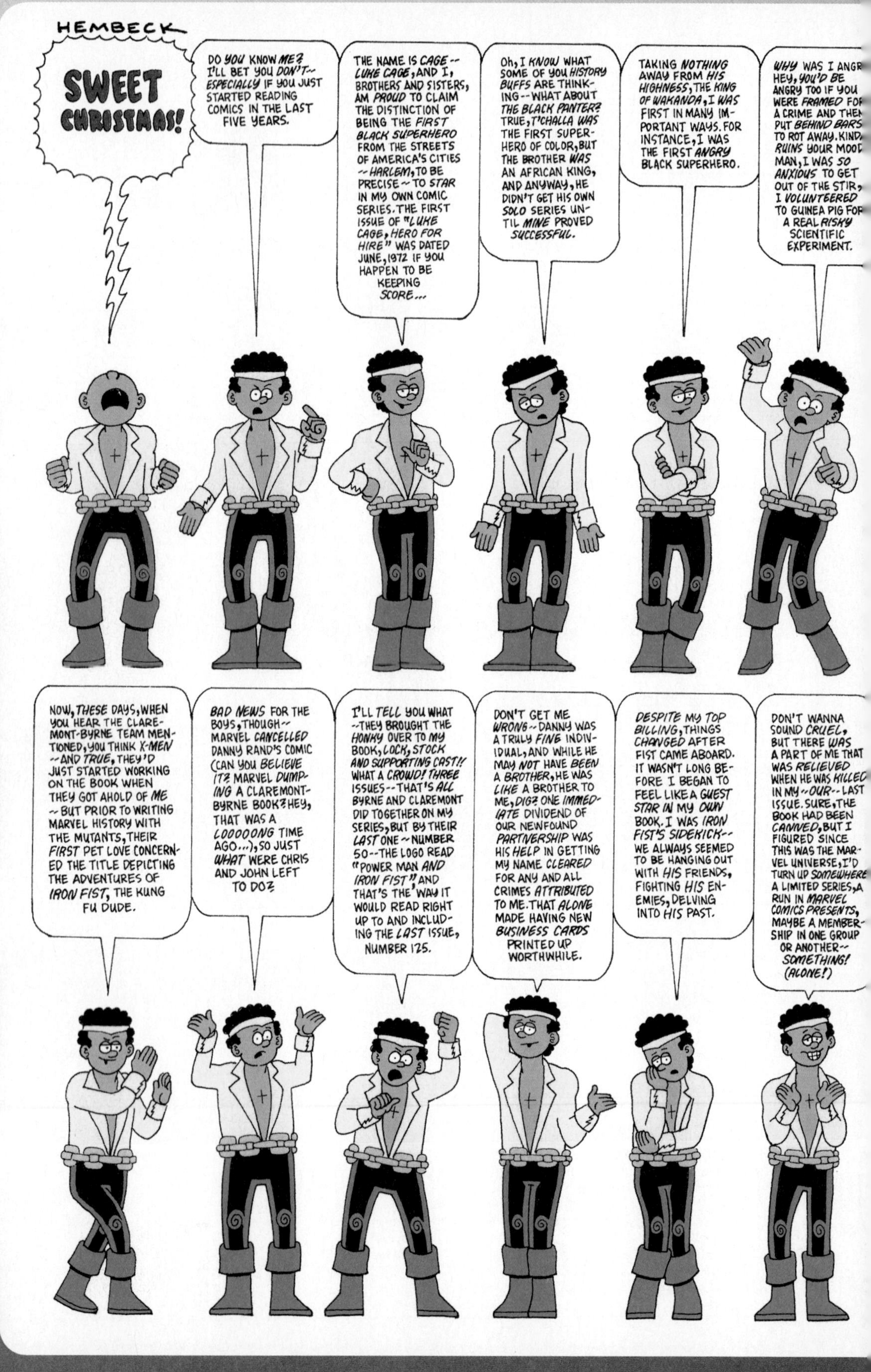
HEMBECK
SWEET CHRISTMAS!
DO YOU KNOW ME? I'LL BET YOU DON'T-- ESPECIALLY IF YOU JUST STARTED READING COMICS IN THE LAST FIVE YEARS.
THE NAME IS CAGE -- LUKE CAGE, AND I, BROTHERS AND SISTERS, AM PROUD TO CLAIM THE DISTINCTION OF BEING THE FIRST BLACK SUPERHERO FROM THE STREETS OF AMERICA'S CITIES -- HARLEM, TO BE PRECISE -- TO STAR IN MY OWN COMIC SERIES. THE FIRST ISSUE OF "LUKE CAGE, HERO FOR HIRE" WAS DATED JUNE, 1972 IF YOU HAPPEN TO BE KEEPING SCORE...
OH, I KNOW WHAT SOME OF YOU HISTORY BUFFS ARE THINKING -- WHAT ABOUT THE BLACK PANTER? TRUE, T'CHALLA WAS THE FIRST SUPERHERO OF COLOR, BUT THE BROTHER WAS AN AFRICAN KING, AND ANYWAY, HE DIDN'T GET HIS OWN SOLO SERIES UNTIL MINE PROVED SUCCESSFUL.
TAKING NOTHING AWAY FROM HIS HIGHNESS, THE KING OF WAKANDA, I WAS FIRST IN MANY IMPORTANT WAYS. FOR INSTANCE, I WAS THE FIRST ANGRY BLACK SUPERHERO.
WHY WAS I ANGR HEY, YOU'D BE ANGRY TOO IF YOU WERE FRAMED FOR A CRIME AND THEN PUT BEHIND BARS TO ROT AWAY. KIND RUINS YOUR MOOD MAN, I WAS SO ANXIOUS TO GET OUT OF THE STIR, I VOLUNTEERED TO GUINEA PIG FOR A REAL RISKY SCIENTIFIC EXPERIMENT.
NOW, THESE DAYS, WHEN YOU HEAR THE CLAREMONT-BYRNE TEAM MENTIONED, YOU THINK X-MEN -- AND TRUE, THEY'D JUST STARTED WORKING ON THE BOOK WHEN THEY GOT AHOLD OF ME -- BUT PRIOR TO WRITING MARVEL HISTORY WITH THE MUTANTS, THEIR FIRST PET LOVE CONCERNED THE TITLE DEPICTING THE ADVENTURES OF IRON FIST, THE KUNG FU DUDE.
BAD NEWS FOR THE BOYS, THOUGH -- MARVEL CANCELLED DANNY RAND'S COMIC (CAN YOU BELIEVE IT? MARVEL DUMPING A CLAREMONT-BYRNE BOOK? HEY, THAT WAS A LOOOOONG TIME AGO...), SO JUST WHAT WERE CHRIS AND JOHN LEFT TO DO?
I'LL TELL YOU WHAT -- THEY BROUGHT THE HONKY OVER TO MY BOOK, LOCK, STOCK AND SUPPORTING CAST!! WHAT A CROWD! THREE ISSUES -- THAT'S ALL BYRNE AND CLAREMONT DID TOGETHER ON MY SERIES, BUT BY THEIR LAST ONE -- NUMBER 50 -- THE LOGO READ "POWER MAN AND IRON FIST," AND THAT'S THE WAY IT WOULD READ RIGHT UP TO AND INCLUDING THE LAST ISSUE, NUMBER 125.
DON'T GET ME WRONG -- DANNY WAS A TRULY FINE INDIVIDUAL, AND WHILE HE MAY NOT HAVE BEEN A BROTHER, HE WAS LIKE A BROTHER TO ME, DIG? ONE IMMEDIATE DIVIDEND OF OUR NEWFOUND PARTNERSHIP WAS HIS HELP IN GETTING MY NAME CLEARED FOR ANY AND ALL CRIMES ATTRIBUTED TO ME. THAT ALONE MADE HAVING NEW BUSINESS CARDS PRINTED UP WORTHWHILE.
DESPITE MY TOP BILLING, THINGS CHANGED AFTER FIST CAME ABOARD. IT WASN'T LONG BEFORE I BEGAN TO FEEL LIKE A GUEST STAR IN MY OWN BOOK. I WAS IRON FIST'S SIDEKICK -- WE ALWAYS SEEMED TO BE HANGING OUT WITH HIS FRIENDS, FIGHTING HIS ENEMIES, DELVING INTO HIS PAST.
DON'T WANNA SOUND CRUEL, BUT THERE WAS A PART OF ME THAT WAS RELIEVED WHEN HE WAS KILLED IN MY -- OUR -- LAST ISSUE. SURE, THE BOOK HAD BEEN CANNED, BUT I FIGURED SINCE THIS WAS THE MARVEL UNIVERSE, I'D TURN UP SOMEWHERE A LIMITED SERIES, A RUN IN MARVEL COMICS PRESENTS, MAYBE A MEMBERSHIP IN ONE GROUP OR ANOTHER -- SOMETHING! (ALONE!)

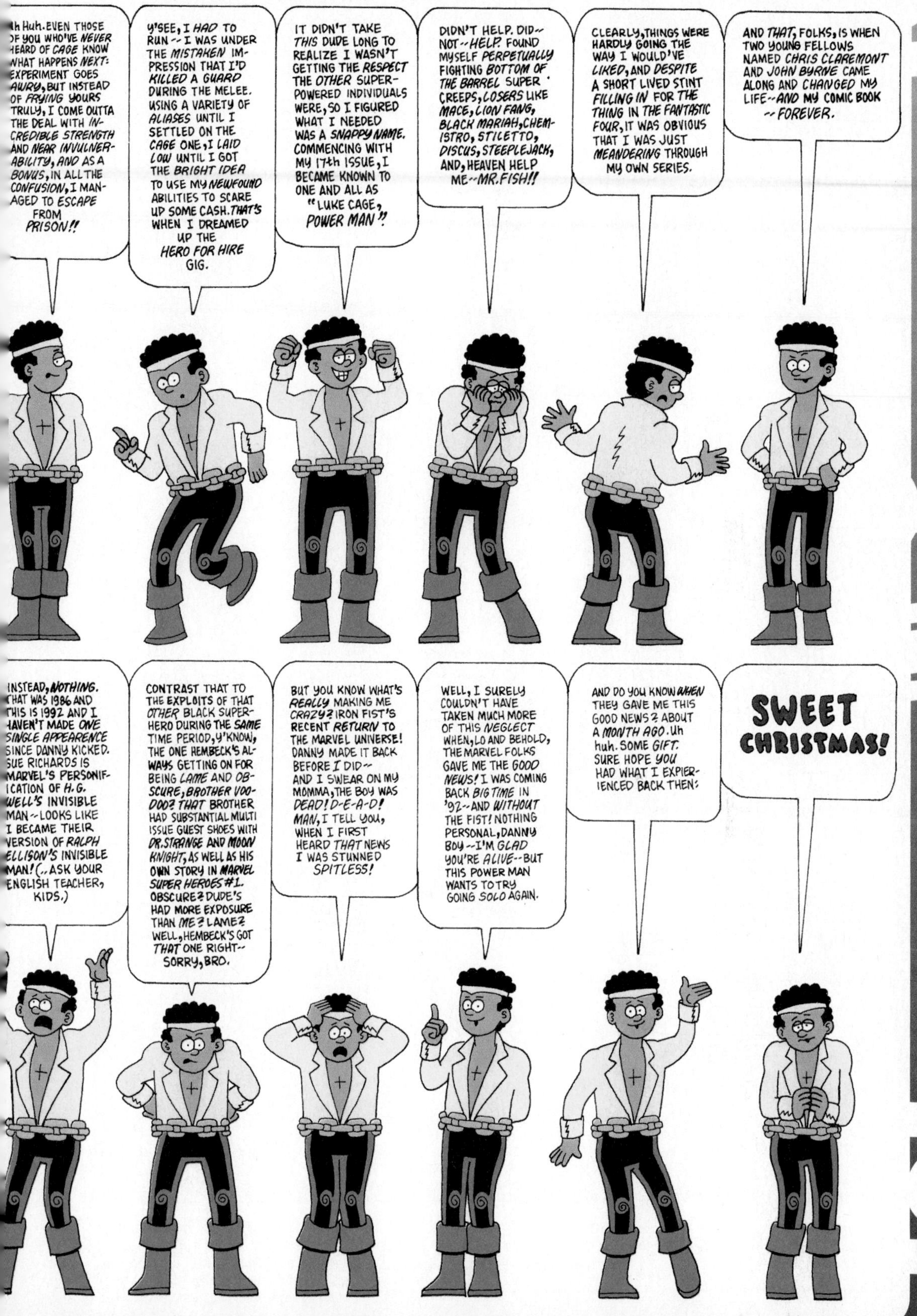
Uh Huh. EVEN THOSE OF YOU WHO'VE NEVER HEARD OF CAGE KNOW WHAT HAPPENS NEXT: EXPERIMENT GOES AWRY, BUT INSTEAD OF FRYING YOURS TRULY, I COME OUTTA THE DEAL WITH INCREDIBLE STRENGTH AND NEAR INVULNERABILITY, AND AS A BONUS, IN ALL THE CONFUSION, I MANAGED TO ESCAPE FROM PRISON!!
Y'SEE, I HAD TO RUN -- I WAS UNDER THE MISTAKEN IMPRESSION THAT I'D KILLED A GUARD DURING THE MELEE. USING A VARIETY OF ALIASES UNTIL I SETTLED ON THE CAGE ONE, I LAID LOW UNTIL I GOT THE BRIGHT IDEA TO USE MY NEWFOUND ABILITIES TO SCARE UP SOME CASH. THAT'S WHEN I DREAMED UP THE HERO FOR HIRE GIG.
IT DIDN'T TAKE THIS DUDE LONG TO REALIZE I WASN'T GETTING THE RESPECT THE OTHER SUPER-POWERED INDIVIDUALS WERE, SO I FIGURED WHAT I NEEDED WAS A SNAPPY NAME. COMMENCING WITH MY 17th ISSUE, I BECAME KNOWN TO ONE AND ALL AS "LUKE CAGE, POWER MAN".
DIDN'T HELP. DID--NOT--HELP. FOUND MYSELF PERPETUALLY FIGHTING BOTTOM OF THE BARREL SUPER CREEPS, LOSERS LIKE MACE, LION FANG, BLACK MARIAH, CHEMISTRO, STILETTO, DISCUS, STEEPLEJACK, AND, HEAVEN HELP ME--MR. FISH!!
CLEARLY, THINGS WERE HARDLY GOING THE WAY I WOULD'VE LIKED, AND DESPITE A SHORT LIVED STINT FILLING IN FOR THE THING IN THE FANTASTIC FOUR, IT WAS OBVIOUS THAT I WAS JUST MEANDERING THROUGH MY OWN SERIES.
AND THAT, FOLKS, IS WHEN TWO YOUNG FELLOWS NAMED CHRIS CLAREMONT AND JOHN BYRNE CAME ALONG AND CHANGED MY LIFE--AND MY COMIC BOOK --FOREVER.
INSTEAD, NOTHING. THAT WAS 1986 AND THIS IS 1992 AND I HAVEN'T MADE ONE SINGLE APPEARENCE SINCE DANNY KICKED. SUE RICHARDS IS MARVEL'S PERSONIFICATION OF H.G. WELL'S INVISIBLE MAN--LOOKS LIKE I BECAME THEIR VERSION OF RALPH ELLISON'S INVISIBLE MAN! (..ASK YOUR ENGLISH TEACHER, KIDS.)
CONTRAST THAT TO THE EXPLOITS OF THAT OTHER BLACK SUPER-HERO DURING THE SAME TIME PERIOD, Y'KNOW, THE ONE HEMBECK'S ALWAYS GETTING ON FOR BEING LAME AND OBSCURE, BROTHER VOODOO? THAT BROTHER HAD SUBSTANTIAL MULTI ISSUE GUEST SHOTS WITH DR. STRANGE AND MOON KNIGHT, AS WELL AS HIS OWN STORY IN MARVEL SUPER HEROES #1. OBSCURE? DUDE'S HAD MORE EXPOSURE THAN ME? LAME? WELL, HEMBECK'S GOT THAT ONE RIGHT--SORRY, BRO.
BUT YOU KNOW WHAT'S REALLY MAKING ME CRAZY? IRON FIST'S RECENT RETURN TO THE MARVEL UNIVERSE! DANNY MADE IT BACK BEFORE I DID--AND I SWEAR ON MY MOMMA, THE BOY WAS DEAD! D-E-A-D! MAN, I TELL YOU, WHEN I FIRST HEARD THAT NEWS I WAS STUNNED SPITLESS!
WELL, I SURELY COULDN'T HAVE TAKEN MUCH MORE OF THIS NEGLECT WHEN, LO AND BEHOLD, THE MARVEL FOLKS GAVE ME THE GOOD NEWS! I WAS COMING BACK BIG TIME IN '92--AND WITHOUT THE FIST! NOTHING PERSONAL, DANNY BOY--I'M GLAD YOU'RE ALIVE--BUT THIS POWER MAN WANTS TO TRY GOING SOLO AGAIN.
AND DO YOU KNOW WHEN THEY GAVE ME THIS GOOD NEWS? ABOUT A MONTH AGO. Uh huh. SOME GIFT. SURE HOPE YOU HAD WHAT I EXPIERIENCED BACK THEN:
SWEET CHRISTMAS!

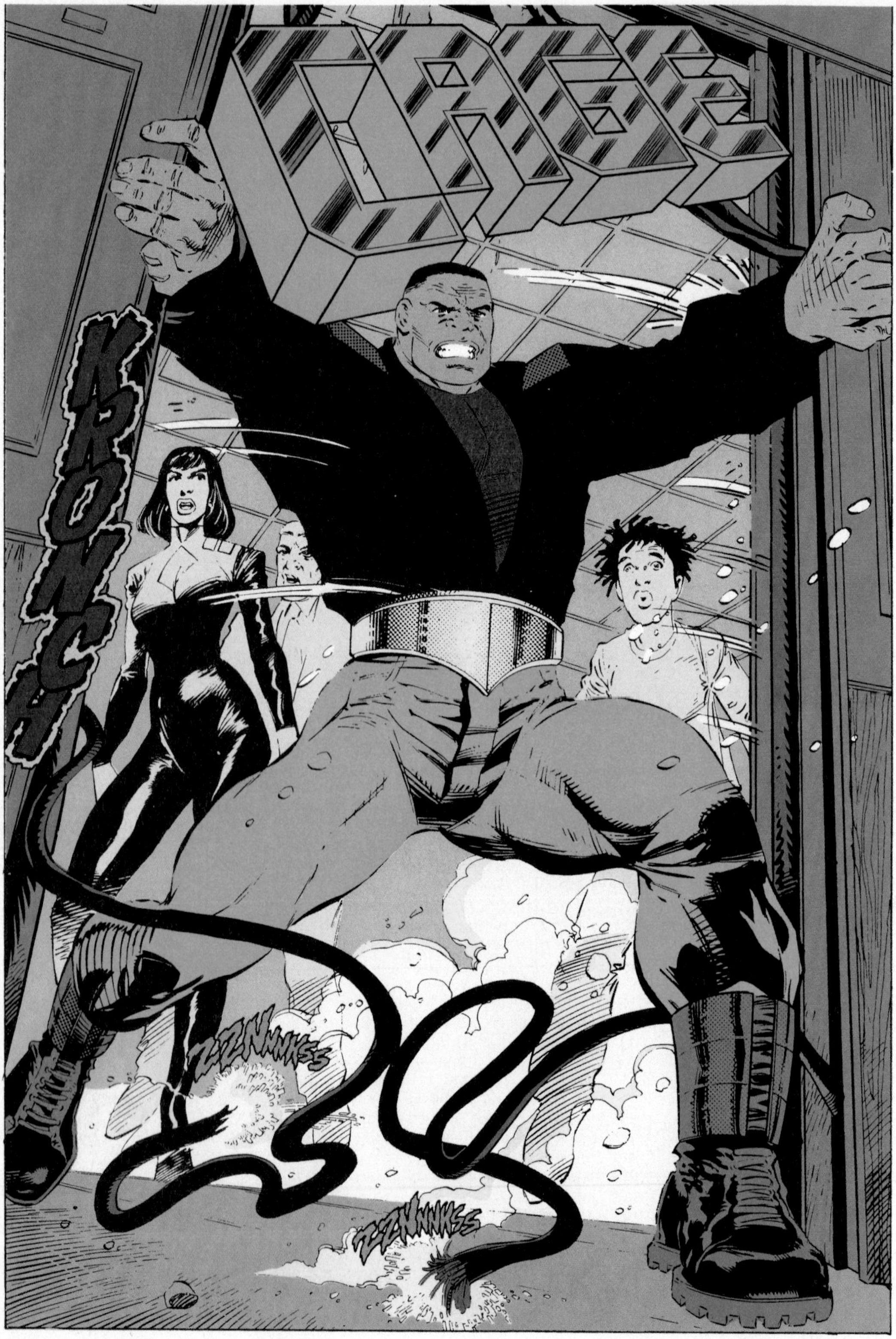
CAGE
KRONCH
ZZNNNKSS
ZZNNNKSS

"Old heroes for hire never die; they return to fight another day. . ."

— ancient comic book industry proverb

February, 1992 marks that day as Luke Cage a.k.a. Hero for Hire, a.k.a. Power Man, hammers his way back into the front ranks of the Marvel Universe with the first issue of a monthly offset comic elegantly entitled, CAGE.

CAGE is the long-awaited return of one of comicdom's most ground-breaking super heroes whose six year absence as a regular has not gone unnoticed by either the Marvel editorial staff or the ranks of fandom.

The splashy debut of LUKE CAGE, HERO FOR HIRE in June, 1972 was followed by an impressive publishing run in which the super heroic exploits of black ex-convict Luke Cage were chronicled. Over the years the title was changed to LUKE CAGE, POWERMAN and then POWER MAN and IRON FIST, in which Cage took on the latter as his crime-fighting partner. All-in-all, the three titles amassed an impressive run of 125 issues, the last released in September, 1986.

The character of Luke Cage was borne out of a time in the 70's during great expansion and experimentation at Marvel. Emerging from the creative crackle was an effort to create super hero characters (and villains, as well) that broke from tradition and expectation. Super heroes with unusual powers, looks, backgrounds and ethnicities began to appear with greater frequency. Cage quickly became the most popular of the black super characters.

By the way, Luke Cage's real name has never been revealed. It's a pseudonym that the character adapted at the very start of the series. Cage, a product of the New York City ghetto, had been framed and wrongly sent to prison. While there, he struck an agreement with a research physiologist who promised to do what he could to get Cage paroled in exchange for Luke's participation in an experiment to test the powers of a chemical agent to fight disease and aging.

A guard who had been Cage's nemesis throughout his prison stay takes control of the experiment and, hoping to kill Cage, pushes the experiment to the max. But rather than having its desired effect, Cage emerges with superhuman strength and steel-hard skin. He flees the island prison, but is assumed dead when guards find his bullet-ridden shirt worn during the escape.

Cage, as fugitive, began a new career, selling his strong-armed services as a crimefighter. He later teamed up with Danny Rand, the Iron Fist, and with his help was able to clear himself of the original charge which landed him in jail.

The original series featured plenty of bang 'em up action and a stable of notable talent behind the carnage. Among the contributors were the likes of Chris Claremont, Archie Goodwin, Len Wein, John Byrne, Steve Engelhart, Mike Zeck, Ron Wilson and Frank Springer.

With a history as rich as this it wasn't a difficult decision to dust off Cage and get him back into the mainstream again. After many months of "redevelopment," the honored task of writing chores was given to Marcus McLaurin whose proposal, according to CAGE editor Kelly Corvese "was the most original." Editor in chief Tom DeFalco gave the go-ahead, Dwayne Turner was selected as penciler and the series was an "all-systems go."

For Corvese and his creative duo, getting the chance to work with a character like Cage was like turning loose three kids in a candy store. The grittiness of the character appealed to all. "Cage has got an inbred nobility — he's wise, with a real street sense," McLaurin says. Turner, hot off the success of his four issue bookshelf Black Panther series, says it most poetically. "Cage is a good character. . .he can touch on everything and yet be touched himself."

McLaurin points out that the character was originally thought to be so unique back in 1972 that he was created to have his own series, rather than having to earn the honor by building a following in other titles. "He was believed to be that strong," he adds. The feeling is still apparent.

Pointing to the tremendous appeal of Cage, Turner notes, "Here's an angry, tough guy with a real attitude and a bad street background. . .very dynamic, very action-oriented."

It's precisely this type of characterization which Turner feels may have been the impetus to get CAGE off the ground. "I think the fact that other forms of media and entertainment have focused attention on these types of characters show that they're viable. . ."

What can we expect for the Cage of the 1990's? "The years have hardened him. He doesn't want a partner, he doesn't want people around," Corvese explains. "But despite his tendency towards isolation and withdrawal, he must come to grips with his obligations to serve. This is part of his fight, his conflict," Turner adds.

From out of this inner conflict a new Cage is emerging. Originally portrayed as an 'act now, think later' type, Cage will be "more of a thinker," according the McLaurin. "He'll learn that he can't run from his past and he will learn that he can change his attitudes."

As his journey is a learning experience for him, it will be one for the reader as well. "The character has been around for so long. . .so well liked, yet so little is known of him. His life before prison has always been a mystery. We're going to address that and we're going to get into family background as well — whatever is necessary and important to the storyline," McLaurin notes.

Heading to Chicago to make a fresh start of things as a hero for hire, Cage forms an alliance of sorts with the *Chicago Spectator*, a newspaper which will help him advertise his services in exchange for the exclusive rights to the stories that his exploits generate. The paper will serve as a clearinghouse for his activities — it will screen the answers to Cage's ads and assign him the cream of the crop — the most challenging and

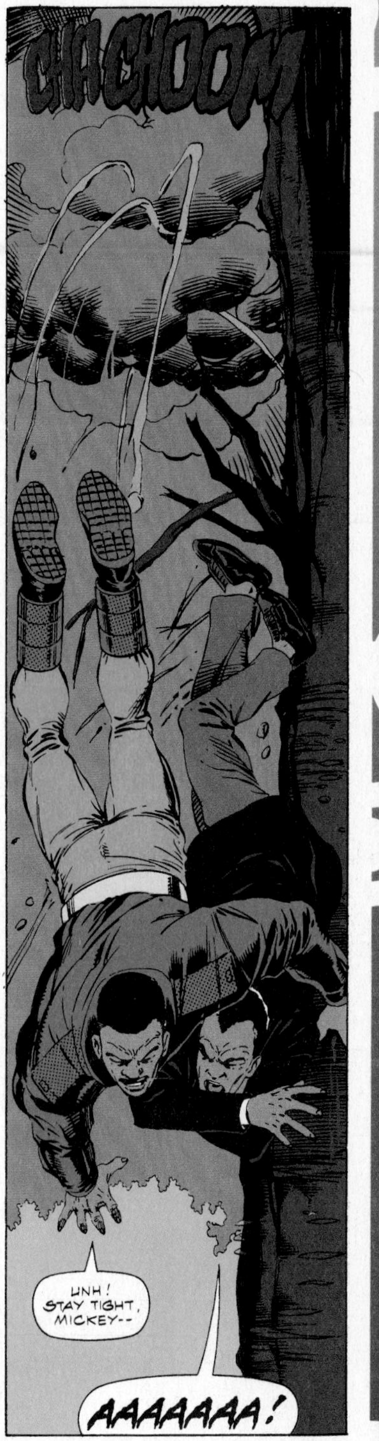
CHACHOOM
UNH! STAY TIGHT, MICKEY--
AAAAAAA!

rewarding for both Luke and the paper.

Cage, however, learns that Chicago leaves a lot to be desired and he will eventually find himself to be a carefully manipulated pawn by influences which are at work to break him. The reasons for his enemies' aggressions are what gives the title its energy.

Look for appearances by some familiar faces, like private investigator Dakota North and villains Tombstone and Nitro, who McLaurin sees as a recurring CAGE bad guy. A new villain, created especially for the series, and going by the name of Hardcore, also promises to cause Cage some sleepless nights.

McLaurin takes a very realistic attitude towards the action in CAGE. "Cage will be fighting villains that match his powers. . .they'll be believable. I see Cage, from the standpoint of power, as being in the league of a Punisher, not Thor," he notes. "Expect to see people get hurt, to see Cage get in trouble for his actions," he adds.

The choice of Chicago as the backdrop for the high-powered action was quite intentional. "This is a city with a history of crime, gang warfare and inner city turmoil," McLaurin says. Penciler Turner will be using lots of photo reference to capture the real flavor of the Windy City. McLaurin has been doing his research by reading Chicago newspapers and following what's been going on in that city. "Some of the story ideas were sparked by real news items," he claims.

Both McLaurin and Turner are intent on avoiding stereotypes that occasionally plagued the original series. "I'm developing characters for the series who are black and not street level, characters that are positive role models for the kids," McLaurin says. "Stereotypes," Turner notes, "are not deserving of the space they're given. Even in real bad neighborhoods, you have families who all work, earn their own way. . .I'll put in that kind of portrayal."

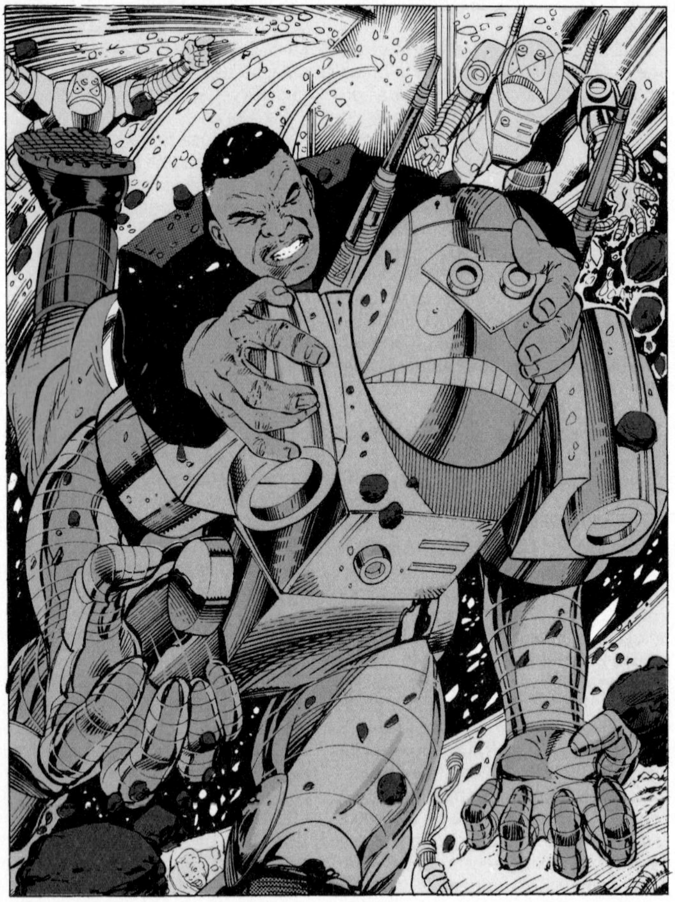

A couple of bonuses await the readers of the new Cage series. First, is the cover design for CAGE #1 which will feature an illustration of the character and the logo printed on clear acetate and laid over the background art, printed on offset comic cover stock. Sounds weird? Imagine a cel of animation and you have the basic idea. And for those of you into double doses of action, you'll be able to catch Cage in the pages of PUNISHER #60-62 as he guest stars in a certain Frank Castle's favorite mag.

So there you have it — Luke Cage for the 90's. A loner hoping to find healing in his seclusion, but finding instead a city intent on preying upon his abilities and good character. New challenges and old memories.

Check it out.

— Nelson Yomtov

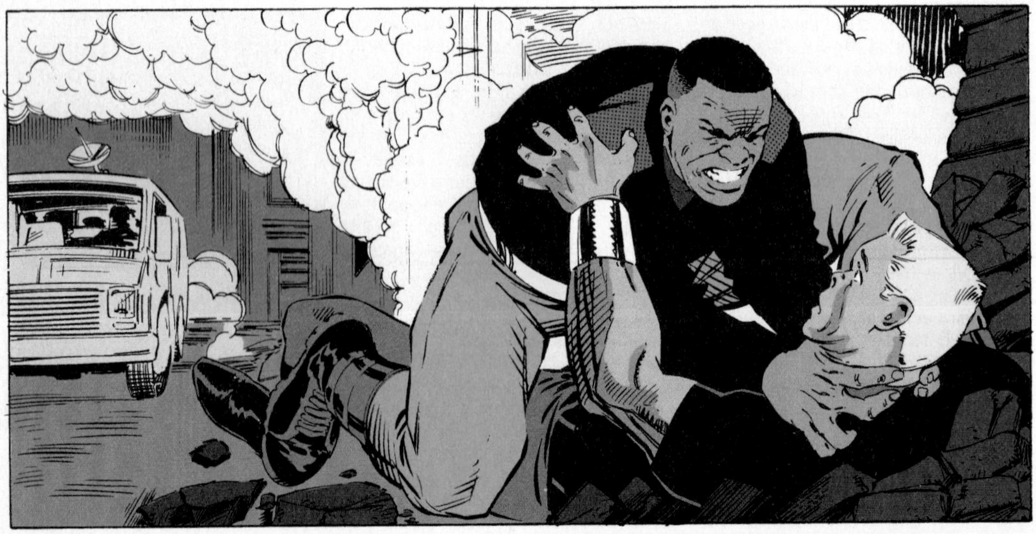

CAGE

Luke Cage is back, in a new city, with a new look, a new supporting cast and a new twist on the "Hero for Hire" concept.

Cage has an agreement with a trashy Chicago tabloid, *The Chicago Spectator*. They'll provide him with a base of operations, a way for people to contact him, and basic operating expenses. In return, they get the story.

He'll be joined by Dakota North, a freelance detective, who will be the brains to Cage's brawn. His cases will involve everything from acting as bodyguard for a rap band to searching for missing persons and industrial espionage.

Cage's main advantage has always been his invulnerability. Now he'll find himself up against technology that can kill him, and people who are more than willing to use it. He'll also be fighting super-foes like "The Hammer" (an offshoot of the X-Factor organization "The Right"), Tombstone (from SPECTACULAR SPIDER-MAN, whose powers parallel Cage's own) and Kickback, an assassin whose legs give him the ability to kill.

Cage's life has been one of violence, poverty and death, and it has left him angry and hard. We'll learn more about Cage's hazy background, particularly when the Maggia sends in a man from his past, the villain called Hardcore, to destroy Cage's life and set him up for their own use.

WRITER Marcus McLaurin	**INKER** Chris Ivy	**IMPRINT** Marvel	**FORMAT** Newsprint offset	**PAGE COUNT** 32
PENCILER Dwayne Turner	**EDITOR** Kelly Corvese	**SHIPPING** February	**FREQUENCY** Monthly	**COVER PRICE** $1.25

MARVEL AGE PREVIEW #2

ANATOMY OF A MAKEOVER: LUKE CAGE

PREVAMP

- Mod 70's haircut
- Yellow silk shirt (easily torn)
- Chains (symbolic)
- Cuffed buccaneer boots (says he's a super hero)

- Bad attitude
- Hangs with Iron Fist
- Favorite phrase: "Sweet Christmas!"

REVAMP

- With-it 80's haircut
- Steel-hard Jacket (not easily worn)
- Belt (functional)
- Huge heavy workman's boots (says he can't run very fast)

- Badder attitude
- Hangs with Dakota North
- Favorite phrase: "Gimme my money — now!"

MARVEL YEAR-IN-REVIEW '92 ARTICLE BY TOM BREVOORT & MIKE KANTEROVICH

CAGE™

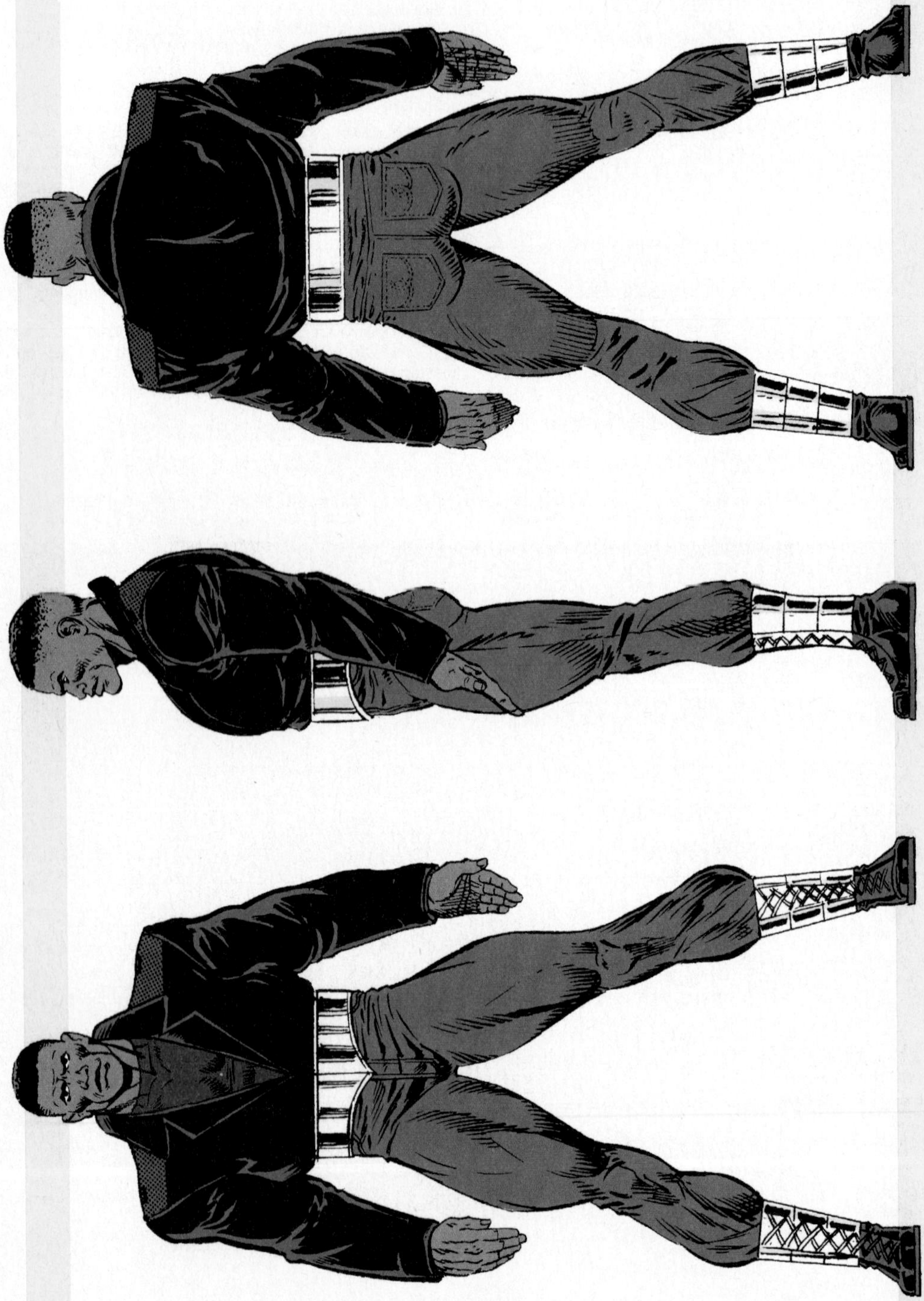

OFFICIAL HANDBOOK OF THE MARVEL UNIVERSE: MASTER EDITION #23
PROFILE ART BY KEITH POLLARD, JOSEF RUBINSTEIN & ANDY YANCHUS

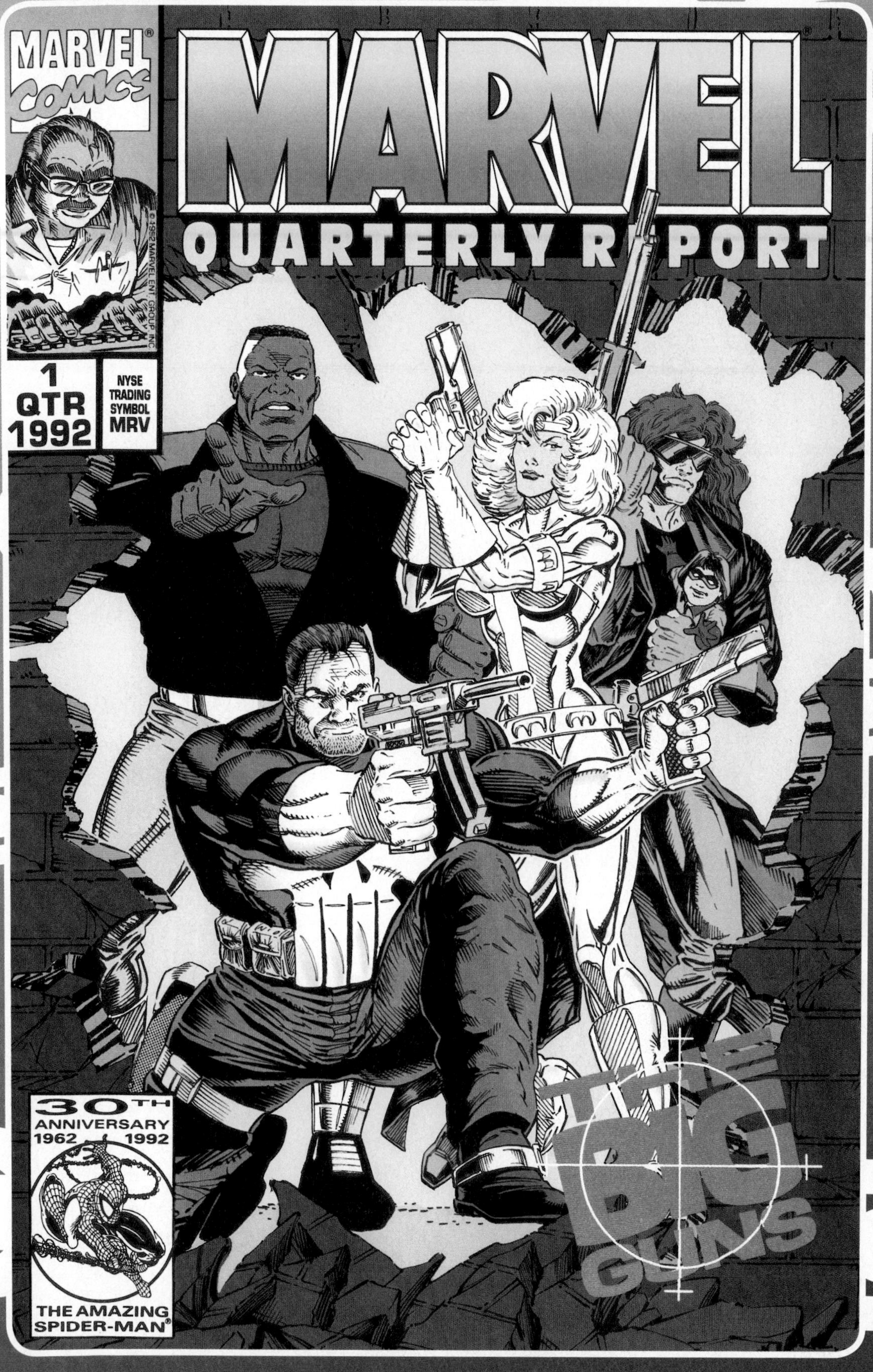
MARVEL COMICS
MARVEL
QUARTERLY REPORT
1 QTR 1992
NYSE TRADING SYMBOL MRV
30TH ANNIVERSARY 1962 1992
THE AMAZING SPIDER-MAN
THE BIG GUNS

MARVEL QUARTERLY REPORT (1992) #1 COVER BY JOHN HEBERT & RODNEY RAMOS

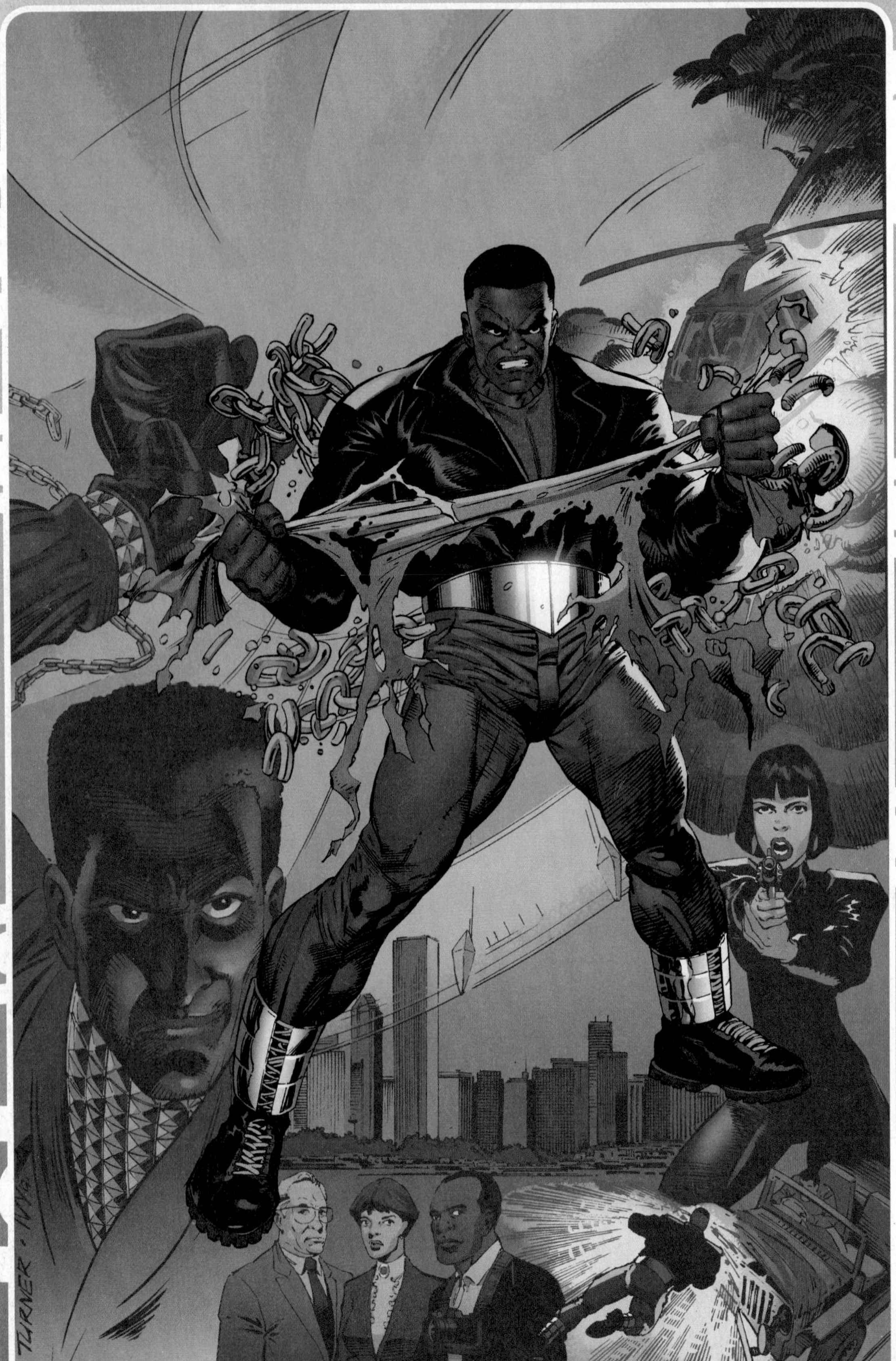
TURNER